T0144199

Deadlock Resolution in Computer-Integrated Systems

Deadlock Resolution in Computer-Integrated Systems

edited by
MengChu Zhou
New Jersey Institute of Technology
Newark, New Jersey, U.S.A.

Maria Pia Fanti
Politecnico di Bari
Bari, Italy

MARCEL DEKKER   NEW YORK

Library of Congress Cataloging-in-Publication Data

Deadlock resolution in computer-integrated systems / edited by MengChu Zhou, Maria Pia Fanti.
 p. cm.
 Includes bibliographical references and index.
 ISBN 0-8247-5368-2 (alk. paper)
 1. Production engineering. 2. Computer integrated manufacturing systems. 3.
 Discrete-time systems. 4. System design. I. Fanti, Maria Pia. II. Title.

TS176.Z53 2004
670'.285--dc22   2004059349

Visit the CRC Press Web site at www.crcpress.com

© 2005 by Marcel Dekker/CRC Press

No claim to original U.S. Government works
International Standard Book Number 0-8247-5368-2
Library of Congress Card Number 2004059349
Printed in the United States of America 1 2 3 4 5 6 7 8 9 0
Printed on acid-free paper

Table of Contents

List of Contributors

B. Benhabib (Chapter 3), benhabib@mie.utoronto.ca
Department of Mechanical and Industrial Engineering, University of Toronto, 5 King's College Road, Toronto, Ontario, M5S 3G8, Canada

Stjepan Bogdan (Chapter 7), stjepan.bogdan@fer.hr
Department of Control and Computer Engineering in Automation, Faculty of Electrical Engineering and Computing (FER), University of Zagreb, Unska 3, HR-10000 Zagreb, Croatia

Thomas O. Boucher (Chapter 2), tboucher@rci.rutgers.edu
Department of Industrial and Systems Engineering, Rutgers University, P. O. Box 909, Piscataway, NJ 08854, USA

Ho Y. Chan (Chapter 15), ckevin@computer.org
Department of Computer Science, University of Southern California Los Angeles, CA 90089, USA

Rocky K. C. Chang (Chapter 15), csrchang@comp.polyu.edu.hk
Department of Computing, The Hong Kong Polytechnic University, Hung Hom, Kowloon, Hong Kong

M. P. Fanti (Chapters 1 and 5), fanti@poliba.it
Dipartimento di Elettrotecnica ed Elettronica, Politecnico di Bari, Bari, Italy

Luca Ferrarini (Chapter 12), ferrarin@elet.polimi.it
Politecnico di Milano, Dipartimento di Elettronica e Informazione, Piazza L. da Vinci 32 - 20133 Milano, Italy

Ayla Gürel (Chapter 7), ayla.gurel@emu.edu.tr
Electrical and Electronic Engineering Department, Eastern Mediterranean University, Famagusta, via Mersin 10, Turkey

MuDer Jeng (Chapter 8), jeng@mail.ntou.edu.tw
Department of Electrical Engineering, National Taiwan Ocean University,
Keelung 202, Taiwan, ROC

Mark Lawley (Chapter 4), malawley@ecn.purdue.edu
School of Industrial Engineering, Purdue University, 1287 Grissom Hall,
West Lafayette, IN 47905, USA

Frank L. Lewis (Chapter 7), flewis@controls.uta.edu
Automation & Robotics Research Institute, The University of Texas at Arlington, 7300 Jack Newell Blvd. S., Fort Worth, Texas 76118, USA

Zhiwu Li (Chapter 10), zhwli@xidian.edu.cn
School of Electro-Mechanical Engineering, Xidian University, Xi'an, China

B. Maione (Chapter 5), maione@poliba.it
Dipartimento di Elettrotecnica ed Elettronica, Politecnico di Bari, Bari, Italy

G. Maione (Chapter 5), gmaione@deemail.poliba.it
Dipartimento di Elettrotecnica ed Elettronica, Politecnico di Bari, Bari, Italy

José Mireles, Jr. (Chapter 7), jmireles@arri.uta.edu
Universidad Autónoma de Ciudad Juárez, Ave. Del Charro 450 Nte., Cd.
Juarez Chihuahua, México, CP 32310

Tadao Murata (Chapter 17), murata@cs.uic.edu
Department of Computer Science, University of Illinois at Chicago, 851 S.
Morgan St., Chicago, IL 60607-7053, USA

Jonghun Park (Chapter 16), j.park@kaist.ac.kr
Department of Industrial Engineering, Seoul National University, San
56-1, Sillim-dong, Gwanak-gu, Seoul, 151-744, Korea

Timothy M. Pinkston (Chapter 13), tpink@charity.usc.edu
Department of Electrical Engineering, University of Southern California,
3740 McClintock Ave., Los Angeles, CA 90089-2562, USA

Luigi Piroddi (Chapter 12), Piroddi@Elet.PoliMi.IT
Politecnico di Milano, Dipartimento di Elettronica e Informazione
Piazza L. da Vinci 32 - 20133 Milano, Italy

A. Ramirez-Serrano (Chapter 3), aramirez@enme.ucalgary.ca
Department of Mechanical & Manufacturing Engineering
University of Calgary, 2500 University Drive, Calgary, Alberta T2N 1N4,
Canada

Elzbieta Roszkowska (Chapter 6), ekr@pwr.wroc.pl
Institute of Engineering Cybernetics, Wroclaw University of Technology,
ul. Janiszewskiego 11/17, 50-372 Wroclaw, Poland

Spyros Reveliotis (Chapter 9), spyros@isye.gatech.edu
School of Industrial and Systems Engineering, Georgia Institute of
Technology, 765 Ferst Drive, Atlanta, GA 30332, USA

Tsuta Tai (Chapter 2), ttai@pfs.com
State Street Corp., 600 College Road East, Princeton, NJ 08540, USA

Mikko Tiusanen (Chapter 17), mikko.tiusanen@tut.fi
Tampere University of Technology, P.O.Box 553, FIN-33101 Tampere,
Finland

B. Turchiano (Chapter 5), turchiano@poliba.it
Dipartimento di Elettrotecnica ed Elettronica, Polytechnic of Bari, Bari,
Italy

Milosh Vladimir Ivanovich (Chapter 14), ivanovic@sub.net.au
Telstra Research Laboratories, Melbourne, Australia

Mathias Weske (Chapter 18), weske@hpi.uni-potsdam.de
Hasso Plattner Institute for Software Systems Engineering at Potsdam
University, Prof.-Dr.-Helmertstr. 2, 14482 Potsdam, Germany

Naiqi Wu (Chapter 11), nqwu@gdut.edu.cn
Department of Mechatronics Engineering, Guangdong University of
Technology, Guangzhou 510090, P. R. China

Xiaolan Xie (Chapter 8), xie@loria.fr
INRIA/Macsi Project and LGIPM, ISGMP-Bat. A, Ile Du Saulcy, 57045
Metz, France

Ali Yalcin (Chapter 2), ayalcin@eng.usf.edu
Industrial and Management Systems Engineering, University of South
Florida, 4202 E. Fowler Avenue, ENB118, Tampa, FL 33620, USA

Adam W. Yeung (Chapter 15), wkyeung@cisco.com
Cisco Systems Inc., 170 West Tasman Drive, San Jose, CA 95134-1700,
USA

MengChu Zhou (Chapters 1, 10 and 11), zhou@njit.edu and
mengchu@ieee.org
Department of Electrical and Computer Engineering, New Jersey Institute
of Technology, 323 MLK Blvd., Newark, NJ 07102, USA and
Laboratory of Complex Systems and Intelligence Science, Institute of
Automation, Chinese Academy of Sciences, P.O. Box 2728, Beijing
100080, P. R. China

Preface

The Aims

This book is edited and written to deal with the research and implementation issues in designing complex computer-integrated systems. These systems include automated production systems, transportation systems, computer operating systems, concurrent software systems, computer networks, distributed database systems, and other automated systems. As technological systems become more complex, automated, distributed, and computing-intensive, deadlock issues facing the researchers and engineers for complex system development become of major significance in both research and practice. Since the 1970s, there have been many studies to model, detect, resolve, and recover from deadlocks and practical applications in the mentioned areas. However, there is no single title that summarizes this important area of research efforts. Deadlock-related issues have been dealt with in some edited volumes and books but were never treated in a systematic and comprehensive manner as in this edited volume. Thus we view this volume as a timely publication to serve well this segment of research and development community that is growing in number and interest.

The Contents

Deadlock is a situation in which there is no system throughput due to inappropriate allocation of resources to concurrent executing processes. More precisely, a deadlock occurs when each element from a set of processes waits for resources held by other elements of the same set. Such phenomena can be observed in computer operating systems, concurrent software systems, automated manufacturing systems, and transportation systems. Their modeling, detection, avoidance, and recovery are very important in improving a system's performance. This book contains 18 chapters that are contributed by prominent researchers in this area. They address one or more of the following research and development subjects:
A. Deadlock prevention approaches including synthesis of deadlock-free models and deadlock-free scheduling;
B. Deadlock detection and recovery methods that allow deadlock to occur with recovery options;

C. Deadlock avoidance that formulates the dynamic control policies that depend upon the system states or at least upon the model structures. In this category, such mathematical and graphical modeling tools as digraphs, Petri nets, and automata are discussed; and
D. Comparison and industrial benchmark studies that compare different approaches.

All these contributions can be classified based on the deadlock modeling approaches they present, the solution types they propose, and applications they seek, as shown in the below table.

Models	Chapter	Solutions	Chapter	Applications	Chapter
Automata	1-4,17	Prevention	1,3,8-10, 13,16,18	Manufacturing /Transportation	1-12
Digraphs	1,5,13, 17	Detection/ recovery	1,3,4,5,8- 11,13,17,18	Communication Network	13, 14
Petri nets	1,6-11, 17	Avoidance	1,2,4,5,7, 11-15,18	Internet	15, 16
Other methods	12,14- 18	Comparison	1,5,12-16, 18	Concurrent Program/Database	17, 18

The editors' introductory chapter "**Introduction to Deadlock Research in Computer-Integrated Systems**" presents fundamental deadlock-research related materials and an up-to-date summary of the present deadlock resolution studies. A typical example from automated manufacturing is offered to illustrate the three primary modeling methods and the related solution approaches: digraphs, automata, and Petri nets. Their advantages and disadvantages are highlighted.

The second chapter "**Deadlock Avoidance in Automated Manufacturing Systems Using Finite Automata and State Space Search**" by Thomas O. Boucher, Tsuta Tai, and Ali Yalcin of Rutgers University, USA, presents an approach to deadlock avoidance based on finite automata. This approach begins from the framework introduced by Ramadge and Wonham (R&W) for modeling and control of discrete event systems (DES) based on formal languages generated by finite automata. They apply this framework to the problem of dynamic scheduling and control of automated manufacturing systems. A typical automated manufacturing system is composed of multiple machines and workstations that perform various operations on a part, and a material handling system that interconnects these machines and workstations. Parts are processed to completion by routing them through various machines and workstations according to their individual process plans. Their presented approach to avoiding deadlock features 1) a simple and natural way of formulating the "requirements model" of the R&W framework from the part routing plans, 2) an ability to handle parts with multiple routing plans within the framework, 3) a solution that guarantees that the resulting controller is both deadlock-free and maximally permissive, and 4) an ability to dynamically reevaluate the controller logic as the active part mix in the manufacturing system changes. The direct application of the R&W framework can involve a large search space as problem size grows. Extensions of their approach have addressed the problems of scalability, state space search, and execution time. They have been accomplished through distributed control and the use of autonomous agents, as well as the introduction of more effective state space search algorithms. These extensions and the relative efficiency of algorithms are also discussed and demonstrated in this chapter.

The third chapter "**Synthesis of Deadlock-free Supervisory Controllers Using Automata**" by A. Ramirez-Serrano, University of Calgary, Canada, and B. Benhabib, University of Toronto, Canada, discusses the automata-based DES-controller synthesis methodologies capable of obtaining deadlock-free supervisors by construction. Namely, the resultant controllers do not require the use of an on-line deadlock detection and recovery mechanism. This chapter reviews R&W control theory and describes its deadlock-free controller yielding characteristics together with other significant properties that can be used for the specification, verification, analysis and synthesis of "correct" DES controllers. Then, the authors review another automata theory, Extended Moore Automata (EMA), which extends the capabilities of R&W theory in controlling more complex systems, e.g., multi-workcell systems producing parts with several alternate processing routes. The probability of encountering deadlocks in such multi-workcell Flexible Manufacturing Systems (FMS) is higher compared with single-workcell systems due to the existing "competition for resources" between the parts that can be processed in several different ways. Even if one is able to identify and detect a deadlock state in an on-line manner, there may be no easy way to resolve it. Thus, when dealing with the control of FMS, it would be beneficial to analyze the controller at hand for possible deadlock states and/or conflicting conditions, identify such states and eliminate them prior to their implementation. As presented in this chapter, the use of individual and independent supervisors for each workcell would reduce the computational complexity when synthesizing the (smaller size) supervisor set and allow for their *a priori* deadlock analysis. Such a deadlock identification method is presented herein based on the use of EMA theory. Naturally, however, an identified deadlock state can only be eliminated by changing the control specifications and constraints imposed by the user of the DES at hand and resynthesis of the supervisor. As an additional practical tool, the authors also present a method to minimize the state-space of the obtained supervisors with respect to the control actions generated at each state of the controller. This minimization methodology can be used for the size reduction of controllers, while preserving their deadlock-free characteristics and the behaviors they enforce.

The fourth chapter "**Deadlock Avoidance and Dynamic Routing Flexibility in Automated Manufacturing Systems**" by Mark Lawley, Purdue University, USA, addresses the deadlock avoidance issues in automated manufacturing systems

(AMS) with dynamic routing flexibility. Dynamic routing arises from three types of system flexibility: machine flexibility, sequence flexibility, and central buffering. Machine flexibility occurs when an operation can be performed on more than one machine. Even though the sequence of operations might be fixed, machine flexibility can generate a large number of potential routes for a part to follow. Sequence flexibility occurs when the set of operations specified by a part's process plan is not completely ordered. Sequence flexibility can also spawn a large number of potential routes for a part to follow. Finally, automated manufacturing systems sometimes use central buffers to alleviate the blocking that occurs when parts finished on one machine await allocation of buffer space on the next. Under central buffering, such parts typically have the option of moving to and awaiting their next allocation at a centrally located buffer, if the buffer is not full. In each of these three cases, the supervisory controller is faced with the task of allocating resources among competing parts when each part has allocation alternatives. These additional degrees of allocation freedom can affect the safety characteristics of the system and must be taken into account when developing deadlock avoidance logic. This chapter summarizes the author's deadlock avoidance research for systems with these types of flexibilities. It discusses the interaction between allocation flexibility and the complexity of safety, presents sub-optimal deadlock avoidance policies for these highly flexible systems, and discusses cases where optimal deadlock avoidance is computationally tractable.

The fifth chapter "**Digraph-Based Techniques for Deadlock Resolution in Automated Manufacturing Systems**" by M. P. Fanti, B. Maione, G. Maione, and B. Turchiano, Politecnico di Bari, Bari, Italy, describes digraph-based methods to face deadlock in AMS. Compared with another popular method, Petri nets, digraphs lend themselves to represent the interactions between jobs and resources (resources allocated to and required by jobs) in an easy and immediate way. Digraphs, indeed, allow a formal characterization of deadlock conditions useful to derive several solving methodologies. The chapter considers different approaches to facing deadlock, consisting of detection/recovery methods and avoidance techniques. Detection/recovery methods require a low computation burden in the detection phase and a dedicated buffer to activate the recovery phase. On the contrary, avoidance techniques need no dedicated hardware and carry out a feedback event-control of the system. The proposed approaches differ in complexity, in the degree of restriction they impose on the free assignment of the system resources to jobs and, consequently, in the production performances they allow. Finally, the proposed framework can be used to deal with the situations in which the deadlock avoidance approaches can be applied in decentralized form, i.e., by partitioning an AMS into subsystems, each controlled by a local controller independently of the other ones. This is particularly useful in cellular manufacturing systems to establish the cells that can be locally controlled and the ones requiring a centralized approach to deadlock avoidance.

The sixth chapter "**Deadlock-Free Supervisory Control for Assembly and Disassembly Systems**" by Elzbieta Roszkowska, Wroclaw University of Technology, Poland deals with a class of processes modeling streams of materials that can join and split, such as in assembly/disassembly systems, at group transport and then individual part processing, or in processes that require temporary meeting of independently routed components. As each such process can be viewed as a set of interacting sequential processes, the processes considered here are called compound processes. By modeling the system dynamics with Petri nets, this chapter investigates the supervisor design problem for ensuring deadlock-free process flow. The required concurrency and use of the same resources by component sequential processes may lead to a compound process that is not realizable. Therefore this chapter presents a model that allows more valuable resources, such as machines, to be released directly after an operation is completed. This is due to the fact that the buffer space required for the products of an operation is allocated together with the machine. Thus, from the viewpoint of deadlock-free process control, we can neglect the problem of machine allocation and only focus on the flow of materials among the buffers. The supervision problem is solved through a joint approach to establishing for each buffer a minimal sufficient capacity and constraining the system dynamics. The resultant supervisor is given in the form of a function that states whether a particular enabled transition or event can take place at a particular state. The underlying idea is that a buffer reserve changes dynamically to ensure that component sequential processes that need to be synchronized can await each other without inducing a deadlock.

The seventh chapter **"Deadlock Avoidance Algorithms and Implementation: A Matrix-Based Approach"** by Jose Mireles, Jr., Universidad Autónoma de Ciudad Juárez, Juarez Chihuahua, México, Frank Lewis, University of Texas at Arlington, Ft. Worth, TX, USA, Ayla Gürel, Eastern Mediterranean University, Famagusta, Turkey, and Stjepan Bogdan, University of Zagreb, Zagreb, Croatia, presents the development of a matrix-based deadlock avoidance supervisory controller for Discrete Event (DE) Systems. The DE controller uses a rule-based matrix dispatching formulation. This matrix formulation makes it direct to write down the DE controller from standard manufacturing tools such as the Bill of Materials or the assembly tree. It is shown that the DE controller's matrix form equations plus its Petri Net marking transition equation together provide a complete dynamical description of DES. This provides a new method for Computer Simulation of DES. On-line deadlock-free firing rules are implemented by the DE matrix controller by performing circular wait analysis for possible deadlock situations, i.e., analyzing the so-called critical siphons and critical subsystems and presence of bottleneck resources. The chapter introduces a matrix-formulated analysis method to identify bottleneck and key resources shared among circular resource loops that lead to deadlock situations. The resultant matrix algorithms are implemented on a robotic Intelligent Material Handling (IMH) cell and its technical information includes the development of the deadlock-free controller in LabVIEW-a graphical programming language developed by National Instruments.

The eighth chapter "**Deadlock Detection and Prevention of Automated Manufacturing Systems Using Petri Nets and Siphons**" by MuDer Jeng, National Taiwan Ocean University, Taiwan, ROC, and Xiaolan Xie, INRIA, Metz, France, discusses Petri net siphon-based approaches for detecting and preventing deadlocks in AMS. Siphons, also named deadlock in some literature, are an important concept in characterizing the deadlock in Petri nets. First, the chapter presents the siphon-based deadlock analysis of AMS modelled by Petri nets. It generalizes the well-known Commoner condition and exploits the notion of potential deadlocks, which are siphons that eventually become unmarked. The chapter then presents a linear programming-based sufficient condition under which a siphon is not a potential deadlock. Using the new sufficient condition, a mathematical programming approach and a mixed-integer programming approach are proposed for checking Petri nets and structurally bounded Petri nets without explicitly generating siphons. The chapter presents stronger results that can be obtained for certain Petri net classes of AMS. These classes of Petri nets include the classical one, asymmetric-choice nets, and some recently proposed classes, e.g., augmented marked graphs, S^3PR, RCN merged nets, ERCN merged nets, and PNR. The chapter finally presents an iterative deadlock prevention approach for S^3PR and discusses some ideas for future research concerning deadlock prevention of other net classes.

The ninth chapter "**Siphon-Based Characterization of Liveness and Liveness-Enforcing Supervision for Sequential Resource Allocation Systems**" by Spyros Reveliotis, School of Industrial & Systems Engineering, Georgia Institute of Technology, Atlanta, GA, USA, deals with one of the most interesting developments from, both, a theoretical and a practical perspective, in the emerging theory of resource allocation systems (RAS), i.e., the characterization of the non-liveness of many RAS classes through the Petri net (PN)-based structural object of empty, or more generally, deadly marked siphon. The work presented in this chapter seeks to develop a general theory that provides a unifying framework for all the relevant existing results, and reveals the key structures and mechanisms that connect the RAS non-liveness to the concept of deadly marked and in certain cases, empty siphon. In this capacity, the presented results allow also the extension of the siphon-based characterization of non-liveness to broader RAS classes, and provide a clear and intuitive explanation for the limitations of the approach. The last part of the work discusses how the derived structural characterization of RAS non-liveness can be combined with some algorithms for detecting empty or deadly marked siphons in a given PN marking, in order to develop analytical liveness sufficiency tests and systematic procedures for the design of liveness-enforcing supervisors (LES). The related computational cost issues are discussed.

The tenth chapter "**Elementary Siphons of Petri Nets for Efficient Deadlock Control**" by Zhiwu Li, Xidian University, Xi'an, China, and MengChu Zhou, New Jersey Institute of Technology, Newark, NJ, USA, prevents a recently proposed novel siphon idea, i.e., elementary and redundant siphons. The latter is linearly dependent upon the former. This provides a new avenue to achieve their non-emptiness control by controlling only the elementary siphons, thus obtaining the desired liveness property of Petri nets. The chapter proves that the number of elementary siphons is bounded by the number of the transitions in a Petri net. It further establishes the results on the siphon control by adding monitors and related arcs to only elementary siphons. The proposed elementary siphon theory is then used to construct two novel deadlock prevention policies that are applied to the S^3PR of two FMS. The chapter illustrates their significant advantages over the previous methods that have to deal with an exponentially growing number of minimal siphons when they add monitors and arcs for the same type of Petri nets.

The eleventh chapter "**Resource-Oriented Petri Nets in Deadlock Prevention and Avoidance**" by Naiqi Wu, Guangdong University of Technology, Guangzhou, China, and MengChu Zhou, New Jersey Institute of Technology, Newark, NJ, USA, develops a finite capacity Petri net called Colored Resource-Oriented Petri Net (CROPN) for the problem of deadlock avoidance in AMS. This model is very concise and relates deadlock to a full circuit in the model. By using the model for AMS in which each machine has an input (output) buffer, this chapter presents necessary and sufficient conditions for deadlock-free and deadlock avoidance policy. This policy is a maximal permission policy. A maximal permission policy in deadlock avoidance may allow blocking to occur in the rule-based scheduling environment. Based on the CROPN, this chapter relaxes the maximal permission policy and presents a new control policy called L-policy by using a sufficient condition so as to reduce blocking. Their applications to a medium size automated manufacturing system are presented. The simulation results illustrate the significant gain in system performance by using the L-policy over a maximally permissive policy under the rule-based scheduling environment. Finally, the concept of CROPN is applied to and the related theory is developed for AGV systems that allow both uni- and bi-directional lanes for deadlock avoidance. One-step look-ahead control policies are presented for such systems.

The twelfth chapter "**The Effect of Modeling and Control Techniques on the Management of Deadlocks in FMS**" by Luca Ferrarini and Luigi Piroddi, Politecnico di Milano, Milano, Italy addresses several deadlock control policies and their performance when the time is considered. To avoid deadlock in FMS, it is necessary to adopt suitable control policies which limit the resource allocation in the system, thus affecting the overall system performance. In spite of the interesting results obtained in the research world, traditionally relegated to untimed models, the problem of deadlock is still conceived by practitioners as a real-time problem, or as a problem due to a bad structured system layout and global organization. However, it is definitely a control problem that can be solved precisely and elegantly from a control system theory perspective, keeping performance optimality in mind also. In the present paper, the authors try to combine the two perspectives, considering both the deadlock avoidance control problem and a more pragmatic, performance-oriented point of view. In particular, the problem addressed here is that of evaluating and comparing the performance of deadlock avoidance control policies applied to FMS, taking into account some of the most common in the literature. This is done considering, first, timed and untimed models, and, second, models of uncontrolled systems, models of systems controlled with imperfect deadlock avoidance algorithms, and deadlock-free controlled systems. Through the definition of suitable indices and reference models, and of suitable analysis and simulation approaches, it is shown how it is possible to design appropriate control schemes tailored to specific purposes. Two different application examples are analyzed in detail, with the help of a commercial simulation package (Arena). Finally, an adaptive algorithm that can learn from system evolution to avoid deadlock is illustrated.

The thirteenth chapter "**Deadlock Characterization and Resolution in Interconnection Networks**" by Timothy Mark Pinkston, University of Southern California, Los Angeles, CA, USA, presents the deadlock modeling and resolution methods for high-performance interconnection networks. Such networks comprise the communication backbone in digital systems at several system levels. For example, at the higher system levels, local-area networks are used in clusters of PCs, networks of workstations and other distributed processing systems which serve as cost/performance-effective alternatives to tightly coupled massively parallel processing systems. At lower levels, networks-on-chip are used to overcome many of the performance limitations of bus-based systems at the chip level. Parallel computing and communication systems require high-performance communication services with high reliability, availability and dependability. The performance of the interconnection network is measured, in part, by packet delivery time from source to destination (i.e., latency) and by the number of packets delivered per unit time (i.e., throughput). In essence, a high-performance network allows the maximum number of packets to make forward progress to their destinations in minimal time. Likewise, the reliability, availability and dependability of a network equally impact the overall "goodness" quality of a system. These attributes are measured, in part, by the network's ability to remain up and running at near normal levels even when unexpected events occur. This chapter presents how various network parameters influence the formation of message blocking and deadlocks in interconnection networks. A model of resource allocations and dependencies is described which allows various types of message blocking to be described precisely, including deadlock. Ways in which a network's susceptibility to deadlock can be reduced are given, and guidelines for designing networks which maximize routing flexibility and resource utilization are also provided.

The fourteenth chapter "**Deadlock Models for a Multi-Service Medium Access Protocol Employing a Slotted Aloha or Q-ary Tree Based Signaling Channel**" by Milosh Vladimir Ivanovich, Telstra Research Laboratories, Melbourne, Australia, presents the deadlock issues in Medium Access Control (MAC) protocols. Such protocols are used for cable modem hybrid fibre/coaxial (HFC) networks, as well as wireless ATM networks. They often utilize a collision-based capacity request signaling channel. This signaling channel typically relies on either the Slotted Aloha or Q-ary Tree multiaccess principles. This chapter studies in detail the performance of a p-persistence Slotted Aloha contention resolution algorithm (CRA), subject to extreme inter-station correlation, by means of a discrete-time Markov chain analysis. It examines, by simulation, the performance of a Q-ary Tree CRA called msSTART (Multi-slot Stack Random Access Algorithm), which was proposed for use in the IEEE 802.14 HFC standard. The performance of the two types of CRA is discussed and contrasted, under what the IEEE 802.14 working group has termed the "disaster scenario", where the entire station population simultaneously requests capacity after a neighborhood-wide power failure, for example. The conditions leading to a deadlock are examined in detail–deadlock being a situation where the time to collision resolution becomes unacceptably high and the system is practically unstable. This chapter analyses several disaster scenario deadlock models and studies the effect of channel error probability, signaling traffic load, and the contention resolution algorithm used. Key factors of the CRAs are identified, with the finding that it is the collision rate but not channel errors, which more strongly governs throughput performance. Further, it is demonstrated that the introduction of an effective priority scheme does not have a significant impact on the stability of the Q-ary Tree based CRA. Three signaling channel schemes introduced in this chapter provide insight into the stability of the MAC after the implementation of priority for different traffic classes. This chapter finds that of the three schemes evaluated, the full Contention Mini-Slot (CMS) sharing scheme employing multiple CMSs per data region extends a MAC protocol's usable load region the furthest.

The fifteenth chapter "**Deadlock-Free TCP Over High-Speed Internet**" by Rocky K. C. Chang, The Hong Kong Polytechnic University, Kowloon, Hong Kong, Ho Y. Chan, University of Southern California, Los Angeles, CA, USA, and Adam W. Yeung, Cisco Systems Inc., San Jose, CA, USA, explores the deadlock phenomena in Transport Control Protocol (TCP) that dominates Internet traffic and presents several algorithms to handle them. A throughout deadlock is reported when TCP is operated on high-speed networks. This deadlock occurs when the Silly Window Syndrome Avoidance Algorithms (SWSAAs) are turned on in both sender and receiver, and the send-receive socket buffer sizes fall in a certain region. The main factor contributing to this problem is that the connection's Maximum Segment Size (MSS), which is used by the SWSAAs, is no longer small when compared with the send-receive socket buffer sizes. Consequently, a TCP sender may not able to compose a MSS segment if its send buffer size is not large enough; similarly, a TCP receiver may not be able to acknowledge since the amount of data received is not large enough when compared with MSS. The result is a deadlock, which can be resolved only by a receiver's 200-ms delayed acknowledgment timer. This chapter proposes a new Adaptive Acknowledgment Algorithm (AAA) to eliminate throughput deadlock while avoiding SWS. Unlike the current delayed acknowledgment strategy, AAA does not rely on the exact value of MSS and the receive buffer size to determine the acknowledgment threshold. This chapter shows that AAA is able to eliminate all throughput deadlocks in a non-congested network. Moreover, to further enhance AAA, it introduces a slow-start-like mechanism in the receiver to account for network congestion, leading to an algorithm called Congestion-Sensitive AAA

(CS-AAA). Extensive simulation results support that CS-AAA's throughput performance significantly exceeds that of AAA, especially when the send buffer size is relatively large.

The sixteenth chapter "**Deadlock Resolution in Large-Scale Internet Computing**" by Jonghun Park, Seoul National University, Seoul, Korea, addresses the deadlock resolution issues in the context of Internet computing. The Internet has revolutionized the way computing is carried out by providing a new medium of information highway. For instance, with the emerging Internet computing infra-structures such as Grid, Peer-to-Peer, and Web services, it has become possible to deploy applications that support various Internet-wide collaborations. Yet, as Internet computing is becoming popular, it also presents a number of new challenges in coordinating resource usage. In particular, the resource allocation protocol that provides clear directives on the acquisition of shared resources is complicated by the inherent characteristics of Internet computing, such as (i) the large-scale application deployment, (ii) the need for co-allocation of distributed resources that span multiple administrative domains, (iii) the lack of means for exchanging information between the independent Internet applications, and finally (iv) the availability of functionally redundant resources. The implication is that the resource allocation method must be decentralized, scalable, and most importantly it should be able to allocate the required resources with minimum time and cost. Recognizing the need for a systematic approach to the resource allocation for large-scale Internet computing, this chapter presents a new scalable resource allocation protocol that can address the characteristics of current Internet computing practices. The proposed protocol is free from deadlock and livelock, and can effectively exploit the available alternative resource co-allocation schemes. Experimental results demonstrate that the proposed protocol yields a significant performance improvement over the existing deadlock prevention protocol. It promises therefore a great future for its eventual deployment.

The seventeenth chapter "**Models used in Static Analysis for Deadlocks of Ada Tasking Programs**" by Mikko Tiusanen, Tampere University of Technology, Tampere, Finland and Tadao Murata, University of Illinois at Chicago, USA, ad-dresses the deadlock modeling and analysis issues encountered in concurrent pro-grams written in Ada. Concurrent programming languages allow software engi-neers to structure a program into smaller communicating entities, called *tasks* in Ada, each with an independent thread of control. With this facility also comes the responsibility of avoiding errors such as deadlocks. Static analysis has been sug-gested as a solution for this: the programs written are analyzed to detect possibilities of deadlocks. This chapter surveys some models that have been used to support static analysis for deadlock detection of Ada tasking programs. The models include Task Flowgraphs (Taylor), Task Interaction Graphs (Clarke and Long), Petri Nets, and Constrained Expressions (Avrunin, Dillon, et al.). These models are illustrated using a common running example to find deadlocks. We shall also consider process algebra on a general level. All the models discussed are shown to be basically equivalent in this context by displaying their relationships to finite state automata.

The equivalence not only provides insight into the models and their relationships, but also gives an opportunity to use the best of the results of any one of the formalisms in any of the others.

The last chapter "**Deadlock Handling in Database Systems**" by Mathias Weske, Hasso Plattner Institute for Software Systems Engineering, Potsdam, Germany, discusses the synchronization of concurrent transactions in database systems. The synchronization using the well-known 2-phase-locking protocol may result in waiting conditions involving database transactions and, in case of circular waiting conditions, deadlock. All transactions involved in a deadlock come to a halt, a clearly very undesirable situation. This chapter characterizes the deadlock problem in database systems using a set of generic deadlock conditions. It shows that a set of transactions encounter a deadlock situation if these conditions are met. This discusses the algorithms based on the following approaches, i.e., deadlock prevention, deadlock avoidance, and deadlock detection. The deadlock detection in distributed database systems is treated in depth. In distributed database systems transactions may span multiple sites. Hence, distributed deadlocks cannot be detected using local knowledge of one site only; on the contrary, sites have to communicate according to deadlock detection algorithms to identify distributed deadlock cycles and to resolve them to allow transactions to resume operation. In this chapter, the deadlock problem in distributed database systems is introduced, and a set of algorithms to detect and resolve distributed deadlocks are presented.

The Audience

The major utility of this book to readers is to serve as a comprehensive reference book that covers what they need for the research, development, and implementation of deadlock-free computer-integrated systems. The readers' needs may include: modeling methods, methods and algorithms for engineering applications, industrial benchmark studies, and research ideas in the deadlock studies for computer-integrated systems. The book is primarily written for researchers and developers in the area of computer-integrated systems especially computer-integrated manufacturing, intelligent transportation systems, operating systems, computer networks, distributed database systems, and concurrent software systems.

The Acknowledgments

The editing of this volume was inspired and assisted by many scholars and specialists working in this area. We would like to thank each of them for intellectual exchanges, valuable suggestions, critical reviews, and kind encouragement. First, we want to thank all the contributing authors who are the subject experts from 14 different countries. It would not be possible without their technical contributions and timely delivery of their chapters. Second, we would like to thank Dr. Robert Kelly, Professor of Electrical and Computer Systems Engineering, Rensselaer Polytechnic Institute; Dr. S. Ramaswamy, Chair of Computer Science Department,

Tennessee Technological University; Dr. Ichiro Suzuki, Professor of Electrical Engineering and Computer Science, University of Wisconsin-Milwaukee; and Dr. Jiacun Wang, Scientific Staff Member, Nortel Networks for their valuable review comments on the book proposal. Also, we would like to thank many pioneers in the subject areas including Dr. N. Viswanadham, Professor of Mechanical and Production Engineering, National University of Singapore; Dr. Yadati Narahari, Professor of Computer Science and Automation, Indian Institute of Science; Dr. Kurt Lautenbach, Professor of Computer Science, University Koblenz; Germany; Dr. Alan Desrochers, Professor of Electrical and Computer Systems Engineering, Rensselaer Polytechnic Institute; and Dr. Frank DiCesare, Emeritus Professor of Electrical and Computer Systems Engineering, Rensselaer Polytechnic Institute. We would thank Mr. Jeff Hall, Production Editor, Ms. Jessica Vakili, Project Coordinator of this book; Dr. Fei-Yue Wang, Professor of Systems and Industrial Engineering, The University of Arizona; and Mr. Zhigang Wang, a doctoral candidate of New Jersey Institute of Technology for their kind help. Finally, we would like to acknowledge the partial research support from New Jersey State Commission on Science and Technology via Multi-lifecycle Engineering Center; New Jersey State via "New Jersey Information Technology Opportunities for the Workforce, Education and Research (NJ I-TOWER)" program; the National Outstanding Young Scientist Research Award from the National Natural Science Foundation of China under Grant No. 60228004; the Key Project on Networked Systems from the National Natural Science Foundation under Grant No.60334020; a Shandong 863 project from Shandong Provincial Government under Grant No. 030335; and a 973 project from the Ministry of Science and Technology of China under Grant No. 2002CB312200.

MengChu Zhou
zhou@njit.edu and mengchu@ieee.org

Maria Pia Fanti
fanti@poliba.it

1

Introduction to Deadlock Research in Computer-integrated Systems

Maria Pia Fanti
Department of Elettrotecnica ed Elettronica, Politecnico di Bari, Bari, Italy.

MengChu Zhou
Department of Electrical and Computer Engineering, New Jersey Institute of Technology, Newark, NJ, USA

1.1 INTRODUCTION

Computer-integrated systems are characterized by a structure in which a set of executing processes share (or compete for) a set of resources, for example, processes running in a multitask operating system, transactions in distributed database systems, concurrent software systems and computer networks, parts produced by automated manufacturing systems, and vehicles competing for the same path in transportation systems. The interacting parts and shared resources are characterized as a resource allocation system that can lead to problems that the isolated execution of a task does not have. Among these problems, we consider deadlock situations: deadlock is a phenomenon in which a system or a part of it remains indefinitely blocked and a set of jobs cannot terminate its task. To demonstrate this condition, we consider a simple and intuitive example of traffic flow along the edges of a square, depicted in Figure 1.1. The boxes represent the cars and the arrows the directions in which they have to move. In this situation, each car of the displayed set is blocked by another car in the same set, occupying the space that it requires. Hence, this situation represents a deadlock.

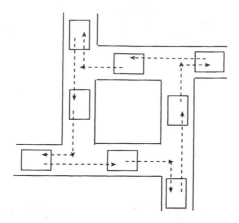

Figure 1.1 : Deadlock condition in traffic flow

Deadlock is a logical condition arising in Discrete Event Dynamic Systems (DEDS) [4] and it is caused by an inappropriate allocation of resources to concurrent executing processes. Deadlock is first addressed by computer scientists developing resource allocation logic in operating systems [7,21,23,25,29]. In particular, Coffman, Elphick and Shoshani [7] give four conditions that must be held for a deadlock to occur:

(i)   "Mutual exclusion," i.e., tasks claim exclusive control of the resource they require;

(ii)   "No preemption," i.e., resources cannot be forcibly removed from the tasks holding them until the resources are used to completion;

(iii) "Wait for condition," i.e., processes hold resources allocated to them, while waiting for additional ones; and

(iv)   "Circular wait," i.e., a circular claim of tasks exists, such that each task holds one or more resources that are being requested by the next task in the claim.

Solving the deadlock problem for generic concurrent systems is a very complicated task, and there is no general solution. Therefore researchers have concentrated on solving the problem for classes of systems coming from specific application domains. Here, as in [36,55,56], we characterize a system of interacting processes with shared resources as a Resource Allocation System (RAS), i.e., a set of concurrently running processes requiring shared resources. Moreover, we suppose that the number of resources in a RAS is limited and resources are characterized as reusable, i.e., their allocation/deallocation to a requesting process does not affect their quality and quantity. In particular, reusable resources can model physical objects (like machines, robots, drives, etc.) which are shared by processes (like parts, vehicles, programs, data, etc.). Moreover, the use of resources is supposed to be sequential, i.e., each process has to acquire resources in a predefined or partially predefined order. The following taxonomy has been introduced [46,55] on the basis of a resource allocation request structure:

(1)   Single Unit RAS (SU-RAS), i.e., at each step of its processing, a part requires a single unit of a single resource for its successive execution;

(2)   Single Type RAS (ST-RAS), i.e., at each step of its processing, a part requires several units of a single resource;

(3)   Conjunctive RAS (C-RAS), i.e., at each step of its processing, a part requires an arbitrary number of units of each resource from a set of resources; and

(4)   Conjunctive/Disjunctive RAS (CD-RAS), i.e., every process stage poses a finite number of alternative conjunctive-type resource requests.

In the last decade, the deadlock issue has attracted much attention in the context of manufacturing systems. In particular, Automated Manufacturing Systems (AMS) are modern production facilities exhibiting a high degree of resource sharing. An AMS consists of a set of workstations, each one capable of processing parts of different kind according to a prescribed sequence of operations. The concept of agile manufacturing has been introduced to satisfy the demand for low volume and high variety products and requires extending flexibility in production to system configuration and control. Therefore a manufacturing system controller that allocates resources in real time without causing deadlock plays a crucial role. In such a context, the strategies for solving deadlock problems are introduced ad hoc and differ from those used in computer operating systems. Indeed, many results on deadlock characterization and resolution have been developed for AMS identified as SU-RAS. More recently, researchers have also addressed the problem in the context of the more general classes of C-RAS and CD-RAS. Modeling an AMS as different classes of RAS, they characterize deadlock and introduce a large number of control strategies. Even if such deadlock resolution policies are oriented toward AMS, they can be applied in different contexts such as transportation systems, railway systems, automated guided systems, storage/retrieval systems.

The aim of this chapter is to present a structured classification of the work about deadlock problems in RAS with particular attention to AMS. The rationality of this choice is the large number of papers in this context and the general applicability of the proposed algorithms. A first selection of papers is made on the basis of the model used to describe the RAS and, in particular, the interaction between jobs and resources. Three modeling methods are singled out: digraphs, automata and Petri nets. There is no conclusive argument making evident the superiority of one of these approaches to another. Indeed, each approach has its own advantages and feeds the researches of many authors which have greatly improved the insight into deadlock phenomena. However, this chapter describes in detail only the contributions that are the most relevant and typical in each of the mentioned approaches. Hence, the chapter is a starting point to approach deadlock in particular classes of RAS and a concise summary of the significant results. Moreover, a simple example is used to help readers clarify the presented strategies. Some basic control strategies are briefly exposed and are applied to the considered system, to give a clear idea of the proposed models and approaches. The chapter is organized as follows: Section 1.2 describes the methods to solve deadlock in RAS, Sections 1.3, 1.4 and 1.5 discuss the main deadlock resolution strategies by using digraphs, automata and PN, respectively. Section 1.6 recalls some comparison studies and, finally, Section 1.7 presents the concluding remarks.

1.2 DEADLOCK RESOLUTION STRATEGIES

This section presents in detail the three methodologies for addressing deadlock problems in SU-RAS: *prevention, detection/recovery* and *avoidance* methods. While for computer applications only bounds on the total number of resources required by each process are known, in AMS of the SU-RAS class, a job requires to visit a predictable sequence of resources for processing. More precisely, each part (job or piece) enters the system and follows a specific working procedure (or production sequence), i.e., an ordered or partially ordered succession of resources necessary to provide the scheduled service (buffer spaces, cutting tools, workstations, transportation vehicles, etc.). Consequently, in SU-RAS the first three conditions given by Coffman *et al.* are always satisfied. Indeed, pieces use resources in an exclusive mode; they hold resources while waiting for the next resources specified by their operation sequence and resources cannot be forcibly removed from the pieces utilizing them until operation completion. Hence deadlock is excluded only if the fourth condition, i.e., the circular wait, fails to hold. More precisely, deadlock occurs if a set of parts or jobs are requesting or waiting for resources held by other parts or jobs in the same set.

1.2.1 Deadlock Prevention

Basic strategies for handling deadlocks are to ensure the violation of at least one of the four conditions necessary for deadlock. In particular, *prevention* methods guarantee that necessary conditions for deadlock cannot be simultaneously satisfied at any point of the RAS dynamic. Moreover, prevention constrains system users and imposes a number of restrictions on interactions between processes and resources so that requests leading to deadlock are never executed. Usually, prevention strategies use information about process resource requirements and demand each process to specify all required resources before transactions begin. The simplest means of preventing deadlock is to outlaw concurrency, but such method is overly conservative, generally leading to significantly low utilization of system resources. The state transitions follow the prescribed rules ensuring that the system is prevented from entering a deadly embrace status. For example, consider the AMS in Fig. 1.2, where part 1 has to follow the routing (L/U, WS_1, WS_2, WS_3, L/U) and part 2 follows the route (L/U, WS_4, WS_2, WS_1, L/U). Since the first three conditions given by Coffman *et al.* [7] are verified, deadlock can be prevented only if the "circular wait" condition is broken. Hence, a simple prevention method can allow the production of Parts 1 and 2 in succession, so that two types of pieces cannot be processed simultaneously. Thus parts flow in only one direction and circular wait never occurs. An advantage of the prevention mechanism is that it requires no knowledge of the system state to realize the deadlock-free control, leading to a straightforward often-simple control law. Such laws have been popular in many practical applications.

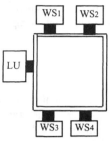

Figure 1.2. A four-workstation AMS.

1.2.2 Deadlock Detection/Recovery

Detection/recovery approaches use a monitoring mechanism for detecting the deadlock occurrence and a resolution procedure for preempting some deadlock resources. When deadlock occurs, the controller detects it and then recovers by terminating some deadlocked processes or by preempting resources from processes. This strategy can in general allow higher resource utilization than a prevention method can offer. It should be used when deadlock is rare and detection and recovery are not expensive and much faster than deadlock is generated.

Consider the previous example. A deadlock detection procedure monitors the system, allows and detects a deadlock occurrence and then a recovery method is employed. For example, suppose that part 1 is in WS_1 and requires WS_2, simultaneously part 2 is in WS_2 and requires WS_1. Such a condition is a deadlock. As a recovery procedure, a central or temporary buffer can be used to accommodate a deadlocked piece so that the system can restart its work.

1.2.3 Deadlock Avoidance

Deadlock avoidance is a strategy that falsifies one or more necessary conditions for deadlock by keeping track of the current state and possible future conditions. This is a dynamic approach that can utilize the knowledge of the current allocation of resources and the future behavior of processes to control the release and acquisition of resources. The main characteristic of the deadlock avoidance strategies is that they work in real time and base the decision on information about the resource status. Indeed, the *state* of a RAS must fully describe the requests and the allocation of the resources at each instant time. Hence, a deadlock controller inhibits or enables events involving resources acquisition or release by using look-ahead procedures so that the system does not reach a deadlock condition. However, to implement a deadlock avoidance algorithm, it is necessary to consider and avoid not only deadlock states but also *unsafe* states, i.e., the states that are not deadlocked but inevitably lead the system to a deadlock. By definition, a state is safe if there exists a sequence of resource acquisition and release operations that allow all the processes in the system to reach completion [3,38,55,56]. Thus, even if deadlock detection can be performed in polynomial time, it is shown that in the general case, the problem of determining the safety of a RAS state is nondeterministic polynomial or NP-complete [2,23,55]. An important consequence is that polynomial deadlock avoidance algorithms must sacrifice flexibility in resource allocation and system performance because they reject some safe state. In particular, Lawley *et al.* [38] single out four properties that a useful deadlock avoidance policy (DAP) must have: (i) correctness: a DAP must guarantee the deadlock-free behavior of the system; (ii) scalability: a DAP must be computationally tractable so that it can be executed in real-time; (iii) operational flexibility: it measures how much a DAP sacrifices system operating flexibility in resource acquisition to achieve scalability; (iv) configurability: a DAP is configurable if the operating constraints that it imposes can be quickly generated for system configurations, i.e., correctness and scalability must be independent of system configuration.

One basic scheme of deadlock avoidance, introduced into the operating system context, is the "banker's algorithm" [21,23]. It manages multiple units of a single resource by requiring that the processes specify their total resource needs at the initiation time. More precisely, the worst case scenario, in which all processes simultaneously require their maximum allowable claims for resources to proceed forward, is assumed. The algorithm refuses the requests of the process that needs resources in excess of the available ones. Such a schema is very simple but it can be too conservative from the resource allocation point of view. Indeed, banker's algorithm does not consider the particular order in which each process acquires and releases resources. Starting from this first procedure, a large number of deadlock avoidance algorithms have been introduced in recent decades to avoid deadlock efficiently. Indeed, deadlock avoidance techniques are considered the most efficient strategies to avoid deadlock in RAS. In particular, deadlock/recovery strategies require continuous monitoring for detecting deadlocks and can lead to a reduction of production rate due to the recovery process. On the other hand, the prevention approaches limit the production flexibility by reducing the variety of the in-process part mix or by imposing the job flow in the same direction. In general, a deadlock avoidance strategy has potential to lead to better resource utilization than a prevention one. A supervisory controller that enables or inhibits the resource allocation in real time can implement each deadlock avoidance policy. When a part is ready to have its next operation performed or to enter the system, the RAS supervisor grants the request. However, the deadlock avoidance policies are different in operational flexibility or complexity and can yield different performance depending on RAS layout.

In any case, whatever may be the technique used to characterize deadlock in RAS, it is necessary to describe the job flow through the system and the dynamic of an allocation/deallocation resource mechanism. Hence, each researcher facing deadlock in RAS, and in particular in AMS, refers to a DEDS model, so that the system state describes the jobs in process, the status of each resource, the interactions between resources and jobs, and the sequence of resources necessary to process each job. The used models can be in the framework of Petri nets, automata and graph theoretic approaches. The following sections discuss the commonly used methods to deal with deadlock problems in AMS characterized as SU-RAS.

1.3 GRAPH THEORETIC APPROACHES

The graphtheoretic approach is a simple and intuitive tool suitable for describing the interactions between jobs and resources [5,14,16,31,32]. This peculiarity allows an efficient deadlock characterization and permits the derivation of detection and avoidance strategies. However, since digraphs are not able to fully model the system dynamics, a Discrete Event System (DES) model is necessary to complete the system behavior description. Among the digraph representations proposed in literature, we describe only one approach based on digraphs. Indeed, the other approaches use similar tools and obtain comparable results.

1.3.1 Definitions and Main Results

In the following, a generic resource is indicated by r_i, with i=1,2,...,R, where R is the number of resources in the system. Moreover, symbol $C(r_i)$ stands for the capacity of r_i, i.e., the maximum number of parts that can contemporaneously hold such a resource. In this way, the complete resource set of the AMS is $R=\{r_i, i=1,2,...,R\}$. To be processed, each job must receive service by some resources from R, in a specified order. Let **w** be such sequence of resources (i.e., the *working procedure*), while let $W=\{\mathbf{w}\}$ indicate the set of all the available working procedures necessary to process the jobs. The considered AMS, processing the set J of jobs, satisfies the following assumptions: (i) working procedures are deterministic, allowing no alternatives for each operation; (ii) no preemption is allowed; (iii) each part can be processed by only one machine at any instant of time, i.e., SU-RAS.

On the basis of graphtheoretic approaches, Wysk, Yang, and Joshi [61], Kumaran, Chang, Cho and Wysk [32], Cho, Kumaran and Wysk [5] and Fanti *et al.* [11,14,16] present algorithms for deadlock detection and avoidance. The important definition and notation on digraphs are summarized in Appendix 1.

Wysk, Yang, and Joshi [61] introduce a graph theoretic approach to characterize deadlock in AMS where each machine can perform only one operation at any instant of time, i.e., $C(r_i)=1$ for $i=1,2,\ldots,R$. In this framework, deadlock is defined as a circular wait situation between several machines and can be shown that the total number of deadlock possibilities for any given manufacturing system is $\sum_{i=2}^{R} \binom{R}{i}$. The authors use a digraph whose nodes represent resources and edges represent all possible transitions of the parts in a system. Moreover, they state that a cycle (or circuit) formed by the part routing is a necessary condition for a deadlock. To better characterize deadlock with necessary and sufficient conditions, Kumaran, Chang, Cho and Wysk [32], Cho, Kumaran and Wysk [5] and Fanti, Maione, Mascolo and Turchiano [14] introduce two digraphs describing the current interactions between jobs and resources. The first digraph (named *system status graph* in [5] and *working procedure digraph* in [14]) synthetically represents all the possible resource allocations. More precisely, the nodes of the digraph represent the resource set of the system and the edge set corresponds to all possible transitions of the parts in the system in the status graph and of the part that can possibly enter the system in the working procedure digraph. The second digraph describes the current interactions between in-process jobs and resources (here named *transition digraph*). It depicts only the next destination of all the parts in the system and is updated dynamically as the system operating condition changes. Hence, the necessary and sufficient condition characterizing deadlock is proved [5,14], i.e., the transition digraph exhibits a cycle. Some more general results are proved in [16] where the resources can serve more jobs at a time. In such a case, it is shown that a deadlock state is associated to a particular strong component of the transition digraph (named *Maximal-weight Zero-outdegree Strong Component-MZSC*). Hence, in this framework a deadlock is a circular wait condition that blocks indefinitely the process of a set of jobs in the system. Obviously, this definition provides for the possibility that the jobs not involved in the deadlock can end their process routes. An example of the system status graph and transition digraph is reported in the following.

Table 1.1. Routes associated with the two in-process jobs.

Jobs	Working procedures
j_1	$\mathbf{w_1}=(r_1, r_2, r_3)$
j_2	$\mathbf{w_2}=(r_3, r_4, r_2, r_1)$

Example 1. A four-workstation AMS with in-process jobs.

Consider the system shown by Figure 1.2. Denote workstation WSi by r_i, $i=1,\ldots,4$. Each resource can process only a job at a time. The resource set is denoted by $R=\{r_1, r_2, r_3, r_4\}$. Table 1.1 defines the working procedures of two in-process parts: j_1 and j_2. Figure 1.3(a) describes the system status graph $D=(N,E)$ where N is the set of nodes corresponding to the resource set $R=\{r_1, r_2, r_3, r_4\}$ and E is the set of edges representing the set of transitions of all jobs in the system. Each node is labeled as (r_i,b) where b represents the machine status: b=j if workstation r_i is occupied by part j, b=0 if r_i is empty. Each edge in E is labeled by e(j,k) where j represents the part identifier and k the transition number of part j or the k-th step in its route. For example, in Figure 1.3(a), label (r_1,1) implies that r_1 is occupied by part 1 while (r_2,0) means that r_2 is empty. In terms of edges e(1,1) represents the first transition of part 1 and e(1,2) represents the second transition of part 1. Figure 1.3(b) illustrates the system status containing only the next destination. Figure 1.3(c) shows a deadlock: job 1 occupies r_1 and requires r_2, and job 2 occupies r_2 and requires r_1.

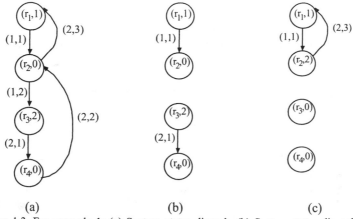

(a)   (b)   (c)

Figure 1.3. For example 1: (a) System status digraph; (b) System status digraph with just next destinations (transition digraph) and (c) Transition digraph exhibiting a deadlock.

From the computational complexity point of view, finding a cycle takes at most $O(|N|+|E|)$ time [52] on a given graph where $|X|$ stands for the cardinality of set X. Consequently, the deadlock detection and recovery schemes introduced in [5,11,14,32] work in polynomial time. Considering that the events important to characterize deadlock occur whenever a job acquires and/or releases a resource, the following events are able to modify the system status graph: (i) a job enters the system, (ii) a job moves from a machine to another, and (iii) a part leaves the system. In order to perform a deadlock detection recovery procedure, the system controller checks if a finished part is involved in a deadlock. If this is the case, the controller moves the part to a special storage buffer and then sequentially moves the other parts. When the deadlock has been solved, i.e., a part leaves a resource involved in the circular wait condition, the job in the storage buffer can be moved to the next machine in its route.

1.3.2 Deadlock Avoidance Policies (DAP)

More efficient strategies based on digraphs are DAPs. In this case a supervisory controller checks for a deadlock before a part moves to the next destination or enters the system. More precisely, when an event has to occur, the controller answers the following question by using a look-ahead procedure of one step: if it happens, will the next state be a deadlock? To answer the question, the supervisor builds the new transition digraph associated with the system state obtained after the event occurrence and checks for a deadlock condition. If the updated transition digraph does not exhibit a deadlock, the controller enables the event. On the contrary, the event is inhibited. This DAP is based on a look-ahead of one step and inhibits an event if and only if (iff) it leads to a deadlock at the next step. As previously pointed out, such a policy can be performed in polynomial time. However, the described DAP can lead the system to unsafe states called impending part flow deadlock states [5]. In such states, immediate transitions of a part are possible, but the system (or a portion of the system) will inevitably terminate in a deadlock after a finite number of transitions or events. The following example illustrates such a situation.

Example 2. A four-workstation AMS with three in-process jobs.

Consider the system described in Example 1. Suppose that it is at such a state that three jobs are in it: j_1, j_2, and j_3. Moreover, the following routes are associated to each job, (r_1, r_2, r_3), (r_3, r_4, r_2, r_1), and (r_4, r_2, r_1), respectively. The transition digraph shown in Figure 1.4 exhibits an impending part flow deadlock. Indeed if j_1 acquires r_2, then r_2, r_3 and r_4 will be in deadlock. On the other hand, if j_3 acquires r_2, then r_1 and r_2 will be in deadlock. In this condition the system is not in a deadlock state, but it will evolve into a deadly embrace in the next step. Such a situation must be avoided.

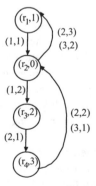

Figure 1.4. System status digraph exhibiting an impending system deadlock.

Unfortunately, impending part flow deadlocks are difficult to detect because it is necessary to explore all the routes of the parts in a system. Indeed, the approaches to solve a deadlock avoidance problem either do not guarantee that the system will never enter deadlock or impending part flow deadlock, or if such a guarantee is provided, it is obtained at excessive computation cost (the required computation is exponential in the size of a RAS configuration). To address this problem, Cho, Kumaran and Wysk [5] present a heuristic procedure verifying, in polynomial time, if there exists an impending part flow deadlock at each event occurrence. The procedure is based on the consideration that impending part flow deadlock occurs because of interactions among cycles having only one node in common. However, the procedure performs a complete look-ahead of the assigned routes and can be tedious and computationally very complex when the number of parts and machines is large.

To overcome this difficulty, Fanti *et al.* [14,16] characterize a particular case of impending part flow deadlock, the Second-Level Deadlock (SLD). The SLD is not a circular wait even if it necessarily evolves into a deadlock in the next step. By determining necessary and sufficient conditions that characterize an SLD occurrence, they prove that the maximally permissive deadlock avoidance policy can be performed in polynomial time by a one step look-ahead strategy if an SLD cannot occur. Moreover, some deadlock avoidance strategies are defined for SU-RAS and are extended to more complex systems including cellular manufacturing [17] and AMS providing assembly operations [18].

Lawley [39,40] uses a digraph named *resource allocation graph* to detect deadlock in $SU^{(n)}$-RAS, which assumes that parts make disjunctive requests at each step of their processing sequences. In other words, $SU^{(n)}$-RAS represents AMS with flexible routing, i.e., every operation of every part type can be performed by a machine in a set of n elements. We do not describe in detail this digraph because it is similar to the transition digraph and the author reaches a similar characterization of deadlock. Moreover, Lawley also establishes the correctness of deadlock avoidance methods for systems with flexible routing and identifies special structures that make the optimally flexible deadlock avoidance algorithm computationally tractable [39].

Finally, a deadlock problem is investigated in [20] using graphs in automated tool sharing systems where different machines use the same tool by automatically transferring them from machine to machine in AMS. A tool allocation graph is defined to provide a compact and precise way to represent tool allocation and request. Moreover, detection and deadlock avoidance policies are proposed for systems with arbitrary tool sequences.

1.4 AUTOMATA APPROACHES

Supervisory control of AMS is a growing area of manufacturing research. One of its essential tasks is to guarantee deadlock-free operation. As an important and efficient formal description of AMS behavior, Finite State Automata are adopted to establish new deadlock avoidance control techniques [33-40,55,56]. In their pioneering work, Reveliotis and Ferreira [55] propose an analytical framework to design deadlock avoidance policies for a subclass of Resource Allocation Systems (SU-RAS). They describe the AMS as a finite state automaton model with static routing. The events of the automaton are: (i) loading a new job; (ii) advancing a partial process job, and (iii) unloading a finished part. The state of the automaton is defined as a vector $\mathbf{q}=[\mathbf{q}_1...\mathbf{q}_k...\mathbf{q}_W]$ where the components of $\mathbf{q}_k$ correspond to the distinct job stages of the k-th working procedure, i.e., $\mathbf{q}_k(h)$ is equal to the number of jobs executing the h-th stage of the k-th working procedure. Assume that L_t is the sum of the lengths of all the working procedures, and $\mathbf{q}$ is a vector of L_t elements. Moreover, the initial and final states correspond to the state $\mathbf{q}_0$ in which the AMS is empty of jobs. The AMS state safety is characterized with the aid of an automata state transition diagram. Therefore, in order to avoid deadlock in the least restrictive way, the system operation should be confined to the maximal communicating set of states, containing $\mathbf{q}_0$. The novelty of the state safety decision problem presented in [55] and in the subsequent work [36-38,56] is that it serves as a framework for the analysis of the correctness of a certain class of deadlock avoidance policies. This class of policies can be formulated as a set of inequalities, which constrain the allocation of system resources at any single instance:

$$\mathbf{A}\,\mathbf{q} \leq \mathbf{f}$$

where $\mathbf{A}$ is an incidence matrix. Each row of $\mathbf{A}$ can be associated with a subset of process stages. Matrix $\mathbf{A}$ and vector $\mathbf{f}$ characterize a particular deadlock avoidance policy. These constraints are static, i.e., they consider only the present status of resource allocation and not its history. Moreover, each policy can be easily synthesized in polynomial time by a supervisory controller.

As an example consider the avoidance policy named Resource Upstream Neighborhood (RUN) policy [55]. Such a control scheme is based on the idea that there are some resources with higher capacity than others in the system from the resource set R that can function as temporary buffers for the jobs that they support. More precisely, the upstream neighborhood of the resource $r_k \in R$ is indicated by $UN(r_k)$ and it is defined as the union of resources that precede r_k in the routing steps that it performs, with the property that every resource r_i in $UN(r_k)$ has capacity $C(r_i) \leq C(r_k)$. The RUN policy requires that the number of jobs in the upstream neighborhood of a resource never exceed the capacity of that resource. Moreover, the policy is proved to be deadlock and RD-free with complexity $O(R \times W \times L^2)$, where L is the maximum number of operations in each working procedure. The efficiency of the control policy has been studied in [33,34].

Example 3. A four-workstation AMS (continued).

Let us consider again the system described in Example 1 with $C(r_i)=1$ for $i=1,3,4$, and $C(r_2)=2$. By previous definitions we obtain: $UN(r_1)=\{r_3,r_4\}$, $UN(r_2)=\{r_1,r_3,r_4\}$, $UN(r_3)=\{r_1\}$, and $UN(r_4)=\{r_3\}$. The RUN policy imposes at most one job in $UN(r_1)$, $UN(r_3)$ and $UN(r_4)$ and at most two jobs in $UN(r_2)$. Since w_1 is composed of three operations and w_2 four, the vector state $q=[q_1 \; q_2]$ has seven elements (we do not consider the stage corresponding to the fictitious resource). More precisely $q_1(h)$ for $h=1,2$ and 3 is equal to the number of jobs executing the h-th operation of w_1 and $q_2(h)$ for $k=1,2,3$ and 4 is equal to the number of jobs executing the h-th stage of w_2. The RUN policy can be expressed by the following linear inequalities:

$$A \, q \leq f$$

with

$$A = \begin{bmatrix} 0 & 0 & 1 & 1 & 1 & 0 & 0 \\ 1 & 0 & 1 & 1 & 1 & 0 & 0 \\ 1 & 0 & 0 & 0 & 0 & 0 & 1 \\ 0 & 0 & 1 & 1 & 0 & 0 & 0 \end{bmatrix} \qquad f = \begin{bmatrix} 1 \\ 2 \\ 1 \\ 1 \end{bmatrix}$$

Each row of the matrix A corresponds to a resource neighborhood and vector f is obtained by the RUN policy specification.

On the basis of the mentioned problem formulation, other deadlock avoidance policies are defined, applicable to different RAS types. More precisely, Reveliotis, Lawley and Ferreira [56] generalize the RUN policy for more complicated resource allocation systems, i.e., for the more general case of conjunctive-RAS models. Based on the same framework, Lawley, Reveliotis and Ferreira [38] define a Resource Order (RO) deadlock avoidance policy. Starting from the idea that parts traveling through the same machines but in opposing directions must at some point be able to pass, the policy orders the machines and each part is categorized according to how it flows with respect to that order. Since the RO policy can be expressed as a set of linear inequalities, its application is very simple and with polynomial complexity. However, to implement RO policy, it is necessary to order the machines and some orders generate more restrictive constraints than others do. Hence, good orders yielding less restrictive constraints are selected through mathematical integer programming. For reasonably sized systems, the problem can be solved to optimality, while for larger systems suboptimal solutions can be obtained. Moreover, this policy can be efficiently generalized to ST-RAS [56]. Supposing that either RUN or RO avoids deadlock, the paper [53] considers the integration of deadlock avoidance control with dynamic policy reconfiguration and job rerouting, in order to accommodate/minimize the disruptive effects of operational contingencies like the following: (i) a resource fails, and (ii) a job arrives which requires immediate processing. To this aim, the RUN and RO policies, expressed as a set of linear inequalities on the system state, use an available policy reconfiguration to accommodate unexpected contingencies with minimal disruption.

In a more formal and generic framework of Ramadge and Wonham [50], Li and Wonham [43] model a DES as a controlled generator G of a formal language $L(G)$ to characterize deadlock. Hence, they investigate the system property of deadlock, defined as a situation in which the system progress is blocked indefinitely, i.e., it is a *total deadlock*. Consequently, the concepts of deadlock-free supervisor and deadlock-free language are introduced and solved.

Using the same framework, Yalcin and Boucher [67] model an AMS as a finite automaton that describes the states of resources and possible part movements. The process plans for different part types are individually modeled as finite automata and are used to define the rules that govern the system. The supervisor restricts events in the system so that the remaining processing requirements of the parts in the AMS can be completed without incurring deadlock. To define the marked sequences of events of the closed-loop system, the algorithm generates the state space and determines the possible control pattern to reach the final state. When more alternative sequences exist, some network flow techniques can be applied to the directed graph representing the automaton state space for the optimal selection of the sequence. The proposed methodology to avoid deadlock is maximally permissive, but requires the analysis of the state space that increases exponentially with the number of resources and the number of process plans. Consequently, this strategy is not suitable for application in real and large AMS.

Ramirez-Serrano and Benhabib [51] consider a multiworkcell AMS, interrelated by common shared resources, and develop a strategy for the synthesis of deadlock-free supervisors to control the workcells individually. Extended Moore Automata (EMA), i.e., finite automata with outputs and inputs, model the behavior of workcells, the set of manufacturing constraints to be imposed on the workcells, and the possible sequences in which parts can be concurrently processed. The supervisors are synthesized for all workcells such that no deadlock can occur, i.e., the system cannot reach a state from which it is impossible to return to the initial state (*partial deadlock* free). They propose an algorithm to identify deadlock states when multiple devices are shared by multiple workcells and synthesize a deadlock-free supervisor for each workcell. The strategy checks for deadlocks for every interrelated combination of workcells and, if deadlock states are found, reconfigures the manufacturing conditions and resynthesizes the corresponding supervisors. Considering the complexity, the proposed approach is less computationally intensive than a traditional approach that synthesizes a global supervisor.

We conclude this section recalling a recent paper [41] where the authors develop the notion of robust supervisory control for AMS with unreliable resources. Moreover, they introduce the important concept of the robustness of a deadlock avoidance policy with reference to the resource failures. In addition, they propose two polynomial control policies that ensure safety of the system while an unreliable resource fails and is repaired.

1.5 PETRI NET APPROACHES

Many researchers use Petri nets (PN) as a formalism to describe AMS [8,68,69] and develop appropriate deadlock resolution methods [1,3,6,9,10,26, 27,45,46,57-60,63-66,68-70]. However, deadlock definitions are different in this framework and can lead to confusion and imprecision. Appendix 2 gives some related notation and definitions considering ordinary PN.

In particular, the following definitions are important to clarify the connection between the deadlock in AMS and the properties of PNs. More precisely, a Petri net PN=(P, T, F, M_0) at the initial marking M_0 is said to be *live* if, no matter what marking has been reached from M_0, it is possible to fire ultimately any transition of the net by progressing through some further firing sequence. Consequently, *liveness* means that, for every reachable state, the model can evolve in such a way that every transition can always fire in the future and, in other words, every system activity can ultimately be carried out [9]. Hence, a live PN guarantees deadlock-free operations. On the other hand, a dead marking or *total deadlock* is a marking M such that no transition is enabled and, translating this idea to the AMS domain, a dead marking represents a state where no piece can move forward.

Moreover, a PN is said to be *deadlock-free* if at least one transition is enabled at every reachable marking. This definition does not guarantee that a circular wait condition involving a part of the system cannot occur. In general, deadlock freeness in PN definition does not prevent a *partial deadlock* between a subset of resources and a subset of in-process parts.

Now, deadlocks are also linked to particular structures of PNs called siphons. More precisely, a subset of places S is called siphon if $^\bullet S \subseteq S^\bullet$; i.e., an input transition is also an output transition of S [44]. A siphon is said to be minimal if it does not contain other siphons. A PN is deadlock-free if no minimal siphon eventually becomes empty.

Next sections present a review of the PN approaches to the AMS deadlock analysis.

1.5.1 Deadlock and PN Liveness

Some of the first investigations on deadlock in AMS are reported in [68] and [69]. They analyze and synthesize PN models for AMS with shared resources so that the PN is bounded, live and reversible. As recalled before, the liveness condition implies the absence of deadlocks and is obtained by adding buffer modules and control places or limiting the number of in-process parts. Hence, in their framework, deadlock is solved using a prevention technique.

Viswanadham, Narahari and Johnson [60] propose deadlock avoidance and prevention techniques. They model the system and job processes by Generalized Stochastic PN. The authors define a deadlock marking as a dead marking. This definition sees a deadlock as a *total deadlock* where no part in the system can complete its route. They propose a deadlock prevention policy, which executes an exhaustive analysis of the reachability graph and considers the graph paths that do not reach a deadlock marking. The reachability analysis technique to arrive at deadlock prevention policies can become infeasible if the state space is very large. Moreover, the avoidance policy introduced in [60] consists in the construction of the reachability graph for a finite number of look-ahead steps to check if the system reaches a deadlock state. If so, the policy avoids the undesirable evolution by controlling events or initiates appropriate recovery procedures if it is necessary.

More efficient deadlock avoidance policies are introduced in [3,57,58]. Using Production Petri nets (PPN), Roszkowska *et al.* describe the AMS consisting of a set of resources $R=\{r_i\}$ with assigned capacity $C(r_i)$. Two places a_{ri} and b_{ri} are assigned to each resource $r_i \in R$: tokens in b_{ri} represent jobs detaining the resource and tokens in a_{ri} indicate available resources of type r_i. For each reachable marking $M \in R(M_0)$ and for each $r_i \in R$, it holds $M(a_{ri})+M(b_{ri})=C(r_i)$. The working procedure to produce a particular product results in a sequence of resource requirements and associates a place-transition sequence with each product type. Places represent individual steps in the sequence of operations necessary to produce a particular part where each step requires a resource. A transition models a releasing or acquiring resources by the parts. Denote the set of job types by Q. If processing a q-type product ($q \in Q$) requires L_q steps, we define the following place and transition sequences:

$$p_q = \{p_q(0), p_q(1),\ldots, p_q(j)\ldots, p_q(L_q), p_q(L_q+1)\}$$

$$t_q = \{t_q(0), t_q(1),\ldots, t_q(j)\ldots, t_q(L_q), t_q(L_q+1)\}$$

Tokens in $p_q(0)$ represent q-type jobs waiting for their processing; those in $p_q(L_q+1)$ indicate completed orders; and those in $p_q(j)$, $j \in \{1, 2,\ldots, L_q\}$, give the currently processed jobs in the j-th step. $t_q(0)$ denotes the arrival of an order to execute a job for product q; firing $t_q(L_q+1)$ indicates the completion of a q-type job; and firing $t_q(j)$, $j \in \{1, 2,\ldots, L_q\}$, means that a q-type job makes transition from the (j-1)-th production step to the j-th step.

The deadlock avoidance policy is defined as a resource allocation policy (Restriction Policy-RP) that selects the enabled transitions to fire. To apply this RP, it is necessary to partition the system resources into two classes: the former collects all the unshared resources, i.e., all the resources required once in only one production sequence; the latter groups the remaining resources (i.e., the shared resources). In this way, for each job-type $q \in Q$, it is possible to split up a place sequence into sub-sequences called zones:

$$p_q = p_q(0) z^1{}_q z^2{}_q \dots z^k{}_q \dots p_q(L_q + 1)$$

Each zone consists of two subzones: $z^k{}_q = s^k{}_q u^k{}_q$ where $s^k{}_q$ represents a subsequence of production steps requiring shared resources and $u^k{}_q$ indicates a subsequence of production steps requiring unshared resources.

The proposed RP allows an enabled transition t to fire only if the following conditions hold true:

(RPA) if, by firing t, a job enters a new zone $z^k{}_q$ in its production sequence, then the capacity of the unshared sub-zone $u^k{}_q$ must exceed the number of jobs currently in the zone $z^k{}_q$;

(RPB) if, by firing t, a job requests a shared resource, then all the resources in the remainder of the zone must be available except the one held by the job.

This RP establishes a simple feedback control law. In general, applying a RP could lead to new situations, named Restricted Deadlocks (RD), in which an indefinite circular wait occurs partly because some transitions are not enabled and partly because some enabled transitions cannot fire owing to the RP. In this case a RP itself helps to form a circular wait, with the same consequence as a deadlock. By using the PPN, it is shown that the RP [3,57] prevents the system from reaching a deadlock or RD and, hence, it is *deadlock-free*. Moreover, their RP is less conservative than existing deadlock avoidance algorithms for computer operating systems because it is based only on resource requirements in the current production sequence zone for each job rather than the entire set of resource requirements. On the other hand, such a policy sometimes appears too conservative because it allows a limited number of jobs in process, resulting in poor system performance. In particular, this holds true when the number of unshared resources is small. However, it remains a simple real time control policy that avoids deadlock and restricted deadlock with little computation required.

Example 4. A four-workstation AMS (continued)

Consider once again the four-machine system without buffers as described in Example 1. There are two job types ($Q=\{1,2\}$) performed, respectively, by the working procedures $\mathbf{w}_1$ and $\mathbf{w}_2$, as shown in Table 1.1 with $L_1=3$ and $L_2=4$. As an example, Figure 1.5 depicts the PPN modeling a type 1 part's process sequence, p_1.

Since only resource r_4 is unshared, the sequence is partitioned as: $p_1=p_1(0)z^1{}_1$ $p_1(4)$, with $z^1{}_1=s^1{}_1=\{r_1,r_2,r_3\}$; $p_2=p_2(0)z^1{}_2z^2{}_2p_2(5)$, with $z^1{}_2=s^1{}_2u^1{}_2=\{r_3\}\{r_4\}$, $z^2{}_2=s^2{}_2=\{r_2,r_1\}$.

Since the capacity of each resource r_i with $i \neq 2$ is equal to 1, the RP allows a job of type 1 to acquire a resource iff each resource of its residual sequence has at least an item at its disposal. On the other hand, a job of type 2 can enter z'_2 only if r_4 is idle and can acquire r_2 (r_1) only if r_1 (r_2, respectively) can accommodate one more job.

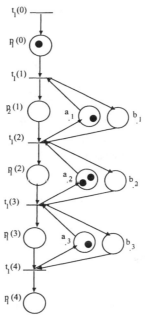

Figure 1.5. The PPN that models type 1 part processing sequence p_1 for Example 4.

Hsieh and Chang [27] use a bottom-up method to synthesize a Controlled Production Petri Net (CPPN) that considers a larger class of AMS where a manufacturing operation may require multiple resources. The CPPN model consists of resource subnets describing resources, job subnets describing processes and exogenous controls. A deadlock state is defined as a state under which a set of jobs are in circular waiting for resources and no operations can go on among them. Hence, to avoid deadlock, it is sufficient to guarantee that each operation be performed infinitely many times, i.e., to keep the system live. To this aim they find the conditions to ensure that the CPPN is live under a control policy and an initial marking. The deadlock avoidance controller includes a sufficient validity test procedure to check whether the execution of a control action is valid to maintain the liveness of the CPPN. If the control fails the test, a valid control action is generated by the validity test. In particular, the validity test algorithm is based on the determination of a sequence of markings leading to an empty system, where every process is finished. The proposed procedure is of polynomial complexity and has good potential for real-time applications. Like the restriction policy [3,57], the drawback of this strategy [27] is that it does not provide a method to apply a maximally permissive deadlock avoidance policy when it is scalable.

Investigating on the field of complex RAS some new contributions address the problem of determining suited deadlock avoidance policies [10,27]. In particular, Ezpeleta *et al.* [10] develop a deadlock avoidance method applicable to systems with the following particular characteristics: production orders are allowed to have assembly/disassembly operations and flexible part routing. The paper adopts a mixed approach based on the computation of the reachability graphs of the different production orders obtained by modeling the system by a PN belonging to the class of Systems of Processes with Resources (S*PR). This class of nets described with more detail in the next section, can model in a natural way both flexible routing and the use of several resources at each processing step. In this framework, a polynomial time complexity adaptation of the Banker's algorithm for deadlock avoidance is proposed.

1.5.2 Deadlock and Siphons

The basic contributions described in the previous section do not characterize deadlock states but just require the PN's liveness. Like [3,57], Xing *et al.* [65] model a production system by using PPN and define a set of transitions in deadlocks as a set of transitions that cannot fire any more because they are not enabled by resource places. To guarantee that all the transitions of the PPN are not in deadlock, they define a PN structure, related to siphons that must not be empty. When the number of any kind of resources is greater than one, the necessary and sufficient conditions are considered which guarantee no occurrence of any deadlock. The peculiarity of this policy with respect to the RP in [3] is that if all the resource capacities are more than one, the policy is maximally permissive because it cannot incur restricted deadlock. However, in the general case, it is of exponential complexity in the numbers of utilization times of each kind of shared resources.

Another important and used model is proposed by Ezpeleta, Colom and Martinez [9] who describe a production system using a particular class of nets called Systems of Simple Sequential Processes with Resources (S^{3}PR). This class of models is a generalization of the one used in [3,27,57,65] since their working procedures allow flexible routing. The deadlock definition in AMS is translated into the liveness definition of the net model. Since the liveness property means that every production process can always introduce in the system new products to be manufactured, the system is deadlock-free if every transition can always fire in the future. In the case that the model is not live, a control policy will constrain the system behavior to a set of states such that whichever state the system reaches, there is always a system evolution. Thus, under the control policy the treatment of each product can reach its final state. Hence, the paper analyzes the liveness of the S^{3}PR net. First of all, they show that a marked S^{3}PR net is live if and only if for each reachable marking from the initial marking, each siphon has at least one token. Considering that a siphon is called minimal iff it includes no other siphon as a proper set, the control policy determines the set of minimal siphons that can be emptied and introduces additional places that constrain the behavior of the system so that no siphon becomes empty, generating no deadlock. It is proved that adding such monitor places creates no new emptiable siphons for S^3PR.

The intuitive meaning of the control prevention policy is as follows. Firing each transition modeling the start of a process needs a token from the added places related to the siphons that may lose all their tokens otherwise. It is proved that the controlled system is live. Moreover, the control policy establishment complexity is strongly conditioned by the complexity of computing the set of minimal siphons. Indeed, the number of siphons is exponential with the number of places in the net. However, the computational effort in order to obtain the set of minimal siphons is not that critical because this computation is carried off-line only once before implementing the deadlock prevention procedure.

Example 5. A four-workstation AMS (continued)

Consider once again the four-machine system without buffers as described in Example 1. Figure 1.6 depicts the S^3PR net modeling the system. The two siphons that can eventually become empty are $S_I = \{r_1, p_1(2), r_2, p_2(4)\}$ and $S_2 = \{r_2, p_1(3), r_3, r_4, p_2(3)\}$. Moreover, Figure 1.6 shows that the introduced additional places V_{S1} and V_{S2} and the added flow relations (the sketched arcs) apply the obtained constraints: S_I and S_2 cannot become empty.

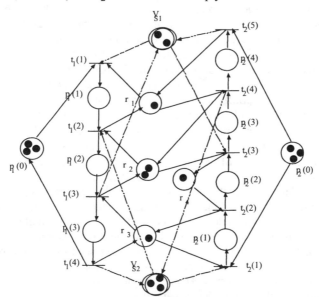

Fig. 1.6. The controlled system of S^3PR modeling the four-machine system of Example 2.

Abdallah and Elmaraghy [1] model AMS by using S^4R nets, which are a generalization of S^3PR nets, and PPN nets. The paper proposes a deadlock prevention policy and a deadlock avoidance policy based on the unsafe marking concept.

Interesting results are derived in [6] where deadlock is analyzed in PNs that can potentially model different discrete event systems. The paper states that a PN subclass, known as Augmented Marked Graphs (AMG), is deadlock-free if no siphon is a potential deadlock where a siphon is a potential deadlock iff it can be emptied. Using a linear programming approach, it is necessary to examine all minimal siphons. Furthermore, the authors show that it is possible to check deadlock freeness without generating all the minimal siphons. Indeed, mathematical programming or Mixed Integer Programming problems find the maximal siphon unmarked of a reachable marking and checks whether there exists a minimal siphon that eventually becomes unmarked. A consequence of these results is that liveness for some particular nets can be checked in polynomial time. Moreover, the proposed methods are applied to PN modeling of manufacturing systems and provide prevention and detection methods. The prevention algorithm is presented in detail in a successive paper [28] where the manufacturing system is modeled by a S^3PR net. The method is an iterative approach consisting of two main stages. The first stage, *siphon control*, adds for each unmarked minimal siphon, a control place to the original net with its output arcs to the sink transitions of the minimal siphon. The second stage, *augmented siphon control*, assures that there are no new unmarked siphons generated due to the control places added at the first stage. The authors show that the resulting control policy is less restrictive than the prevention method proposed in [9].

Starting from the basic results obtained in [6], Park and Reveliotis establish in [46] that AMG, for example S^3PR nets, can effectively model the controlled behavior of a class of sequential RAS under algebraic polynomial deadlock avoidance policy control. Hence, RUN and RO policies can be improved. More precisely, the AMG-based framework has the capability of enhancing the flexibility of any existing algebraic DAP and enriching the space of effectively computable algebraic DAP with new policy instantiations. In [46], a novel framework using PN structural analysis is provided for analyzing the correctness of any tentative algebraic deadlock avoidance policy.

The above-mentioned approaches successfully address the deadlock avoidance problem primarily in the context of SU-RAS. Recently, Park and Reveliotis [47] have shown that the empty siphon can be the deadlock-interpreting mechanism even in the case of CD-RAS. On the basis of the results obtained in [46], they provide a complete PN-based structural characterization of CD-RAS liveness through a new siphon construct that effectively extends the notion of an empty siphon to a non-ordinary generalization of S^3PR and S^4R nets called System of Simple Sequential Processes with General Resource Requirements, denoted by S^3PGR^2. The paper investigates the liveness properties of S^3PGR^2 nets and establishes their strong relationship to the development of a new siphon construct, called the deadly marked siphon. The paper exploits the derived siphon-based liveness characterization of CD-RAS, in order to develop a sufficiency test for the correctness of CD-RAS DAP that can be expressed as a set of invariant imposing control places, superimposed on the PN modeling the original RAS behavior.

Finally, in a subsequent work Park and Reveliotis [48] synthesize a liveness-enforcing supervision which is scalable and correct for CD-RAS that present un-controllability with respect to: (i) the timing of some requested resource alloca-tions; i.e., these allocations will take place as long as the requested resources are available, (ii) the routing of certain jobs that, after some processing stages, might request special treatment or rework. In addition, the paper addresses the accom-modation in the liveness-enforcing supervision synthesis problem of forbidden state specifications.

On the basis of the siphon analysis approach, some mixed models are intro-duced to improve the controller synthesis and the model potentiality. To this pur-pose, we recall the paper [15] that compares PN and digraph models to solve dead-lock in AMS. The paper indicates a tight connection between the two approaches to the deadlock problem, building a unitary framework that links graph-theoretic and PN models and results. In particular, it is shown that iff there is an unmarked siphon in the PN modeling the system, then the transition digraph contains a par-ticular subdigraph structure. Finally, it shows how avoidance policies derived from digraphs can be implemented by controlled PNs.

In the same context, papers [22] and [42] deal with deadlock avoidance for a large class of multiple reentrant flow-lines using S^3PR nets to explore the exact relationship among circular waits, siphons and deadlock situations. A novel ma-trix-based model of AMS is employed which, together with the PN marking tran-sition equation, provides a complete dynamical description for the manufacturing system. The matrix framework is very convenient for computer simulation as well as for supervisory controller design. The introduced deadlock avoidance scheme is based either on a critical siphon that becomes empty or on a wait relation graph exhibiting a circular wait condition. Based on these structures, the matrix equa-tions of the controller are written in *(min, +)* algebra and a minimally restrictive control policy is synthesized. The originality of this method consists in the use of the matrix-based model of discrete event manufacturing systems utilized in con-junction with the Petri net model and the digraphs to synthesize a job-sequencing controller with resource allocation. The approach leads to an efficient and simple design of a supervisory controller to avoid deadlock.

1.5.3 Deadlock and Circuits

A Petri net model, called Resource Oriented Petri Net (ROPN), is developed by Wu [63]. The resource-oriented model mainly describes the dynamic of the resource allocation instead of the production processes of operations in the system. In this proposed framework, just one place is necessary to model a resource. More precisely, the authors define a ROPN=$(P,T,\mathbf{I},\mathbf{O},M,K)$ where K: $P \rightarrow \{0,1,2,\ldots\}$ is a capacity function in which K(p) represents the number of tokens that place *p* can hold. In this framework, transition t∈ *T* in an ROPN is enabled if for all p∈ *P*,

$$M(p) \geq I(p,t) \tag{10.1}$$

and

$$K(p) \geq M(p) - I(p,t) + O(p,t) \tag{10.2}$$

In ROPN, when (10.1) is satisfied, we say that t is process-enabled. Moreover, if (10.2) is satisfied, we say that t is resource-enabled.

It is assumed that: (i) each machine has one output buffer with finite capacity, (ii) no job visits the same machine consequently, and (iii) there is a load-unload station with infinite capacity. Parts in the system are represented by the tokens. To distinguish different processes, colors [30] are introduced into the ROPN, resulting in Colored ROPN (CROPN). Because of the equivalence between deadlock in the AMS and liveness in the CROPN, the sufficient and necessary conditions for deadlock occurrence are proved. Before introducing the deadlock avoidance policy proved in [63,64], the following definitions are necessary: (i) regarding transitions and places as nodes of the net, a *circuit* is a path from a node to the same node where every transition and node appears once except for the last one; (ii) symbol c_i indicates a *production process circuit* (PPC) if it is a *circuit* in the CROPN that does not contain the place p_0 representing the load/unload station; (iii) in ROPN a subnet formed by a number of PPCs is said to be an interactive PPC subnet if every PPC in the subnet has common places and transitions with at least one other PPC in the subnet, and the subnet is strongly connected. Denote by c^n an interactive PPC formed by n PPCs; t is said to be an input transition of an interactive subnet c^n if t is not in c^n and its output place is in c^n. $T_I(c^n)$ denotes the set of the input transitions of c^n; (iv) we call intercircuit input transitions (IIT) the input transitions belonging to two PPCs. Now, the L-policy [64] is recalled.

L-condition: L-condition holds for PPC v and marking M iff there is at least a nonshared free space available in v at M.

L-policy: L-policy is a control policy under which (1) L-condition holds for any c in c^n after t's firing if t∈ $T_I(c^n)$ is selected to fire; and (2) L-condition holds for any c in subnet c^{n-1} of c^n after IIT's firing if it is external to c^{n-1} and selected to fire.

It is proved that a CROPN controlled by the *L-policy* is live. The following example shows their application.

Example 6. A four-workstation AMS with buffers (continued).

The CROPN of Fig. 1.7 models the system described in Example 1. In this case we consider each machine provided with an output buffer of capacity equal to 1. A type 1 part can be released into the system from p_0 to p_1 by firing $t_1(I)$. A type 2 part enters the system from p_0 to p_4 by firing $t_2(I)$. When a type 1 part is completed by Machine 3, it goes back to p_0 through $t_1(O)$. On the other hand, when a type 2 part is completed by Machine 1, it goes back to p_0 through $t_2(O)$. The

CROPN contains two PPCs: $c_1=(p_1(I),t_1,p_1(O),t_{12},p_2(I),t_2,p_2(O),t_{21})$ and $c_2=(p_2(I),t_2,p_2(O),t_{23},p_3(I),t_3,p_3(O),t_{34},p_4(I),t_4,p_4(O),t_{42})$.

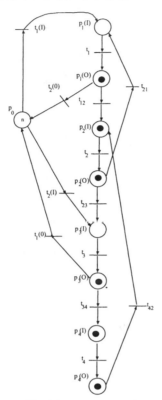

Fig. 1.7. A resource oriented Petri net.

These two PPCs form an interactive subnet c^2 with IIT=$\{t_{12}, t_{42}\}$ and $T_I(c^2)=\{t_1(I), t_2(I)\}$. Suppose that the CROPN is at the marking shown in Figure 1.7, where only places $p_1(I)$ and $p_2(I)$ are empty and the others in c^2 are full with the token in $p_1(O)$ representing a type-1 part and token in $p_3(O)$ representing a type 2 part. In this marking, transitions $t_1(I)$ and $t_2(I)$ are resource- and process-enabled but they are inhibited by the control law. Indeed, since there is only one nonshared free space available in c_1 and c_2, firing $t_1(I)$ or $t_2(I)$ leads to a deadlock.

We remark that the benefits of this model with respect to the S^3PR nets and the PPN are its simplicity and its capacity for modeling each resource with finite capacity by using only one place. Indeed, it results in an efficient tool to model the dynamic of AMS and to describe the interaction between jobs and resources. Since in scheduling an AMS two things should be avoided: deadlock and starvation, this control law provides a good opportunity to prevent starvation or to improve resource utilization while avoiding deadlocks [64]. By using a conservative policy for deadlock avoidance, the number of parts allowed in the system leads the AMS to starvation and low resource utilization. On the other hand, a maximally permissive policy can introduce blocking. The paper [64] takes a novel approach and proposes a slightly more restrictive policy than the maximal one. Such a policy gives clear advantages over the maximally permissive policy in a rule-based scheduling environment.

Table 1.2. A summary of digraph/automaton-based deadlock control methods

Ref.	Model	Methods to characterize deadlock	Policy	Types of RAS	Complexity	Routing
55	Automata	State safety and reachability graph	AV	SU-RAS	$O(R \times W \times L^2)$	Static
38	Automata	State safety and reachability graph	AV	SU-RAS	$O(L_t \times M^2)$	Static
56	Automata	State safety and reachability graph	AV	C-RAS ST-RAS	$O(R \times W \times L^2)$ $O(L_t \times M^2)$	Static
67	Automata in Ramadge-Wonham framework	State safety and reachability graph	AV	SU-RAS	Exponential	Static
51	Extended Moore Automata	Fully reachable automaton	AV	SU-RAS	Polynomial	Static
61,62	Digraphs	Cycles	AV DT	SU-RAS	$O(\min (J, R))$	Static
5,32	Digraphs	Cycles	AV DT	SU-RAS with unit capacity	Polynomial	Static
11-18	Digraphs	Cycles and strong components	AV DT	SU-RAS	$O(J \times E)$	Static
39	Automata and digraphs	Digraphs and knots	AV DT	SU-RAS	$O(L_n \times R^2)$	Flexible

J= number of jobs in process
W= number of available working procedures
L= maximal working procedure length
L_n= number of processing alternatives for every stage of every working procedure
L_t= cumulative number of operations of all the working procedures
R= number of resources in the system
E= number of edges in the defined digraph
AV=AVOIDANCE
DT=DETECTION

1.6 COMPARISON AND BENCHMARK STUDIES

Tables 1.2 and 1.3 summarize the main approaches to deal with deadlock in AMS using digraphs, automata, and Petri nets. The first column of each table lists the references and the second denotes the model used to describe a system and the interactions between jobs and resources. Moreover, the third column exhibits some key words to show the used approach to characterize deadlock and the following shows whether a detection/recovery, avoidance or prevention strategy is defined. Finally, the last three columns exhibit the RAS type considered in the model, the complexity of the proposed solution algorithm and if it allows flexible routings, respectively.

Table 1.3. A summary of PN-based deadlock control methods.

Re-fer.	System model	Methods to characterize deadlock	Policy	Type of RAS	Complexity	Routing
60	PN	Reachability graph	PRE AV	SU-RAS	Exponential	Static
3,57 58	PPN (Production Petri nets)	Liveness	PRE	SU-RAS	Polynomial	Static
27	CPPN (Controlled PPN)	Liveness	AV	SU-RAS	Polynomial	Static
65	PPN (Production Petri nets)	Liveness	AV	SU-RAS	Exponential	Static
9	PN S^3PR	Liveness and siphons	PRE	SU-RAS	Exponential	Flexible
1	PN S^4R	Liveness and siphons	PRE AV	CD-RAS	Exponential	Flexible
6, 28	PN	Liveness, Siphons and integer programming	DE PRE	SU-CRAS	Polynomial	Static
41	PN	Siphons and digraphs	AV	SU-RAS	Polynomial	Static
15	S^3PR	Siphons and digraphs	AV	SU-RAS	Polynomial	Flexible
46, 47	S^3PGR^2 net	Liveness and siphons	AV	CD-RAS	Polynomial	Flexible
63, 64	Resource-Oriented PN	Liveness and circuits	AV	SU-RAS	O(R)	Flexible

Comparing different approaches, digraphs appear very simple and intuitive instruments. They are able to fully characterize allocations and de-allocations of resources in SU-RAS. They allow researchers to characterize deadlock conditions and propose efficient deadlock detection/recovery and deadlock avoidance strategies. Their main drawback is that they are not suited to describe more complex RAS such as CD-RAS or ST-RAS. Moreover, digraphs do not model the complete RAS dynamics. Hence, it is necessary to use DEDS models (automata or PN) to describe the RAS behavior. For this reason, some efficient deadlock avoidance policies derived from digraphs are put into a PN framework [15].

Based on automata, efficient deadlock avoidance strategies of polynomial complexity are defined [55,56]. Since these policies are expressed by linear inequalities, they are easy to apply and suitable for supervisory control implementation. On the other hand, classical models in the Ramadge-Wonham framework provide some techniques based on the analysis of the reachability graph. Owing to their exponential complexity, these techniques are not suited to real-time implementation in large AMS.

Finally, PNs result in a complete and powerful instrument that models the system dynamic and allows the introduction of new deadlock resolution techniques. Moreover, PNs provide a suitable framework where policies obtained by digraphs and automata can be implemented. However, a drawback of PN approaches is that the method utilized to characterize and resolve deadlock is related to the limited classes of PN describing computer-integrated systems. For example, the presence of an unmarked siphon is a necessary and sufficient condition for deadlock only if PNs of the class of S^3PR nets model the system.

Referring to the specific application of the various schemes, a crucial problem is what policy must be applied to a given RAS to obtain good performance indices. The problem of selecting an appropriate deadlock resolution strategy for a given RAS configuration has been given very limited consideration in literature. On the other hand, it is hard to evaluate a priori which technique is the most suitable for global performance improvement. The first selection must be based on the type of RAS under study. While few policies can be applied to CD-RAS and T-RAS, a large number of strategies can manage SU-RAS. If the SU-RAS enjoys the conditions for which the maximal permissive policy to avoid deadlock has polynomial complexity, then it must be applied. If the layout of the system is complex and impending part flow deadlock can occur, then the choice can be difficult and can be based on the computational complexity of the various schemes. In addition, to evaluate the impacts of the strategies on the system performance, simulation results can be analyzed [49]. In particular, Wysk *et al.* compares avoidance and detection/recovery strategies on the basis of performance indices evaluated through simulated experimentation on some randomly generated system configuration [62]. Several deadlock control methods are compared for a particular distributed system using stochastic Petri nets in [70].

Moreover, Reveliotis [54] undertakes an analytical investigation of the problem of selecting optimal deadlock resolution strategy for buffer space allocation in a simple AMS. The author develops an analytical formulation for selecting the optimal deadlock resolution strategy that maximizes the system throughput and identifies the conditions under which each of the two strategies, i.e., prevention/avoidance and detection/recovery, is the optimal selection for the considered system.

In addition, the avoidance algorithms can be distinguished based on the effects of the constraints they impose on the freedom in resource allocation. Referring to this algorithm characterization, Fanti, Maione, Mascolo and Turchiano [12,13] compare the performances of deadlock avoidance policies given in [3,14]. Moreover, Ferrarini, Piroddi and Allegri [19] evaluate and compare the performance of deadlock avoidance control policies by means of a simulation study. Some indices are proposed to assess the structured properties of AMS with respect to deadlock occurrence and their performance. Different deadlock avoidance control algorithms are considered among the most common in literature, i.e., one in [3], and the Banker's algorithm. They show how it is possible to design appropriate control schemes tailored to specific purposes through the definition of suitable indices and reference models and of suitable analysis of simulation results.

1.7 CONCLUSIONS

This chapter presents a tutorial survey of deadlock control methods that are particularly suitable for automated manufacturing systems (AMS), but that can be efficiently applied in other computer-integrated systems and networks. The used models and deadlock solution techniques are presented in their *historical* evolution so that the reader can follow the development of the resolution methods in the past 10 years. Indeed, starting from the analysis of deadlock in operating systems, the solution policies have been specialized for AMS and for resource acquisition structures, which are increasingly complex. The development of solution strategies shows that the tractable avoidance techniques are the most promising policies to avoid deadlock while achieving the desired system performance. Hence, research studies have focused especially on these strategies.

Among many approaches, digraphs are a powerful and intuitive means to model interactions between jobs and resources in simple resource allocation systems (RAS). They allow us an easy deadlock characterization and the synthesis of some flexible and permissive avoidance policies. On the other hand, automata approaches provide scalable and correct deadlock avoidance policies. Finally, as derived from a large body of research results, Petri Nets (PN) offer a complete and formal model able to describe fully the system dynamics and to introduce deadlock avoidance and prevention policies. Moreover, using particular PN models (e.g., S^3PR and S^3PGR^2 nets), the siphon characterization of deadlock allows us to obtain PN-based supervisory control theory to avoid deadlock in several type RAS modeling complex AMS. To sum up, approaching a deadlock problem by means of different tools, the past research efforts led to a deep understanding of this phenomenon and to a satisfactory number of available solving techniques.

Future research should continue to investigate efficient and high-performance deadlock avoidance policies fit to complex RAS such as conjunctive/disjunctive RAS. Different strategies and deadlock avoidance policies to improve performances of real systems should be compared and recommended to industrial use. Moreover, deadlock and blocking problems must be considered in systems with unreliable resources. Future research should analyze the robustness of relevant deadlock resolution strategies with respect to unreliable resource failures.

APPENDIX 1- BASIC DIGRAPH DEFINITIONS AND PROPERTIES

A digraph is denoted by $D=(N,E)$ where N is the set of vertices and E is the set of edges [24]. The *outdegree of* a vertex $r \in N$ is the number of edges from E

having *r* as their starting node. Analogously, the *indegree of r* is the number of edges having *r* as their ending node. A *path* is a subdigraph of D composed by an alternating sequence of distinct vertices and arcs. If D contains a path from r_i to r_m, r_m is said to be *reachable* from r_i. Moreover if r_m (r_i) is reachable from r_i (r_m), r_i and r_m are said to be *mutually reachable*. A *cycle* of D is a nontrivial path in which all vertices are distinct except for the first and last ones. A subdigraph $\mu=(N_\mu,E_\mu)$ of D is *strong* if every two vertices from N_μ are mutually reachable in μ. Finally, a *strong component* of D is a maximal strong subdigraph, i.e., no larger strong subdigraph (with more nodes and more edges) contains it. This implies that each strong subdigraph of D is contained in exactly one of its strong components.

APPENDIX 2- ORDINARY PETRI NETS

An ordinary (marked) Petri net is a bipartite digraph $PN=(P,T,F,M)$ where *P* is a set of places and *T* is a set of transitions [44]. The set of arcs $F \subset (P \times T) \cup (T \times P)$ is the flow relation. Given a PN and a node $x \in P \cup T$, the set $\bullet x=\{y \in P \cup T: (y,x) \in F\}$ is the preset of x and $x \bullet =\{y \in P \cup T: (x,y) \in F\}$ is the post-set of x. Similarly, if $S \subseteq P \cup T$, $\bullet S = \cup_{x \in S} \bullet x$ and $S \bullet = \cup_{x \in S} x \bullet$. The set of places *S* is a siphon iff $\bullet S \subseteq S \bullet$, and it is a trap iff $S \bullet \subseteq \bullet S$.

The state of a PN is given by its marking M: $P \rightarrow N$ where N is the set of non-negative integers. M is described by a $|P|$-vector and M(p) represents the number of tokens pictured by dots in place $p \in P$.

A PN structure can be described by two matrices **O** and **I** of non-negative integers of dimension $|P| \times |T|$. The typical entries of **O** and **I** for an ordinary Petri net are given by:

$\mathbf{O}(p,t)=1$ if $(t,p) \in F$ else $\mathbf{O}(p,t)=0$

$\mathbf{I}(p,t)=1$ if $(p,t) \in F$ else $\mathbf{I}(p,t)=0$

Matrix **O-I** is called the incidence matrix. A transition $t \in T$ is enabled at a marking M iff $\forall p \in \bullet t, m(p)>0$. It is denoted as M[t>. Firing an enabled transition t yields a new marking M', denoted as M[t>M' where $\forall p \in P$, M'(p)=M(p)-$\mathbf{I}(p,t)+\mathbf{O}(p,t)$. M' is reachable from M iff there exists a firing sequence $\sigma=t_1 t_2 \ldots t_n$ such that $M[t_1>M_1[t_2>M_2 \ldots M_{n-1}[t_n>M'$. It is denoted as M[$\sigma$>M'. The set of markings reachable from M in PN is denoted R(M).

Given a marked Petri net $PN=(P, T, F, M_0)$, a transition $t \in T$ is live iff $\forall M \in R(M_0)$, there exists $M' \in R(M)$ s.t. M'[t>, and $t \in T$ is dead at $M \in R(M_0)$ iff there exists no $M' \in R(M)$ s.t. M'[t>. A marking $M \in R(M_0)$ is a dead marking or a total deadlock iff $\forall t \in T$, t is dead. Finally, a marked PN is weakly live or deadlock-free iff $\forall M \in R(M_0)$, there exists $t \in T$ s.t. M[t>, and it is live iff $\forall t \in T$, t is live.

REFERENCES

1. I.B. Abdallah and A. Elmaraghy. Deadlock Prevention and Avoidance in FMS: A Petri Net based Approach. Int. J. Advanced Manufacturing Technology, 14: 704-715, 1998.
2. T. Araki, Y. Sugiyama, and Kasami, Complexity of the deadlock avoidance problem. Proceedings of 2nd IBM Symposium on the mathematical Foundations of computer Science, Tokyo, Japan, 1977, 229-257.
3. Z.A. Banaszak and B.H. Krogh, Deadlock Avoidance in Flexible Manufacturing Systems with Concurrently Competing Process Flows. IEEE Trans. on Robotics and Automation, 6: 724-734, 1990.
4. C.G. Cassandras and S. Lafortune. Introduction to Discrete Event Systems, Kluwer Academic Publisher, Boston, 1999.
5. H. Cho, T.K. Kumaran, and R.A. Wysk. Graph-Theoretic Deadlock Detection and Resolution for Flexible Manufacturing Systems. IEEE Trans. on Robotics and Automation, 11: 413-421, 1995.
6. F. Chu and X. Xie. Deadlock Analysis of Petri Nets Using Siphons and Mathematical Programming. IEEE Trans. On Robotics and Automation, 13: 793-804, 1997.
7. E.G. Coffman, M.J. Elphick, and A. Shoshani. System Deadlocks. ACM Computing Surveys, 67-78, 1971.
8. A.A. Desrochers and R.Y. Al-Jaar. Applications of Petri Nets in Manufacturing Systems. IEEE Press. New York 1995.
9. J. Ezpeleta, J.M. Colom, and J. Martinez. A Petri Net Based Deadlock Prevention Policy for Flexible Manufacturing System. IEEE Transactions on Robotics and Automation, 11: 173-184, 1995.
10. J. Ezpeleta, F. Tricas, F. Garcia-Vallés, and J.M. Colom. A Banker's Solution for Deadlock Avoidance in FMS with Flexible Routing and Multi-Resource States. IEEE Trans. on Robotics and Automation. 18: 621-625, 2002.
11. M.P. Fanti, G. Maione, and B. Turchiano. Digraph-Theoretic Approach for Deadlock Detection and Recovery in Flexible Production Systems. Studies in Informatics and Control, 5: 373-383, 1996.
12. M.P. Fanti, B. Maione, S. Mascolo, and B. Turchiano. Performance of Deadlock Avoidance Algorithms in Flexible Manufacturing Systems. Journal of Manufacturing System,. 15: 164-178, 1996.
13. M.P. Fanti, B. Maione, S. Mascolo, and B. Turchiano. Low-Cost Deadlock Avoidance Policies for Flexible Production Systems. Int. J. on Modeling and Simulation, 17: 310-316, 1997.
14. M.P. Fanti, B. Maione, S. Mascolo, and B. Turchiano. Event-based feedback control for deadlock avoidance in flexible production systems. IEEE Trans. Robotics Automat.13: 347-363, 1997
15. M.P. Fanti, B. Maione, and T. Turchiano. Comparing Digraph and Petri net Approaches to Deadlock Avoidance in FMS Modeling and Perform-

ance Analysis. IEEE Transactions on Systems, Man, and Cybernetics, Part B, 30: 783-798, 2000.

16. M.P. Fanti, B. Maione, and B. Turchiano. Event Control for Deadlock Avoidance in Production Systems with Multiple Capacity Resources. Studies in Informatics and Control, 7: 343-364, 1998.

17. M.P. Fanti, G. Maione, and B. Turchiano. Distributed Event-Control for Deadlock Avoidance in Automated Manufacturing Systems. Int. Journal of Production Research, 39:1993-2021, 2001.

18. M.P. Fanti, G. Maione, and B. Turchiano. Design of Supervisors Avoiding Deadlock in Flexible Assembly Systems. Int. Journal of Flexible Manufacturing Systems, 14:157-175, 2002.

19. L. Ferrarini, L. Piroddi, and S. Allegri, A comparative performance analysis of deadlock avoidance control algorithms for FMS. Journal of Intelligent Manufacturing. 10:569-585, 1999.

20. N.Z. Gebraeel and M.A. Lawley. Deadlock Detection, Prevention, and Avoidance for Automated Tool Sharing Systems. IEEE Trans. on Robotics and Automation. 17:342-356, 2001.

21. E.M. Gold. Deadlock Prediction: Easy and Difficult Cases. SIAM Journal of Computing. 7:320-336, 1978.

22. A. Gurel, S. Bogdan, and F.L. Lewis. Matrix Approach to Deadlock-Free Dispatching in Multi-Class Finite Buffer Flowlines. IEEE Transactions on Automatic Control, 45:2086-2090, 2000.

23. A.N. Habermann. Prevention of System deadlocks. Commun. ACM, 12: 373-378, 1969.

24. F. Harary, R.Z. Norman, and D. Cartwright. Structural Models: An Introduction to the Theory of Directed Graphs. John Wiley & Sons, Inc. New York, 1965.

25. R.C. Holt. Some Deadlock Properties of Computer Systems. ACM Computing Surveys, 6:176-196,1972.

26. F. Hsieh. Reconfigurable Fault Tolerant Deadlock Avoidance Controller Synthesis for Assembly Processes. Proceedings of 2000 IEEE Int. Conf. On Systems, Man and Cybernetics, 3045-3050, 2000.

27. F. Hsieh and S. Chang. Dispatching-Driven Deadlock Avoidance Controller Synthesis for Flexible Manufacturing Systems. IEEE Trans. on Robotics and Automation, 10:196-209, 1994.

28. Y. Huang, M. Jeng, X. Xie, and S. Chung. Deadlock Prevention Policy Based on Petri Nets and Siphons. Int. J. Prod. Res., 39:283-305, 2001.

29. S.S. Isloor, and T.A. Marsland, The deadlock problem: An overview. Comput., 58-78, 1980.

30. K. Jensen. Colored Petri Nets, Basic Concepts, Analysis Methods and Practical Use. Vol I EATS Monography and Theoretical Computer Science, Springer Verlag, New York, 1992.

31. C.O. Kim and S.S. Kim. An Efficient Real-Time Deadlock-Free Control Algorithm for Automated Manufacturing Systems. Int. J. Prod. Res., 35: 1545-1560, 1997.

32. T.K. Kumaran, W. Chang, H. Cho, and R.A. Wysk, A Structured Approach to Deadlock Detection, Avoidance and Resolution in Flexible Manufacturing Systems. Int. J. Prod. Res., 32: 2361-2379, 1994.

33. M.A. Lawley and J. Mittenthal. Order Release and Deadlock Avoidance Interactions in Counter-Flow System Optimization. Int. J. Prod. Res., 37: 3043-3062, 1999.

34. M.A. Lawley, S. Reveliotis, and P. Ferreira. The Application and Evaluation of Banker's Algorithm for Deadlock-Free Buffer Space Allocation in Flexible Manufacturing System. Int. Journal of Flexible Manufacturing Systems, 10: 73-100, 1998.

35. M.A. Lawley, S. Reveliotis, and P. Ferreira. Design Guidelines for Deadlock Handling Strategies in Flexible Manufacturing Systems. Int. Journal of Flexible Manufacturing Systems, 9:5-30, 1997.

36. M.A. Lawley, S. Reveliotis, and P. Ferreira. Flexible Manufacturing System Structural Control and the Neighborhood Policy, Part 1. Correctness and scalability. IIE Transactions, 29: 877-887, 1997.

37. M.A. Lawley, S. Reveliotis, and P. Ferreira. Flexible Manufacturing System Structural Control and the Neighborhood Policy, Part 2. Generalization, Optimization, and Efficiency. IIE Transactions, 29:889-899, 1997.

38. M.A. Lawley, S.A. Reveliotis, and P.M. Ferreira. A correct and Scalable Deadlock Avoidance Policy for Flexible Manufacturing Systems. IEEE Transactions on Robotics and Automation, 14:796-809, 1998.

39. M.A. Lawley. Deadlock Avoidance for Production Systems with Flexible Routing. IEEE Trans. on Robotics and Automation. 15: 497-509, 1999.

40. M.A. Lawley. Integrating Flexible Routing and Algebraic Deadlock Avoidance Policies in Automated Manufacturing Systems. Int. J. Prod. Res., 38: 2931-2950, 2000.

41. M.A. Lawley and W. Sulistyono. Robust Supervisory Control Policies for Manufacturing Systems with Unreliable Resources. IEEE Transactions on Robotics and Automation, 18:346-359, 2002.

42. F.L. Lewis, A. Gürel, S. Bogdan, A. Doganalp, and O.C. Pastravanu, Analysis of Deadlock and Circular Waits Using Matrix Model for Flexible Manufacturing Systems. Automatica, 34: 1083-1100, 1998.

43. Y. Li and W.M. Wonham, Deadlock Issues in Supervisory Control of Discrete- Event Systems. Proceedings of the 22nd Annual Conference on Information Sciences and Systems, Princeton, NJ, 57-63, 1988.

44. T. Murata. Petri Nets: Properties, Analysis and Applications. Proc. IEEE, 77:541-580, 1989.

45. Y. Narahari and N. Viswanadham. A Petri Net Approach to the Modelling and Analysis of Flexible Manufacturing Systems. Annals of Operations Research, 3:449-472, 1985.

46. J. Park and S.A. Reveliotis. Algebraic Synthesis of Efficient Deadlock Avoidance Policy for Flexible Manufacturing Systems. IEEE Trans. on Robotics and Automation, 16:190-195, 2000.

47. J. Park and S.A. Reveliotis. Deadlock Avoidance in Sequential Resource Allocation Systems with Multiple Resource Acquisitions and Flexible Routings. IEEE Trans. on Automatic Control, 46:1572-1583, 2001.

48. J. Park and S.A. Reveliotis. Liveness-Enforcing Supervision of Resource Allocation Systems with Uncontrollable Behavior and Forbidden States. IEEE Trans. on Robotics and Automation, 18, 234-239, 2002.

49. S.E. Ramaswamy and S.B. Joshi. Deadlock-free Schedules for Automated Manufacturing Workstations. IEEE Trans. on Robotics and Automation, 12:391-400, 1996.

50. P.J. Ramadge and W.M. Wonham. Supervisory Control of a Class of Discrete Event Processes. SIAM Journal on Control and Optimization, 25:206-230, 1987.

51. A. Ramirez-Serrano and B. Benhabib. Supervisory Control of Multi-Workcell Manufacturing Systems with Shared Resources. IEEE Transactions on Systems, Man, and Cybernetics, Part B, 30: 668-683, 2000.

52. E.M. Reingold, J. Nievergelt and N. Deo. Combinatorial algorithms: Theory and Practice. Englewood Cliffs, NJ: Prentice-Hall, 1997.

53. S.A. Reveliotis. Accommodating FMS Operational contingencies through Routing Flexibility. IEEE Transactions on Robotics and Automation, 15: 328-339, 1999.

54. S.A. Reveliotis. An Analitical Investigation of the Deadlock Avoidance detection and Recovery Problem in Buffer-Space Allocation of Flexibility Automated Production Systems. IEEE Transactions on Systems, Man, and Cybernetics-Part B: Cybernetics, 30: 799-811, 2000.

55. S.A. Reveliotis and P.M. Ferreira. Deadlock Avoidance policies for Automated Manufacturing Cells. IEEE Transactions on Robotics and Automation. 12:845-857, 1996.

56. S.A. Reveliotis, M.A. Lawley, and P.M. Ferreira. Polynomial-Complexity Deadlock Avoidance Policies for Sequential Resource Allocation Systems. IEEE Trans. on Automatic Control, 42: 1344-1357, 1997.

57. E. Roszkowska. Deadlock Avoidance in Concurrent Compound Pipeline Processes. Archiwum Informatyki Teoretycznej I Stosowanej, 2:227-242, 1990.

58. E. Roszkowska and J. Jentink. Minimal Restrictive Deadlock Avoidance in FMSs. Proceedings of European Control Conference ECC'93, 2: 539-544, 1993.

59. W. Sulistyono and M. Lawley. Deadlock Avoidance for Manufacturing Systems with Partially Ordered Process Plans. IEEE Trans. On Robotics and Automation, 17: 819-832, 2001.

60. N. Viswanadham, Y. Narahari, and T.L. Johnson. Deadlock Prevention and Deadlock Avoidance in Flexible Manufacturing Systems using Petri Net Models. IEEE Trans. on Robotics and Automation, 6:713-723, 1990.

61. R.A. Wysk, N.S. Yang, and S. Joshi. Detection of Deadlocks in Flexible Manufacturing Cells. IEEE Trans. on Robotics and Automation, 7:853-859, 1991.

62. R.A. Wysk, N.S. Yang, and S. Joshi. Resolution of Deadlocks in Flexible Manufacturing Systems: Avoidance and Recovery Approaches. J. of Manufacturing Systems, 13:128-138, 1994.

63. N.Q. Wu. Necessary and Sufficient Conditions for Deadlock-Free Operation in Flexible Manufacturing Systems Using a Colored Petri Net Model. IEEE Trans. on Systems, Man, and Cybernetics, Part C, 29:192-204, 1999.

64. N.Q. Wu and M.C. Zhou. Avoiding Deadlock and Reducing Starvation and Blocking in Automated Manufacturing Systems. IEEE Transactions on Robotics and Automation, 17, 658-669, 2001.

65. K.Y. Xing, B.S. Hu, and H.X. Chen. Deadlock Avoidance Policy for Petri Net modeling of Flexible Manufacturing Systems with Shared Resources. IEEE Trans. on Automatic Control, 41:289-295, 1996.

66. H.H. Xiong and M.C. Zhou. A Petri Net Method for Deadlock-Free Scheduling of Flexible Manufacturing Systems. International Journal of Intelligent Control and Systems, 3:277-295, 1999.

67. A. Yalcin and T.O. Boucher. Deadlock Avoidance in Flexible Manufacturing Systems Using Finite Automata. IEEE Trans. on Robotics and Automation, 16, 424-429, 2000.

68. M.C. Zhou and F. DiCesare. Parallel and Sequential Mutual Exclusions for Petri net Modeling of Manufacturing Systems with Shared Resources. IEEE Transactions on Robotics and Automation, 7:515-527, 1991.

69. M.C. Zhou, F. DiCesare, and A.A. Desrochers. A Hybrid Methodology for Synthesis of Petri Nets for Manufacturing Systems. IEEE Transactions on Robotics and Automation, 8: 350-361, 1992.

70. M.C. Zhou. Deadlock Avoidance Methods for a Distributed Robotic System: Petri Net Modeling and Analysis. Journal of Robotic Systems, 12:177-187, 1995.

2

Deadlock Avoidance in Automated Manufacturing Systems Using Finite Automata and State Space Search

Ali Yalcin
University of South Florida, Tampa, FL, USA.

Tsuta Tai
State Street Corp., Princeton, NJ, USA.

Thomas O. Boucher
Rutgers University, New Brunswick, NJ, USA.

ABSTRACT

An approach to deadlock avoidance based on finite automata is reviewed in this chapter. This approach begins from the framework introduced by Ramadge and Wonham (R&W) for modeling and control of discrete event systems based on formal languages generated by finite automata. We apply this framework to the problem of dynamic scheduling and control of automated manufacturing systems.

A typical automated manufacturing system is composed of multiple machines and workstations that perform various operations on a part, and a material handling system that interconnects these machines and workstations. Parts are processed to completion by routing them through various machines and workstations according to their individual process plans. After processing is complete, the part leaves the system. Deadlock occurs when parts enter a "circular wait" condition where, in order to continue processing, a set of two or more parts require resources that are held by parts of the same set.

Our approach to avoiding deadlock is unique in the following contributions: (1) a simple and natural way of formulating the "requirements model" of the R&W framework from the part routing plans, (2) an ability to handle parts with multiple routing plans within the framework, (3) a solution that guarantees that the resulting controller is both deadlock-free and maximally permissive, and (4) an ability to dynamically reevaluate the controller logic as the active part mix in the manufacturing system changes.

The direct application of the R&W framework can involve a large search space as problem size grows. Extensions of our approach have addressed the problems of scalability, state space search, and execution time. This has been accomplished through the introduction of more effective state space search algorithms. These extensions and the relative efficiency of algorithms are also discussed and demonstrated in this chapter.

2.1 INTRODUCTION

A deadlock occurs in a manufacturing system when a set of two or more parts require resources that are held by parts of the same set. This situation results in a "circular wait" condition, in which parts are unable to release resources until they are granted requested resources, which are held by other parts in the set. The goal of deadlock avoidance is to ensure that this condition never occurs.

In a manufacturing context, the relationship between a part and the resources it requires is encapsulated in the "routing plan" of the part. The routing plan describes the sequence of resources required to completely manufacture the part. The routing plan can be represented as a digraph in which the nodes are resources and the arcs indicate precedence and the order in which resources are acquired. When several parts are in the manufacturing system simultaneously, the union of their routing graphs may contain circuits, which are indicators of potential deadlocks. In deadlock avoidance, an instance of these circuits is not allowed to occur during the execution of the manufacturing plan.

Automated manufacturing systems must avoid deadlock because a deadlock condition will halt further processing of the parts. If this happens, manual intervention will be required to clear the deadlock and reset the system. This is undesirable because it requires designing human intervention into the normal operation of the system and can result in introducing errors when resetting the state of the controller. It is more desirable that the system controller is designed such that it has the ability to avoid the deadlock condition entirely. However, system controllers must respond to changing conditions in real time. Therefore, deadlock avoidance in automated manufacturing systems is a real time problem and algorithms implemented for that purpose must execute quickly.

An important consideration in deadlock avoidance is the permissiveness of the deadlock avoidance algorithm. Algorithms that do not reject any deadlock-free path are said to be maximally permissive and, when compared with algorithms that are not maximally permissive, lead to better utilization of system resources [1]. However, maximally permissive algorithms come at a price of increased state space size and computation time and may not be applicable to real time control of large systems.

The remainder of this chapter describes an approach to deadlock avoidance using finite automata. The next section describes the basic modeling approach. This is followed by a description of its application in manufacturing. Finally, we discuss the application of the model for real time control and describe the execution times encountered in implementation.

2.2 FINITE AUTOMATA AND CONTROL

In this section we describe the basic modeling approach. It is based on the use of finite automata and the theory of control for discrete event systems developed by Ramadge and Wonham (R&W) [2].

A symbol σ represents an event in a system. A string ω is a finite sequence of events that take place in a system. An alphabet Σ is a finite set of symbols. A language L is a set of strings from some alphabet. A finite automaton is formally defined by a five-tuple:

$$G=(\Sigma, Q, \delta, q_o, Q_m),$$

where Q is the set of states q, Σ is a finite alphabet of events, $\delta: \Sigma \times Q \rightarrow Q$ is the transition function, $q_o \in Q$ is the initial state and $Q_m \subset Q$ is the set of marked (final) states. Generally δ is a partial function defined for some $\Sigma(q) \subset \Sigma$. G can also be represented as a directed graph with node set Q and an edge $q \rightarrow q'$ labeled by σ for each (σ, q, q') such that $q' = \delta(\sigma,q)$. Throughout this chapter we will represent initial states with a double circle and final states with a filled circle.

$L(G) = \{\omega| \omega \in \Sigma^*, \delta(\omega,q_0) \in Q$ is defined$\}$, where ω is a string and Σ^* is the set of all strings over the alphabet Σ. In other words L(G) is the set of all possible sequences of events (strings) which take the initial state to some reachable state in Q.

$L_m(G) = \{\omega| \omega \in \Sigma^*, \delta(\omega,q_0) \in Q_m\}$. $L_m(G)$ is the marked language generated by G which represents the sequence of events that take the initial state to some marked (final) state, Q_m.

For the finite automaton G, $Q_a = \{q \in Q \mid (\exists w \in \Sigma^*) \; \delta(w,q_o)=q\}$, i.e., the set of all the states that can be reached from the initial state is called the accessible states subset. Also, for the finite automaton G, $Q_{ca} = \{q \in Q \mid (\exists w \in \Sigma^*) \; \delta(w,q)=Q_m\}$, i.e., the set of all the states q from which some marked (final) state can be reached is called the co-accessible states subset. The finite automaton G is said to be "trim" if it is accessible ($Q= Q_a$) and co-accessible ($Q= Q_{ca}$).

In the R&W theory of supervisory control, the uncontrolled behavior of the plant is modeled by a finite automaton. That finite automaton is modified to accept control. This is done by defining a set of events, $\Sigma_c \subseteq \Sigma$, which accept control. Those that are uncontrollable are represented by Σ_u, and $\Sigma = \Sigma_u \cup \Sigma_c$. A supervisor is an agent that enables or disables controllable events in the plant such that the language generated satisfies some specifications. Formally the supervisor consists of a finite automaton S and an output function Ψ(control pattern). $S=(S,\Psi)$, where:

$S=(\Sigma, X, \xi, x_0, X_m)$ and
$\psi:\Sigma \times X \rightarrow (0:\text{disable},1:\text{enable})$ such that $\psi(\sigma,x)= 0$ or 1 if $\sigma \in \Sigma_c$ and 1 if $\sigma \in \Sigma_u$.

The finite automata model of the supervisor, S, is defined from a behavioral specification for the plant. We refer to the behavioral specification as the "requirements model." The supervisor finite automata model and the plant are coupled to form a closed loop system. Assume that at a given time the plant is in state q_i and the supervisor is in state x_j. A set of events $\sigma \in \Sigma$ can occur in the uncontrolled process in state q_i. According to the state x_j only a subset of the $\sigma \in \Sigma_c$ may be permitted. The supervisor generates a control pattern ψ. This concept of a closed loop system is illustrated in Figure 2.1.

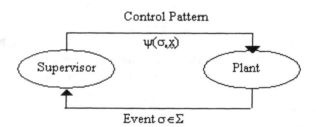

Figure 2.1 Closed loop coupled system.

The closed loop system is denoted by S/G. Two languages generated by S/G are of interest. $L(S/G)= L(S) \cap L(G)$ is the sequences of events of the closed loop system. These are all the possible sequences of events that will transition the system among allowable states. However, if the controller is given some specific final state, called the marked state, only the subset of L(S/G) that allows the system to evolve to that final state is appropriate. $L_m(S/G)= L_m(S) \cap L_m(G)$ is the marked sequences of events of the closed loop system; i.e., it is the set of all strings that allows the system to evolve from its current state to the marked state.

2.3 APPLICATION TO DEADLOCK AVOIDANCE IN MANUFACTURING

2.3.1 Plant Model

In our application of finite automata to deadlock avoidance [3,4], the plant model is based on the manufacturing system resources and their states. Resources may be machines, robots, transporters, and other equipment used to process parts. In our modeling framework we constrain each resource to have unit capacity. The plant model describes the possible states of the plant and the transitions that link those states. An example of a plant is shown in Figure 2.2, where the plant is composed of three resources, two machines and a robot. The plant model, or finite automata, is shown is Figure 2.3. Each state of the FA, shown as a circle, is defined by a 3-tuple, {M1, M2, R1}. The symbol "i" indicates the idle state and "b" indicates the working state.

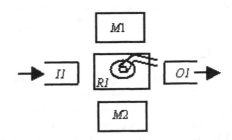

Figure 2.2 A manufacturing cell.

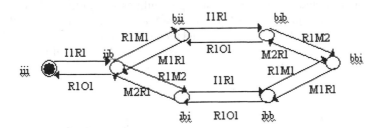

Figure 2.3 Finite automata of Figure 2.2 [From Ref. 3].

The transition arcs that connect the states are labeled with the events that cause a change in state. These events are the alphabet from which strings (sequences) of events may be formed. Thus, δ(I1R1, iii)=iib and δ(I1R1 R1M1 I1R1, iii)=bib. The events are described by the notation I1R1, R1M1, etc., where the 2-tuple describes the source and destination of the movement of a part. We can now describe the components of the plant model, $G=(\Sigma, Q, \delta, q_o, Q_m)$, as follows:

$\Sigma=(I1R1, R1M1, R1M2, M1R1, M2R1, R1O1)$

$Q=(iii, iib, bii, ibi, bib, ibb, bbi)$

	iii	bii	ibi	iib	bbi	bib	ibb
iii	–	–	–	$I1R1$	–	–	–
bii	–	–	–	$M1R1$	–	$I1R1$	–
ibi	–	–	–	$M2R1$	–	–	$I1R1$
$\delta = $ iib	$R1O1$	$R1M1$	$R1M2$	–	–	–	–
bbi	–	–	–	–	–	$M2R1$	$M1R1$
bib	–	$R1O1$	–	–	$R1M2$	–	–
ibb	–	–	$R1O1$	–	$R1M1$	–	–

For a manufacturing plant, the initial state is the idle state and, after all production is completed, the plant is idle again. Therefore, $q_o=(iii)$ and $Q_m=(iii)$.

2.3.2 Requirements Model

The requirements model will specify the behavioral requirements of the plant. We define these requirements based on the required sequence of operations needed to process parts through the plant. This is given by the part process plan, which, for a specific plant design, is converted to a part "routing plan." The routing plans are modeled as finite automata. The model of each routing plan explicitly depicts the possible routes a part may take for complete processing. This facilitates modeling parts with alternate sequencing, parts that may visit a machine more than once, and alternate machining possibilities within the cell. Figure 2.4 depicts the process plans for two part types: A and B. Part A is a part that has alternate sequencing. It has to visit M1 and then M2 for completion but can do this in any order. Part B is a part that needs to visit M1 and M2. Therefore, there is no flexibility associated with part B.

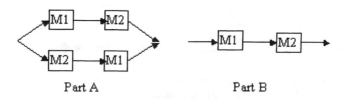

Part A   Part B

Figure 2.4 Part routing plans [From Ref. 3].

The finite automaton model for each process plan will be used in synthesizing the requirements model for the cell. Figure 2.5 depicts the finite automata models of part types A and B. For each part type model, there is a state associated with each resource the part may visit. There are also two additional nodes denoted by subscripts "i" and "f" which are the initial and final states of the automaton. The subscript "i" indicates that the part is in the input buffer; the subscript "f" indicates that the part has gone to the output buffer. Let A and B be the state sets for parts A and B, respectively. The arcs that connect these states are the possible part movements in the cell that transfer the parts in process from one resource to another. Formally, for each part type manufactured in the cell, we have a finite automaton model; e.g., part type A, $A=(\Sigma, A, \delta_A, a_i, a_f)$ and part type B, $B=(\Sigma, B, \delta_B, b_i, b_f)$. The language generated by the finite automaton model of a part type, for example part A, is described as: $L(A) = \{\omega| \ \omega \in \Sigma^*, \ \delta(\omega,a_0) \in A \}$, where ω is a string and Σ^* is the set of all strings over the alphabet Σ. Among the strings in this language, those that take the initial state to a final state, namely $\delta(\omega,a_0)= a_f$, are the sequences of events which complete the processing of the part.

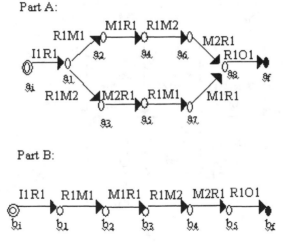

Figure 2.5 Finite automata for part types A and B [From Ref. 3].

2.3.3 Requirement Model Synthesis

The supervisor will restrict events in the cell so that the remaining processing requirements of the parts in the system can be completed. These processing requirements are determined from the individual process plans of the parts. The supervisor is dynamic and changes as parts are scheduled to be loaded into the cell. When the scheduler informs the supervisor that a part is available to enter the cell, S, the requirement model is synthesized by shuffling (denoted by symbol "||")

[2] the finite automata models for the parts already in the cell and the part queued in the input buffer for processing. Shuffling is done to obtain all the possible sequences for finishing the remaining processing requirements of the parts currently in the cell and the part queued in the input buffer. In order to keep track of which part is moved, we will modify event names to include the part identifier also. We have used part names identical with the part types for illustrative purposes. These names should be assigned so that they can uniquely identify the parts in the cell. For example "M1R1, A" corresponds to part A being moved from M1 to R1. Consider a point in time when part A is still being processed in machine 1 and part B is released to the cell (placed in the input buffer) for processing. The current states of finite automata models for parts A and B are a_2 and b_i, respectively. We generate $S = A \| B$ as shown in Figure 2.6. Formally, the supervisor S consists of a finite automaton S and an output function Ψ. $S = (S, \Psi)$, where $S = (\Sigma, X, \xi, x_0, X_m)$ and $\psi : \Sigma \times X \to (0:\text{disable}, 1: \text{enable})$ such that $\psi(\sigma, x) = 0$ or 1 if $\sigma \in \Sigma_c$ and 1 if $\sigma \in \Sigma_u$. In this application, all events are controllable events.

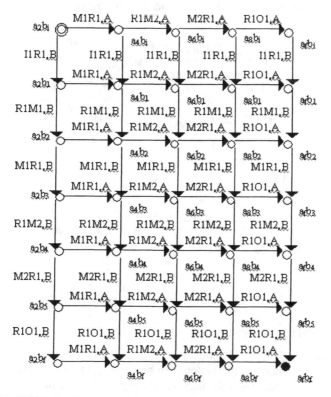

Figure 2.6 Transition graph of the shuffle of parts A and B from initial state $a_2 b_i$ [From Ref. 3].

Note that, in Fig. 2.6, the initial state of S is $x_0 = a_2b_i$. This is the combined current states of the individual parts in the cell and parts scheduled to enter the cell. The control pattern of the supervisor only takes into consideration the remaining processes when deciding on a sequence of events. The final state of S, $X_m = a_fb_f$ is the combined final states of the parts.

2.3.4 The Coupled System

The coupled supervised discrete event process is defined as:

$$S/G = (\Sigma, \ Q \times X, \ \delta \times \xi, \ x_0 \times q_c, X_m \times \Omega_m)$$

where q_c is the current state of the plant model. The transition graph for S/G is shown in Figure 2.7, below:

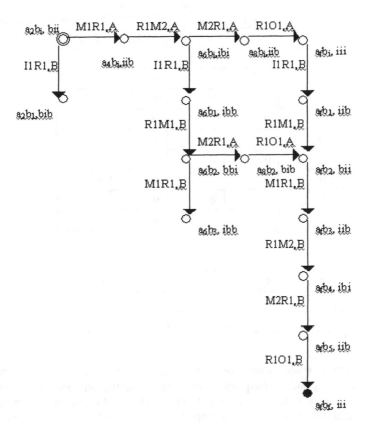

Figure 2.7 Transition graph of the coupled cell [From Ref. 3].

From the transition graph we can determine:

$L_m(S/G)$= [(M1R1,A R1M2,A M2R1,A R1O1,A I1R1,B R1M1,B M1R1,B R1M2,B, M2R1,B R1O1,B), (M1R1,A R1M2,A I1R1,B R1M1,B   M2R1,A R1O1,A M1R1,B R1M2,B M2R1,B R1O1,B)].

The language $L_m(S/G)$, the marked sequences of events of the closed loop system, takes the coupled system from an initial state to the combined final state where all parts in the system are processed and unloaded. Therefore, all the strings in $L_m(S/G)$ are deadlock-free execution sequences.

A supervisory control pattern that restricts the cell to executing sequences only in $L_m(S/G)$ guarantees deadlock-free control and full processing of all the parts in the cell. The control pattern, Ψ, for the supervisor synthesized above is shown in Table 2.1.

Table 2.1 Supervisory control pattern, Ψ.

	I1R1	R1M1	M1R1	R1M2	M2R1	R1O1
a_2b_i	0	0	1	0	0	0
a_4b_i	0	0	0	1	0	0
a_6b_i	1	0	0	0	1	0
a_6b_1	0	1	0	0	0	0
a_6b_2	0	0	0	0	1	0
a_8b_i	0	0	0	0	0	1
a_8b_2	0	0	0	0	0	1
a_fb_i	1	0	0	0	0	0
a_fb_1	0	1	0	0	0	0
a_fb_2	0	0	1	0	0	0
a_fb_3	0	0	0	1	0	0
a_fb_4	0	0	0	0	1	0
a_fb_5	0	0	0	0	0	1
a_fb_f	0	0	0	0	0	0

Source: Ref. 3.

We can make some observations concerning Table 2.1. At the time the new part (part type B) is queued for production, it can enter the cell since the robot is idle (a_2b_i, bii). However the loading event I1R1 is disabled by the control pattern in state a_2b_i. If this event is allowed to happen, the cell would be deadlocked as can be seen in Figure 2.7. The deadlock situation arises because part B is on the robot and it can only go to M1. However M1 is occupied by part A, and part A needs the robot to move it from M1 to M2. When the supervisor is in state a_6b_i, I1R1 is enabled along with M2R1. At this point either of these events can take place depending on which event happens first in the cell. This is the reason why there are two separate sequences for $L_m(S/G)$. Also in state a_6b_2, M1R1 is disabled to prevent another deadlock situation.

2.4 IMPLEMENTATION ISSUES

Finite automata models tend to grow exponentially in state space as problem size grows. Since our application is in real-time control, we have been evaluating ways of implementing this model that reduce state space size and improve computational speed. One preliminary observation to make is that, in systems where there is one material handler, it is unnecessary to include that resource in the routing plan. When the robot is allowed to move a part, the execution sequence will include the acquisition and deposition of the part. This reduces the state space for a given cell size. However, real time computation ultimately depends on designing algorithms that will execute quickly, which has been accomplished to a considerable extent. This effort is briefly described in this section and references are given to documents containing more details.

2.4.1 The Basic Algorithm

The basic algorithm takes the part routing plans and the plant model as inputs. The requirements model is then formed as previously shown in Figure 2.6. The coupling of the requirements model with the plant model is done using a file that relates the state of each part to its contribution to the state of the plant. This is called the "part process plan/plant state file." An example for parts A and B is shown in Figure 2.8. These files are constructed by combining the part states of Figure 2.5 with the corresponding plant states of Figure 2.3. The plant states are the tuple (M1 M2 R1).

Node	Plant State		Node	Plant State
a_i	(000)		b_i	(000)
a_1	(001)		b_1	(001)
a_2	(100)		b_2	(100)
a_3	(010)		b_3	(001)
a_4	(001)		b_4	(010)
a_5	(001)		b_5	(001)
a_6	(010)		b_f	(000)
a_7	(100)			
a_8	(001)			
a_f	(000)			

Figure 2.8 Part process plan/plant state lists for parts A and B.

The part process plan/plant state list is used in order to identify illegal states. Illegal states are states in which more than one part is occupying the same machine. These states are identified by taking the bitwise logical AND of the plant states corresponding to the nodes of the process plans that are being shuffled. If the logical AND does not return a zero, the state is not legal. So, for example, plant_state(a_2) AND plant_state(b_1) = (1 0 0) AND (0 0 1) = (0 0 0) is legal. In that state ($a_2 b_1$), part A is on M1 and part B is on R1. However, plant_state(a_2) AND plant_state(b_2) = (1 0 0) AND (1 0 0) = (1 0 0) is not legal. In this state both part A and part B would be occupying M1 simultaneously.

Determining illegal nodes as described above is analogous to the coupling process described in Section 2.3.4. Instead of using the coupled system transition matrix ($\delta \times \xi$) to check if an event is enabled, a simple AND operation determines if the state that will be reached after executing the event is physically possible in the cell. The completion of this process yields an untrimmed graph like that of Figure 2.7.

As explained in Section 2.3.4, the marked language of the coupled system, $L_m(S/G)$, determines the control pattern for each state of the system. A depth first search (DFS) algorithm [5], which is widely used in finding routes through directed graphs, is used to determine the marked language of the coupled model.

Shuffling the finite automata models of all the possible remaining states of parts each time a new part enters the cell generates a large state space when many parts are being simultaneously considered for processing. In order to further reduce the size of the state space, we use the already existing coupled system model to determine the new event sequences that allow all the parts in the cell to be completely processed. The state space of the coupled system is smaller when compared with the state space of the supervisor obtained by shuffling all the remaining states of parts in the cell. We have formally proven elsewhere that using the coupled system for generating the supervisor is not more restrictive (will not restrict the marked language) then the supervisor obtained by the methodology described in Section 2.3.4 [4]. Therefore, this approach to state space reduction saves computational time without restricting the marked language of the coupled system. C language source code for implementing the algorithm described in this section is documented in [6].

2.4.2 Depth First Search Algorithm with Partial State Space Search

As previously described, the role of the supervisor is to evaluate a request for the movement of a part and to either allow or disallow the request in consideration of whether or not allowing the request will result in either an illegal state or a deadlock state. In constructing the digraph of Figure 2.7, all the possible routes through the digraph from the current state to the marked state are evaluated. However, it is clear that knowledge of all the legal and deadlock-free execution sequences is not required in order to evaluate whether or not the move is allowed.

It is only necessary to find one path from the current state to the final state in order to conclude that the requested move can be allowed. In effect, evaluating a partial digraph can reduce execution time.

In designing an algorithm for a reduced state space search, we combine the bitwise logical AND to determine illegal states with the depth first search algorithm. The current part is advanced until an illegal state is reached. The algorithm then rolls back to the prior legal state and another part is selected and advanced. An important advantage of this approach is that it is a "one pass" algorithm. We do not need to explore all the routes in the digraph. The search algorithm is a recursive function that always tries to reach the final state, the so-called Depth First Search [5]. The idea of DFS is to traverse the digraph as deep as possible. If the algorithm reaches a state and cannot move forward, the algorithm will backtrack and try another path recursively. The algorithm stops when it reaches the final (marked) state of the digraph. The details of the implementation of the algorithm are described in [1] and C language source code for implementation is documented in [6].

2.4.3 Partial Deadlock Detection Algorithm

The partial state space search algorithm is enhanced by applying a partial deadlock detection algorithm (PDDA) to further reduce the search space. The PDDA is a one-step look-ahead algorithm that detects a circular wait condition (a partial deadlock) in a directed graph. A resource allocation graph (RAG) is defined as RAG=(U,α) where U, the set of nodes, is the set of resources (machines and buffers) and $\alpha\{(u, v): u, v \in U\}$, the set of directed edges, represents the set of events in the current processing stage of each part in the system that take the part to the machine required by its next processing stage. A modified resource allocation graph (MRAG) is created as follows:

1. Let $U' \subseteq U$ be the set of nodes without outgoing arcs. These nodes correspond to resources that are not occupied in the current state. Combine all $u \in U'$ into one node u_i which also includes the output buffer.

2. Modify the arcs in RAG such that, in the resource pairs that define each arc $(u,v) \in \alpha$, replace all instances of $u \in U'$ with u_i. In addition, reverse the direction of all arcs.

This process, which has worst case complexity $O(\alpha)$, results in MRAG=$\{U',\alpha'\}$. The algorithm that detects partial deadlocks is a DFS performed on MRAG. During the search, the nodes are numbered as they are reached from the initial node u_i. If all nodes in MRAG are numbered, then there is no partial deadlock. A numbered node is indicative of a resource occupied by a part that is going to move to an idle machine through the execution of the current moves of the parts in the cell. If all nodes are not numbered, there exist a set of at least two nodes not connected to the initial node of the search indicating a partial deadlock. A typical program list of such an algorithm is as follows:

PDD Algorithm:

Input: *MRAG*= {*U*',α`}
Output: Partial deadlock, no deadlock
Begin
Integer *i*
Procedure *DFS* (*v,u*); !vertex *u* is the parent of vertex *v*
Begin
Number (*v*):=*i*:=*i*+1 !number each vertex with increasing integers
For *w* in the adjacency list of *v DO*
       Begin
       If *w* is not yet numbered then
             Begin
             Construct arc *v->w*
             DFS (*w,v*);
             END
   END;
END;
i:= 0;
DFS (*u_i*,0); !search starts from *u_i*
If |*U*'| = *i* then exit with no deadlock, else exit with partial deadlock
END;

To illustrate this procedure, consider the example in Figure 2.9. The move being considered is loading *Part1* on to *M1*. The processing requirements of all the parts in the cell are also listed in Figure 2.9. The associated RAG and MRAG are illustrated in Figure 2.10. In the RAG, each resource is modeled by a node, and each edge represents a move associated with a part from its currently held resource to a resource it requires next for processing. In the MRAG, the output buffer is the only resource included in *u_i*, and direction of each edge is reversed. The PDDA will expand *u_i* and number *M4*. Expanding *M4* generates *M2*, and expanding *M2* generates no new nodes, terminating the DFS. The algorithm reports partial deadlock since there are 5 nodes in MRAG, but only 3 are numbered.

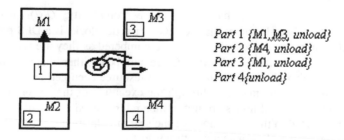

Part 1 {M1, M3, unload}
Part 2 {M4, unload}
Part 3 {M1, unload}
Part 4{unload}

Figure 2.9 Four machine cell example.

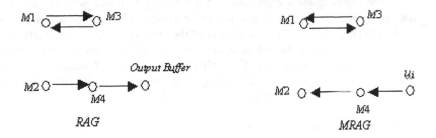

Figure 2.10 RAG and MRAG for example problem in Figure 2.9.

The difference between the deadlock detection approach described in Section 2.4.2 and the approach that incorporates PDDA is depicted in Figure 2.11. The numbers next to each edge indicate the move associated with that part number. The edges that do not lead to new nodes correspond to "illegal" moves as described in Section 2.4.1. While the approach in Section 2.4.2 will continue the search until all *nodes A, B, C and D* are expanded and all the edges are explored, a search enhanced by the described PDDA will terminate at *node A* since this node has a partial deadlock between *part 1* and *part 2* and the system cannot reach the final state when there is a partial deadlock among a subset of parts in the system.

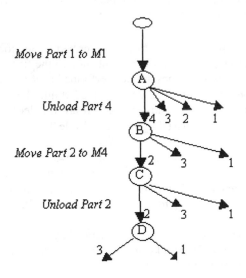

Figure 2.11 Search space from the current state of the cell depicted in Figure 2.9.

The computational complexity of the PDDA is linear with $U^`$ and $\alpha^`$ in MRAG or $O(U^`+\alpha^`)$. Each node can only be numbered once and each edge in the graph is examined once. The complexity of the algorithm increases linearly as the number of machines in the cell increases. For example, a 4-machine cell can have at most 5 vertices, and a 6-machine cell can have at most 7 vertices. A detailed description of the algorithm with examples is given in [1,7,8] and C language source code is documented in [9].

2.4.4 Computational Experiences

A randomized experimental design is used in order to gain more insight into the computational requirements of the deadlock avoidance algorithms described in Sections 2.4.1, 2.4.2 and 2.4.3. The experimental design uses the randomly generated process plans for cell sizes of 4, 6, 8, and 10 machines per cell. The processing times are generated from UNIF(10,15) for each operation. Fifty random part arrivals are generated for each cell size for the cases of single and multiple routing for each algorithm. In order to compare the steady state computational requirements, computations associated with the first and last 10 part arrivals are disregarded. All the experiments were conducted on a computer with a 400-MHz Pentium II processor and 128-MB RAM. We are interested in the size of the state space searched (nodes expanded) and computation time between an event request and the decision to enable/disable the event.

Three different algorithms are implemented to demonstrate the incremental reductions associated with time and state space.

Algorithm 1: This is the basic algorithm as described in Section 2.4.1 and determines all deadlock-free paths from the current state to the final state. It is important to note that these computations are not performed every time there is a move request by a part, but only when a new part is loaded into the cell. Move requests associated with parts that are already in the cell are enabled/disabled by simply looking up the value of Ψ from a table similar to Table 2.1.

Algorithm 2: This is the partial state space search with the depth first search algorithm as described in Section 2.4.2. The computation is performed every time there is a part move request, whether it is associated with a new part being loaded into the cell or associated with a part that is already in the cell.

Algorithm 3: This is the algorithm that is augmented by partial deadlock detection as described in Section 2.4.3. Similar to Algorithm 2, the computations are executed every time there is a request to move a part.

Tables 2.2, 2.3 and 2.4 summarize the experimental results associated with the implementation of the three algorithms mentioned above. For Algorithm 1, only the results for 4 and 6 machine cells are tabulated. For larger cell sizes, this algorithm was not practical for multiple routing, where state space size grows exponentially. The most basic step of graph searching is the *node generation,* which is computing the representation code of an adjacent node from its parent. The new successor is said to be *generated,* and its parent is said to be *explored.* Another important step is the *node expansion,* which consists of generating all successors of a given parent node. The parent is then said to be *expanded.* The experimental results focus on the number of nodes expanded and the CPU time.

All three tables indicate the exponential state space increase for the maximum number of nodes expanded. In the multiple routing case for Algorithms 2 and 3, the searches were not as long as the single routing case. This is attributed to the fact that in the multiple routing cases, due to the availability of machining options, the algorithm finds paths to the final state without running into deadlock, therefore expanding fewer nodes. Considering multiple routing options has provided additional paths that resolved the deadlocks in the system. This, in turn, has decreased the length of the searches to find deadlock-free paths.

In the implementation results of Algorithm 2 shown in Table 2.3, a closer look at the longest searches reveals that moves that result in failures (no path to the final states were found) are associated with the longest searches. This is quite intuitive since the search explores the complete legal state space before a failure is reported. For the 2376 searches considered, only 30 searches were longer than the average 231150 nodes expanded. For the 30 searches, 24 of them resulted in failures. These observations clearly indicate that moves that lead to deadlocks result in the longest searches. This is the major motivating factor for incorporating partial deadlock detection in Algorithm 3.

Table 2.2 Number of nodes expanded and computation time of Algorithm 1.

	4 Machines	6 Machines
Single Routing		
Max. Nodes Expanded	218	5776
Avg. Nodes Expanded	98	1953
Max. CPU Time(sec)	<1	2
Avg. CPU Time(sec)	< 1	<1
Multiple Routing		
Max. Nodes Expanded	1072	118112
Avg. Nodes Expanded	486	35604
Max. CPU Time(sec)	<1	304
Avg. CPU Time(sec)	<1	44

Table 2.3 Number of nodes expanded and computation time of Algorithm 2.

	4 Machines	6 Machines	8 Machines	10 Machines
Single Routing				
Max. Nodes Expanded	11	45	1869	421857317
Avg. Nodes Expanded	3	4	18	231150
Max. CPU Time(sec)	<1	<1	<1	6826
Avg. CPU Time(sec)	<1	<1	<1	4
Multiple Routing				
Max. Nodes Expanded	12	26	42	912617
Avg. Nodes Expanded	4	5	5	1088
Max. CPU Time(sec)	<1	<1	<1	25-26
Avg. CPU Time(sec)	<1	<1	<1	<1

Table 2.4 Number of nodes expanded and computation time of Algorithm 3.

	4 Machines	6 Machines	8 Machines	10 Machines
Single Routing				
Max. Nodes Expanded	11	19	396	2696157
Avg. Nodes Expanded	3	3	6	3975
Max. CPU Time(sec)	<1	<1	<1	212
Avg. CPU Time(sec)	<1	<1	<1	<1
Multiple Routing				
Max. Nodes Expanded	12	25	42	68
Avg. Nodes Expanded	4	5	6	9
Max. CPU Time(sec)	<1	<1	<1	<1
Avg. CPU Time(sec)	<1	<1	<1	<1

Results shown in Table 2.4, for Algorithm 3, indicate that for the single routing case, the maximum number of nodes generated still grows exponentially with increasing cell size. On the other hand, average response time is under 1 second for all cell sizes. For the multiple routing case, due to the ability to process parts on alternate resources, finding a deadlock free path does not require as lengthy a search.

Table 2.5 shows the comparison of the maximum number of nodes expanded between Algorithms 1 and 2. The difference is due to enabling an event when a path is found from the current state to the final state (Algorithm 2), instead of generating all deadlock-free paths from the current state to the final state (Algorithm 1).

Table 2.5. Comparison of maximum number of nodes expanded between Algorithm 1 and Algorithm 2.

	Algorithm 1	Algorithm 2	Percent Reduction
Single Routing			
4-machine Cell	218	11	95%
6-machine Cell	5776	45	99%
Multiple Routing			
4-machine Cell	1070	11	99%
6-machine Cell	118112	26	99%

Table 2.6 shows the advantage of using partial deadlock detection (Algorithm 3). As the cell size increases, the reduction in the number of nodes expanded to disable/enable a requested event increases. This is due to the fact that even if two resources are occupied by partially deadlocked parts, there are still many parts in the system that need to be considered and possibly continue or finish processing, increasing the legal state space to be searched. Detecting partial deadlocks eliminates the necessity to expand the remaining legal nodes further along the path. In the multiple routing case, due to the existence of many alternate machining options, not many deadlocks were encountered. However, in the 10-machine cell, the detection of partial deadlocks considerably decreased the search space required to find deadlock-free paths.

Table 2.6 Comparison of maximum number of nodes expanded between Algorithm 2 and Algorithm 3.

	Algorithm 2	Algorithm 3	Percent Reduction
Single Routing			
4-machine Cell	11	11	0%
6-machine Cell	45	19	58%
8-machine Cell	1869	396	79%
10-machine Cell	421857317	2696157	99.4%
Multiple Routing			
4-machine Cell	12	12	0%
6-machine Cell	26	25	4%
8-machine Cell	42	42	0%
10-machine Cell	912671	68	99.9%

2.5 SUMMARY

In this chapter we described an approach to modeling deadlock avoidance in manufacturing systems based on the framework introduced by Ramadge and Wonham for modeling and control of discrete event systems. This approach to avoiding deadlock is unique in the following contributions: (1) a simple and natural way of formulating the "requirements model" of the R&W framework from the part routing plans, (2) an ability to handle parts with multiple routing plans within the framework, (3) a solution that guarantees that the resulting controller is both deadlock-free and maximally permissive, and, (4) an ability to dynamically reevaluate the controller logic as the active part mix in the manufacturing system changes.

In this chapter, we also reviewed three algorithms for deadlock avoidance in automated flexible manufacturing systems and presented computational results of the implementation of these algorithms in single capacity automated manufacturing cells. In the first algorithm, we couple the requirements model, based on the routing plans of the parts, with the plant model finite automaton. Following that, we use a depth first search algorithm to generate the marked language. This implementation generates all deadlock-free paths for the processing of the parts in the system, but it is computationally cumbersome for systems consisting of more than six resources where multiple part routing plans are used. In the second algorithm, we have decreased the search space required for maximally permissive deadlock avoidance using a partial search of the state space, which determines a single deadlock-free path from the current state of the system to the final state. The third algorithm was motivated by the results from the second algorithm, where it was observed that the longest search spaces were associated with deadlocks and that early detection of deadlocks would decrease the search space. The third algorithm incorporates the intelligence of partial deadlock detection. This algorithm is still maximally permissive, capable of dynamic routing flexibility and requires much less computation than the other two algorithms to find deadlock-free paths.

REFERENCES

1. A. Yalcin. Architectures for Automated Flexible Manufacturing Cells with Routing Flexibility. PhD Dissertation, Rutgers University, 2000.
2. P.L. Ramadge and W.M. Wonham. Supervisory Control Of A Class Of Discrete Event Processes. SIAM J. Control and Optimization, 25:206-230, 1987.
3. A. Yalcin and T.O. Boucher. Deadlock Avoidance in Flexible Manufacturing Systems Using Finite Automata. IEEE Transactions on Robotics and Automation, 16-4:424-429, 2000.

4. T.O Boucher, A. Yalcin, and T. Tai. Dynamic Routing and the Performance of Automated Manufacturing Cells. IIE Transactions on Design and Manufacturing, 32-10:975-988, 2000.
5. R.E. Tarjan. Depth First Search and Linear Graph Algorithm. SIAM Journal of Computing, 1:146-160, 1972.
6. A. Yalcin, T. Tai, and T.O. Boucher. Source Codes of Controller Implementations for Automated Manufacturing Cells. Ind. Eng. Dept., Rutgers Univ., Pisctaway, NJ, Working Paper #00-103, 2000.
7. T. Tai and T.O. Boucher. An Architecture for Scheduling and Control in Flexible Manufacturing Systems Using Distributed Objects. IEEE Transactions on Robotics and Automation, 18-4:452-462, 2002.
8. A. Yalcin. Deadlock Avoidance in Automated Flexible Manufacturing Cells Using Partial Deadlock Detection. International Journal of Operations and Quantitative Management, 9-1:21-33, 2003.
9. T. Tai and T.O. Boucher. Scheduling with Distributed Objects: Source Code and Experimental Trials. Ind. Eng. Dept., Rutgers Univ., Piscataway, NJ, Working Paper #01-119, 2001.

3

Synthesis of Deadlock-free Supervisory Controllers Using Automata

Dr. A. Ramirez-Serrano
University of Calgary, Calgary, Alberta, Canada

Dr. B. Benhabib
University of Toronto, Toronto, Ontario, Canada

Abstract

Discrete event modeling techniques such as Automata and Petri nets are often used to describe systems, whose underlying continuous aspects do not play a significant role in determining their behavior. These modeling techniques for Discrete-Event Systems (DES) usually result in abstract models with large number of states where every system state is considered to change instantaneously with the occurrence of certain events. The largeness of the state-space together with specific discrete-event phenomena, such as deadlocks, often limit the applicability of formal DES controller design methodologies for industrial applications.

An issue of great practical concern in the control of (DES) manufacturing and communication systems is the synthesis and implementation of deadlock-free supervisory controllers. A DES deadlock is loosely defined as *"a condition in which one or more events await for another event in the same set to execute before they can be triggered."* Since events taking part in a deadlock cannot execute, the corresponding devices responsible for triggering them cannot be released and the associated resources cannot be used (until the deadlock is resolved). Many solutions have been proposed over the years for the identification, detection of and recovery from deadlocks in DESs discussed in various chapters of this Book. This chapter, on the other hand, will discuss automata-based DES-controller synthesis methodologies capable of obtaining deadlock-free supervisors by construction. Namely, the resultant controllers do not require the use of an on-line deadlock detection and recovery mechanism.

Automata and formal-language based supervisory-control theories of DESs, pioneered by the work of Professors Ramadge and Wonham (R-W), aim to design supervisors in such a way that the physical process coupled to its supervisor behaves deadlock-free according to logical constraints. Herein, we review R-W control theory and describe its deadlock-free controller yielding characteristics together with other significant properties that can be used for the specification, verification, analysis and synthesis of correct DES controllers. Subsequently, we review another automata theory, extended moore automata (EMA), that extends the capabilities of R-W theory in controlling significantly more complex systems, for example, multiworkcell systems producing parts with several alternate processing routes.

In the context of multiworkcell flexible manufacturing systems (FMSs), where resources may be shared among workcells for the production of parts, the operation of more than one workcell comprising the system may be stalled due to an event in "circular waiting." The probability of encountering deadlocks in such multi-workcell systems is higher compared with single-workcell systems due to the existing "competition for resources" between the parts that can be processed in several different ways. Even if one is able to identify and detect a deadlock state in an on-line manner, there may be no automatic way or immediate way to resolve it. Thus, when dealing with the control of FMSs, it would be beneficial to analyze the controller at hand for possible deadlock states and/or conflicting conditions, identify such states and eliminate them prior to their implementation. As also presented in this chapter, the use of individual and independent supervisors for each workcell, for a multiworkcell manufacturing system, would reduce the computational complexity when synthesizing the (smaller size) supervisor set and allow for their a priori deadlock analysis.

Using EMA theory in this chapter, a deadlock identification methodology for manufacturing workcell systems is described where deadlocks are identified in an off-line fashion, i.e., after the controller set has been synthesized, but before it is implemented. The deadlock identification methodology presented herein gives users the opportunity to identify and correct any possible conflict, thus, avoiding possible manufacturing delays and the use of on-line deadlock detection and recovery mechanisms. The deadlock identification methodology can be applied in many manufacturing control contexts such as in systems where the control specifications (temporarily) change, and to single- and multiworkcell systems, as described in the chapter. As an additional important and practical characteristic of the supervisor synthesis methodology and deadlock identification methodology here described, we present a methodology to minimize the state-space of the obtained supervisors with respect to the control actions generated at each state of the controller. This state-space minimization methodology can be used for the reduction of controllers (preserving their deadlock-free characteristics and behaviors they enforce) targeted to be used on single- and multiworkcell systems. We show how EMA-based controllers having these and other characteristics are suitable to be used in industrial applications employing computer-integrated systems. The chapter, however, does not provide a methodology on how to modify the controllers if potential deadlocks are identified. Nevertheless, the proposed technique provides users with the means to identify which manufacturing conditions allow such undesired states. Therefore, users may decide which manufacturing specifications or production conditions to modify and/or eliminate in order to obtain the supervisors that will control the system without deadlocks.

Finally, assuming a DES is described by an automaton, the chapter also describes how automata and their associated tools are used to determine if each admissible supervisor event sequence (trajectory) has the desired properties. Typical desired properties which are especially described are: *stability* (e.g., state convergence), *correct use of resources* (e.g., mutual exclusion), and *desirable dynamic behavior* (e.g., no deadlocks).

3.1 DESCRIPTION OF R-W CONTROL THEORY RELATED TO DEADLOCK-FREE CONTROL

3.1.1 Discrete Event Systems and Automata Theory

Competitive manufacturing strategies require the use of automated production systems which can be reconfigured and reprogrammed with efficiency. Such systems are expected to provide manufacturers with rapid-response capability, by being flexible enough to cope with frequent changes in customer demands [1]. In this context, the utilization of flexible manufacturing workcells (FMCs) has been advocated for low-volume, high-variety production. An FMC is defined herein as a system comprising automatic processing machines typically serviced by robotic material-handling devices working under the control of a supervisor [2]. These types of systems can be seen as systems that evolve by the occurrence of asynchronous discrete events. DESs encompass a wide variety of physical systems. They include manufacturing systems, traffic systems and communication networks. Typically, the processes associated with these systems are thought of as discrete (in time and space) and asynchronous (event-driven rather than time-driven). DESs in general and manufacturing systems in particular have been commonly modeled using automata.

This chapter gives a brief introduction to the definition of DESs and their representations using language and automata theory. It describes how DESs can be viewed as generators of a formal language and how, by adjoining a control structure, it is possible to control the language generated by a DES within certain limits.

In the academic literature, FMCs have been modeled as DESs utilizing a variety of formal control theories, most notably by PNs [3-7] and Ramadge-Wonham Automata theory [8]. This literature has also advocated the use of PCs for the direct control of FMCs, in an *open hardware architecture environment*. However, upon examining the current state of industrial control, one notes the wide use of programmable logic controllers (PLCs) for the control of FMCs and other production facilities [9-13].

In this section, we describe a formal methodology to synthezise supervisors for FMCs and other DES systems based on R-W supervisory control theory. The control methodologies described here can be implemented using a hybrid PC/PLC supervisory-control system as described in [14].

Automata and formal-language based supervisory-control theories of DESs, pioneered by the work of Professors Ramadge and Wonham (R-W), aim to design supervisors in such a way that the physical process coupled to its supervisor behaves deadlock-free according to logical constraints. A supervisor is a term used to describe a type of controller that observes the system's execution and at each state it enables/disables events. That is, supervisors do not enforce events; they simply allow or prevent them from occurring. In turn the system itself is the one responsible for executing an event from the set of enabled events.

Controlled Automata

The attractiveness of R-W controlled automata theory lies in its high expressive power and in the primary characteristic that the supervisory design technique guarantees the control strategy to be correct (conflict- and deadlock-free) by construction [8]. R-W theory provides a systematic approach that does not require iterating through phases of trial, analysis, and redesign.

State Explosion

As a result of the complexity, heterogeneity, and the nondeterministic nature of manufacturing workcells and other DES systems that arise naturally as the number of resources (e.g., machines) and jobs/parts increases, the use of traditional DES techniques is limited in practical applications. The inevitable DES exponential state-explosion problem that arises in discrete state nature models is generally used to synthezise context-dependent supervisors. Thus, in a typical manufacturing environment, for example, the effectiveness of the control strategy is limited. Efforts to overcome the combinatorial control-state-space problems associated with the state-explosion problem have resulted in modular, decentralized, and hierarchical controllers, though with limited success [15-16]. Traditionally, the monitoring capabilities of this theory are also limited, which limit its use in practical applications. These and other limitations have been in some way solved by using EMA. Herein we advocate the use of EMA for the synthesis of deadlock-free controllers for manufacturing systems.

Discrete Event Systems

DESs are dynamic systems that have a discrete state space, where the change from one state to another is driven by the occurrence of events at discrete time instants. Events are considered instantaneous in time and their occurrence is considered to take place at unpredictable time instances. At a specific state of a DES, where there may be more than one event that can occur, the DES is considered to select just one of the possible events in accordance with some internal (hidden) mechanism proprietary to the system. Normaly, it is assumed that two or more events cannot occur simultaneously. Within a manufacturing workcell, the internal state-change mechanism may be defined as a set of rules that select the next event to occur. In this sense, the operation of the DES is said to be non-deterministic. However, in DES theory, it is assumed that the event set that can occur at every state of a DES is deterministic in the sense that, at every state of the DES, every possible event takes the system to a different state.

Discrete event systems and their supervisors are in general represented using automata. Each state comprising an automaton represents a particular state of the system at hand. Transitions between states represent the events that change the state of the system. The state-event evolution of DESs is also modelled and analyzed using automata/language theory.

Automata Theory

Considered as the foundation of modern computational theory, automata theory provides a set of formal tools to model and study the logical behavior of DESs. In such a theory, a DES is considered a generator of a language described by an automaton that represents the evolution of the DES. One of the basic concepts in automata theory is that of finite-state machines. A finite-state machine, or automaton, is an abstract representation of a sequential process, where the model uses the notion of states and transitions: states are used to symbolize the discrete status of a process or a system, while transitions symbolize the occurrence of events that change the process or system from one state to another. An automaton is usually defined as a quintuple [17]: $\{\Sigma, Q, q_0, \delta(q, \sigma), F\}$. In this quintuple, Σ is a finite input alphabet, where each symbol represents an event, Q is a finite set of states, $q_0 \in Q$ is the initial state, δ is the state transition function defined as $\delta : Q \times \Sigma \rightarrow Q$, $\sigma \in \Sigma$ is an element or symbol of the input alphabet, and $F \subseteq Q$ is a set of final states where each state in the set "F" may represent the completion of the process. An automaton can be graphically represented using a state-transition diagram, where each node denotes a specific state in the set Q and each arc labeled with an element from the input alphabet denotes a transition from one state to another, as shown in Figure 3.1. In this sense, each transition may represent an event that the automaton processes, or an event that the DES executes. Figure 3.1 represents an automaton having two states: states 0 and 1, where state 0 is the initial state and state 1 is the final state. The input alphabet of this automaton comprises two symbols labeled as α and β.

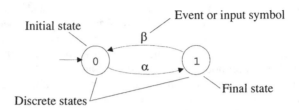

Figure 3.1. Automaton: an example.

A sequence of input symbols are called a string and a set of strings are called a language. These concepts are similar to a spoken language, which is composed of letters, words and sentences. Given a finite automaton, **G**, and a string, *s*, it is said that *s* is accepted by **G** if and only if **G** reaches a final state, $q \in F$, after sequentially processing every symbol comprising *s*. A language, L, is said to be accepted by G if all strings $s \in L$ are processed by **G**. The language accepted by **G** is denoted as L(**G**). For example, the string $\alpha\beta\alpha$ is accepted by the automaton of Figure 3.1, but the string $\alpha\alpha$ is not accepted since after processing the (first) symbol α the automaton reaches state 1, where β is the only possible event that can occur.

A language is *regular* if there exists a finite automaton, i.e., an automaton with a finite number of states that accepts such a language. In control only finite automata and, thus, regular languages are considered for practical purposes.

Automata can be used in the modeling of DESs, where languages are viewed as a representation of the behavior of the system, i.e., languages represent the possible set of activities that can occur within the system. Since automata can be used to describe a system through a set of mapping functions, it is possible to use such functions to derive a system's behavior and synthesize controllers as will be described in the following sections.

Moore Automata

Automata theory, as described above, can only be used for processing or generating languages. It cannot be used for processing inputs, as defined by their state transition function, and generating outputs. An automaton with outputs, on the other hand, is able to transform an input string into an output string, where output strings are formed by symbols comprising an output alphabet. This characteristic is necessary for the effective modeling and control of DESs that interact with their environment by providing outputs after executing events. A workcell controller, for example, may need to generate control commands (outputs) according to information received from the system under its control.

There exist two types of automata that generate outputs: (i) Moore and (ii) Mealy. Moore automata (MA) generate their outputs as a direct mapping between their states and their output alphabet. Mealy automata define their outputs as a mapping between their transitions and their output alphabet. Both, Moore and Mealy automata have been proven to be equivalent [17-18]. Herein Moore automata are selected as the tool to synthesize deadlock-free supervisors since its output function is simpler and can be used to explicitly specify the control commands generated by a DES controller depending on the global state of the system.

Moore automata are formally defined as a sixtuple [18], $\{\Sigma, Q, q_0, \delta(q, \sigma), \Delta, \omega\}$, where Σ, Q, q_0, and δ have the same meanings as in automata theory; Δ is the finite output alphabet; and ω is the output function, which maps, one-to-one, the current state to its associated output, $\omega : Q \rightarrow \Delta$. An illustrative example showing the characteristics of a MA is depicted in Figure 3.2, using a two-state automaton, where the output alphabet comprises two symbols, $\Delta = \{a, b\}$, since the outputs generated at states 0 and 1, defined by the output function, are $\omega(0) = a$ and $\omega(1) = b$, respectively.

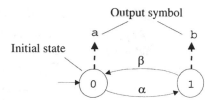

Figure 3.2. Moore automata: an example.

One must note, however, that MA are suitable only for the modeling, analysis and control of single-input/single-output systems. Moore automata have been used to synthesize controllers for various single-input/single-output systems. In [17], a simulated example of a MA-based supervisor that can control the traffic flow of automobiles at a street intersection is described. Control is enforced by changing the state of the traffic light by control signals represented by the outputs of the MA. In the control of many DESs, where several subsystems (e.g., individual resources) have to be controlled, it is necessary to extend the structure of MA to accept multiple inputs and generate multiple outputs. Thus making possible the control of diverse DES configurations, such as systems sharing resources, cooperating DES, and distributed plants, just to name a few.

3.1.2 Ramadge-Wonham Controlled Automata Theory

The problem of supervisory control of DESs modeled as automata has been extensively studied since Ramadge and Wonham's initial work in the area [8]. The key idea of supervisory control is that some executable DES events may be enabled or disabled when desired. By influencing the feasibility of events at certain times, it may be possible to achieve the desired behavior of the system.

In R-W control theory, the formal structure of a DES to be controlled is that of an automaton that generates a given language by executing a sequence of events. The mode of operation of a DES can be described as follows: starting from the initial state, the DES executes a sequence of events according to its state transition function. Upon the occurrence of an event, the event symbol is said to be generated by the DES. In this sense, the DES generates a string of event symbols over the event alphabet Σ. The set of all strings that can be generated by the DES defines a language that represents the uncontrolled, or free, behavior of the DES. The event set that a DES can execute, Σ, is partitioned into two disjoint subsets, Σ_c and Σ_u, which denote the controllable and uncontrollable events, respectively. Controllable events can be disabled at any time, while uncontrollable events cannot.

If L denotes the language generated by an automaton, and $\overline{L}$ denotes the prefix closure of L given by $\overline{L} = \{s \mid sx \in L\}$, where s is a prefix of a string comprising L, then the language K is said to be controllable if any prefix s of a string in K concatenated with an uncontrollable event, $e \in \Sigma_u$, for which the string "se" belongs to L, is another prefix of a string in K: formally, K is controllable if it satisfies the following expression:

$$\overline{K} \Sigma_u \cap L \subseteq \overline{K}. \tag{1}$$

If the language K is controllable, then there exists a supervisor, which guarantees that the closed-loop behavior of the DES is within the desired behavior, K, i.e., *the supervisor is correct by construction*. Moreover, if every string in K takes the system from its initial state to a final or *marker* state [8], then the system is deadlock-free. A marker state is interpreted as a state where the system reaches its objective, e.g., the production of a given set of parts or the successful transmission of a given signal.

If there is a string in K such that the system reaches a nonmarker state, after executing the sequence of events represented by such string, and no controllable or uncontrollable event will ever occur at such state, then the system is said to be in a deadlock state. A control function f specifies which events within the set Σ_c are enabled, i.e., allowed to occur at each state of the DES. It is evident that events in the set Σ_u are always enabled. Control of a DES is performed by changing the set of enabled events at every state of the DES based on the event history. In R-W control theory, DESs are not forced to execute events, instead they are allowed to freely execute any event from the set of enabled events. Thus, as described before, the DES controller is called a *supervisor*. In R-W control theory the supervisor synthesis methodology can be described in general terms using two steps:

Step 1:   The uncontrolled behavior of the system and the control specifications to be imposed are both described using individual automata. These two automata are, in turn, constructed by combining individual automata, each one representing either a physical component of the system, i.e., a machine, or a specific constraint to be imposed on the free-behavior of the DES. Two operations are used to obtain these automata: the *shuffle* and the *synch* operations, respectively. These two operations are standard for the specification of control problems involving the coordination and synchronization of several DESs. The result of the shuffle operation on two languages, L_1 and L_2, is defined as a language, L_3, consisting of all possible *interleavings* (shuffles) of strings of L_1 with string of L_2. The result of the *synch* operation, on the other hand, is defined as the language consisting of all strings that are obtained as a result of a synchronization of the common events comprising languages L_1 and L_2.

Step 2:   The *synch* operation is used to combine the languages generated by the composed system's automaton and the state machine representing the overall control specifications. Through an iterative process consisting of combining *supremal* controllable sublanguages, in conjunction with the control specifications, a (controllable) language is obtained. An automaton that accepts this language is then obtained and used as the supervisor, where the supervisor is seen as a recognizer of the particular language which describes the system's desired closed-loop behavior. If the obtained automaton is *trim*, i.e., every state comprising the automaton is *reachable* and *coreachable* as defined in [8], then the system under the control of the supervisor is guaranteed to be deadlock-free.

The R-W supervisory control theory has led to the development of several methodologies such as modular, hierarchical and hybrid techniques [19-20]. The R-W theory has also been used for the control of DESs under partial observation [21], where partial observation refers to situations in which the system to be controlled may execute events that are not observable by the supervisor. In order to deal with the timing aspects of many DESs and to study their performance, other authors have extended R-W control theory by including timing information into the modeling and control schemes [22].

3.2 EMA CONTROL

In contrast to traditional automata control, in this section EMA is introduced as a novel tool to synthesize deadlock-free controllers for a greater class, in terms of complexity, of DESs. Herein EMA is defined and the modeling of DES systems is described. Subsequently deadlock-free supervisor synthesis techniques are introduced.

3.2.1 EMA and Its Logic Operations

Definition of EMA

As described in the previous section, Moore automata are finite-state machines that can generate single outputs derived from their current state. In contrast EMA, first proposed in [23], are suitable for environments where several inputs and outputs are required for the proper control of DESs. In [24], EMA were proposed in combination with R-W automata theory to synthesize deadlock-free supervisors and, in [25], they were used for the control of workcells processing parts having alternative routes. EMA are defined as a sixtuple [26]:

$$
\text{EMA} = \{\left(\prod_{i \in I_1} \Sigma_i\right), Q, q_{0_t}, \delta^*(q, \sigma^*), \left(\prod_{i \in I_2} \Delta_i\right), \omega^*\}, \tag{2}
$$

where

$\prod_{i \in I_1} \Sigma_i$: is a set of finite-size input vectors, obtained by n-1 Cartesian products
  on input alphabets Σ_i: $\prod_{i \in I_1} \Sigma_i = \Sigma_1 \times \Sigma_2 \times \cdots \times \Sigma_n$. Thus, each element in $\prod_{i \in I_1} \Sigma_i$ is an n-tuple $(\sigma_1, \ldots, \sigma_n)$, where $\sigma_i \in \Sigma_i$ for $1 \le i \le n$.
  Herein, such elements are referred to as multi-input vectors. In the control of DESs the controllability (or uncontrollability) of these elements must be defined in terms of the controllability of the individual elements comprising every input alphabet, Σ_i;

Q: is a finite set of states;

q_0:   is the initial state;

δ^* :   is the extended partial transition function defined as $\delta^* : Q \times \prod_{i \in I_1} \Sigma_i \to Q$.
  This function defines the next state for each state and multi-input vector

pair, (q, σ^*), where $\sigma^* \in \prod_{i \in I_1} \Sigma_i$ and $q \in Q$. If $\delta^*(q, \sigma^*)$ is defined, it is denoted as $\delta^*(q, \sigma^*)$!, and if it is not defined, it is denoted as $\neg \delta^*(q, \sigma^*)$!;

$\prod_{i \in I_2} \Delta_i$: is a finite-size output vector set, obtained by m-1 Cartesian products on output alphabets Δ_i: $\prod_{i \in I_2} \Delta_i = \Delta_1 \times \Delta_2 \times \cdots \times \Delta_m$. Herein, the elements of $\prod_{i \in I_2} \Delta_i$ are referred to as multi-output vectors; and,

ω^* : is the extended output function which defines the multi-output vector generated at each state. Mathematically, it is defined as $\omega^* : Q \rightarrow \prod_{i \in I_2} \Delta_i$.

EMA can be used as controllers, herein referred to as EMA-based supervisors, that can read (receive) several inputs in a vector form, ($\prod_{i \in I_1} \Sigma_i$), and issue several control commands abstractly represented by their outputs, ($\prod_{i \in I_2} \Delta_i$). Namely, the multi-input vectors are used as monitoring information, or input signals, which change the global state of the DES under control. In turn, multi-outputs enable/disable machines to process specific part types and/or to perform specific operations depending on the current global state of the plant.

EMA can be represented in a state-table or in a state-diagram form. Herein the state-diagram representation is used since it provides a visual description of the behavior of the modeled DES. In a state-diagram form, circles, directed arrows, and dashed-line arrows represent states, transitions, and outputs of an EMA, respectively, as in Figure 3.3.

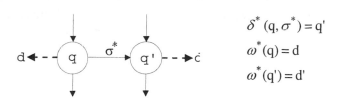

$$\delta^*(q, \sigma^*) = q'$$
$$\omega^*(q) = d$$
$$\omega^*(q') = d'$$

Figure 3.3. Illustrative state-diagram representation of EMA.

In general, DESs are man-made systems that have a deterministic behavior. Thus, here we are only concerned with deterministic EMA. An example of a deterministic DES is a manufacturing workcell that, regardless of what event it executes at every state, it is always possible to identify its current state by keeping track of its event history. The tools needed to combine EMA for the specification of control problems are described in the following subsections.

Input and Output Languages

In contrast to ordinary automata, which can only generate one language, an EMA is capable of generating two types of languages [26]: the *input* and *output* languages. For a particular EMA, the input and output languages are referred to as L_{in}(EMA) and L_{out}(EMA), respectively. L_{in}(EMA) is defined as the set of multi-input strings, x, accepted by the automaton, $\{x | \delta^*(q_0, x)!\}$. The output language L_{out}(EMA) is defined as the set of strings formed by the successive catenation of the multi-output vectors obtained at the visited states after processing every multi-input string comprising the input language. Formally:

$$L_{out}(EMA) = \{v | v = \omega_{cat}^*(\delta^*(q_0, x)) \ \wedge \ x \in L_{in}(EMA)\}, \qquad (3a)$$

where

v: is an output string generated by EMA, $v \in L_{out}(EMA)$;

x: is a multi-input string comprising multi-input vectors; and

ω_{cat}^*: denotes the string v formed by the successive catenation of the multi-output vectors obtained at the visited states after processing a multi-input string x. That is, if $x \in L_{in}(EMA)$, then $\omega_{cat}^*(\delta^*(q_0, x)) \in L_{out}(EMA)$ for $x = \sigma_1^* \sigma_2^* \cdots \sigma_n^*$, where $\sigma_i^* \in (\prod_{i \in I_i} \Sigma_i)$ such that $v = \omega_{cat}^*(\delta^*(q_0, x)) = \omega^*(q_0) \ \omega_{cat}^*(\delta^*(q_0, \sigma_1^*)) \cdots \omega_{cat}^*(\delta^*(q_{n-1}, \sigma_n^*))$. ω_{cat}^* can be recursively defined   on   two   multi-input   strings x and s as $\omega_{cat}^*(\delta^*(q_0, x)) \bullet (\omega_{cat}^*(\delta^*(\delta^*(q_0, x), s)))$, where $\bullet$ denotes the catenation of two strings x and s such that $x \bullet s = xs$, and $xs \in L_{in}(EMA)$.

In the special case, when x, in (3a), is equal to the null string, ε, then the output string is simply:

$$v = \omega^*(q_0). \qquad (3b)$$

Expressions (3a) and (3b) completely define the output language, L_{out}(EMA), generated by EMA in terms of the input language, L_{in}(EMA), and the extended output function, ω^*.

Next we describe the basic logic operations required to combine automata and obtain a global representation of two or more automata models.

Logic Operations on EMA

Herein, we describe four logic operations (on EMA languages) that allow us to describe complex DESs in terms of simpler ones as well as to synthesize "correct" DES supervisors. Although, these logic operations are based on traditional automata operations, as those included in [27], they are recent and valuable extensions necessary for the control of complex flexible-manufacturing systems, which would not be possible using other techniques. An example of the type of complex systems that the following operations allow us to control is a *reconfigurable FMC*, which may share resources with other FMCs for the production of parts having alternative processing routes [24, 28].

(*i*) The shuffle operation

The shuffle operation on EMA yields an automaton that accepts all possible interleavings (shuffles) of strings (words) of the input language generated by all the EMA upon which the operation is being applied. Thus, the obtained automaton represents the coordinated behavior of several EMA. Let the interleaving of two languages, L_1 and L_2, defined as *interleave*$[L_1, L_2]$, generate a new language, L_3, defined as:

$$L_3 = interleave[L_1, L_2] = \{x_1 y_1 x_2 y_2 \cdots x_k y_k \mid k \text{ is arbitrary}, x_1 x_2 \cdots x_k \in L_1 \text{ and } y_1 y_2 \cdots y_k \in L_2\}, \tag{4}$$

where some strings x's and y's may be empty, i.e., ε. Based on (4) and on the R-W shuffle operation developed for controlled automata [8], the shuffle operation, $\otimes$, on two EMA, EMA$_1$ and EMA$_2$, is then defined as [26]:

$$\text{shuffle\_EMA} = \text{EMA}_1 \otimes \text{EMA}_2 =$$
$$\{ \bigcup_{n=1,2} (\textstyle\prod \Sigma)_n, Q, q_0, \delta^*(q, \sigma^*), \prod_{n=1,2} (\textstyle\prod \Delta)_n, \omega^* \}. \tag{5}$$

where

$\bigcup_{n=1,2} (\prod \Sigma)_n$: is the finite multi-input vector set defined as the union of the multi-input vector sets within EMA$_1$ and EMA$_2$: $\bigcup_{n=1,2} (\prod \Sigma)_n = \left(\prod_{i \in I,} \Sigma_i \right)_1 \cup \left(\prod_{i \in I,} \Sigma_i \right)_2$;

Q: is the Cartesian product of Q_1 and Q_2, $Q_1 \times Q_2$, which defines all possible global states of shuffle_EMA. A global state q is defined as a pair: $(q_{i_1} \in Q_1, q_{j_2} \in Q_2)$, where q_{i_1} refers to state *i* of EMA$_1$ and q_{j_2} refers to state *j* of EMA$_2$. If Q_1 and Q_2 are finite, then shuffle_DES is also finite. The number of all possible global states (cardinality of Q) is obtained as: $|Q| = \prod |Q_i|$;

q_0:   is the initial global state, $q_0 = (q_{0_1}, q_{0_2}) \in Q$;

$q \in Q$: is a global state as defined above: $q \in (q_{i_1} \in Q_1, q_{j_2} \in Q_2)$;

σ^*:   is a multi-input vector: $\sigma^* \in \bigcup_{n=1,2} (\prod \Sigma)_n$. In order to distinguish one multi-input vector from another, the input vector k of EMA_t is represented as $\sigma^*_{k_t}$;

δ^*:   is the extended partial transition function. $\delta^*(q, \sigma^*)$ maps, one-to-one,

$\quad Q \times \bigcup_{n=1,2} (\prod \Sigma)_n$ to Q

$\quad$ such that: $\delta^*((q_{i_1}, q_{j_2}), \sigma^*_{k_t}) = (\delta_1^* \times \delta_2^*)[(q_{i_1}, q_{j_2}), \sigma^*_{k_t}]$

$$\delta^*((q_{i_1}, q_{j_2}), \sigma^*_{k_t}) = \begin{cases} \delta_1^*(q_{i_1}, \sigma^*_{k_t}) \times \{q_{j_2}\} & \text{if } \delta_1^*(q_{i_1}, \sigma_{k_t})! \text{ and } t = 1 \\ \{q_{i_1}\} \times \delta_2^*(q_{j_2}, \sigma^*_{k_t}) & \text{if } \delta_2^*(q_{j_2}, \sigma_{k_t})! \text{ and } t = 2 \\ \varnothing & \text{otherwise.} \end{cases}$$

where $\varnothing$ represents the empty set, e.g., no transition can occur from state q_{i_1} under $\sigma^*_{k_1}$;

$\prod_{n=1,2} (\prod \Delta)_n$: is the set of multi-output vectors. $\prod_{n=1,2} (\prod \Delta)_n$ contains the multi-output vector for each global state in shuffle_DES. $\prod_{n=1,2} (\prod \Delta)_n$ is obtained by performing a Cartesian product on the output sets within EMA_1 and EMA_2, including the null output, ε:

$\quad \prod_{n=1,2} (\prod \Delta)_n = \{ (\prod_{i \in I_1} \Delta_i)_1 \cup \varepsilon \} \times \{ (\prod_{i \in I_2} \Delta_i)_2 \cup \varepsilon \}$; and

ω^*:   is the extended output function that defines the multi-output at each global state in shuffle_DES: $\omega^* : Q \rightarrow \prod_{n=1,2} (\prod \Delta)_n$. ω^* is obtained using the set Union function ($\cup$) on the individual states composing each global state:

$\quad \omega^*(q \in Q) = \omega^*(q_{i_1}, q_{j_2}) = [\omega_1^*(q_{i_1}) \cup \omega_2^*(q_{j_2})] \in \prod_{n=1,2} (\prod \Delta)_n$.

If the multi-input sets comprising EMA_1 and EMA_2, $(\prod_{i \in I_1} \Sigma_i)_1$ and $(\prod_{i \in I_1} \Sigma_i)_2$, respectively, are not disjoint, i.e., $(\prod_{i \in I_1} \Sigma_i)_1 \cap (\prod_{i \in I_1} \Sigma_i)_2 \neq \varnothing$, then the automaton obtained after applying the shuffle operation on EMA_1 and EMA_2 is nondeterministic. However, this is not the case if the common multi-input vectors only perform selfloop transitions, i.e., transitions that point to the same state from which they exit. If $\left(\prod_{i\in I_1}\Sigma_i\right)_1$ and $\left(\prod_{i\in I_1}\Sigma_i\right)_2$ are disjoint, i.e., $\left(\prod_{i\in I_1}\Sigma_i\right)_1 \cap \left(\prod_{i\in I_1}\Sigma_i\right)_2 = \varnothing$, then the obtained automaton is deterministic.

(*ii*) The meet operation

The meet operation is used to combine several EMA with common multi-input vectors into a single EMA. The common set of multi-input vectors of two EMA is first obtained by performing an intersection set operation over their multi-input vector sets, $\left(\prod_{i\in I_1}\Sigma_i\right)_1$ and $\left(\prod_{i\in I_1}\Sigma_i\right)_2$. The EMA are then combined by performing a synchronization of their common multi-input vectors. Based on [8], the meet operation, $\oplus$, for two EMA, EMA_1 and EMA_2, is defined as [26]:

$$\text{meet\_EMA} = EMA_1 \oplus EMA_2 =$$
$$\{\cap_{n=1,2}(\textstyle\prod\Sigma)_n ,Q, q_0, \delta^*(q,\sigma^*), \prod_{n=1,2}(\textstyle\prod\Delta)_n , \omega^*\}. \quad (6)$$

where

Q, q_0, q, σ^*, $\prod_{n=1,2}(\prod\Delta)_n$, and ω^* are defined as in (5), whereas now $\sigma^* \in \cap_{n=1,2}(\prod\Sigma)_n$;

$\cap_{n=1,2}(\prod\Sigma)_n$: is the finite multi-input vector set defined as: $\cap_{n=1,2}(\prod\Sigma)_n = \left(\prod_{i\in I_1}\Sigma_i\right)_1 \cap \left(\prod_{i\in I_1}\Sigma_i\right)_2$. If $\cap_{n=1,2}(\prod\Sigma)_n = \varnothing$, then EMA_1 and EMA_2 have no common multi-input vectors. Thus, there is no synchronization to be performed and the resulting automaton is an empty EMA, i.e., an automaton with one state and zero transitions; and

δ^* : is the extended transition partial function defined as, $\delta^* : Q \times \cap_{n=1,2}(\prod\Sigma)_n \rightarrow Q$ with $\delta^* = \delta_1^* \times \delta_2^*$:

$$\delta^*((q_{i_1}, q_{j_2}), \sigma_k^*) = \quad (7)$$
$$\begin{cases} (\delta_1^*(q_{i_1}, \sigma_k^*) \in Q_1, \delta_2^*(q_{j_2}, \sigma_k^*) \in Q_2) & \text{if } \delta_1^*(q_{i_1}, \sigma_k^*)! \wedge \delta_2^*(q_{j_2}, \sigma_k^*)! \\ \varnothing & \text{if } \neg\delta_1^*(q_{i_1}, \sigma_k^*)! \vee \neg\delta_2^*(q_{j_2}, \sigma_k^*)! \end{cases}.$$

(*iii*) The shuffle-meet operation (disjunction operation)

The EMA shuffle and meet operations yield an EMA that either represents the coordinated or the synchronized behavior of the models upon which the operation is being applied to, respectively, but not both. Herein, the *disjunction* operation, which merges the shuffle and meet operations to yield an automaton that represents the behavior of several EMA inter-related with common events, is described – namely, an EMA having the following two properties:

$$\left(\prod_{i\in I_1} \Sigma_i\right)_1 \cap \left(\prod_{i\in I_1} \Sigma_i\right)_2 \neq \varnothing, \text{ and (EMA}_1 \text{ and EMA}_2 \text{ have common multi-inputs)} \quad (8a)$$

$$\left(\prod_{i\in I_1} \Sigma_i\right)_1 \neq \left(\prod_{i\in I_1} \Sigma_i\right)_2 .\text{(EMA}_1 \text{ and EMA}_2 \text{ have uncommon multi-inputs)} \quad (8b)$$

The automaton obtained by the disjunction operation, thus, represents the behavior of several DESs evolving independently while synchronizing their common actions. Based on the work initiated by Ramadge and Wonham [8], the disjunction operation ($\vee$) on two EMA, EMA$_1$ and EMA$_2$, having the properties defined in (8), is defined as [28]:

$$\text{EMA}_1 \vee \text{EMA}_2 = \{\textstyle\bigcup_{n=1,2}\left(\prod\Sigma\right)_n, Q_1 \times Q_2, (q_{0_1}, q_{02}), \overline{\delta}^*, \overline{\Delta}, \overline{\omega}^*\}, \quad (9)$$

where

$\bigcup_{n=1,2}\left(\prod\Sigma\right)_n$, $Q_1 \times Q_2$, and (q_{0_1}, q_{02}) are defined as in (5);

$\overline{\delta}^*$: is the extended transition partial function defined as the combination of the shuffle and meet operations. If a transition (multi-input vector) belongs to both EMA, EMA$_1$ and EMA$_2$, then the EMA meet operation is used, otherwise the shuffle operation is used. Formally:

If $\sigma^*_{k_t} \notin \{\prod_{i\in I_1} \Sigma_i\}_1 \cap \{\prod_{i\in I_1} \Sigma_i\}_2$, i.e., the multi-input $\sigma^*_{k_t}$ is not a common transition, then the EMA shuffle operation is applied:

$$\overline{\delta}^* = \begin{cases} \delta_1^*(q_{i_1}, \sigma^*_{k_t}) \times \{q_{j_2}\} & \text{if } \delta_1^*(q_{i_1}, \sigma^*_{k_t})! \text{ and } t = 1 \\ \{q_{i_1}\} \times \delta_2^*(q_{j_2}, \sigma^*_{k_t}) & \text{if } \delta_2^*(q_{j_2}, \sigma^*_{k_t})! \text{ and } t = 2 \\ \varnothing & \text{otherwise.} \end{cases}$$

If $\sigma^*_{k_t} \in \{\prod_{i\in I_1} \Sigma_i\}_1 \cap \{\prod_{i\in I_1} \Sigma_i\}_2$, i.e., the multi-input $\sigma^*_{k_t}$ is a common transition, then

$\sigma^*_k = \sigma^*_{k_t}$, and the EMA meet operation is applied:

$$\overline{\delta}^* = \begin{cases} (\delta_1^*(q_{i_1}, \sigma^*_k) \in Q_1, \delta_2^*(q_{j_2}, \sigma^*_k) \in Q_2) & \text{if (see No. 1 below)} \\ \varnothing & \text{if (see No. 2 below)} \end{cases}$$

$$\text{No.1}:\ \delta_1^*(q_{i_1},\sigma_k^*)!\wedge\delta_2^*(q_{j_2},\sigma_k^*)!$$

$$\text{No.2}:\ \neg\delta_1^*(q_{i_1},\sigma_k^*)!\vee\neg\delta_2^*(q_{j_2},\sigma_k^*)!$$

$\overline{\Delta}$: is the set of multi-output vectors generated by both EMA$_1$ and EMA$_2$ defined as: $\overline{\Delta} = \left(\prod_{i\in I_2}\Delta_i\right)_1 \cup \left(\prod_{i\in I_2}\Delta_i\right)_2$; and

$\overline{\omega}^*$: is the multi-output function defined as:

$$\overline{\omega}^* = \omega_1^* \vee \omega_2^* =$$

$$=\{\omega_1^*(q\in Q_1)\cup\omega_2^*(q\in Q_2)\}\ \cap\ \{\{\textstyle\prod_{i\in I_1}\Delta_i\}_1\cap\{\textstyle\prod_{i\in I_1}\Delta_i\}_2\}.$$ That

is, the output function only generates outputs that can be generated by both EMA$_1$ and EMA$_2$.

For compactness, the disjunction operation applied to a set of EMA is represented herein as: $\underset{k\in I_3}{\mathbf{V}}\ \text{EMA}_k$, where **V** is the disjunction operator and I_3 is a non-empty index set that represents the set of EMA to which the operator is being applied to. For example, when the disjunction operation is used to combine EMA$_1$, EMA$_3$ and EMA$_5$, then, $I_3 = \{1,3,5\}$, and, thus,

$$\underset{k\in I_3}{\mathbf{V}}\ \text{EMA}_k = \text{EMA}_1 \vee \text{EMA}_3 \vee \text{EMA}_5.$$

The EMA *shuffle, meet* and *disjunction* operations satisfy the associative and commutative properties. For example, if A, B, and C are three EMA, then A⊗(B⊗C) = (A⊗B)⊗C and A⊗B = B⊗A. This is true for the meet and disjunction operations as well, e.g., A∨(B∨C) = (A∨B)∨C.

(*iv*) The natural projection on EMA input languages
A natural projection (NP) is an operation that allows the user to erase some undesirable symbols (events) from every string comprising a given language. (This operation is useful for the analysis of individual resources comprising the controlled plant). The NP on languages, defined for regular automata in [29], is described herein for EMA input languages.

Let $L_{in}(\text{EMA}_1)$ and $L_{in}(\text{EMA}_2)$ be defined over different multi-input alphabets, $\{\prod_{i\in I_1}\Sigma_i\}_1$ and $\{\prod_{i\in I_1}\Sigma_i\}_2$, respectively, where it is allowed that:

$$\bigcap_{t=1}^{2}(\textstyle\prod_{i\in I_1}\Sigma_i)_t = \{\textstyle\prod_{i\in I_1}\Sigma_i\}_1 \cap \{\textstyle\prod_{i\in I_1}\Sigma_i\}_2 \neq \varnothing. \tag{10}$$

Also, let $L_{in}(\text{EMA}^*)$ be defined over the multi-input alphabet comprising EMA$_1$ and EMA$_2$:

$$\bigcup_{n=1,2}(\Pi\Sigma)_n = \{\Pi_{i\in I_1}\Sigma_i\}_1 \cup \{\Pi_{i\in I_1}\Sigma_i\}_2. \tag{11}$$

The NP for EMA is then defined as [28]:

$$NP_{EMA_t} : L_{in}(EMA^*) \rightarrow L_{in}(EMA_t) \qquad (t = 1, 2) \tag{12}$$

according to $NP_{EMA_t} : (\varepsilon) = \varepsilon,$

$$NP_{EMA_t} : (\sigma^*) = \begin{cases} \varepsilon & \text{if } \sigma^* \notin \{\Pi_{i\in I_t}\Sigma_i\}_t \\ \sigma^* & \text{if } \sigma^* \in \{\Pi_{i\in I_t}\Sigma_i\}_t \end{cases},$$

where ε is the null symbol.

By using the concatenate property of multi-input vectors, NP_{EMA_t} can be recursively defined on multi-input strings $x \in L_{in}(EMA^*)$, where $x = \sigma_1^*\sigma_2^*...\sigma_n^* \mid \sigma_i^* \in \bigcup_{n=1,2}(\Pi\Sigma)_n$ as:

$$NP_{EMA_t}(x\sigma^*) = NP_{EMA_t}(x)\, NP_{EMA_t}(\sigma^*). \tag{13}$$

Thus, the action of NP_{EMA_t} on a string x, belonging to the language $L_{in}(EMA^*)$, is simply erasing all occurrences of σ^*, when $\sigma^* \in \{\bigcup_{n=1,2}(\Pi\Sigma)_n - (\Pi_{i\in I_1}\Sigma_i)_t\}$, where $(\Pi_{i\in I_1}\Sigma_i)_t$ is the set of events that can occur within the DES of interest (e.g., a workcell machine), modeled by EMA_t. The NP, thus, represents the relationship between the input languages accepted by EMA^* and EMA_t. The definition of the NP on two EMA can be easily extended to several EMA, $L_{in}(EMA_t)$, $t = 1$ to n, by allowing $\bigcap_{t=1}^{n}(\Pi_{i\in I_1}\Sigma_i)_t \neq \emptyset$, and defining $L_{in}(EMA^*)$ over the multi-input alphabet $\bigcup_{t}^{n}(\Pi_{i\in I_1}\Sigma_i)_t$ (namely, extending (10) and (11)).

3.2.2 Using EMA in the Modeling Process

Similar to traditional automata, EMA can be used to model manufacturing devices (i.e., machines), communication systems, and other DESs [14]. System specifications, processing routes, and production constraints can also be represented (modeled) using EMA [24-26, 28]. In this section, we describe how EMA are used to describe these and other DESs.

Machines and other devices

The behavior of a machine in a production environment can be represented by the language accepted by its corresponding EMA model, where the multi-input vectors represent the set of (processes) transitions that can occur: $\sigma^* = (\sigma \in \Sigma_1,$ $\sigma \in \Sigma_2, \ \sigma \in \Sigma_3) \in \prod_{i \in I_1} \Sigma_i$. Each alphabet, Σ_1, Σ_2 and Σ_3, is used to represent physical events, part types and operations (jobs), respectively. Specifically, lowercase Greek letters represent the elements of Σ_1, uppercase italic bold Latin letters represent the elements of Σ_2, and integer numbers comprise the elements of Σ_3. In a manufacturing plant model, each triplet of symbols in σ^*, thus, represents the part type that is affected by the occurrence of the physical event and the operation being performed on it. Herein, device or resource models are represented as M_i, where the subscript i represent the machine/resource identification number.

In the graphical representation of manufacturing or other devices, controllable multi-input vectors, which can be enabled/disabled at will by a supervisor, are identified with a tic in their transition arrows ($\longmapsto$). The multi-output vector of a particular state is used to represent the controllable physical events that are (or need to be) disabled at that state. In case no multi-input need to be disabled, an empty multi-output, (-), is defined. As an example, Figure 3.4 shows an EMA model that represents a basic device such as a robotic manipulator or a lathe which is capable of performing operation No. 5 on part type A, with I_i, W_i, and D_i representing the idle (initial state), working, and down states, respectively. (Again the subscript i is used as a generalization to represent the machine/resource identification number.) The symbols α, β, λ, and μ represent the events start of operation, ending of operation, machine failure, and repair of machine, respectively. The symbols (#) and (-) represent a "don't_care" condition.

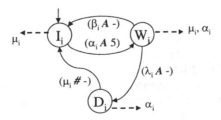

Figure 3.4. Basic production resource model.

Constraints

Constraint models can be used to represent manufacturing rules needed to produce parts within workcells or to represent the constraints to be imposed on communication networks, just to name a couple of examples. Models used to define the size of a buffer or to specify the order in which machines will be repaired (in case more than one breaks down) are typical examples that may occur in a manufacturing environment. In these models, herein represented as $SPEC_i$, multi-input and multi-output vectors are interpreted in the same manner as described before [26].

Routes

Manufacturing processing routes and the steps (protocol) needed to transmit a message in a communications network are other types of entities that can be represented in a similar way using EMA. When synthesizing a supervisor, one has to consider the possible routing problems, such as deadlocks and device overflowing that may arise when two or more entities, probably of the same type but using different routes, are being produced or administered by the system concurrently. In manufacturing, for example, a part-route model represents the full set of alternative production sequences for that part. In production environments the movements of entities (e.g., parts) within a DES are described using a *route model*. Thus, a route model is not a necessary DES but the parts' evolution can be described using DES terminologies.

The need to use route models arises from the need to describe the behavior of a DES in terms of the movement that occurs inside the system itself.

In order to address and solve deadlocks, device overflowing, and other problems that arise in DES, in [25, 26] it was proposed to use *advance route models* (ARM) that can trace the processing history of each individual part flowing in a workcell. By being able to trace the part/job history, it is possible to find and avoid potential problems in an effective way. ARMs can also be employed in non-manufacturing scenarios where it is necessary to trace the history of every entity flowing within a DES.

ARMs are constructed using a three-step process. First, for every part type, an EMA *basic route model* (BRM) that represents all its alternative routes is constructed. An example BRM model is shown in Figure 3.5 (For a route type X, this model is denoted by BRM_X.). All multi-input vectors which affect the specific route type at hand must be included in its BRM_X model. Figure 3.5 represents an entity that has two alternative processing routes as defined by the two cycles: $B_0B_1B_2B_3B_0$ and $B_0B_1B_2B_4B_0$.

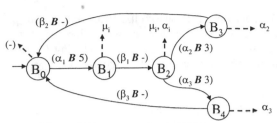

Figure 3.5. An example of a BRM.

Second, for each BRM, an ARM that represents the concurrent processing of several entities having the same route set is constructed. For route type X, its ARM_X is obtained by performing $(n-1)$ shuffle operations on the corresponding BRM_X, where n is the maximum number of entities of type X that the system can concurrently process [26]:

$$ARM_X = BRM_{X_1} \otimes BRM_{X_2} \otimes \cdots \otimes BRM_{X_n} . \qquad (14)$$

The language accepted by ARM_X tracks the processing history of entities by observing the global states in the automaton ARM_X.

Some global states in ARM_X may be "unsafe" and need to be "trimmed" in order to prevent them from occurring. An unsafe state is a state that prevents some or all parts currently being processed from proceeding to completion, e.g., a state where a deadlock occurs. (In [26], the conditions that a state comprising an ARM must satisfy in order to be a safe state are formally defined and the *safe operation* used to obtain safe ARMs is described in detail). The construction of the safe ARM, ARM_X^s, represents the third and final step in the route modeling process:

$$ARM_X^s = safe\ (ARM_X). \qquad (15)$$

3.2.3 Synthesis of Deadlock-free Supervisors

In this section, we describe how EMA are used to synthesize deadlock-free supervisors. This section describes the process of manufacturing workcells, but similar steps can be used to obtain supervisors for other types of DES.

Modeling

In order to synthesize a workcell supervisor, all pertinent EMA models must be first generated and combined to represent (i) the global (unconstrained) behavior of the workcell, **CELL**, (ii) the set of manufacturing constraints to be imposed on the global behavior of the workcell, **SPEC**, and (iii) all possible sequences in which parts can be concurrently processed within the system, **PARTS**, respectively. For a DES comprising n machines, producing k different part types while satisfying p manufacturing constraints, the corresponding three models are generated as follows [28, 30]:

$$\mathbf{CELL} = \mathbf{M}_1 \otimes \mathbf{M}_2 \otimes \cdots \otimes \mathbf{M}_n, \tag{16}$$

$$\mathbf{SPEC} = \mathbf{SPEC}_1 \oplus \mathbf{SPEC}_2 \oplus \cdots \oplus \mathbf{SPEC}_p, \tag{17}$$

$$\mathbf{PARTS} = \mathbf{ARM}_A^s \otimes \mathbf{ARM}_B^s \otimes \cdots \otimes \mathbf{ARM}_k^s. \tag{18}$$

The global models generated in Expressions (16) to (18) yield specific languages, namely, the *behavior*, $L_{in}(\mathbf{CELL})$, the *constraint*, $L_{in}(\mathbf{SPEC})$, and the *processing* languages, $L_{in}(\mathbf{PARTS})$, respectively, which describe the uncontrolled behavior of the FMC, the global system's constraint, and the concurrent processing of parts, respectively.

Synthesis of supervisors

In order to control a workcell, according to the information provided by the three languages described above, the automaton **CTRL** that represents the overall control strategy is generated by using the EMA meet operation on the **CELL**, **SPEC** and **PARTS** models [26]:

$$\mathbf{CTRL} = \mathbf{CELL} \oplus \mathbf{SPEC} \oplus \mathbf{PARTS}. \tag{19}$$

CTRL is an EMA that restricts the language generated by **CELL**, i.e., the free behavior of the system, to only those strings that can also be generated by **SPEC** and **PARTS**, simultaneously: $L_{in}(\mathbf{CTRL}) = L_{in}(\mathbf{CELL}) \cap L_{in}(\mathbf{SPEC}) \cap L_{in}(\mathbf{PARTS})$. Control execution is performed by **CTRL** by generating a new set of controllable events for disablement, i.e., multi-outputs, or for enablement, multi-inputs, respectively, after an event causes the workcell to change state. Thus, the controlled behavior of **CELL** consists exactly of the set of strings of $L_{in}(\mathbf{CELL})$ that survive under the supervision of **CTRL**.

3.3 Flexibility Provided by EMA for Reconfigurable Deadlock-Free Systems

Recent investigations have shown that EMA can be effectively used for the deadlock-free control of reconfigurable systems. Manufacturing plants are one such example where changes in the production system are required when production modifications are introduced. EMA have also been used for the deadlock-free control of systems sharing resources [28] and for cooperating systems (e.g., two or more manufacturing plants producing a single product).

In this section, we present a recent and novel methodology for the control of systems that are allowed to undergo changes without the need to modify the original (nominal) controller. Herein we refer to this type of systems as reconfigurable DESs. The two types of changes that will be discussed are (i) changes in the part type set produced, and (ii) the introduction of new machines into the system on a temporary basis. The control synthesis processes presented here allow to reconfigure DESs either on an *on-line* or *off-line* basis.

EMA not only can be used for the control of reconfigurable systems but can also cope with traditional DES control problems such as the state-explosion problem as shown in [26] where a state-space minimization algorithm is described and an illustrative example is presented. Section 4 of this chapter describes such state-space minimization technique in detail.

EMA also allows the implementation of DES supervisors using industrial controllers (e.g., programmable logic controllers) in a transparent way to the user as described in [14], where a complete description of the methodology and software tools that have been developed are presented.

3.3.1 Deadlock-Free Control of Reconfigurable DESs

General problem statement

It is well known that diverse DESs such as manufacturing workcells may provide redundancy for those components of the system that are subject to failures with higher than acceptable rates. These redundant components may be permanently embedded in the nominal system or may be added as needed on a temporary basis. In the past, a common approach has been to provide redundancy only for those components that are critical. These components are, then, considered during the supervisor synthesis process, and therefore, embedded in the controller. On a more recent approach, redundancy has been used on a standby basis where operation is switched from an original to its redundant component when needed. Herein DESs are seen as systems that have two types of redundancy: (i) *operation redundancy*, where machines have the capability to perform operations performed by other machines comprising the system and/or the capability to perform operations that are not presently required, and (ii) *standby redundancy*, where new devices can be introduced on a temporary basis to accommodate changing requirements. These two types of redundancies have several advantages, some of which are to: generate new products that were not originally produced; remove bottlenecks; increase throughput; increase capacity and production speed; distribute workload and resolve deadlocks.

Although redundancy can have a significant positive impact on the utilization of DESs, their implementation is not a common practice due to the fact that there exists no (systematic) methodology to control such expanding systems. Namely, since system requirements cannot be always predicted one cannot synthesize supervisors capable of coping with changing requirements. Here we address the problem of DES supervision when the control specifications change (temporarily). This type of systems is referred to as temporarily expanded/reconfigurable DESs [28, 31].

Proposed approach for the deadlock-free control of reconfigurable DESs

Traditionally, the function of a supervisor is to coordinate the various elements comprising the DES for the accomplishment of a predetermined desired set of jobs using a predetermined set of resources. Herein, these set of jobs to be performed and the resources used are referred to as *nominal jobs/resources*, and the supervisors controlling such (nominal) systems are referred to as *nominal supervisors*. During the nominal-supervisor synthesis process, it is assumed that the complete set of events that can be executed by the system is *observable*. Namely, the synthesized supervisor is able to recognize and process each and every event, and provide adequate control signals after every event occurrence. If a supervisor can respond to an event, such an event is noted to be an *observable event*. Herein, a supervisor that can observe every event in a system is said to be *complete*, otherwise it is said to be *incomplete*. Incomplete supervisors are, thus, incapable of responding to a subset of events that the plant under its control can generate. The set of events to which an incomplete supervisor cannot respond to is defined as the *unobservable* event set. If a plant has unobservable events, then the system is said to be *partially observable*, otherwise, it is *completely observable*. The control of partially observed systems has been addressed in the literature. However, the control of systems which are allowed to change from being completely observable to partially observable, or vice versa, such as reconfigurable manufacturing plants, has not been addressed in the literature. Current supervisor synthesis methodologies assume that the job mix remains constant and only consider systems that are not allowed to expand or contract. In practice, however, the job or product mix changes over time, new jobs are required to be processed while, other (nominal) jobs may be temporarily or permanently discontinued.

One can take several approaches in addressing the control of temporarily-expanded systems. In one approach, the nominal supervisor is resynthesized while considering the new plant (i.e., including its new specifications) as the new system, e.g., nominal and new resources/jobs are considered together. The resynthesized supervisor naturally is complete: the supervisor can respond to any event generated by the expanded plant. However, the time required to resynthesize the supervisor and rewire the complete system may be a serious limitation. A second approach is to synthesize a nominal supervisor together with a set of standby supervisors, where each standby supervisor is designed to control the plant according to specific extensions (e.g., based on forecasting). A third approach involves the synthesis of a nominal and a complementary supervisors. Once synthesized, the nominal/complementary supervisor pair is used to concurrently control the expanded plant without deadlocks. If the plant returns to its nominal specification set, then the complementary supervisor is discarded. Herein, we describe the use of a *nominal/complementary supervisor pair* and how such a pair can effectively control a DES without deadlocks [e.g., 31].

The nominal supervisor is responsible for controlling the behavior of the nominal system, while the complementary supervisor is targeted to either (*i*) control the flow of jobs when they follow any one of the routes that have been temporarily added into their nominal space route due to the introduction of new resources, or (*ii*) control the flow of a set of a priori unplanned job types within the nominal plant. This approach presents several primary advantages over other methodologies, some of which are:

(i) The plant can be expanded without any restrictions and resynthesis of the nominal supervisor is not necessary; and

(ii) The supervisory tasks are distributed, thus, the two supervisors controlling the expanded system are simpler than a global supervisor enforcing the same desired deadlock-free behavior.

The nominal supervisor is synthesized using the methodology described in Section 2. The process to synthesize the complementary supervisor depends on how the nominal system is to be expanded. If the nominal plant is expanded to carry out a new set of jobs, then the complementary supervisor synthesis process described in Section 3.3 is used [30]. If, however, the nominal DES is expanded by introducing new resources, then the complementary supervisor synthesis process follows the approach described in Section 3.4 [31]. Before describing these synthesis processes, the following section will first introduce the necessary notation.

3.3.2 Notation and Definitions

Nominal and complementary supervisors

The automata representing both the nominal and the complementary supervisors are defined as:

$$\mathbf{CTRL}_{\text{nom}} = \{ \Sigma, Q, q_0, \delta^*(q, \sigma^*), \Delta, \omega^* \}, \text{ and} \tag{20}$$

$$\mathbf{CTRL}_{\text{com}} = \{ \Gamma, X, x_0, \xi^*(x, \gamma^*), \Lambda, \varphi^* \}, \text{ respectively,} \tag{21}$$

where Σ and Γ are finite sets of events (i.e., multi-input vectors); $\Sigma \cap \Gamma \neq \varnothing$; Σ is the event set observable by $\mathbf{CTRL}_{nom}$ and Γ is the event set observable by $\mathbf{CTRL}_{com}$; Q and X are finite sets of states; q_0 and x_0 are the initial states; δ^* and ξ^* are the extended transition functions defined as $\delta^* : Q \times \Sigma \rightarrow Q$ and $\xi^* : X \times \Gamma \rightarrow X$, respectively; q and x are states such that $q \in Q$ and $x \in X$; σ^* and γ^* are multi-input vectors, $\sigma^* \in \Sigma$ and $\gamma^* \in \Gamma$; Δ and Λ are finite sets of multi-output vectors generated by $\mathbf{CTRL}_{nom}$ and $\mathbf{CTRL}_{com}$, respectively. The sets Δ and Λ may satisfy the relationship $\Delta \cap \Lambda \neq \varnothing$, namely, there may be events that can be disabled by either supervisor; and, ω^* and φ^* are the extended output functions defined as $\omega^* : Q \rightarrow \Delta$ and $\varphi^* : X \rightarrow \Lambda$, respectively.

Observable and unobservable event sets

When a plant is expanded, the nominal supervisor, $\mathbf{CTRL}_{nom}$, which was originally complete, becomes incomplete, i.e., not all events generated by the expanded system are observable by $\mathbf{CTRL}_{nom}$. As proposed in [31], these new events, unobservable by $\mathbf{CTRL}_{nom}$, would be observable and, thus, controllable by the complementary supervisor, $\mathbf{CTRL}_{com}$. From (20) and (21), the complete set of events that can occur within the expanded system is defined as:

$$\Omega = \Sigma \cup \Gamma. \tag{22}$$

The set Ω can be furthermore divided into two disjoint sets: (1) the set of events generated by job-processing devices such as lathes, milling machines and database query systems, Ω_p, and (2) the set generated by transporting devices such as robots, conveyors and network transmission lines, Ω_t. Thus, $\Omega = \Omega_p \cup \Omega_t$.

The set of events unobservable by the nominal supervisor, Σ_u, is defined as the set of events observable by both supervisors minus those observable by the original (nominal) supervisor:

$$\Sigma_u = \Omega - \Sigma. \tag{23}$$

The set Σ_u, thus, represents the set of new events that were added into the system when it was expanded. Similarly, the set of events unobservable by the complementary supervisor, $\mathbf{CTRL}_{com}$, is defined as:

$$\Gamma_u = \Omega - \Gamma. \qquad (24)$$

The three previous Expressions (22) to (24) impose that every event within the expanded plant must be observable by at least one supervisor. This condition is referred to as the *global observability* condition [31]. In DESs, the global observability condition is a natural assumption since users always have a complete knowledge regarding the set of jobs the system is producing/handling and the set of operations (processes) that can be executed by the plant, regardless of how the job's flow is controlled.

3.3.3 Supervisory Control of Expanded Plants when Handling a Priori Unplanned Set of Jobs

In this section, the supervisory control of plants, whose control-specifications change (temporarily) based on the arrival of a priori unplanned jobs/parts is described [30, 32]. Such unplanned jobs/parts will be referred herein as *new job/part types*. When a new set of job types are introduced into the plants the system generates new events.

Control methodology

Although the arrival of new job/part types into a DES has been considered in diverse areas such as workcell formation and production scheduling, it has not been considered in the control literature. For example, several authors have proposed methodologies to design manufacturing plants while considering the arrival of new part types. In [33], for example, Seifoddini considered the probabilistic nature of the product mix for the machine workcell formation. In these and other similar studies, however, the production routes of new part types were considered to be known in advance. Namely, the processing requirements for each of the new incoming job/part types are known (e.g., based on forecasting) well before system design/formation. In industrial systems, the processing requirements of new job types may not be known a priori, i.e., not known when the nominal supervisor is synthesized.

As described previously, a nominal/complementary supervisor pair has been proposed for the control of plants handling nominal and new job/part types that randomly arrive into the plant [32]. The nominal supervisor is designed to exclusively control the flow of nominal job/part types, while the complementary supervisor is designed to exclusively control the flow of new job/part types. The supervisors, uncoupled with respect to the set of job types they control, are used concurrently. When the last job/part within the set of new job/part types exits the system, the complementary supervisor is discarded and the FMC is again exclusively controlled by the nominal supervisor.

The nominal supervisor is synthesized, as described in the following section, following the same methodology first introduced in Section 2, while the complementary supervisor is synthesized following a similar but novel process [30, 32]. The synthesis methodology is performed in such a way that each supervisor comprising the nominal/complementary supervisor pair has control only over a subset of events that can occur within the expanded system. Although each supervisor is incomplete after passing a deadlock-state analysis check, the supervisory controllers are able to control the expanded plant without deadlocks.

Synthesis of the nominal supervisor

The synthesis of nominal workcell supervisors is performed as described in Section 2. For a system comprising n machines, processing k different nominal job types while satisfying p production/manufacturing constraints, the (nominal) supervisor, $\mathbf{CTRL}_{nom}$, is, thus, synthesized as described by Expressions (16) to (19), thus:

$$\mathbf{CTRL}_{nom} = \mathbf{CELL} \oplus \mathbf{SPEC} \oplus \mathbf{PARTS}. \tag{25}$$

Synthesis of the complementary supervisor

Herein (as in [32]), it is assumed that the processing/handling routes and the system constraints required to process the new job/part types are given. Furthermore, it is also assumed that, after having been programmed/configured, the corresponding resources can indeed be used for the handling/production of these job/part types. Subsequently, the complementary supervisor, $\mathbf{CTRL}_{com}$, is synthesized as if the corresponding plant devices were to manipulate only the new job/part types. In order to accomplish this, first, the set of new-job processing routes and the corresponding production/manufacturing-constraint models are constructed as described below [30]:

New-job/part route models: The job route model for each new job/part type is constructed in the same way as the nominal job route models, where only events (i.e., transitions) pertaining to the new job/part type being modeled are considered in its model.

New-job/part system-constraint models: These models specify how the new job/part types are to be produced/handled by the expanded system. All multi-input vectors that can take place in the system, except the ones exclusively affecting the nominal job/part types, must be included in the transition structure of these models.

Second, for each resource required for the production/handling of the set of new job/part types, the corresponding resource models are redefined as follows [30]:

Redefined resource models: Based on the operations that resources can perform on new job/part types, the corresponding resource models are redefined by assuming these machines are exclusively used for the production/handling of the new job types.

As an example of a redefined resource model, let us consider the nominal resource model shown in Figure 3.4. Figure 3.6 represents the same (redefined) physical machine illustrated in Figure 3.4 where now the redefined resource model is also used to perform Op_4 on the new job/part type N. Some of the transitions comprising the redefined resource model, i.e., $(\alpha_1 N 4)$, $(\beta_1 N -)$ and $(\lambda_1 N -)$, represent new transitions, i.e., unobservable by $\mathbf{CTRL}_{nom}$. Similarly, the transitions $(\alpha_1 A 5)$, $(\beta_1 A -)$, and $(\lambda_1 A -)$ defined in Figure 3.4 will be unobservable by $\mathbf{CTRL}_{com}$.

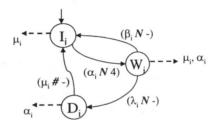

Figure 3.6. Redefined resource model: an example.

As the last step of the synthesis process, with the above three sets of new models (i.e., redefined resources, new-job/part routes, and new-job/part system-constraint models), the complementary supervisor is obtained using the same procedure used to synthesize the nominal supervisor [32]. For a set of k new job/part types requiring p new system constraints and n new resources, the complementary supervisor is synthesized according to the three expressions below:

$$\mathbf{CELL}_{new} = \mathbf{M}_{1-new} \otimes \mathbf{M}_{2-new} \otimes \cdots \otimes \mathbf{M}_{n-new},$$
$$\mathbf{SPEC}_{new} = \mathbf{SPEC}_{1-new} \oplus \mathbf{SPEC}_{2-new} \oplus \cdots \oplus \mathbf{SPEC}_{p-new}, \tag{26}$$
$$\mathbf{PARTS}_{new} = \mathbf{ARM}^s_{A-new} \otimes \mathbf{ARM}^s_{B-new} \otimes \cdots \otimes \mathbf{ARM}^s_{k-new}, \text{ and}$$

$$\mathbf{CTRL}_{com} = \mathbf{CELL}_{new} \oplus \mathbf{SPEC}_{new} \oplus \mathbf{PARTS}_{new}, \tag{27}$$

where $\mathbf{M}_{i\text{-new}}$ represents the redefined model for resource i; $\mathbf{SPEC}_{i\text{-new}}$ represents the i'th resource constraint needed to produce the new job/part types; and $\mathbf{ARM}_{i\text{-new}}^{s}$ represents the safe concurrent processing of the new job/part type i obtained as described in Section 2.2 taking into account only the set of machines that is used for the processing of the new jobs/parts.

Deadlock analysis

After the individual deadlock-free nominal and the complementary supervisors have been synthesized, both supervisors are used independently but concurrently to control the (expanded) plant. Each supervisor, as mentioned before, however, can only observe a subset of the event set that can occur within the expanded system. Thus, a multi-output generated by $\mathbf{CTRL}_{nom}$ may implicitly disable an event allowed to occur by $\mathbf{CTRL}_{com}$ and vice versa, taking the system into a deadlock state. Thus, in order to check for deadlocks, the concurrent disablement of events by the nominal/complementary supervisor pair must be analyzed by comparing the set of events disabled by one supervisor with the set of events enabled by the other supervisor [32]. If the system is determined to be deadlock-free, then the plant can produce the set of new and nominal job/part types as required, otherwise, it cannot. The process used to check for deadlock states is described next.

First, the behavior enforced on the expanded plant by the supervisor pair is specified by constructing the automaton $\mathbf{CTRL}_{nom\lor com}$, (i.e., $\mathbf{CTRL}_{nom}\lor\mathbf{CTRL}_{com}$), refer to Section 2.1. All events that can occur within the expanded system are observable by $\mathbf{CTRL}_{nom\lor com}$. Thus, the automaton $\mathbf{CTRL}_{nom\lor com}$ is complete and the behavior enforced on the system can be analyzed using this automaton. The analysis process is carried out as follows [30, 32]: at each state of $\mathbf{CTRL}_{nom\lor com}$, the set of transitions defined is compared with the set of outputs generated. If the set of transitions is a subset of the state's corresponding outputs, then this state is a deadlock state, otherwise, it is not.

Since the explicit disablement of a physical event may implicitly disable multiple multi-input vectors from occurring, this must be taken into account when determining if a set of multi-input vectors is a subset of the generated outputs. For this, the set of multi-input vectors, at a specific state, is defined as a subset of the outputs generated at the same state according to the following expression [30]:

$$\{\sigma^{*}\in\mathbf{CTRL}_{nom\lor com}\,|\,\delta^{*}(q,\sigma^{*})!\}\leq\{\omega^{*}(q)\}, \tag{28}$$

where the symbol $\leq$ is used to indicate that the disablement of a set of multi-input vectors by the disablement of a physical event has been considered. For example, the disablement of the physical event α_{1} implicitly disables events $(\alpha_{1}\,A\,5)$ and $(\alpha_{1}\,B\,1)$. If Expression (28) holds, then state q is a deadlock state, otherwise, it is not.

3.3.4 Supervisory Control of Expanded Workcells when Utilizing New Machines

In the previous section, we considered the first type of DES redundancy discussed previously: *operation redundancy*. In this section, we now consider the second type of redundancy: *standby redundancy*. Thus here we consider the control of DESs that have been temporarily expanded by the introduction of new resources. Herein we describe the methodology recently presented in [31], which allows FMCs to be expanded and still be controlled without modifying the nominal setup. The methodology employs a nominal/complementary supervisor pair as described in the following subsections. In order to use the newly introduced resources, the nominal resources may also need to perform new tasks. A robot forming part of a nominal manufacturing plant (e.g., a workcell) may need to be reprogrammed in order to move jobs to the new resources as in Figure 3.7. These new tasks, performed by the nominal resources also need to be monitored and controlled. The introduction of new resources may also increase the route space of nominal jobs/parts. Namely, nominal jobs may undergo operations on new resources, which increases the number of possible ways in which these jobs/parts can be produced/handled, as shown in Figure 3.8.

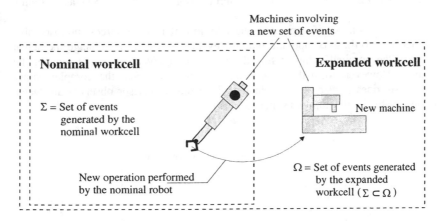

Figure 3.7. Nominal and expanded system.

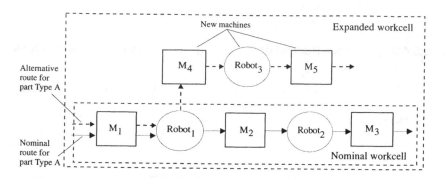

Figure 3.8. A manufacturing system expanded by the introduction of new resources.

In order to effectively control the expanded system, the nominal/complementary supervisor pair has to enable/disable nominal and new events, which the nominal and new DES resources can perform, according to the new production/handling conditions. Similar to the methodology used to control DESs producing/handling new job/part types, the nominal supervisor is responsible for controlling the behavior of the nominal plant, while the complementary supervisor controls the flow of jobs when they follow any of the routes that have been added into their nominal route space by the introduction of new resources as in Figure 3.9.

In the context of expansion via addition of new resources, unobservable events refer to those comprising the new event set, which may change the actual state of the nominal system while the nominal supervisor does not register the change. However, from the *global observability condition*, the complementary supervisor does register such a change, since this supervisor observes all events unobservable by the nominal supervisor [30, 31].

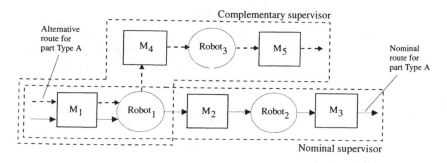

Figure 3.9. Nominal/complementary supervisor pair controlling an expanded plant.

If an (unobservable) event does indeed change the state of the nominal system, it will be required to change the state of the nominal supervisor in order to bring it to the state that represents the real state of the nominal plant. In this way, the nominal supervisor can continue enforcing the desired behavior on the nominal plant according to the current (real) state of the (nominal) system. Herein we describe the novel methodology to perform such a state change on the nominal supervisor, when required, by using a *virtual sequence of events* generated by the complementary supervisor as described in [31].

Restrictions on the new-machine control methodology

Due to the introduction of new resources, jobs/parts may enter and/or exit the nominal system at an a priori unplanned entrance and/or exit points, as shown in Figure 3.8. When a job enters or exits the nominal plant in a non-nominal fashion, such events may take the nominal system to an undesired state, i.e., a state where a system constraint imposed on the nominal plant is not satisfied. Thus, in order to simplify the problem of controlling an expanded plant when new resources are introduced, the following two restrictions are imposed on the systems to be controlled:

Restriction 1: Once a job/part exits the nominal system, it is not allowed to re-enter the (nominal) plant and no jobs/parts are allowed to enter the plant from a point different from its original (nominal) entrance point.

Restriction 2: When using an unplanned exit point, a part may exit the nominal plant in two possible ways: (i) removed by a "nominal" resource, e.g., by a robot, which have been (re) programmed to perform such an operation; or (ii) removed by a new resource. In order to correctly control the expanded plant, the complementary supervisor must, thus, monitor all resources (nominal and new) that can remove jobs from the resources where the jobs may choose to follow a nominal or a new (added) route.

The above two restrictions may restrict the user's freedom on how the nominal plant can be expanded. They provide, however, the conditions that allow the synthesis of a nominal/complementary supervisor pair that will properly control the expanded plant without violating any of the system constraints imposed on the nominal plant. These restrictions also guarantee deadlock-free control, as will be described later.

Control methodology

The supervisory control architecture that is proposed in [31] for the control of systems that are temporarily expanded by the introduction of new resources is schematically shown in Figure 3.10.

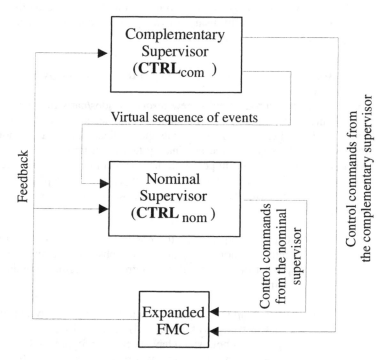

Figure 3.10. Supervisory control architecture when new machines are introduced into the nominal workcell.

The nominal supervisor and the complementary supervisor at their corresponding states enable a set of controllable events that the expanded plant is allowed to execute. At a given plant state, an event would occur based on one of the following two conditions:

Condition 1:   If the event is observable by both supervisors, $CTRL_{nom}$ and $CTRL_{com}$, then the expanded plant can only execute this event if it is enabled by both supervisors. (An event is observable by both supervisors if the resource enabled to execute it is under the control of both supervisors). For example, Machine M_1 in Figure 3.9 is controlled by both supervisors.

Condition 2: If the event is observable by only one supervisor, then it can be executed only if enabled by the corresponding controlling supervisor, i.e., by the supervisor capable of observing the event. For example, Machine M_3 in Figure 3.9 is controlled only by one supervisor.

When an event occurs (no matter which event), the plant informs both supervisors of such occurrence. Based on this information, the supervisors will take one of the following three actions:

Action 1: If both supervisors have observed the event, both will change their respective new states.

Action 2: If only the nominal supervisor has observed the event, only this supervisor will change its state.

Action 3: If only the complementary supervisor has observed the executed event, the complementary supervisor will first change its state. Subsequently it will determine, via its mask or observation function, if the event that just occurred has changed the state of the nominal plant. If such a change has indeed occurred, the complementary supervisor will generate a sequence of *virtual events* by means of its mask function to be sent to the nominal supervisor. The set of virtual events is assumed to be immediately processed by the nominal supervisor, which will change its state to the state that represents the (real) current status of the nominal plant.

The two restrictions regarding parts' entrance and exit from the plant, described above, allow us to synthesize a complementary supervisor where nominal events, unobservable by $\mathbf{CTRL}_{com}$, would not change the state of the resource set controlled by $\mathbf{CTRL}_{com}$. Thus, there is no need for the nominal supervisor to generate virtual event sequences.

Synthesis of the nominal supervisor

The EMA-based nominal supervisor, $\mathbf{CTRL}_{nom}$, is synthesized as was described in Section 3.3 to control the nominal plant.

Synthesis of the complementary supervisor

The complementary supervisor is defined as a pair, (S, M):

$$\mathbf{CTRL}_{com} = (S, M), \tag{29}$$

where $S = \{\Gamma, X, x_0, \xi^*(x, \gamma^*), \Lambda, \varphi^*\}$ is an EMA-based supervisor, and M is a mask function. The main purpose of M is to take the nominal supervisor to a state that represents the real state of the nominal plant, whenever an event unobservable by $CTRL_{nom}$ changes the state of the nominal plant. Mathematically M is defined as:

$$M:(\Gamma, Q, X) \rightarrow \Sigma^*, \tag{30}$$

where, Σ^* denotes the set of all finite strings $s = \sigma_1 \cdots \sigma_n$ that can be formed using elements from Σ, including the empty string, ε. A string $s \in \Sigma^*$ generated by M is referred to as a virtual string or virtual event sequence. For example, $M(\gamma^*, q, x) = s$ is interpreted as follows: a virtual string s, i.e., an event sequence observable by $CTRL_{nom}$, is generated by $CTRL_{com}$, when $CTRL_{nom}$ is at state $q \in Q$ and $CTRL_{com}$ is at state $x \in X$, after observing the event $\gamma^* \in \Gamma$, which is unobservable by $CTRL_{nom}$. If the event γ^* is observable by $CTRL_{nom}$, then the virtual sequences generated by $CTRL_{com}$ is a null or empty string, $s = \varepsilon$. This is because $CTRL_{nom}$ does not need to be informed by $CTRL_{com}$ of the occurrence of event γ^*. The pair (S, M) is obtained as described in the following subsections.

Automaton S

Similar to the synthesis of the nominal supervisor in order to construct the automaton S, three sets of models are required:

Resource models:

(i) *New resource models*: Models for the added new resources are constructed using the same methodology used to construct nominal resource models: for a set of g resources, this process generates a set of g new resource models, $M_{new-1}, \ldots, M_{new-g}$. For the system shown in Figure 3.9, the models for M_4, M_5 and Robot$_3$ represent new resource models.

(ii) *Redefined nominal resource models*: Models for each redefined nominal resource are constructed by considering the new operations that they must perform: for a set of $h \leq n$ redefined nominal resources, this process generates a set of h redefined resource models, $M_{redefined-i}$, $i \in h$. For the system shown in Figure 3.9, the new model for Robot$_1$ represents a redefined resource model.

(iii) *Unchanged nominal resource models*: If the capabilities of nominal resources do not need to be redefined although the new alternative route of a nominal job uses these resources, the corresponding unchanged nominal resource models still need to be used in the synthesis process of the complementary supervisor. This model will be denoted as before, M_1, ..., M_n. Again for the system of Figure 3.9 the model for M_1 represents an unchanged nominal resource model.

Job-route models:

New job-route models will include partial processing sequences of the nominal routes: each of these models will be denoted as $ARM^s_{i\text{-new}}$.

System-constraint models:

There will be new and redefined system constraints, $SPEC_{new-i}$ and $SPEC_{redefined-i}$, respectively. The new constraint models must only affect the set of processes taking place in the new resources. Each redefined system constraint model, on the other hand, is constructed by incorporating into the manufacturing constraint to be redefined the set of new events in the form of selfloop transitions and by removing from the same constraint model the set of nominal events that is of no interest to the complementary supervisor, i.e., events affecting nominal jobs which do not use new resources [30].

Once all the corresponding models have been built, the automaton S is synthesized as follow:

$$CELL_{com} = (M_{new-1} \otimes \ldots \otimes M_{new-g}) \otimes (M_{redefined-1} \otimes \ldots \otimes M_{redefined-h}) \otimes (M_1 \otimes \ldots \otimes M_n),$$
$$SPEC_{com} = (SPEC_{new-1} \oplus \ldots \oplus SPEC_{new-i}) \oplus (SPEC_{redefined-1} \oplus \ldots \oplus SPEC_{redefined-i}),$$
$$PARTS_{com} = ARM^s_{1\text{-new}} \otimes ARM^s_{2\text{-new}} \otimes \cdots \otimes ARM^s_{k\text{-new}}, \text{ and} \qquad (31)$$

$$S = CELL_{com} \oplus SPEC_{com} \oplus PARTS_{com} = \{\Gamma, X, x_0, \xi^*(x, \gamma^*), \Lambda, \varphi^*\}. \qquad (32)$$

Mask function

The methodology to construct the mask function, which will generate a virtual sequence of events that will take the nominal supervisor to a state that represents the real state of the nominal plant, is illustrated in Figure 3.11 which shows a sequence of events, t_n, that take the nominal supervisor to its current state, q, and subsequently an unobservable event, $\gamma_c^* \in \Sigma_u$, occurs. After the occurrence of

event γ_c^*, however, the nominal supervisor remains in this state, q, which does not

represent the real state of the nominal plant, i.e., State q'. (The subscript c in γ_c^* is

used to denote a state change of the nominal plant by the occurrence of the event

$\gamma^* \in \Sigma_u$).

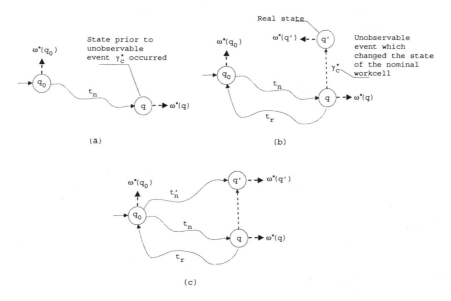

Figure 3.11. Proposed methodology to change the state of the nominal supervisor: (a) a sequence of events t_n take the nominal supervisor to its current state, (b) an unobservable event, γ_c^*, occurs, and (c) a sequence of events, $t_r t_n'$, take the nominal supervisor to the real state of the nominal plant.

In order to bring the nominal supervisor to State q', first, the nominal supervisor is reset (i.e., taken to its initial state), as in Figure 3.11b. This is performed by having the nominal supervisor process the event sequence t_r. Subsequently, the nominal supervisor is taken to State q' by sending to the nominal supervisor a virtual event sequence, t_n', for its processing, as in Figure 3.11c. The above process is carried out using six sequential steps [31].

Step 1: Obtain the sequence of events t_n

Obtain a sequence of events (string), t_n, that can be used to take the nominal supervisor from its initial state, q_0, to its current state, q, as in Figure 3.11a. The sequence t_n can be anyone of the many possible sequences that can take **CTRL**$_{nom}$ from its initial state to its current state, including the latest recorded event set. If the sequence t_n is obtained by using the recorded history of **CTRL**$_{nom}$, the process of finding t_n is automatic. However, keeping track of the nominal plant's history may require a considerable amount of memory.

In [31] it is proposed to obtain t_n using the extended transition function, $\delta^*(q, \sigma^*)$, defined in **CTRL**$_{nom}$. Any set of events of the many possible is sufficient. This approach can be time consuming rather than being memory intensive, however, it can be used to obtain t_n either in an on-line or off-line fashion. Formally, the string t_n is obtained by finding a sequence:

$$\delta^*(q_0, \sigma_0^*) \rightarrow \delta^*(q_1, \sigma_1^*) \rightarrow \delta^*(q_2, \sigma_2^*) \rightarrow \ldots \rightarrow \delta^*(q_n, \sigma_n^*) = q, \quad (33)$$

where q_0 is the initial state, q_1 is the state that can be reached from State q_0 by processing event σ_0^*, etc. Using a short notation, Expression (33) can be written as: $q_0 \xrightarrow{t_n} q$ or as $\delta^*(q_0, t_n) = q$, where

$$t_n = \sigma_0^* \sigma_1^* \ldots \sigma_n^*. \quad (34)$$

Step 2: Obtain the sequence of events t_r

Obtain a sequence of events, t_r, that will take the nominal supervisor from its current state, q, to its initial state, q_0, as in Figure 3.11b. That is, the sequence t_r resets the nominal supervisor. The sequence t_r can be obtained by tracking back the state-event sequence defined by δ^* and registering the corresponding events as the process continues until the initial state, q_0, is reached. Many t_r strings can be obtained, however, anyone can be used. Formally, the string t_r is obtained by finding a sequence:

$$\delta^*(q_0, \sigma_0^*) \leftarrow \delta^*(q_1, \sigma_1^*) \leftarrow \ldots \leftarrow \delta^*(q_{n-1}, \sigma_{n-1}^*) \leftarrow \delta^*(q_n, \sigma_n^*) \leftarrow q. \quad (35)$$

Using a short notation, Expression (35) can be written as $q \xrightarrow{t_r} q_0$ or as $\delta^*(q, t_r) = q_0$, where

$$t_r = \sigma_n^* \, \sigma_{n-1}^* \ldots \sigma_1^* \, \sigma_0^*. \tag{36}$$

Step 3: Obtain the sequence of events t_c

Obtain a sequence of events, t_c, that took the complementary supervisor from its initial state, x_0, to its current state, x, as in Figure 3.12a, where State x corresponds to State q'. Similar to Step 1, many t_c strings can be obtained; however, only one is needed. Formally, the string t_c is obtained by finding a sequence:

$$\xi^*(x_0, \gamma_0^*) \rightarrow \xi^*(x_1, \gamma_1^*) \rightarrow \ldots \rightarrow \xi^*(x_c, \gamma_c^*) = x. \tag{37}$$

Using a short notation, Expression (37) can be written as $x_0 \xrightarrow{t_c} x$, or as $\xi^*(x_0, t_c) = x$, where

$$t_c = \gamma_0^* \, \gamma_1^* \ldots \gamma_c^*. \tag{38}$$

The last event symbol in (38), $\gamma_c^* \in \Sigma_u$, represents the unobservable event that changed the state of the nominal workcell without the nominal supervisor registering it.

Step 4: Identify the last observable (processor[†]) event, γ^*

In order to determine a virtual string of events that can take the nominal supervisor from its initial state to the state that represents the real state of the nominal plant, it is necessary to determine which nominal resource was the last resource visited by the job/part before it exited the nominal plant (using an unplanned exit point). One can identify the last visited nominal resource if the processor event, $\gamma^* \in \Omega_p$, observable by both supervisors, $\gamma^* \in \Sigma \cap \Gamma$, that took

---

[†] A processor event is executed by a processing resource, while a transporting event is executed by a transporting resource.

CTRL$_{com}$ to a state where the unobservable event, γ_c^*, was allowed to occur, is identified. Such observable processor event, $\gamma^* \in \Omega_p$, is identified as follow: (i) erase the last symbol in the string t_c, Step 3, to obtain a new sequence t_c'; and (ii) examine the set of outputs, $\varphi^*(x')$, generated by the automaton S, after processing the string t_c', as in Figure 3.12b:

$$\xi^*(x_0, t_c') = x'$$

$$\Rightarrow \quad \varphi^*(x') = \{\text{set of events disabled after processing } t_c' \}. \tag{39}$$

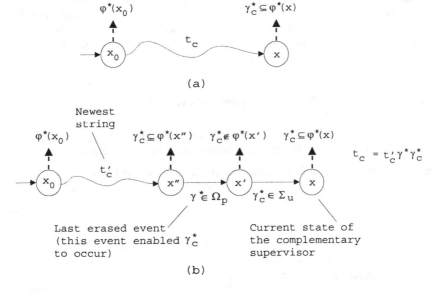

(a)

(b)

Figure 3.12. (a) A string of events that took the complementary supervisor to its current state, and (b) a string of events, t_c', which enabled the unobservable event γ_c^* to occur.

If the unobservable event $\gamma_c^* \in \Sigma_u$ does not lie within the set of outputs, $\gamma_c^* \notin \varphi^*(x')$, meaning that **CTRL**$_{com}$ does not disable the event γ_c^* after processing string t_c', then continue erasing events from t_c, until a string t_c' that takes

$\mathbf{CTRL}_{com}$ to a state, x'', where the event γ_c^* is disabled, $\gamma_c^* \subseteq \varphi^*(x')$, is found, as in Figure 3.12b. The last erased event is the processor event, $\gamma^* \in \Omega_p$, that we are looking for.

Step 5: Obtain the sequence of events t_n'

Find the observable processor event, γ^*, identified in Step 4, in the event sequence t_n (obtained in Step 1) by starting from its last event symbol. Subsequently, obtain the string t_n' by replacing the event γ^* that was found with the event sequence $\sigma_1^* \sigma_2^*$, where σ_1^* represents a resource-failure event and σ_2^* represents a resource-repair event. Here, it is assumed that whenever a resource fails, the job/part being processed is considered a scrap job and therefore discarded. By assuming this, the job/part is automatically removed from the nominal plant and thus, the nominal supervisor can keep track of the system's state where the corresponding job/part has been removed.

Step 6: Obtain the virtual sequence of events, $t_r t_n'$

The last step is to obtain the virtual sequence of events, generated by the mask function at state q. For the specific state-pair (q, x) being analyzed, the virtual event sequence is defined as the concatenation of strings t_r and t_n' :

$$M(\gamma_c^*, q, x) = t_r t_n'. \tag{40}$$

The action of the mask function is interpreted as follows: when an unobservable event that changed the state of the nominal plant has occurred, reset the nominal supervisor and immediately take it to the state that represents the real state of the nominal plant. The reset action is performed by the virtual substring t_r, while the virtual substring t_n' takes the supervisor from its initial state to the real state of the nominal system.

Now that the complementary supervisor has been synthesized, it can be used concurrently with the nominal supervisor to control the temporarily expanded system.

Deadlocks

Because of the introduction of new resources that bring new events into the system, the expanded system may reach a deadlock state. By definition, the nominal and complementary supervisors are individually conflict- and deadlock-free. Moreover, when used together, it is guaranteed that their concurrent actions will never take the expanded plant into a deadlock state. That is, the control methodology described above guarantees that the system is deadlock-free. To illustrate this, let us subdivide a job's/part's route into three possible subroutes, Figure 3.13: (i) *nominal-new*; (ii) *purely-nominal*; and, (iii) *purely-new* routes, [31].

(i) Nominal-new subroute

When a part is on its nominal-new subroute, its flow is controlled by the concurrent actions of the two supervisors comprising the supervisor-pair. Since the set of redefined manufacturing constraint models and the corresponding set of nominal constraint models specify the same behavior on the parts' processing routes, these two sets of constraints are never in conflict. Moreover, since every event occurring within this subroute is observable by both supervisors, a part can only be processed by a machine, or moved by a transporting device, only if both supervisors allow it. This guarantees a deadlock-free flow during this sub-route.

(ii) Purely-nominal subroute

When a part is on its purely-nominal subroute, its flow is controlled only by the nominal supervisor. Since the events occurring during this subroute are neither observable nor affected by $CTRL_{com}$, the part's flow is not affected by the actions of the complementary supervisor. Thus, the parts' evolution will never be in a deadlock since the nominal supervisor itself is deadlock-free.

(iii) Purely-new subroute

When a part is on its purely-new subroute its flow is controlled only by the complementary supervisor which itself is deadlock-free. The events occurring during this phase are not observable by $CTRL_{nom}$. Some of these events, however, may change the state of the nominal workcell without the nominal supervisor registering such a change. These are events that change a part's route from its nominal-new subroute to its purely-new subroute. When this happens the complementary supervisor, via its mask function, takes $CTRL_{nom}$ to the real state of the nominal workcell. In this way, the nominal supervisor is informed of the removal of the job/part from the nominal workcell and, thus, $CTRL_{nom}$ can continue enforcing the desired deadlock-free behavior.

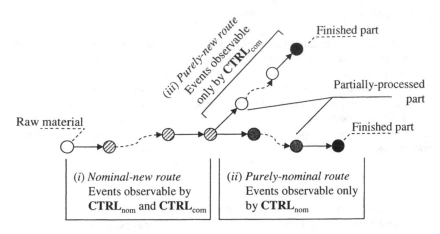

Figure 3.13. Job/part subroutes.

3.4 EMA DESs State-Space Minimization Technique

As mentioned previously the state-space of EMA-based supervisors can be significantly reduced following the methodology proposed in [26]. In this section, we describe such methodology.

Since, in general, EMA-based supervisors have equivalent states (to be explicitly defined in the following subsection), they can be minimized (i.e., reduced in their number of states) by considering the set of outputs generated at each state. The literature on the minimization of automata has primarily considered the search for minimal automata that accepts the same input language as its nonminimized counterpart [17]. A state-space reduction technique for automata-based supervisors was proposed in [34] based on exploiting the symmetry of many DESs. Such methodology, however, is applicable only to a specific class of DESs, where the languages, representing individual components of the specific system to be modeled, exhibit *symmetry* properties based on the notions of group theory. In [8], the *Quotient Structure Theorem* was introduced for the reduction of the state-space of supervisors while preserving their control actions. In such a methodology, the simplification of the supervisor is based on a projection of the supervisor into an equivalent supervisor which is referred to as a quotient supervisor. Quotient supervisors, however, can be furthermore reduced using intuitive or adhoc approaches.

In contrast to these approaches, here we describe a novel minimization algorithm for EMA supervisors based on their output language, $L_{out}(\mathbf{CTRL})$ [26]. The approach obtains supervisors with a state-space smaller than the state-space obtained using other methodologies. Moreover, based on the supervisor's extended output function, ω^*, the obtained state-space is minimal.

3.4.1 Definitions

Before describing the state-space minimization methodology, some definitions are first introduced [26].

(i) *Equivalent states* are defined as those that generate identical outputs:
$$\text{if} \quad q, q' \in Q \wedge q \neq q' \wedge \omega^*(q) = \omega^*(q') \quad \Rightarrow \quad q \sim q'. \tag{41}$$

(ii) *State-class* is defined as a group of states that satisfies the following three conditions:
1. All states in the same state-class are equivalent,
2. Any two states in different state-classes produce different responses, and
3. Transitions between equivalent states do not change the response of the EMA.

(iii) *Redundant states* are defined as those that belong to a state-class comprising more than one state.

(iv) *Isomorphic-EMA* is defined based on the concept of isomorphic graphs from graph theory: Let $M = EMA_1$ and $N = EMA_2$. M and N are isomorphic, if N can be obtained from M by relabeling the states, the multi-input, and the multi-output vectors of M, in such a way that there exists a one-to-one correspondence between the extended transition functions δ_1^* and δ_2^*, and the extended output functions ω_1^* and ω_2^*.

3.4.2 Minimization Process

The state-space minimization algorithm for EMA-based DESs controllers is based on the elimination of all redundant states from the corresponding isomorphic EMA supervisor thus, the elimination process is discussed first.

Elimination of redundant states

The elimination process for redundant states consists of two general steps: (i) grouping states into state-classes, and (ii) elimination of all redundant states.

Let $M = EMA_1$ and $q_i, q_j \in Q$, $q_i \neq q_j$ be states belonging to the same state-class. The EMA obtained by merging the states q_i, and q_j in M (i.e., eliminating the redundant state q_i) is defined as:

$$\hat{M} = \{\textstyle\prod_{i \in I_1} \Sigma_i, \hat{Q}, q_0, \hat{\delta}^*(q, \sigma^*), \textstyle\prod_{i \in I_2} \Delta_i, \hat{\omega}^*\}, \tag{42}$$

where $\hat{Q}$, defined as $\hat{Q} = Q - q_i$, is the finite set of states that survive after reduction. If q_0 belongs to a state-class with redundant states, then q_0 is the state that survives after the elimination of the redundant state q_i; $\hat{\omega}^* = \omega^* (q \in \hat{Q})$ is the extended output function of $\hat{M}$, and $\hat{\delta}^* (q \in \hat{Q}, \sigma^*)$ is the extended state transition function. $\hat{\delta}^*$ in (42) is obtained by considering the following four cases, as shown in Figure 3.14:

Case (i): if $q', q \in \hat{Q}$, and $\delta^* (q, \sigma^*) = q'$, then $\hat{\delta}^* (q, \sigma^*) = q'$.

   Namely, $\forall q \in \hat{Q}$ all transitions $\sigma^* \in \prod_{i \in I_1} \Sigma_i$ not leading to the state to be eliminated, q_i, remain unchanged, e.g., transitions σ_5^*, and σ_6^*, including the selfloop transition σ_7^*, in Figure 3.14a, where we assume $\omega^* (q_j) = \omega^* (q_i)$, thus, $q_j \cdot q_i$.

Case (ii): if $q \in \hat{Q}$ and $\delta^* (q, \sigma^*) = q_i$, then $\hat{\delta}^* (q, \sigma^*) = q_j$.

   In this case, all transitions coming out of a state $q \in \hat{Q}$ and leading to the state q_i are redirected in such a way that now they come out from their original state and lead to a state in the same state-class, e.g., q_j. Transitions σ_2^* and σ_4^* in Figure 3.14a satisfy this condition.

Case (iii): if $q \in \hat{Q}$ and $\delta^* (q_i, \sigma^*) = q$, then $\delta^* (q_i, \sigma^*) = q$ is changed to $\hat{\delta}^* (q_j, \sigma^*) = q$.

   Namely, transitions coming out of the state q_i and leading to a state $q \in \hat{Q}$ are shifted in such a way that now such transitions come out from a state belonging to the same state-class as q_i and lead to their original state, e.g., transitions σ_1^* and σ_3^* in Figure 3.14a, and

Case (iv): if $\delta^* (q_i, \sigma^*) = q_i$ then, such transitions are shifted to q_j: $\hat{\delta}^* (q_j, \sigma^*) = q_j$.

   This case considers all selfloop transitions, not considered in Case (i), occurring at the state q_i. Such transitions are shifted to q_j, e.g., transition σ_8^* in Figure 3.14a.

Applying the above definitions to the EMA shown in Figure 3.14a, the corresponding reduced EMA shown in Figure 3.14b is obtained.

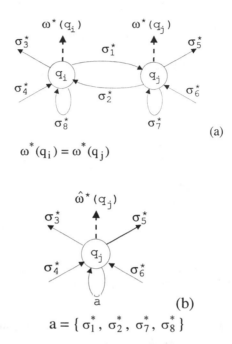

Figure 3.14. A minimization example: (a) original EMA, (b) minimized EMA.

State-space minimization algorithm

The algorithm to minimize EMA-based supervisors consists of two basic steps: (i) obtaining an isomorphic EMA supervisor, and (ii) eliminating all the redundant states from this isomorphic EMA.

Step (i) Obtaining the isomorphic EMA

In general, when redundant states are eliminated, a nondeterministic EMA is obtained [30]. In order to avoid obtaining such a nondeterministic EMA, when applying the reduction algorithm to eliminate redundant states, an isomorphic EMA must be first generated through the following three-step procedure, as shown in Figure 3.15:

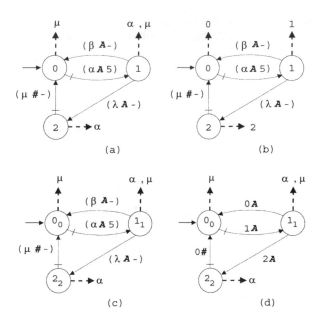

Figure 3.15. (a) Resource model, (b) resource control model (RCM), (c) state relabeled
supervisor, and (d) isomorphic supervisor.

(a)   Based on the device models used to synthesize the supervisor **CTRL**, *Re-
       source Control Models* (RCM) are created. RCMs are defined as models
       that generate as outputs integer numbers that indicate the current state of
       each device. These outputs are used by the minimized supervisor to monitor
       the workcell. Figure 3.15b shows the RCM for the basic device model
       shown in Figure 3.15a.

(b)   The states in **CTRL** are relabeled in such a way that each one represents the
       global (logical) state of the workcell. This is obtained by attaching a multi-
       digit subscript to each state label. Each digit comprising the subscript indi-
       cates the current state of a particular machine. Assuming that the supervisor
       for a FMC comprising only one machine is identical to the EMA shown in
       Figure 3.15a, the relabeled supervisor would then be as the one shown in
       Figure 3.15c, where each state-subscript denotes the state of the machine
       (i.e., the state of the workcell.)

(c)   The last step is to relabel multi-input vectors in **CTRL** in such a way that
       each multi-input transition represents the workcell's global state to which

the transition is leading to, as well as the part type that is affected by such transition. The new label, thus, consists of the subscript of the relabeled state the transition is leading to concatenated with the symbol representing the part type affected by the occurrence of such transition. The part type affected by the corresponding transition is obtained from the transition structure in **CTRL**. Herein, the isomorphic EMA **CTRL** is referred to as isom-**CTRL**. Figure 3.15d shows the isomorphic EMA supervisor for the relabeled supervisor shown in Figure 3.15c.

Step (ii) Eliminating all the redundant states

In order to eliminate the redundant states and obtain the minimal supervisor, herein referred to as isôm - **CTRL**, Expression (42) is applied to isom-**CTRL**.

The time complexity function, f(n), of the algorithm to eliminate redundant states is a function of s, n and m for a specific EMA, where s is the cardinality of the multi-input vector set, n is the number of states, and m is the number of state-classes. Considering the worst-case scenario, for each of the two basic steps of the minimization algorithm, it is known that f(n) is of the order $O(n^2 + sn^3)$.

From a theoretical point of view, the advantages of multi-input vectors allow us to have a compact representation of both the workcell open-loop behavior and its corresponding control strategy. They also allow us to reduce, to a minimum, the state-space of the supervisor based on an equivalence criterion on ω^*. This makes potentially large state-space supervisors implementable. By monitoring multi-input vectors, the supervisor is able to know without ambiguity the set of processes that are taking place in the DES and what job/part types are being affected by such operations and, thus able to perform better control decisions as to which set of processes must be disabled. This type of input also provides the means to discover omissions, contradictions and ambiguities within the models.

From a practical point of view, multi-input vectors allow the control actions of the minimized supervisors to be fully determined based on the current global state of the DES without considering how such a state was reached. Thus, by using multi-input vectors, it is possible to synthesize memory-less supervisors that will force workcells to behave in accordance to a set of desired manufacturing constraints while processing jobs/parts with alternative processing routes regardless of the past history of the DES.

Our experience indicates that the proposed state-space minimization methodology normally generates supervisors of smaller size than the ones obtained using other methodologies. Considering the manufacturing workcell example presented in [8] as an illustration, the above state-space minimization methodology generated a minimal supervisor comprising 4 states, while the quotient supervisor presented in [8] comprised 6 states. Another illustrative example of the above state-space minimization process is presented in [26], where a supervisor for a 3-Machine-1-Buffer system is synthesized and the obtained controller (comprising 29 states) is minimized to a supervisor comprising 6 states. In [26] it is shown that the minimized supervisor enforces the same behavior on the system as the original controller.

Output languages

In order to show that **CTRL** and isôm - **CTRL** enforce the same behavior on the given DES, one can prove that their output languages are identical [26], namely,

$$L_{out}(\textbf{CTRL}) = L_{out}(\text{isom-}\textbf{CTRL}), \text{ and} \tag{42a}$$
$$L_{out}(\text{isom-}\textbf{CTRL}) = L_{out}(\text{isôm -}\textbf{CTRL}). \tag{42b}$$

CONCLUSIONS

A novel automata-based methodology has been presented for the modeling of resources, job/part routes, and DES constraints. The shuffle and the meet logic operations for the synthesis of EMA supervisors have also been described. These concepts allow us to synthesize correct (deadlock- and conflict-free) EMA supervisors that have the ability to explicitly generate control commands and control FMCs processing parts with multiple routes. The EMA supervisors are minimized with respect to their number of states without affecting the behavior enforced on the (controlled) DES.

Exemplary EMA-based supervisors have been successfully implemented using PLC technology [14]. While intensive research has focused on the control of DES, many of these projects have been purely theoretical and lack the implementation of the corresponding DES controller. The implementation methodology of formal DES-theory-based supervisors can be achieved using EMA. Furthermore, EMA based controllers can be applied to industrial DES, as experimental results have shown in a laboratory.

REFERENCES

[1]   L. O'Connor, "Agile Manufacturing in a Responsive Factory", *ASME, Mechanical Engineering*, Vol. 116, No. 7, p. 54, 1994.

[2]   B. Benhabib, C.Y. Chen, and W.R. Johnson, "An Integrated Manufacturing Workcell Management System", *ASME, Journal of Manufacturing Review*, Vol. 2, No. 4, pp. 266-276, 1989.

[3]   K.P. Valavanis, "On the Hierarchical Modeling Analysis and Simulation of Flexible Manufacturing Systems with Extended Petri Nets", *IEEE Transactions on Systems, Man, and Cybernetics*, Vol. 20, No. 1, pp. 94-100, 1990.

[4]   K.A. D'Souza and S.K. Khator, "A Survey of Petri Net Applications in Modeling Controls for Automated Manufacturing Systems", *Computers in Industry*, Vol. 24, No. 1, pp. 5-16, 1994.

[5]   H. Van Brussel, Y. Pen, and P. Valckenaers, "Modeling Flexible Manufacturing Systems Based on Petri Nets", *CIRP Annals, Manufacturing Technology*, Vol. 42, No. 1, pp. 42-47, 1993.

[6]   J.M. Proth and V.M. Savi, "A Modular Petri Nets Approach for Modeling Complex Manufacturing Systems", *8th International Conference on CAD/CAM, Robotics and Factories of the Future*, France, pp. 1783-1790, 1992.

[7]   M.C. Zhou and A.D. Rubbi, "Applications of Petri Net Methodology to Manufacturing Systems", in *Computer Control of Flexible Manufacturing Systems*, Edited by Joshi B.B. and Smith J.S., Chapman & Hall, pp. 207-230, 1994.

[8]   P.J.G. Ramadge and W.M. Wonham, "Supervisory Control of a Class of Discrete Event Systems", SIAM, *Journal of Control and Optimization*, Vol. 25, No. 1, pp. 206-230, January 1987.

[9]   G.L. Batten Jr., *Programmable Controllers: Hardware, Software and Applications*, 2nd Edition, McGraw-Hill, New York, 1994.

[10] G. Michel, *Programmable Logic Controllers: Architecture and Applications*, John Wiley & Sons, Toronto, 1990.

[11] Filer and Leinenon, *Programmable Controllers and Designing Sequential Logic*, Saunders College Publishing, Toronto, 1992.

[12] D. Robinson, "The Soft Option", *IEE Review,* Vol. 43, No. 5, pp. 214, September 1997.

[13] A.J. Crispin, *Programmable Logic Controllers and their Engineering Applications*, McGraw-Hill, Toronto, 1990.

[14] A. Ramirez-Serrano, S.C. Zhu, S.K.H. Chan, S.S.W. Chan, M. Ficocelli, and B. Benhabib, "A Hybrid PC/PLC Architecture for Manufacturing-System Control - Theory and Implementation", *Journal of Intelligent Manufacturing (JIMS)*, Vol. 13, No. 4, pp. 261-281, August 2002.

[15] Lin F. and W.M. Wonham, "Decentralized Supervisory Control of Discrete-Event Systems", *Information Science*, Vol. 44, pp. 199-224, 1988.

[16] Wong K.C. and W.M. Wonham,, "Hierarchical Control of Discrete-Event Systems", *Discrete-Event Systems: Theory and Applications*, Vol. 3, No. 3, pp. 241-273, 1996.

[17] J. Carol and D. Long, *Theory of Finite Automata: with introduction to formal languages*, Prentice Hall, Englewood Cliffs, New Jersey, 1989.

[18] J.E. Hopcroft and J.D. Ullman, *Introduction to Automata Theory, Languages, and Computation*, Addison Wesley, 1979.

[19] R.A. Williams, B. Benhabib, and K.C. Smith, "A DES-Theory-Based Hybrid Supervisory Control System for Manufacturing Systems", *SME Journal of Manufacturing Systems*, Vol. 15, No. 2, pp. 71-83, 1996.

[20] M. Fabian and R. Kumar, "Mutually Non-blocking Supervisory Control of Discrete-Event Systems", *International Conference on Decision and Control*, pp. 2970-2975, San Diego, CA, December 1997.

[21] S. Takai, T. Ushio, and S. Kodama, "Static-State Feedback Control of Discrete Event Systems under Partial Observation", *IEEE Transactions on Automatic Control*, Vol. 40, No. 11, pp. 1950-1954, November 1995.

[22] B.A. Brandin and M.W. Wonham, "Supervisory Control of Timed Discrete Event Systems", *IEEE Transactions on Automatic Control*, Vol. 39, No. 2, pp. 329-342, February 1994.

[23] N. Duan, S.R.T. Kumara, and D.J. Madeiros, "EMM-Network Model for FMS Modeling, Simulation and Control", *Second Annual Conference on AI, Simulation and Planning in High Autonomy Systems*, Cocoa Beach, FL, pp. 253-262, April 1991.

[24] A. Ramirez, C. Sriskandarajah, and B. Benhabib, "Control of Flexible-Manufacturing Workcells Using Extended Moore Automata", *IEEE International Conference on Robotics and Automation*, Detroit, MI, May 12-14, pp. 120-125, 1999

[25] A. Ramirez-Serrano, S.C. Zhu and B. Benhabib, "Moore Automata for the Supervisory Control of Robotic Manufacturing Workcells", *Journal of Autonomous Robots*, Vol. 9, No. 1, pp. 59-69, July 2000.

[26] A. Ramirez-Serrano, C. Sriskandarajah and B. Benhabib, "Automata-Based Modeling and Control Synthesis for Manufacturing Workcells with Part-Routing Flexibility", *IEEE Transactions on Robotics and Automation*, Vol. 16, No. 6, pp. 807-823, December 2000.

[27] C.G. Cassandras and S. Lafortune, *Introduction to Discrete Event Systems*, Kluwer Academic Publishers, Boston, MA, 1999.

[28] A. Ramirez-Serrano and B. Benhabib, "Supervisory Control of Multi-Workcell Manufacturing Systems with Shared Resources", *IEEE Transactions on Systems, Man and Cybernetics: Part B, Cybernetics*, Vol. 30, No. 5, pp. 668-683, October 2000.

[29] F. Lin and M.W. Wonham, "On Observability of Discrete Event Systems", *Journal of Information Sciences*, Vol. 44, No. 3, pp. 174-198, 1988.

[30] A. Ramirez-Serrano, "Extended Moore Automata for the Supervisory Part-Flow Control of Virtual Manufacturing Workcells", Ph.D. Thesis, Department of Mechanical and Industrial Engineering, University of Toronto, November 2000.

[31] A. Ramirez-Serrano and B. Benhabib, "Supervisory Control of Reconfigurable Flexible-Manufacturing Workcells — temporary addition of resources", *Int. Journal Computer Integrated Manufacturing*, Vol. 16, No. 2, pp. 93-111, 2003.

[32] A. Ramirez-Serrano and B. Benhabib, "Supervisory Control of Flexible-Manufacturing Workcells that Allow the Production of A priori Unplanned Part Types", *IEEE International Conference of Systems, Man and Cybernetics*, Nashville, pp. 2127-2131, October 8-11, 2000.

[33] H. Seifoddini, "A Probabilistic Model for Machine Cell Formation", *SME Journal of Manufacturing Systems*, Vol. 9, No. 1, pp. 69-75, 1990.

[34] J.M. Eyzel and J.E.R. Cury, "Exploiting the Symmetry in the Synthesis of Supervisors for Discrete Event Systems", *American Control Conference*, Philadelphia, PA, pp. 244-248, June 1998.

4

Deadlock Avoidance and Dynamic Routing Flexibility in Automated Manufacturing Systems[1]

Mark Lawley
Purdue University, West Lafayette, IN, USA.

4.1 INTRODUCTION

Many automated manufacturing systems support routing flexibility. Routing flexibility arises when a part being manufactured has some choice regarding its next required machine tool. With flexible routing, the part can act opportunistically based on the current allocation of machine capacity across the system. This improves system performance by increasing the chances that a part can proceed to its next processing step, resulting in reduced machine blocking and increased system production rate.

Routing flexibility can arise due to machine flexibility and/or sequence flexibility. Machine flexibility occurs when a part operation can be performed on more than one machine, while sequence flexibility occurs when the set of operations specified by a part's process plan is not completely ordered. Machine flexibility requires some level of resource redundancy and is therefore most likely to be supported in larger systems. On the other hand, sequence flexibility is more a function of part design and process planning and is most useful for complex parts with many required operations. Both types of flexibility have the

---

[1] Material presented here is taken from Lawley (1999, 2000) and Sulistyono and Lawley (2001), with the permission of the International Journal of Production Research (http://www.tandf.co.uk/journals/tf/00207543.html) and IEEE. See references at end of chapter.

potential to generate a combinatorial number of routes. For example, a part with n unordered processing steps and k alternatives at every step can potentially follow $n!(k^n)$ routes through the system (the $n!$ due to sequence flexibility, and the k^n due to machine flexibility).

Clearly, sophisticated control software is required to exploit the advantages of flexible routing. This software should allow parts to take full advantage of the flexibility supported while assuring that the system remains deadlock-free. Deadlock analysis techniques and the resulting deadlock avoidance policies (DAP) have typically required route enumeration. As noted above, this is a significant disadvantage that must be overcome for these highly flexible systems.

This chapter will review deadlock analysis and avoidance techniques that support full flexibility while avoiding full route enumeration. It starts by providing a very brief review of the most relevant literature on the performance aspects of flexible routing. The chapter then presents a review of the author's deadlock avoidance results and techniques for systems with machine flexibility and sequencing flexibility.

4.2 PERFORMANCE ADVANTAGES OF FLEXIBLE ROUTING

Many researchers have investigated the performance of systems with flexible routing. Overall, authors report significant improvements in the typical system performance measures. For example, to quote Lin and Solberg (1991) "Under certain reasonable circumstances, the throughput can be improved around 10% over that which occurs with fixed process plans, and average flow time is reduced by a similar factor." Researchers such as Benjaafar and Ramakrishnan (1996), Chen and Chung (1996), Benjaafar, Talavage, and Ramakrishnan (1995), and Upton and Barash (1988) have investigated and proposed measures that attempt to quantify the amount of routing flexibility that a system exhibits.

Benjaafar and Ramakrishnan (1996) propose a measure that relates the number of alternatives at each stage of a part's processing to part waiting time. Their objective is to provide a flexibility measure that managers can use to predict system performance. Based on simulation results, they observe that (1) system performance measures tend to improve with increasing flexibility; (2) the benefits of flexibility are of the diminishing kind, that is, most benefits are achieved by introducing a limited amount of flexibility; and (3) distributing flexibility among part stages is more important than the total number of possible sequences, and thus, every part stage should possess some flexibility.

Chen and Chung (1996) investigate a measure they call routing flexibility utilization that quantifies the utilization of alternate routes. Their simulation results lead them to observe that (1) the benefits of flexibility follow the law of diminishing returns; and (2) when processing times exhibit low variance, system components are more fully utilized if the FMS has no flexible routing. Benjaafar, Talavage, and Ramakrishnan (1995) verify the positive effects of flexible routing on system performance, as do Hutchinson and Pflughoeft (1994), and

Shmilovoci and Maimon (1992). A common observation is that dispatching rules become less important as routing flexibility increases.

4.3 AVOIDANCE FOR SYSTEMS WITH MACHINE FLEXIBILITY

This section presents results dealing with machine flexibility. The basic assumption is that each part requires a sequence of operations where each operation can be performed by a set of machines, thus distributing flexibility among part stages. The chapter presents two approaches, the first being the application of algebraic avoidance policies developed for systems with single routes (these require route enumeration), and the second based on fundamental deadlock analysis.

4.3.1 Route Enumeration, Equivalent States, and Switching Heuristic

This section summarizes methods presented in Lawley (2000) for enumerating a small subset of routes that is used to develop a method for dynamically switching routes under the supervision of an algebraic DAP. We assume the process plan to specify the set of machines that can perform each part operation and that the sequence of operations is completely ordered. μ is the set of machines and C_u represents the capacity of machine, $M_u \in \mu$. Π is the set of part types produced where each $\pi_i \in \Pi$ is represented as an ordered set of processing stages $\pi_i = \langle p_{i1}, p_{i2}, ..., p_{i|\pi_i|} \rangle$. μ_{ik} denotes the subset of machines that can perform the kth operation for π_i. $\Re g_i$ is the route generator, for π_i and is defined as the ordered set of μ_{ik}'s for $k=1...|\pi_i|$, $\Re g_i = \langle \mu_{i1}, \mu_{i2}, ..., \mu_{i|\pi_i|} \rangle$. $\Re_i = \{\rho_{ij} : \rho_{ij} \in \{\mu_{i1} x \mu_{i2} x ... x \mu_{i|\pi_i|}\}\}$ is the complete set of routes for π_i, the cross-product $\Re g_i$. We assume that any route of $\Re_i$ can be feasibly executed.

This section demonstrates a method, based on Taguchi's orthogonal arrays (Taguchi, 1989), for quickly enumerating a small sub-set of routes, the cover referred to as $\Re c_i$, that can be broken apart and recombined to generate any route of $\Re_i$. The cover is used to generate DAP constraints. The method guarantees that the cover exhibits the following properties:

1) The cover is dense, that is, every pair $(M_u, M_v) \in \{\mu_{ik} x \mu_{i,k+c} : k=1...(|\pi_i|-1), c=1... (|\pi_i|-k)\}$ appears in at least one route of the cover;

2) The cover is balanced, that is, the pairs (M_u, M_v) and (M_u, M_w) appear with the same frequency in the cover.

To see the advantage of these properties, suppose $p_{i,k+c}$ can be served by n alternative machines. Then denseness guarantees that p_{ik} has at least n different routes to follow, one leading to each alternative. Thus, if $M_v \in \mu_{i,k+c}$ is down or becomes a bottleneck, all parts of type i in stages preceding k+c can be assigned to routes that avoid M_v. Further, if p_{ik} is being processed on $M_u \in \mu_{ik}$ and $M_v, M_w \in \mu_{i,k+c}$, then, in a dense and balanced cover, p_{ik} has as many routes leading to M_v as to M_w. These two properties together guarantee that the routes for π_i are evenly distributed over the sets $\langle \mu_{i1}, \mu_{i2}, ..., \mu_{i|\pi_i|} \rangle$, which prevents any particular machine from having too much constraining influence in the DAP.

For example, suppose $\Pi = \{\pi_1, \pi_2\}$, $\mu = \{M_1, M_2, M_3, M_4, M_5, M_6, M_7, M_8\}$, $\Re g_1 = \langle \{M_1, M_2\}, \{M_3, M_4\}, \{M_5, M_6\}, \{M_7, M_8\} \rangle$, and $\Re g_2 = \langle \{M_1, M_8\}, \{M_2, M_3\}, \{M_5, M_7\}, \{M_4, M_6\} \rangle$. The number of possible routes for π_i is 2^4 for a total of 2^5 routes. Dense and balanced covers for π_1 and π_2 are given in Table 4.1. Note that $\Re_i$ has a total of 16 routes and that $\Re c_i$ enumerates half of these. Table 4.2 records the frequency with which each pair $(M_u, M_v) \in \{\mu_{ik} \times \mu_{i,k+c} : i=1,2; k=1,2,3; c=1...(4-k)\}$ appears in the cover and thus demonstrates that the covers are indeed dense and balanced.

Table 4.1   Route covers for π_1 and π_2.

ρ_{11}	1	3	5	7	ρ_{21}	1	2	5	4
ρ_{12}	1	3	5	8	ρ_{22}	1	2	5	6
ρ_{13}	1	4	6	7	ρ_{23}	1	3	7	4
ρ_{14}	1	4	6	8	ρ_{24}	1	3	7	6
ρ_{15}	2	3	6	7	ρ_{25}	8	2	7	4
ρ_{16}	2	3	6	8	ρ_{26}	8	2	7	6
ρ_{17}	2	4	5	7	ρ_{27}	8	3	5	4
ρ_{18}	2	4	5	8	ρ_{28}	8	3	5	6

Table 4.2   Frequency of machine pairs in routes of the cover.

$\Re c_1$	3	4	5	6	7	8	$\Re c_2$	2	3	5	7	4	6
1	2	2	2	2	2	2	1	2	2	2	2	2	2
2	2	2	2	2	2	2	8	2	2	2	2	2	2
3			2	2	2	2	2			2	2	2	2
4			2	2	2	2	3			2	2	2	2
5					2	2	5					2	2
6					2	2	7					2	2

Dense and balanced route covers are easily enumerated using Taguchi's orthogonal arrays (Taguchi, 1989). For demonstration, we consider the case where $|\mu_{ik}|$ is constant. For the case where $|\mu_{ik}|$ is not constant, please refer to Lawley (2000). Suppose, for example, that $|\pi_i| = 4$ and $|\mu_{ik}| = 2$. A dense and balanced cover is constructed by selecting any four columns from the orthogonal array $L_8(2^7)$, given in Table 4.3, and placing these in any order. Each row represents a route, and we assign machines accordingly. Suppose we select columns 1, 2, 3, and 4, and put them in that order. The first row (1,1,1,1) represents the assignment of machines to the first route, and so the first route contains the first machine of μ_{i1}, the first machine of μ_{i2}, and so forth. The second row (1,1,1,2) represents the assignment of machines to the second route, and so the second route contains the first machine of μ_{i1}, the first machine of μ_{i2}, the first machine of μ_{i3}, and the second machine of μ_{i4}, etc. The orthogonal array used is a function of redundancy and route length. For additional information on choosing the appropriate array, see Lawley (2000).

Table 4.3 $L_8(2^7)$ orthogonal array.

1	2	3	4	5	6	7
1	1	1	1	1	1	1
1	1	1	2	2	2	2
1	2	2	1	1	2	2
1	2	2	2	2	1	1
2	1	2	1	2	1	2
2	1	2	2	1	2	1
2	2	1	1	2	2	1
2	2	1	2	1	1	2

The next step is to develop a method for switching between routes in the cover, so that a part following one route can change to another when such a change is desirable. We assume that every part must be assigned to follow exactly one route from its cover. We let p_{ijk} represent a part of type i in the kth stage of jth route of $\Re c_i$, and X_{ijk} be the number of p_{ijk}'s in the current system state. Variables for the previous example include:

$$p_{11}: \{X_{111}, X_{121}, X_{131}, X_{141}, X_{151}, X_{161}, X_{171}, X_{181}\}$$
$$p_{12}: \{X_{112}, X_{122}, X_{132}, X_{142}, X_{152}, X_{162}, X_{172}, X_{182}\}$$
$$p_{13}: \{X_{113}, X_{123}, X_{133}, X_{143}, X_{153}, X_{163}, X_{173}, X_{183}\}$$
$$p_{14}: \{X_{114}, X_{124}, X_{134}, X_{144}, X_{154}, X_{164}, X_{174}, X_{184}\}$$

and similar sets for p_{21}-p_{24}.

Further, we let Ω_u be the set of variables associated with the parts processed by M_u, that is, $\Omega_u = \{X_{ijk} : M_u$ is the kth machine of the jth route of $\Re c_i\}$. In the example system, the variable sets for M_1 and M_2 are as follows:

$$\Omega_1 = \{X_{111}, X_{121}, X_{131}, X_{141}, X_{211}, X_{221}, X_{231}, X_{241}\}$$
$$\Omega_2 = \{X_{151}, X_{161}, X_{171}, X_{181}, X_{212}, X_{222}, X_{252}, X_{262}\}$$

The system state is the collection of all of these variables into a single vector, χ. The state provides information on the number of parts in the system, their current machine location, and the routes they are following. The length of the state vector is the sum of the lengths of all routes in the covers of all part types. Figure 4.1 illustrates a state for the example system.

The system state can change in two ways. First, state transition can occur in the usual way, through single step advancement of parts. That is, a new part enters the system, a part advances one step in its route, or a part leaves the system. State transition can also occur through route reassignment without any movement of parts. In Figure 4.1, the state has $X_{111}=2$ and $X_{121}=X_{131}=X_{141}=0$.

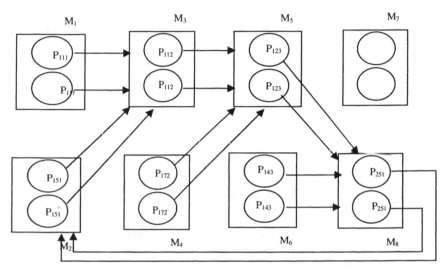

$$\chi = \langle\, X_{111},X_{121},...,X_{181};\ \ X_{112},X_{122},...,X_{182};\ X_{113},X_{123},...,X_{183};\ X_{114},X_{124},...,X_{184};$$
$$X_{211},X_{221},...,X_{281};\ \ X_{212},X_{222},...,X_{282};\ X_{213},X_{223},...,X_{283};\ X_{214},X_{224},...,X_{284}\,\rangle^{\mathrm{T}}$$

$$\chi' = \langle\, 20002000\,;\,20000020\,;\,02020000\,;\,00000000;\,00002000\,;\,00000000\,;$$
$$00000000\,;\,00000000\rangle^{\mathrm{T}}$$

Figure 4.1   Possible state for example system.

Clearly, the state can be changed by switching the route assignment, with any assignment of parts to routes on M_1 being feasible so long as $X_{111}+X_{121}+X_{131}+X_{141}=2$. The complete set of constraints for the example is:

$(M_1)\ \ X_{111}+X_{121}+X_{131}+X_{141}=2;\quad X_{211}+X_{221}+X_{231}+X_{241}=0$

$(M_2)\ \ X_{151}+X_{161}+X_{171}+X_{181}=2;\quad X_{212}+X_{222}+X_{252}+X_{262}=0$

$(M_3)\ \ X_{112}+X_{122}+X_{152}+X_{162}=2;\quad X_{232}+X_{242}+X_{272}+X_{282}=0$

$(M_4)\ X_{132}+X_{142}+X_{172}+X_{182}=2;\quad X_{214}+X_{234}+X_{254}+X_{274}=0$

$(M_5)\ X_{113}+X_{123}+X_{173}+X_{183}=2;\quad X_{213}+X_{223}+X_{273}+X_{283}=0$

$(M_6)\ X_{133}+X_{143}+X_{153}+X_{163}=2;\quad X_{224}+X_{244}+X_{264}+X_{284}=0$

$(M_7)\ X_{114}+X_{134}+X_{154}+X_{174}=0;\quad X_{233}+X_{243}+X_{253}+X_{263}=2$

(M_8) $X_{124}+X_{144}+X_{164}+X_{184}=0;$ $X_{251}+X_{261}+X_{271}+X_{281}=2.$

The constraints partition the variables into equivalence classes. Each class is associated with a given machine and represents the routing assignment of a set of parts at that machine. If ξ_u represents the equivalence classes associated with M_u, then for the example problem, we have:

M_1: $\xi_1=\{\xi_{11},\xi_{12}\}$ $\xi_{11}=\{X_{111}, X_{121}, X_{131}, X_{141}\}$ $\xi_{12}=\{X_{211}, X_{221}, X_{231}, X_{241}\}$

M_2: $\xi_2=\{\xi_{21},\xi_{22}\}$ $\xi_{21}=\{X_{151}, X_{161}, X_{171}, X_{181}\}$ $\xi_{22}=\{X_{212}, X_{222}, X_{252}, X_{262}\}$

M_3: $\xi_3=\{\xi_{31},\xi_{32}\}$ $\xi_{31}=\{X_{112}, X_{122}, X_{152}, X_{162}\}$ $\xi_{32}=\{X_{232}, X_{242}, X_{272}, X_{282}\}$

M_4: $\xi_4=\{\xi_{41},\xi_{42}\}$ $\xi_{41}=\{X_{132}, X_{142}, X_{172}, X_{182}\}$ $\xi_{42}=\{X_{214}, X_{234}, X_{254}, X_{274}\}$

M_5: $\xi_5=\{\xi_{51},\xi_{52}\}$ $\xi_{51}=\{X_{113}, X_{123}, X_{173}, X_{183}\}$ $\xi_{52}=\{X_{213}, X_{223}, X_{273}, X_{283}\}$

M_6: $\xi_6=\{\xi_{61},\xi_{62}\}$ $\xi_{61}=\{X_{133}, X_{143}, X_{153}, X_{163}\}$ $\xi_{62}=\{X_{224}, X_{244}, X_{264}, X_{284}\}$

M_7: $\xi_7=\{\xi_{71},\xi_{72}\}$ $\xi_{71}=\{X_{114}, X_{134}, X_{154}, X_{174}\}$ $\xi_{72}=\{X_{233}, X_{243}, X_{253}, X_{263}\}$

M_8: $\xi_8=\{\xi_{81},\xi_{82}\}$ $\xi_{81}=\{X_{124}, X_{144}, X_{164}, X_{184}\}$ $\xi_{82}=\{X_{251}, X_{261}, X_{271}, X_{281}\}$

Thus, for a given system state, χ^t, these constraints can be more compactly expressed as follows:

$$\sum_{X_{ijk}\in\xi_{uv}} X_{ijk} = \sum_{X_{ijk}\in\xi_{uv}} X^t_{ijk} \quad u=1...|\mu|, v=1...|\xi_u|$$

We refer to these as $A\chi = A\chi^t$, and define a pair of state vectors, χ^s and χ^t, to be equivalent iff

$$A\chi^s = A\chi^t \tag{1}$$

It is easy to show that A defines an equivalence relation on the system state space and that A is totally unimodular. This implies that given a system state, say χ^t, the set of solutions to the linear program (LP) relaxation of $A\chi=A\chi^t$ is the set of all states equivalent to χ^t. Thus, if the system is in state χ^t and we change the routes of a set of parts without moving any part, the resulting state will be a solution to the above LP.

Up to this point we have illustrated how to generate a small set of routes and how to switch between those routes. We will conclude this section of the chapter by showing how to integrate these functions with algebraic DAPs.

An algebraic DAP is a set of integer linear constraints on the system state that guarantees deadlock-free operation. We denote an algebraic DAP as $B\chi^t \le f(C)$ where, B is a binary constraint matrix, χ^t is desired a state vector, and $f(C)$ is a function of system capacity. In deciding whether to allow a certain part to move forward, the resulting state, χ^t, is submitted to the DAP. If χ^t satisfies the constraints, then the DAP admits the state and the part is allowed to move forward, otherwise the state is rejected and the part is not allowed to move. Two families of algebraic DAPs have been developed and are presented in the literature. Lawley, Reveliotis, and Ferreira (1997) develop the resource upstream neighborhood (RUN) policy, which avoids deadlock by applying a capacity reservation scheme based on the intuition that high capacity machines can be treated as central storage buffers for parts that require their services. Lawley, Reveliotis, and Ferreira (1998) develop the resource order (RO) policy, which is based on the intuition that parts flowing in opposite directions through the same set of machines must at some point be able to pass. Both policies define convex regions of FMS operation that are guaranteed to be deadlock-free. Further, both generate families of DAPs since the machines must be ordered to generate constraints. With at least $|\mu|!$ different orders available, it is possible to generate a large number of different constraint sets, any one of which guarantees deadlock-free operation. For more detailed information, the reader is referred to Lawley, Reveliotis, and Ferreira (1997, 1998).

The fact that RUN and RO generate families of DAPs is a major advantage since operational flexibility can be improved by using several different DAPs together in disjunction. In this case, a state can be allowed if it is accepted by at least one DAP from among a set of DAPs. If $\{B_q\chi \le f_q(C) : q=1,2,...,K \}$ represents a set of DAPs, a state vector χ will be admissible if and only if there exists $k \in \{1,2,...,K\}$ such that $B_k\chi \le f_k(C)$. This situation is easily modeled as a disjunctive set of linear constraints, that is, we define a binary indicator variable Y_k such that $Y_k=1 \Rightarrow$ if $B_k\chi \le f_k(C)$. Then χ is admitted by at least one DAP if and only if there exists a solution to the following:

$$B_q\chi \le f_q(C) + \omega(1-Y_q) \quad q=1...K \tag{2}$$

$$\sum_{q=1}^{K} Y_q = 1 \tag{3}$$

Constraint set (3) is included to help control the size of the feasible region of these constraints, since it is sufficient for χ to satisfy one of the K DAPs. ω is a vector of upper bounds on $B_q\chi$.

All of these can now be combined into a single mathematical program as follows:

$$\min f(\chi)$$
subject to

$$A \chi = A \chi^t \tag{1}$$

$$B_q \chi \leq f_q(C) + \omega(1-Y_q) \qquad q=1...K \tag{2}$$

$$\sum_{q=1}^{K} Y_q = 1 \tag{3}$$

$$\chi \in Z^+ \qquad Y_q \in \{0,1\} \tag{4}$$

χ^t is the desired state that results from advancing a chosen part, and χ is the variable vector. Constraint set (1) assures state equivalence, (2) guarantees dead-lock-free operation, and (3) expresses that it is sufficient for χ to satisfy one of the K DAPs. A solution is a state vector equivalent to χ^t that satisfies at least one of the DAPs and is therefore acceptable. Thus, the part would be advanced and the route assignment would be updated.

Lawley (2000) presents a polynomial heuristic for solving this program, which consists of two parts, H1 and H2. H1 changes the route of the advancing part by indexing through the set of machines to which the part can advance, and for each machine, indexing through all possible route assignments for the part on that machine. Each possible route assignment is submitted to each of the K DAPs. If a DAP accepts, the acceptable state is returned, the system is updated to that state, and the heuristic is terminated. If a DAP rejects, a tuple consisting of the rejected state, the rejecting DAP, and the set of variables in violated constraints of the DAP, is inserted into a list, VIOLATION, which is used in H2. It is easy to show that it is polynomial.

If H1 fails to accept, then H2 searches for equivalent states that are DAP admissible. It first sorts VIOLATION in ascending order using the number of variables appearing in violated constraints as the key. It then iteratively removes and tests these tuples. Step 1 removes the next tuple and retrieves its state, DAP, and variable list. Step 2 then generates an equivalent state, using (1), that minimizes the sum of variables appearing in violated constraints of the DAP. Minimizing these variables produces an equivalent state that comes as close as possible to satisfying the previously violated constraints, although there is no guarantee that previously satisfied constraints will not be violated. This equivalent state is then submitted to the corresponding DAP, which either accepts or rejects. If the DAP accepts, the new state is returned, the system is updated to that state, and the heuristic is terminated. Otherwise, the heuristic continues. (For more information on this heuristic, the reader is referred to Lawley (2000).)

Lawley (2000) studies the interactive effect of this heuristic and DAP disjunction (using RO) on system flexibility and performance on four randomly generated systems using discrete event simulation. A partial summary of the results for four systems is given in Table 4.4. This table gives the total number of part blocks that were resolved in each simulation run that used both H1 and H2, and the number of unblocks provided by each. For example, the first row represents a run of 4000 parts through system 1 using a single DAP. During this run, a total of 3608 blocking situations were resolved though route reassignments. H1 was responsible for 3078 of these, while H2 resolved 530 of the situations that H1 failed to resolve. Overall, when both H1 and H2 are applied together, 83% of blocking resolution is attributable to H1, while 17% is attributable to H2.

This section has presented a method that uses algebraic DAPs developed for systems with single routes to avoid deadlock in systems with machine flexibility. This approach is advantageous because it takes advantage of previous work without requiring extensive analysis of the deadlock structure of these more complex systems. In contrast, the next section will develop avoidance methods that are based on the detailed analysis of deadlock and safety in systems with machine flexibility.

Table 4.4   Relative blocking resolution of H1 vs. H2.

System	DAP	Number Unblocks			%Unblocks	
		Total	H1	H2	%H1	%H2
1	Single	3608	3078	530	0.85	0.15
	Single	3533	2983	550	0.84	0.16
	Mult.	3705	3150	555	0.85	0.15
	Mult.	3723	3195	528	0.86	0.14
2	Single	3664	2795	869	0.76	0.24
	Single	4246	3244	1002	0.76	0.24
	Mult.	4731	3602	1129	0.76	0.24
	Mult.	4803	3690	1113	0.77	0.23
3	Single	3446	2788	658	0.81	0.19
	Single	3294	2679	615	0.81	0.19
	Mult.	3881	3537	344	0.91	0.09
	Mult.	3724	3442	282	0.92	0.08
4	Single	3616	3046	570	0.84	0.16
	Single	3603	3048	555	0.85	0.15
	Mult.	4247	3516	731	0.83	0.17
	Mult.	3994	3224	770	0.81	0.19
					0.83	0.17

Note: Each row represents a single production run of 4000 parts running under H1+H2.

4.3.2 Deadlock Avoidance in Systems with Machine Flexibility

This section presents a summary of the detailed safety analysis presented in Lawley (1999) for systems in which every operation of every part type is supported by n machines (we refer to these systems as $SU^{(n)}$-RAS). We initially assume that every machine has a single unit of buffer capacity and then extend the results to mixed capacity systems where some machines, possibly all, have two or more units of buffer capacity (where buffer capacity is assumed to be the total number of physical locations at a machine where a part can sit or be held). Near the end of the section, we discuss systems with central buffers.

Let μ be the set of system machines and P be the set of parts in the system. Let p_{ik} represent a part of type i in its kth stage of processing, and let μ_{ik} represent the set of machines able to perform the operation required of p_{ik}. We often use "p_i" to represent a part of type i without specifying its current processing stage, and we use $|p_i|$ to denote the number of processing steps required by a part of type i. The part $p_{i,|p_i|}$ is terminal since it is in its final processing stage. Terminal parts finish and exit the system without additional resource allocation and can therefore be ignored. In the following, we assume that $\mu_{ik} \cap \mu_{i,k+1} = \varnothing$. We justify this assumption by noting that if two successive operations can be performed on the same machine, then the operations can be combined into a single operation.

The resource allocation graph (RAG) is defined as a pair $\{\mu, \alpha\}$ where $\alpha = \{(M_u, M_v) : M_u, M_v \in \mu$ and M_u holds p_{ik} with $M_v \in \mu_{i,k+1}\}$. A subdigraph of RAG, $\{\mu', \alpha'\}$, is *induced* when $\mu' \subset \mu$ and $\alpha' = \{(M_u, M_v) : (M_u, M_v) \in \alpha$ and $M_u, M_v \in \mu'\}$. $\{\mu', \alpha'\}$ forms a *knot* in RAG if $\forall M_u \in \mu'$, $R(M_u) = \mu'$, where $R(M_u)$ is the set of all nodes reachable from M_u in RAG. In other words, a set of nodes, μ', forms a knot in RAG when, for every node in μ', the set of nodes reachable along arcs in RAG is exactly μ'. Figure 4.2 demonstrates the RAG for an single capacity system (SCS) with four machines. Note, for example, that p_1 is occupying M_1 and needs next to visit either M_2 or M_4. Further note that the allocation shown in (b) contains a knot consisting of M_1, M_2, and M_4, while that of (a) contains no knot. Theorem 4.1 establishes that a knot in RAG is necessary and sufficient for deadlock in the SCS (for proof see Lawley, 1998).

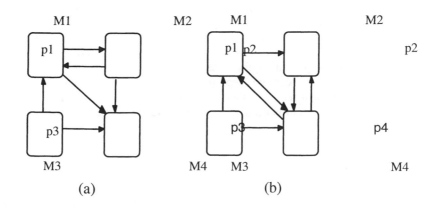

(a) (b)

Figure 4.2   Example resource allocation graphs, © 1999 IEEE.

Theorem 4.1   A knot in RAG is necessary and sufficient for deadlock in the

SCS.

Thus, to detect deadlock, we need only detect a knot in RAG. This is easily accomplished using the knot detection algorithm provided in Lawley (1999), which is $O(n|\mu|^2)$.

We say that a deadlock avoidance policy is *optimal* if it permits every safe allocation and rejects only those that are unsafe (where an allocation state represented by RAG is safe precisely when there exists a sequence of resource allocations that completes all currently processing parts). Lawley (1998) establishes that safety, and thus optimal deadlock avoidance, is NP-complete in the $SU^{(n)}$–RAS. This result, together with polynomial knot detection, implies the existence of deadlock-free unsafe states, leading to Theorem 4.2.

Theorem 4.2 A necessary condition for the NP-completeness of optimal deadlock avoidance is the existence of deadlock-free allocation states that are unsafe.

This result is easily seen if we consider the two questions:
(i) Is an allocation state deadlock-free?   (ii) Is an allocation state safe?

As just shown, (i) is polynomial and (ii) is NP-complete. Thus, these are different questions. Clearly, safe implies deadlock-free. If the questions are different, then deadlock-free must not imply safe. Only the existence of allocation states that are both deadlock-free and unsafe can account for this situation. Thus, if optimal deadlock avoidance is NP-complete, deadlock-free unsafe states exist.

Theorem 4.2 is an essential tool for proving the polynomial complexity of optimal deadlock avoidance for special cases, for if we can show that deadlock-free unsafe states do not exist for some special case, then all resource allocation states are either safe or deadlock. To determine whether a given allocation results in a safe or unsafe allocation state, we need only check the resulting state for the existence of deadlock, a polynomial computation.

We now demonstrate a deadlock-free unsafe state. Consider the system of Figure 4.3. This system has five machines, each of unit capacity. Machines M_1, M_2, M_4, and M_5 hold parts p_1, p_2, p_3, and p_4, respectively. Machine M_3 holds no part, and each part has two processing alternatives for its next step. Suppose that after finishing their next processing steps (the ones that could be performed on M_3), parts p_1 and p_2 will require either M_4 or M_5. Further, suppose that after finishing their next processing steps (the ones that could be performed on M_3), parts p_3 and p_4 will require either M_1 or M_2. Then, if any part advances, a knot results and the system is deadlocked. Since the state given is deadlock-free, we have a deadlock-free unsafe state.

Lemmas 4.3 and 4.4 provide additional characterization for deadlock states and deadlock-free unsafe states. Theorem 4.5 establishes three methods of avoiding deadlock for SCS.

Lemma 4.3 In an SCS where every processing stage of every part type has n processing alternatives, the minimum number of parts required for deadlock is n+1.

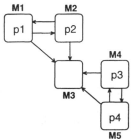

Figure 4.3   Deadlock-free unsafe state for $SU^{(n)}$-RAS,
© 1999 IEEE.

Lemma 4.4 If each part has n processing alternatives, then at least 2n parts and (2n+1) machines are necessary in a deadlock-free unsafe state.

Theorem 4.5 Deadlock-free operation is guaranteed when (i) at most n parts are allowed in the system at one time; (ii) at most (2n-1) parts are allowed in the system at one time coupled with single step look-ahead for knots in RAG; and (iii) $|\mu|$ is even and n=($|\mu|/2$) coupled with single step look-ahead for knots in RAG.

Figure 4.4 provides a realistic example. This cell consists of four machines, $\mu=\{M_1,M_2,M_3,M_4\}$, which we assume to be single capacity, and produces four part types, $\{p_1,p_2,p_3,p_4\}$ each with two processing steps and with respective machine sets $\langle\{M_1,M_3\},\{M_2,M_4\}\rangle$, $\langle\{M_2,M_4\},\{M_1,M_3\}\rangle$, $\langle\{M_4,M_3\}, \{M_2,M_1\}\rangle$, and $\langle\{M_2,M_1\}, \{M_4, M_3\}\rangle$. Since n=2, at least three parts are required for deadlock. Applying Theorem 4.5(i) would avoid deadlock by allowing at most n=2 parts in the system at once. Theorem 4.5(ii) would allow at most (2n-1)=3 parts, coupled with single step look-ahead for deadlock. Finally, since n=$|\mu|/2$, Theorem 4.5(iii) tells us that this system has no deadlock-free unsafe states, and thus single step look-ahead for deadlock, with no restriction on the number of parts in the system, guarantees deadlock-free operation. For this system, we can let any new part enter the system just so long as it does not cause a knot in RAG. This approach provides optimal flexibility.

These properties are easily extended to systems where some machines have multiple units of buffer capacity. We refer to systems in which some machines have multiple units of buffer capacity, while others have only single units as mixed capacity systems (MCS). Again, let μ be the set of system machines, and note that $\mu = \mu' \cup \mu''$, where μ' (μ'') is the set of single (multiple) capacity machines. Let RAG be defined as before. A *capacitated* knot in RAG is a knot in which every machine forming a node in the knot is filled to capacity with non-terminal parts. We present a set of lemmas and theorems corresponding to those of SCS.

Theorem 4.6   A capacitated knot in RAG is necessary and sufficient for deadlock in the MCS.

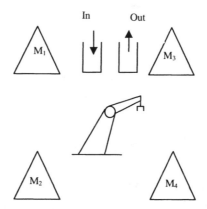

Figure 4.4   SCS illustrative example, © 1999 IEEE.

Only minor modifications of the knot detection algorithm presented in Lawley (1999) are required to detect capacitated knots, and therefore, detecting deadlock in the MCS is polynomial. Further, it is easy to show that Theorem 4.2 continues to hold, and thus the complexity of optimal deadlock avoidance for the MCS is NP-complete. (For further details, please see Lawley (1999).)

Lemma 4.7   In an MCS where every part has n processing alternatives at every stage, at least $(n+1)C_{min}$ parts are necessary for deadlock, where C_{min} is the minimum machine capacity.

Lemma 4.8   Let $\mu_{(i)}$ be a subset of i machines with minimal accumulated capacity, $C_{(i)}$, that is, the summed capacity of $\mu_{(i)}$ does not exceed the summed capacity of any other subset of i machines from μ. Then, in an MCS where every part has n processing alternatives at every stage, at least $C_{(n+1)}$ parts are necessary for deadlock.

These two lemmas establish lower bounds for the number of parts that are required for an MCS to deadlock. We now establish similar bounds for the number of parts required for deadlock-free unsafeness. Theorem 4.11 establishes several operational conditions for maintaining deadlock-free operation in MCSs.

Lemma 4.9 If $\mu' = \emptyset$, then deadlock-free unsafe states do not exist in the $SU^{(n)}$-RAS.

Lemma 4.10 Let $\mu_{(i)}$ and $C_{(i)}$ be defined as given in Lemma 4.8 and assume that $\mu' \neq \emptyset$. Then at least $(C_{(2n+1)}-1)$ parts are necessary for unsafeness.

Theorem 4.11 Deadlock-free operation is guaranteed when (i) at most $(C_{(n+1)} - 1)$ parts are allowed in the system at one time; (ii) at most $(C_{(2n+1)} - 2)$ parts allowed in the system at one time coupled with single step look-ahead for deadlock; (iii) at most n full machines are allowed at one time; (iv) at most 2n-1 full machines are allowed coupled with single step look-ahead for deadlock; and (v) $\mu' = \emptyset$ coupled with single step look-ahead for deadlock.

We now demonstrate how to apply these results. Consider a system of 12 machines, each with 2 units of capacity. There are two input/output stations where parts arrive and leave the system. Parts are transported between machines by a single part transporter. We will suppose that the system produces 100 different part types, with no apparent structure to the routes other than that each stage of each part type has two processing alternatives. If each part type has at least two processing steps, then at least $2^2 = 4$ different routes per part type are possible, and there are at least 400 different routing possibilities. Clearly, avoidance methods based on explicit route enumeration and analysis would be computationally difficult to apply. The methods developed in this work are easy to apply since they require only the number of alternatives at each step.

The total system capacity (not including the transporter) is 24 parts. Applying Theorem 4.11 (i) (v) provides the following deadlock avoidance methods: (i) guarantees that no deadlock will occur if the controller allows no more than $C_{(2+1)}-1=6-1=5$ parts into the system at once; (ii) guarantees that no deadlock-free unsafe states will be encountered, and thus single step look-ahead for capacitated knots in RAG will avoid deadlock if the controller allows no more than $C_{(5)}-2=10-2=8$ parts into the system at once; (iii) guarantees deadlock-free operation if the controller allows no more than n=2 full machines at once. Thus, the controller can allow up to $2(2)+(12-2)=14$ parts into the system at once; (iv) guarantees that no deadlock-free unsafe states will be encountered and thus single step look-ahead for capacitated knots in RAG will avoid deadlock if the controller allows no more than 2n-1=3 full machines at once. Thus, the controller can allow up to $3(2)+(12-3)=15$ parts into the system at once; and finally, because there are no single capacity machines, (v) guarantees that there are no deadlock-free unsafe states, and thus single step look-ahead for capacitated knots in RAG, with no limit on the number of parts, will avoid deadlock for this system. This controller is optimally flexible since it allows any part entry or part movement that does not cause a capacitated knot in RAG.

We now investigate deadlock in systems with a finite central buffer that can be revisited after every processing stage. We make no assumptions about the capacity of the central buffer other than that it is finite.

Definition 4.12 An MCS is *buffered*, BMCS, if there exists a central finite capacity buffer, represented as β, that parts can revisit after every processing step and at which no processing takes place.

In the BMCS, $(M_u, M_v) \in \alpha$ implies $(M_u, \beta) \in \alpha$, that is, each machine holding a part has a corresponding arc to the central buffer in the RAG, since each part can next visit the central buffer (see Figure 4.5). Furthermore, an arc $(\beta, M_v) \in \alpha$ if and only if β holds a part, p_{ik}, and $M_v \in \mu_{i,k+1}$. Note that β does not belong to any μ_{ik}, since it performs no processing function. Lemmas 4.13 and 4.14, and Theorem 4.15 characterize deadlock and optimal deadlock avoidance for the $SU^{(n)}$-RAS with a central buffer.

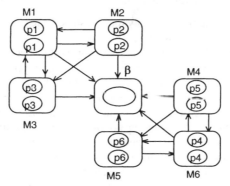

Figure 4.5 $SU^{(n)}$-RAS with a central buffer, © 1999 IEEE.

Lemma 4.13 Let k_1 be a capacitated knot in the RAG of a BMCS, then $\beta \in k_1$.

Lemma 4.14 The RAG of a BMCS has a capacitated knot if and only if every $M_u \in R(\beta) \neq \varnothing$ is filled to capacity.

Theorem 4.15 In the $SU^{(n)}$-RAS with a central buffer, deadlock-free unsafe states do not exist.

By Theorem 4.15, optimal deadlock avoidance is computationally tractable for the $SU^{(n)}$-RAS with a central buffer. It is not necessary to treat the central buffer in any special way, it is only necessary to avoid states exhibiting a capacitated knot. Furthermore, the central buffer need hold only a single part. Finally, detecting a capacitated knot for this case is much easier since we need only check $R(\beta)$ to see if it contains free capacity.

This section has presented both sub-optimal and optimal deadlock avoidance approaches for systems where every operation has some machine flexibility. As noted earlier, these methods require no route enumeration, which significantly reduces their implementation complexity over methods requiring route enumeration or methods in which the sequence of operations is captured in the structure of a Petri net. The following section presents similar types of results for systems with sequencing flexibility.

4.4 SAFETY ANALYSIS FOR SYSTEMS WITH SEQUENCE FLEXIBILITY

This section presents results that describe the fundamental complexity of the deadlock avoidance problem for systems with sequencing flexibility and then provides a selection of special cases. We begin by noting that it is easy to establish that deadlock is equivalent to a knot in the RAG, and that the knot detection algorithm presented in the previous section applies to these systems. Furthermore, although the safety problem remains NP-complete (see Sulistyono and Lawley, 2001 for a detailed proof), there are interesting structures on the partial orders of operations that render safety equivalent to detection (eliminate the possibility of deadlock-free unsafe states). This section will present several of these structures. Our goal is to investigate and understand how precedence between part operations affects the complex interactions that arise among parts competing for limited resources. For more details, the reader is referred to Sulistyono and Lawley (2001). We first require some additional formalism.

Let Θ_i represent the set of operations required by p_i, that is, $\Theta_i = \{o_{i1}, o_{i2}, ..., o_{in_i}\}$, and Ω_i be the partial order defined for Θ_i, that is, $\Omega_i = \{\langle o_{ij}, o_{ik} \rangle \mid o_{ij} < o_{ik}, o_{ij}$ must precede $o_{ik}\}$. We assume Θ_i and Ω_i are given by the process plan for p_i. Let $\varphi_{im} \subseteq \Omega_i$ be the set of "remaining precedence" arcs, the precedence remaining on the operations of a partially completed part. Let $\Sigma_i = \{ o_{ij} : \langle o_{ij}, o_{ik} \rangle \in \Omega_i \}$, i.e., Σ_i is the set of operations required by p_i that must precede at least one other operation.

We consider the following special cases important because they can eventually help integrate process planning and control, that is, if process plans can be developed that integrate the structures discussed below, then safety can be assured through single-step look-ahead for deadlock, and the system can be controlled in a more flexible manner. Furthermore, if the partial orders of remaining operations required by the current set of parts in a manufacturing system satisfy one of these partial order structures, then single step look-ahead keeps the system safe as long as new parts are not introduced. Thus, it might be possible to design flexible process plans that are perhaps close to one or more special cases. Then by placing priority on those part operations that are predecessors to other operations, that is, scheduling and dispatching so as to eliminate precedence within the system as quickly as possible, the system can be brought to a state in which the precedence constraints of remaining operations of each part satisfy some special case. Then the system will have reached a region of its state space where safety is polynomial, the deadlock avoidance policies become more flexible, and scheduling and dispatching methods have more leeway to optimize system performance. Finally, we note that these are the cases we have found and others, perhaps highly relevant ones, no doubt remain to be identified. We hope our work will inspire other researchers in this direction.

Our first result indicates that when there is no precedence, safety is polynomial. We recognize that the result of Theorem 4.16 is rarely directly applicable, since we always expect to have some precedence on the operations of a set of part types. However, it provides important insight into the effect of precedence on the complexity of safety. It also provides an important base case from which more applicable results can flow.

Theorem 4.16 Let $\Omega_i = \{\langle o_{ij}, o_{ik}\rangle \mid o_{ij} < o_{ik}\}$ be the partial order for part type p_i. Then, if $\Omega_i = \varnothing$ for all i, that is, there are no precedence requirements, then deadlock-free unsafe states do not exist and safety is polynomial.

Corollary 4.17 Let Π_A represent the set of parts that are allocated machine capacity in a given allocation state. Let $\varphi_{im} \subseteq \Omega_i$ be the set of remaining precedence requirements for $p_{im} \in \Pi_A$. If $\varphi_{im} = \varnothing \ \forall p_{im} \in \Pi_A$, then single step look-ahead for deadlock guarantees safe operation.

Corollary 4.17 states that when the system reaches a state where each partially completed part in the system has satisfied all precedence constraints on its operations and those remaining can be performed in any order, then deadlock-free unsafe states cannot arise unless new parts are introduced into the system. Thus, once such a state is attained, optimal deadlock avoidance is possible until new parts with precedence constraints are introduced into the system. Corollary 4.17 gives rise to the idea of a "switching" policy that uses a sub-optimal deadlock avoidance approach while parts in the system have a good deal of remaining precedence. After sufficient precedence is eliminated, the system switches to the more flexible single step look-ahead for deadlock to finish off the remaining operations. When new parts are introduced to the system, the controller switches back to the sub-optimal policy, and so forth. It is currently unclear what properties such a switching policy would have to satisfy, and thus this is one direction of future research.

We now establish a lower bound on the number of parts in a deadlock-free unsafe state one step from deadlock that are requesting an available resource to perform an operation that is the source of precedence.

Lemma 4.18 Let M_u be a requested and available machine in state s_o, a deadlock-free unsafe state one step from deadlock. Further, let $\Pi_u^{s_o} = \Pi_{u1}^{s_o} \cup \Pi_{u2}^{s_o}$ be the set of parts requesting M_u, where $p_i \in \Pi_{u1}^{s_o}$ requires M_u for an operation that is the source of a precedence and $p_k \in \Pi_{u2}^{s_o}$ requires M_u for an operation that is not the source of a precedence. Then, $|\Pi_{u1}^{s_o}| \geq 2$.

Lemma 4.18 can be used to strengthen Corollary 4.17 as follows: let $\Pi_A = \Pi_{A1} \cup \Pi_{A2}$ where Π_A is the set of parts allocated resources in the system, Π_{A1} is the set of parts that have some precedence constraints associated with their remaining operations, and Π_{A2} is the set of parts that has no precedence constraints associated with remaining operations. Then deadlock-free unsafe states cannot arise as long as $|\Pi_{Al}| < 2$. Lemma 4.18 also provides important insight that leads to the following theorems.

Theorem 4.19 Let $\Sigma = \bigcup_{\forall i} \Sigma_i$. Note that Σ is the set of all operations across all part types that must precede at least one other operation. Recall that μ_{ij} is the set of machines that can be used to perform operation o_{ij}. Then if $\bigcap_{o_{ij} \in \Sigma} \mu_{ij} = \varnothing$, deadlock-free unsafe states do not exist, that is, safety is polynomial.

Theorem 4.20 Suppose that $\Sigma_u \subseteq \Sigma$, such that all operations in Σ_u can use a common machine, say M_u, that is, $M_u \in \bigcap_{o_{ij} \in \Sigma_u} \mu_{ij}$. Let $\Lambda_u = \{ o_{ik} : o_{ij} \in \Sigma_u$ and $\langle o_{ij}, o_{ik} \rangle \in \Omega_i$ for some $i \}$ be the set of immediate successors of operations in Σ_u. Then if $\bigcap_{o_{ik} \in \Lambda_u} \mu_{ik} \neq \varnothing$, deadlock-free unsafe states do not exist, that is, safety is polynomial.

Theorem 4.19 and Theorem 4.20 provide conditions that can be developed into guidelines for process planners responsible for assigning operations to machines. By Theorem 4.19, if every operation that is the source of precedence can be assigned to a different machine, then deadlock-free unsafe states will not exist, and safety can be guaranteed through single-step look-ahead for deadlock. Theorem 4.20 states that if some set of operations that are the source of precedence must be assigned to the same machine, then if their successors can be assigned some common machines, deadlock-free unsafe states will not exist. Based on these results, one direction for future work is to formulate these conditions into an operation/resource assignment problem.

4.5 CONCLUSION

This chapter has presented a selection of the author's research in flexible routing for both machine flexibility and sequence flexibility. We first presented methods for applying algebraic DAPs to systems with machine flexibility. These methods support dynamic routing assignment and DAP disjunction without requiring extensive route enumeration or deadlock analysis. We then presented several approaches for deadlock avoidance based on the detailed analysis of deadlock and safety in systems with machine flexibility. These methods are advantageous in that they require no route enumeration. Finally, we presented a selection of results from the author's work on flexible sequencing. We hope these results provide the foundation for future research in developing guidelines for system design and control and for process planning. Of the three areas, flexible sequencing is least developed.

REFERENCES

Benjaafar, S., Talavage, J., and Ramakrishnan, R., 1995, The effect of routeing and machine flexibility on the performance of manufacturing systems. *International Journal of Computer Integrated Manufacturing*, **8**(4), 265-276.

Benjaafar, S. and Ramakrishnan, R., 1996, Modelling, measurement and evaluation of sequencing flexibility in manufacturing systems. *International Journal of Production Research*, **34**(5), 1195-1220.

Chen, I. and Chung, C., 1996, An examination of flexibility measurements and performance of flexible manufacturing systems. *International Journal of Production Research*, **34**(2), 379-394.

Hutchinson, G. and Pflughoeft, K., 1994, Flexible process plans: their value in flexible automation systems. *International Journal of Production Research*, **32**(3), 707-719.

Lawley, M., Reveliotis, S., and Ferreira, P., 1997, Flexible manufacturing system structural control and the neighborhood policy: parts 1&2, *IIE Transactions*, **29**(10), 877-899.

Lawley, M., Reveliotis, S., and Ferreira, P., 1998, A correct and scalable deadlock avoidance policy for flexible manufacturing systems, *IEEE Transactions on Robotics and Automation*, **14**(5), 796-809.

Lawley, M., 1998, NP-completeness proofs for safe buffer space allocation in automated manufacturing systems, Research Memorandum 98-07, School of Industrial Engineering, Purdue University, West Lafayette, IN, USA.

Lawley, M., 1999, Deadlock avoidance for production systems with flexible routing, *IEEE Transactions on Robotics and Automation*, **15**(3), 497-510.

Lawley, M., 2000, Integrating routing flexibility and algebraic deadlock avoidance policies in automated manufacturing systems, *International Journal of Production Research*, 38(13).

Lin, G. and Solberg, J., 1991, Effectiveness of flexible routing control, *International Journal of Flexible Manufacturing Systems*, **3**, 189-211.

Shmilovici, A. and Maimon, O., 1992, Heuristics for dynamic selection and routing of parts in an fms. *Journal of Manufacturing Systems*, **11**(4), 285-296.

Sulistyono, W. and Lawley, M., 2001, Deadlock avoidance for manufacturing systems with partially ordered process plans, **17**(6); 819-832.

Taguchi, G., 1989, *Taguchi Methods Design of Experiments*, Dearborn, MI: American Supplier Institute.

Upton, D. and Barash, M., 1988, A grammatical approach to routing flexibility in large manufacturing systems. *Journal of Manufacturing Systems*, **7**(3), 209-221.

5

Digraph-Based Techniques for Deadlock Resolution in Automated Manufacturing Systems

M.P. Fanti, B. Maione, G. Maione, B. Turchiano
Dipartimento di Elettrotecnica ed Elettronica, Politecnico di Bari, Bari, Italy.

5.1 INTRODUCTION

Deadlock is a circular wait situation in which some jobs (parts) in a set remain indefinitely blocked because each of them requests access to a resource held by some parts in the same set; in this case, any further job flow is inhibited. This condition may arise in production systems with a high level of resource sharing, such as automated manufacturing systems (AMS), consisting of a set of workstations performing different operations and of a material handling system carrying parts among workstations. Both workstations and transport devices are under control and supervision of one or several computers that are in charge of properly managing all the resources, preventing the system from reaching any deadlock condition.

The strategies that face deadlock are generally classified in three different groups: prevention methods, detection/recovery approaches and avoidance techniques. Some static policies can prevent deadlock occurrence by limiting the flexibility in resource utilization. Detection/recovery does not prevent deadlock conditions, but it monitors the system state to detect deadlock occurrences and restores the system operation by proper recovery procedures. Finally, avoidance prevents circular waits from occurring by using a proper on-line feedback control of resource allocation. Generally, prevention techniques lead to poorer performances than detection/recovery and avoidance methods. On the other hand, detection/recovery asks for dedicated hardware to perform the recovery phase.

The methods proposed in the technical literature to solve a deadlock problem are mainly based on three different types of formal tools to model the interactions between jobs and resources. They lead to different characterizations of deadlock states and to different solving procedures. Most of the approaches use Petri nets (PN) for their modular and systematic structure and because they are a unified tool for modeling, analysis, simulation and control of concurrent processes [1,3,4,16,20,27,28]. Other methods are founded on finite-state automata descriptions of the production system [17,18,21,25]. Finally, some approaches use models based on graph-theoretic tools [2,8,9,12,29,30]. Although these models are less general and less popular than PN-based ones, they appear more synthetic because they just represent the information necessary for deadlock characterization [10].

This chapter deals with graph-based approaches to deadlock resolution. The starting point is a unitary framework for modeling the production process and for characterizing deadlock states and some particular situations similar to deadlocks, named second-level deadlocks. This characterization is the basis of both detection/recovery and avoidance policies. Finally, the same theoretic results allow us to establish decentralized avoidance approache, by properly partitioning the production system into subsystems that can be controlled locally, i.e., each independently of the other ones. The technique is particularly useful for cellular manufacturing systems composed of several independent subsystems called cells [11], and leads to improved performance measures and flexibility in resource allocation. While the presented graph-based framework is very natural and intuitive in a single-unit resource allocation paradigm, it becomes hard to generalize to more complex and arbitrary resource allocation schemes. In these cases, other tools such as PN models can be more effective in obtaining supervisory controllers to avoid deadlock [22]. However, deadlock has been characterized also using digraph tools for AMS with conjunctive resource service, where at each stage a part can require a single unit of an arbitrary number of resource types [13,14].

This chapter is organized as follows. Section 5.2 introduces the graph-theoretic model of AMSs and Section 5.3 characterizes deadlock and second level deadlock states. Section 5.4 describes a detection/recovery approach based on the results previously established. In Section 5.5 some deadlock avoidance policies are explained and compared. Finally, Section 5.6 defines a decentralized approach to deadlock avoidance and Section 5.7 draws some concluding remarks.

5.2 THE MODEL

An AMS is composed of a set of resources such as machining stations, multiple-slot buffers, automated guided vehicle (AGV) systems provided with several trucks, robots, inspection and measuring stations, all under computer control to process a set J of jobs. In the following, r_i, with $i=1,2,\ldots,R-1$, indicates a generic resource while $C(r_i)$ stands for the capacity of r_i, i.e., the maximum number of parts that can contemporaneously hold such a resource. Moreover, we consider a further fictitious resource r_R to model the system output. So, we assume that each part acquires r_R as it leaves the system. This way, the complete resource set of the AMS is $R=\{r_i, i=1,2,\ldots,R\}$. We also assume $C(r_R)=\infty$, i.e., there is no restriction on jobs leaving the system.

To be processed, each job in J must receive service by some resources from R, in a specified order. Let **w** be such sequence of resources (i.e., the *working procedure*), while let $W=\{\mathbf{w}\}$ indicate the set of all the working procedures necessary to process the jobs in J. Obviously, r_R is the last resource in each working procedure.

From a theoretic point of view, the AMS can be modeled as a discrete-event dynamical system (DEDS) [6], where jobs acquire and release resources on the occurrence of some events, such as the arrival of a new job to the system (1-type event) and the progress of a job from a resource to another or the departure of a job from the system (2-type event). A label $\sigma_1=(j,\mathbf{w})$ describes a 1-type event, where $j \in J$ and $\mathbf{w} \in W$, respectively, denote the job entering the system and the assigned working procedure. Moreover, the label $\sigma_2=\{j,r_m,r_p\}$ characterizes a 2-type event involving the move of a job j from r_m to r_p. Obviously the DEDS state **q** (system state) must encapsulate information on the AMS operating conditions, concerning the set $J_q \subseteq J$ of jobs in process, the corresponding working procedures and their *residual working procedures*, i.e., the sequence of resources necessary for each $j \in J_q$ to complete its processing, including the resource currently held. In the following, we use $HR(j)$ and $SR(j)$ to denote, respectively, the resource detained and that required by $j \in J_q$ in the current state **q**, i.e., respectively, the first and the second resources in the residual working procedure pertaining to j. Moreover, if $SR(j) \neq r_R$, then $TR(j)$ indicates the third resource in such a residual working procedure. Finally, we say that a resource r_i is *busy* in the state **q** if the number of jobs holding it equals $C(r_i)$, so that r_i is currently unavailable. Obviously, if r_m is busy, any part $j \in J_q$ requiring it as a next resource is *blocked*.

The previous definitions and notations allow us to build two digraphs representing the interactions between jobs and resources in a concise and useful way. The former, denoted by $D_W=(N,E_W)$ and named *working procedure digraph*, represents all the resources pertaining to each working procedure from W in their specific sequence. Going into details, the vertex set coincides with the resource set, i.e., $N=R$. Moreover, the edge $e_{im}=(r_i,r_m)$, directed from r_i to r_m, is in $E_W \subset N \times N$ iff (if and only if) r_m immediately follows r_i in some $w \in W$. In this case, e_{im} can be labeled by the working procedures generating it. Obviously, digraph D_W only depends on the mix characteristics and does not vary as the state $\mathbf{q}$ changes. On the contrary, the second digraph $D_{Tr}(\mathbf{q})=[N,E_{Tr}(\mathbf{q})]$, named *transition digraph*, depends on the current DEDS state. As shown by the adopted notation, while the vertex set N still coincides with the resource set and is fixed, the edge set $E_{Tr}(\mathbf{q})$ changes as $\mathbf{q}$ is updated. In particular, $E_{Tr}(\mathbf{q})$ is a subset of E_W defined as follows: an edge e_{im} from E_W is in $E_{Tr}(\mathbf{q})$ if a part $j \in J_{\mathbf{q}}$ holds r_i in the state $\mathbf{q}$ and requires r_m as next resource. In opposition to D_W, the transition digraph only describes the current interactions between jobs in progress and resources, by exhibiting the resources currently held by each job from $J_{\mathbf{q}}$ and that required by the same job in the next step of its working procedure. To complete the definition of the transition digraph, let us observe that, if the capacity of r_i is greater than one, a single edge $e_{im} \in E_{Tr}(\mathbf{q})$ may represent several parts, all detaining r_i and requesting r_m. To encapsulate this piece of information in the transition digraph, let us associate the following weight to each edge $e_{im} \in E_{Tr}(\mathbf{q})$:

$$a_{\mathbf{q}}(e_{im}) = \text{Card}\{j \in J_{\mathbf{q}} : HR(j) = r_i \text{ and } SR(j) = r_m\} \tag{1}$$

where Card(.) stands for "cardinality of ...". In other words, $a_{\mathbf{q}}(e_{im})$ equals the number of parts that holds r_i and request r_m as next resource. Obviously, $a_{\mathbf{q}}(e_{im})=0$ means that e_{im} is not in $E_{Tr}(\mathbf{q})$.

The transition digraph can be easily updated on the occurrence of any 1-type or 2-type event. Namely, on the occurrence of a 1-type event $\sigma_1=(j,\mathbf{w})$ leading the DEDS from a state $\mathbf{q}$ to $\mathbf{q}'$, the updated edge set $E_{Tr}(\mathbf{q}')$ and the edge weights are given by

$$a_{\mathbf{q}'}(e_{mp}) = a_{\mathbf{q}}(e_{mp}) + 1 \tag{2}$$

$$E_{Tr}(\mathbf{q}') = E_{Tr}(\mathbf{q}) \cup \{e_{mp}\} \tag{3}$$

where r_m and r_p are, respectively, the first and the second resource in $\mathbf{w}$. If the occurring event is 2-type, specified by the label $\sigma_2=\{j,r_m,r_p\}$, two cases are in order. If $r_p \neq r_R$, putting $r_n=TR(j)$, then we get:

$$a_{\mathbf{q}'}(e_{mp}) = a_{\mathbf{q}}(e_{mp}) - 1 \tag{4}$$
$$a_{\mathbf{q}'}(e_{pn}) = a_{\mathbf{q}}(e_{pn}) + 1 \tag{5}$$
$$E_{Tr}(\mathbf{q}') = E_{Tr}(\mathbf{q}) \cup \{e_{pn}\} - \{e_{mp}\} \quad \text{if } a_{\mathbf{q}}(e_{mp}) = 1 \tag{6}$$
$$E_{Tr}(\mathbf{q}') = E_{Tr}(\mathbf{q}) \cup \{e_{pn}\} \quad \text{if } a_{\mathbf{q}}(e_{mp}) > 1 \tag{7}$$

On the other hand, if $r_p=r_R$, then the updating equations became

$$a_{\mathbf{q}'}(e_{mp}) = a_{\mathbf{q}}(e_{mp}) - 1 \tag{8}$$
$$E_{Tr}(\mathbf{q}') = E_{Tr}(\mathbf{q}) - \{e_{mp}\} \quad \text{if } a_{\mathbf{q}}(e_{mp}) = 1 \tag{9}$$
$$E_{Tr}(\mathbf{q}') = E_{Tr}(\mathbf{q}) \quad \text{if } a_{\mathbf{q}}(e_{mp}) > 1 \tag{10}$$

Note that the weights of the edges not appearing in the updating equations are not modified by the event occurrence.

Example 5.1.

To clarify the previous definitions and notations, let us consider a system composed by three double-capacity workstations r_2, r_3, r_4, and a single-capacity workstation r_1, organized to produce parts according to working procedures $\mathbf{w}_1 = (r_1, r_2, r_3, r_1, r_4, r_5)$ and $\mathbf{w}_2 = (r_1, r_3, r_4, r_1, r_3, r_5)$, where r_5 is the fictitious resource (R=5). So, Figure 5.1 depicts the corresponding working procedure digraph where r_5 is not shown, for the sake of brevity. Now, suppose the system is in a state $\mathbf{q}$ and let Table 5.1 describe working procedures ($\mathbf{w}$) and resources held and required (HR and SR) by parts in $J_q = \{j_1, j_2, j_3, j_4\}$. Figure 5.2 shows the corresponding transition digraph $D_{Tr}(\mathbf{q})$, where dark and white nodes represent, respectively, busy and not busy resources and weights label the corresponding edges. Note that the jobs j_2 and j_3, respectively holding r_2 and r_3, are blocked, because they require busy resources, respectively r_3 and r_1, for their next operation steps. If j_1 releases r_1 and acquires r_2, then the new state $\mathbf{q}'$ is represented by $D_{Tr}(\mathbf{q}')$ in Figure 5.3, as $TR(j_1)=r_3$ in state $\mathbf{q}$.

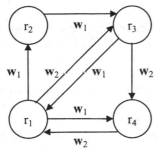

job	j_1	j_2	j_3	j_4
w	$\mathbf{w}_1$	$\mathbf{w}_1$	$\mathbf{w}_2$	$\mathbf{w}_1$
HR	r_1	r_2	r_3	r_3
SR	r_2	r_3	r_1	r_4

Figure 5.1. Working procedure digraph.   Table 5.1. Jobs in state $\mathbf{q}$.

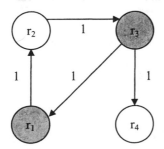
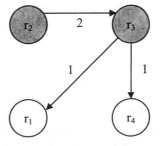

Figure 5.2. Transition digraph $D_{Tr}(\mathbf{q})$. Figure 5.3. Transition digraph $D_{Tr}(\mathbf{q}')$.

5.3   DIGRAPH CHARACTERIZATION OF DEADLOCK

The transition digraph provides the information necessary to formally characterize and detect deadlock occurrence. As already mentioned in the introduction,
deadlock is caused by a circular wait condition, where parts in a set require access
to resources held by other parts in the same set. The following definition formal-
izes this intuitive concept.

Definition 1. $q \in Q$ is a deadlock state if there exist two non-empty subsets $J_D \subseteq J_q$
and $R_D \subseteq R$, satisfying the following properties:
D1a) J_D is the maximal subset of J_q such that $HR(J_D)=R_D$;
D1b) $SR(J_D) \subset R_D$;
D1c) all the resources in $SR(J_D)$ are busy.

The meaning of Definition 1 can be easily explained. Namely, the set J_D collects jobs requiring resources only held by jobs in the same set. Each of such resources is busy, so that jobs in J_D are permanently and mutually blocked. Obviously, such a circular wait condition persists indefinitely because no element in J_D
can progress in its working procedure.

The properties invoked by Definition 1 can be easily tested using the transition digraph. To this aim, let us introduce a particular subdigraph of $D_{Tr}(q)$, named
maximal-weight zero-outdegree strong component" (MZSC). For standard digraph
figures the reader can refer to [15].

Definition 2. Let $\mu=(N_\mu,E_\mu)$ be a strong component of $D_{Tr}(q)$. We call μ an MZSC
of $D_{Tr}(q)$ if the following properties hold true:
D2a) *Maximal-weight:* all the resources from N_μ are busy;
D2b) *Zero-outdegree:* all the edges of $D_{Tr}(q)$ outgoing from vertices of N_μ belong
      to E_μ.

There is a simple connection between deadlocks and MZSCs, as established
by the following proposition, proven in [7].

Proposition 1. q is a deadlock state iff there exists at least one MZSC in $D_{Tr}(q)$.

The following example clarifies the meaning of such a result.

Example 5.2.
Let us consider the system of Example 5.1 in a state q, with $J_q = \{j_1, j_2, j_3, j_4, j_5, j_6\}$ such that $HR(j_1) = r_1$, $SR(j_1) = r_3$, $HR(j_2) = r_2$, $SR(j_2) = r_3$, $HR(j_3) = r_3$, $SR(j_3) = r_1$, $HR(j_4) = r_3$, $SR(j_4) = r_4$, $HR(j_5) = HR(j_6) = r_4$, $SR(j_5) = SR(j_6) = r_1$. The transi-

tion digraph $D_{Tr}(\mathbf{q})$ of Figure 5.4 shows that $HR(J_D) = R_D$ and $SR(J_D) = \{r_1, r_3, r_4\}$ $\subset R_D$, where $J_D = J_\mathbf{q}$ and $R_D = \{r_1, r_2, r_3, r_4\}$, and that all the resources in $SR(J_D)$ are busy. Moreover, the transition digraph contains an MZSC μ, with $N_\mu = \{r_1, r_3, r_4\}$ and $E_\mu = \{e_{13}, e_{31}, e_{34}, e_{42}\}$ (see Figure 5.4). Obviously, no job from J_D can progress to its next resource, so that $\mathbf{q}$ is a deadlock state. On the contrary, if one of the two jobs in r_4, say j_6, were not present, the system would be in a state $\mathbf{q}^*$, which is not a deadlock. Namely, the corresponding transition digraph $D_{Tr}(\mathbf{q}^*)$ does not contain any MZSC because r_4 is not busy (see Figure 5.5).

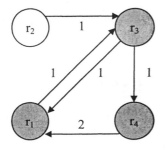
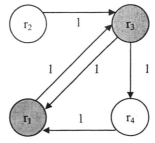

Figure 5.4. A MZSC in $D_{Tr}(\mathbf{q})$.   Figure 5.5. Digraph $D_{Tr}(\mathbf{q}^*)$.

Obviously, if $D_{Tr}(\mathbf{q})$ contains a MZSC, at least one of its cycles has all vertices busy. So, defining the *capacity of a cycle* as the sum of the capacities of all its vertices and denoting with C_0 the minimum capacity of all the cycles of D_W ($C_0 = \infty$ if D_W is acyclic), if the condition

$$\text{Card}(J_\mathbf{q}) < C_0 \tag{11}$$

holds true, then $\mathbf{q}$ cannot be a deadlock state.

To fully understand some approaches to deadlock resolution proposed in the next sections, we must define and illustrate another situation that, even if it is not an actual deadlock, inevitably leads to a deadlock state in the near future. Such a condition, called second-level deadlock, is established by the following definition.

Definition 3. $\mathbf{q} \in Q$ is a *second-level deadlock* state (SLD) if it is not a deadlock state and there exist two non-empty subsets $J_S \subseteq J_\mathbf{q}$ and $R_S \subseteq R$, satisfying the following properties:
D3a) $HR(J_S) \subseteq R_S$, $SR(J_S) \subseteq R_S$;
D3b) the set J_S collects all the jobs holding resources from R_S, i.e., J_S is the maximal subset of $J_\mathbf{q}$ such that $HR(J_S) \subseteq R_S$;
D3c) for any $j \in J_S$ that is not blocked in the state $\mathbf{q}$, the occurrence of the 2-type event $(j, HR(j), SR(j))$ leads to a deadlock state $\mathbf{q}'$, with $J_D \subseteq J_S$.

The meaning of Definition 3 is easily clarified. In fact, the conditions of the above Definition 3 characterize a situation where each job from J_S is either blocked, because it requires access to a busy resource held by other jobs in J_S, or determines a deadlock on acquiring the next resource in its residual working procedure. Obviously, in this case deadlock certainly occurs unless the jobs in J_S hold indefinitely the resources currently taken, not progressing in their working procedure. This situation is very similar to a deadlock state: thus, any effective deadlock avoidance policy must prevent the system from reaching deadlocks, SLDs, and any other similar condition of impending deadlock.

A necessary condition for an SLD occurrence can be stated using another digraph $D^2{}_W=(N^2,E^2{}_W)$, called *second level digraph*. To build $D^2{}_W$, let $\Gamma=\{\gamma_1,\gamma_2,...,\gamma_K\}$ be the complete set of all the cycles of D_W and set N^2 associate a vertex $n^2{}_v\in N^2$ with each element $\gamma_v\in\Gamma$ ($v=1,...,K$). Moreover, for each $s,v\in\{1,...,K\}$, let the edge $e^2{}_{vs}=(n^2{}_v,n^2{}_s)$ belong to $E^2{}_W$ iff the following conditions hold true:

(a) $\gamma_v = (N_v, E_v)$ and $\gamma_s = (N_s, E_s)$ have only one vertex in common (say r_m) with capacity $C(r_m)=1$;

(b) there exists a working procedure $w\in W$ including resources r_i, r_m and r_p in strict order of succession, with $e_{im}\in E_v$ and $e_{mp}\in E_s$.

Now, let $\gamma^2{}_n=(N^2{}_n,E^2{}_n)$ be a cycle in $D^2{}_W$ (second-level cycle) and $\Gamma_n=\{\gamma_{n_1},\gamma_{n_2},...,\gamma_{n_P}\}$ be the set of cycles of D_W corresponding to the vertices in $N^2{}_n$. We define the capacity of the second-level cycle $\gamma^2{}_n$ as the sum of the capacities of all the resources in the cycles from Γ_n:

$$C(N^2{}_n) = C(\bigcup_{s=1}^{P} N_{ns}) \tag{12}$$

Finally, let us consider the following particular subset of second-level cycles:

$$\Gamma^2 = \{\gamma^2{}_n \text{ of } D^2{}_W\text{: there exists a vertex } r_m\in N \text{ such that } C(r_m)=1 \text{ and } N_s\cap N_v=\{r_m\} \text{ for each } s,v\in\{n_1,n_2,...,n_P\}\} \tag{13}$$

Using these notations, the following proposition states a necessary condition for SLD occurrence [8,9]:

Proposition 2. If **q** is an SLD state, then there exists a second-level cycle γ^2_n in Γ^2 such that the following condition holds true

$$\text{Card}(J_q) \geq C(N^2_n)-1 \tag{14}$$

Example 5.3.

Referring again to the system of Example 5.1, we remark that the working procedure digraph contains the following cycles (see Figure 5.1): $\gamma_1 = (\{r_1, r_3\}, \{e_{13}, e_{31}\})$, $\gamma_2 = (\{r_1, r_4\}, \{e_{14}, e_{41}\})$, $\gamma_3 = (\{r_1, r_2, r_3\}, \{e_{12}, e_{23}, e_{31}\})$, $\gamma_4 = (\{r_1, r_3, r_4\}, \{e_{13}, e_{34}, e_{41}\})$, $\gamma_5 = (\{r_1, r_2, r_3, r_4\}, \{e_{12}, e_{23}, e_{34}, e_{41}\})$. According to the definition of second-level digraph, we associate nodes n^2_v to cycles γ_v ($v=1,\dots,5$) and edges $e^2_{12}, e^2_{21}, e^2_{32}$ in E^2_W. Hence, in the second-level digraph in Figure 5.6, we identify the cycle $\gamma^2_1 = (\{n^2_1, n^2_2\}, \{e^2_{12}, e^2_{21}\})$, with $C(N^2_1) = C(N_1 \cup N_2) = C(r_1)+C(r_3)+C(r_4) = 5$. Note that $\Gamma^2 = \{\gamma^2_1\}$. Now, let us suppose that the system is in state **q**, with $J_q = \{j_1, j_2, j_3, j_4\}$ such that $HR(j_1) = HR(j_2) = r_3$, $SR(j_1) = SR(j_2) = r_1$, $TR(j_1) = TR(j_2) = r_4$, $HR(j_3) = HR(j_4) = r_4$, $SR(j_3) = SR(j_4) = r_1$, $TR(j_3) = TR(j_4) = r_3$. The solid lines of Figure 5.7 show the current digraph $D_{Tr}(\mathbf{q})$, whereas the dashed lines represent the "second transitions" in the residual working procedures of the unblocked jobs from J_q. It is easy to recognize that **q** is an SLD state. In fact, if one of the jobs in r_3 (j_1 or j_2) acquires r_1, then a deadlock identified by cycle γ_2 occurs; similarly, if one of the jobs in r_4 (j_3 or j_4) acquires r_1, then a deadlock corresponding to the cycle γ_1 occurs.

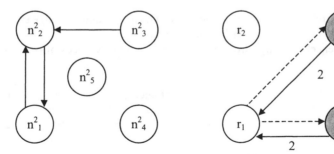

Figure 5.6. Second level digraph.   Figure 5.7. Second level deadlock.

5.4   DEADLOCK DETECTION AND RECOVERY

The idea of detection/recovery techniques [19,29,30] is to let the system evolve without any prevention/avoidance mechanism, allowing it to reach deadlock states. In this case, first, a detection procedure identifies the jobs and the resources involved in the deadlock condition. Second, a suitable recovery procedure breaks the circular wait and brings the system to a safe state, restoring the normal operating conditions. To this aim, one of the deadlocked jobs is transferred to a dedicated buffer, and a control policy rules the allocation of the resources involved until deadlock is resolved. At that point, the job in the buffer can be reinserted in the production process.

Deadlocks can be detected in real time searching for MZSCs by a depth first search (DFS) in the transition digraph $D_{Tr}(\mathbf{q})$ [7]. To this aim, the detection algorithm has to keep memory of the transition digraph and to update it according to the state transition rules related to 1-type or 2-type events. In fact, this algorithm has to check if, in state $\mathbf{q}$ next to the occurred event, the transition digraph $D_{Tr}(\mathbf{q})$ includes any MZSC and, in this case, it must identify the jobs and the resources involved.

The core of the detection procedure is an algorithm performing a DFS to find strong components [24]. This algorithm can be adapted to search for MZSCs [7] as follows. If j is the job involved in the last event leading to state $\mathbf{q}$, the algorithm successively examines three conditions, according to Definition 2, as depicted in the left part of the flowchart in Figure 5.8:

<u>D1</u>: First, it searches for a strong component of $D_{Tr}(\mathbf{q})$ containing HR(j), say μ;
<u>D2</u>: Second, it verifies that all vertices in μ are busy;
<u>D3</u>: Third, it checks whether from each vertex in μ only vertices of μ are reachable.

In particular, a detailed and optimized implementation of the search for an MZSC is in [7]. As described in [7], the algorithm goes through a limited number of steps in which it successively visits all vertices in the MZSC, progressing through all edges belonging to the MZSC. At each step, the algorithm updates a list of visited vertices, by inserting the last visited one in the list if it is a new one and is busy, and then evaluates the adjacent vertices (depth search). Then, the same check is performed on each of the adjacent vertices until the root of the search, HR(j), is reached. So, at the same time, the DFS verifies the strong connection, the zero outdegree and the busy properties of the MZSC.

In synthesis, the proposed detection method has a low computational burden since the DFS is performed in O(e) time, where e=Card($E_{Tr}(\mathbf{q})$) is the number of edges in the transition digraph [7,24]. Another efficient algorithm to detect dead-lock occurrence is described in [26].

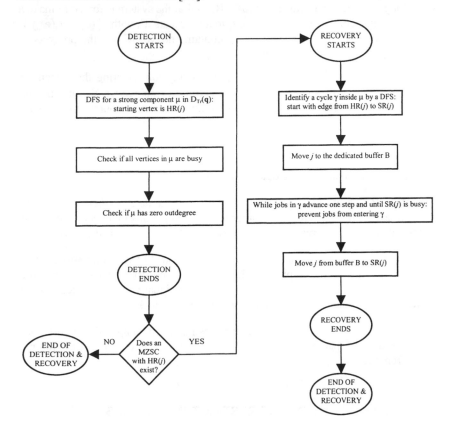

Figure 5.8. Detection/Recovery flowchart.

In case job j gets blocked by a busy resource and no such MZSC exists, j waits in a queue until the resource is free (idle or empty); otherwise, the recovery procedure starts. On the other hand, once an MZSC, say μ, has been detected, the recovery procedure starts the following four steps (see right part of the flowchart of Figure 5.8):

<u>R1</u>: Identification of a cycle $\gamma=(N_\gamma, E_\gamma)$ inside μ, containing an edge $e_{im}=(r_i, r_m)$ where $r_i=HR(j)$ and $r_m=SR(j)$. This is performed by a DFS on the subdigraph μ, starting with vertex r_i and edge e_{im}, in $O(e+v)$ time, where v is the number

of vertices in the transition digraph because only one cycle is identified [7,24].

R2: Job j is moved to a dedicated buffer B, so that the system is forced to make a transition from the deadlock state $\mathbf{q}$ to a new state $\mathbf{q}$', with $a_{q'}(e_{im})=a_q(e_{im})-1$. The new transition digraph $D_{Tr}(\mathbf{q}')$ contains no MZSC and the progress of any job to r_i becomes feasible.

R3: A restriction policy is applied to prevent any job, entering the system or moving from a resource $r_n \notin N_\gamma$, from getting a resource $r_p \in N_\gamma$ until the end of recovery. This allows jobs detaining and requiring resources in N_γ to advance one step ahead in their residual working procedures.

R4: When a state $\mathbf{q}^*$ is reached such that r_m is not busy, job j can be moved from B back to r_m, the restriction policy at step R3 is removed, the recovery procedure terminates and the detection starts once again.

If a job j_2 is blocked by a busy resource and the detection/recovery procedure is in execution, triggered by another job j_1, then j_2 waits in a queue the end of the procedure. When the recovery is over, j_2 is awakened and calls the detection.

In fact, at the end of the recovery procedure, an MZSC might still exist in the resulting transition digraph. So, the detection/recovery is repeated to force deadlocked jobs to advance one more step in the residual working procedures. In this way, we guarantee that jobs are never indefinitely blocked.

In conclusion, the recovery procedure has no added computational costs, but only needs a unit-capacity buffer, usually in a central location, to host the job removed from the cycle γ.

5.5 DEADLOCK AVOIDANCE RESTRICTION POLICIES

The characterization of deadlock and SLD states allows us to define three policies for deadlock avoidance, named *restriction policies* (RP) RP-A, RP-B and RP-C (see RP1, RP3 and RP4 in [9]). They differ from each other in computational complexity and restrictions imposed on resource allocation. All the policies avoid deadlock by preventing the occurrence of any MZSC in the transition digraph. In particular, they perform feedback control laws, using the knowledge of state $\mathbf{q}$ to inhibit or enable 1-type and 2-type events, in real time. A 1-type event $\sigma_1=(j,\mathbf{w})$ is inhibited if the RP prevents j from entering the system and a 2-type event $\sigma_2=(j,r_m,r_p)$ is inhibited if the control policy does not allow j to acquire r_p. Denoting by Σ the set of all the possible events, we define the control rules for 1-type and 2-type events as a function

$$f: \Sigma \times Q \rightarrow \{0,1\}. \qquad (15)$$

where $f(\sigma,\mathbf{q})=0$ means that, with the system in the state $\mathbf{q}$, the control law prevents the event σ from occurring; on the contrary, $f(\sigma,\mathbf{q})=1$ indicates that the event σ is enabled.

The simple idea behind the first policy (RP-A) consists of binding the number of jobs in process by a value lower than the minimum cycle capacity C_0 of D_W. Indeed, this prevents any cycle (and so any of the strong subdigraphs in D_W) from having all its resources busy. In this way, no MZSC can arise in the transition digraph, for any reachable state $\mathbf{q}$. Hence, RP-A controls only 1-type events (new job inputs) and requires feedback of state information only concerning the number of in-progress jobs. With a more formal notation, RP-A can be expressed by the following function, controlling 1-type events only.

RP-A

For any $\sigma_1 \in \Sigma$:

$$f_A(\sigma_1, \mathbf{q}) = 0 \qquad \text{if } \mathrm{Card}(J_\mathbf{q}) = C_0 - 1 \tag{16.1}$$
$$f_A(\sigma_1, \mathbf{q}) = 1 \qquad \text{in the other cases} \tag{16.2}$$

For any $\sigma_2 \in \Sigma$:

$$f_A(\sigma_2, \mathbf{q}) = 1 \qquad \text{in all cases} \tag{16.3}$$

If, on one hand, RP-A is very simple and requires limited information on the system state, on the other hand it limits the system flexibility; for example, if D_W contains a cycle of capacity 2 ($C_0=2$), RP-A allows only one piece at a time in the system.

The next RP, named RP-B, improves the control flexibility by allowing a less restrictive management of resources. To this aim, it governs both 1-type and 2-type events by ruling job entering and job transitions from resource to resource. The aim of this policy is to limit freedom in resource allocation as little as it can, by inhibiting only events immediately leading to a deadlock state. So, if $\mathbf{q}$ is the current state and a job requires a resource, the policy performs a one-step look-ahead to determine the new state $\mathbf{q}'$ resulting from the event occurrence and the corresponding transition digraph. If $D_{Tr}(\mathbf{q}')$ contains an MZSC, the piece movement is inhibited, otherwise it is enabled. Policy RP-B can be expressed by the following function.

RP-B

For any $\sigma_i \in \Sigma$, with i=1,2:

$$f_B(\sigma_i, \mathbf{q}) = 0 \qquad \text{if } D_{Tr}(\mathbf{q}') \text{ contains an MZSC} \tag{17.1}$$
$$f_B(\sigma_i, \mathbf{q}) = 1 \qquad \text{in the other cases} \tag{17.2}$$

RP-B is the least restrictive policy one can find [6,9]. However, in some cases it is not applicable because it might cause a situation similar to a deadlock, called *restricted deadlock* (RD). This happens when an indefinite circular wait occurs partly because some pieces are blocked and partly because the RP itself prevents some transitions from occurring. As proven in [9], the prevention of an SLD occurrence guarantees that RP-B does not lead to any RD state. Hence, falsifying one or more of the necessary conditions for an SLD occurrence is an effective means to avoid RD. On this basis, putting

$$C^2_0 = \min_{\gamma^2_n \in \Gamma^2} C(N^2_n) \tag{18}$$

(with $C^2_0 = \infty$ if Γ^2 is empty) we define a new RP by introducing a constraint on Card(J_q). In fact, as pointed out by Proposition 2, RD cannot occur if the system contains ($C^2_0 - 2$) jobs at the most. Therefore, the new policy, RP-C, modifies RP-B by controlling the 1-type events to limit the number of in-process jobs.

RP-C

For any $\sigma_1 \in \Sigma$:

$f_C(\sigma_1, \mathbf{q}) = 0$ \qquad if $D_{Tr}(\mathbf{q'})$ contains an MZSC *OR* Card(J_q) = $C^2_0 - 2$(19.1)

$f_C(\sigma_1, \mathbf{q}) = 1$ \qquad in the other cases \hfill (19.2)

For any $\sigma_2 \in \Sigma$:

$f_C(\sigma_2, \mathbf{q}) = 0$ \qquad if $D_{Tr}(\mathbf{q'})$ contains an MZSC \hfill (19.3)

$f_C(\sigma_2, \mathbf{q}) = 1$ \qquad in the other cases \hfill (19.4)

If D^2_W is acyclic or, more generally, Γ^2 is empty, the optimal policy RP-B can be applied without risking RD. Moreover, we remark that D^2_W is acyclic in many practical situations. For example, a first case occurs if the capacity of each resource in the AMS is greater than one. A second case occurs when each unit-capacity resource exhibits an indegree or an outdegree lower than two in D_W. This is the typical situation of a single machine equipped with an input or an output buffer. In both previous cases, indeed, there are no cycles in D_W sharing only one unit-capacity vertex.

For what concerns the computational complexity of the proposed RPs, we distinguish between on-line and off-line costs; the former are related to the real-time algorithms, while the latter characterize the off-line computations, performed once, before the proper real-time control.

The off-line cost is small in the case of RP-A; namely, this policy requires the computation of C_0 only, that is a polynomial-complexity problem, requiring $O(v^3)$ operations, where v=Card(N). On the other hand, the on-line costs of RP-A are due to the real-time updating of Card(J_q) only.

RP-B demands no off-line computations while the on-line algorithm is in two steps. The first one transforms $D_{Tr}(\mathbf{q})$ into $D_{Tr}(\mathbf{q'})$ with few operations according to the procedure described in section 2. The second step searches for MZSCs in $D_{Tr}(\mathbf{q'})$ using the detection algorithm of section 4, based on the depth-first search and consisting of $O(e)$ operations, with $e=Card(E_{Tr}(\mathbf{q}))$.

Implementing RP-C requires the off-line detection of the cycles from D_W and D^2_W. Building D^2_W needs $O[(c_1)^2 l]$ operations, where l indicates the sum of the lengths of all the working procedures and c_1 is the number of cycles in D_W. Furthermore, generating the cycles of D^2_W and the set Γ^2 requires $O\{[c_1+Card(E^2_W)](c_2+1)\}$ and $O(c_1 c_2 v)$ operations respectively, where c_2 indicates the number of cycles in D^2_W. Finally, RP-C needs the same on-line computations as RP-B and the updating of $Card(J_q)$.

5.6 DECOMPOSITION STRATEGIES OF DEADLOCK AVOIDANCE POLICIES

As previously noted, the approaches to deadlock avoidance mainly differ in the computational costs and in the strictness they impose on the resource allocation freedom. So, a nontrivial question regards the choice of a proper avoidance policy resulting from the best compromise between computational costs and flexibility. As shown in [5], the simplest policies usually result in poorer system flexibility and, hence, in reduced production performances. However, in contrast with this consideration, for particular layouts of the system, simple restriction policies may also guarantee good performance figures. Limiting the analysis to RP-A, RP-B and RP-C, it is obvious that, when applicable, RP-B is the best restriction policy because it is minimally restrictive in resource allocation. On the other hand, if the digraph D_W consists of one cycle only, then RP-A can lead almost to the same performances as RP-B, even if its implementation is easier. Finally, if D_W contains more cycles and the set Γ^2 is not empty, RP-B cannot be used while RP-A could be too restrictive. In this case, the only suitable policy is RP-C.

To improve the flexibility of the deadlock avoidance policies, we propose an approach of performing a distributed control [11]. The main idea consists of partitioning the system resources in subsets, called subsystems, each of which can be controlled locally, i.e., independently of the other ones. Thus, each local controller is in charge of ruling resource allocation and deallocation of only one subsystem and makes decisions on events inhibition by only using information on parts and resources in the same subsystem. This way, one can choose a suitable avoidance policy for each subsystem so that the behavior of the complete AMS results in better performance measures. For example, as remarked above, if digraph D^2_W of the complete system leads to a nonempty set Γ^2, policy RP-B cannot be applied. However, if the AMS is decomposed in independent subsystems, such a policy could be used for some of them, while RP-A and RP-C may rule resource allocation for the remaining subsystems. Obviously, this approach allows the production system to exhibit better performance indices than centralized control. Moreover, since the RPs are applied to smaller systems, the overall on-line computational charge is reduced and the flows of information and commands between controllers and plant are less intensive. The following subsections show how to decompose the system to obtain an efficient distributed control.

The system partition

According to the previous results, the strong components of $D_{Tr}(\mathbf{q})$ play a crucial role in deadlock occurrence. We start observing that, since $D_{Tr}(\mathbf{q})$ is a sub-digraph of D_W, any strong component of $D_{Tr}(\mathbf{q})$ is always contained in a strong subdigraph of D_W. Moreover, a strong subdigraph of D_W is always part of a strong component of the same digraph [15]. In addition, if D_W contains H strong components $H_k=(N_k,E_k)$ for k=1,...,H, the subsets N_k represent a partition of N and the resource r_R results in a trivial strong component $H_H=(\{r_R\},\varnothing)$ consisting of one resource only and no edge. These considerations lead to the following proposition.

Proposition 3. Let $\mu=(N_\mu,E_\mu)$ be an MZSC of $D_{Tr}(\mathbf{q})$. Then there exists only one strong component $H_k=(N_k,E_k)$ of D_W containing μ, i.e., such that $N_\mu \subseteq N_k$ and $E_\mu \subseteq E_k$.

Propositions 1 and 3 lead to the fundamental remark that each deadlock involves a resource set belonging to only one strong component of D_W. Moreover, there is another consequence. Namely, let us denote by J_k a subset of J_q collecting jobs holding resources from N_k in the state $\mathbf{q}$. So, if $D_{Tr}(\mathbf{q})$ contains just one MZSC, then there exists a set J_k containing all the deadlocked jobs. Analogously, if $D_{Tr}(\mathbf{q})$ exhibits several MZSCs, then each of them corresponds to a deadlocked area in the manufacturing system. In other words, in this case the system experiences some concurrent and independent deadlocks, one for each MZSC. All the deadlocked jobs concurring in each of these local deadlocks are contained in a set J_k.

This result implies that, to avoid deadlock, the whole system can be decomposed in H subsystems, each one corresponding to a strong component H_k of D_W and each one controlled locally and independently of the other ones.

Now, let us focus our attention on a subsystem, say the k-th one with $k \in \{1,2,...,H-1\}$, to establish the graph-theoretic tools necessary to state its local control law. Obviously, any trivial subsystem, such as the one representing the fictitious resource, does not require any control law. Moreover, the dynamic interactions between jobs in J_k and resources in N_k can be described by a transition digraph $D_k(\mathbf{q})=[N_k^*,E_k(\mathbf{q})]$. Such a digraph must also describe jobs that hold resources from N_k and require resources in other subsystems for their next operation step. Namely, the other subsystems are considered as "outer environment" of the k-th subsystem such jobs leave on their next transition. According to these considerations, the vertex set N_k^* must be defined as $N_k^*=N_k\cup\{n_0\}$, where the single node n_0 represents all the resources in subsets other than N_k.

Analogously, an edge e_{im} from E_k is in $E_k(\mathbf{q})$ if there exists a job $j\in J_k$ holding a resource $r_i\in N_k$ and requiring $r_m\in N_k$ as a next resource. Moreover, if a job j from J_k holds $r_i\in N_k$ and requires a resource r_m belonging to a different strong component H_h ($h\neq k$), then there exists an edge $e^*_{i0}\in E_k(\mathbf{q})$ outgoing from r_i and ending in n_0.

As remarked in the previous section, the applicability of RP-B depends on the properties of the second-level digraph. Now, we can extend to D^2_W the same partitioning procedure used for D_W. Namely, all the vertices of a second-level cycle represent cycles belonging to only one strong component of D_W. So, we build a second-level digraph D^2_k for each strong component H_k, independently of the other subsystems, and check whether the corresponding subset Γ^2_k is empty.

To sum up, the proposed decomposition of the whole system in subsystems allows us to apply the results on deadlock characterization, restricted deadlock and deadlock avoidance to each subsystem. In particular, the previous discussion leads to the following propositions:

(a) $\mathbf{q}$ is a deadlock state iff there exists at least one MZSC in some $D_k(\mathbf{q})$ for $k\in\{1,\ldots,H{-}1\}$.

(b) Necessary condition for $\mathbf{q}$ to be a deadlock state is that there exists a subsystem corresponding to a strong component H_k and containing C_k jobs in process at least (i.e. $\mathrm{Card}(J_k)\geq C_k$), where C_k is the minimum capacity of the cycles from H_k.

(c) Necessary condition for $\mathbf{q}$ to be an RD under RP-B is that there exists a subsystem corresponding to a strong component H_k with the set Γ^2_k not empty and having more than $C^2_k{-}2$ jobs in process (i.e., $\mathrm{Card}(J_k)\geq C^2_k{-}1$), where C^2_k is the minimum capacity of the cycles from Γ^2_k.

The distributed control policy

A distributed control policy consists of a set of local and autonomous controllers, each in charge of ruling resource allocation for a subsystem, on the basis of local information. The first step to define a local controller is establishing the events under its domain. In particular, relevant events for a subsystem H_k are the ones that involve allocation of resources from N_k. More precisely, these events are defined as follows:

(a) If a job $j\notin J_k$ requires a resource r_m of N_k, the corresponding event denoted with

(j,r_m) is considered as a 1-type event for the subsystem H_k. Namely, it represents a job that "enters" the strong component H_k;

(b) If $j \in J_k$ requires a resource r_m of N_k, then $\sigma_2 = (j,r_m)$ is a 2-type event for the subsystem H_k and represents the move of j from the resource it currently holds to r_m.

As previously pointed out, the decentralized approach allows us to choose a different control policy for each subsystem. Here we limit our attention to the three policies reviewed in Section 5.5, indicated by f_h, with $h \in \{I,II,III\}$. Now, let f_h be applied to subsystem H_k. So, denoting with σ_i a local event for H_k and with $\mathbf{q}$ the state information only concerning the parts that currently hold resource from N_k, i.e., the jobs from J_k, the notation $f_h(\sigma_i,\mathbf{q})=0$ ($=1$) means that, with the subsystem in the state $\mathbf{q}$, event σ_i is inhibited (enabled). In other words, each local controller is in charge of avoiding deadlock in one subsystem and all the local controllers work concurrently. In this way, each subsystem H_k can use a deadlock avoidance strategy that guarantees the best compromise between complexity and performance. To this aim, a proper choice must consider the following suggestions:

Case 1: If H_k consists of one cycle only, then RP-A can be suitably applied. Namely, in such a case this simple control rule guarantees high flexibility in resource allocation and leads to performance measures very similar to those allowed by RP-B.

Case 2: If H_k contains more cycles and Γ^2_k is empty, then RP-B is applicable and allows the best performances because it is minimally restrictive.

Case 3: If H_k contains more cycles and Γ^2_k is not empty, then RP-C should be applied.

Case 4: If H_k consists of one vertex only (it is a trivial strong component), then no control is needed because such a subsystem cannot exhibit any deadlock.

In conclusion, the deadlock avoidance strategy can be synthesized in the following steps:

Step 1: Determine the strong components of D_W, say H_k for $k=1,\ldots,H$.

Step 2: Determine the digraph D^2_k and the set Γ^2_k associated to each strong component H_k.

Step 3: Following the previous suggestions, select the local RP to apply to each subsystem H_k.

Step 4: Each RP is applied independently of the other ones.
In this context, the events involving the transition of a job from a subsystem to another require a particular remark. So, let $\sigma=(j,r_m)$ be one of such events,

where j belongs to a subset J_k and $r_m \in N_h$ with $k,h \in \{1,\ldots,H\}$ and $k \neq h$. Although σ is a 2-type event for the complete system, it must be considered just as a 1-type event for H_h, so that it is controlled by the RP chosen for such a subsystem.

Example 5.4.

Consider a system consisting of 10 resources (R=11) where $C(r_3)=C(r_8)=1$ and the remaining resources have capacities equal to 2. The system produces a job mix according to the working procedures $w_1 = (r_2, r_3, r_1, r_7, r_8, r_9, r_{11})$, $w_2 = (r_1, r_2, r_4, r_5, r_6, r_{11})$, $w_3 = (r_5, r_4, r_6, r_4, r_9, r_{10}, r_8, r_7, r_{11})$. Figure 5.9 shows the corresponding working procedure digraph that contains four strong components: $H_1 = (N_1, E_1) = (\{r_1, r_2, r_3\}, \{e_{12}, e_{23}, e_{31}\})$, $H_2 = (\{r_4, r_5, r_6\}, \{e_{45}, e_{46}, e_{54}, e_{56}, e_{64}\})$, $H_3 = (\{r_7, r_8, r_9, r_{10}\}, \{e_{78}, e_{87}, e_{89}, e_{9,10}, e_{10,8}\})$ and finally, the trivial strong component corresponding to the fictitious resource $H_4 = (\{r_{11}\}, \varnothing)$. Let the system be in a state **q**, with $J_q = J_1 = \{j_i \mid i=1,\ldots,5\}$ and with the transition digraph $D_1(\mathbf{q}) = (N^*_1, E_1(\mathbf{q}))$ exhibited by Figure 5.10. Resources r_1, r_2, r_3 are busy in the state **q** and the strong component H_1 of D_W is also a strong component of $D_1(\mathbf{q})$. However, while jobs j_i for $i=1,2,3,5$ hold resources in N_1 and require resources in the same set, as shown by edge e^*_{20}, j_4 holds r_2 and needs a resource not in N_1 for its next operation. So, the strong component H_1 of $D_1(\mathbf{q})$ has outdegree equal to one and **q** is not a deadlock state. On the contrary, if j_4 required r_3 as next resource, then H_1 would have outdegree equal to zero and it would be a MZSC of $D_1(\mathbf{q})$. The second-level digraphs associated with the three nontrivial strong components are shown by Figure 5.11. In the sequel, we identify each of the corresponding subsystem with the same symbols as the associated strong components H_1, H_2 and H_3, respectively.

The system layout allows the application of a distributed deadlock avoidance approach, using three different control policies. In particular, since the first strong component, named H_1, contains only one cycle, i.e., $\gamma_1 = (\{r_1, r_2, r_3\}, \{e_{12}, e_{23}, e_{31}\})$, RP-A can be suitably applied to it, with $C_0 = C_1 = C(r_1)+C(r_2)+C(r_3) = 5$. Hence, the first controller rules the incoming jobs, on the basis of the number of jobs in process within the first subsystem. The second subsystem H_2 contains three cycles: $\gamma_2 = (\{r_4, r_5\}, \{e_{45}, e_{54}\})$, $\gamma_3 = (\{r_4, r_6\}, \{e_{46}, e_{64}\})$ and $\gamma_4 = (\{r_4, r_5, r_6\}, \{e_{45}, e_{56}, e_{64}\})$. Since D^2_2 is acyclic (see Figure 5.11), Γ^2_2 is empty, so that no RD can arise if RP-B is applied. On the contrary, the third subsystem H_3 has to be controlled by RP-C because it is subject to RDs involving the critical unit-capacity resource r_8. Namely, D^2_3 consists of the cycle γ^2 belonging to Γ^2_3 and composed of two nodes (n^2_5 and n^2_6) involving resources r_7, r_8, r_9 and r_{10}. Consequently, we obtain $C^2_3 = C(r_7)+C(r_8)+C(r_9)+C(r_{10}) = 7$. Hence, RP-C controls acquisition and releasing of each resource of the third cell and limits the number of in-process parts in H_3 to $C^2_3-2 = 5$. Finally, the trivial strong component $H_4 = (\{r_{12}\}, \varnothing)$ does not need any deadlock control.

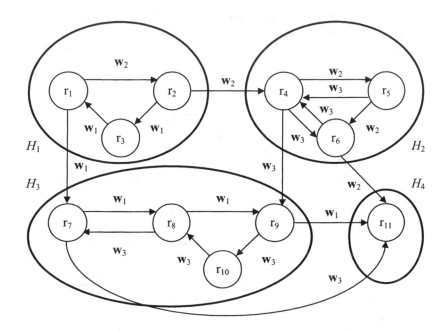

Figure 5.9. Strong components in the working procedure digraph.

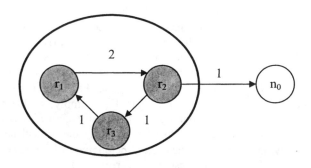

Figure 5.10. Strong components in the transition digraph.

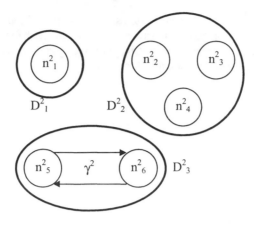

Figure 5.11. Second-level digraphs related to the strong components.

Concluding this section, we remark that the obtained general results are particularly suitable to cellular manufacturing systems that do not exclude intercell flow [23] and every part can be processed in one cell with few intercell movements. In this case, the method determines the cells that can be controlled independently and the ones that must be controlled jointly, in order to avoid deadlock.

5.7　CONCLUDING REMARKS

The methods that face deadlock described in the previous sections have a common base in the digraph representation of the interactions between jobs and resources and in the corresponding characterization of deadlock and SLD states. Such a digraph-based representation of AMS appears more concise than other models because it only describes the information necessary for deadlock characterization. The developed framework allows a deep knowledge of the mechanisms generating deadlocks and, consequently, leads to the definitions of the detection/recovery and avoidance strategies illustrated in this chapter. Moreover, starting from the same theoretical base, further policies can be easily derived. The various approaches that face deadlock problems differ in complexity and in the degree of restrictions they impose on the free assignment of resources to jobs. Generally, the best compromise between such requirements depends on the particular layout of the AMS, and, more precisely, on the structure of the working procedure digraph. To guarantee better flexibility in such a choice, Section 5.6 describes a decomposition strategy to deadlock avoidance that allows us to partition the production system into subsystems, each controlled independently of the other ones. This way, a particular strategy can be adopted for each subsystem, chosen by analyzing the peculiarities of its working procedure digraph. Some suggestions to drive these choices are also formulated.

REFERENCES

1. ZA Banaszak, BH Krogh. Deadlock Avoidance in Flexible Manufacturing Systems with Concurrently Competing Process Flows. IEEE Trans Rob and Autom 6 (6): 724-734, 1990.

2. H Cho, TK Kumaran, RA Wysk. Graph-Theoretic Deadlock Detection and Resolution for Flexible Manufacturing Systems. IEEE Trans Rob and Autom 11 (3): 413-421, 1995.

3. F Chu, X Xie. Deadlock Analysis of Petri Nets Using Siphons and Mathematical Programming. IEEE Trans Rob and Autom 13 (6): 793-804, 1997.

4. J Ezpeleta, JM Colom, J Martinez. A Petri Net Based Deadlock Prevention Policy for Flexible Manufacturing Systems. IEEE Trans Rob and Autom 11 (2): 173-184, 1995.

5. MP Fanti, B Maione, S Mascolo, B Turchiano. Performance of Deadlock Avoidance Algorithms in Flexible Manufacturing Systems. J Manuf Syst 15 (3): 164-178, 1996.

6. MP Fanti, B Maione, G Piscitelli, B Turchiano. System Approach to Design Generic Software for Real-Time Control of Flexible Manufacturing Systems. IEEE Trans Syst, Man, and Cybern, Part A: Systems and Humans 26 (2): 190-202, 1996.

7. MP Fanti, G Maione, B Turchiano. Digraph-Theoretic Approach for Deadlock Detection and Recovery in Flexible Production Systems. Studies in Informatics and Control 5 (4): 373-383, 1996.

8. MP Fanti, B Maione, S Mascolo, B Turchiano. Event Based Feedback Control for Deadlock Avoidance in Flexible Production Systems. IEEE Trans Rob and Autom 13 (3): 347-363, 1997.

9. MP Fanti, B Maione, B Turchiano. Event Control for Deadlock Avoidance in Production Systems with Multiple Capacity Resources. Studies in Informatics and Control 7 (4): 343-364, 1998.

10. MP Fanti, B Maione, B Turchiano. Comparing Digraph and Petri net Approaches to Deadlock Avoidance in FMS. IEEE Trans Syst, Man, and Cybern, Part B: Cybernetics 30 (5): 783-797, 2000.

11. MP Fanti, G Maione, B Turchiano. Distributed Event-Control for Deadlock Avoidance in Automated Manufacturing Systems. Int J Prod Res 39 (9): 1993-2021, 2001.

12. MP Fanti, G Maione, B Turchiano. Design of Supervisors Avoiding Deadlock in Flexible Assembly Systems. The Intern Journ of Flex Manuf Syst 14 (2): 153-171, 2002.

13. MP Fanti. A Colored Timed Petri Net Model to Manage Resources in Complex Automated Manufacturing Systems. Proceedings of IEEE International Conference on Robotics and Automation, Washington, USA, 2002.

14. MP Fanti, B Turchiano. Deadlock Analysis in Automated Manufacturing Systems with Conjunctive Resource Service. Proceedings of IEEE International Conference on Robotics and Automation, Taipei, Taiwan, 2003.

15. F Harary, RZ Norman, D Cartwright. Structural Models: An Introduction to the Theory of Directed Graphs. New York: John Wiley & Sons, Inc., 1965.

16. FS Hsieh, SC Chang. Dispatching-Driven Deadlock Avoidance Controller Synthesis for Flexible Manufacturing Systems. IEEE Trans Rob and Autom 10 (2): 196-209, 1994.

17. M Lawley, S Reveliotis, P Ferreira. Design Guidelines for Deadlock Handling Strategies in Flexible Manufacturing Systems. Int J Flex Manuf Syst 9 (1): 5-30, 1997.

18. M Lawley, S Reveliotis, P Ferreira. The Application and Evaluation of Banker's Algorithm for Deadlock-Free Buffer Space Allocation in Flexible Manufacturing Systems. Int J Flex Manuf Syst 10 (2): 73-100, 1998.

19. YT Leung, GJ Sheen. Resolving Deadlocks in Flexible Manufacturing Cells. J Manuf Syst 12 (4): 291-304, 1994.

20. FL Lewis, A Gürel, S Bogdan, A Doganalp, O. Pastravanu. Analysis of Deadlocks and Circular Waits using a Matrix Model for Flexible Manufacturing Systems. Automatica 14 (9): 1083-1100, 1998.

21. Y Li, WM Wonham. Deadlock Issues in Supervisory Control of Discrete-Event Systems. Proceedings of the 22nd Annual Conference on Information Sciences and Systems, Princeton, NJ, 1988, pp. 57-63.

22. J Park, SA Reveliotis. Deadlock Avoidance in Sequential Resource Allocation Systems with Multiple Resource Acquisitions and Flexible Routings. IEEE Trans Automat Contr 46 (10): 1572-1583, 2001.

23. D Rajamani, N Singh, YP Aneja. Design of Cellular Manufacturing. Int J Prod Res 34: 1917-1924, 1996.

24. EM Reingold, J Nievergelt, N Deo. Combinatorial Algorithms: Theory and Practice. Englewood Cliffs, NJ: Prentice-Hall, Inc., 1977.

25. SA Reveliotis, PM Ferreira. Deadlock Avoidance Policies for Automated Manufacturing Cells. IEEE Trans Rob and Autom 12 (6): 845-857, 1996.

26. SA Reveliotis, MA Lawley, PM Ferreira. Polynomial-Complexity Deadlock Avoidance Policies for Sequential Resource Allocation Systems. IEEE Trans Automat Contr 42 (10): 1344-1357, 1997.

27. N Viswanadham, Y Narahari, TL Johnson. Deadlock Prevention and Deadlock Avoidance in Flexible Manufacturing Systems Using Petri Net Models. IEEE Trans Rob and Autom 6 (6): 713-723, 1990.

28. KY Xing, BS Hu, HX Chen. Deadlock Avoidance Policy for Petri-Net Modeling of Flexible Manufacturing Systems with Shared Resources. IEEE Trans Automat Contr 41 (2): 289-295, 1996.

29. RA Wysk, NS Yang, S Joshi. Detection of Deadlocks in Flexible Manufacturing Cells. IEEE Trans Rob and Autom 7 (6): 853-859, 1991.

30. RA Wysk, NS Yang, S Joshi. Resolution of Deadlocks in Flexible Manufacturing Systems: Avoidance and Recovery Approaches. J Manuf Syst 13 (2): 128-138, 1994.

6

Deadlock-Free Supervisory Control for Assembly and Disassembly Systems

Elzbieta Roszkowska
Wroclaw University of Technology, Wroclaw, Poland.

Abstract

This chapter deals with a class of processes modeling streams of materials that can join and split, such as in assembly/disassembly systems, at group transport and then individual part processing, or in processes that require temporary meeting of independently routed components. As each such process can be viewed as a set of interacting sequential processes, the processes considered here are called *compound processes*. The dynamics of the system are represented with an ordinary PN, and the problem studied is the design of a supervisor for ensuring deadlock-free process flow. The necessary concurrency and the possible use of the same resources by component sequential processes result in a compound process that might not be realizable if the number of units of a particular resource is less than some minimal value. Therefore we propose a model that allows more valuable resources, such as machines, to be released directly after an operation is completed. This is due to the fact that the buffer space required for the products of an operation is allocated together with the machine. Thus, from the viewpoint of deadlock-free process control, we can neglect the problem of machine allocation and only focus on the flow of materials between the buffers. The supervision problem is solved through a joint approach to establishing for each buffer a minimal sufficient capacity, dependent on the processes' structure, and constraining the system dynamics. The proposed supervisor is given in the form of a function that states whether a particular enabled transition is admissible or inadmissible at a particular state. The concept underlying its development assumes a dynamic buffer reserve, which ensures that component processes that need to be synchronized can await each other without inducing a deadlock.

6.1 INTRODUCTION

Most of the research devoted to deadlock problems in automated manufacturing systems has employed various models that represent concurrent sequential processes, typical for job flow in flexible manufacturing systems (FMS). A broader view of FMS, and particularly of flexible assembly systems (FAS), reveals more complex relations among the flow of materials. From control point of view, the basic difference between these two types of systems is that unlike in machining, operations at assembly stations involve mating one or more components, which may require a "meeting" of separately transported objects or partitioning compound transport units into elements that undergo further transport/processing individually. This difference is significant when developing the control logic for an FAS and implies new requirements for handling of deadlocks.

The primary transport objects in an FAS are the base components of the product and the parts to be mounted on them. The way in which the items are presented and delivered to the workstations depends on the assembly technology. Some of the options include [1, 2]:

Assembly Kitting. All of the parts that are required to make one assembly, including the base component, are kitted on one pallet that travels between the workstations until the assembly is complete.

Palletized Trays. The component parts that make up one or more assemblies are palletized. The base component is fixtured onto a separate pallet. The pallets containing the components are routed between the workstations as needed and remain in the system until empty. The pallets containing the base components are routed through the system each time an assembly is built.

Magazines. Individual part types or small products that are presented in higher volume are loaded into a magazine, e.g., a mould or a frame, which is able wholly or partially to maintain the orientation of the objects. Magazines are used both as units for transport through the assembly and containers of parts that are delivered to individual workstations and replaced when used up. In some cases, assembly is performed directly in the magazines, which then act to support the products against the operation stresses.

Feeders. Special or programmable feeders store and feed in small bulk parts, such as screws, at the workstations. The components can arrive bunkered in containers and then are oriented by the feeding equipment, or in magazines that have been loaded somewhere else in the system.

The types and the organization of material handling equipment for flexibly automated assembly systems are discussed in detail in, e.g., [1, 2, 3, 4, 5]. The assembly of a complex product can in many cases be divided up into a series of subassemblies that can often be common to several product families and built in separate, dedicated system units. Thus, from the viewpoint of the system layout, the transportation task can be divided up into transport of components to the system, transport of the base component through the assembly and transport of finished products for further assembly. In fact the division will not always be reflected physically in three separate transport systems, as in many cases it will be possible to use the same transport devices for several of the tasks. The most common are conveyor belts with or without pallets, automated guided vehicles (AGV), handling robots, and some combination of these. For example, a conveyor system might be used for routing a pallet containing the base component between the workstations, while material handling AGVs would deliver palletized components to the workstations. If vehicles are utilized for component parts transport, the items are typically arranged in magazines and delivered in higher volume to the relevant assembly station or intermediate stores, from which things are extracted as required. This often means that advanced handling equipment will be needed at individual stations to take the items from the magazines. Another solution is that handling robots will also deal with the job of transporting base components. In this type of plant, the magazines are usually placed between stations to perform as a buffer store.

The objects to be transported in the assembly system can also be part of the assembly equipment or the tools. For example, at printers and disk drives production [1], depending on which variant of the product is to be made, two particular pallets are moved from the store to the robot workstations. One of the pallets principally carries the tools (grippers, circular feeders, etc.) required by the job, while the other contains the components to be used in the assembly. During assembly of heavy products in the car industry it can sometimes be attractive to move both the product and the assembly device. In the spot-welding of car bodies, for example, it is often the case that both the welding robot and the product are mobile.

It follows that one of the basic features that has to be taken into account when abstracting the flow of materials in this type of manufacturing systems is the "fork/join" character of the processes. At an early stage of the research into the deadlock avoidance in production material flow, a taxonomy was proposed [6] that classified discrete manufacturing processes by means of a three-parameter vector $[\alpha, \beta, \gamma]$. The parameters can take one of the following values: $\alpha = l$ or $\alpha = g$, depending on whether a process consists of a linearly or a partially ordered set of operations; $\beta = s$ or $\beta = g$, depending on whether an operation requires a single resource or an arbitrary number of resource types; and $\gamma = u$ or $\gamma = g$, depending on whether a single unit of a resource is involved in an operation or an arbitrary number of units. A process with $\alpha = l$ is *sequential*, while a process with $\alpha = g$ is *compound* and represents a concurrent execution of component sequential processes. These processes are specified by independent paths of operations in the graph representing their partial order, where vertices that have more than one input or output arc correspond to component processes' synchronization points. The abstraction is used to model the flow of materials where independently processed items can be joined together and undergo further processing as a whole (e.g., to make an assembly or for a common transport), or material units can be split up so that their components will follow separate routes (e.g., at disassembly or separate processing of parts delivered in magazines), as well as to model the flow of objects that require a temporary meeting (e.g., independently routed pallets with the base components and pallets with parts to be mounted onto the base).

Another class of systems, the *PO-RAS*, that also deals with a partial order of operations, was introduced in [7] as an extension of an earlier proposed taxonomy of resource allocation systems (*RAS*) [8]. We note that although in both *PO-RAS* and [*g*, ∗, ∗] a partially ordered set of operations is used to define a process, there is a substantial difference between these classes. In *PO-RAS*, an operation that has more than one successor can be compared to a procedure in a computer program ended with the *case* instruction that allows only one of the successors to be executed next. This implies that a process of this class is sequential and its single execution involves the operations that lie on one of the paths in the operation graph. In [*g*, ∗, ∗] the partial order is used to model a compound process, where a sequential component process can split into two or more concurrently executed component processes, or a number of concurrent processes can join into one sequential process. In the graph depicting the partial order of operations, the former situation is represented by a vertex that has more than one successor, while the latter situation is represented by a vertex that has more than one predecessor.

Such networks have been relatively intensively researched in the framework of stochastic discrete event models (see, e.g., [9, 10, 11, 12] and the references therein), while there are few theoretical results concerning the deterministic supervisory control for that class of processes. The problem of deadlock avoidance and the design of a supervisory controller for flexible assembly systems, based on the model where parts can be joined (but not split) was discussed in [13, 14, 15]. In this chapter we consider a similar problem, but address it for the processes that can both fork and join, called here *compound processes*. The starting point is our earlier results presented in [16, 17, 18]. As will be demonstrated in the sequel, the possibility of deadlock avoidance in the considered class of systems depends on their structure and the capacity of the resources. In other words, as compared with concurrent sequential processes, we encounter here a new control problem, the problem of process realizability.

In the following section we develop a PN model of a system of compound processes, whose dynamics is studied in the sequel. In Section **6.3** we concentrate on the realizability problem, and in Section **6.4** we analyze the reasons of deadlocks between sequential processes that need to be synchronized. The supervisory control for compound processes is developed in two steps. In Section **6.5**, through establishing a certain minimal capacity for each buffer, that depends on the structure of a compound process, we ensure that deadlocks can be avoided with a simple policy if only single copies of sequential processes are allowed in the system. A general solution for the deadlock avoidance problem, that allows multiple instantiations of processes, is developed in the following two sections. In Section **6.6** we give the intuition underlying the concept of the supervisory control, and in Section **6.7** we present its formal description. The dynamics of the so constrained system are analyzed in Section **6.8** and final proofs for the correctness of the proposed method are given in Section **6.9**.

6.2   THE MODEL

As mentioned in the previous section, we will use the abstraction of a compound process to model streams of materials that can join and split, such as in assembly/disassembly systems, at group transport and individual part processing, in processes that require temporary meeting of independently routed components, etc. Before developing a formal model of such a system, let us consider the following example:

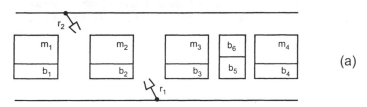

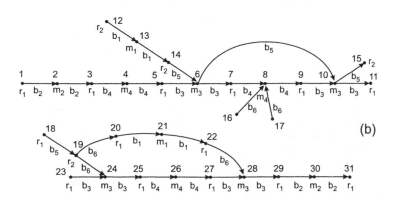

Figure 6.1: Illustration for Example 1. (a) A flexible assembly cell and (b) a diagram of the material flow.

Example 1 Figure 6.1(a) presents the structure of an example assembly cell that consists of four workstations, m_1, m_2, m_3, m_4, with buffers b_1, b_2, b_3, b_4, respectively, two individual buffers b_5 and b_6 accessible for the manipulators of both m_3 and m_4, and two handling robots r_1 and r_2. The robots transport materials from/to the system input/output and between buffers. Pallets with base components are handled by robot r_1 and placed in buffers b_2, b_3, or b_4, while trays with subassemblies and unpalletized components are handled by robot r_2 and placed in buffers b_1, b_5 or b_6. The flow of material objects in the cell is depicted in Figure 6.1(b). The graph consists of two disjoint subgraphs corresponding to two compound processes π_1 and π_2. The vertices represent technological and transport operations, and the edges represent material units at a particular stage of their route. The symbols placed next to a vertex and its input and output arcs denote the resources required for the corresponding operation which are: the machine, and the buffers to store the material units (pallets, trays, and unpalletized components) before and after the operation. Operations 1-11 and 23-29 involve base components of π_1 and π_2, respectively. $1, 3, 5, 7, 9, 11, 23, 25, 27, 29, 31$ are transports of base components, operations $12, 14, 15$ correspond to the transport of trays with subassemblies, and operations $18, 20, 22$ correspond to the transport of unpalletized components. Vertex 13 represents mounting of a subassembly; vertices 6, 10 represent mounting of subassemblies carried on pallets onto base components; and operations 24, 28 represent mounting of unpalletized components onto base components. Operation 21 is performed exclusively on unpalletized components. In transport operation 18 two components are handled at a time, one of which is mounted onto a base component in workstation m_3, while the other is further transported to m_1.

In order to ensure possibly efficient machine utilization, it is assumed that buffers for parts that leave a machine are allocated together with a machine when an operation starts. This means, for example, that a robot cannot start a transport operation until there is free space in the buffer where the transported part should be placed. Such an approach is also justified for assembly operations, which typically are much shorter than those in the machining processes. Since the machines (that is, the processors of the machines) are released by the completion of the operations, as the products are placed in the buffers, the processing/transport of the material objects can be viewed as transient, and an operation execution as a single event. An occurrence of such an event does not change the state of the machine, as it has to be idle in order to start an operation and it is idle again as soon as the operation is completed. Thus the processors are always available eventually. Consequently, from the viewpoint of deadlock-free process control, we can neglect the problem of machine allocation and only focus on the flow of materials between the buffers. This also implies that in the case of an operation concerning a single object that is supposed to occupy the same buffer before and after the operation, it is not necessary to distinguish between the pre-operation and the post-operation stage, but consider them as one stage associated with the continuous use of a particular buffer. Thus, when specifying the processes discussed in Example 1 it is sufficient to limit the information on their structure and resource requirement to that depicted in Figure 6.2(a). In general, we will assume that a system of compound processes is characterized by the following parameters:

Definition 1 A specification of a system of compound processes is a fourtuple $sc = (G, B, \beta, c)$, where $G = (T, E, \succ)$ is an acyclic directed graph with vertex set T, edge set E, and incidence function $\succ: E \to T \times T$, whose vertices and edges model, respectively, *operations* and *parts* (i.e., material unit types that take part in the operations), B is the set of *buffers* used to store part units, $\beta : E \to B$ is the *buffer dedication function*, and $c : B \to \{1, 2, ...\}$ is the *buffer capacity function*.

Note that we do not require that graph G be connected. Thus, it may consist of a number of subgraphs, each of which is connected, but any two of them are not con-

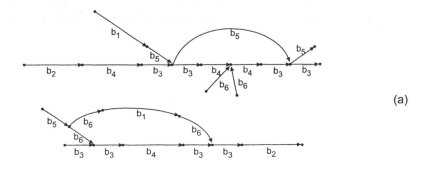

(a)

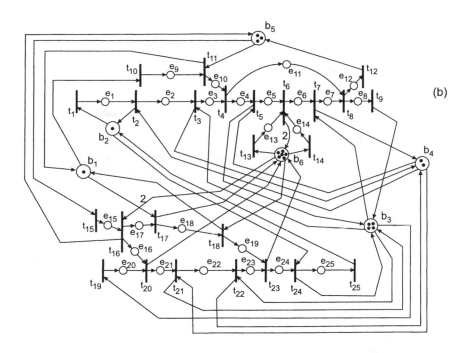

(b)

Figure 6.2: Specification *sc* of the compound processes depicted in Figure 6.1 and the corresponding PN $N(sc)$. It is assumed that the capacity of the buffers is given by $\beta(b_1) = \beta(b_2) = 1$, $\beta(b_3) = 4$, $\beta(b_4) = 2$, $\beta(b_5) = 3$, $\beta(b_6) = 6$.

nected with each other, specifying a group of concurrent compound processes. The dynamic model of a system of compound processes with a particular specification sc will be defined as a mapping of sc onto a particular PN $N(sc)$. The class of PNs constituted by all systems $N(sc)$ that can be specified according to Definition 1 will be denoted with N.

Definition 2 A system of compound processes specified by sc is a PN $N = N(sc) = (P, T, F, w, M_0)$ such that:

1. $P = E \cup B$ is the place set, T is the transition set.

2. $F = F^e \cup F^b$ is the arc set such that[1]

   (a) $F^e = \{(t, e)) \mid coord^1 \succ (e) = t\} \cup \{(e, t)) \mid coord^2 \succ (e) = t\}$

   (b) $F^b = \{(b, t) \mid f(b, t) - f(t, b) > 0\} \cup \{(t, b) \mid f(t, b) - f(b, t) > 0\}$
       where: $f(b, t) = |\{(t, e) \in F^e \wedge \beta(e) = b\}|$ is the number of output parts of operation t stored in buffer b, $f(t, b) = |\{(e, t) \in F^e \wedge \beta(e) = b\}|$ is the number of input parts of operation t stored in buffer b.

3. w is the *arc weight function* given by $\forall (x, y) \in F^e$, $w(x, y) = 1$ and $\forall (x, y) \in F^b$, $w(x, y) = f(x, y) - f(y, x)$.

4. M_0 is the initial marking given by $M_0(e) = 0$, and $M_0(b) = c(b)$.

An example PN $N \in N$, system $N(sc)$ corresponding to specification sc depicted in Figure 6.2.a, is given in Figure 6.2.b. Note that N is a class of pure PNs, that is, for each $t \in T$, $p \in P$, $(p, t) \notin F$ if $(t, p) \in F$ and $(t, p) \notin F$ if $(p, t) \in F$. We will extend relation F_e to F_e^* as follows:

Definition 3 $F_e^* \subseteq E \cup T \times E \cup T$ is the transitive closure of relation F_e.

In other words, $(x, y) \in F_e^*$ if there exists a path in N from vertex x to vertex y, that does not include any buffer place $b \in B$. We will denote in the standard way the sets ${}^\bullet t$ and $t^\bullet$ of input and output places of transition t, respectively. The dynamics of N will be described with two functions, φ and δ, expressing the standard rules for the evolution of marking M.

Definition 4 Let M be the set of all functions $P \to \{0, 1, \ldots\}$. $\varphi : M \times T \to \{enabled, disabled\}$ is the *enabling function* given by $\varphi(M, t) = enabled$ iff $\forall p \in {}^\bullet t$, $M(p) \geq w(p, t)$. $\delta : M \times T \to M$, the *next-marking function*, is a partial function defined for each (M, t) such that $\varphi(M, t) = enabled$. The new marking $M' = \delta(M, t)$ is given by $M'(p) = M(p) - w(p, t)$ if $p \in {}^\bullet t$, $M'(p) = M(p) + w(t, p)$ if $p \in t^\bullet$, and $M'(p) = M(p)$ otherwise.

---

[1]Recall that *coord* is a mathematical term used to denote the function that extracts elements of a vector; for $X = (x_1, x_2, \ldots, x_n)$ and $i \in \{1 \ldots n\}$, $coord^i X = x_i$.

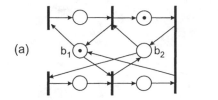 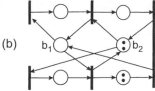

Figure 6.3: A compound process run in a system with buffer capacity: (a) $c(b_1) = c(b_2) = 1$, and (b) $c(b_1) = 1$, $c(b_2) = 2$. In case (a) the system is not realizable and a deadlock cannot be avoided. In case (b) the system is realizable, yet a deadlock marking still can be reached.

6.3 REALIZABILITY PROBLEM

Unlike independent sequential processes where with an appropriate policy it is always possible to avoid deadlocks, not all systems of compound processes are realizable.

Definition 5 System $N \in N$ is *realizable* iff there exists a firing sequence $z = t_1 t_2 \ldots t_{|T|}$ such that $M_0[z > M_0$ and each transition $t \in T$ occurs in z exactly once.

In general, the realizability of a particular system N depends on its structure and the capacity of the buffers. It is trivial to note that an operation can never be enabled if n of its input or output parts require the same buffer b and the capacity $c(b) < n$. However, as can be easily demonstrated (see Figure 6.3), even if each input or output part of an operation should be placed in a different buffer, the operation may be dead at the initial marking. The unique distinction between the systems of compound processes where deadlocks can be avoided and those where they cannot poses a formal decision problem.

Theorem 1 Let *Realizability of N* be a decision problem defined by the question: given a system $N \in N$, is N realizable? The problem is NP-complete in the strong sense.

<u>Proof.</u> An analogical theorem has been proved for a model of compound processes considered in [18, 19]. It is not hard to demonstrate (therefore we will omit it here) that this model and system N can be reduced each to other. Thus the results obtained in the references also prove Theorem 1. □

The complexity of the realizability problem not only implies that it is practically impossible to give an easily verifiable condition for determining in each case of N whether or not it is realizable, but also that any deadlock avoidance policy addressed for the whole class of realizable systems N would require an NP-hard algorithm, thus would be practically useless.

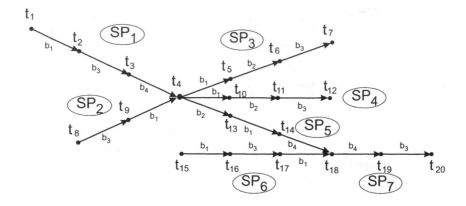

Figure 6.4: Specification of an example compound process. The process can be viewed as a set of seven sequential processes synchronized at operations t_4 and t_{18}

Theorem 2 Let $\psi : R(M_0) \times T \rightarrow \{admissible, inadmissible\}$ be a supervisor able to restrict the behavior of any realizable system $N \in \mathbf{N}$ so that the operation of N is deadlock-free. The calculation of values of ψ poses an NP-hard problem.

Proof. Assume that there exists supervisor ψ and an algorithm that calculates values of ψ in polynomial time $O(s(N))$, where $s(N)$ is the size of N. Since a system that is not realizable has the same general structure as a realizable one, it is possible to apply ψ to any system $N \in \mathbf{N}$ and control the execution of the processes so that each transition $t \in T$ is fired at most once. If N is realizable then in $|T|$ steps the initial marking is restored. If N is not realizable, then in less than $|T|$ steps a deadlock occurs. It follows that there exists an algorithm with polynomial complexity $|T| \, O(s(N))$ able to solve the realizability problem. Since this contradicts the thesis of Theorem 1, the assumption is false, which proves Theorem 1. $\square$

The fact established in Theorem 2 indicates that a deadlock-free control can only be developed for a subclass of N distinguished by imposing some conditions on the parameters of N that are sufficient, but stronger than necessary for the realizability of the system. Since a particular class of systems requires the control specific for that class, the problem of deadlock avoidance in compound processes requires a joint approach to constraining N to a subclass $N' \subset \mathbf{N}$ of realizable processes, and constraining the dynamics of N' so that the resulting system is reversible and live.

6.4 DEADLOCKS IN SYNCHRONIZED PROCESSES

Note that a compound process can be viewed as a set of sequential processes (SP) synchronized at operations that have more than one input or output parts, called *nodes* in the sequel. Each SP starts with an input operation or a node, and ends with an output operation or a node. For example, Figure 6.4 presents the specification of a process that consists of seven sequential processes: SP_1, from t_1 to t_4, SP_2, from t_8 to t_4, SP_3, from t_4 to t_7, SP_4, from t_4 to t_{12}, SP_5, from t_4 to t_{18}, SP_6, from t_{15} to t_{18}, and SP_7, from t_{18} to t_{20}. The final products of SPs that end with an output operation leave the system, while the final products of the other SPs are node input parts. Parts that are not final products correspond to intermediate products of SPs. For clarity of the drawing, Figure 6.4 presents the specification sc of the example system rather than PN model $N(sc)$, that requires depicting all arcs connecting transitions with buffer places. The reader can easily picture the corresponding dynamic system. Fragments of this net will be presented in Figure 6.5.

In a system of independent (not synchronized) sequential processes, deadlocks can be avoided by ensuring that each process can eventually accomplish its last operation, which allows it to terminate and release all the resources it has possessed. The same applies to those SPs that do not end with a node, such as SP_3, SP_4, and SP_7. Otherwise, the buffer allocated for the last operation of an SP can only be released as a result of firing the node ending the processes. A node transition cannot fire until at least one unit of each of its input parts is available. Thus, while waiting for the remaining final products, those that have already been produced block the respective buffers, which may disable other SPs to run to completion. Moreover, unlike in independent processes, a single event associated with firing a node may initiate two or more sequential processes at a time. This can be another reason for a deadlock, as the new initiated processes can block each other.

If in the example system the capacity of buffer b_1 is $\beta(b_1) = 1$, then transition t_4 is dead at the initial marking, as two of the output parts of t_4 require b_1. Thus, let us assume that $\beta(b_1) = 2$, and let $\beta(b_2) = \beta(b_3) = \beta(b_4) = 1$. We will consider four firing sequences that end up in a deadlock. The first deadlock is typical for a system of independent sequential processes, while the remaining three are specific for synchronized SPs. Figure 6.5 depicts fragments of system $N(sc)$ that are involved in a deadlock.

1. $M_0[t_1, t_8, t_{15} > M$ (Figure 6.5(1)). Since at marking M both buffer b_1 and buffer b_3 are filled to capacity, processes SP_1, SP_2, and SP_6 block one another, hence a deadlock occurs.

2. $M_0[t_8, t_9, t_{15}, t_{16}, t_{17} > M$ (Figure 6.5(2)). At marking M processes SP_2 and SP_6 already have their final products, yet in order to terminate they require a unit of the final products of SP_1 and of SP_5, respectively. Since at marking M buffer b_1 is filled to capacity, it is impossible to fire transition t_1, so the final product of SP_1 cannot be produced. Thus process SP_5 cannot start, which makes it impossible to fire t_{18}. Consequently, buffer b_1 can never be released.

3. $M_0[t_1, t_2, t_3, t_8, t_9, t_{15}, t_{16}, t_{17} > M$ (Figure 6.5(3)). At marking M processes SP_1 and SP_2 already have their final products, so all input parts of t_4 are present. Since t_4 has only one input part located in b_1 and two of the output parts of t_4 require this buffer, an additional space unit is necessary to fire t_4. However, this space is currently used by an input part of t_{18}, so b_1 cannot be released

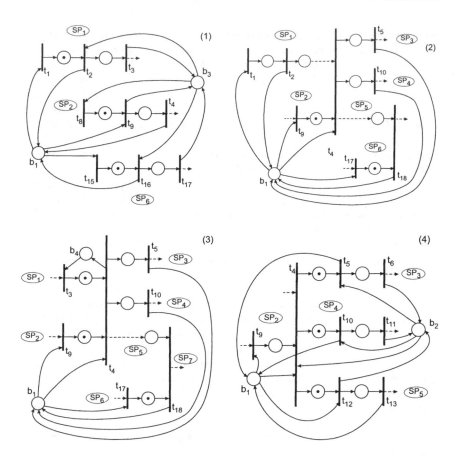

Figure 6.5: Examples of deadlocks occurring in system $N(sc)$ specified in Figure 6.4.

until t_{18} fires. Since t_{18} requires the final product of SP_5, and SP_5 starts from t_4, a deadlock occurs.

4. $M_0[t_1,t_2,t_3,t_8,t_9,t_4 > M$ (Figure 6.5(4)). Firing of t_4 allows processes SP_1 and SP_2 to terminate and initiates processes SP_3, SP_4, and SP_5. Thus, units of all output parts of t_4 are present in the system. Two of the parts are located in b_1, which can be released if SP_1 or SP_2 obtains space in buffer b_2. The third part is located in b_2, which can be released if SP_3 obtains space in buffer b_1. Since both b_1 and b_2 are filled to capacity, a deadlock occurs.

Note that only single instantiations (or copies) of SPs were considered above, while in general multiple instantiations of each sequential process can run concurrently. The approach to the development of the supervisory control for compound processes proposed in this work consists of two steps. First, through establishing for each buffer a certain minimal capacity that depends on the structure of a compound process, we will ensure that deadlocks can be avoided with a simple policy if only single copies of SPs are allowed in the system. Next, for the subclass of systems N with buffer capacity greater than or equal to the minimal, we will propose a policy that allows multiple instantiations of SPs and constrains the dynamics of the processes so that the resulting system is reversible and live.

6.5 MINIMAL BUFFER CAPACITY

The deadlocks discussed in the previous section could be avoided if SPs were able to run to their last stage one at a time (no deadlocks in case (1)), the lack of buffer space due to storing final products did not prevent SPs from starting or proceeding (no deadlocks in case (2)), additional buffer space was provided for each node that requires more space in a particular buffer for its output parts than for its input parts (no deadlocks in case (3)), and the SPs that start from the same node did not block each other due to the fact that the first intermediate products of some SPs (output parts of the node) and the second intermediate products of other SPs use the same buffers (no deadlocks in case (4)). If we allow only one copy of each SP to be present in the system then these requirements can be satisfied by providing sufficient buffer capacity established as follows.

Definition 6 For a system $N \in N$, let $T^N = \{t \in T : |{}^{\bullet}t \cap E| > 1 \vee |t^{\bullet} \cap E| > 1\}$ be the set of operations, called nodes, that have more than one input part or more than one output part. Let $E^N = E_{in}^N \cup E_{out}^N$ be the union of the set of input node-parts $E_{in}^N = {}^{\bullet}T^N \cap E$ and the set of output nodeparts $E_{out}^N = (T^N)^{\bullet} \cap E$. Let $B^N = \{\beta(e) \mid e \in E_{in}^N \cup E_{out}^N\}$ be the set of buffers used for storing node parts, and let $B^{nN} = \{\beta(e) \mid e \in E - E^N\}$ be the set of buffers used for storing non-node parts. The minimal buffer capacity is given by $v(b) = v'(b) + v''(b)$, where:

$$v'(b) = \begin{cases} 1 & \text{if } b \in B^{nN} - B^N \\ max_{t \in T^N} w(b,t) & \text{if } b \in B^N - B^{nN} \\ max_{t \in T^N} w(b,t) + 1 & \text{if } b \in B^{nN} \cap B^N \end{cases}$$

$$v''(b) = |\{e \in E_{in}^N \wedge \beta(e) = b\}|$$

Note that for each buffer b, $v(b) \geq 1$. If b is used to store exclusively non-node parts, then $v(b) = v'(b) = 1$. If b is supposed to store exclusively node parts, then $v(b) = max_{t \in T} w(b,t) + v''(b)$, and if both node and non-node parts, then $v(b) = max_{t \in T} w(b,t) + v''(b) + 1$. $v''(b)$ is the number of SPs whose final products are to be stored in buffer b.

Example 2 For system N given in Figure 6.2 we obtain: $T^N = \{t_4, t_6, t_8, t_{16}, t_{18}, t_{20}, t_{23}\}$, $E_{in}^N = \{e_3, e_5, e_7, e_9, e_{13}, e_{14}, e_{15}, e_{16}, e_{20}, e_{19}, e_{23}\}$, $E_{out}^N = \{e_4, e_6, e_8, e_{11}, e_{12}, e_{16}, e_{17}, e_{21}, e_{24}\}$, $E^N = E_{in}^N \cup E_{out}^N = \{e_3, e_4, e_5, e_6, e_7, e_8, e_9, e_{11}, e_{12}, e_{13}, e_{14}, e_{15}, e_{16}, e_{17}, e_{18}, e_{20}, e_{21}, e_{22}, e_{23}, e_{24}\}$, $B^N = \{b_3, b_4, b_5, b_6\}$, $B^{nN} = \{b_1, b_2, b_4\}$, $v(b_1) = 1 + 0 = 1$, $v(b_2) = 1 + 0 = 1$, $v(b_3) = 0 + 4 = 4$, $v(b_4) = 1 + 1 = 2$, $v(b_5) = 0 + 3 = 3$, $v(b_6) = 2 + 4 = 6$,

It is not hard to notice that the minimal buffer capacity $v(b)$ is sufficient for the realizability of system N.

Property 1 Each system N such that $\forall b \in B$, $c(b) \geq v(b)$ is realizable.

Proof. If only a single copy of each SP is allowed in the system, then the final products of all SPs can be stored in $v''(b)$ units of buffers b required by the products and there remains $v'(b)$ free space units in each buffer b. Since for each transition t, $v'(b) \geq w(b,t)$, then there is enough space for the output products of any operation. Moreover, if a particular buffer is used for storing both the first intermediate product (a node output part) and the second intermediate product of an SP, then $v'(b) \geq w(b,t) + 1$. Thus, any SP that starts with an input operation of the compound process can become active and run to its last stage. Moreover, the final product of the SP can await the other products with which to be joined without preventing other SPs from proceeding. If all final products that end at the same node are present then the node can fire and again each of the new SPs can run to completion. For example, a firing sequence generated according to this rule in the compound process specified in Figure 6.4 can include: all transitions of SP_1 but t_4, next all transitions of SP_2, next the remaining transitions of SP_3 and SP_4, next the remaining transitions of SP_5 but t_{18}, next all transitions of SP_6, and finally the remaining transitions of SP_7. Consequently, if $\forall b \in B$, $c(b) \geq v(b)$, then it is possible to fire each transition exactly once, which proves that system N is realizable. $\square$

The subclass of systems N with buffers b such that $c(b) \geq v(b)$ will be denoted with NV. The requirement that the capacity of buffers should be at least equal to $v(b)$ may be over-restrictive for the realizability of a particular system N. For example, it can be easily noticed that in the system considered in Figure 6.2, $c(b_6) = 6$ is more than necessary, as $c(b_6) = 2$ is sufficient if we allow at most one instantiation of each component process to be present in the system at one time. Nevertheless, we will adopt function $v(b)$ in the proposed form and concentrate on the subclass $NV \subset N$ for two reasons. As will be demonstrated in the following section, for such a class we will be able to develop a closed-form formula for transition admissibility, whose construction would be much more complicated for a smaller buffer capacity. Moreover, in order to provide a possibly high concurrency of the material flow, buffers with some greater capacity are generally required. Thus NV includes most of the systems that can be considered in practice when establishing the parameters of N from the system performance point of view. We note as well that the constraint $c(b) \geq v(b)$ is still relatively weak, as the problem of the optimal deadlock-free process control in class NV remains NP-hard (see the discussion in the next section).

6.6 SUPERVISORY CONTROL

Taking into account the structure of systems $N \in NV$, in order to avoid deadlocks it is necessary and sufficient to constrain the dynamics of N so that the resulting system is reversible. The optimal (i.e., the least restrictive) way to achieve this goal is to forbid a marking change $M[t> M'$ if and only if marking M' is not safe, that is, $M_0 \notin R(M')$. This, however, poses a problem of distinguishing between safe and unsafe markings, which has been proved to be NP-complete in SU-RAS [20, 21]. Since, as follows from the structure of N and the definition of $v(b)$, the SU-RAS constitutes a special subclass of NV, the safety problem is also computationally hard for the NV class of compound processes. This justifies the approach to the development of a supervisor ψ based on a compromise between the complexity of computing the admissibility of transitions - values of ψ, and the level of restriction that the function imposes. Since a supervisor based on sufficient conditions causes that some safe state changes are forbidden, the control we are looking for must ensure that not only physical deadlocks are avoided, but also that, due to the unreachability of certain safe states, no logical deadlocks are induced or a component process can never start. In other words, the logic underlying the restriction of the dynamics of system N must provide that for each component process there exists a reachable state such that the process can become active, and that for each state reachable in the restricted system, all active copies of SPs can eventually terminate through a sequence of state changes qualified as admissible by the supervisor (i.e., not through any sequence of safe states, as some of those states may become unreachable).

Definition 7 For system N, let $\psi : R(M_0) \times T \to \{admissible, inadmissible\}$ be a partial function defined for all pairs (M,t) such that $\varphi(M,t) = enabled$. Let $R(M,\psi)$ be the set of all markings M_n such that there exists an execution sequence $\sigma = M_1 t_1 \ldots t_{n-1} M_n, M_1 = M$, and $\forall i = 1..n-1, \psi(M_i,t_i) = admissible$. ψ is a supervisor for N if: (i) for each $t \in T$, there exists $M \in R(M_0,\psi)$ such that $\psi(M,t) = admissible$, and (ii) for each marking $M \in R(M_0,\psi), M_0 \in R(M,\psi)$.

A general idea underlying the development of the proposed supervisor ψ is based on two assumptions, A0 and A1, as given below.

Proposition 1 Function ψ is a supervisor for any system $N \in NV$ if it ensures that: (A0) at the initial marking each enabled transition is admissible, and (A1) for each marking $M \in R(M_0,\psi) - \{M_0\}$ and each admissible firing sequence z such that $M_0[z> M$, there exists transition t such that t is admissible at M and the number of the occurrences of transition t in sequence z is $k(z,t) < k_{max}$, where $k_{max} = max_{\tau \in T} k(z,\tau)$.

Proof. If (A0) holds, then condition (i) in Definition 7 holds. If (A1) holds, then for each $M \in R(M_0,\psi) - \{M_0\}$ it is possible to construct an admissible execution sequence $\sigma = M_1 t_1 M_2 t_2 \ldots t_{n-1} M_n$ such that $M_1 = M$ and for each $z_i = z t_1 t_2 .. t_i, i = 1,2..n-1, k(z_i,t_i) < k_{max}$. Since at each occurrence of any transition t_i in σ the value $k(z_i,t_i)$ increases, then ultimately marking M_n is reached such that for each $t \in T$, $k(z_n,t) = k_{max}$. Since $M_n \in R(M_0,\psi)$ and (A1) does not hold at M_n, then $M_n = M_0$. Consequently, condition (ii) in Definition 7 holds, which proves that ψ is a supervisor for system N. $\square$

The requirement for buffer capacity $c(b) \geq v(b)$ is sufficient for that in each system $N \in NV$, each input transition is enabled at the initial marking M_0. Thus, when developing the supervisor we can also assume that each input transition is admissible at M_0, that is, implement requirement (A0) in ψ. The intuition underlying the control that ensures (A1) is discussed below and the formalization of this concept will be presented in the following section.

Recall that if there is no more than a single active copy of each SP, then the minimal buffer capacity $v(b)$ ensures that the final product of each copy can await the other products to be joined with, without disabling other SPs. This implies that for the correct process flow it is sufficient to provide that no deadlocks occur among the SPs that are at intermediate stages of execution. The same approach can be employed in the case when multiple instantiations of the processes are present in the system, but only with respect to one copy of each SP. Thus, additional control is required to prevent the other copies from the activity that could deprive the selected copies of their potential to start, progress, and terminate. To provide this, we will assume that the latter copies are privileged to share the $v(b)$ part of the buffer space, while the former copies should share the remaining $c(b) - v(b)$ space units, and only use the $v(b)$ part when it is possible to ensure that the space can be released if needed for a privileged copy.

In order to implement this idea, we introduce the notion of *buffer reserve* $\eta(M,b) = v'(b) + nf(M,b)$. $nf(M,b)$ is the number of SPs that use buffer b for their final products, but have no such products at marking M. Note that at the initial marking no SP is active and the number of SPs that use buffer b for their final products is $v''(b)$. Thus, $\eta(M_0,b) = v'(b) + v''(b) = v(b)$, and at any reachable marking $M \in R(M_0)$, $\eta(M,b) \geq v'(b)$ and $\eta(M,b) \leq v(b)$. The value of the reserve is decreased by one when the first final product of each particular SP that uses b is placed in the buffer, and increased by one when the last final product becomes consumed and b contains no more final products of this process.

Intuitively, if for each $b \in B, M(b) \geq \eta(M,b)$, then there is sufficient buffer space for each uncompleted privileged copy to obtain a unit space for its final product, and for each SP that currently has no copy, to generate a privileged one. Note that once the privileged copy of an SP terminates, that is, either the final product leaves the system or is consumed by the node operation that ends the SP, a new copy can become privileged. Therefore a basic objective of the supervisory control should be to ensure that each privileged process instantiation is able to attain its last stage. To achieve this, we will want to maintain buffer reserve such that $\forall b \in B, M(b) \geq \eta(M,b)$, and allow a break of the reserve only when it is possible to restore it. The proposed control is based on the following assumptions.

As privileged, we will consider any copy of each SP that ends with a non-node output transition, and the most advanced copy of each SP that ends with a node. Thus we will also consider as privileged all transitions that can cause the progress or generate such copies. A non-node transition t is privileged if there is no node on the path from t to an output transition or when no place e on the path from t to the nearest node is marked. A node transition t is privileged if the same applies to all paths starting from t. At marking M, a copy of an SP can progress or new copies of SPs can be generated, that is, a non-node transition t or node transition t, respectively, can fire if:

1. At the new marking M', for each buffer $b \in {}^\bullet t \cup t^\bullet$, the buffer reserve is maintained, that is, $M'(b) \geq \eta(M',b)$, or

2. t is privileged and the progressing copy or each of the new generated copies can run to completion due to that no buffer that will be used by the copies is filled to capacity.

In the following section, in the framework of the PN model of the system of compound processes, we present more precisely the concept discussed above, and in Sections **6.8-6.9** we give the required proofs.

6.7 THE SUPERVISOR

In order to describe the admissibility conditions, for each transition t we will distinguish specific subsets of transitions $TZ(t) \subseteq T$, places $EZ(t) \subseteq E$, and buffers $BZ(t) \subseteq B$, called operation zones, part zones, and buffer zones of t, respectively. Similarly as in Definition 6, we will assume that vertex t is a node if it has more than one input or output arc, and a non-node otherwise. t is an input vertex if it has no predecessors in relation F_e, and an output vertex if it has no successors. t' is an immediate successor of t if there exists part $e \in E$ such that $e \in t^\bullet \cap {}^\bullet t'$.

Definition 8 Let $t \in T$ be a transition in system N such that t has no more than one immediate successor. Let $d = t_1 e_1 \ldots t_n e_n t_{n+1}$ be the path in N from vertex $t = t_1$ to vertex t_{n+1} such that t_{n+1} is a node or an output vertex, and for each $i = 1..n$, t_i is not a node. The zones of t are defined as follows: *operation zone* $TZ(t) = \{t_1, t_2, \ldots, t_n\}$; *part zone* $EZ(t) = \{e_1, e_2, \ldots, e_n\}$; *buffer zone* $BZ(t) = \{\beta(e_2), \beta(e_3), \ldots, \beta(e_n)\}$.

Definition 9 Let $t \in T$ be a transition in system N such that t has more than one immediate successor. The zones of t are defined as follows: *operation zone* $TZ(t)$ is the union of $\{t\}$ and operation zones $TZ(t')$ of all non-node immediate successors t' of t; *part zone* $EZ(t)$ is the union of set $t^\bullet \cap E$ and part zones $EZ(t')$ of all immediate non-node successors t' of t; *buffer zone* $BZ(t) = \{\beta(e) \mid e \in EZ(t)\} - (t^\bullet \cap (B^N - B^{nN}))$.

Note that Definitions 8 and 9 imply that operation zone $EZ(t)$ contains the output parts of all transitions t' such that $t' \in TZ(t)$, including t, while buffer zone $BZ(t)$ contains the buffers used to store all parts $e \in EZ(t)$ except the buffers that store the output parts of t, if t is a non-node, and except the buffers that are used exclusively by nodes, if t is a node. Such a definition will be useful to give in a concise form one of the conditions regarding the transition admissibility. For the same purpose we will introduce the following notion.

Definition 10 For each transition $t \in T$, *node zone* of t is $EZ^{-1}(t) = \{e \mid e \in EZ(t) \wedge \exists t' \in T^N, (e,t) \in F_e^*\}$.

Stated another way, part e is in the node zone of t, $EZ^{-1}(t)$, if there exists a path in N from t to e and from e to some node t', that contains only non-node transitions and part places $e \in E$. The following two examples illustrate the introduced notions.

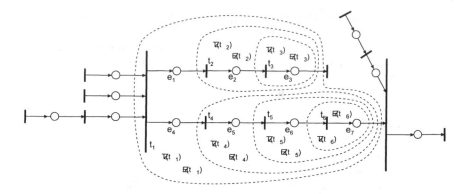

Figure 6.6: The structure of operation and part zones associated with node transition t_1 and with the transitions comprised by $TZ(t_1)$.

Example 3 Figure 6.6 shows the structure of zones associated with node transition t_1, and of the zones associated with transitions comprised by $TZ(t_1)$. For the sake of clarity of the drawing we do not present a complete example system N, but a subnet of N that does not contain buffer places and the corresponding arcs.

Example 4 For system N given in Figure 6.2, we can distinguish the following example zones (note that t_1, t_2, t_3, t_{17}, and t_{23} are non-node transitions, while t_4 and t_{16} are nodes).

$TZ(t_1) = \{t_1, t_2, t_3\}$, $EZ(t_1) = \{e_1, e_2, e_3\}$, $EZ^{-1}(t_1) = EZ(t_1)$, $BZ(t_1) = \{b_4, b_3\}$.

$TZ(t_2) = \{t_2, t_3\}$, $EZ(t_2) = \{e_2, e_3\}$, $EZ^{-1}(t_2) = EZ(t_2)$, $BZ(t_2) = \{b_3\}$.

$TZ(t_3) = \{t_3\}$, $EZ(t_3) = \{e_3\}$, $EZ^{-1}(t_3) = EZ(t_3)$, $BZ(t_3) = \emptyset$.

$TZ(t_4) = \{t_4, t_5, t_6, t_7\}$, $EZ(t_4) = \{e_4, e_5, e_6, e_7, e_{11}\}$, $EZ^{-1}(t_4) = EZ(t_4)$, $BZ(t_4) = \{b_4\}$. Note that $b_3, b_5 \notin BZ(t_4)$ as $b_3, b_5 \in t_4^{\bullet}$ and $B^N - B^{nN} = \{b_3, b_5, b_6\}$ (see Example 2), hence $b_3, b5 \in t_4^{\bullet} \cap (B^N - B^{nN})$.

$TZ(t_8) = \{t_9, t_{12}\}$, $EZ(t_8) = \{e_8, e12\}$, $EZ^{-1}(t_8) = \emptyset$. $BZ(t_8) = \emptyset$.

$TZ(t_{17}) = \{t_{17}, t_{18}, t_{19}\}$, $EZ(t_{17}) = \{e_{18}, e_{19}\}$, $EZ^{-1}(t_{17}) = EZ(t_{17})$, $BZ(t_{17}) = \{b_6\}$.

$TZ(t_{16}) = \{t_{16}\} \cup TZ(t_{17})$, $EZ(t_{16}) = \{e_{16}, e_{17}\} \cup EZ(t_{17})$, $EZ^{-1}(t_{16}) = EZ(t_{16})$, $BZ(t_{16}) = \{b_1\}$. Again, $b_6 = \beta(e_{16})$, yet $b_6 \notin BZ(t_{16})$ as $b_6 \in t_{16}^{\bullet} \cap (B^N - B^{nN})$.

$TZ(t_{23}) = \{t_{23}, t_{24}\}$, $EZ(t_{23}) = \{e_{24}, e_{25}\}$, $EZ^{-1}(t_{23}) = \emptyset$, $BZ(t_{23}) = \{b_2\}$.

The buffer reserve discussed in the previous section is defined formally as follows.

Definition 11 For each marking $M \in R(M_0)$ and each buffer $b \in B$, buffer reserve
$\eta(M, b) = v'(b) + |\{e \mid \beta(e) = b \wedge e \in E_{in}^N \wedge M(e) = 0\}|$.

Using the notions defined above, we will propose a supervisor for systems $N \in NV$.

Proposition 2 For system $N \in NV$, let t be a transition enabled at marking M, and let $M' = \delta(M, t)$. Function $\psi(M, t) = admissible$ if and only if at least one of the two following conditions holds:

   I. $\forall b \in {}^\bullet t \cup t^\bullet, M'(b) \geq \eta(M', b)$

  II. (a) $\forall b \in BZ(t), M'(b) > 0$, and

       (b) $\forall e \in EZ^\dashv(t), M(e) = 0$.

Note that if transition t fires under condition (II), then place $e \in t^\bullet$ becomes marked and there is no other marked place e' in zone $EZ^\dashv(t)$. It follows that no transition in $TZ(t)$, but possibly $t' \in e^\bullet$ is enabled. Moreover, since e is marked, then no transition t'' such that $e \in EZ^\dashv(t'')$ can fire under condition (II). Thus, the copy of SP associated with place e becomes privileged, as no other copy of the same SP can progress.

We will denote system N supervised by function ψ with symbol N_ψ. In the sequel, when referring to condition (I) or condition (II) we will mean the conditions given above. The dynamics of N_ψ is analyzed in the following section and in Section **6.9** we prove that ψ is a correct supervisor for system N.

6.8 MARKING EVOLUTION IN SYSTEM N_ψ

Let $\sigma = M_0 t_0 M_1 t_1, \ldots t_{i-1} M_i \ldots$ be any execution sequence such that M_0 is the initial marking and for each $i \geq 0$, $M_i \in R(M_0, \psi)$. With each i, we will associate buffer reserve $\eta_i(b) = \eta(M_i, b)$, $b \in B$, and two strings of parts, Q_i and U_i.

Definition 12 For an execution sequence $\sigma = M_0 t_0 M_1 t_1, \ldots t_{i-1} M_i \ldots$, strings $Q_i = Q(M_i)$ and $U_i = U(M_i)$ are defined as follows.

1. Q_0 is an empty string. Q_{i+1} is obtained from Q_i by: (i) adding at the end of Q_i any permutation of all parts $e \in t_i^\bullet - E_{in}^N$, and (ii) removing the first entry of each part e such that $e \in {}^\bullet t_i - E_{in}^N$.

2. U_0 is an empty string. U_{i+1} is obtained from U_i by: (i) adding at the end of U_i any permutation of all parts $e \in t_i^\bullet \cap E_{in}^N$, and (ii) removing the first entry of each part e such that $e \in {}^\bullet t_i \cap E_{in}^N$.

3. For each buffer $b \in B$, $q(M_i, b) = q_i(b)$ is the number of entries e in Q_i such that $\beta(e) = b$, and $u(M_i, b) = u_i(b)$ is the number of entries e in U_i such that $\beta(e) = b$.

Clearly, each part e can only occur in one of the strings: string Q_i, if $e \in E - E_{in}^N$, and string U_i, if $e \in E_{in}^N$. The number of the occurrences of e is equal to $M_i(e)$, that is, the number of tokens in place e. Since new entries are added at the end of Q_i or U_i, the tokens appear in the strings in the order of their production. Using the new notions we will follow the evolution of the marking in system N guarded by supervisor ψ. Note that for each $i = 1, 2, \ldots$

$$c(b) = M_i(b) + q_i(b) + u_i(b) \tag{1}$$

When transition t_i fires, then the number of tokens in b changes by $M_{i+1}(b) - M_i(b) = f(t_i, b) - f(b, t_i)$. The tokens removed from b are added as entries e to Q_i or U_i, and the tokens added to b cause the removal of entries e from Q_i or U_i, depending on the type of entry. Thus, no more entries other than $f(b,t)$ are added to Q_i. It follows that

$$q_{i+1}(b) - q_i(b) \leq M_i(b) - M_{i+1}(b) \tag{2}$$

When a new entry e s.t. $\beta(e) = b$ is added to string U_i, then $u_{i+1}(b) = u_i(b) + 1$. Similarly, when entry e is removed from U_i, then $u_{i+1}(b) = u_i(b) - 1$. This corresponds to appearing a new token in place $e \in E_{in}^N$, and disappearing a token, respectively. Thus, $u_i(b)$ can be viewed as a counter that gives the total number of all copies of all entries e in string U_i associated with buffer b. Unlike $u_i(b)$, the value of $\eta_i(b)$ (see Definition 11) changes only when for some e such that $\beta(e) = b$, $M_i(e) = 0$ and a new token is produced, or when $M_i(e) = 1$ and the token located in e is consumed. In the former case, each such token contributes to decreasing $\eta_i(b)$ by 1, in the latter case, to increasing $\eta_i(b)$ by 1. Thus, $\eta_i(b)$ observes only the fact of whether there exists part e in string U_i and, contrary to $u_i(b)$, increases when the last copy of e disappears, and decreases when the first copy of e appears in U_i. Since $\eta_0(b) = v(b)$, from Definition 6 and by Definitions 11 and 12 we have

$$v(b) - \eta_i(b) = |\{e \mid e \text{ occurs in } U_i \wedge \beta(e) = b\}| \tag{3}$$

Since $(v(b) - \eta_i(b))$ counts only a single copy of each entry type, we can introduce an additional counter to capture the remaining copies. The value of the counter increases when entries e are added to U_i and there is already a copy of e, and decreases when entries e are removed from U_i and there remains another copy of e. Formally, we obtain that

$$u_{i+1}(b) - u_i(b) = (v(b) - \eta_{i+1}(b)) - (v(b) - \eta_i(b)) + x_{i+1}(b) - y_{i+1}(b) \tag{4}$$

where

$$x_{i+1}(b) = |\{e \mid \beta(e) = b \wedge e \in t_i^\bullet \cap E_{in}^N \wedge M_i(e) > 0\}| \tag{5}$$

$$y_{i+1}(b) = |\{e \mid \beta(e) = b \wedge e \in {}^\bullet t_i \cap E_{in}^N \wedge M_i(e) > 1\}| \tag{6}$$

From (4)

$$\eta_{i+1}(b) - \eta_i(b) = u_i(b) - u_{i+1}(b) + x_{i+1}(b) - y_{i+1}(b) \tag{7}$$

Using (7) we will calculate the value of $\eta_i(b)$ reached through any execution sequence $\sigma = M_0 t_0 M_1 t_1, \ldots t_{i-1} M_i$. Note that

$$\eta_i(b) = \eta_0(b) + (\eta_1(b) - \eta_0(b)) + (\eta_2(b) - \eta_1(b)) + \ldots + (\eta_i(b) - \eta_{i-1}(b)) \tag{8}$$

Thus, from (7) and (8)

$$\eta_i(b) = \eta_0(b) + u_0(b) - u_i(b) + X_i(b) - Y_i(b) \tag{9}$$

where

$$X_i(b) = \sum_{l=1}^{i} x_l(b), \quad Y_i(b) = \sum_{l=1}^{i} y_l(b) \tag{10}$$

Since $\eta_0(b) = \eta(M_0, b)$, by Definition 11, $\eta_0(b) = v(b)$. From this, (9), and (1)

$$u_i(b) = v(b) - \eta_i(b) + X_i(b) - Y_i(b) \tag{11}$$

$$q_i(b) = c(b) - v(b) - M_i(b) + \eta_i(b) - (X_i(b) - Y_i(b)) \tag{12}$$

Using formula (12), we will follow the changes in the use of buffer b. Let us consider any execution sequence $\sigma = M_0 t_0 M_1 \ldots M_k t_k M_{k+1} \ldots M_n t_n M_{n+1}$ s.t. $M_k(b) \geq \eta_k(b)$ and $\forall i = k+1..n$, $M_i(b) < \eta_i(b)$. Since the inequality $M_k(b) \geq \eta_k(b)$ changes to $M_{k+1}(b) < \eta_{k+1}(b)$ then $b \in {}^\bullet t \cup t^\bullet$ and, by Proposition 2, transition t_k is not admissible under condition (I). Thus t_k fires under condition (II). It follows that $\forall e \in t^\bullet \cap E_{in}^N$, $M_k(e) = 0$. Thus, from (5), $x_{k+1}(b) = 0$. Moreover since for each $i = k+1..n$, $M_i(b) < \eta_i(b)$ then each transition t_i, $i = k..n-1$ s.t. $b \in {}^\bullet t_i \cup t_i^\bullet$ fires under condition (II). Thus,

$$\forall i = k..n-1, \ x_{i+1}(b) = 0, \quad \text{and} \quad \forall i = k..n-1, \ X_{i+1}(b) = X_k(b) \tag{13}$$

Consequently

$$\forall i = k..n-1, \ X_{i+1}(b) - Y_{i+1}(b) \leq X_i(b) - Y_i(b) \tag{14}$$

From (12) and (14)

$$\forall i = k+1..n, \ q_i(b) + M_i(b) - \eta_i(b) \geq q_k(b) + M_k(b) - \eta_k(b) \tag{15}$$

Since $M_k(b) \geq \eta_k(b)$ and $\forall i = k..m-1$, $M_{i+1}(b) < \eta_{i+1}(b)$, then from (15)

$$\forall i = k..m-1, \ q_{i+1}(b) > q_k(b) \tag{16}$$

Formula (16) implies that when the inequality $M_k(b) \geq \eta_k(b)$ changes to $M_{k+1}(b) < \eta_{k+1}(b)$, the number of entries e s.t. $\beta(e) = b$ increases from $q_k(b)$ to $q_{k+1}(b)$, and remains greater than $q_k(b)$ for each $i > k$ such that $M_i(b) < \eta_i(b)$.

Note that for each $i = k+1..n$, $q_i(b) > q_k(b)$, yet not necessarily for each $i = k..n-1$, $q_{i+1}(b) > q_i(b)$. When $q_{i+1}(b) \leq q_i(b)$ then, from Definition 12, t_i is not a node transition. Thus, from Definitions 11 and 12, and Formula (13)

$$u_i(b) \leq u_{i+1}(b) \quad \text{and} \quad y_{n+1}(b) = 0 \quad \text{and} \quad x_{n+1}(b) = 0 \tag{17}$$

From (17) and (11)

$$\eta_{i+1}(b) - \eta_i(b) \leq 0 \tag{18}$$

From (17), (18) and (12)

$$M_{i+1}(b) - M_i(b) \geq q_i(b) - q_{i+1}(b) \tag{19}$$

It follows that if t_i fires under condition (II) and $q_{i+1}(b) \leq q_i(b)$, then

$$M_{i+1}(b) \geq M_i(b) \tag{20}$$

Assume now that at marking M_{n+1}, in string Q_{n+1} the number of the entries e such that $\beta(e) = b$ decreases to the initial or a smaller value, that is,

$$q_{n+1}(b) = q_k(b) - z, \quad z \geq 0 \tag{21}$$

From (12) and (10)

$$q_n(b) - q_{n+1}(b) = M_{n+1}(b) - \eta_{n+1}(b) + x_{n+1}(b) - y_{n+1}(b) - M_n(b) + \eta_n(b) \tag{22}$$

From (21), (22), and since $M_n(b) < \eta_n(b)$

$$q_n(b) - q_k(b) + z < M_{n+1}(b) - \eta_{n+1}(b) + x_{n+1}(b) - y_{n+1}(b) \tag{23}$$

Since $z \geq 0$ and $q_n(b) > q_k(b)$, from (23)

$$0 < M_{n+1}(b) - \eta_{n+1}(b) + x_{n+1}(b) - y_{n+1}(b) \tag{24}$$

Since, from (16) and (21), $q_{n+1}(b) < q_n(b)$, then t_n is not a node transition. Thus, from (5) and (6)

$$0 \leq x_{n+1}(b) \leq 1, \quad y_{n+1}(b) = 0 \tag{25}$$

From (24) and (25), we obtain that

$$M_{n+1}(b) \geq \eta_{n+1}(b) \tag{26}$$

The conducted analysis shows that the buffer reserve gets broken (i.e., at some marking M_{k+1}, the inequality $M_k(b) \geq \eta_k(b)$ changes to $M_{k+1}(b) < \eta_{k+1}(b)$) due to an excessive number $q_{k+1}(b) - q_k(b)$ of tokens in places e that represent intermediate parts whose units are stored in buffer b. Only then when no such excessive tokens are present in the system (i.e., at some marking M_{n+1}, $q_{n+1}(b) \leq q_k(b)$), the reserve of buffer b is restored (i.e., we obtain again $M_{n+1}(b) \geq \eta_{n+1}(b)$). Note that to achieve this goal, it is sufficient to reduce the number of intermediate products of SPs that use buffer b (i.e., the value of $q_{n+1}(b)$), while the number of the processes' final products stored in b (i.e., the value of $u_{n+1}(b)$) does not influence directly the fact of whether the buffer reserve is maintained (i.e., whether $M_{n+1}(b) \geq \eta_{n+1}(b)$).

6.9 THE PROOF

As established in Proposition 1, the defined admissibility function ψ is a supervisor for system N if it satisfies conditions (A0) and (A1). Loosely speaking, the conditions require that at the initial marking, each enabled transition be admissible, and at each reachable marking $M \neq M_0$ exist an admissible transition that fired less times than some other transition. In order to prove that the proposed supervisor ensures these requirements, we will distinguish two complementary cases of the marking, $\mathcal{M}^0$ and $\mathcal{M}^{\neg 0}$, where

$$M \in \mathcal{M}^0 \quad \text{if} \quad M \in R(M_0, \psi) \quad \text{and} \quad \forall b \in B, M(b) \geq \eta(M, b)$$

$$M \in \mathcal{M}^{-}0 \quad \text{if} \quad M \in R(M_0, \psi) \quad \text{and} \quad \exists b \in B, M(b) < \eta(M, b)$$

In the following two subsections, we consider separately these two cases. Note that marking $M_0 \in \mathcal{M}^0$. Thus, condition (A0) is considered in Section **6.9.1**, where we prove as well that condition (A1) holds in the first case of the marking. In Section **6.9.2**, using the results obtained in Section **6.8**, we demonstrate that (A1) is also satisfied for each marking $M_0 \in \mathcal{M}^0$.

6.9.1 Case 1: $M \in \mathcal{M}^0$

The objective of this subsection is to demonstrate that the admissibility conditions of supervisor ψ, established in Proposition 2, imply the required properties (A0) and (A1) of system N_ψ in the first case of the marking. The following lemma shows that for each $M \in \mathcal{M}^0$, condition (II.b) of Proposition 2 implies condition (II.a), and Lemma 2, that this, in turn, implies condition (A0). Since the initial marking $M_0 \in \mathcal{M}^0$ and condition (II.b) is satisfied at M_0, this proves that (A0) holds, that is, each transition enabled at M_0 is also admissible. In Lemma 3 we prove that at each reachable marking $M \in \mathcal{M}^0$ there exists a *head transition* that satisfies the assumption of Lemma 1, and that it also implies the satisfaction of condition (A1).

Lemma 1 In system N_ψ, for each marking $M \in \mathcal{M}^0$ and each transition enabled at M, if $\forall e \in EZ(t)$, $M(e) = 0$, then $\forall b \in BZ(t)$, $M'(b) = \delta(M, t) > 0$.

Proof. If $b \in BZ(t)$, then by Definitions 8 and 9, $b \in B^N \cap B^{nN}$. Thus, by Definition 6, $v'(b) = 1 + max_{t' \in T} w(b, t') > w(b, t)$. From Definition 6 and 11, $\eta(b) \geq v(b) - v''(b) = v'(b)$. Since $M \in \mathcal{M}^0$, then $M(b) \geq \eta(b)$. Thus, $M(b) \geq v'(b) > w(b, t)$. Since $M'(b) = M(b) - w(b, t)$, then $M'(b) > 0$. $\square$

Lemma 2 System N_ψ satisfies condition (A0) of Proposition 1.

Proof. Let t be any input transition in N_ψ. We need to demonstrate that t is admissible at the initial marking M_0. Note that for each $b \in B$, $M_0(b) = c(b) \geq v(b) \geq w(b, t)$. Thus, t is enabled at M_0. To demonstrate that t is admissible, consider condition (II) of Proposition 2. Since, from Definition 11, $\eta(M_0, b) = v(b)$, then $M_0(b) \geq \eta_0(b)$. As for each $e \in E$, $M_0(e) = 0$ then t satisfies the assumption of Lemma 1. Consequently, for each $b \in BZ(t)$, $M' = \delta(M, t) > 0$, which proves that condition (II.a) holds. Since $\forall e \in E$, $M_0(e) = 0$ and $EZ^{-1}(t) \subseteq EZ(t) \subseteq E$, t satisfies condition (II.b) at marking M_0. Thus, t is admissible at M_0. $\square$

To prove the following lemma, we will distinguish a subset of *head transitions* $H(M) \subseteq T$, $M \in R(M_0)$, defined as the set of all transitions $t \in T$ such that $\forall e \in E$, if $(t, e) \in F_e^*$, then $M(e) = 0$.

Lemma 3 In system N_ψ, for each marking $M \in \mathcal{M}^0$ there exists a transition that satisfies condition (A1) of Proposition 1.

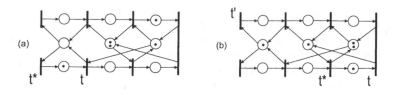

Figure 6.7: Examples illustrating the proof of Lemma 4.

Proof. Let z be any firing sequence such that $M_0[z > M$ and $M \in \mathcal{M}^0$. We need to demonstrate that there exists transition t_{ad} that is admissible at M and occurs in z less times than some other transition t^*. It is not hard to notice that at each marking reachable in system N, $H(M)$ is not empty. Moreover, if $M \neq M_0$, there exists transition $t \in H(M)$ with at least one place $e \in {}^\bullet t$ such that $M(e) > 0$. Let t be a transition that satisfies this condition at marking M. There are two possible cases (see Figure 6.7 for an example): (a) for each $e \in {}^\bullet t$, $M(e) > 0$, or (b) there exists transition $t' \in H(M)$ such that $(t', t) \in F_e^*$ and for each $e \subset {}^\bullet t'$, $M(e) > 0$. Clearly, in case (a), $t_{ad} = t$ is enabled and its predecessor t^* fired one more time than t, while in case (b), $t_{ad} = t'$ is enabled and $t^* = t$ fired more times than t'. To prove that t_{ad} is admissible at M, we will show that condition (II) of Proposition 2 holds. Note that t_{ad} is a head transition, thus for each $e \in EZ(t_{ad})$, $M(e) = 0$. Since $EZ^{-1}(t) \subseteq EZ(t)$ and $t_{ad} \in H(M)$, then t_{ad} satisfies condition (II.b). Since $M \in \mathcal{M}^0$ and $t \in H(M)$, then t_{ad} satisfies the assumptions of Lemma 1. It follows that $\forall b \in BZ(t_{ad})$, $M'(b) > 0$. Thus t_{ad} satisfies condition (II.a). Consequently, transition t_{ad} is admissible. $\square$

6.9.2 Case 2: $M \in \mathcal{M}^{-0}$

In Section **6.8** it was demonstrated that when transition t_{i-1} fires under condition (II), then the resulting marking $M_i \in \mathcal{M}^{-0}$ due to that an "excessive" entry $e \in t_{i-1}^\bullet$ to string Q_{i+1} is produced. The following lemma proves that when such an entry is produced, that is, transition t_i fires under condition (II), then transition t such that $e \in {}^\bullet t$ is admissible under condition II at marking M_{i+1}. To illustrate this situation, let us return to Figure 6.6. If, for example, t_1 fires under condition (II), then at the resulting marking both t_2 and t_4 are admissible. Similarly, if t_4 fires under condition (II), then t_5 becomes admissible. In Lemma 5 we prove that t remains admissible at each marking M_m, $m > i$, at least as long as e is the last entry in string Q_m, that has been produced under condition II. Finally, Lemma 6 demonstrates that the previous results imply that condition (A1) holds for each marking $M \in \mathcal{M}^{-0}$.

Lemma 4 In system N_ψ, for each execution sequence $\sigma = M_0 t_0 M_1 \ldots t_{i-1} M_i \ldots$, if transition t_{i-1} fires under condition (II) of Proposition 2, then each immediate non-node successor t of t_{i-1} is admissible under condition (II) at marking M_i.

Proof. Assume that t_{i-1} has an immediate non-node successor t. Since t_{i-1} fires under condition (II), then $\forall b \in BZ(t_{i-1})$, $M_i(b) > 0$ and $\forall e \in EZ(t)^{-1}$, $M_{i-1}(e) =$

0. Since $^\bullet t \subseteq BZ(t_{i-1})$, transition t is enabled at M_i. Moreover, since t is a non-node successor of t_{i-1}, then, from Definitions 8-9, $BZ(t) \subseteq BZ(t_{i-1})$ and $BZ(t)$ does not contain buffer $b' = \beta(e)$ such that $e \in t^\bullet$. If t fires, changing the marking to M_{i+2}, then the only buffer whose marking can decrease is b'. Thus, $\forall b \in BZ(t)$, $M_{i+1}(b) = M_i(b) > 0$, that is, t satisfies condition (II.a). If $EZ^\dashv(t) = \emptyset$ (as in the case of transition t_2 in Figure 6.6) then the lemma holds. Otherwise (as in the case of transition t_4 in Figure 6.6)), we need to consider condition (II.b). Since t_{i-1} fires under condition (II), then $\forall e \in EZ^\dashv(t_{i-1})$, $M_{i-1}(e) = 0$. As only the marking of $e \in t_{i-1}^\bullet$ can increase when t_{i-1} fires, we have that $\forall e \in EZ^\dashv(t_{i-1}) - t_{i-1}^\bullet$, $M_i(e) = 0$. Since $EZ^\dashv(t) \subset EZ^\dashv(t_{i-1}) - t_{i-1}^\bullet$ then $\forall e \in EZ^\dashv(t)$, $M_i(e) = 0$, which proves condition (II.b). Consequently, each immediate non-node successor t of t_{i-1} is admissible at M_i. $\square$

Lemma 5 Let $\sigma = M_0 t_0 \ldots t_i M_i \ldots M_n t_n M_{n+1}$ be any execution sequence in system N_ψ such that: (a) t_n is admissible under condition (I) of Proposition 2, or (b) t_n is admissible under condition (II) and $\forall b \in B$, $q_{n+1}(b) \leq q_n(b)$. If there exists transition $t \neq t_n$ that is admissible under condition (II) at marking M_n, then t is admissible at marking M_{n+1}.

Proof. Since transition t is admissible at M_n under condition (II), it is evident that at marking M_{n+1}, t is enabled and condition (II.b) holds. Since t is admissible at M_n, then (II.a) holds at marking M_{n+1} if $\forall b \in BZ(t)$, $M_{n+1}(b) \geq M_n(b)$. Consider any buffer $b \in BZ(t)$. If $b \notin {}^\bullet t_n$, then $M_{n+1}(b) \geq M_n(b)$. Otherwise, in case (a), since t_n fires under condition (I), then $M_{n+1}(b) \geq \eta_{n+1}(b) \geq v'(b)$. If $b \in BZ(t)$ then $b = \beta(e)$ and $e \in EZ(t)$. If $e \notin E_{in}^N$, then by Def 6, $v'(b) > 0$. Thus, $M_{n+1}(b) \geq M_n(b)$. Otherwise $e \in E_{in}^N$. Since $t \neq t_n$ and $\forall e \in EZ(t)$, $M_n(e) = 0$, then $M_{n+1}(e) = 0$. By Definition 11, $\eta_{n+1}(b) \geq v'(b) + 1$. Thus, again $M_{n+1}(b) \geq M_n(b)$. In case (b), by formula (20) derived in Section **6.8**, $M_{n+1}(b) \geq M_n(b)$. $\square$

Lemma 6 In system N_ψ, for each marking $M \in \mathcal{M}^{\dashv 0}$, there exists a transition that satisfies condition (A1) of Proposition 1.

Proof. Let $\sigma = M_0 t_0 M_1 \ldots t_k M_{k+1} \ldots t_{n-1} M_n$ be any execution sequence s.t. $M_n = M$. To prove the lemma, we need to demonstrate that there exists transition t that is admissible at M_n and occurs in σ less times than some other transition. Since $M \in \mathcal{M}^{\dashv 0}$, then there exists buffer b s.t. $\eta_n(b) < M_n(b)$. As follows from the discussion in Section **6.8** and Formula (16), in particular, this implies that string Q_n contains entry e s.t. $\beta(e) = b$ and e was produced by a transition that fired under condition (II) of Proposition 2. Thus, out of all the entries in Q_n, we can select one that was produced last, say by transition t_k. Since e is an entry in Q_k, then there exists a non-node transition t s.t. $e \in {}^\bullet t$. By Lemma 4, t is admissible at M_{k+1}. Since e is the last entry in Q_n produced under condition (II) then for each $i = k+1..n$, e is an entry in each Q_i, $M_i(b) < \eta_i(b)$, and $M_i(e) = 1$. Thus, transition t is enabled at each marking M_i. Moreover, since e is the last part in Q_n produced under condition (II), each transition t_i, $i \in k+1..n-1$ either fires under condition (I) or each of its output parts $e' \in t_i^\bullet$ is an entry to string U_{i+1}. Note that in the latter case $\forall b \in B$,

$q_{i+1}(b) \leq q_i(b)$. Thus, by Lemma 5, transition t is admissible at each marking M_i, $i = k+1..n$. Since $M_n(e) = 1$, then transition t_k occurs more times in sequence σ than t. Consequently, transition t satisfies condition (A1) of Proposition 1. $\square$

Now we can formulate the final result of this work.

Theorem 3 Function ψ established in Proposition 2 is a deadlock avoidance supervisor for each system $N \in NV$.

Proof. By Lemma 2, system N satisfies condition (A0) of Proposition 1. By Lemma 3 and Lemma 6, condition (A1) holds in the case of $M \in \mathcal{M}^0$ and in the case of $M \in \mathcal{M}^{-0}$, respectively. Since this exhausts the set of reachable markings, by Proposition 1, the theorem holds. $\square$

6.10 CONCLUSION

This chapter deals with the class of compound processes that model streams of materials that can join and split, such as in assembly/disassembly systems, at group transport and then individual part processing, or in processes that require temporary meeting of independently routed components. The dynamics of the system were represented with an ordinary PN N, and the problem studied was the design of a supervisor for ensuring the deadlock-free process flow. The model views each operation as a single event whose result is a change of the number and the location of the material objects, called parts, involved in the operation.

Since parts can be split and joined, avoiding deadlocks in a compound process requires both ensuring the eventual availability of the permanent resources required for each operation (buffer space for each part), and the synchronization of the part production in each component sequential process. The necessary concurrency of these processes and the possible use of the same buffers result in a compound process that might not be realizable if the capacity of a particular buffer is less than some minimal value. Therefore we solve the supervision problem through, first, establishing the so-called minimal buffer capacity $v(b)$ for each buffer $b \in B$, that depends on the processes' structure and gives a value sufficient for the possibility of deadlock-free process flow, and, second, addressing the control problem for the subclass of systems with the capacity of buffers greater than or equal $v(b)$.

The proposed supervisor is given in the form of a function that states whether a particular enabled transition is admissible at a particular state of the system. The concept underlying its development assumes the introduction of a buffer reserve whose value changes dynamically and ensures the availability of a unit buffer space for one unit of the final product of each sequential component process. The avoidance of deadlocks in the component sequential processes is due to a policy assuming that an operation is admissible if at the moment there is enough resources to let its product undergo all the remaining operations in the process and await the products of the other sequential processes with which they interact. The general idea is formally described and the behavior of the system with so restricted dynamics is analyzed.

An important result of the analysis is that the broken buffer reserve can be restored when the sequential processes that caused the break attain their last stage. This implies that processes that are awaiting other processes to be synchronized with do not induce deadlocks. Based on the definitions of the notions describing the supervisory control concept and using the results of the analysis, we prove formally that the proposed supervisor ensures the required behavior of the system. The presented ideas can be further developed in future works by associating the introduced general synchronization concept based on the dynamic buffer reserve with other deadlock avoidance policies for systems of sequential processes.

REFERENCES

[1] M.M. Andreasen and T. Ahm. Flexible Assembly Systems IFS Publications, Springer-Verlag, 1988.

[2] D.N. Hall and K.E. Stecke. Design problems of flexible assembly systems. In K. E. Stecke and R. Suri, editors, Proc. 2nd ORSA/TIMS Conf. on FMS: Operations Research Models and Applications, 1986, pp 145–156.

[3] P. Valckenaers, H. Van Brussel, L. Bongaerts, and F. Bonneville. Programming, scheduling, and control of flexible assembly systems. Computers in Industry, V26(N3):209–218, 1995.

[4] J. Wyns. Reference architecture for Holonic Manufacturing Systems - the key to support evolution and reconfiguration. PhD thesis, K.U. Leuven, Belgium, 1999.

[5] http://www.mech.kuleuven.ac.be/pma/project/goa/testb1.html.

[6] E. Roszkowska and Z. Banaszak. Problems of deadlock handling in pipeline processes. In: Computer and Information Sciences VI. Elsevier Science Publishers, 1991, pp 1185–1194.

[7] J. Ezpeleta, F. Tricas, F. Garcia-Valles, and J.M. Colom. A banker's solution for deadlock avoidance in FMS with flexible routing and multi-resource states. IEEE Transactions on Robotics and Automation, 18(4):621–625, 2002.

[8] M. Lawley, S. Reveliotis, and P. Ferreira. Design guidelines for deadlock handling strategies in flexible manufacturing systems. Int. J. of Flexible Manufacturing Systems, pp 5–30, 1997.

[9] V.S. Kouikoglou. Optimal rate allocation in unreliable assembly/disassembly production networks with blocking. In Proc. 1999 IEEE Int. Conf. Robotics & Automation, 1999, pp 1126–1131.

[10] C. Paik and D. Tcha. Throughput equivalencies in fork/join queueing networks with finite buffers and general service times. Int. Journal of Production Research, 33(3):695–703, 1995.

[11] Y. Dallery, Z. Liu, and D. Towsley. Equivalence, reversibility, symmetry and concavity properties of fork/join networks with blocking. Journal of the ACM, 41(5):903–942, 1994.

[12] Y. Dallery, Z. Liu, and D. Towsley. Equivalence relations in queueing models of fork/join networks with blocking. Performance Evaluation, 10:233–245, 1989.

[13] M.P. Fanti, B. Maione, and B. Turchiano. Design and implementation of supervisors avoiding deadlocks in flexible assembly systems. In Proc. of IEEE-SMC Multiconf. Computat. Eng. in Systems Applications, CESA'98, 1998.

[14] M.P. Fanti. Event-based controller to avoid deadlock and collisions in zone-control AGVs. Intl. J. Product. Res., 40(6):1453–1478, 2002.

[15] M.C. Zhou, Z. Wang, and D.L. Guo. Deadlock avoidance in a five-robot-five-assembly-line system: Petri net modeling and analysis. In IFAC Workshop on Discrete Event System Theory and Applications in Manufacturing and Social Phenomena (91'DES), 1991, pp 123–128.

[16] Z. Banaszak and E. Roszkowska. Deadlock avoidance in pipeline concurrent processes. Podstawy Sterowania (Foundations of Control), 18:3–17, 1988.

[17] E. Roszkowska. CAST-Tools for automatic FMS dynamics models synthesis. In Computer Aided Systems Theory - EUROCAST'91, volume 585 of Lecture Notes on Computer Science, pp 412–421, Springer-Verlag, 1992.

[18] E. Roszkowska and R. Wojcik. Problems of process flow feasibility in FAS. In: CIM in Process and Manufacturing Industries, Oxford: Pergamon Press, 1993, pp 115–120.

[19] E. Roszkowska. Supervisory control for deadlock avoidance in compound manufacturing processes. IEEE Trans. on Sys. Man Cybern., Part A, 34:52–64, 2004.

[20] J.Blazewicz, D.P. Bovet, J. Brzezinski, G. Gambosi, and M. Talamo. Optimal centralized algorithms for store-and-forward deadlock avoidance. IEEE Trans. on Computers, 43:1333–1338, 1994.

[21] M.A. Lawley and S.A. Reveliotis. Deadlock avoidance for sequential resource allocation systems: hard and easy cases. The Intl. Jrnl. of FMS, 13(4):385–404, 2001.

7

Deadlock Avoidance Algorithms and Implementation, a Matrix Based Approach

José Mireles, Jr.
Universidad Autónoma de Ciudad Juárez, Chihuahua, México.

Frank L. Lewis
The University of Texas at Arlington, Texas, USA.

Ayla Gürel
Eastern Mediterranean University, Gazi Magosa Mersin, Turkey.

Stjepan Bogdan
University of Zagreb, Zagreb, Croatia.

7.1 INTRODUCTION, MOTIVATION AND OBJECTIVES

This chapter presents a deadlock avoidance matrix-based supervisory controller for discrete event (DE) systems. The formulation of this matrix-based controller makes it direct to write it down from standard manufacturing tools such as the bill of materials or the assembly tree. It is shown that the DE controller's matrix form equations plus the petri net (PN) marking transition equation together provide a complete dynamical description of DE systems (DES). Deadlock-free dispatching rules are derived by performing circular wait (CW) analysis in matrix form for possible deadlock situations. An analysis of the so-called critical siphons, certain critical subsystems and structured bottleneck resources is shown. This analysis is needed for the development of a DE controller (DEC) that guaranties deadlock-free dispatching by limiting the work-in-progress (WIP) in certain critical subsystems associated with each CW. Such policy is the least restrictive dispatching policy that avoids deadlock. A demonstration is provided implementing the matrix-based DE controller for deadlock-free on a 3-robot, 2-machine reentrant flow-line. Technical information given includes the development of the deadlock-free controller in LabVIEW®.

The objectives of this chapter are

1. To describe the DEC formulation, including the relationship of this DEC formulation with PNs.

2. To illustrate an implementation of the DEC on an intelligent material handling (IMH) robotic workcell. Technical information includes the development of the controller in a graphical environment, LabVIEW.

3. To show the analysis and computation in matrix notation of circular waits, their critical siphons and certain critical subsystems needed to implement a deadlock-free DEC.

4. To show the integration of CW analysis and deadlock-free dispatching rules into an augmented DEC matrix formulation that limits the WIP in the critical subsystems.

5. To illustrate an implementation example of this deadlock avoidance DEC on a 3 robot IMH robotic workcell. A detailed exposition of the development of the DEC for the workcell is given, including all steps needed for its implementation. Technical information includes this implementation in a graphical environment, LabVIEW.

The content of this chapter as follows:

Section 7.2 contains the introduction of matrix formulation into DES. Section 7.3 defines the structure of the DEC matrix formulation, including its relationship with Petri Nets and its use to define a complete dynamical description of DES. Section 7.4 shows an implementation of the DE matrix controller on a 3-robot, 2-machine reentrant flow-line. This section also covers the DEC conflict resolution strategy, including its three levels of its intelligent control structure and technical information for its implementation on a graphical environment, LabVIEW. Section 7.5 shows the constructions based on matrices needed to yield efficient deadlock avoidance algorithms. These constructions are calculated by performing CW analysis among resources, which, if dispatching is not properly sequenced, CW might contain critical siphons that generally lead to deadlock conditions. Section 7.5 also shows both, PN and matrix notations to identify such constructions needed for deadlock analysis. This policy is defined in terms of the matrix constructions from section 7.4. Also, the second part of Section 7.5 shows an implementation example of this deadlock avoidance policy in a 3-robot, 2-machine reentrant flow-line.

7.2 MATRIX FORMULATION FOR DE SYSTEMS

A problem in Flexible Manufacturing Systems [*Buzacott et al. 86*] or DES is job sequencing when some resources are shared. While some resources manipulate or machine single parts in DES, others manipulate or machine multiple parts for several products in the manufacturing process. If jobs are not correctly sequenced in the latter case, serious problems in the performance of the DES can be obtained, including **blocking** and system **deadlock**. Therefore, it is very important that the DE controller properly sequences jobs and assigns resources.

Many approaches exist to control the resource dispatching sequences in manufacturing systems, including first-in-first-out (FIFO), first-buffer-first-serve (FBFS), last-buffer-first-serve (LBFS), earliest-due-date (EDD), least-slack (LS), and others [*Panwalkar et al 77*]. Rigorous analysis for some of these algorithms has been done for the case of unbounded buffer lengths. For instance, [*Kumar et al. 92-95*] has shown that LBFS yields bounded buffer stability in the case of a single part reentrant flow-line (RF), However, in actual manufacturing systems, the buffer lengths are usually finite, which introduces the possibility of system deadlock. Moreover, little rigorous work has been done for dispatching in multipart RF (MRF) with finite buffers. In this chapter we provide a technique for avoiding deadlock in MRF with finite buffers by restricting the WIP in certain *critical subsystems* related to siphon structures. This is a rigorous notion related to the idea of 'CONWIP' [*Spearman et al. 90*]. All computations are performed using straightforward matrix algorithms, including computation of the critical subsystems, for any RFL in a certain general class.

For analysis, modeling and control of manufacturing systems, one of the tools that is extensively used is PN [*Peterson 81, Murata 89, Desrochers 90, Krogh et al. 91, Zhou et al. 92-96, Pastravanu 94b*]. Though PN have proven very useful in analysis and control of manufacturing systems, it can be difficult to draw a PN directly from the manufacturing bill of materials (BOM) [*Elsayed et al. 94*], or assembly tree [*Wolter et al. 92a-b*]. In contrast, this DEC matrix-based formulation can directly written down from the BOM or the partial assembly tree. In addition, the DEC formulation can easily be modified if there are changes in product requirements or resources available, making the control of the workcell more flexible and re-configurable. It can be shown that this DEC is a formalized version of both the *top-down* and the *bottom-up* PN design approaches [*Desrochers 90, Zhou et al. 92-93, Jeng et al. 95*].

PN cannot provide a mathematically complete dynamical description of DES. The PN marking transition equation provides a partial description, but it is incomplete in that it has not yet been demonstrated how to determine the allowable firing vector [*Peterson 81*]. It will be shown that the DEC equations presented herein plus the PN marking transition equation provide together a complete dynamical description of a DES. This allows one to control an actual workcell using the DEC logic, and to simulate on a computer the time behavior of the controlled system using the DEC equation plus the PN marking transition equation.

This chapter presents the development and implementation of an augmented DEC for multipart reentrant flow lines that is based on the decision-making matrix formulation introduced in [*Lewis 92, Lewis et al. 93ab*], and its implementation is shown in [*Mireles et al. 01ab*]. Important features of this matrix formulation are that it uses a logical algebra, not the Max/Plus algebra [*Cofer et al. 92*], and that it can be described directly from standard manufacturing tools that detail product requirements, job sequencing [*Warfield 73, Eppinger 90, Steward 62-81ab*] and resource requirements [*Kusiak et al. 90-92*].

We make the following three assumptions which define the sort of discrete-part manufacturing systems that can be described by Petri nets:

No preemption. A resource cannot be removed from a job until it is complete;

Mutual exclusion. A single resource can be used for only one job at a time;

Hold while waiting. A process holds the resources already allocated to it until it has all resources required to perform a job.

In addition to these assumptions, we assume there are no machine failures and that the system is regular, i.e. no structured bottleneck resources associated [*Gurel et al. 00, Mireles et al. 02abc, Section 7.5.5*], and that the system is ordinary (from the corresponding ordinary PN [*Murata 89*].)

7.3 MATRIX-BASED DISCRETE EVENT CONTROLLER

A novel DEC for manufacturing workcells was described in [*Lewis et al. 93-94, Mireles et al. 01a*], and has been in constant development [*Pastravanu et al. 94a, Huang 95, Tacconi et al. 97*]. This DEC is based on matrices, and it was shown to have important advantages in design, flexibility and computer simulation.

We show that the formulated DEC allows commensurate advantages in actual implementation on a practical robotic cell [*Mireles et al. 01a-b, Mireles et al. 02b*]. Following the same notation used in [*Lewis et al. 93b*], the definition of the variables of the Discrete Event System is as follows. Let v be the set of tasks or jobs used in the system, r the set of resources that implement/perform the tasks, u the set of inputs or parts entering the DES and y the set of outputs or finished parts/products of the DES. The DEC Model State Equation is then described as

$$\bar{x} = F_v \otimes \bar{v} \oplus F_r \otimes \bar{r} \oplus F_u \otimes \bar{u} \oplus F_{uc} \otimes \bar{u}_C \tag{1}$$

where: $\bar{x}$ is the task or state logical vector, F_v is the job sequencing matrix, F_r is the resource requirements matrix, F_u is the input matrix, F_{uc} is the conflict resolution matrix, and u_c is a conflict resolution vector. This DEC equation is performed in the AND/OR algebra. That is, symbol $\otimes$ represents logical "AND" multiplication, and symbol $\oplus$ represents logical "OR" addition, and the over-bar means logical negation.

From the model state equation, four interpretations can be obtained:

1. The job sequencing matrix F_v reflects the states to be launched based on the current finished jobs. It is the matrix used by [*Steward 81ab*] and others [*Whitney 91*].
2. The resource requirement matrix F_r represents the set of resources needed to fire possible job states. It is the matrix used by [*Kusiak et al. 90-92*].
3. The input matrix F_u determines initial states to fire for input parts to the system.
4. The conflict resolution matrix F_{uc} prioritizes states launched from the external dispatching input u_C, which has to be derived via some decision making algorithm [*Panwalkar et al. 77, Graves 81*].

The state logic obtained from the state equation is used to calculate the jobs to be done (or task commands), to release resources, and to inform about the final products produced by the system. These three important features are obtained by using the three equations:

Start Equation (task commands) $v_S = S_v \otimes x$ (2)

Resource Release Equation $r_S = S_r \otimes x$ (3)

Product Output Equation $y = S_y \otimes x$ (4)

where S_v, S_r, and S_y are the **job start matrix**, **resource release matrix**, and the **job release matrix**, respectively. Figure 7.1 shows the DEC based on the matrix formulation as used to control job sequences and resource assignment of a workcell. Subscript "s" on the vectors v and r denotes "start." Thus, v and r are outputs from the workcell measured by sensors, while v_s and r_s are commands to the workcell to begin jobs or set resources as "released."

The relationship of these matrices with PNs is shown in Section 7.3.1.

7.3.1 Matrix Analysis of Petri-Nets

The PN is a valuable tool in flexible manufacturing modeling for deadlock analysis and control [*Murata 89, Xing 96*]. In particular, structural constructions defined in PN notation, such as *siphon* and *trap* structures are very useful in characterizing deadlock conditions in systems [*Ezpeleta 95*]. We show next the relationship between PN structures and our matrix formulation structures.

There is a very close relationship between the DEC just described and PNs. The incidence matrix [*Peterson 81*] of the PN is obtained by defining the activity completion matrix and the activity start matrix by

Activity Completion Matrix $F = [F_u \quad F_v \quad F_r \quad F_y]$ (5)

Activity Start Matrix $S = [S_u^T \quad S_v^T \quad S_r^T \quad S_y^T]^T$ (6)

Then, the PN's incidence matrix is defined as

$$M = S^T - F = [S_u^T - F_u, \ S_v^T - F_v, \ S_r^T - F_r, \ S_y^T - F_y]$$ (7)

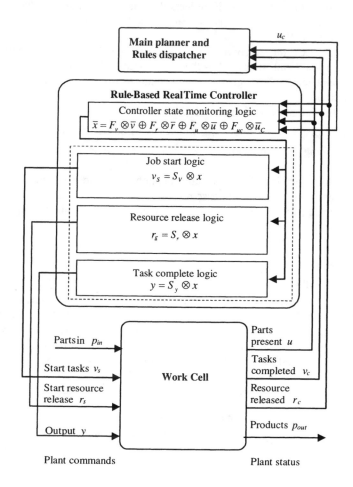

Figure 7.1. Matrix formulation DES controller.

If we define X as a set containing the elements x (the state controller vector from Equation (1)), and A as the set of activities containing the vectors v and r, i.e. $(A = \begin{bmatrix} v \\ r \end{bmatrix})$, then it can be shown that (A, X, F^T, S) is a PN ([*Pastravanu et al. 94ab*] and Section 7.2.). This allows one to directly draw the PN of a system given the matrices F and S.

The elements of matrices F and S, which are "zero" or "one," can be related directly with a PN as shown in Figure 7.2. In fact, F^T is the PN input incidence matrix and S is the PN output incidence matrix. The $F_{v\ i,j}$ (i,j elements of F_v) which are set to "one," state that to fire transition x_i, the job v_j needs to be finished; the $F_{r\ i,j}$ elements set to "one," indicate that to fire transition x_i, the resource r_j needs to be available; the $S_{v\ i,j}$ elements set to "one," indicate that to start job v_j, the transition x_i needs to be finished; and, the $S_{r\ i,j}$ elements are set to "one" to indicate that the resource r_i is released after the transition x_j is finished.

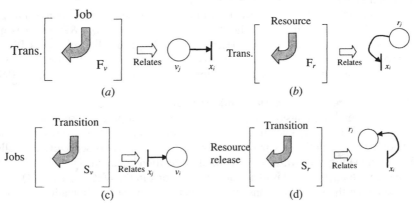

Figure 7.2. Relationship of the matrices with PN: (*a*) job-sequencing matrix F_v, (*b*) resource requirement matrix F_r, (*c*) job start matrix S_v, (*d*) resource release matrix S_r.

7.3.1.1   PN Marking Transition Equation

It is common in PN theory [*Murasta 89*] to represent in matrix form the sets of function arcs I and O, as described in Section 7.1. This is, $I_{ij} = 1$ if place j is an input place of transition i, and $O_{ij} = 1$ if place j is an output place of transition i, with all the other elements set to 0. Matrix I represents the inputs to the transitions, and O the outputs from the transitions. Then, the **PN incidence matrix** is defined as

$$W = O - I .\tag{8}$$

For instance, its matrix form in terms of activity completion and activity start matrices was introduced in Equation (7), so that $W = M$.

Let m(t) denote the PN marking vector m at time t. In terms of the PN incidence matrix, one can write the *PN marking transition equation*

$$m(t_2) = m(t_1) + W^T \tau = m(t_1) + (O - I)^T \tau \qquad (9)$$

where $t_1 < t_2$, and τ is a vector denoting which transitions have fired between times t_1 and t_2; element $\tau_i = n_i$ if the i-th transition has fired n_i times in the interval.

This matrix transition equation can be constructed using this DE matrix formulation. If the marking vector $m(t)$ from a PN is defined as

$$m(t) = [u(t)^T, \ v(t)^T, r(t)^T, u_D(t)^T]^T \qquad (10)$$

for a specific time iteration t, then the PN marking transition equation [*Murata 89, Peterson 81*] is

$$m(t+1) = m(t) + M^T x = m(t) + [S^T - F]x(t). \qquad (11)$$

Unfortunately, this equation is *not* a complete description of a PN since it does not take into account the order of firing of the transitions, or whether a given transition can actually fire at any point in time. Thus, the matrix approach to PN has yielded some valuable insight [*Buzacott et al. 86, Murata 89*], but was not extended to provide a complete description of the firing dynamics of a PN. A complete dynamical description in matrix form is presented in Section 7.3.2. But first, we present matrix development of important behavioral constructions of PNs.

7.3.2 Complete Dynamical Description for DES

The marking transition Equation (11) provides a partial description [*Peterson 1981*], but it is not known in the literature how to generate the allowable firing vector $x(t)$. This deficiency is repaired by using the matrix-based DEC controller Equation (1) together with the PN marking transition equation. The key is to note that the vector $x(t)$ in (11) is identical to the vector x in the DEC Equation (1).

To put the DEC equations into a format convenient for simulation, one may write (2-1) as $\overline{x} = F \otimes \overline{m}$ or

$$x(t) = \overline{F} \oplus \overline{\overline{m}}(t) = \overline{[F_u \quad F_v \quad F_r \quad F_{uc}]} \oplus \overline{\overline{[u \quad v \quad r \quad u_c]}}(t) \qquad (12)$$

The double negation over $m(t)$ is used since we are assuming that the system is ordinary, i.e., only one resource-job type is needed at a time to fire a transition (associated with ordinary PNs, see section 7.2) So, for every member a_k of the vector $m(t)$, the double negation is used to obtain "one" if $a_k \geq 1$ (i.e., resources are available, or jobs completed), or "zero" if $a_k = 0$ (i.e. no resources are available).

To be able to provide a complete dynamical description of the system, one has to incorporate the ***time durations*** of the jobs and the time required for resource releases. We do this by analyzing the transient *Timed Place PN* [*López-Mellado et al. 96*].

Since the duration time of jobs vary for different machines or resources, equation (11) must be divided in two parts, so that we can distinguish properly in the marking vector pending and finished jobs. Therefore, $m(t)$ is split into two vectors, one representing all available resources and current finished jobs, the available marking vector m_a, and the other showing the jobs in process, the pending marking vector m_p. In this way, we are able to keep track of the status of all pending jobs. Note that only the available resources and finished jobs m_a are allowed to be used to fire transitions. Then, the overall marking vector is defined by

$$m(t) = m_a(t) + m_p(t)$$

(13)

Splitting $m(t)$ into two vectors means that the PN marking transition Equation (11) must also be split into two equations. The first part of the equation, representing the pending marking vector, is

$$m_p(t+1) = m_p(t) + S^T x(t)$$

(14)

This equation adds all new jobs into the vector m_p. This vector also contains any unfinished jobs currently in process.

The other part of the equation, representing the available marking vector, is

$$m_a(t+1) = m_a(t) - F x(t)$$

(15)

This equation takes away tokens from m_a corresponding to which transitions they are used to fire. Note that adding (14) and (15) gives (11).

When a transition fires, the tokens go into the pending vector $m_p(t)$, where they stay until the job is finished. Then, the token is moved into $m_a(t)$, where it may be used to fire subsequent transitions. Therefore, to keep track of jobs in progress, it is necessary now to move tokens from $m_p(t)$ to $m_a(t)$, when jobs are completed.

In real applications on actual manufacturing processes, we will be sensing the expiration of such finished jobs by either using sensors (e.g., proximity, tactile, etc.) or via notification from the machines or resources. We shall discuss this issue further in our implementation section.

For the purposes of computer simulation, on the other hand, we must find a way to keep track of time lapsed in the processing of jobs. To keep track of the time duration of jobs, we may identify the time required for all jobs or resources by creating a vector *Time*. *Time* will have the same size as the marking vector m(t) in (2-10) and may be defined as

$$Time = [O, vtimes^T, rtimes^T, O]^T,$$

(16)

where $vtimes^T$ is the vector containing the average duration times of each job in v, and $rtimes^T$ is a vector containing the times needed by each resource in r to become ready to work after being released.

Equation (12) may use only the available marking vector m_a to generate valid transition vectors x. The pending marking vector m_p has to be analyzed at each discrete event iteration to check whether or not any pending jobs are finished. The corresponding completed jobs are then moved into m_a. However, for deadlock avoidance purposes, both m_a and m_p should be considered. The use of marking m_p is explained in the deadlock sections. Then, to keep track of the times remaining in each job during computer simulations, we introduce a small constant sample period, t_{sample}. We also define a second vector of the same size as *Time*, and compatibly partitioned, which we call T_{pend}. This vector contains the time remaining for each job, and for each resource release. T_{pend} is initially set equal to zero. When any token appears in m_p, the corresponding entry of T_{pend} is set equal to the job duration entry from the duration vector *Time*. Then, each time there is a discrete event iteration, we subtract t_{sample} from every time in T_{pend}. When any entry of T_{pend} becomes zero or negative, it means that the corresponding job is finished, or resource has been released. Then, the corresponding entry of m_p is decremented and the corresponding entry of m_a is incremented. The job or resource is now available to fire subsequent transitions.

This procedure is easy to write in equation form for the case where there can be only one token in each place. This means that only one job is allowed to be serviced at a time by each resource (e.g., only one job per machine at any given time). In this case, one may write

$$T_{pend}(t+1) = diag\{ m_p(t) \} [T_{pend}(t) - t_{sample}] + diag \{S^T x(t)\} \ Time$$
(17)

where $diag\{S^T x(t)\}$ is a diagonal matrix formed by writing the elements of vector $\{.\}$ on the diagonal of a matrix. The last term adds the entire time duration needed for the job to T_{pend} for any jobs newly fired at time $t+1$. The first term decreases by t_{sample} the times left on every pending job or resource release. The finished jobs are obtained by checking whether any element from T_{pend} is less than or equal to zero, indicating jobs just finished.

Jobs that are finished must be moved from m_p to m_a. To write this in equation form, define a third vector m_{finish} of the same dimension as and compatibly partitioned with *Time*. Whenever any element from T_{pend} becomes less than or equal to zero, the corresponding element of the expiration vector m_{finish} is set equal to "one" (all other elements are set to zero). Then, the marking vectors can be updated by

$$m_p(t+1) = m_p(t) - m_{finish}(t), \text{ and}$$
(18)

$$m_a(t) = m_a(t) + m_{finish}(t).$$
(19)

Finally, one computes (2-22).

In summary, one discrete event iteration consists of computing $x(t)$ using (2-19), then using (2-24), then determining m_{finish}, and using (2-25), (2-26), and finally (2-22) again. A graphical representation of this process is shown in Figure 7.3.

If there exists more than one token in each place, i.e., more than one job may be accomplished simultaneously by one resource, then (17)-(19) must be modified in a straightforward manner, by expanding vectors for as many as pending jobs are in place. Similar equations were used in simulations presented by [*Tacconi et. al 97*], who did not include deadlock-free dispatching supervision. This is to be detailed in deadlock sections.

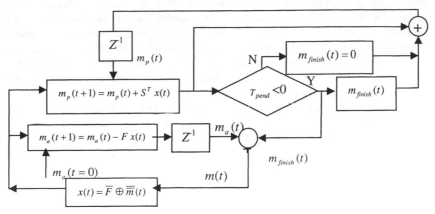

Figure 7.3. Graphical dynamics of PN markings.

Thus, a *complete dynamical description* of the DES is provided by the PN marking eq. (2-11), which is decomposed into Equations (14) and (15), plus the DEC equation (12). The job time durations are added using (17)-(18). This allows one to use these equations to fully simulate the controlled workcell shown in Figure 7.1.

7.4 SIMULATION AND IMPLEMENTATION OF THE DEC

This section provides the simulation and implementation of the matrix DEC for the supervision of an intelligent material handling (IMH) cell from the University of Texas at Arlington's Automation & Robotics Research Institute (ARRI). Then, we show that the actual implementation and the simulated system give commensurate results. The IMH cell is a multipart reentrant flow-line (MRF) system. The objective of this chapter is to show the versatility of the system developed with this matrix formulation. This DEC permits implementing different methodologies for conflict resolution, as well as optimization of the resource assignment and part throughput. Technical information given includes the development of the DEC in LabVIEW and its simulation using MATLAB®.

7.4.1 Intelligent Material Handling (IMH) Cell Description

The IMH cell at the University of Texas at Arlington's ARRI is composed of three robots, three conveyors, ten sensors and two simulated machines. Different configuration of reentrant flow-line problems can be accomplished with this structure. The image and part flow-line for a specific layout structure of the IMH cell are depicted in Figures 7.4 and 7.5.

For this specific layout structure, the robot defined as R1, a CRS robot, can perform four different tasks. Two tasks relate to picking up parts types A and B from the *Input-parts* area, which are to be placed in the conveyor denominated B1. The other two tasks relate to picking up final products A and B from conveyor B3 and placing them in the output area. A PUMA robot, R2, performs three different tasks: pick up parts A from conveyor B1 to place them in M1 (machine one), pick up parts B from conveyor B1 to place them in conveyor B2, and pick up parts A from M1 to be placed in conveyor B2. The Adept robot, R3, also performs three different tasks: pick up parts A from conveyor B2, to place them in conveyor B3, pick up parts B from conveyor B2 to place them in M2 (the machine two), and pick up parts B from M2 to be placed in conveyor B3.

Then, for this layout, three robots manipulate two different parts while two of them manipulate reentrant flow of parts. Machines M1 and M2 are simulated by activating valve-air cylinders controlled from a PC.

This configuration of the IMH cell is a MRF problem, shown in flow-line form (without showing transportation jobs, conveyor jobs) in Figure 7.6. All robotic resources are shared and manipulate two part types A and B.

Figure 7.4. Picture of the IMH-cell from ARRI.

The DEC matrices in Equation (1) (some of them shown in Figure 7.7), can be directly written down by considering Figures 7.6 and 7.8, which show both job sequencing and resource assignment. Also, it has been demonstrated in [*Harris et al. 01*], that DEC's matrices can be derived for automatic planning using polynomial-time algorithms, once providing assembly trees and resource requirements matrix [*Murata 89*].

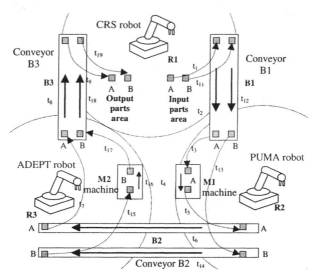

Figure 7.5. Layout of the IMH-cell from ARRI.

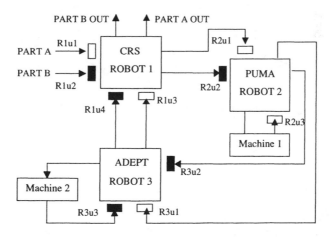

Figure 7.6. Multipart reentrant flow-line problem.

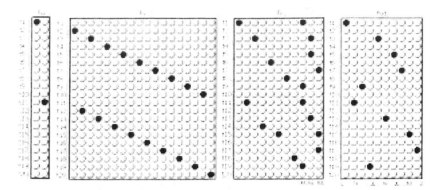

Figure 7.7. Set of matrices F_u, F_v, F_r and F_{uc}.

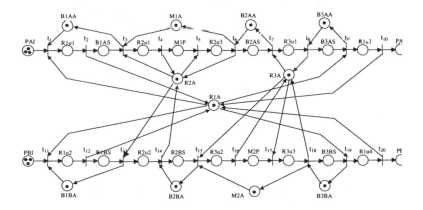

Figure 7.8. Petri net associated with the layout of the IMH-cell.

The PN from Figure 7.8 shows two linear paths representing the job sequences to manufacture products for the IMH cell layout. The size of the matrices F_v, F_r, F_u, and F_{uc} for this specific design/structure are 20x18, 20x11, 20x2 and 20x10, respectively. Following the design directions from [*Lewis et al. 94*], and considering the order of the columns of F_u as {PAI, PBI}, F_v as {R1u1, R1u2, B1AS, B1BS, R2u1 ,R2u2, M1P, B2BS, R2u3, R3u2, B2AS, M2P, R3u1, R3u3, B3AS, B3BS, R1u3, R1u4}, and F_r as {B1AA, B1BA, M1A, B2BA, B2AA, M2A, B3AA, B3BA, R1A, R2A, R3A}, we obtain the set of matrices shown in Figure 7.7 (black and gray circles, respectively, indicate "1" and "0" in matrices.) F_{uc} is the conflict resolution matrix constructed from columns on F_r containing more than one token. This means that resources corresponding to those columns from F_r are shared resources. Then, for each token on these columns, one column is constructed in F_{uc} having only one token in the corresponding position for each repeated token in F_r. The use of this conflict resolution matrix is explained in Section 7.4.3.

The sparse position of ones in matrices depends on the order one enumerates transitions, and the number of jobs and resources present in the design/system. The nomenclature used in the PN is as follows: "PxI" means input parts 'x', "RXuY" means jobs 'Y' is been accomplished by robot 'X', "BxyS" means that path for product type 'y' in buffer (or conveyor) 'x' is busy, "MxP" means machine 'x' is busy, "BxyA" means that path for product type 'y' in buffer (or conveyor) 'x' is available, "MxA" means machine 'x' is available, "RxA" means that robot 'x' is available.

In similar fashion matrices S_u, S_r, S_v and S_{ud} are written down as shown in [*Lewis et al. 94, Huang 95, Tacconi et al. 97*]. The PN associated with the IMH cell layout, which models the sequence of operations of the robots, conveyors and machines, is depicted in Figure 7.8 This PN, as noted earlier, was drawn directly from the DEC matrices F and S. This PN shows two linear paths representing the job sequences to manufacture products A and B. The upper linear path contains the operations associated with part A. Between these linear paths the shared robot resources R1, R2 and R3 are located. Outside the two linear paths, the machine and conveyor resources are located. Note that instead of having three different resources for the conveyors B1, B2 and B3, six different resources are used. This is because of the two different materials paths on each conveyor. For example, conveyor B1 has paths B1A and B1B, which are denoted in the PN as B1AA and B1BA when they are available, and denoted as B1AS and B1BS when they are carrying material.

7.4.2 Simulation of DES

Once having the matrices generated via standard industrial engineering structures such as bill of materials, assembly tree, and resource requirements matrix, a complete dynamical description is obtained via Equations (2-9) and (2-12)-(2-19). Using these Equations, one can perform computer simulations of the workcell like those provided by [*Tacconi et al. 97*]. The time history of the simulation of the IMH cell using augmented last buffer fast-serve (ALBFS) conflict resolution strategy [*Mireles et al. 01b*] is shown in Figure 7.9 This simulation shows an ideal time history development of jobs. We mean ideal time by considering that each time duration of robotic and conveyor jobs endure exactly the same time.

In our simulation, machine job times are fixed for every machine. These machines are remained pending until the "machined" part is released. We considered machining times 6.4 and 4.5 seconds for M1 and M2, respectively. We believe these short machining times provide more diversity in the conditions or states of the cell while in operation, allowing different noticeable process time of products for different dispatching rules.

Figure 7.9 shows a graph representing the discrete events occurring in the workcell. All possible job-events of the workcell are shown on the right side of the graph. For example, the upper row shows R1u1, which is the time history of the robot R1 (the CRS robot) accomplishing job one, i.e., every "high" level in this event represents R1 performing job one. When the signal is low, the robot is not performing job one.

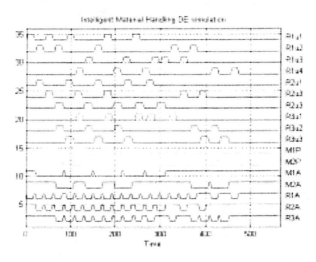

Figure 7.9. Simulation of the workcell using ALBFS conflict resolution.

From Figure 7.9, if we analyze the events/jobs having R1u3 and R1u4 titled on its right side, which are the last jobs needed to manufacture products A and B shown in PN of Figure 7.8, we can see that the DEC prefers to machine products B rather than products A. Five products B are manufactured after running the cell for 365 seconds, while five products A are manufactured in 475 seconds, a 110 seconds of difference. By changing the conflict resolution strategy u_c one can change the order of importance that the DEC assigns to manufacture the products, i.e., one might give preference to products A over B, or give them the same "level" of importance. For proper dispatching rule selection, see [*Panwalkar 77, Kumar 94*].

7.4.3 Conflict Resolution Strategies

One of the strengths of the matrix-based DEC is that different shared resources conflict resolution strategies can be implemented by suitably computing u_c, the conflict resolution input. From the job flow and resource requirement information as contained in Figure 7.6, we are able to formulate the matrices needed for our DEC. But one must be careful, since the marking transition equation does not identify or distinguish the tasks used by each resource (i.e., each robot or machine), it is possible that more than one task is fired for a single available resource.

For example, if transitions t_3 and t_{13} fire at the same discrete event, both jobs R2U1 and R2U2 for R2 are dispatched (i.e., robot R2, PUMA robot, can pick up part A or part B from conveyor B1), which is impossible. Therefore, a conflict resolution strategy for the shared resources must be used. By adding an extra matrix, F_{uc}, one can administrate or sequence the desired jobs.

Note that the last three columns of F_r correspond to the shared resource RxA's, or robots 'x' available (R1A, R2A and R3A.) If we take a look at Figure 7.7, we see that there exist more than one 'one' in each of these columns. This means that while using Equation (1), we can fire several transitions for a single robot availability (i.e., a single robot is used for more than one job). Since it is not possible for a robot to accomplish two jobs at the same time, by adding an extra matrix called conflict resolution matrix, F_{uc}, we can control which job we want to be fired depending on the specific situation in the cell.

F_{uc} is constructed by creating a new column for each 'one' appearing in F_r for the shared resources. By doing this, every time we get a conflict in any of our robot resources, we simply set to 'one' the corresponding element from the marking vector u_c which corresponds to the desired job from the shared resource, and set the other elements to 'zero'. For example, if we set to 'one' the marking corresponding to first column of F_{uc}, and set to 'zero' the next three markings, we guarantee that only our transition t_1 will be fired. This is, R1A will be assigned to job R1u1, and any other job from R1 will be excluded. This set of dispatching rules is a set of messages generated from the supervisor via conflict resolution input u_c, shown in Figure 7.1. A complete detailed firing rule example using F_{uc} is shown in [*Lewis et al 94*].

Shared-resource dispatching in multi path reentrant flow-lines is not an easy topic. Some techniques are given in [*Kumar 93*]. The following is the conflict resolution used in the IMH cell for layout from Figure 7.5 It is an augmented version of the last-buffer-first-serve LBFS, we call it ALBFS, modified for multi path systems. The following conflict resolution logic generates proper u_c using ALBFS to properly dispatch jobs. To understand this dispatching rule, we use the following constructions. From **current marking vector** m, we calculate first an **intermediate marking vector** m_i, which might contain conflicts. Define $m_x(y: z)$ as a function that obtains the marking corresponding to the resource (or job) z from the column of matrix y, where m_x can be markings m_i or m, and y can be matrices F_r or F_{uc}. Notice that $m(F_{uc}: RxUy)$ corresponds to the marking of u_c that dispatches robotic job "y" from robotic resource "x."

Depending on the way one selects the conflict resolution strategy to generate u_c, different dispatching rules can be selected. These fall mainly into two categories: Buffer and Part/Machine [*Panwalkar et al. 77, Lewis et al. 93a*]. Examples of the buffer category are: first-buffer-first-serve, last-buffer-first-serve, shortest non-full queue, shortest remaining capacity, and shortest queue next. Examples of the part/machine category are: shortest imminent operation time, largest imminent operation time, shortest remaining processing time, largest remaining processing time, machine with least work and least slack time.

if m_i (F_r: R1A)<0; (i.e., resource R1 requested more than once)
    if (m_i(F_{uc}: R1U4)==0) (i.e., job R1U4 was dispatched)
        m(F_{uc}: R1U1) = 0; m(F_{uc}: R1U2) = 0; m(F_{uc}: R1U3) = 0; m(F_{uc}: R1U4) = 1;
    else if (m_i(Fuc: R1U3)==0)
        m(F_{uc}: R1U1) = 0; m(F_{uc}: R1U2) = 0; m(F_{uc}: R1U3) = 1; m(F_{uc}: R1U4) = 0;
    else if (m_i(F_{uc}: R1U1)==0)
        m(F_{uc}: R1U1) =1; m(F_{uc}: R1U2) = 0; m(F_{uc}: R1U3) = 0; m(F_{uc}: R1U4) = 0;
    else
        m(F_{uc}: R1U1) = 0; m(F_{uc}: R1U2) = 1; m(F_{uc}: R1U3) = 0; m(F_{uc}: R1U4) = 0;
    end
end
if m_i (F_r, R2A)<0;
    if (m_i(F_{uc}: R2U3)==0)
        m(F_{uc}: R2U1) = 0; m(F_{uc}: R2U2) = 0; m(F_{uc}: R2U3) = 1;
    else if (m_i (Fuc: R2U1)==0)
        m(F_{uc}: R2U1) = 1; m(F_{uc}: R2U2) = 0; m(F_{uc}: R2U3) = 0;
    else
        m(F_{uc}: R2U1) =0; m(F_{uc}: R2U2) = 1; m(F_{uc}: R2U3) = 0;
    end
end
if m_i (F_r, R3A)<0;
    if (m_i(F_{uc}: R3U3)==0)
        m(F_{uc}: R3U1) = 0; m(F_{uc}: R3U2) = 0; m(F_{uc}: R3U3) = 1;
    else if (m_i(F_{uc}: R3U2)==0)
        m(F_{uc}: R3U1) = 0; m(F_{uc}: R3U2) = 1; m(F_{uc}: R3U3) = 0;
    else
        m(F_{uc}: R3U1) =1; m(F_{uc}: R3U2) = 0; m(F_{uc}: R3U3) = 0;
    end
end

7.4.4   Implementation of the DEC on the IMH Cell

The DEC was implemented using Equations (1)-(7), (11), and (12) in Lab-VIEW graphical programming environment. In LabVIEW, we can sequence and control different processes at the same time. The processes we are interested in are jobs implemented in manufacturing processes, like robotic jobs, machining jobs and transferring parts using conveyors. One big problem is to synchronize such processes and control different robotic and machine jobs. This problem can be solved by using this matrix formulation. In comparison with Figure 7.1, in Figure 7.10 we try to represent inside the dashed lines the DEC implemented in a PC to control the IMH cell. This PC-based IMH controller has three serial ports that interact with the three robots which sequence the jobs. It also has a DAQ card that receives digital signals from capacitive proximity sensors, which sense the status of parts in conveyors, and sends digital signals to activate machine jobs.

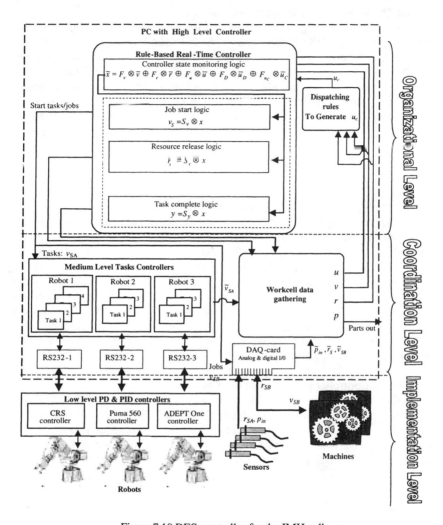

Figure 7.10 DES controller for the IMH-cell.

7.4.4.1 Three Levels of Intelligent Control

Note that in Figure 7.10 one can find the three levels of intelligent control depicted in [*Saridis 88-95, Antsaklis et al. 92*]. The first level is organization, which is the highest level of intelligence and in our case is our DES controller structure, the matrix formulation. The second level of intelligence is the coordination level. This level contains a set of independent modules that are composed by robot programming sentences encrypted in VAL-like commands [*Shimano 79, Larson 83*] (VAL: Victor's Assembly Language, from its creator Victor Sheinman). These program modules define the jobs to be done by the robots (i.e. sequence of VAL commands needed to command robots to perform pick and place tasks.) Then, once the task or job is selected by the intelligent organization level, the coordination level sequence the steps needed for each of these jobs. So, for the case of robotic jobs, the IMH cell's coordination level sends commands sequentially to the appropriate robot to accomplish the desired task.

The main purpose of our implementation is to present the advantages and great potential of the organization level, the DEC's matrix formulation, i.e. the controller that decides which jobs to fire and/or dispatch. The last level of intelligence is the execution level, which is accomplished by the controllers of the robots. For the IMH cell controller, after each independent robot-controller receive each VAL-like command via serial port, the robot-controllers accomplish low level control calculations and strategies such as interpolation, **proportional derivative (PD) control, proportional integrate derivative (PID) control**, fuzzy logic control, neural network control or any other low level control strategy to manipulate the robotic arms.

7.4.4.2 DE Controller in Graphical Environment

The purpose of this section is to explain the development of the DES controller using LabVIEW [*Mireles et al. 01ab*]. The key equations of the matrix formulation, once all matrices F and S are defined, are the transition equation (11) and the allowable marking vector (10). As stated in the first sections, this equations use logical AND and OR matrix algebra, replacing the multiplication by logic AND and addition by logic OR. Figure 7.11 shows the graphical development of Equations (10) and (11). The internal FOR loop on this Figure 7.12 is showing the label "MULTOA(X,Y)," which obtains the allowable marking vector, while the external part relates the marking transition Equation (11). The input parameters to this diagram are F, S', $m(t)$, and *iterations*. "*Iterations*" variable came from Equation (11). The term $m(t+1)$ from (11) receives the next marking vector. But if *iterations* is set to 2, the diagram will calculate the marking vector as if $m(t+2)$ were used in (11).

The entire diagram from Figure 7.12 is used as a single LabVIEW-block (or function) in the drawing for the DEC shown in Figure 7.13. The LabVIEW block for the drawing from Figure 7.12 is shown in Figure 7.11, which represents the marking transition Equation (11).

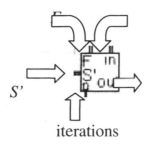

Figure 7.11. Block of marking transition Equation (2).

External FOR loop

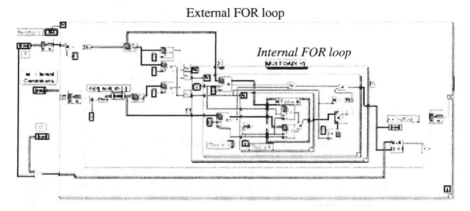

Figure 7.12. Graphical development of the allowable marking vector.

In Figure 7.13, the circle for the DES IMH cell controller is shown. On the left of the WHILE "Main loop," the set of matrices F and S are depicted. The "Fix Uds" LabVIEW-block function is also found inside the Main loop. This block is depicted in Figure 7.14, and actualizes the states a_k of the marking vector $m(t)$ related with the conflict resolution states, it set all $m(t)$ Fuds to "one", i.e., all robotic jobs are "available" for activation. Later, if a conflict is detected on any of the robots, a conflict resolution block will deactivate undesirable states that were activated by "Fix Uds." Inside the main loop, an internal loop is used to determinate the allowed marking vector using marking transition Equation (11). If any of the states a_k is less than zero, i.e., one or more of the resources are required to perform more than one job, then the conflict resolution subroutine is accomplished.

Therefore, an internal case loop is used to change the marking vector as discussed in the conflict resolution section.

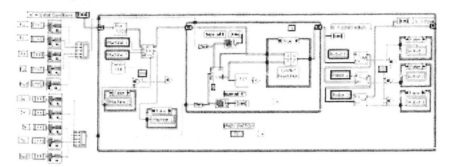

Figure 7.13. Graphical development of the controller.

Initial states of

marking vector   the
marking vector

Figure 7.14. Block "Fix Uds" initializes conflict resolution states.

By applying the conflict resolution strategy used in our simulations, the real IMH cell DES output behaves as shown in Figure 7.16 This Figure was obtained in real-time directly from our DEC implementation in the graphical environment, LabVIEW. Figure 7.15 shows the discrete duration of the robotic jobs. Notice that the time duration of the real IMH workcell presented in the simulation run, is in terms of discrete event intervals, while the simulation shown Figure 7.9 is in terms of time. In comparison, only small deviations between our previous simulation and the real system behavior are noticed. The differences are due to the phenomena produced by the differences in time duration of the jobs. Since the PC-machine is constantly interacting with the robots and ordering them different jobs, i.e., accomplishing coordination level of intelligence, this time interaction varies depending on which jobs are fired at a specific moment causing the robotic job durations to vary. However, by having more computational power or implementing the coordination level of intelligence directly on the robots and not in the same PC-machine, this phenomenon can be reduced.

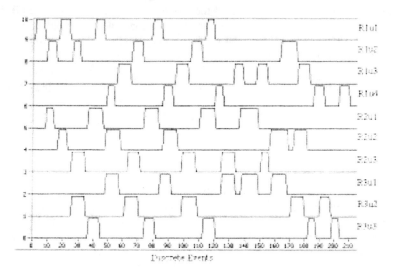

Figure 7.15. Implementation of the real IMH workcell using ALBFS conflict resolution.

In summary, the key equations of the matrix formulation, once all matrices *F* and *S* are defined, are the transition equation (11) and the allowable matrix vector (10). A conflict resolution strategy is used in the internal loop of Figure 7.13, which block diagram shows label "conflict resolution." After the internal loop is finished, the final conditions of the marking vector are obtained for the next DE. At this time, we are able to send appropriate job tasks to resources. Figure 7.11 shows the LabVIEW block implementation of equations (9) and (10). The algorithm used in this block is the corresponding MATLAB algorithm MULTOA(X,Y) used by [*Tacconi et al. 97*], which obtains the allowable marking vector for the next DE iteration. The input parameters to this block are *F*, S^T, *m(t)*, and *iterations*. "*iterations*" variable came from equation (11). The term *m(t+1)* from (11) receive the next marking vector. But if *iterations* is set to 2, the diagram will calculate the marking vector as if *m(t+2)* were used in (11).

Also, by applying the conflict resolution strategy ALBFS, the IMH cell DES behaves as shown in Figure 7.15. This Figure was obtained in real-time directly from our DEC implementation in the graphical environment, LabVIEW. This Figure shows the discrete time duration of the robotic jobs. Notice that the time duration of the real IMH workcell run is in terms of discrete event intervals, while the simulation shown on Figure 7.9 is in terms of time. The total discrete time duration differs by 12 seconds, but what we believe is important is their consistency in the dispatching sequence. In this figure, the event times for the machines are not shown since we administrated the "machining" time duration by controlling the activation of air-pressure valves from the PC DAQ card. We allowed exact time duration of such jobs and we allowed the machines to remain pending until the corresponding robotic job releases the part from the machine (as we did in simulations). Notice in Figure 7.15 that all same robotic jobs have different time durations from each other, particularity of real manufacturing systems.

In comparison, only small deviations between our previous simulation and the real system behavior are noticed. The differences are due to the phenomena produced by the differences in time duration of the jobs.

7.5   Matrix Analysis of Deadlock Internal Structures in MRF Systems

In this section, we present a least restrictive deadlock-free dispatching policy for MRF systems. MRF systems are described and defined in Section 7.5.1. The techniques suggested for supervision of deadlock avoidance are generally based on two tools, graphic-net theory (of circular waits among resources) and PNs. That is, proposed approaches for deadlock avoidance in MRF systems use either one, or the other approach. An advantage of the matrix framework from Section 7.2, is that these tools can be described in matrix form, such that they can be combined for analysis of deadlock in MRF systems. This means that the matrix framework presented in section 7.2 for DES yields computationally efficient algorithms for analyzing the structures of MRF systems and determining constructions needed for deadlock-free dispatching and supervision. Regular systems lack second level deadlock constructions on its structural composition. We present rigorous analysis of deadlock structures for MRF systems, how to develop deadlock-free notions, and identification of a system's regularity using matrices. Two main approaches for deadlock avoidance are used: a one-step look-ahead technique, and other integrating supervisory network to the PN system.

In this section, we also show an example illustrating these constructions.

7.5.1 Multipart Reentrant Flow-Line (MRF) System Definitions.

A MRF system is defined considering the following assumptions, which basically define the sort of discrete-part manufacturing systems that can be described by a PN:

- No preemption. A resource cannot be removed from a job until it is complete.
- Mutual exclusion. A single resource can be used for only one job at a time.
- Hold while waiting. A process holds the resources already allocated to it until it has all resources required to perform a job.
- We assume there are no machine failures.
- Each job uses only one resource.
- After each resource executes one job, it is released immediately.
- Parts flow through a deterministic routing path.

MRF systems having assumptions just described are discussed in the rest of this chapter. Slight differences in assumptions are discussed in later chapters. For purposes of the analysis of these MRF systems, a PN model for MRF systems will be introduced below [*Gurel et al. 00*].

For a certain general class of MRF systems, define $P = \overline{P} \cup PI \cup PO$, with $\overline{P} = R \cup J \cup P_o$, where the places in R, J, P_o, PI and PO respectively represent the availability of resources, jobs, pallets, input of parts, and output of products. Let $\eta = |\overline{P}|$. The transitions represent decisions or rules for the starting/completion of jobs and assignment/release of resources.

In the PN model of an MRF system, a path that starts with a place in PI and terminates in a place in PO is called a ***part-path***. Associated with part-path $j \in \Pi$ is the sequence of job places J^j so that $J = \cup_j J^j$. Let the set of transitions along part-path j be $x_1^j, x_2^j, \ldots, x_{L_j}^j$. Part-path j may have a place in P_o, denoted as r_0^j, which means that each part entering the cell is fixed during its job sequence (i.e., deterministic routing). Therefore $r_0^j \in {}^\bullet x_1^j$, $r_0^j \notin {}^\bullet x_i^l$, $i \neq 1$, and $r_0^j \in x_{L_j}^j{}^\bullet$, $r_0^j \notin x_i^j{}^\bullet$, $i \neq L_j$. Places in PI and PO have, respectively, no input transitions and no output transitions. Places in R always occur off the part-paths, with $R = R_{ns} \cup R_s$, where R_{ns} and R_s are the sets of *non shared and shared* resource places. Denote by $R(J_i^j)$ the resource used for job J_i^j. For any $r \in R$, define the *job set of r* as $J(r) = r^{\bullet\bullet} \cap J$, and for any set $Q \subset R$, let $J(Q) = \cup_{r \in Q} J(r)$.

The existence of an available resource, an available pallet, an ongoing job, a part in or a product out is indicated by tokens in their respective places. It is assumed that places in PI are always marked and places in PO are always empty. The marking m: $\overline{P} \rightarrow Z$, where Z is the set of non-negative integers, represents the distribution of tokens in the places of set $\overline{P}$. The initial marking m_0 assigns tokens only to places in R such that $m_0(p) \neq 0$ if and only if $p \in R$. Denote by $\{N, m_0\}$ a PN N with initial marking m_0. Let Reach(m) denote the set of all markings **reachable** from m. A transition is *dead* with respect to m if there exists no $m' \in$ Reach(m) that enables it. A place p is said to be *dead* if $m(p) = 0$ and there exists no $m' \in$ Reach(m) such that $m'(p) > 0$.

The following architecture defines the formal specifications for the type of MRF systems considered in the remaining of this chapter.

Definition [MRF]. Define MRF as the class of multipart reentrant flow-line systems with PN N satisfying the following properties [*Gurel et al. 00*]:

$\forall p \in \overline{P}, {}^\bullet p \cap p^\bullet = \varnothing$;

$\forall k \in \Pi, x_1^{k\bullet} \cap \overline{P} \backslash J = \varnothing$ and ${}^\bullet x_{L_i}^k \cap \overline{P} \backslash J = \varnothing$;

$\forall J_i^k \in J, |R(J_i^k)| = 1$ and $R(J_i^k) \neq R(J_{i+1}^k)$;

$$\forall J_i^k \in J, |J_i^{k\ \bullet}|=1;$$

$$\forall t_i^k \in J, |{}^\bullet t_i^k \cap J|\le 1;$$

$R_s \ne \varnothing.$

There are no self loops; each part-path has a well-defined beginning and an end; every job requires one and only one resource; there are no choice jobs and no assembly jobs; and there are shared resources. For MRF systems, for any $r \in R$, $J(r)$ $= r^{\bullet\bullet} \cap J = {}^{\bullet\bullet}r \cap J$ and $R(J_i^k) = J_i^{k\ \bullet\bullet} \cap R = {}^{\bullet\bullet}J_i^k \cap R.$

7.5.1.1 Deadlock in MRF Systems

The following define the notions of deadlock for the above MRF systems.

Definition [part-path deadlock]. Given an MRF system with corresponding PN $\{N, m_0\}$, part-path j is said to be deadlocked at any $m \in \text{Reach}(m_0)$ if some job-enabled transition x_i^j is dead at m.

Obviously, a deadlocked part-path is permanently disabled, and depending on the system structure it may disable other paths as well (in case the system has routing paths and/or assembly). For any part-path j, define a sequence of jobs $\bar{J}^j \subset J^j$ from part-path j such that, for $|\bar{J}^j| > 1$, if $J_i^j \in \bar{J}^j$, then $\{J_{i-1}^j, J_{i+1}^j\} \cap \bar{J}^j \ne \varnothing$. Let $M_{\bar{J}^j}^m \subset \text{Reach}(m)$ denote the set of markings reachable from m via a sequence of markings $\{m^i\}$ such that $m^i(\bar{J}^j) \le m(\bar{J}^j)$, for all i.

Definition [system deadlock]. Given a system of class MRF and with PN $\{N, m_0\}$, N is said to be deadlocked at any $m \in \text{Reach}(m_0)$ if at least one of the following holds:

-   Some part-path is deadlocked at m.

-   For some $j \in \Pi$, there exists some $\bar{J}^j$ with $m(\bar{J}^j) > 0$ such that, at every $m' \in M_{\bar{J}^j}^m$ with $m'(\bar{J}^j) = 0$, some part-path is deadlocked.

Consider now a dispatching policy U for the system of $\{N, m_0\}$, and let $M_U \subset \text{Reach}(m_0)$ denote the set of all markings reachable from m_0 under U.

Definition. A *dispatching policy* U is said to be deadlock-free if N is not deadlocked at any $m \in M_U$.

For a class of MRF systems and considering definitions described above, deadlock can occur only if there is a *circular wait relation* among the resources [*Deitel 84, Jeng 95, Gurel et al. 00*]. Circular wait relations are ubiquitous in reentrant flow-lines and in themselves do not present a problem. However, if a circular wait relation develops into circular blocking, then one has deadlock. But, as long as dispatching is carefully performed, the existence of circular wait relations presents no problem for *regular systems* [*Gurel et al. 00*]. The definition of a *"regular system"* is given later (in Section 7.5.5.1).

7.5.1.2 Circular Waits: Simple Circular Waits and Their Unions

In this section we present a digraph matrix procedure to identify all circular waits (CW) present in MRF systems. CWs are special wait relationships among resources and are key structures for deadlock structures. The following are the formal definitions.

Definition [*wait for relationship*]. Given a set of resources R, for any two resources $r_i, r_j \subset R$, r_i is said to wait for r_j, denoted $r_i \rightarrow r_j$, if the availability of r_i is an immediate requirement to release r_j, or equivalently, if there exists at least one transition $x \in \bullet r_j \cap r_i \bullet$.

Definition [*circular waits*]. Circular waits among resources are a set of resources $r_a, r_b, \ldots r_w$, which wait relationships among them are $r_a \rightarrow r_b \rightarrow \ldots \rightarrow r_w$, and $r_w \rightarrow r_a$.

Definition [*simple circular waits*]. The simplest CW C is such that, for some appropriate re labeling, one has $r_1 \rightarrow r_2 \rightarrow \ldots \rightarrow r_q$, with $r_i \neq r_j$ for $i \neq j$. This will be referred to as a *simple CW, sCW*.

To identify such sCW, a wait relation **digraph** [*Harary 72*] of resources has to be constructed first. A digraph $D=(R,A)$, where $R=\{r_1, r_2, r_3 \ldots, r_i\}$ is the set of nodes and $A=\{a_{ij}\}$ is the set of edges, with a_{ij} drawn if $r_i \rightarrow r_j$ (in other words, each a_{ij} represents all transitions in $\bullet r_j \cap r_i \bullet$). The **digraph of resources** corresponding to the system is easily obtained from the matrix formulation by getting

$$W = (S_r F_r)^T. \tag{20}$$

Each "one" in the w_{ij} elements from W, represents that the digraph has an arc from resource i to resource j. The procedure we followed to calculate all sCW is a similar approach to the string algebra used by [*Wysk 91, Hyenbo et al. 95*]. This approach takes advantage of numeric characters to facilitate multiplication of matrices. The number of rows of the resulting matrix of this approach/algorithm is the number of sCW, and its columns correspond to the resources present in the system. In this matrix, an entry of "one" in position (i,j) means that resource j is included in the ith sCW.

Unfortunately, to be able to analyze the MRF system and its possible deadlock structures, we need to identify all CWs, not just the simple CWs. A reason is that shared resources among sCW may compose other deadlock structures, which must be considered in our deadlock-free dispatching rule. A detailed explanation of these reasons is given in Section 7.5.4. Then, the entire set of CWs are the sCW plus circular waits composed of unions of non disjoint sCW (unions through shared resources among sCW). In Figure 7.16, we show a LabVIEW diagram that calculates all CWs from the sets of all sCW; it uses a Gurel algorithm from [*Lewis et al. 98*] encrypted in MATLAB script code which uses matrices for efficiency of computations. Using this diagram/code, we obtain two resulting *matrices*, C_{out} and G. C_{out} provides the set of resources which compose every CW (in rows), that is, an entry of "one" on every (i,j) position means that resource j is included in the ith CW. G provides the set of composed CWs (rows) from unions of sCW (columns), that is, an entry of "one" on every (i,j) position means that j^{th} sCW is included in the ith composed CW. In Section 7.5.5.1 one can find the resulting matrices for a given example.

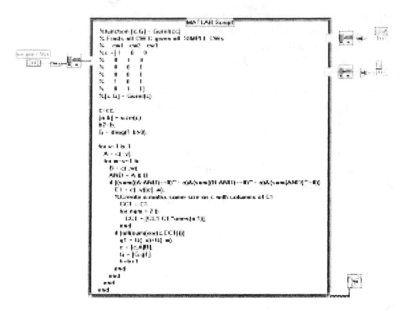

Figure 7.16. Gurel's algorithm that identifies all CWs from sCW.

7.5.1.3 Deadlock Analysis: Identifying Critical Siphons and Critical Subsystems

In this section, we apply PN and matrix-based notions to calculate specific PN-place sets associated with each CW. The determination of these sets is required so that we can identify possible *circular blocking* (CB) [*Ezpeleta et al. 95, Xing et al. 96, Lewis et al. 98, Gurel et al. 00*] phenomena or deadlock situations. After computing the sets, we will provide computationally efficient matrix-based algorithms for a least restrictive deadlock-free dispatching policy. These sets are highly tied to *siphons* associated with each CW. A siphon set has a behavioral property that if it is token-free under some marking, then it will remain token-free under each successor marking. Such property may leads to CB, i.e., deadlock. Formally speaking, CB is defined as follows.

Circular blocking is a situation where, for a CW $C=\{r_i\}$ one has the following:

$$m(C)=0; \text{ and for every } r_i \in C, \forall \mathbf{J}_i^j \in J(r_i) \text{ if } m(\mathbf{J}_i^j) \neq 0, \text{ then } \mathbf{J}_i^j{}^\bullet \in C^\bullet.$$

Under these conditions, C is said to be in a CB.

Three important sets associated with the CWs C are the *siphon-job* sets $J_s(C)$, the *critical siphons*, $S_c(C)$, and *critical subsystems*, $J_o(C)$. The critical siphon of a CW is the smallest siphon containing the CW. A set of places S are a *siphons* if and only if for all places $p_i \in S$ one has $\bullet p_i \subset U_j \{p_i \bullet\}$ for some $\{p_j\} \subset S$. Note from Figure 7.4a, that if the critical siphon ever becomes empty, the CW can never again receive any tokens. That is, the CW has become a CB. The siphon-job set, $J_s(C)$, is the set of jobs which, when added to the set of resources contained in

CW C, yields the critical siphon. The critical siphons of that CW C are the conjunction of sets $J_s(C)$ and C. The critical subsystems of the CW C are the *job sets* $J(C)$ from that C not contained in the siphon-job set $J_s(C)$ of C. That is $J_o(C) = J(C) \setminus J_s(C)$. The job sets of CW C are defined by $J(C) = \cup_{r \in C} J(r)$, for $J(r) = r^{\bullet \bullet} \cap J$, where J is the set of all jobs.

7.5.1.4 Identification of Deadlock Structures in Matrix Form

We now provide computational tools to determine the siphon-job sets $J_s(C)$, the critical siphons, $S_c(C)$, and critical subsystems, $J_o(C)$, for every CW C. To determine such sets, we need to calculate the set of *adding* transitions $T_C^+ = {}^{\bullet}C \setminus C^{\bullet}$ and *clearing* transitions $T_C^- = C^{\bullet} \setminus {}^{\bullet}C$. T_C^+ are the set of transitions that, when fired, add tokens to the CW C. On the contrary, T_C^- are the set of transitions that, when fired, subtract tokens from C. ${}^{\bullet}C$ and $C^{\bullet}$ are the set of *input* and *output* transitions from C. These sets of transitions are important in keeping track of the tokens inside every CW C, and hence in determining the status of tokens inside the critical siphon.

In order to implement efficient real-time control of the DES, we need to compute these sets in matrix form. Thus, the intermediate quantities ${}^{\bullet}C$ and $C^{\bullet}$ in matrix form for each CW are denoted ${}_dC$ and C_d, respectively, computed as,

$$_dC = C_{out} \, S_r, \text{ and} \tag{21}$$
$$C_d = C_{out} \, F_r^{\mathrm{T}}. \tag{22}$$

Now, we are able to calculate the adding transitions $T_C^+ = {}^{\bullet}C \setminus C^{\bullet}$ in matrix form

$$T_p = {}_dC - ({}_dC \wedge C_d), \tag{23}$$

and the clearing transitions $T_C^- = C^{\bullet} \setminus {}^{\bullet}C$ in matrix form

$$T_m = C_d - (C_d \wedge {}_dC), \tag{24}$$

where operation $A \wedge B$ represents an element-by-element logical AND operation between matrices A and B.

Important note. For each circular wait, these matrix forms contain the set of transition vectors T_C^+ and T_C^- arranged in the rows of matrices T_p and T_m, respectively. That is, an entry of "one" on every (i,j) position in matrix T_p (T_m), means that j^{th} transition is a T_C^+ (T_C^-) transition belonging to that i^{th} composed CW.

In terms of these constructions, matrix form sets are described next, indicating "one" on every entry (i,j) for places that belong to that set existing in every i^{th} CW. The job sets described earlier for each CW C, $J(C)$, in matrix form (for all CWs arranged in rows) are described by

$$J_C = {}_dC \, F_v = C_d \, S_v^{\mathrm{T}}. \tag{25}$$

The **siphon-job** sets are defined for each ith CW C_i as $J_s(C_i) := J(C_i) \cap {}^{\bullet}T_C^+$.
In matrix notation, we can obtain them for all CWs by

$$J_s = T_p \, F_v. \tag{26}$$

There is a shortcut way to identify these **siphon-job sets** without calculating T_p. However, later we will need construction T_p to identify presence/absence of critical resources. This shortcut way in matrix form is

$$J_s = J_C \wedge (\overline{C_d \, F_v}). \tag{27}$$

This mathematical shortcut facilitates the calculation of these sets only if the system fulfills conditions presented in the beginning of Section 7.4.4.

The **critical subsystems**, defined as $J_o(C_i) = J(C_i) \backslash J_s(C_i)$, in matrix form for all CWs C_i are obtained by

$$J_o = J_C \wedge (C_d \, Fv). \tag{28}$$

Such representation is similar of that presented by [*Lewis et al. 98*]. In their work, the authors present another way to calculate the critical subsystems from the **p-invariant** covering job sets, not belonging to the critical siphon job set.

7.5.2 Deadlock Avoidance

In terms of the constructions just given in earlier sections, we now present a minimally restrictive resource dispatching policy that guarantees absence of deadlock for MRFs. To efficiently implement in real time a DEC with this dispatching policy, we use matrices for all computations. We consider the case where the system is **regular**, that is, it cannot contain critical resources (the so-called bottleneck resources or **key resources** [*Xing 96, Gurel et al. 00*]) existing in second level deadlock structures [*Fanti et al. 97-01*]. Section 7.5.4 describes a mathematical test to verify that the MRF system is regular. If that is not the case, we can still use this matrix formulation, but with a different dispatching policy designed for systems containing second-level deadlock structures.

7.5.2.1 Deadlock-Free Dispatching Policy in MRF Systems

In this section, we consider dispatching for regular MRF systems. A matrix test for a system's regularity is given in the next section. In [*Lewis et al. 98*], a minimally restrictive dispatching policy for regular systems was given. This policy avoids deadlock for the class of MRF systems considered in this chapter. To understand this policy, note that, for this class of systems, a deadlock is equivalent to a CB.

The following five results are provided in [*Lewis et at. 96, and Gurel et al. 00*]. We need these results and the constructions involved in those results, as well as the constructions derived in previous sections, to be able to identify all deadlock constructions needed for implementing deadlock DE supervisors.

Theorem 4.2.1 Given $\{N, m_0\}$ and any $m \in \text{Reach}(m_0)$, the following are equivalent.

- There exists a job-enabled dead transition at m.
- There exists a dead resource place $r \in R$ at m.
- There exists a CB at m.
- The result stated next characterizes further the situation described by Theorem 1.

Theorem 4.2.2 Given $\{N, m_0\}$, a CW C is in a CB at any $m \in \text{Reach}(m_0)$ if and only if $m(S_C)=0$.

Now, define $M_F = \{m \in \text{Reach}(m_0) \mid m(S_C)=0$, for some CW $C\}$, i.e., the set of reachable markings with CB. Clearly form Definition 2, there is some deadlocked part-path at any $m \in M_F$. The theorem stated next lays the ground work for proving the subsequent two results.

Theorem 4.2.3. If a given system $\{N, m_0\}$ is a regular system, then at any $m \in \text{Reach}(m_0) \backslash M_F$, there exists at least one transition that is enabled to fire without resulting in any CB.

This result says that given a regular system $\{N, m_0\}$, if at any marking reached there is no CB, then there always exists at least one transition that is enabled to fire without causing CB. This means that part-flow will continue provided CB is avoided.

In order to satisfy the condition of Theorem 4.2.3, a policy is required that results in a *pull behavior* between some local subsystems defined by the critical siphons, namely the critical subsystems, $J_o(C)$ [*Gurel et al. 00*]. These notions are similar to those explored in [*Perkins and Kumar 95*], where the concept of "head machines" was used to partition a flow-line into subsections. Assuming that jobs are dispatched singly, the notion of dispatching priority can be defined as follows: given two activated jobs J_i^j and J_l^k, J_i^j is said to be dispatched with priority over J_l^k, denoted pri(J_i^j)>pri(J_l^k), if whenever both jobs are requested simultaneously J_i^j is given preference. Given two job sets S_1 and S_2, the notation pri(S_1)<pri(S_2) means that every job in S_2 is dispatched with priority over every job in S_1. That is, when two jobs are requested simultaneously, one in S_1 and the other in S_2, the job in S_2 is preferred.

Now, whenever any $J_i^j \in J(C)$ is dispatched $m(S_C)$ changes as follows: receipt of a token by a place (i) in $J_N(C)$ leaves $m(S_C)$ unchanged; (ii) in $\hat{J}_S(C)$ increases $m(S_C)$ by one; and (iii) in $\hat{J}_Q(C)$ reduces $m(S_C)$ by one. This is significant in devising deadlock-free dispatching priorities.

The foregoing analysis leads to the following multi part LBFS dispatching rule that is more general than the uniform LBFS policy of [*Lu and Kumar 91*]. It effectively keeps the WIP in every critical subsystem $J_0(C)$ as small as possible, thus guaranteeing absence of deadlock and it is easy to implement.

Theorem 4.2.4 Consider a regular system of class MRF with PN $\{N, m_0\}$. Suppose an LBFS dispatching policy is defined such that, whenever a multitude of jobs $\{ J_i^j \} \subset J(C)$, are activated simultaneously, they are dispatched according to the following:

-   set pri($\hat{J}_Q(C)$)<pri($J_S(C) \cup \hat{J}_N(C)$), and
-   do not dispatch any $J_i^j \in \hat{J}_Q(C)$ if $m(\hat{J}_Q(C) \cup \hat{J}_N(C)) = m_0(C)-1$.

Then, deadlock will not occur.

Stated next is a generalized kanban strategy that not only avoids deadlock, but also allows for improvement of percent utilization of the resources.

Theorem 4.2.5 Given a regular system of class MRF with PN $\{N, m_0\}$, any dispatching policy U is deadlock-free if and only if, for all $m \in M_U$, when assigning dispatching priorities to a multitude of simultaneously activated jobs $\{ J_i^j \}$, it disallows dispatching of any J_i^j whenever there is some CW C such that $J_i^j \in \hat{J}_Q(C)$ and $m(\hat{J}_Q(C) \cup \hat{J}_N(C)) = m_0(C)-1$.

The theorem formulates a dispatching policy that provides the most permissive policy that avoids deadlock. Specifically, keeping $m(C)$ as close to 1 as possible maximizes the WIP in the critical subsystem $J_0(C)$ and hence percent utilization of the resources. For instance, this is similar to having a general permissible set of jobs in J_o for each CW C_i.

Then, by summarizing previous results, there is a CB if and only if there is an empty CW, and is only possible (for regular systems) iff the corresponding critical siphon is empty. By construction, this is equivalent to all jobs of the circular wait being in the critical subsystem (CS). In terms of PN, there is a deadlock iff all tokens of the CW are in the CS.

Therefore, the key to deadlock avoidance is to ensure that the WIP in the CSs is limited to one less job than the total number of initial tokens in the CW (i.e., the total number of resources available in the CW). Due to the necessity and sufficiency of all the conditions just outlined, this MAXWIP policy is the *least restrictive* policy that guarantees absence of deadlock. It is very easy to implement. Preliminary off-line computations using matrices are used to compute the CSs. A supervisor is assigned to each CS who is responsible for *dynamic dispatching* by counting the jobs in that CS and ensuring that they do not violate the following condition, for each CW C_i,

$$m(J_o(C_i)) < m_o(C_i). \tag{29}$$

That is, the number of enabled places contained in the CS for each C_i must not reach the total number of resources contained in that C_i.

7.5.3 Implementation Rules for Deadlock-Free Dispatching

For the implementation of the DECs in this work, and differing from the definition of sets considered in [*Huang et al. 96, Lewis et al. 98, Gurel et al. 00*], *we are considering row vectors instead of column vectors* (this is needed to separate properly sets contained in each CW C_i.) That is, matrix form sets having "ones" on every entry (i,j) indicate places that belong to that set existing in every i^{th} row CW.

In our implementation example, in every DE iteration, we use FBFS dispatching policy. Generally, FBFS maximizes WIP and machine percent utilization. However, it is known that FBFS often results in deadlock. Therefore, we combine FBFS with our deadlock avoidance test (29) [*Mireles et al. 02abc*]. Thus, before we dispatch the FBFS resolution, we examine the marking outcome with our deadlock policy. If this resulting outcome does not satisfy (29), then the algorithm denies or *pre-filters* in real time the firing and we apply again the FBFS conflict resolution strategy for the next possible allowable firing sequence. Therefore, using FBFS while permitted, we will try to satisfy in most of the current status of the cell the case $m(J_o(Ci)) = m_o(Ci)-1$. The latter condition is the so called MAXWIP policy, defined in [*Huang et al. 96*].

The dispatching policy for case one has a regular system follows three main steps:

First, based on the structure of the system defined by matrices F and S, we use (4-9) to obtain for all CWs its corresponding critical subsystems, $J_o(CW)$. In matrix form (having all CWs), J_o^{mxn} has m rows as CWs, and n columns as total # resource-jobs in the system.

Second, for every DE iteration, one must calculate from the current marking vector, $m_{current}$, the corresponding possible successor-marking vector, $m_{possible}$. Equation (11), which can be split into Equations (14) and (15) provide this possible successor $(m_a(t+1) = m_{possible}, m_a(t) = m_{current})$. However, for a given $m_{current}$ vector, since it is possible to have enabled more than one transition $r_s\bullet$, for r_s be a shared resource, marking $m_{possible}$ can have negative elements due to (15). That is, it is possible that the marking vector $m_{possible}$ has negative number(s) in the $r(t)$ section from the general marking vector $m(t+1)$ from (11), if more than one resource job, $v(t)$, are attempted to fire requesting a single-shared resource, $r(t)=r_s$ (verify from (10) that $r(t)$ is part of $m(t)$, as well as $v(t)$ and $u_c(t)$). That is why the marking $m_{possible}$ has to be "filtered" by a conflict resolution dispatching policy to deny negative elements (any viable dispatching rule can be used.) This can be seen as an extra loop which filters marking $m_{possible}$. Refer to Figure 7.17 and identify this feedback loop in the conflict resolution block (having feedback control signal as u_c).

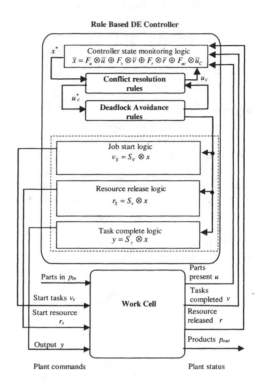

Figure 7.17. Matrix formulation DEC.

We "filter" negative numbers from m_{possible} by setting to zero the non desired resource-job elements in vector $u_c(t)$ from the current marking vector m_{current}. $u_c(t)$ is strategically preset full of ones in m_{current} before one starts every new DE iteration (set of these three steps), and readjusted after the calculation of m_{possible} having negative numbers to solve any possible conflict on shared resources. This is how we are able to calculate another m_{possible} vector lacking negative numbers.

Third, once selected the candidate m_{possible}, to avoid deadlock, one must verify the condition $m(J_o(C_i)) < m_o(C_i)$ for every CW C_i. This can be accomplished by extracting from marking m_{possible} the $v(t)$ vector (from 2-10), defined as v_{possible}, and performing

$$\|J_{oi} \wedge v_{\text{possible}}\| < \|C_{\text{out}i}\|, \tag{30}$$

for J_{oi} be i^{th} row vector from J_o, $C_{\text{out}i}$ be the ith row (or i^{th} CW) vector from C_{out}, and $\|V\|$ be the Σv_i, for v_i be the ith element of vector V.

If for any DE iteration, (30) does not hold, one must eliminate the resource job from v_{possible} that is attempting to cause circular blocking in that i^{th} CW. This elimination can be accomplished by a *high order conflict resolution among different machines* (notice that for this case, this resolution is not among jobs from a single resource/machine, but among jobs from different resources/machines). The jobs that might attempt to cause deadlock problems are found by

$$v_{\text{problem}i} = (v_{\text{possible}} - (v_{\text{possible}}{}^\wedge v_{\text{current}}))^\wedge J_{oi} \tag{31}$$

This is a high-order conflict resolution strategy that has to be accomplished among elements from each $v_{\text{problem}i}$, and the chosen resource job not to be fired must be cleared (set to zero) from u_c from m_{current} and the second step restarted. This yields an extra feedback loop between the "deadlock avoidance" and the "conflict resolution" blocks from Figure 7.17

To be prepared for this high-order conflict resolution strategy for the DEC implementation, one must decide among strictly trap-job sets contained in vectors J_{oi} (for each ith CW). That is, one must decide among resource jobs contained in i^{th} row from J_{Qs} when the following condition holds

$$\|J_{o_{\text{possible}_i}}\| >= \|C_{\text{out}i}\|, \tag{32}$$

for $\|J_{o_{\text{possible}_i}}\|$ be the number of jobs contained in J_o present in the current v_{possible} vector from the ith CW. In words, Condition (32) verifies condition $m(J_o(\text{CW})) < m_o(\text{CW})$ for the attempted firing vector v_{possible}, and if (32) holds, resolution among jobs in vector $v_{\text{problem}i}$ has to be solved. Such resource jobs are contained in the same i^{th} row from J_{Qs}.

7.5.4 Deadlock Analysis for MRF Systems and Supervisory Net structures

This section highlights the importance of the analysis of interconnections of circular waits in MRF systems. Proofs of this analysis are developed in terms of analysis of initial markings for each CW C, $m_0(C)$. We show the importance of considering deadlock structures not only related to each simple circular wait (sCW), but also deadlock structures from composed unions of sCW. Also, this section shows that the deadlock policies described in previous sections can lead to the development of a supervisory network (SN) structure. This SN is developed by adding a set of new places and arcs to the PN system structure, which "supervises" the system, without the need of one-step look-ahead technique used in Section 7.5.2. Each place keeps track of tokens from the critical subsystem $J_0(C_i)$ of the corresponding CW C_i.

The following refinements are needed later for the definition and development in matrix form of SN structures, as well as for the definition of critical resources (present in second level deadlock structures), and identification of system regularity.

These sets indicate "one" on every entry (i,j) for places that belong to that set existing in every i^{th} CW, C_i.

The **trap-job** set for every i^{th} CW C_i, defined as $J_Q(C_i) = J(C_i) \cap T_C^{-\bullet}$, is computed in the ith row of the matrix

$$J_Q = T_m S_v^{T}. \tag{33}$$

The **siphon-trap-job** sets, $J_{SQ}(C_i) = J_s(C_i) \cap J_Q(C_i)$, are the intersection of the siphon-job and trap-job sets, which in matrix notation, they are

$$J_{SQ} = J_s \wedge J_Q \tag{34}$$

The **strictly siphon-job** set is defined as $\hat{J}_s (C_i) = J_s(C_i) \backslash J_{SQ}(C_i)$, which in matrix form is

$$J_{Ss} = J_s - (J_s \wedge J_{SQ}) \tag{35}$$

The **strictly trap-job** set is defined as $\hat{J}_Q (C_i) = J_Q(C_i) \backslash J_{SQ}(C_i)$, which in matrix form it is

$$J_{Qs} = J_Q - (J_Q \wedge J_{SQ}) \tag{36}$$

The **neutral-job** set is defined as $J_N(C_i) = J(C_i) \backslash (\hat{J}_s (C_i) \cup \hat{J}_Q (C_i))$, which in matrix form is

$$J_N = J_C - [J_C \wedge (J_{Ss} + J_{Qs})] \tag{37}$$

The **strictly neutral-job** set is defined as $\hat{J}_N (C_i) = J_N(C_i) \backslash J_{SQ}(C_i)$, which in matrix form is

$$J_{Ns} = J_C - (J_C \wedge J_{SQ}) \tag{38}$$

The earlier described **critical subsystems**, $J_o(C_i)$, which are needed in our deadlock-free algorithm, can also be defined from these quantities for all CW by

$$J_o = J_{Qs} \vee J_{Ns}. \tag{39}$$

Once the mathematical analytical constructions are calculated, it can be shown that constructions siphon sets $Js(C)$, and critical subsystems $J_o(C)$ are disjoint sets, as shown in Figure 7.18.

To define supervisory network structures, and for the calculation of critical resources, and regularity test for MRF systems, we need to identify the **precedent transitions** $T_{pre}(C_i)$ and the **posterior transitions** $T_{pos}(C_i)$ for the associated critical subsystem for each CW C_i. Precedent and posterior transitions are defined as

$$T_{pre}(C_i) = {}^{\bullet}\hat{J}_Q (C_i) = {}^{\bullet}J_o(C_i) \setminus J_o(C_i)^{\bullet},$$ which, once they are fired, will augment by 1 the number of tokens in the critical subsystem associated to C_i, and

$$T_{pos}(C_i) = {}^{\bullet}\hat{J}_s (C_i) = J_o(C_i)^{\bullet} \setminus {}^{\bullet}J_o(C_i),$$ which, once they are fired, will diminish by 1 the number of tokens in the critical subsystem associated to C_i.

$$T_{pre} = (J_o S_v) - [(J_o S_v) \wedge (J_o F_v^{T})], \text{ and} \tag{40}$$
$$T_{pos} = (J_o F_v^{T}) - [(J_o S_v) \wedge (J_o F_v^{T})]. \tag{41}$$

The next sections use later these constructions for formal definitions and development of computationally efficient structures needed for online supervision and deadlock avoidance.

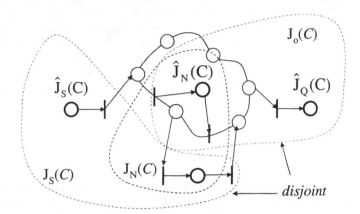

Figure 7.18. Notice that constructions siphon sets Js(*C*), and critical subsystems $J_o(C)$ are disjoint.

7.5.5 Second Level Deadlock in MRF Systems

There is a certain structural case in MRF systems which requires extreme care in deadlock-avoidance dispatching. This case occurs where there exist the so called **Second Level Deadlock** (SLD) [*Fanti et al. 97-01*] structures in the system. SLD exist on the presence of **critical resources**, known as bottlenecks [*Gurel et al. 00*], and key resources [*Xing 96*]. Profr. Ayla Gurel refers to bottleneck resources as the structured-placed bottleneck resources, not the well known timed bottleneck resources. These structures are identified by analyzing interconnectivities in circular wait relationships and its siphons [*Xing 96, Gurel et al. 00*] and/or by accomplishing digraph connectivity-analysis on resources and jobs [*Fanti et al. 97-01*]. We now define these critical resource structures using matrices.

7.5.5.1 Regularity Test: Identifying Critical and Key Resources

To define critical resources, we must determine the presence of **cyclic circular wait** (CCW) loops in the DE system. These specify a particular sharing among circular waits that needs special attention for deadlock-free dispatching [*Xing 96, Gurel et al. 00*], and are a requisite for existence of critical resources. These are structured-placed bottlenecks (among CWs). Specific structures are defined next in terms of precedent and posterior transitions, matrices (40) and (41). To identify whether if the system has **cyclic circular wait** (CCW) loops, let C_i and C_j be two circular waits with

$$T_{pos}(C_i) \cap T_{pre}(C_j) \neq \varnothing \text{ and } T_{pre}(C_i) \cap T_{pos}(C_j) \neq \varnothing. \tag{42}$$

If that is the case, then we got a CCW. The matrix test to find CCW loops among all CWs is

$$C_{CW} = (T_{pre} \ T_{pos}{}^T) \wedge (T_{pre} \ T_{pos}{}^T)^T. \tag{43}$$

If we define $\| C \| = \Sigma c_{ij}$, for c_{ij} be the (i,j) element of matrix C, then, if $\|C_{CW}\| > 0$ we have an *irregular* system, otherwise, the system is *regular*. If we have CCW loops, C_{CW} is a symmetric matrix having non-zero elements in each ccw_{ij}, for i^{th} CW (indicated by row i from C_{CW}) and j^{th} CW (column) be respectively C_i and C_j.

The transitions that interconnect such CCWs are needed to define critical resources. We can use matrix C_{CW} and the precedent and posterior matrix transitions T_{pre} and T_{pos} to identify such transitions.

$$\hat{T}_{pre} = (C_{CW} \ T_{pos}) \wedge T_{pre} \tag{44}$$

$$\hat{T}_{pos} = (C_{CW} \ T_{pre}) \wedge T_{pos} \tag{45}$$

We call them the *cyclic precedent* and *cyclic posterior* transitions, (44) and (45) respectively. The definition of a *critical CW* is as follows: Given PN N, and its initial marking m_o, let $\{C_i, C_j\}$ be a CCW such that $|C_i \cap C_j| = 1$ and let $C_i \cap C_j = \{r_b\}$. If $T_{pos}(C_i) \cap T_{pro}(C_j) \subset r_b{}^{\bullet}$ and $T_{pos}(C_j) \cap T_{pre}(C_i) \subset r_b{}^{\bullet}$, then $\{C_i, C_j \}$ is said to be a *critical CW* and r_b is called its *critical resource* (structured-placed bottleneck resource [*Gurel et al. 00*]). If in addition $m_o(r_b) = 1$, then r_b is called *key resource*.

Then, since we already identify the cyclic precedent and cyclic posterior transitions for all CCW in the system, we can proceed to identify the critical resources using the following straightforward matrix formula

$$Res_{CW} = (\hat{T}_{pos} \ F_r) \wedge (\hat{T}_{pre} \ F_r) \tag{46}$$

Res_{CW} provides, for each CW, the set of critical resources shared with other CWs in one or more CCW. If this matrix is zero, there are no critical resources and hence no key resources. Section 7.5.6 shows an example identifying irregular systems.

7.5.6 Deadlock-Free Implementation in MRF Systems

With the purpose of showing the flexibility of this matrix approach, consider two possible PN structures A and B, shown respectively in Figures 7.19 and 7.20, which can be implemented in the IMH cell of ARRI to "manufacture" two products. We use term "manufacture" because our machines are simulated machines.

However, our resources are real robotic systems which we intend to perform the MRF sequence problem. By applying steps from Sections 7.3 and 7.4, we will show that one of these systems is irregular. Then, we implement the deadlock-free dispatching in the regular system. The Fv, SvT, Fr and SrT matrices for these PN systems are shown in LabVIEW discrete format in Figures 7.21 and 7.22. In the LabVIEW discrete representation of matrices, each black circle is a 'one' and the others are "zero."

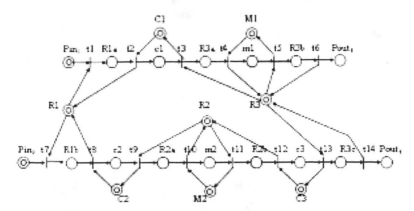

Figure 7.19. Petri Net system structure A.

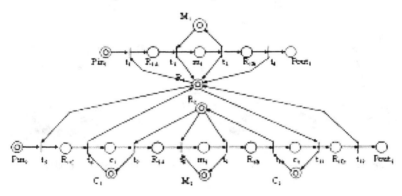

Figure 7.20. Petri Net system structure B.

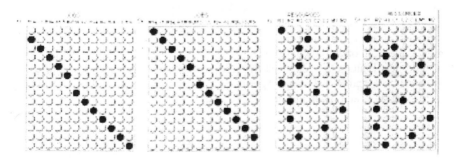

Figure 7.21. $F_v S_v^T, F_r S_r^T$ matrices for system A (in LabVIEW discrete format).

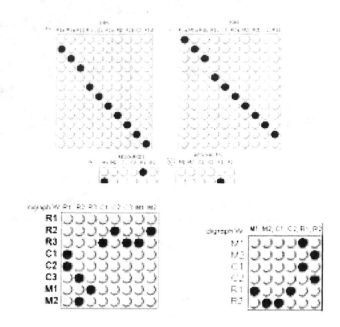

Figure 7.23. Resulting W matrices for system A (left) and system B (right).

Figure 7.24. Simple circular waits for system A (left) and system B (right).

7.5.6.1 Determination of Circular Waits

Taking advantage of the fact that LabVIEW can use MATLAB script code, we created a small program that uses matrices S_r^T and F_r^T, to internally calculate the digraph matrix W, (20), and use MATLAB script code to get the matrix containing the sCW, for both systems [*Mireles et al. 02b*]. Also, in LabVIEW, we can represent each program in a single block function, which can be used inside diagram code from other programs. Later, we will show the entire LabVIEW diagram containing all interconnected block functions. The digraph of resources, W matrix, for systems A and B is shown in Figure 7.23. The output matrix contains all sCW from systems A and B and they are shown in Figure 7.26.

From the number of rows in matrices from Figure 7.26, we can see that we found two sCW in system A, and three sCW in system B. System A has one sCW composed by R3 and M1 and other composed of resources R2 and M2. System B has one sCW composed of M1 and R1, other composed of M2 and R2, and the third one composed of resources C1, C2, R1 and R2.

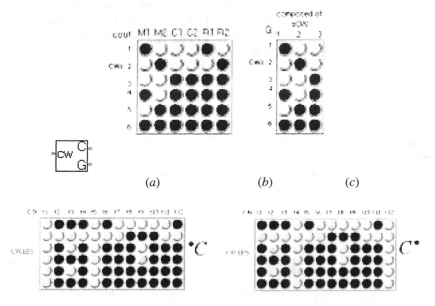

(a)   (b)   (c)

Figure 7.26. $^\bullet C$ and $C^\bullet$ for every CW cycles for system B.

The next step is to use Gurel's algorithm to calculate matrix C_{out} (algorithm shown in Figure 7.16). For our system A, C_{out} is equal to matrix sCW, and G matrix is a 2x2 identity matrix. That means that there is no shared resource interconnecting any sCW, and that the system does not have composed circular waits. At this point, we can say that there are no critical resources in system A, because critical resources are resources that interconnect CW or sCW (if we continue performing the analysis for system A, we will get this conclusion. That is, system A does not have critical resources, and so system A is regular). But, even if we have shared resources among sCW, that does not guarantee we have critical resources in the system. That is why we offer the matrix test (42). For system B, Figure 7.25(a) and 7.25(b) show the resulting matrices C_{out} and G, respectively. Also, Figure 7.25(c) shows the block representation of Gurel's algorithm/diagram from Figure 7.16, showing output matrices, C_{out} and G, on its right side. We remind the reader that G provides the set of composed CWs (rows) from unions of sCW (columns), that is why, as an example from system B, the set of resources of composed CW C_4 (composed of resources on 4th row of C_{out}) contains the resources from sCW C_1 (1st column of G) and sCW C_3 (3rd column of G). System B has a total of six CWs, three sCW (first three rows of C_{out}) and three composed of unions of such sCW (last three rows of C_{out}).

7.5.6.2   Verifying Absence of Critical Resources, Regularity Test

At this point, we need to verify whether if system B has a critical resource. For that, we follow the procedure in Section 7.5.2. First, we calculate the input and output transitions for every CW in matrices $_dC$ and C_d, Equations (2) and (3). For system B, these set of transitions are shown in Figure 7.26.

Once found, the input and output transitions for each cycle or CW, we proceed to calculate the adding, clearing transitions and the job sets, T_p, T_m and J_C respectively, by using Equations, (4), and (6). T_p and T_m are needed to calculate the siphon-job and trap-job sets, and with these constructions, we calculate the critical subsystems for each CW of the system. Matrix J_o contains all critical subsystems for all CWs of the system. Figure 7.27 shows the LabVIEW diagram code that implements Equations, (2)-(9), and (33)-(39). Figure 7.28 shows resulting matrices from Equations (32)-(42), for system B.

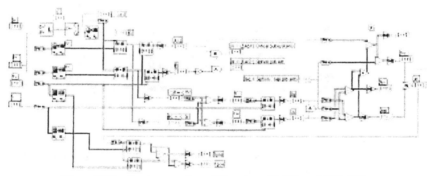

Figure 7.27.   Implementation of Equations (2)-(9), and (33)-(39).

We present in Figure 7.29 the adding, clearing and the intersection of input and output transitions for the first CW shown in the first row of C_{out} (composed of resources M_1 and R_1). This result is obtained by combining resulting matrices from Figure 7.26 and matrices T_p and T_m (denoted as "T+" and "T-", respectively, in Figure 7.28).

The last step is described in Section 7.5.4, which provides the formulation to identify possible critical resources using the matrices we just got. Applying Equations, (40) and (41), the corresponding precedent and posterior transitions for each CW are contained in matrices T_{pre} and T_{pos}, respectively, and shown in Figure 7.30.

If Equation (42) is satisfied, we got a cyclic circular wait composed of two or more CWs. For system B, Condition (42) is TRUE for the case $i=2$ and $j=3$ or $j=4$. Figure 7.31 a) shows the resulting matrix test C_{CW}. We can see that we had just found that for system B, CW C_2 is connected with CWs C_3 and C_4 through a critical resource. This means that C_2 can be described as C_i and that CW_3 and CW_4 can be described as C_j as defined in Condition (42).

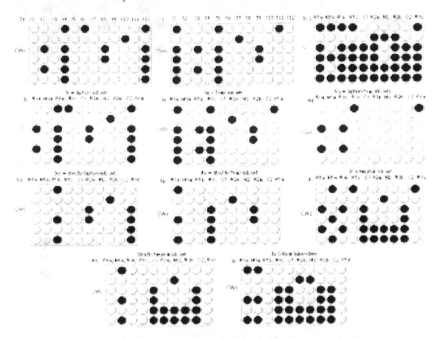

Figure 7.28. Resulting matrices from Equations (4)-(9), and (33)-(39) for system B.

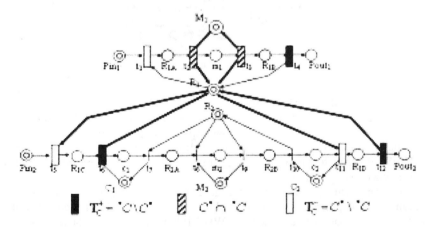

Figure 7.29. Result from the first row of the two matrices.

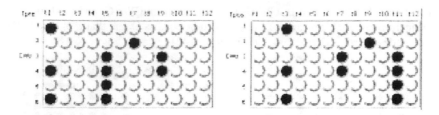

Figure 7.30. T_{pre} and T_{pos} matrices.

The calculated Res_{CW} matrix is shown in Figure 7.31 b). We can see that the shared critical resource for our system B is R_2, which relates C_2, C_3 and C_4. Since $m_o(R_2) = 1$, R_2 is a key resource. We conclude system B is an irregular system.

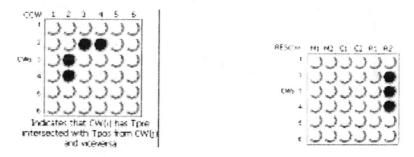

Figure 7.31.   (a) C_{CW} matrix (left), (b) Res_{CW} matrix (right).

Figure 7.32.   Resulting matrix J_o for system A.

7.5.6.3 Implementation of Deadlock–Free Dispatching

Once proven that system A is a regular system, to implement the deadlock-free dispatching rule, we proceed to follow steps shown in Section 7.5.3. First, we calculate the critical subsystems matrix J_o. Such matrix can be found by using the LabVIEW diagram shown in Figure 7.27. Figure 7.32 shows the resulting J_o matrix for system A.

Further discussion will refer to Figure 7.33, which shows the LabVIEW diagram containing the main loop of the DE real-time controller implemented at ARRI. The input parameters to the main WHILE loop are shown in the left side of the figure. The input parameters are matrices F and S, critical subsystems and initial marking vectors.

Matrices F and S are concatenated by the blocks near the denoted circles (A) and (B) using a LabVIEW concatenation function block. Notice that two extra matrices were added to such matrices F and S, F_y and F_x. Matrix F_y is the output matrix of the system, and matrix F_x is an extra matrix needed to facilitate the control of firing transitions and number of tokens in the DEC system. They do not alter the matrix formulation, the deadlock-free dispatching policy, or all calculations contained in this chapter.

For the implementation of this DEC, the critical subsystems are an input parameter to the main loop. This means that the critical subsystems are precalculated before the DE controller loop starts. The denoted circle (C) refers to the block shown in Figure 7.33, which calculates the sCW of the system. Then, the block near to denoted circle (D), uses these sCW in matrix form, and matrices F_v, F_r, S_v, and S_r, to calculate the siphon-job sets, the critical subsystems and the number of resources associated for each CW. Notice that system A does not contain any composed circular waits, but this block, near denoted circle (D), calculates them internally (if any) and verifies that the system is regular.

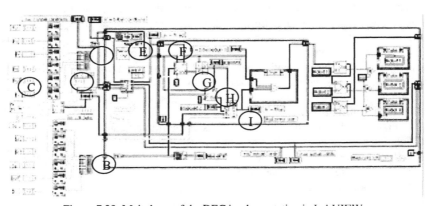

Figure 7.33. Main loop of the DEC implementation in LabVIEW.

The other input parameters to the main WHILE loop are the initial marking vectors of the DE system. Two marking vectors are used, the one defined in (2-10) with the addition of vectors $y(t)$ and $x(t)$ (the output marking vector, and the extra marking vector needed for matrix F_x), and a *sensors* marking vector. The sensors marking vector was included to facilitate the control of information provided from the sensors in the simulated machines M1 and M2. The detail of this implementation will be published in a technical paper. Again, these extra vectors do not need any further mathematical explanation which might add complication to the current analysis.

The main loop performs the second and third steps described in Section 7.5.3. Before we start performing these steps, the DEC has to update the marking vector depending on the information provided by the sensors in the cell. This is accomplished by the block below remark circle (E), inside the main WHILE loop. After the refinement of the sensor marking vector is made, steps two and three are applied inside the internal WHILE loop having denoted marks (F)-(I).

The second step is performed in remarks (F), (G) and (H). Equations (11) and (12) are accomplished inside the block below remark circle (F). This block receives $m_{current}$ and obtains a candidate $m_{possible}$ (as described in the first part of the second step of Section 7.5.3). Then, block over remark circle (G) filters the $m_{current}$, depending on the first outcome $m_{possible}$ for the case it needs to perform conflict resolution on shared resources. That is, for the case $m_{possible}$ has negative numbers. The resulting vector from block denoted (G) will be a new $m_{current}$ vector that will not lead any conflict on the subsequent outcome vector $m_{possible}$. Equations (11) and (12) are accomplished again in block denoted with remark circle (H) and the resulting vector is a marking $m_{possible}$ without any negative numbers.

The third step is performed in remark (I). Block denoted in remark (I) verifies Condition (30) and applies Equation (31), if necessary. That is, it compares subset marking vector $v_{possible}$ with each of J_o, and, if necessary, calculates the resource jobs that attempt to cause a deadlock problem, $v_{problem i}$. If necessary, the same block performs a high-order conflict resolution strategy. If that is the case, a TRUE signal is activated to perform a second iteration of the entire sequence of steps in Section 7.5.3, but with a new filtered marking vector $m_{current}$ having "zeros" on the non desired jobs on its $u_c(t)$ vector (as detailed in the second step of Section 7.5.3). Otherwise, it uses the resulting $m_{possible}$ marking from denoted block (H) as the resulting firing marking vector.

Figure 7.34 shows the Discrete Events of the implementation run for system A. This Figure was obtained in real-time directly from our DE implementation in LabVIEW. In the Figure 7.34, the discrete duration of the robotic jobs are shown. Every line represents a discrete event for every robotic job, and it has only two states, high and low (or ON and OFF), meaning executing a robotic job, and not executing such a robotic job, respectively. Notice that for every robot/resource (R1x, R2x and R3x), only one robotic job goes high at any time.

7.6 Conclusions

In this chapter, we presented the development of a deadlock avoidance supervisory DEC for multipart reentrant flow-line systems, which were defined in Section 7.5.1. This DEC uses a rule-based matrix dispatching formulation, and it was described in Section 7.3. Using this matrix-based approach, on-line deadlock-free dispatching rules were implemented by the DE matrix controller. This was accomplished by analyzing circular waits for possible deadlock situations while analyzing the so-called critical siphons, certain critical subsystems and the presence of bottleneck resources. This analysis was developed in matrix format in Section 7.5.4. We also presented a matrix formulation that identifies bottleneck and key resources shared among circular resource loops that lead to second level dead-lock structures. In addition to deadlock-free dispatching rules, conflict resolution strategies are implemented by the DEC in a reentrant flow-line. This is accomplished thanks to the matrix-based deadlock structures developed in Sections 7.5.4, and 7.5.5. Technical information given included the development of the deadlock-free controller implemented in LabVIEW. We envision that further research on second level deadlock structures having bottleneck resources as well as shared resource conflict resolution strategies will be performed.

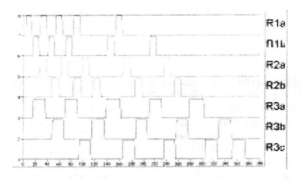

Figure 7.34. Results of the implementation of the DEC in LabVIEW.

References

[1] Antsaklis P.J. and K.M. Passino. *"An Introduction to Intelligent and Autonomous Control Systems."* Kluwer, Boston, MA. 1992.

[2] Banaszak Z.A. and B.H. Krogh. "Deadlock Avoidance in Flexible Manufacturing Systems with Concurrently Competing Process Flows." *IEEE Trans. Robotics and Automation*, RA-6, pp. 724-734. December 1990.

[3] Buzacott J.A. and D.D. Yao. "Flexible Manufacturing Systems: A Review of Analytical Models." *Management Sci. 7*, pp. 890-905, 1986.

[4] Campos, R., J. Mireles, A. Ramírez, E. López, and F. Lewis "A Controller-Observer Scheme for a Robotic Cell", *IEEE International Conference on Systems, Man and Cybernetics*, Washington, D.C., USA. October 5-8, 2003.

[5] Cofer D.D. and V.K. Garg. "A Timed Model for the Control of Discrete Event Systems Involving Decisions in the Max/Plus Algebra." *Proc. Of the 31st Conf. On Decision and Control*, pp. 3363-3368, 1992.

[6] Cohen G., D. Dubois, J.P. Quadrat, and M. Voit. "A Linear-System-Theoretic View of Discrete-Event Processes and its Use for Performance Evaluation in Manufacturing." *IEEE Trans. Automat. Control,* vol. AC-30, no.3, 1985, pp. 210-220.

[7] Cohen G., P. Moller, J.-P. Quadrat, and M. Voit. "Algebraic Tools for the Performance Evaluation of Discrete Event Systems." *Proc. IEEE*, vol. 77, no. 1, pp. 39-58. Jan. 1989.

[8] Desrochers A.A. *"Modeling and Control of Automated Manufacturing Systems,"* IEEE Computer Society Press. Washington D.C. 1990.

[9] Elsayed E.A. and T.O. Boucher. *"Analysis and Control of Production Systems."* 2nd Ed., Prentice-Hall, Englewood Cliffs, NJ. 1994.

[10] Ezpeleta S.D., J. M. Colom, and J. Martinez. "A Petri Net Based Deadlock Prevention Policy for Flexible Manufacturing Systems." *IEEE Trans. Robotics and Automation*, RA-11, pp. 173-184. April 1995.

[11] Fanti M.P., B. Maione, S. Mascolo, and B. Turchiano. "Event-Based Feedback Control for Deadlock Avoidance in Flexible Production Systems." *IEEE Transactions on Robotics and Automation*, Vol. 13, No. 3, June 1997.

[12] Graves S.C. "A Review of Production Scheduling." *Operations Research*, vol. 29, no. 4, pp. 173-184, 1981.

[13] Gurel A., S. Bogdan, and F.L. Lewis. "Matrix Approach to Deadlock-Free Dispatching in Multi-Class Finite Buffer Flowlines." *IEEE Transactions on Automatic Control*. Vol. 45, no. 11, p. 2086-2090,Nov. 2000.

[14] Harary F. *"Graph Theory."* Addison-Wesley Pub. Co., MA, 1972.

[15] Hsieh F.-S. and S.-C. Chang. "Dispatching-Driven Deadlock avoidance controller Synthesis for Flexible Manufacturing Systems." *IEEE Trans. Robotics and Automation*, RA-11, pp. 196-209, April 1994.

[16] Huang Hsiang-Hsi, F.L. Lewis, and D. Tacconi. "Deadlock Analysis Using a New Matrix-Based Controller for Reentrant Flow Line Design." *Proceedings of the 1996 Industrial Electronics, Control, and Instrumentation. IEEE IECON 22nd International Conference.* Vol. 1. pp. 463-468, 1996.

[17] Hyuenbo C., T.K. Kumaran, and R.A. Wysk. "Graph-Theoretic Deadlock Detection and Resolution for Flexible Manufacturing Systems." *IEEE Transactions on Robotics and Automation*, vol. 11, no. 3, pp. 413-421, 1995.

[18] Jeng M.D. and F. DiCesare. "Synthesis Using Resource Control Nets for Modeling Shared-Resource Systems." *IEEE Trans. Robotics and Automation*, RA-11, pp. 317-327, June 1995.

[19] Krogh B.H. and L.E. Holloway. "Synthesis of Feedback Control Logic For Discrete Manufacturing Systems," *Automatica*, vol. 21, no. 4, pp. 641-651, 1991.

[20] Kumar S. and P.R. Kumar. "Performance Bound for Queueing Networks and Scheduling Policies." *Technical report, Coordinated Science Lab., U. of Illinois, Urbana, IL.* 1992.

[21] Kumar P.R. "Re-entrant lines." *Queueing Systems: Theory and Applications.* Switzerland. vol. 13, pp. 87-110, 1993.

[22] Kumar, P.R. "Scheduling Semiconductor Manufacturing Plants." *IEEE Control Systems Magazine*, vol. 14, issue 6. pp. 33-40, December 1994.

[23] Kumar P.R. and S.P. Kumar. "Stability of Queueing Networks and Scheduling Polices." *IEEE Trans. In Automatic Contrl*, vol. 40, no. 2, pp. 251-260, Feb. 1995.

[24] Kumaran T.K., W. Chang, N. Cho, and R.A. Wysk. "A Structured Approach to Deadlock detection, avoidance, and solution in Flexible Manufacturing Systems." *Int. Journal Prod. Res.*, vol. 32, pp. 2361-2379, 1994.

[25] Kusiak A. and J. Ahn. "A Resource-Constrained Job Shop Scheduling Problem with General Precedence Constraints." *Working paper No.* 90-03, Dept. Ind. Eng., Univ. Iowa, Iowa City, IA. 1990.

[26] Kusiak A. and J. Ahn. "Intelligent Scheduling of Automated Machining Systems." *Computer Integrated Manufacturing Systems*, vol. 5, no. 1, Feb. 1992, pp. 3-14. UK.

[27] Larson T.M. "Robotic Control Language." *Advances in Instrumentation.* Vol.38, Part 1. *Proceedings of the ISA International Conference and Exhibit. ISA.* 1983, pp. 665-675. Research Triangle Park, NC, USA.

[28] Lewis F. L. "A Control System Design Philosophy for Discrete Event Manufacturing Systems." *Proc. Int. Symp. Implicit and Nonlinear Systems*, pp. 42-50, Arlington, TX. 1992.

[29] Lewis F.L., H.-H. Huang, and S. Jagannathan. "A Systems Approach to Discrete Event Controller Design for Manufacturing Systems Control." *Proceedings of the 1993 American Control Conference* (IEEE Cat. No.93CH3225-0). American Autom. Control Council. Evanston, IL, USA. vol. 2., pp. 1525-1531, 1993a.

[30] Lewis F.L., O.C. Pastravanu, and H.-H. Huang. "Controller Design and Conflict Resolution for Discrete Event Manufacturing Systems." *Proceedings of the 32nd IEEE Conference on Decision and Control* (Cat. No.93CH3307-6). IEEE. New York, NY, USA. Part vol. 4, pp. 3288-3293, 1993b.

[31] Lewis F.L. and H.-H. Huang. "Control System Design for Flexible Manufacturing Systems, in (A. Raouf and M. Ben Daya)" *Flexible Manufacturing Systems: Recent Developments*, Elsevier. 1994.

[32] Lewis F.L., H.-H.Huang, O.C. Pastravanu, and A. Gürel. "A Matrix Formulation for Design and Analysis of Discrete Event Manufacturing Systems with Shared Resources". *1994 IEEE International Conference on Systems, Man, and Cybernetics. Humans, Information and Technology* (Cat. No .94CH3571-5). New York, NY, USA. IEEE. Part vol. 2, 1994, pp. 1700-1705.

[33] Lewis F.L., A. Gurel, S. Bogdan, A. Docanalp, and O.C. Pastravanu. "Analysis of Deadlock and Circular Waits using a Matrix Model for Flexible Manufacturing Systems." *Automatica*, vol. 34, no. 9, pp. 1083-1100, Sept. 1998.

[34] López-Mellado E., "Simulation of Timed Petri Net Models." *Systems, Man and Cybernetics, 1995. Intelligent Systems for the 21st Century.*, IEEE International Conference, vol. 3, pp. 2270–2273, 1995.

[35] Mireles J. and F.L. Lewis, "On the Development and Implementation of a Matrix-Based Discrete Event Controller." *MED01, Proceedings of the 9th Mediterranean Conference on Control and Automation.* Published on CD, reference MED01-012. Dubrovnik, Croatia, June 27-29, 2001a.

[36] Mireles J. and F.L. Lewis. "Intelligent Material Handling: Development and Implementation of a Matrix-Based Discrete Event Controller." *IEEE Transactions on Industrial Electronics.* Vol. 48, issue 6, Dec. 2001b.

[37] Mireles J., Jr., Lewis F.L., and Gurel A., "Deadlock Avoidance for Manufacturing Multipart Reentrant Flow Lines Using a Matrix-Based Discrete Event Controller," *Int. J. Production Research, Vol. 40, No. 13, pp. 3139-3166*, 2002a.

[38] Mireles J., Jr., and Lewis F.L., "Implementation of a Deadlock Avoidance Policy for Multipart Reentrant Flow Lines Using a Matrix-Based Discrete Event Controller," *Conference ASME DSCD Robotics 2002*, New Orleans, Nov. 2002b.

[39] Mireles J., Jr., and Lewis F.L., "Deadlock Analysis and Routing on Free-Choice Multipart Reentrant Flow Lines Using a Matrix-Based Discrete Event Controller," *IEEE Conference on Decision and Control 2002*, Las Vegas, Dec. 2002c.

[40] Mireles, J., Jr.; and Lewis F.L., "Blocking Phenomena Analysis for Discrete Event Systems with Failures or Preventive Maintenance Schedules," *11th Mediterranean Conference on Control MED03, IEEE-CSS*, CD-ROM Proceedings DNBI 85-7665-0-86785-766-503, paper T4-008. RA, Rhodes Greece. June 2003.

[41] Murata T. "Petri Nets: Properties, Analysis and Applications." *Proceedings of the IEEE*, vol.77, no.4, pp. 541-80. USA. April 1989.

[42] Panwalkar S.S. and W. Iskander. "A Survey Of Scheduling Rules," *Operations Research*, vol. 26, pp. 45-61. 1977.

[43] Pastravanu O.C., A. Gürel, F.L. Lewis and H.-H. Huang. "Rule-Based Controller Design Algorithm For Discrete Event Manufacturing Systems." *Proceedings of the 1994 American Control Conference* (Cat. No.94CH3390-2). IEEE. New York, NY, USA. Part vol.1, pp.299-305, 1994.

[44] Pastravanu O.C., A. Gürel and F.L. Lewis. "Petri Net Based Deadlock Analysis in Flowshops with Kanban-Type Controllers." *10th ISPE/IFAC International Conference on CAD/CAM, Robotics and Factories of the Future CARs & FOF `94. Information Technology for Modern Manufacturing.* Conference Proceedings. OCRI Publications. Kanata, Ont., Canada. pp.75-80, 1994.

[45] Peterson J.L. *"Petri Net Theory and the Modeling of Systems."* Prentice-Hall. Englewood Cliffs, NJ, USA. 1981.

[46] Saridis G.N. "On the Theory of Intelligent Machines: A Survey." *Proceedings of the 27th Conference on Decision and Control.* Austin, TX USA, Dec. 1988.

[47] Saridis G.N. "Architectures of Intelligent Controls." *Intelligent Control Systems*, M.M. Gupta and N. Sinha, Eds. Piscataway, NJ: IEEE Press, ch. 6, 1995.

[48] Shimano B. "VAL: A Versatile Robot Programming and Control System." *Proceedings 3, COMPSAC79, the IEEE Computer Society's Third International Computer Software & Applications Conference*, Nov. 5, Chicago IL, pp. 878-883, 1979.

[49] Steward D.V. "On an Approach to Techniques for the Analysis of The Structure of Large Systems of Equations." *SIAM Review*, vol. 4, no. 4, pp. 321-342. 1962.

[50] Steward D.V. "The Design Structure System: A Method for Managing the Design of Complex Systems." *IEEE Trans. On Engineering Management*, vol. EM-28, no. 3, pp. 71-74, 1981.

[51] Steward D.V. *"Systems Analysis and Management: Structure, Strategy, and Design."* New York: Petrocelli Books, 1981.

[52] Spearman M.L., D.L. Woodruff, and W.J. Hopp, "CONWIP: a Pull Alternative to Kanban." *Int. J. Production Research*, vol. 28, no. 5, pp. 879-894, 1990.

[53] Tacconi D.A. and Lewis F.L. "A New Matrix Model for Discrete Event Systems: Application to Simulation." *IEEE Control Systems Magazine*, vol. 17 issue: 5, pp. 62-71., Oct. 1997.

[54] Wolter, J., S. Chakrabarty, J. Tsao. "Mating Constraint Languages for Assembly Sequence Planning." Proceedings. 1992 IEEE International Conference on Robotics And Automation (Cat. no. 92CH3140-1). Los Alamitos, California: *IEEE Computer Soc. Press*, vol 3. pp. 2367-2374. 1992,

[55] Wolter, J., S. Chakrabarty, and J. Tsao. "Methods of Knowledge Representation for Assembly Planning." *Proc. NSF Design and Manuf. Sys. Conf.*, pp. 463-468, 1992.

[56] Wysk, R. A., N. S. Yang and S. Joshi. "Detection of Deadlocks in Flexible Manufacturing Cells." *IEEE Trans. Robotics Automat.*, RA-7, pp. 853-859. 1991.

[57] Xing K.Y., K.L. Xing, J.M Li, and B.S. Hu. "Deadlock Avoidance Controller for a class of Manufacturing Systems." *Proceedings of the 1996 IEEE International Conference on Robotics and Automation*,   pp. 220-204. 1996.

[58] Zhou M., F. DiCesare. "Parallel and Sequential Mutual Exclusion for Petri Net modeling of Manufacturing Systems with Shared Resources." *IEEE Trans. Robotics and Automation*, vol. 7, no. 4, pp. 550-527. 1992.

[59] Zhou M., F. DiCesare. *"Petri Net Synthesis for Discrete Event Control of Manufacturing Systems"*, Norwell, Massachusetts: Kluwer, 1993.

[60] Zhou M. "Generalizing Parallel and Sequential Mutual Exclusions for Petri Net Synthesis of Manufacturing Systems", *IEEE Simposium on Emerging Technologies & Factory Automation*, vol. 1, 49-55. 1996.

8

Deadlock Detection and Prevention of Automated Manufacturing Systems Using Petri Nets and Siphons

MuDer Jeng
Department of Electrical Engineering , National Taiwan Ocean University, Taiwan, ROC.

Xiaolan Xie
INRIA/Macsi Project and LGIPM, ISGMP-Bat. A, Metz, France.

This chapter discusses, in three parts, Petri net(PN) siphon based approaches for detecting and preventing deadlocks in automated manufacturing systems. First, the chapter addresses the deadlock analysis of automated manufacturing systems modelled by PNs. It generalizes the well-known Commoner condition and exploits the notion of potential deadlocks, which are siphons that eventually become unmarked. The chapter then presents a linear programming-based sufficient condition under which a siphon is not a potential deadlock. Using the new sufficient condition, a mathematical programming approach and a mixed-integer programming approach are proposed for checking ordinary PNs and structurally bounded PNs, respectively, without explicitly generating siphons. In the second part of the chapter, stronger results are obtained for various PN models of a wide range of automated manufacturing systems. The classes of systems that we focus on are the classical net class, asymmetric-choice nets, as well as some recently proposed classes, including augmented marked graphs, S^3PR, RCN merged nets, ERCN merged nets, and PNR. The third part of the chapter presents an iterative deadlock prevention approach for S^3PR based on the above results.

8.1 INTRODUCTION

PNs become more and more popular for modelling automated manufacturing systems(AMS). The increasing interest in PNs is stimulated by their modelling power and a mathematical arsenal supporting the analysis of the modelled systems. Unfortunately some fundamental problems remain open. One of them is the detection and prevention of deadlocks, which is an important issue in designing AMSs.

The purpose of this chapter is to exploit the potential of siphons for the above issue. It is known that any unmarked siphon remains unmarked [4, 17]. This implies that transitions connected to it can no longer be realized. However, besides well-known results for free-choice nets based on the so-called Commoner conditions, there is hardly any efficient algorithm for checking deadlock-freeness of large PN models. We present an analysis based on potential deadlocks, which are siphons that eventually become unmarked. As will be presented, a PN without potential deadlocks is deadlock-free. A sufficient condition is shown to determine whether a PN has potential deadlocks. Its verification is based on linear programming. Since this approach is based on siphons and linear programming, its computational efficiency is relatively insensitive to the initial marking and it is expected to be more efficient than classical state enumeration approaches.

However, the number of siphons to check quickly grows beyond practical limits. To circumvent this problem, based on the above sufficient solution, it will be shown that it is possible to check deadlock-freeness without explicitly generating siphons by using mathematical programming(MP) approaches. In particular, it will be shown that a mixed-integer programming(MIP) approach can be used to verify structurally bounded PN models. Although mixed-integer programming problems are NP-hard, the MP and MIP formulations open a new way of checking deadlock-freeness. Further, numerical results for randomly generated PN models of up to 184 transitions and 194 places are very encouraging.

The concept of potential deadlocks turns out to be very powerful for analyzing PN models of automated manufacturing systems and for control of such systems. In this chapter, we investigate a wide range of PN models of manufacturing systems including asymmetric choice nets, augmented marked graphs, resource control net (RCN) merged nets, Simple sequential process with resource (S^3PR), extended resource control net (ERCN) merged nets, and process nets with resources (PNR). All these nets take into account resource constraints and resource interactions. Some of them are constructed using bottom-up synthesis approaches or modular approaches. For all these nets, the concept of potential deadlocks is used to characterize properties such as reversibility and liveness. These properties are much stronger than the deadlock-freeness checked for general PNs.

Another area where the concept of potential deadlocks plays an important role is the deadlock prevention control of manufacturing systems. We show in this chapter how this concept can be used to design efficient deadlock prevention control policies. We present a two-stage control policy that uses mathematical programming to find potential deadlocks and add control places to the original model to prevent such potential deadlocks from occurring. The basic idea is to decide the number of initial tokens of each control place such that no siphons in the controlled net can be unmarked.

Closely related to this chapter are existing techniques for deadlock detection. Among them is the classical reachability analysis [4, 17, 18]. The major drawback of this technique is the state space explosion problem, which prevents it from being applicable to even PNs of medium size. A linear algebraic approach was proposed in [20] for deadlock analysis. The major problem of this approach is the large number of linear equation systems to consider. It is worth mentioning that efforts were made in [20] to reduce the number of equation systems to consider. Other related works concern deadlock avoidance and prevention. Partial simulation is used in [21] for the deadlock avoidance control. This approach does not guarantee the avoidance of deadlocks. deadlock avoidance problem has also been considered in [1, 2, 8] in the context of manufacturing systems. Especially, siphon-based approaches were proposed in [2] for deadlock avoidance and in [8] for deadlock prevention.

This chapter is organized as follows: Section 8.2 introduces basic notions and properties of PNs. Section 8.3 is devoted to the detection of potential deadlocks by using a linear programming approach. Section 8.4 presents mathematical programming approaches. Section 8.5 presents manufacturing applications. Sections 8.6-8.9 apply the siphon-based analysis to a wide range of PN models of manufacturing systems, including asymmetric choice nets, augmented marked graphs, RCN-merged nets, S^3PR, ERCN merged nets, and PNR. Section 8.10 is devoted to siphon-based techniques for deadlock prevention control of manufacturing systems. Concluding remarks are summarized in Section 8.11.

8.2 BASIC DEFINITIONS AND PROPERTIES

Consider an ordinary PN $N = (P, T, F, M_0)$ where P is the set of places, T is the set of transitions, $F \subseteq (P \times T) \cup (T \times P)$ is the set of directed arcs, and $M_0 : P \to IN$ is the initial marking, where IN is the set of non-negative integers. The set of input (resp. output) transitions of a place p is denoted by ${}^\bullet p$ (resp. $p^\bullet$). Similarly, the set of input (resp. output) places of a transition t is denoted by ${}^\bullet t$ (resp. $t^\bullet$). For any subset of places S, ${}^\bullet S$ (resp. $S^\bullet$) denotes the set of transitions with at least one output (resp. input) place belonging to S.

A transition t is said to be enabled or firable at M_0 if for all $p \in {}^\bullet t$, $M_0(p) \geq 1$. A transition may fire if it is enabled. The new marking M' is obtained by removing one token from each of its input places and by putting one token to each of its output places. This process is denoted by $M[t > M'$. Extension to firing sequences is denoted by $M[\quad > M'$, where   is a sequence of transitions that brings M to M'. The set of all markings reachable from M_0 is denoted by $R(M_0)$.

The incidence matrix $C = [c_{ij}]$ is such that $c_{ij} = 1$, if $t_j \in {}^\bullet p_i \backslash p_i^\bullet$; $c_{ij} = -1$, if t_j $\in p_i^\bullet \backslash {}^\bullet p_i$; $c_{ij} = 0$, otherwise. For any M such that $M_0[\ >M$, $M = M_0 + C\vec{\sigma}$ where $\vec{\sigma}$, called the *firing count vector*, is a vector whose i-th entry denotes the number of occurrences of t_i in   . A non-negative integer vector $y \neq 0$ such that $Cy=0$ is called a *t-invariant*. A t-invariant y is minimal if there does not exist a t-invariant x such that $x \leq y$. Similarly, a non-negative integer vector $x \neq 0$ such that $x^T C = 0$ is called a *p-invariant*.

A transition t is said to be *live* if for any $M \in R(M_0)$, there exists a sequence of transitions firable from M which contains t. A PN is said to be live if all the transitions are live. A PN is said to be *deadlock-free* if at least one transition is enabled at every reachable marking. A place p is said to be *bounded* if there exists a constant K such that $M(p) \leq K$ for all $M \in R(M_0)$. A PN is said to be bounded if all the places are bounded. It is said to be *structurally bounded* if it is bounded whatever the initial marking is. A PN is said to be *reversible* if, for any M in $R(M_0)$, M_0 is reachable from M.

Classical classes of PNs include state machines, marked graphs, free-choice nets, asymmetric nets and mono-T-semiflow nets. *State machines* are PNs such that $t \in T: |t^\bullet| = |{}^\bullet t| = 1$. *Marked graphs* are PNs such that $p \in P: |p^\bullet| = |{}^\bullet p| = 1$. *A free-choice net* or FC net is a PN such that $p \in P: |p^\bullet| > 1 \Rightarrow {}^\bullet(p^\bullet) = \{p\}$. *An asymmetric choice net* or AC net is a PN such that $p_1, p_2 \in P: p_1^\bullet \cap p_2^\bullet \neq \varnothing \Rightarrow$ $p_1^\bullet \subseteq p_2^\bullet$ or $p_1^\bullet \supseteq p_2^\bullet$. A mono-T-semiflow net is a structurally bounded net with a unique T-invariant that includes all transitions.

A subset of places S is called a *siphon* if ${}^\bullet S \subseteq S^\bullet$, i.e. any input transition of S is also an output transition of S. It is called a *trap* if $S^\bullet \subseteq {}^\bullet S$. A siphon (resp. trap) is said to be *minimal* if it does not contain other siphons (resp. traps). The PN of Figure.8.1 has 4 siphons: {p2, p3, p4, p5}, {p1, p3, p4}, {p1, p3, p4, p5}, {p1, p2, p3, p4, p5} and 4 traps: {p2, p3, p4, p5}, {p1, p2, p3}, {p1, p2, p3, p4}, {p1, p2, p3, p4, p5}. Among them, {p2, p3, p4, p5} and {p1, p3, p4} are minimal siphons and {p2, p3, p4, p5} and {p1, p2, p3} are minimal traps. Efficient computation algorithm for determination minimal siphons and traps can be found in [26].

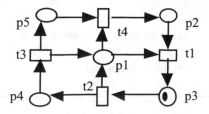

Figure. 8.1. A PN.

The following property [4, 17, 18] shows the importance of siphons and traps in the detection of deadlocks.

Property 2.1: (a) A siphon S free of tokens at a marking remains token-free. Furthermore, all transitions connected to S are not live. (b) A trap marked by a marking remains marked. (c) For any marking such that no transition is enabled, the set of empty places forms a siphon.

In the following, a marking M such that no transition is enabled is called *dead marking*. A siphon S that eventually becomes empty is called *potential deadlock*. From Property 2.1(c) and from the definition of minimal siphons,

Property 2.2: A PN is deadlock-free if no minimal siphon eventually becomes empty.

Condition of Property 2.2 holds if every siphon contains a trap marked by M_0, i.e. the Commoner condition holds. Another condition proposed in [15] is based on the invariant-controlled siphons defined as follows: A siphon S is *invariant-controlled* if there exists a vector x such that $x^T C = 0$, $x^T M_0 > 0$ and $x[p] \leq 0$, $p \notin S$. Commoner condition is sufficient but not necessary and it does not hold for PN models of many systems with shared resources and are usually difficult to check. The PN of Figure 8.1 is a counter-example. Commoner condition does not hold since siphon S = {p1, p3, p4} does not contain any trap. S is invariant-controlled with $x = [1, 0, 1, 0, -1]^T$ and hence, the PN is deadlock-free.

In general, deadlock-freeness does not imply liveness. Exceptions include marked graphs and mono-T-semiflow nets [5]. For some other important classes of PNs including FC nets and AC nets, liveness can still be checked by means of siphons and traps.

Property 2.3: An FC net is live iff every siphon contains a marked trap.

Property 2.4: An AC net is live if every siphon contains a marked trap.

8.3 DEADLOCK ANALYSIS USING SIPHON

This section addresses the deadlock analysis of general PNs. We first present conditions under which a siphon is not a potential deadlock. We then show that these conditions can be expressed as a linear system of the initial marking. This provides a tool to analyze the structural deadlock-freeness of general PNs.

8.3.1 Detection of Potential Deadlocks

From Property 2.2, a PN is deadlock-free if no siphon is a potential deadlock. Clearly,

Property 3.1: Any siphon which contains a marked trap is not a potential deadlock.

From the basic definition, a siphon S is a potential deadlock iff f(S) = 0 where

$$f(S) = \min\{M(S) \mid M \in R(M_0)\} \tag{1}$$

where $M(S)$ is the total number of tokens in S, i.e., $M(S) = \sum_{p \in S} M(p)$. Due to the large number of reachable markings, problem (1) is difficult to solve. To avoid the explicit enumeration, we consider another quantity $F(S)$ defined as follows:

$$F(S) = \min\{M(S) \mid M = M_0 + CY, M \geq 0, Y \geq 0\} \tag{2}$$

where C is the incidence matrix and M and Y are vectors of real numbers. Relation $M = M_0 + CY$ is usually called *the state equation*. From the basic theory of PNs, any reachable marking M fulfills the state equation, but the converse is not true. This implies $F(S) \leq f(S)$. Hence any siphon S such that $F(S) > 0$ is not a potential deadlock.

Property 3.2: A PN is deadlock-free if for each minimal siphon S, either it contains a marked trap or $F(S) > 0$.

Note that problem (2) is a linear programming problem and can be solved in polynomial time. From an extensive numerical experimentation [6], imposing integrity constraints to M and Y as it is usually done in the literature does not significantly improve the sufficient condition of Property 3.2. However, it significantly increases the computational complexity of $F(S)$.

Example 3.1: Consider the PN of Figure 8.1. It has two minimal siphons S_1 = {p1, p3, p4} and S_2 = {p2, p3, p4, p5}. S_2 is also a marked trap but S_1 does not contain any trap. Solving problem (2) with $S = S_1$, we obtain $F(S_1) = 1$,which implies the deadlock-freeness of the net. Since the net is an augmented marked graph to be introduced in Section VII, Property 7.6 implies that the potential-deadlock-freeness of this net implies liveness and reversibility.   □

Note that conditions of Property 3.2 are sufficient but not necessary for the deadlock-freeness of PNs. The AC net of Figure 8.2(a) is a counter-example. It is live, bounded and reversible. $M = [0, 0, 0, 2, 0, 0, 0, 1]^T$ and $Y = [0, 0, 2, 0, 2, 2]^T$ satisfy the state equation. At M, siphon {a, b, c} is unmarked. Hence $F(\{a, b, c\}) = 0$.

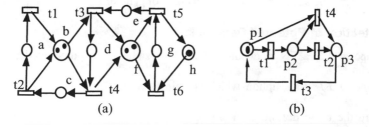

(a)   (b)

Figure 8.2. Two counter-examples.

This disturbing situation is the consequence of the spurious marking M [7], which is a solution of the state equation, but is not a reachable marking. We notice that at the spurious marking M, trap {e, f, g} marked by M_0 becomes unmarked. A natural way to reduce the number of spurious markings would be to impose constraints $M(D) \geq 1$ for all minimal traps D that are marked by M_0. Also due to spurious markings, a siphon S that contains a trap marked by M_0 can become unmarked at a spurious marking. In the PN of Figure 8.2(b), the only siphon S = {p1, p2, p3} is also a trap. The net is deadlock-free. However, M = $[0, 0, 0]^T$ and Y = $[1, 0, 1, 1]^T$ satisfy the state equation, leading to F(S) = 0.

8.3.2 Deadlock-Free Initial Markings

This subsection shows that the sufficient conditions of property 3.2 can be expressed as a system of linear inequalities of the initial marking. Nevertheless, we notice that for a given initial marking, the most efficient way to check the deadlock-freeness is still to use the results of the previous section.

From property 3.1, a siphon S which contains a trap is not a potential deadlock if $M_0(Q(S)) \geq 1$ where Q(S) denotes the maximal trap of S. This condition is also necessary if S is itself a trap. For any other siphon S, F(S) = 0 implies that system (4) has a solution:

$$M_0(p) + c_p Y \geq 0, p \in P - S; M_0(p) + c_p Y = 0, p \in S; Y \geq 0 \qquad (4)$$

where c_p denotes the row corresponding to place p of the incidence matrix C. System (4) can be expressed in matrix form : $C1Y \geq - M1_0$, $C2Y = - M2_0$, $Y \geq 0$ where C1 and C2 correspond to places in P - S and S respectively. According to Farkas-Minkowski's Lemma [16], it has a solution iff system (5) has no solution:

$$u^T C1 + v^T C2 \leq 0, u^T M1_0 + v^T M2_0 < 0, u \geq 0. \qquad (5)$$

From the basic theory of convex set [19], any solution of system $u^T C1 + v^T C2 \leq 0$ with $u \geq 0$ can be expressed as a nonnegative linear combination of a finite set of solutions of the same system, commonly called *generators*. Let K(S) be a set of generators. Clearly, F(S) = 0 and system (5) has no solution iff:

$$u^T M1_0 + v^T M2_0 \geq 0, [u,v] \in K(S) \qquad (6)$$

Property 3.3: A PN is deadlock-free if $M_0(Q(S)) \geq 1$ holds for any minimal siphon S such that $Q(S) \neq \emptyset$ and conditions (6) do not hold for all other minimal siphons.

Example 3.1 (continued): For simplicity, let $m_i = M_0(p_i)$. Siphon S_1 does not contain any trap. The matrices of system (5) are : $u = [u_2, u_5]^T$, $v = [v_1, v_3, v_4]^T$, $M1_0 = [m_2, m_5]^T$, $M2_0 = [m_1, m_3, m_4]^T$,

$$
C1 = \begin{bmatrix} -1 & 0 & 0 & 1 \\ 0 & 0 & 1 & -1 \end{bmatrix},
$$

$$
C2 = \begin{bmatrix} -1 & 1 & 1 & -1 \\ 1 & -1 & 0 & 0 \\ 0 & 1 & -1 & 0 \end{bmatrix}.
$$

$K(S_1)$ contains two solutions $[u_2, u_5, v_1, v_3, v_4]^T = [1, 0, 1, 2, 1]$ and $[0, 1, -1, -1, 0]$. As a result, $F(S_1) = 0$ iff $m_2 + m_1 + 2m_3 + m_4 \geq 0$ and $m_5 - m_1 - m_3 \geq 0$. Since the first relation is always true, $F(S_1) > 0$ iff $m_5 - m_1 - m_3 < 0$. Since siphon S_2 is also a trap, it is not a potential deadlock iff $m_2 + m_3 + m_4 + m_5 \geq 1$. Hence the PN is deadlock-free if $m_2 + m_3 + m_4 + m_5 \geq 1$ and $m_5 - m_1 - m_3 < 0$. For this net, the conditions are necessary as well. As a matter of fact, for any initial marking such that $m_5 - m_1 - m_3 \geq 0$, sequence $(t2t3t4)^{m3}(t3t4)^{m4}t4m1+m3$ leads to a dead marking.   □

Let us notice that finding the set $K(S)$ of generators is rather tedious. In practice, at least for problems of a small size, condition (6) can be directly derived from system (4) by algebraic manipulations. The direct approach consists in (i) writing down the state equation; (ii) setting the marking of every place in the siphon under consideration to zero; (iii) solving the related equations; (iv) replacing the solution in the remaining inequality constraints; (v) simplifying the inequality system to obtain the final linear system.

Example 3.2: Minimal siphons of the PN of Figure 8.3 are: $S_1 = \{p4, p5\}$, $S_2 = \{p6, p7\}$, $S_3 = \{p1, p2, p3\}$, $S_4 = \{p1, p3, p6\}$, $S_5 = \{p1, p2, p7\}$. S_1, S_2, and S_3 are also traps. S_4 and S_5 do not contain any trap. For simplicity, let $m_i = M_0(pi)$.

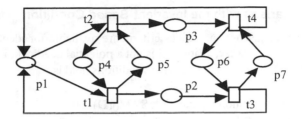

Figure 8.3. A Petri Net.

$F(S_4) = 0$ implies that $M(p)=0$ $p \in S_4$ and $M(p) \geq 0$ $p \notin S_4$ for some M satisfying the state equation. Solving the state equations $M(p) = 0$ for all $p \in S_4$ gives : $y_1 = m_1 + m_6 + 2m_3 + y_2$, $y_3 = m_6 + m_3 + y_2$, $y_4 = m_3 + y_2$. Substituting these results into the remaining state equations leads to : $M(p_2) = m_2+m_1+m_3$, $M(p_4) = m_4-m_1-m_6-2m_3$, $M(p_5) = m_5+m_1+m_6+2m_3$, $M(p_7) = m_7+m_6$. Hence $F(S_4) = 0$ iff $m_4-m_1-m_6-2m_3 \geq 0$ or equivalently, $F(S_4) > 0$ iff $m_4-m_1-m_6-2m_3 < 0$.

Similarly, $F(S_5) > 0$ iff $m_5 - m_1 - m_7 - 2m_2 < 0$. Combining with constraints related to S_1, S_2 and S_3, the PN is deadlock-free if : $m_4 + m_5 > 0$, $m_6 + m_7 > 0$, $m_1 + m_2 + m_3 > 0$, $m_1 + m_6 + 2m_3 > m_4$, $m_1 + m_7 + 2m_2 > m_5$. The first three conditions are also necessary. We show by contradiction the necessity of the last two conditions. Let us assume that the net is deadlock-free and

$$m_4-m_1-m_6-2m_3 \geq 0. \tag{7}$$

Since the net is a mono-T-semiflow net, the deadlock-freeness implies its liveness and no siphon is eventually token-free. From (7), if $m_1 > 0$, sequence $t1^{m_1}$ leads to a marking M with $M(p1) = 0$ which fulfills (7). For this reason, we assume without loss of generality $m_1=0$. Let us distinguish three cases: *Case 1:* $m_6=0$. Since S_2 and S_4 are not token-free, $m_7>0$ and $m_3 > 0$. Sequence $t4t1t3t1)^{m_3}$ is fireable, thanks to (7) and a marking in which S_4 is token-free is reached. This contradicts the liveness. *Case 2:* $m_6>0$, $m_2 > 0$. Sequence $t3t1)^{m_6}$ leads to a marking M with $M(p6) = 0$ which fulfills (7). Hence there exists a marking reachable from M such that S_4 is token-free. This contradicts the liveness. *Case 3:* $m_6 > 0$, $m_2 = 0$. Since S_3 and S_5 are not token-free, $m_7>0$ and $m_3 > 0$. Sequence $t4t1t3t1)^{m_3}$ $t3t1)^{m_6}$ is fireable and a marking in which S_4 is token-free is reached. This contradicts the liveness ☐

8.3.3 Comparison with the Invariant-Based Condition

From the above discussion, various criteria are available for identifying potential deadlocks. To summarize, a siphon S is not a potential deadlock, i.e., $M(S) > 0$ for all $M \in R(M_0)$, if one of the following conditions hold is:

C1 (Commoner condition): a trap $D \subseteq S / M_0(D) > 0$;

C2 (Invariant-control): $x / x^T C = 0, x^T M_0 > 0, x[p] \leq 0, p \notin S$;

C3: $x / x^T C \geq 0, x^T M_0 > 0, x[p] \leq 0, p \notin S$;

C4 (State-equation control) : $F(S) > 0$ with $F(S) = \min\{M(S) \mid M = M_0 + CY, M \geq 0, Y \geq 0\}$;

C5 : $F''(S) > 0$ with $F''(S) = \min\{M(S) \mid M = M_0 + CY, M \geq 0\}$.

    Property 3.4: (i) C2 $\Leftrightarrow$ C5; (ii) C3 $\Leftrightarrow$ C4; (iii) C5 $\Rightarrow$ C4; (iv) if the net is consistent, then C2 $\Leftrightarrow$ C3 $\Leftrightarrow$ C4 $\Leftrightarrow$ C5.

    Proof: To prove (i), $F''(S)=0 \Leftrightarrow -c_p Y = M_0(p), p \in S; -c_p Y \leq M_0(p), p \notin S$. According to Farkas-Minkowski's Lemma, $F''(S) = 0 \Leftrightarrow \nexists x / -x^T C = 0, x^T M_0 < 0, x[p] \geq 0, p \notin S \Leftrightarrow \nexists x / x^T C = 0, x^T M_0 > 0, x[p] \leq 0, p \notin S$. As a result, C2 $\Leftrightarrow$ C5.

    To prove (ii), $F(S)=0 \Leftrightarrow -c_p Y = M_0(p), p \in S; -c_p Y \leq M_0(p), p \notin S; Y \geq 0$. According to Farkas-Minkowski's Lemma, $F(S) = 0 \Leftrightarrow \nexists x / -x^T C \geq 0, x^T M_0 < 0, x[p] \geq 0, p \notin S \Leftrightarrow \nexists x / x^T C \geq 0, x^T M_0 > 0, x[p] \leq 0, p \notin S$. As a result, C3 $\Leftrightarrow$ C4.

    The proof of (iii) is obvious.

    To prove (iv), it is enough to show that $F''(S) = 0 \Rightarrow F(S) = 0$. Since the net is consistent, there exists a t-invariant $W > 0$ such that $C.W = 0$. $F''(S)=0 \Rightarrow Y / M(S) = 0, M = M + CY, M \geq 0 \Rightarrow M(S) = 0, M = M + C(Y + kW), M \geq 0, Y + kW \geq 0$ with $k = \max\{-Y[t] / W[t], t \in T\} \Rightarrow F(S)=0$.   Q.E.D.

    This property shows that the state-equation based condition is stronger than the invariant-based condition and these conditions are equivalent for consistent nets. However, it will be shown in the next section that the state-equation based condition can be checked without explicitly generating siphons.

8.4 MATHEMATICAL PROGRAMMING APPROACHES

The linear programming approach requires the examination of all minimal siphons. Its efficiency depends on the number of minimal siphons. Unfortunately, it is wellknown that the total number of minimal siphons (traps) grows quickly beyond practical limits and that, in the worst case, it grows exponentially in the number of nodes. One way to reduce the complexity of the linear programming approach is to find efficient algorithms for generating minimal siphons that do not contain traps without generating other siphons. Unfortunately, to the best of our knowledge, such an algorithm does not exist. Furthermore, we believe that the number of such siphons still grows exponentially in the number of nodes. In the following, we exploit the above results and show that it is possible to check dead-lock-freeness without generating minimal siphons.

8.4.1 Token-Free Siphons at a Given Marking

This subsection presents conditions for checking whether there exist siphons un-marked at a given marking M. Let S be the maximal siphon empty at M, i.e., $p \notin S, p / M(p) > 0$. The classical algorithm for determining S proceeds as follows. First it removes all places marked by M. It removes all transitions that do not have any input place and their output places. The latter step is repeated until no more nodes can be removed. It can be checked that the remaining places form the maximal siphon S that is not marked by M.

Although S can be determined in polynomial time by the above algorithm, we show that it is the solution of an integer programming problem. For this pur-pose, let us introduce the following indicators:

$$v_p = 1\{p \notin S\}, z_t = 1\{t \notin S^{\bullet}\}.$$

Clearly, any p with $v_p = 1$ and any t with $z_t = 1$ will be removed if the classi-cal algorithm is used. Since S is a siphon, $v_p = 0 \Rightarrow z_t = 0, \ t \in p^{\bullet}$ and $z_t = 1 \Rightarrow v_p = 1, \ p \in t^{\bullet}$ which lead to:

$$z_t \geq \sum_{p \in {}^{\bullet}t} v_p - |{}^{\bullet}t| + 1, t \in T \qquad (8)$$

$$v_p \geq z_t, (t, p) \in F \qquad (9)$$

$$v_p, z_t \in \{0, 1\} \qquad (10)$$

Property 4.1 [6]: Any siphon corresponds to a solution of linear system (8)-(10) and the converse holds.

An immediate implication of this property is that the maximal siphon S empty at a given marking M can be determined by the following integer pro-gramming problem and there exist siphons empty at M iff G(M) < |P|.

$$G(M) = \text{Minimize} \sum_{p \in P} v_p \ \text{ s.t. constraints (8-10) and}$$

$$v_p \geq 1\{M(p) > 0\}, p \in P. \qquad (11)$$

8.4.2 A Mathematical Programming Approach

The previous subsection naturally leads to the MP problem :

$$G^{MP} = \text{Minimize} \sum_{p \in P} v_p$$

s.t. constraints (8-11), $M = M_0 + CY$, $M \geq 0$, $Y \geq 0$.

Property 4.2: There exists a siphon S such that $F(S) = 0$ iff $G^{MP} < |P|$. Hence the PN is deadlock-free if $G^{MP} = |P|$.

From the counter-examples of Figure 8.2, $G^{MP} = |P|$ is sufficient but not necessary for deadlock-freeness of PNs. Since it was shown in Section 8.3 that $F(S)$ can be equal to 0 even if siphon S contains a trap marked by M_0, the MP approach is less powerful than the linear programming approach of Section III in the sense of correct identification of deadlocks. However, it does not require the determination of all minimal siphons.

The main difficulty in solving problem MP is the nonlinearity of constraint (11). Efficient algorithms for solving MP for general nets are subject of future research. In the following, we limit ourselves to structurally bounded nets and show that MP can be transformed into a MIP problem.

8.4.3 Structurally Bounded Nets

The key for transforming (11) into linear constraints is the structural bound defined as follows: $SB(p) = \max\{M(p) \mid M = M_0 + CY, M \geq 0, Y \geq 0\}$. Note that structural bounds can be determined by using any LP software. We assume $SB(p) > 0$ for all p since $SB(p) = 0$ implies that transitions connected to p are never enabled. Constraint (11) can be rewritten as follows:

$$v_p \geq M(p) / SB(p), \ p \in P \tag{12}$$

and problem MP becomes a MIP problem:

$$G^{MIP} = \text{Minimize} \sum_{p \in P} v_p$$

s.t. (8-10), (12), $M = M_0 + CY$, $M, Y \geq 0$.

8.4.4 Characteristics of Minimal Siphons

Problem MP or MIP intends to find the maximal siphon unmarked at a reachable marking. However, in view of Property 2.2, we only need to check whether there exists a minimal siphon that eventually becomes unmarked. This section shows that some characteristics of minimal siphons can be easily incorporated in the MP or MIP formulation to narrow the solution space.

A transition t is called an AC-type transition if its input places p_1, p_2, ..., $p_{|{\bullet}t|}$ can be labeled in such a way that: $p_1^{\bullet} \subseteq p_2^{\bullet} \subseteq ... \subseteq p_{|{\bullet}t|}^{\bullet}$.

Property 4.3: Any minimal siphon S contains at most one input place of an AC-type transition t.

An immediate consequence of this property is that constraint (8) can be strengthened as follows: $z_t = \sum_{p \in {\bullet}t} v_p - |{\bullet}t| + 1$, for all AC-type transitions t. Clearly, Property 4.3 holds for any transition of an AC net. As a result, the new constraint applies to each transition of an AC net. It is worth mentioning that Property 4.3 holds as well for extended nonself controlling nets [3].

Property 4.4: Let S be a minimal siphon and let p and q be two places such that $p^{\bullet} \subseteq q^{\bullet}$. Then $q \in S \Rightarrow p \in S$.

Property 4.4 implies that: $v_p + v_q \geq 1$. Furthermore, if $z_t = 1$ for some $t \in p^{\bullet}$, i.e., $t \notin S^{\bullet}$, $p \notin S$ and $q \notin S$. Hence, $v_p + v_q \geq 1 + z_t$, $t \in p^{\bullet}$ and p, q $/ p^{\bullet} \subseteq q^{\bullet}$. A case of interest of Property 4.4 is $|p^{\bullet}| = 1$ and $|q^{\bullet}| > 1$ which corresponds to a shared resource. The property can be easily generalized as follows.

Property 4.5: Let Q be a set of places $\{p_1, p_2, ..., p_k\}$ such that $p_1^{\bullet} \subseteq p_2^{\bullet} \subseteq ... \subseteq p_k^{\bullet}$. Then any minimal siphon contains at most one place in Q and $\sum_{p \in Q} v_p \geq |Q| - 1 + z_t$, $t \in p_1^{\bullet}$.

8.4.5 Some Results on AC and FC Nets

From [3], for any minimal siphon S of an AC net, it holds that (i) $|S \cap {\bullet}t| \leq 1$; (ii) the subnet induced by S and ${\bullet}S$ is strongly connected. Furthermore,

Property 4.6: For any minimal siphon S of an AC net that contains a trap D marked at M_0, $M(S) \geq M_0(D) > 0$, $M / M = M_0 + CY$, $Y \geq 0$.

Property 4.7: For a consistent AC net, any minimal siphon S that contains a trap is a trap and generates a state-machine component, i.e., $|{\bullet}t \cap S| = |t^{\bullet} \cap S| = 1$, $t \in S^{\bullet}$. Hence, $M(S) = M_0(S)$, $M / M = M_0 + CY$.

Property 4.8: Let (N, M_0) be an AC net such that every siphon contains a marked trap. Then $G^{MP} = |P|$. If it is structurally bounded, then $G^{MIP} = |P|$.

Since the counter-example of Figure 8.2(a) is an AC net, $G^{MP} = |P|$ or $G^{MIP} = |P|$ is sufficient but not necessary for deadlock-freeness of AC nets.

Property 4.9: Let (N, M_0) be an FC net. Then $G^{MP} = |P|$ iff (N, M_0) is live. If the net is structurally bounded, then $G^{MIP} = |P|$ iff (N, M_0) is live.

Note that it has been proved that the liveness of structurally bounded FC nets can be checked in polynomial time. Hence, Property 4.9 is not of any practical significance in terms of liveness identification of FC nets. However, it does provide support for the efficiency of the MP and MIP approaches.

8.5 APPLICATIONS

PNs of this section are structurally bounded. Deadlock-freeness is checked by solving problem MIP using the IBM commercial software package OSL (Optimization Subroutine Library) on an IBM workstation RISC System /6000 320 H. Note that the siphon-based approach proposed in this paper is also applied to property checking of PN models of real-life semi-conductor manufacturing systems [13, 27].

8.5.1 An Automated Manufacturing System

Figure 8.4 is the model of an automated manufacturing system composed of four machines, two robots, two buffers of capacity 3 and an assembly cell. It is taken from [25] where it was shown, using a synthesis method, to be live, reversible and bounded if $2 \leq M_0(p1) \leq 4$. Problem MIP is solved for $1 \leq M_0(p1) \leq 20$. The CPU time ranges from 1 to 3 seconds. $G^{MIP} = |P| = 25$, i.e. the net is deadlock-free, for $1 \leq M_0(p1) \leq 8$. Since this net is an augmented marked graph introduced later in Section 8.7, Property 7.4 implies that it is live and reversible for $1 \leq M_0(p1) \leq 8$. If $M_0(p1) \geq 9$, sequence $(t1t3t5t2t4t6)^3t7t8t1t3t5t2t1t3t10t8$ leads to a total deadlock.

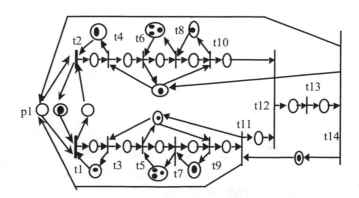

Figure 8.4. A manufacturing system (from [25]).

8.5.2 Job-Shop Like Systems

Consider a manufacturing system which is composed of a set of resource types R = $\{R_1, R_2, ..., R_n\}$ and produces a set of part types P = $\{P_1, P_2, ..., P_m\}$. There are H_j resources of type R_j. Each part of type P_i requires K_i operations (or operation steps, to be precise) and C_i resources $\{r_{ij}, 1 \leq j \leq C_i\} \subseteq R$. A resource of type r_{ij} is needed to start B_{ij}-th operation and is released at the end of E_{ij}-th operation where $1 \leq B_{ij} \leq E_{ij} \leq K_i$. The number of parts of type P_i in the system is limited to U_i due to, for example, the number of automated guided vehicles (AGVs) available.

The PN model is straightforward. Each part type P_i is represented by an elementary circuit $\{p_{i,0} t_{i,0} p_{i,1} t_{i,1} \cdots p_{i,K_i} t_{i,K_i} p_{i,0}\}$ in which $p_{i,j}$ for $1 \leq j \leq K_i$ represents the j-th operation, $t_{i,j-1}$ its beginning and $t_{i,j}$ its completion. $p_{i,0}$ contains initially U_i tokens and places $p_{i,j}$ for $1 \leq j \leq K_i$ are initially empty of tokens. Each type R_j of resources is represented by a place R_j containing initially H_j tokens. For each resource r_{ij}, an arc connects resource place r_{ij} to transition $t_{i,B_{ij}-1}$ and another arc connects $t_{i,E_{ij}}$ to r_{ij}. An example of two part types and three resource types is given in Figure 8.5.

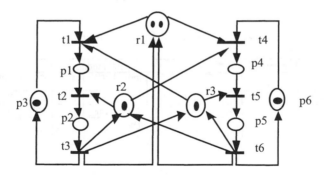

Figure 8.5. A job-shop like system.

To evaluate the performance of the MIP approach, we randomly generate H_j on $[1, \overline{H}]$, K_i on $[\underline{K}, \overline{K}]$, U_i on $[1, \overline{U}]$. For each resource type R_j, we randomly generate a subset of part types and, for each part type P_i in this subset, B_{ij} and E_{ij} are randomly generated as well.

Extensive numerical experimentations have been conducted. The PN models are too big to be presented. Let us notice that most of the randomly generated models are such that $G^{MIP} < |P|$. In each of the experimentations, the vector Y of the optimal solution is always an integer vector and a feasible firing sequence with Y as firing count vector is always found. This implies that the generated PN models such that $G^{MIP} < |P|$ are not deadlock-free. This confirms the efficiency of MIP approach in terms of deadlock detection.

To demonstrate the computational efficiency of the MIP approach, we show four typical PN models in Table 8.1. The following remarks can be made. First, PNs up to 200 places and 200 transitions can be checked in a small amount of time. For example, it takes only 44 CPU seconds to check PN PN3 that contains 194 places, 184 transitions and 578 directed arcs. Larger examples have not been tested due to the inefficient representation of PN models by means of incidence matrix. It seems that the computational efficiency depends on the structural bounds of places. For example, although PN4 is smaller than PN3, it takes 121 CPU seconds to check PN4 while it takes only 44 CPU seconds for PN3. To explain this phenomenon, notice that there can be up to 3 resources and 10 parts of the same type in PN4 while there can be only 1 resource and 5 parts of the same type in PN3. Since there is usually a small number of resources of the same type in most real-life systems (due to high resource costs and the tendency to reduce the WIP levels), we believe that the MIP approach can be used to check much larger systems. An efficient representation of PN models becomes crucial.

TABLE 8.1 Typical models.

	resource		part				PN models				
PN	m	$\overline{U}$	n	$\overline{H}$	$\underline{K}$	$\overline{K}$	|P|	|T|	|F|	G	CPU
#1	5	10	10	2	2	6	34	24	108	13	2"
#2	10	1	20	1	3	10	158	148	514	20	10"
#3	10	1	25	5	3	10	194	184	578	28	44"
#4	20	3	10	10	3	10	87	67	356	21	121"

8.6 ASYMMETRIC CHOICE NETS

This section begins a series of studies of a wide range of PN models of manufacturing systems. We will show in Sections VI-IX that stronger properties can be characterized using siphons for most meaningful PN models. Especially, it will show that reversibility and liveness can be established using siphons, a concept introduced to characterize deadlock-freeness.

This section focuses on the liveness of asymmetric choice nets, which form an important class of PNs. Let us recall that an asymmetric choice net or AC net is an ordinary PN such that $p_1^{\bullet} \cap p_2^{\bullet} \neq \varnothing \Rightarrow p_1^{\bullet} \subseteq p_2^{\bullet}$ or $p_1^{\bullet} \supseteq p_2^{\bullet}$ for all $p_1, p_2 \in P$. As pointed out in Section II, an AC net is live if every siphon contains a marked trap. It is known [14] that an AC net is live iff it is place-live, i.e., for each reachable marking M_1 and for every place p, there exists $M \in R(M_1) / M(p) > 0$. However, this condition is difficult to check. The purpose of this section is to provide easily checkable conditions for the liveness. The main result is the following property:

Property 6.1 [6]: An asymmetric choice net is live iff no minimal siphon is a potential deadlock.

From the analysis of Section 8.3, We have:

Property 6.2: An asymmetric choice net is live if for each minimal siphon S, either it contains a marked trap or F(S) > 0.

From their definition, asymmetric nets can be used to model manufacturing systems in which (i) each product requires only one additional resource at a time; (ii) whenever a product has to choose one among several possible manufacturing processes, either no shared resource is involved in this choice or the same set of shared resources is needed for any choice. Requirement (i) does not exclude the possibility of a product holding several resources at the same time. The following examples are such systems.

Example 6.1: The PN of Figure 8.6(a) is the model of a manufacturing system with two products. Product P1 has two manufacturing processes and the choice is made in place p2. Product P2 has one manufacturing process. p6 is an unshared resource. Tokens in p10 and p11 correspond to shared resources. The minimal siphons are {p5, p6}, {p1, p10, p9} and {p4, p11, p7, p8, p9}. All of them are traps. Hence the PN is live iff each of the three siphons contains a token. It is worth noticing that the PN is not bounded, which makes it impossible to apply most deadlock detection techniques.

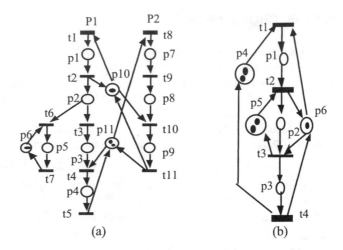

Figure 8.6. PN models of manufacturing systems.

The PN of Figure 8.6(b) is the model of a manufacturing system given in [23]. Liveness and reversibility were proved under conditions specified in terms of sequential mutual exclusion. The PN is an AC net with four minimal siphons S_1 ={p1, p2, p3, p4}, S_2 = {p2, p5}, S_3 = {p1, p6, p3}, and S_4 = {p3, p5, p6}. The first three siphons are traps. By expressing $F(S_4) = 0$ in terms of the initial marking, it can be shown that $F(S_4) > 0$ iff $M_0(p5) + M_0(p6) > M_0(p4)$. It can be checked that this condition is also necessary for deadlock-freeness. Finally, the net is live iff $M_0(p5)+M_0(p6) > M_0(p4)$, $M_0(S_1) > 0$, $M_0(S_2) > 0$, $M_0(S_3) > 0$. □

8.7 AUGMENTED MARKED GRAPHS

In this section, we present an extension of marked graphs, called augmented marked graphs, which can be used for modelling real-life systems with shared resources. It will be shown that siphons can be used to establish liveness and reversibility of augmented marked graphs. Details on proofs of the results can be found in [6].

8.7.1 Definition

An augmented marked graph is a PN N with an initial marking M_0 composed of two sets P and R of places and a set T of transitions and satisfying the following conditions:

H1.   The net G obtained by removing the places in R is a marked graph;

H2. To each place $r \in R$ are associated $k_r > 1$ pairs of transitions denoted by $D^r = \{(a_{r1}, b_{r1}), \ldots, (a_{rk_r}, b_{rk_r})\}$ where $a_{ri}, b_{ri} \in T, i \in N_r = \{1, \ldots, k_r\}$. Furthermore, $r^{\bullet} = \{a_{r1}, \ldots, a_{rk_r}\}, {}^{\bullet}r = \{b_{r1}, \ldots, b_{rk_r}\}, a_{ri} \neq a_{rj}$ and $b_{ri} \neq b_{rj}$ $i \neq j \in N_r$, and there exists an elementary path O_{ri} in G connecting a_{ri} to b_{ri} if $a_{ri} \neq b_{ri}$;

H3. Each elementary circuit in G is marked by M_0;

H4. Every place in R is marked by M_0 and no path O_{ri} is marked by M_0.

PNs of Figures 8.2(a), 8.3, 8.4 and 8.5 are augmented marked graphs. In the following, we call places in R *resource places*. According to the above assumptions, all resources are initially available. A token in a resource place r is used for the firing of a transition a_{ri}, it then moves along path O_{ri}, and returns to place r after the firing of b_{ri}.

8.7.2 Properties

Since any place p in P has one input transition and one output transition, by abuse of notation, we denote by ${}^{\bullet}p$ and $p^{\bullet}$ its input transition and its output transition.

Property 7.1: Each resource place $r \in R$ together with the places in the paths O_{ri} forms a p-invariant and $M \in R(M_0)$,

$$M(r) + \sum_{i \in N_r} \sum_{p \in O_{ri}} M(p) = M_0(r) + \sum_{i \in N_r} \sum_{p \in O_{ri}} M_0(p).$$

Property 7.2: An augmented marked graph is reversible if it is live.

Property 7.3: Let $<N, M_0>$ be a live PN satisfying assumptions H1, H2, H3. Let $M^* \geq 0$ be a marking such that $<C1>, Y \in IN^{|T|}$ such that $M^* = M_0 + CY$, and $<C2>$ no place in paths O_{ri} is marked by M^*. Then M^* is reachable from M_0 and $M^*(r) > 0, r \in R$.

Property 7.4: An augmented marked graph is live iff it does not contain any potential deadlock.

The implications of Properties 7.1, 7.2 and 7.4 are obvious. Concerning Property 7.3, since H4 does not hold, some resources are not free initially and the net is not an augmented marked graph. Nevertheless, Property 7.3 ensures that it is possible to make all resources free provided the net is live and conditions C1 and C2 hold. From the analysis of Section III,

Property 7.5: An augmented marked graph is live and reversible if for each minimal siphon S containing at least one resource place, either it contains a marked trap or F(S) > 0.

Example 7.1: The PN of Figure 8.6(b) is an augmented marked graph if $M_0(p1) = M_0(p2) = M_0(p3) = 0$. It is live and reversible iff $M_0(p5) + M_0(p6) > M_0(p4)$, $M_0(p4) > 0$, $M_0(p5) > 0$ and $M_0(p6) > 0$.   □

Let us note that Property 7.4 can be easily generalized as follows:

Property 7.6: Let <N, M_0> be a PN satisfying assumptions H1, H2 and H3. If there exists a marking $M^* \geq 0$ satisfying conditions C1 and C2, then <N, M_0> is live iff it does not contain any potential deadlock. Furthermore, M^* is a home state, i.e. $M^* \in R(M)$ for all $M \in R(M_0)$.

8.7.3 Modelling Manufacturing Systems

From the definition of augmented marked graphs, they can be used to model manufacturing systems in which (i) every product has a single manufacturing process, i.e., the operations needed to produce it can be described by an acyclic graph in which nodes with multiple input arcs correspond to assembly operations and nodes with multiple output arcs correspond to disassembly operations; and (ii) each operation requires a given set of shared resources. The following example presents such a system.

Example 7.2: The PN model of a job-shop like system of Section 8.5.2 is an augmented marked graph. As a result, it is live and reversible iff it does not have potential deadlocks. Furthermore, since it is structurally bounded, the MIP approach can be used to check liveness and reversibility. Consider the PN of Figure 8.5. It has one minimal siphon S = {p2, p5, r2, r3} that does not contain a trap. Commoner condition does not hold and S is not invariant-controlled whatever the initial marking. Consider an initial marking such that $M_0(p) > 0$, $p \in$ {p3, p6, r1, r2, r3} and $M_0(p) = 0$, $p \in$ {p1, p2, p4, p5}. By expressing F(S) = 0 in terms of initial marking, it can be shown that F(S) = 0 iff $M_0(p3) \geq M_0(r3)$, $M_0(p6) \geq M_0(r2)$, $M_0(r1) \geq M_0(r2) + M_0(r3)$. It can be checked that these conditions are necessary and sufficient for the existence of deadlocks. If one of these conditions does not hold, the PN is live and reversible.

Systems with multiple manufacturing processes can still be modelled by augmented marked graphs provided that the choice of the manufacturing process is made at the beginning and prior to the start of the first operation. In the PN model of such a system, the places that model the choice of manufacturing processes can be considered as resource places. Figure 8.7 is the PN model of a product with two manufacturing processes. Process 1, i.e., t1p1t2p2t3, requires two operations while process 2, i.e. t4p4t5, requires only one operation. The choice of the manufacturing processes is made in place p3.

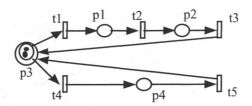

Figure 8.7. Two manufacturing processes.

8.8 RESOURCE CONTROL NETS AND THEIR INTEGRATION

In this section, siphons are used to characterize the properties of some integrated nets obtained using the modelling methodology proposed in [11], which is re-source oriented and is modular. The main steps of this methodology include the modelling of the dynamic behavior of each resource using PNs, and the integration of resource net modules by taking into account interactions or synchronizations among resources. Each resource is modelled using resource control nets(RCN) and the integration is realized through merging of common transitions and common transition subnets.

8.8.1 Definitions

Definition 8.1: A RCN is a strongly connected state machine $G = (P, T, F, M_0)$ in which there exists one and only one place $p_r \in P$, called *resource place*, such that $M_0(p_r) \neq 0$. The remaining places $p \in P - \{p_r\}$ are called *operation places*.

Definition 8.2: A *transition subnet* $G' = (P', T', F', M'_0)$ of a PN G is a subnet of G such that input transitions and output transitions of any place $p \in P'$ are transitions in T'. In other words, the places of a transition subnet are local.

Definition 8.3: A PN $G = (P, T, F, M_0)$, obtained by merging n RCN's $\{G_s \mid G_s = (P_s, T_s, F_s, M_{s0}), s = 1, \ldots, n\}$ through common transitions and common transition subnets, is a net such that: $P = P_1 \cup \ldots \cup P_n$, $T = T_1 \cup \ldots \cup T_n$, $F = F_1 \cup \ldots \cup F_n$, $M_0(p) = M_{s0}(p)$ if $p \in P_s$. Clearly, in the integrated model G, the common elements of any two RCNs form a transition subnet. In the following, G will be called an *RCN-merged net*.

Figure 8.8 is obtained by merging 7 RCNs. Places p1, p4, p7, p8, p9, p12 and p15 are resource places and the other places are operation places.

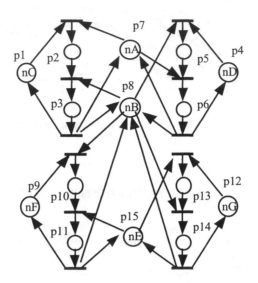

Figure 8.8. An example.

By construction, an RCN-merged net is state machine decomposable. Each RCN is a state machine component. The total number of tokens in any state machine component (i.e., any RCN) remains constant whatever transition firings. As a result,

Property 8.1: An RCN-merged net is conservative and structurally bounded.

In the following, additional restrictions concerning the merging of RCNs are considered.

Restriction A. At each common transition, there exists at most one input place that is an operation place.

Restriction B. Common transition subnets should not include resource places.

Restriction C. The PN G* derived from the integrated model G by removing the resource places is an acyclic graph.

Restriction C is motivated by the fact that the net G*, obtained by removing resource constraints, models flows of material or information. These flows are usually acyclic and situations of Figure 8.9 should not happen. Unfortunately, restriction C rules out the possibility of rework and resource failures. Extensions for taking into account local loops can be found in [13].

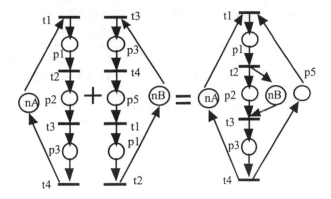

Figure 8.9. A model that does not satisfy restriction C.

8.8.2 Properties

Reversibility of an RCN-merged net can be easily checked using siphons, properties usually used to characterize deadlocks.

Theorem 8.1. Suppose that restrictions A, B and C hold. Then G is reversible iff no siphon of G can become empty.

The basic idea of the proof is as follows. Starting from any reachable marking, by suspending the source transitions of G^*, the other transitions can only be fired a finite number of times. A marking M such that only source transitions might fire is reached. The proof is completed by showing that $M \neq M_0$ implies the existence of an empty siphon.

Example 8.1: Consider the PN of Figure 8.8. It has three minimal siphons that do not contain marked traps: $S1 = \{p8, p3, p6, p11, p14, p15, p7\}$, $S2 = \{p8, p3, p6, p11, p14, p15, p5\}$ and $S3 = \{p8, p3, p6, p11, p14, p10, p7\}$. From Property 3, the condition of Theorem 1 holds if $F(S1) > 0$, $F(S2) > 0$ and $F(S3) > 0$. After some algebraic manipulations, it can be shown that $F(S1) > 0$ iff

$$(nE > nG) \vee (nA > nC) \vee (nB > nF + nD), \tag{13}$$

$F(S2) > 0$ iff

$$(nE > nG) \vee (nB > nF), \tag{14}$$

and $F(S3) > 0$ iff

$$(nA > nC) \vee (nB > nD). \tag{15}$$

It can be shown that conditions (13-15) are necessary as well. We notice that they are less restrictive than the following condition obtained in [11] by using circular-wait: $((nA > nC) \vee (nB > nF + nD)) \wedge ((nE > nG) \vee (nB > nF + nD))$. The superiority of siphon-based approach will be confirmed later.   □

Under the reversibility, the RCN-merged net G is deadlock-free iff the initial marking is not a dead marking, i.e., at least one transition can fire. Furthermore, the liveness of the integrated model reduces to its potential liveness, a property easier to check.

Theorem 8.2. Suppose that restrictions A, B and C hold, then G is live and reversible iff no siphon of G can become empty and if every transition can fire at least once, i.e., if every transition is potentially firable.

The following results can be used to check the potential firability of the transitions.

Restriction D. At any common transition, there is at most one output place that is an operation place.

Theorem 8.3. Suppose that restrictions A, B, C and D hold, any transition in G is potentially firable.

It can be checked that the net of Figure 8.8 satisfies restriction D. As a result, it is live and reversible iff conditions (13-15) hold.

Consider now the case where restriction D does not hold. The verification of the potential firability becomes more difficult as firing any transition not fulfilling restriction D creates parallel processes. One solution to checking the potential firability of a given transition t is to check whether a sequence of transitions containing t can be found either by explicit enumeration or heuristic search. Structural properties of the RCN-merged nets are used in [12] to check the potential firability of RCN-merged nets.

8.8.3 Siphon, Circular Structures and Circular wait

The notions of circular structure and circular wait were used in [11] for analyzing liveness of RCN-merged nets. The purpose of this section is to show a relation between siphons and these notions.

First, a *circular structure* is a set of places $CS = \{p_1, p_{s_1r}, p_2, p_{s_2r}, \ldots, p_k, p_{s_kr}\}$ such that $p_1 \in G_{s_k}$, $p_{i+1} \in G_{s_i}$, $1 \le i < k$, and p_i and p_{s_ir} share at least one common transition. A *circular wait* is defined by a set of circular structures CS_1, $\ldots$, CS_m and a reachable marking M such that:

$$\sum_{p \in P_{ox}} M(p) = M(p_{xr}), \ x \in W$$

where W is the set of RCNs involved in the circular structures and P_{ox} is the set of operation places of RCN G_x that belong to the circular structures.

Theorem 8.4. Suppose that restrictions A, B and C hold. If there exists a siphon that can become empty, then (i) there exists a reachable marking M and a circular structure $\{p_1, p_{s_1r}, p_2, p_{s_2r}, \ldots, p_k, p_{s_kr}\}$ such that $M(p_i) > 0$ and $M(p_{s_ir}) = 0$; and (ii) there exists a circular wait.

From Theorem 8.4, the existence of a siphon that can become empty implies the existence of a circular wait. However, the converse is not true. A counter-example is given in Figure 8.10. The reachable marking $M = [0\ 1\ 0\ 0\ 1\ 0]^T$ and the circular structure {p2, p4, p5, p1} form a circular wait. However, the net is live and reversible. It can be checked using results of this paper. First, restriction D holds, which implies that every transition is potentially firable. There are two minimal siphons {p1, p2, p3} and {p4, p5, p6}. Each of them is a marked trap as well. Hence, by Theorem 8.2, the RCN-merged net is live and reversible.

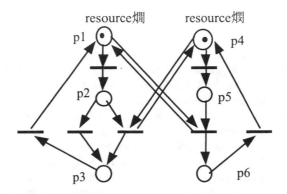

Figure 8.10. A counter-example.

From the above comments, we conclude that the results in this section are stronger than those of [11]. Furthermore, siphon-based conditions can be checked using Property 3.2 or mathematical programming techniques presented earlier. Finally, the reversibility of RCN-merged nets is also established. Below we present a sub class of RCN-merged nets called S³PR.

8.8.4 S³PR nets

This class of S³PR nets has been proposed by Ezpeleta *et al.* [8]. An S³PR is defined as the union of a set of nets N_i sharing common places, called *resource idle places* (also called *resource places* in this paper) P_{Ri}, such that $N_i = (P_i \cup \{p_i^0\} \cup P_{Ri}, T_i, F_i)$ where (1) $P_i \neq \phi$, $p_i^0 \notin P_i$; (2) N_i' is a strongly connected state machine where $N_i' = (P_i \cup \{p_i^0\}, T_i, F_i')$ is the resultant net after P_{Ri} is removed from N_i; (3) every circuit of N_i' contains the place p_i^0 and (4) any two N_i' are composable when they share a set of common resource idle places. In the above definition, p_i^0 is called the *process idle place* and P_i is called the set of *operation places*. We shall call N_i' a *process net*. An S³PR has a constraint that only one shared resource is allowed at each operation state, i.e., a place in P_i is marked. In addition, the resource used in a state is released when the system moves to the next state. Figure 8.8 is also an S³PR net with four process nets and three resource places nA, nB, nE.

It can be easily shown that an S³PR net is also an RCN-merged net that satisfies restrictions A, B, C and D. As a result:

Theorem 8.5. An S³PR net is live and reversible iff no siphon in it can become unmarked.

8.8.5 Extensions

It is well-known that state machines cannot represent parallel activities and synchronization. As a result, the RCN-based modular approach cannot represent manufacturing systems with assembly/disassembly operations. The extension proposed here is based on the notion of parallel blocks.

Definition 8.4: A *parallel block* is PN with one source transition, called *fork*, and one sink transition, called *join*, together with $k > 1$ independent unmarked state machines connecting the fork to the join.

Definition 8.5: An *ERCN* is a PN derived from an RCN by iteratively replacing transitions by parallel blocks.

By construction, an ERCN is state-machine decomposable. A state-machine component can be derived from the initial RCN by choosing one and only one branch for each parallel block. As a result, it is conservative and hence structurally bounded. Further, using the transformation rules proposed in [4], it can be shown that an ERCN is live and reversible.

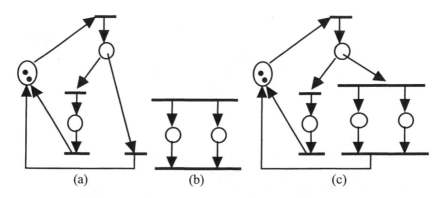

Figure 8.11. (a) An RCN, (b) a parallel block, (c) an ERCN.

As in RCN-merged nets, the integration of ERCN modules is done by merging common transitions or common transition subnets.

Definition 8.6: A PN $G = (P, T, F, M_0)$, obtained by merging n ERCNs $\{G_s \mid G_s = (P_s, T_s, F_s, M_{s0}), s = 1, \ldots, n\}$ through common transitions and common transition subnets, is a net such that: $P = P_1 \cup \ldots \cup P_n$, $T = T_1 \cup \ldots \cup T_n$, $F = F_1 \cup \ldots \cup F_n$, $M_0(p) = M_{s0}(p)$ if $p \in P_s$. Clearly, in the integrated model G, the common elements of any two ERCNs form a transition subnet. In the following, G will be called an *ERCN-merged net*.

Figure 8.12 is an example of ERCN-merged nets. It allows us to illustrate the approach of this paper. The net is obtained by merging 3 ERCNs. Places p1, p10, and p11 are resource places and the other places are operation places. ERCN A and C are merged through subnet {t2, p3, t3, t7, p8, t8}, B and C through subnet {t3, p4, t4, t6, p7, t7}, and A and B through {t3, t7}.

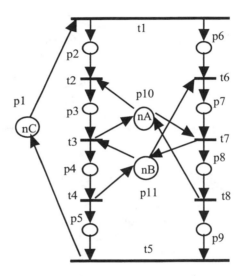

Figure 8.12. An ERCN-merged net.

Results of RCN-merged nets are extended in [22] to the ERCN-merged nets under similar restrictions with restriction A replaced as follows:

Restriction A. At each common transition, any ERCN either contains all input places that are operation places or it does not contain any such input place.

8.9 PROCESS NETS WITH RESOURCES

A much broader class of nets than S^3PR and augmented marked graphs is presented in this subsection. It is called the class of process nets with resources

(PNR). The relationship of PNR, S³PR, RCN-merged nets, ERCN-merged nets, and augmented marked graphs is shown in Figure 8.13. It should be noted that each of these net classes partially overlaps with the classical class of AC nets.

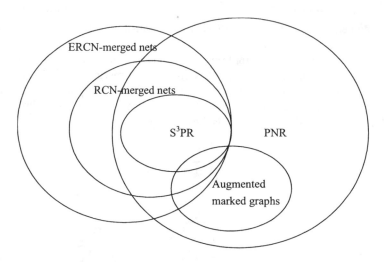

Figure 8.13. Relationship of the models presented.

Modeling manufacturing systems using PNR is a bottom-up approach. To construct a PNR, we first specify the process flows of each part type in the system using a so-called *process net* without the consideration of the resource require-ments. Then, *resource places* denoting the availability of resource types are added to the process nets such that for each resource place, the input and output transi-tions of the resource place generate a *transition subnet*.

8.9.1 Process Nets

Definition 9.1: A process net $G = (P, T, F, M_0)$ is a consistent, conservative, strongly connected, and live PN that satisfies the following three conditions:

Condition I: G contains exactly one place p_o called the *job place* such that $M_0(p_o) = k > 0$, and $M_0(p) = 0$, $\forall p \in P$ such that p (called *operation places*) $\neq p_o$.

Condition S: The resultant net G^* after removing p_o from G is acyclic, i.e., every circuit in G includes p_o, and all output transitions of p_o are source transitions of G^*.

Strong Reversibility: Under a *firing policy X* that inhibits the firing of transi-tion t, $\forall t \in p_o\bullet$, we can always return to M_0 starting from any marking $M \in R(M_0)$.

A process net denotes the process flows of a part type. The initial marking in the job place represents the number of raw parts. A process net can model far more complex process flows that those in prior work. For example, the process flow models for S^3PRs, RCN merged nets, ERCN merged nets, and augmented marked graph are state machines (i.e., RCN), subclasses of free-choice (FC) nets (i.e., ERCN), and marked graphs, respectively. That is, they are all subclasses of FC nets, which are sufficient to model the process flows in many systems.

Consider the implications of the above conditions of a process net in manufacturing. Consistency, conservativeness, strong-connectedness, and liveness are common and meaningful assumptions. Condition I is justified since the initial condition is usually that the system does not contain unfinished parts. Tokens in the job and operation places represent raw parts ready and parts being processed, respectively. Strong reversibility is also reasonable in manufacturing since an unfinished part will finish processing if enough resources are available and does not depend on the arrival of a new part in the future. From the manufacturing viewpoints, Condition S is the strongest restriction of all the above conditions. Under this condition, we cannot model local process cycles because each circuit in G contains p_o, the place where tokens are initially located. We also notice that Condition S has been assumed or implied in many prior work's.

Considering the conditions of process nets, the identification of consistency, conservativeness, and strong-connectedness is easy because these are all structural conditions that can be checked using linear algebraic techniques. In addition, it is not difficult to check the liveness of a process net or to construct a live process net because of the arguments explained below. First of all, it is easy to check the liveness of small or simple process nets. Second, using refinement techniques, we can construct a large or complex live process net. Last, since interactions among resources have not yet been considered, when given a large or complex process net, we can usually verify its liveness using reduction rules. In the following, we will discuss how strong reversibility can be checked by presenting a necessary and sufficient condition for strong reversibility based on the siphons.

Proposition 9.1: Under conditions I and S, a strongly connected and conservative net G is strongly reversible iff $M(Q) - M(p_o) > 0$, for all siphon Q and for all reachable marking $M \neq M_0$.

The above property can be transformed into a sufficient condition for strong reversibility. By replacing the reachability condition by the state equation, the above property implies that strong reversibility holds if $\beta(Q) > 0$ for all siphons Q with

$$\beta(Q) = \min\{M(Q) - M(p_o) \mid M = M_0 + CY, M \geq 0, Y \geq 0, M(p_o) \leq M_0(p_o) - 1\}.$$

It can be easily proved that   (Q) > 0 for any siphon Q that contains a P-invariant $X \geq 0$ in the sense that $XC = 0$ and $X(p) = 0$, $\forall p \notin Q$. Further, the mixed integer programming (MIP) technique presented earlier can be easily adopted to check this sufficient condition without explicitly generating siphons.

8.9.2 PNRs

A PNR considers the resource requirements of a manufacturing system by adding so-called *resource places*, representing the availability of resource types, to process nets. The concept of transition subnets [11] is used for connecting transitions of process nets to resource places.

Definition 9.2: A transition subnet $G_s = (P_s, T_s, F_s, M_{0s})$ of a net $G = (P, T, F, M_0)$ satisfies $(\bullet P_s \cup P_s \bullet) \cap (T - T_s) = \varnothing$ and $\forall p \in P_s$, $M_{0s}(p) = 0$.

From the above definition, a transition subnet of a process net does not contain the job place. Furthermore, due to Condition S of a process net, a transition subnet of a process net has source and sink transitions. As a result, we can generate a transition subnet by its source and sink transitions as follows:

Definition 9.3: In a set of process nets, a transition subnet generated by two sets of transitions T_1 and T_2 is the circuit-free union of all initially unmarked paths from T_1 to T_2.

Definition 9.4: A PNR G is the resultant net after a set of resource places is added to a set of process nets such that for each resource place p_{rx}, $p_{rx} \bullet$ and $\bullet p_{rx}$ generate a transition subnet G_x satisfying the following two conditions: (i) $M_0(p_{rx}) \neq 0$ and $M_0(p) = 0$, $\forall p \in P_x$; and (ii) p_{rx}, G_x and the connected arcs form a conservative net, called *resource net*.

The first condition above is reasonable in manufacturing since in the initial state the system is usually empty of unfinished parts and all resources are free. The second condition is obviously necessary for manufacturing resources.

Example 9.1: Figure 8.15 is a PNR (the job places and resource places are denoted as double circles) after four resource places are added to the two process nets G_1 and G_2 in Figure 8.14. The four resource nets of the PNR can be easily derived.□

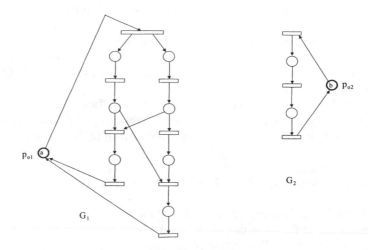

Figure 8.14. Two process nets.

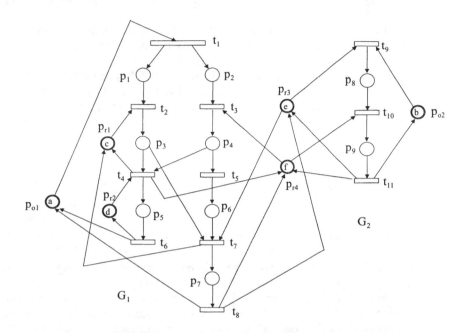

Figure 8.15. A PNR with two process nets and four resource places.

8.9.3 Properties of PNR

In the following, we extend the concepts of strong reversibility and firing policy X for process nets to those for PNRs. Then we present a necessary and sufficient condition for strong reversibility of PNRs. As a result, this condition is a sufficient condition for reversibility of PNRs.

Definition 9.5: A PNR G is strongly reversible iff under firing policy X that inhibits the firing of transition t, $\forall t \in p_o \bullet$, $\forall p_o \in P^J$, where P^J is the set of all job places, we can always return to M_0 starting from any marking $M \in R(M_0)$.

Theorem 9.1: A PNR G is strongly reversible iff G does not contain any siphon Q such that

$$\exists M \in R(M_0), M(p) < M_0(p), \forall p \in Q \cap P^J, \text{ and } \sum_{p \in Q \backslash P^J} M(p) = 0 \quad (SR).$$

The above theorem can be transformed into a sufficient condition for strong reversibility. By replacing the reachability condition by the state equation, the

above property implies that strong reversibility holds if   (Q) > 0 for all siphons Q
with   (Q) = min{M(Q\P^J) | M = M$_0$ + CY, M ≥ 0,Y ≥ 0, M(p) ≤ M$_0$(p) −1, ∀p ∈
Q∩P^J}.

It can be easily proved that   (Q) > 0 for any siphon Q that contains a P-
invariant. Further, the MIP technique can be easily adopted to check this sufficient
condition without explicitly generating siphons.

Example 9.2: Consider the net in Figure 8.15. It has one minimal siphon Q$_1$
= {p$_4$, p$_7$, p$_9$, p$_{r3}$, p$_{r4}$} that does not contain a P-invariant. The condition of Theorem 9.1 holds if   (Q$_1$) > 0.   (Q$_1$) = 0 iff there exist M ≥ 0 and Y = (y$_1$, y$_2$, y$_3$, y$_4$,
y$_5$, y$_6$, y$_7$, y$_8$, y$_9$, y$_{10}$, y$_{11}$)^T ≥ 0 such that M = M$_0$ + CY, M(p) = 0, ∀p ∈ Q$_1$, M(p) ≥
0, ∀p ∉ Q$_1$. Solving the equations leads to y$_3$ = y$_4$ + y$_5$, y$_7$ = y$_8$, y$_{10}$ = y$_{11}$, y$_5$ = y$_7$ +
f, and y$_9$ = y$_{10}$ + e. Replacing them into the last relation and after some algebraic
manipulations, it can be shown that   (Q$_1$) > 0 if

$$(a < f) \lor (b < e). \tag{16}$$

It can be shown that the above condition is necessary as well. If condition
(16) does not hold, a ≥ f and b ≥ e. Then the sequence t$_9$^{e}(t$_1$t$_3$t$_5$)^{f}t$_1$$^{a-f}t_2$$^{\max\{c,\,a\}}$ leads to
a total deadlock where σ^k denotes the *k*-th repetition of σ. According to Theorem
9.1, the net is strongly reversible iff condition (16) holds.

Note that a PNR G is reversible if G is strongly reversible. Since reversibility plus potential firability (L1 liveness) for each transition imply liveness, it is
sufficient to check the potential firability of each transition in a PNR to verify its
liveness due to Theorem 9.1.

Theorem 9.2: A PNR G is live and strongly reversible iff G contains no siphons fulfilling condition SR and each transition is potentially firable.

As a result, the liveness problem is reduced to the potential firability problem. The latter is much simpler to check than the former. Therefore, given a PNR
G, we only need to check its process nets one by one for potential firability of
every transition. For each process net G$_i$, we allocate all resources to G$_i$ since we
are only interested if each transition in G$_i$ can fire once. That is, we prohibit the
firing of any transition that is not in G$_i$ starting from the initial marking. This leads
to the so-called *isolated process net*. The verification of the potential firability of
isolated process nets is addressed in [14]. The potential firability of all transitions
of the PNR net of Figure 8.15 can be easily proved by finding for each transition a
firing sequence and hence the net is live and reversible.

8.10 DEADLOCK PREVENTION CONTROL

The aforementioned MIP deadlock analysis can be used for deadlock prevention
control. This section introduces such a deadlock prevention control policy [9] for
S^{3}PR. The policy iteratively utilizes the MIP method to find an unmarked siphon,
and consists of two stages: *siphon control* and *augmented siphon control*. At the

siphon control stage, each unmarked siphon of the initial net is controlled by adding the output arcs of a control place to the sink transitions of the siphon. At the augmented siphon control stage, each unmarked siphon generated from the first stage is controlled by adding the weighted output arcs of a control place to some source transitions of the resultant net after all initially marked places of the initial net are removed. This latter stage assures that no further unmarked siphons will be generated. This control policy guarantees that the final controlled net is live and reversible.

The following notation is used to describe the policy.

- $N^0 = (P^0, T^0, F^0)$ is an S^3PR;
- $N^1 = (P^1, T^1, F^1)$ is the net obtained after the siphons control stage where the control places are denoted as dashed circles,
- $N^2 = (P^1 \cup \{P_{AC(S)}\}, T^2, W^2, F^2)$ is the net obtained after the augmented siphons control stage, where $P_{AC(S)}$ is a control place, denoted as a double-dashed circle. Note that N^1 is always an ordinary net while N^2 may be a generalized net.
- $OP(r)$ is the set of operation places requiring resource r.
- R is the set of resource places.
- $O(S)$ is the set of operation places, called *stealing places*, denoted as shaded circles; such places require resources and are not in a siphon S.

8.10.1 Siphon Control

To prevent each minimal siphon S_i of N^0 from becoming unmarked, a control place p_{ci} is added as follows Figure 8.16:

1. Determine the set of resource places $\{r_1, r_2, \cdots \}$ of S_i.
2. Determine the set of stealing places $O(S_i) = \{p_1, p_2, \cdots \}$ that require resources $\{r_1, r_2, \cdots \}$ and that are not in S_i.
3. For each stealing place p of S_i, (i) $\forall t \in \bullet p$, add an arc from p_{ci} to t if t does not have an input place that is a stealing place, i.e., if $\bullet t \cap O(S_i) = \emptyset$; and (ii) $\forall t \in p\bullet$, add an arc from t to p_{ci} if $t\bullet \cap O(S_i) = \emptyset$.
4. $M_0(p_{ci}) = \displaystyle\sum_{r \in S \cap R} M_0(r) - 1.$

From *Theorem* 10.1 below, $M_0(p_{ci}) \geq 1$.

Theorem 10.1: Any minimal siphon S such that $\exists M = M_0 + CY$ and $M(S) = 0$ contains at least two resource places.

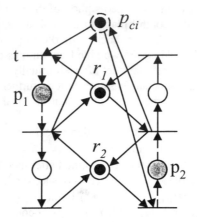

Figure 8.16. A siphon control place.

At the end of this stage, the resultant net N^1 is obtained by

(1) Choosing a set of minimal siphons $\{S_1, S_2, \cdots, S_n\}$ such that $\exists\ M = M_0 + CY / M(S_i) = 0$;

(2) Adding a control place p_{ci} to each siphon S_i such that S_i can not be unmarked, so that no siphon of N^0 can become unmarked.

N^1 has the following properties:

Theorem 10.2: N^1 is an RCN-merged net.

Theorem 10.3: N^1 is live and reversible if and only if no siphon in N^1 can become unmarked.

Unfortunately, the condition of *Theorem 10.3* does not always hold. Siphons of the net N^1 can still become unmarked. An example is illustrated in Figure 8.17. Using the above steps, we can obtain the net N^1 in Figure 8.18 after adding control places p_{c1} and p_{c2} to the net N^0 in Figure 8.17. We find out that N^1 has a new siphon $\{p_4, p_5, p_6, p_8, p_9, p_{10}, p_{c1}\}$.

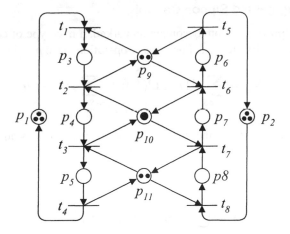

Figure 8.17. An example of N^0.

Therefore, additional control places should be added to N^1 such that no siphons become unmarked. This results in the augmented siphons control stage.

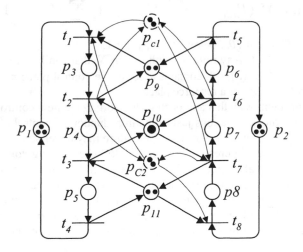

Figure 8.18. An example of N^1.

8.10.2 Augmented Siphon Control

In order to prevent S from becoming unmarked, a new type of control places will be introduced. First, let us define, for any operation place $p \notin S$,

$$N_p = \sum_{p_{ci} \in S} 1\{p \in O(S)\} + \sum_{r \in S \cap R} 1\{p \in OP(r)\}$$

N_p corresponds to the number of control place tokens and resource places tokens in S held by a token in p.

A straightforward method to prevent each new siphon S from becoming unmarked is to introduce a control place $P_{AC(S)}$ as follows:

Determine the set $O(S)$ of stealing places, i.e.,

(1) $O(S) = \bigcup_{p_{ci} \in S} O(S_i) \bigcup_{r \in S \cap R} OP(r) \setminus S$

(2) For each stealing place p of S, (i) $\forall\, t \in \bullet p$, let p' be the input operation place of t. Add an arc $(P_{AC(S)}, t)$ of weight $N_p - N_{p'}$ if $N_p > N_{p'}$; and (ii) $\forall\, t \in p\bullet$, let p'' be the output operation place of t. Add an arc $(t, P_{AC(S)})$ of weight $N_p - N_{p''}$ if $N_p > N_{p''}$.

(3) $M_0(P_{AC(S)}) = \sum_{p_{ci} \in S} M_0(p_{ci}) + \sum_{r \in S \cap R} M_0(r) - 1.$

From *Theorem 10.4* below, $M_0(P_{AC(S)}) \geq 1$.

Theorem 10.4: Any minimal siphon S in N' that can become unmarked, i.e., $\exists\, M = M_0 + CY / M(S) = 0$, contains at least one control place p_{ci}, and either one more control place p_{cj} or a resource place.

The problem with this approach is that adding the new control place can still create new deadlock situations just as the introduction of control places at the end of the first stage. Therefore, the above procedure may never stop.

In order to avoid creating new deadlocks when adding control place $P_{AC(S)}$, we adopt a conservative policy. Whenever a token leaves a process idle place p_{0j} by firing a source transition t (in the sense that all resource and control places are removed), we assign to $P_{AC(S)}$ the maximal number N_{p^*} of control tokens it may eventually need (see Figure 8.19). While the token moves to an operation place p, it keeps the maximal number of control tokens it may still need before returning to p_{0j}.

For this purpose, we define the following weights:

$$N_p = \begin{cases} \displaystyle\sum_{p_{ci} \in S} 1\{p \in O(S_i)\} + \sum_{r \in S \cap R} 1\{p \in OP(r), \text{ if } p \notin S\} \\ 0, \hspace{6cm} \text{otherwise .} \end{cases}$$

For all transitions *t* and operation places *p*,

$$W_t = \max_{p \in \Gamma_t} N_p \text{ and } W_p = \max_{p' \in \Gamma_p} N_{p'}$$

where Γ_x is the set of operation places *p* in the same process net with the process idle place p_{oj} such that there exist a path in the process net from node *x* to *p* not containing p_{oj}. W_t represents the maximal number of control tokens to associate with the operation place token generated by firing *t*. Clearly, we have:

$$W_t = W_p, \forall t \in \bullet p$$
$$W_p = \max\{N_p, \max_{t \in p\bullet} W_t\}.$$

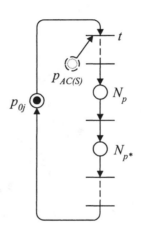

Figure 8.19. An augmented siphon control place.

Figure 8.20 is an example that allows us to illustrate the definitions of N_p, W_t, and W_p. In this example, assume p_A, p_B, p_C, and $p_D \in O(S)$, p_{c1}, r_1, and $r_2 \in S$, and p_{01}, $p_{02} \notin S$.

Based on the above definition, $N_{p_A} = N_{p_D} = 2$ (i.e., if $t_{n-1}(t_{m-1})$ fires, then place $p_A(p_D)$ obtains two resource tokens), and $N_{p_B} = N_{p_C} = 1$. Hence, $W_{t_1} = \max\{N_{p_A}, N_{p_B}\} = 2$ in the process net starting at t_1 and ending at t_{n+1}. As the same reasons, $W_{t_2} = 2$.

Formally speaking, the control place $P_{AC(S)}$ for each siphon *S* can be defined as follows:

(1) Determining   the   set $O(S)$ of   stealing   places,
    i.e., $O(S) = \bigcup_{p_{ci} \in S} O(S_i) \bigcup_{r \in S \cap R} OP(r) \setminus S$.

(2) For all source transition t (in the sense that all resource and control
    places are removed), i.e., $\forall\, t \in p_{0j}\bullet$ for some process idle places p_{0j},
    such that $W_t > 0$, add an arc $(P_{AC(S)}, t)$ of weight W_t.

(3) For all transition t that is not a source transition, let p be its input
    operation place. Add an arc $(t, P_{AC(S)})$ of weight $W_p - W_t$ if $W_p > W_t$.

(4) $M_0(P_{AC(S)}) = \sum_{p_{ci} \in S} M_0(p_{ci}) + \sum_{r \in S \cap R} M_0(r) - 1 \geq 1$.

For example in Figure 8.20, the obtained weight of arc (P_{AC}, t_1) is equal to 2,
the weights of arcs (t_n, P_{AC}) and (t_{n-1}, P_{AC}) are both equal to 1 (i.e.,
$W_{P_A} > W_{t_n}, W_{P_A} = 2, and\ W_{t_n} = 1$), and $M_0(P_{AC}) = 4$. Similarly, the weight
of arc (P_{AC}, t_2) is equal to 2, the weight of arc (t_m, P_{AC}) is equal to 1, the weight of
arc (t_{m-1}, P_{AC}) is equal to 1.

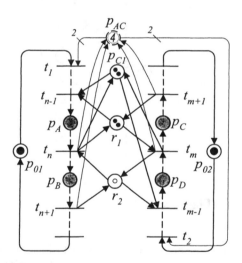

Figure 8.20. An augmented siphon control net.

In order to prevent all siphons of N^1 from becoming unmarked, more control
places are added to N^1 to obtain net N^2 in the following way:

(1) Choosing a set of minimal siphons $\{S^1, S^2, \cdots, S^b\}$ of N^1 such that $\exists$
    $M = M_0 + CY / M(S^i) = 0$;

(2) Adding a control place $P_{AC(S)}$ for each siphon S^i such that S^i cannot
    become unmarked so that no siphon of N^1 can become unmarked.

The final controlled net N^2 has the following properties:

Theorem 10.5: N^2 is live and reversible.

8.10.3 The Algorithm

The steps of the above two stages can be summarized using a deadlock prevention algorithm as presented later. First, since the algorithm uses the MIP approach to obtain maximal siphons unmarked at some markings, the following algorithm is adopted to obtain an unmarked minimal siphon from each unmarked maximal siphon.

Algorithm 1. Unmarked Minimal Siphons from a Maximal Siphon S

Step 1: $V = \varnothing$, where V is the set of places already checked;

Step 2: Choose a place $p^* \in S\backslash V$;

      Step 2.1: set $V = V \cup \{p^*\}$;

      Step 2.2: $S' = S - \{p^*\}$; /* remove p^* from the siphon */

      Step 2.3: While $\exists$ source transition t of S', remove all output places of t in S' (i.e., $t\bullet \cap S'$);

      Step 2.4: If $S' \neq \varnothing$, then $S = S'$;

Step 3: Go to step 2.

End of Algorithm

Consider the example in Figure 8.17. A siphon $S = \{p_2, p_4, p_5, p_6, p_9, p_{11}\}$ is obtained by MIP. If p_2 or p_4 is removed, then no *source transitions* exist in the subnet of N^0 generated by S and shown in Figure 8.21. When p_5 is removed (i.e., t_4 is a source transition), all of the places will be removed. Thus, p_5 belongs to an unmarked minimal siphon. Similarly p_6, p_9, p_{10}, and p_{11} also belong to the unmarked minimal siphon. As a result, an unmarked minimal siphon $\{p_5, p_6, p_9, p_{10}, p_{11}\}$ is obtained by this algorithm. For convenience, the places in an unmarked minimal siphon are represented as slashed circles.

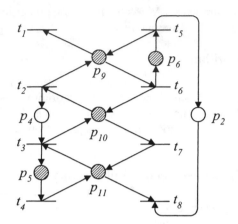

Figure 8.21. A subnet of N^0 generated by a siphon.

The deadlock prevention algorithm is presented as follows:

Algorithm 2: Deadlock Prevention
/*** Siphon Control *****/**
Step 1: Apply MIP on N^0 to obtain a maximal siphon.
Step 2: *IF* there exists such a siphon,
THEN
Step 3: Apply Algorithm 1 to obtain a minimal siphon,
Step 4: Add a control place p_{ci} to N^0,
Step 5: $\quad M_0(p_{ci}) = \sum_{r \in S \cap R} M_0(r) - 1,$
Step 6: For each stealing places p of S_i,
- $\forall\, t \in \bullet p$, add an arc from p_{ci} to t if t does not have an input place that is a stealing place,
- $\forall\, t \in p\bullet$, add an arc from t to p_{ci} if $t\bullet \cap O(S_i) = \varnothing$,
Step 7: Add a new constraint, $\sum M_0(p) \le M_0(p_{ci})\ \forall p \in O(S_i)$, to the original MIP problem,
Step 8: Go to Step 1.
ELSE
Step 9: Obtain N^1,
    - While $\exists$ redundancy control places p_{ci} of N^1, remove all such places in N^1.
Step 10: $V = \varnothing$.
Step 11: Apply MIP to N^1 to obtain a maximal siphon.
Step 12: *IF* there does not exist such a siphon,
THEN go to Step 19,
ELSE

Step 13: Apply Algorithm 1 to obtain a minimal siphon.
/***** **Augmented Siphon Control** *****/
Step 14: Add a control place $P_{AC(S)}$ to N^1 such that $V = V \cup \{P_{AC(S)}\}$.
Step 15: For all source transitions t (in the sense that all resource and control places are removed), add an arc $(P_{AC(S)}, t)$ of weight W_t.
Step 16: For all transitions t that are not source transitions, add an arc $(t, P_{AC(S)})$ of weight $W_p - W_t$ if $W_p > W_t$.
Step 17: Add a new constraint, $\sum M_0(p) \leq M_0(P_{AC(S)}) \ \forall p \in O(S_i)$, to the MIP problem of N^1.
Step 18: Go to Step 11.
Step 19: Obtained $N^2 = N^1 \cup V$.
Step 20: Stop.
End of Algorithm

Example 10.1: Figure 8.22 is an example taken from [24]. The system is an S^3PR that can be blocked when $m_0(p_8) \geq 3$. Specifically, when $m_0(p_8) = 3$, a deadlock state can be reached by firing $t_7 t_8 t_7 t_8 t_7$. The net is also called a *generalized sequential mutual exclusion* (GSME). □

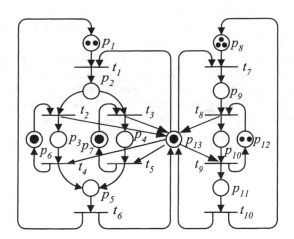

Figure 8.22. An example of S^3PR.

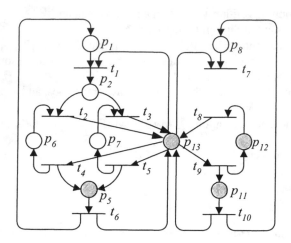

Figure 8.23. A maximal siphon of the GSMC.

In Figure 8.22 we obtain an *unmarked maximal siphon* by which the subnet generated is shown in Figure 8.23, i.e., $v_{pi} = 0$ for $i=1, 2, 5, 6, 7, 8, 11, 12$, and 13. From the maximal siphon, an *unmarked minimal siphon* $\{p_5, p_{11}, p_{12}, p_{13}\}$ can be obtained. Hence, we can find out that t_7 is a *sink transition*, $\{p_9, p_{10}\} \in O(S)$, and $M_0(p_{c1}) = M_0(p_{12}) + M_0(p_{13}) - 1 = 2$. After a control place p_{c1} is added, as shown in Figure 8.24, the resultant net is live because no further unmarked siphons are found. As a result, we can conclude that this example needs only the *siphons control* stage and the controlled net is live and reversible. That is, the control policy is optimal or maximally permissive for this example.

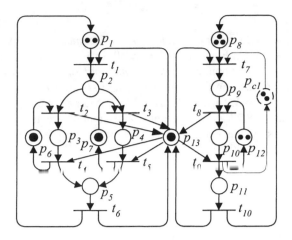

Figure 8.24. A GSME and its control place.

In spite of the fact that the resultant net after the siphons control stage is deadlock-free for this example, the following example shows that a deadlocked situation can occur after the siphons control stage.

Example 10.2: Figure 8.25 is an example taken from [8]. This is a production system where two types of processes execute concurrently and share a set of common resources. The system model is an S^3PR. □

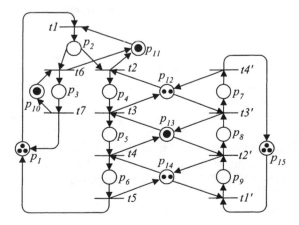

Figure. 25. An S^3PR with deadlocks (from [8]).

In Figure 8.25 we obtain an *unmarked maximal siphon* by which the subnet generated is shown in Figure 8.26, i.e., $v_{pi}=0$ for $i = 1, 2, 3, 6, 7, 8, 12, 13$, and 14. From the maximal siphon, an *unmarked minimal siphon* $\{p_6, p_8, p_{13}, p_{14}\}$ can be obtained. Hence, we can point out that *t3* and *t1'* are *sink transitions*, $\{p_5, p_9\} \in O(S)$, and $M_0(p_{c1}) = M_0(p_{13}) + M_0(p_{14}) - 1 = 2$. After a control place p_{c1} is added, as shown in Figure 8.27(a), further unmarked siphons are found. In this example, three iterations in the siphons control stage are required. Other iterations are shown in Figure 8.27(b) and (c).

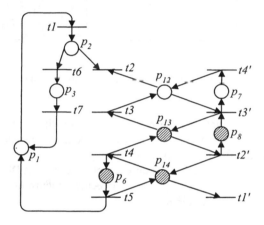

Figure 8.26. A maximal siphon.

After the siphons control stage, three control places p_{c1}, p_{c2} and p_{c3} and the associated arcs added to the net such that no siphons in N^0 can become unmarked (see Figure 8.28). Nevertheless, a new unmarked maximal siphon $\{p_5, p_6, p_7, p_8, p_{12}, p_{14}, p_{c1}, p_{c2}, p_{c3}\}$ is found in N^1 (due to the control places). From this siphon, an unmarked minimal siphon $\{p_6, p_7, p_{12}, p_{14}, p_{c1}, p_{c3}\}$ can be obtained (shown in Figure 8.29). Thus, in the augmented siphons control stage, first, we remove all resource and control places of N^1 (Figure 8.28) and we obtain two source transitions *t1* and *t1'*. Second, we obtain $\{p_4, p_5, p_8, p_9\} \in O(S)$, $W_{t1} = W_{t1'} = 2$, and weights of arcs $(P_{AC}, t1)$ and $(P_{AC}, t1')$ are both equal to 2.

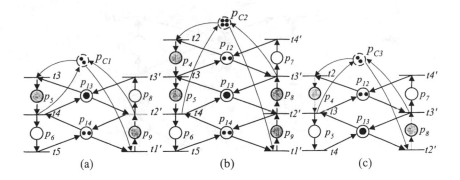

Figure 8.27. Adding control places at the siphon control stage.

Since $W_{t3} = W_{t4} = W_{t3'} = W_{t2'} = 1$, weights of arcs $(t3, P_{AC})$, $(t4, P_{AC})$, $(t3', P_{AC})$, and $(t2', P_{AC})$ are all equal to 1. Since $W_{t6} = 0$, weight of arc $(t6, P_{AC})$ is equal to 2.

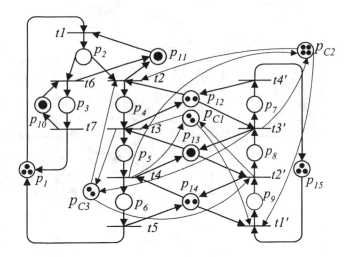

Figure 8.28. The net after the siphon control stage.

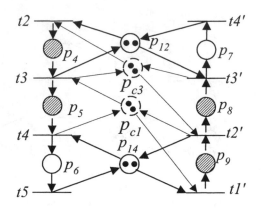

Figure 8.29. A new unmarked siphon.

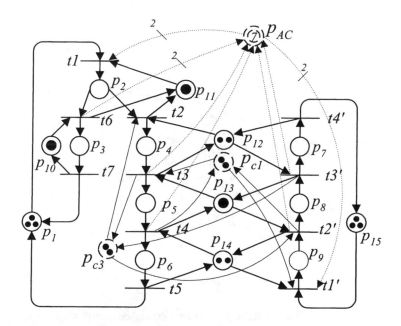

Figure 8.30. A final controlled net.

Next, $M_0(P_{AC}) = M_0(p_{c1}) + M_0(p_{c3}) + M_0(p_{12}) + M_0(p_{13}) + M_0(p_{14}) - 1 = 7$. After a control place P_{AC} is added, the resultant net is shown in Figure 8.30, where there are no siphons that can become unmarked. Based on *Theorem 10.5*, the net is live and reversible. Notice that p_{c2} is a redundant control place and is removed.

8.10.4 Optimality and Extension of the Policy

If after the first stage, no new unmarked siphon is generated, the two-stage control policy is optimal since all the states that are forbidden by this policy are deadlocked states. Note that if both stages are required, this policy is suboptimal. Nevertheless, an experimental study shows that this policy is more permissive than the policy proposed in [8], which can be viewed as exploiting only the augmented siphon control stage with unity arc weights. For example, refer to a comparison in table 8.2. Both policies add three control places to the original net of Figure 8.25. The system controlled by the two-stage policy allows *four parts* being processed at the same time. Since *t1* and *t1'* transitions can fire at the same time, this system can load two parts for processing for each transition. However, the system controlled by the policy in [8] cannot handle this situation since their system allows either *t1* or *t1'* to fire. Thus, it is allowed that only *two parts* being processed at the same time. A rigorous proof of this argument will be a topic for further study. An extension of this method to handling a larger net class, called ES^{3}PR, is reported in [10].

Table 8.2. Comparison with the controlled net of Figure 8.6 in [8].

	The controlled system of figure 6				The controlled system of figure 30		
	$V_{si}\bullet$	$\bullet V_{si}$	$m_{0A}(V_{si})$		$p\bullet$	$\bullet p$	$M_0(p_i)$
V_{s1}	{t1, t1'}	{t3, t6, t3'}	2	p_{c1}	{t3, t1'}	{t4, t2'}	2
V_{s2}	{t1, t1'}	{t4, t6, t2'}	2	p_{c3}	{t2, t2'}	{t3, t3'}	2
V_{s3}	{t1, t1'}	{t4, t6, t3'}	4	p_{AC}	{2t1, 2t1'}*	{t3, t4, t6, t3', t2'}	7

*Note: "2t1" denotes that the number of arcs from p to *t1* is 2, and Vsx represents the control places in [8].

8.11 CONCLUSIONS

This chapter has investigated the deadlock analysis and prevention of PNs. The deadlock analysis was based on potential deadlocks which are siphons that eventually become unmarked. A linear programming-based sufficient condition under which a siphon is not a potential deadlock was proposed. Based on this sufficient condition, a mathematical programming approach and a mixed-integer programming approach were proposed for checking general PNs and structurally bounded PNs.

We have investigated a wide range of PN models of automated manufacturing systems including asymmetric choice nets, augmented marked graphs, RCN merged nets, S^{3}PR, ERCN merged nets, and process nets with resources. All these nets take into account resource constraints and resource interactions. For all these nets, the concept of potential deadlocks is used to characterize properties such as reversibility and liveness. These properties are much stronger than the deadlock-freeness checked for general PNs.

We have also shown in this chapter how the concept of potential deadlock can be used to design efficient deadlock prevention control policies of automated manufacturing systems. A two-stage control policy is presented, which adopts the concept of adding control places and deciding their initial markings to prevent potential deadlocks. This control policy guarantees that the final controlled net is live and reversible.

REFERENCES

[1] Z.A. Banaszak, and B.H. Krogh, "Deadlock Avoidance in Flexible Manufacturing Systems with Concurrently Competing Process Flows," *IEEE Trans. Robot. Automat.*, vol. 6, pp. 724-734, 1990.

[2] K. Barkaoui and I. Ben Abdallah, "An Efficient Avoidance Control Policy in FMS Using Structural Analysis of Petri Nets," in Proc. IEEE SMC Conf., San Antonio, Texas, 1994.

[3] K. Barkaoui, J.M. Couvreur, and C. Dutheillet, "On the Liveness in Extended Non-Self-Controlling Nets," in *Advances in Petri Nets 1995*, LNCS 935, Springer-Verlag, 1995.

[4] G.W. Brams, *Réseaux de Petri: Théorie et Pratique,* MASSON, 1983.

[5] J. Campos, G. Chiola and M. Silva, "Ergodicity and Throughput Bounds of Petri Nets with Unique Consistent Firing Count Vector," *IEEE Trans. Software Eng.*, vol. 17, pp. 117-125, 1991.

[6] F. Chu and X.L. Xie. "Deadlock analysis of Petri Nets using siphons and mathematical programming," *IEEE Trans. Robot. Automat.*, vol. 13, pp. 793-804, 1997.

[7] J.M. Colom and M. *Silva, "Improving the Linearly Based Characterization of P/T Nets,"* in *Advances in Petri Nets 1990*, LNCS 483, Springer-Verlag, 1991.

[8] J. Ezpeleta, J.M. Colom, and J. Martinez, "A Petri Net Based Deadlock Prevention Policy for Flexible Manufacturing Systems" *IEEE Trans. Robot. Automat.*, vol. 11, pp. 173-184, 1995.

[9] Y.S. Huang, M.D. Jeng, X.L. Xie, and S.L. Chung, "A Deadlock Prevention Policy Based on Petri Nets and Siphons," *International Journal of Production Research*, Vol. 39 (2), pp. 283-305, January 2001.

[10] Y. S. Huang, M. D. Jeng, X. L. Xie, and S. L. Chung, "A Deadlock Prevention Policy for Flexible Manufacturing Systems Using Siphons," *Proceedings of IEEE International Conference on Robotics and Automation*, Seoul, Korea, 2001.

[11] M.D. Jeng and F. DiCesare, "Synthesis Using Resource Control Nets for Modeling Shared-Resource Systems," *IEEE Trans. Robot. Automat.*, vol. 11, pp. 317-327, 1995.

[12] M.D. Jeng and X.L. Xie, "Analysis of Modularly Composed Nets by Siphons," *IEEE Trans. on Systems, Man and Cybernetics, part A*, 29(4), pp. 399-405, 1999.

[13] M.D. Jeng and X.L. Xie, "Modeling and Analysis of Semiconductor Manufacturing Systems with Degraded Behavior Using Petri Nets and Siphons," *IEEE Trans. Robot. Automat.*, 17/5, 576-588, 2001.

[14] M.D. Jeng, X.L. Xie, and M.Y. Peng, "Process Nets with Resources for Manufacturing Modeling and Their Analysis," *IEEE Trans. on Robotics and Automation*, vol. 18/6, pp. 875-889, 2002.

[15] K. Lautenbach and H. Ridder, "Liveness in Bounded Petri Nets which are Covered by T-Invariants," in *Advances in PNs 1994*, LNCS 815, Springer-Verlag, 1994.

[16] M. Minoux, *Programmation Mathématique: théorie et algorithme*, Dunod, Paris, 1983.

[17] T. Murata, "Petri Nets: Properties, Analysis and Applications," *Proceedings of IEEE*, vol. 77, pp.541-580, 1989.

[18] J.-M. Proth and X.-L. Xie, *Petri Nets: A Tool for Design and Management of Manufacturing Systems*, John Wiley & Sons, 1996.

[19] R.T. Rockafellar, *Convex Analysis*, Princeton, NJ: Princeton University Press, 1972.

[20] E. Teruel, J.M. Colom, and M. Silva, "Linear Analysis of Deadlock-Freeness of Petri Net Models," in Proc. 2nd European Control Conference, Groningen, The Netherlands, 1993.

[21] N. Viswanadham, Y. Narahari, and T.L. Johnson, "Deadlock Prevention and Deadlock Avoidance in Flexible Manufacturing Systems Using Petri Net Models," *IEEE Trans. Robot. Automat.*, vol. 6, pp. 713-723, 1990.

[22] X.L. Xie and M.D. Jeng, "ERCN-merged Nets and Their Analysis Using Siphons," *IEEE Trans. on Robotics and Automation*, 15(4), pp. 692-703, 1999.

[23] M.C. Zhou and F. Dicesare, "Parallel and Sequential Mutual Exclusions for Petri Net Modeling of Manufacturing Systems with Shared Resources," *IEEE Trans. Robot. Automat.*, vol. 7, pp. 515-527, 1991.

[24] M. C. Zhou and F. DiCesare, *Petri Net Synthesis for Discrete Event Control of Manufacturing Systems* Boston, MA: Kluwer, 1993.

[25] M.C. Zhou, F. Dicesare, and A.A. Desrochers, "A Hybrid Methodology for Synthesis of Petri Net Models for Manufacturing Systems," *IEEE Trans. Robot. Automat.*, vol. 8, pp. 350-361, 1992.

[26] E.R. Boer and T. Murata, "Generating basis siphons and traps of Petri Nets Using the Sign Incidence Matrix", IEEE Transactions on Circuits and Systems I: Fundamental Theory and Applications, Vol. 41, 4, pp. 266-271, April 1994.

[27] M.D. Jeng, X.L. Xie, and S.W. Chou. "Modeling, Qualitative Analysis, and Performance Evaluation of the Etching Area in an IC Wafer Fabrication System using Petri Nets," *IEEE Trans. on Semiconductor Manufacturing*, 11(3), pp. 358-373, 1998.

9

Siphon-based characterization of liveness and liveness-enforcing supervision for sequential resource allocation systems

Spyros A. Reveliotis
Georgia Institute of Technology, Atlanta, GA, USA

Abstract – One of the most interesting developments from, both, a theoretical and a practical perspective, in the emerging theory of resource allocation systems (RAS), is the characterization of the non-liveness of many RAS classes through the Petri net (PN)-based structural object of empty, or more generally, deadly marked siphon. The work presented in this chapter seeks to develop a general theory that provides a unifying framework for all the relevant existing results, and reveals the key structures and mechanisms that connect the RAS non-liveness to the concept of deadly marked – and in certain cases, empty – siphon. In this capacity, the presented results allow also the extension of the siphon-based characterization of non-liveness to broader RAS classes, and provide a clear and intuitive explanation for the limitations of the approach. The last part of the work discusses how the derived structural characterization of RAS non-liveness can be combined with some algorithms for detecting empty or deadly marked siphons in a given PN

---

[1]The first part of this chapter (Sections 9.1-9.3) was originally published in *S.A. Reveliotis, "On the Siphon-based Characterization of Liveness in Sequential Resource Allocation Systems", 24th International Conference on Application and Theory of Petri nets, Eindhoven, the Netherlands, June 2003*, while some of the key ideas underlying Section 9.4 were originally presented in *J. Park and S. A. Reveliotis, "Deadlock Avoidance in Sequential Resource Allocation Systems with Multiple Resource Acquisitions and Flexible Routings", IEEE Trans. on Automatic Control, vol. 46, no. 10, 1572-1583, 2001*.

marking, in order to develop analytical liveness sufficiency tests and systematic procedures for the design of liveness-enforcing supervisors (LES).

9.1 Introduction

One of the major breakthroughs underlying our capability to systematically evaluate the liveness of various resource allocation system (RAS) configurations, and to synthesize effective and computationally efficient liveness-enforcing supervisors for non-live RAS, is the formal characterization of the non-liveness of the Petri net (PN) sub-classes modelling the behavior of these environments, through the formation of a particular PN structural object, known as *empty* or, more generally, *deadly marked siphon*[2] [1]. This type of results can be originally traced in the seminal work of Ezpeleta and his colleagues [2], that provided a siphon-based characterization for (non-)liveness in *Single Unit (SU)* RAS [3], i.e., a sequential RAS sub-class in which processes execute in (partially) ordered sequences of stages, with each stage requiring for its support the exclusive allocation of one unit from a single resource type. More specifically, [2] established that in the class of SU-RAS, non-liveness can be interpreted through the development of *empty* siphons in the system reachability space. Similarly, the work of [4] established that the development of reachable empty siphons is also the cause for non-liveness in *Augmented Marked Graphs (AMG)*, a RAS model that generalizes the class of SU-RAS by introducing task parallelism, through the presence of merging and splitting transitions. The role of empty siphons for the non-liveness of single-unit RAS with merging and splitting transitions was subsequently investigated more extensively in [5]. At the same time, the work of [6] established that the behavior of an SU-RAS under the control of a class of liveness-enforcing supervisors (LES) expressed by a set of linear inequality constraints on the RAS state – known as *algebraic* LES – can be modelled as an AMG, and therefore, the aforementioned results of [4] provide a structural test for assessing the LES correctness. Beyond its theoretical value, this finding is of considerable practical significance since the work of [4] provides also computational sufficiency tests for the non-existence of reachable empty siphons, that take the convenient form of mathematical programming (MP) formulations polynomially sized, in terms of variables and constraints, with respect to the underlying PN model. More recently, this entire set of results, originally developed in the context of SU-RAS, has been generalized to the broader RAS class involving *Conjunctive (C)* [3] resource allocation, i.e., to RAS environments that engage an arbitrary set of resources, each of them at an arbitrary level of units, for the support of a single process stage [7, 8]. In the C-RAS operational context, the new PN structural object characterizing the non-liveness of the RAS behavior is that of *deadly marked* siphon, while its presence is detected on a *modified* reachability space, that constitutes a projection of the original PN reachability space to a subspace defined by a subset of the components of the net marking vector [7]. The work in [7] developed also MP-based sufficiency tests for

---

[2]All technical concepts are systematically introduced in the later parts of this chapter.

the non-existence of deadly marked siphons in the aforementioned modified reachability space, and therefore, it offers computational tools for developing algebraic LES for this broader class of RAS behavior. Finally, some additional works that have investigated the role of the PN siphon structure in the liveness of sequential resource allocation, are those presented in [9, 10, 11, 12, 13].

As it is evident from the above discussion, currently, all the existing results on siphon-based characterization of liveness in sequential RAS have been developed in a rather fragmented fashion, each of them pertaining to a RAS sub-class characterizing a particular type of RAS behavior. Furthermore, the detailed study of their development would reveal that, while they are based on formal and rigorous technical arguments, they fail to provide an explicit and intuitive characterization of the underlying key mechanism that links the non-liveness of the considered RAS classes to the presence of some empty or deadly marked siphons. Hence, the work presented in this chapter seeks to develop a general theory that

- will provide a systematic explanation of the relationship between the RAS non-liveness and the presence of deadly marked – and in the case of SU-RAS, empty – siphons;

- will offer, thus, a unifying framework for interpreting all the relevant results existing in the literature;

- will allow the extension of the existing results to broader and/or other RAS behaviors;

- will eventually enable a systematic methodology for establishing correct and live behavior in the considered RAS classes, through a *decomposition* that differentiates between (a) the design of the involved process flows, and (b) the synthesis of a supervisor that manages the allocation of the system resources to the concurrently executing process instances in a way that preserves the system liveness.[3]

Our approach is based on the identification of a minimal set of requirements for the structure of the RAS processes and their behavior, which when met, will allow the attribution of any experienced RAS non-liveness to the development of deadly marked siphons in the modified reachability space of the RAS-modelling PN. Two concepts that are shown to play a central role in this minimal set of requirements are those of the process *quasi-liveness* and *reversibility*. These properties essentially imply that the execution logic underlying the various process flows is inherently consistent, and therefore, any non-liveness of the PN modelling the overall RAS behavior can be attributed to the competition of the concurrently executing processes for the finite system resources. A third requirement

---

[3]It must be mentioned at this point, that while the present chapter was in the review process, reference [14] was published, with a set of results quite similar to the research program outlined above. It is emphasized that these two works were developed simultaneously and independently, and throughout the subsequent development, we point out the similarities and differences among them.

that appears in the subsequent results, and it is necessary in order to connect the non-liveness of the process-resource net to the presence of deadly marked siphons, is that of *acyclic process flows*, i.e., the developed results pertain to RAS in which the various processes do not present re-circulating loops among their different stages.[4]

The rest of the chapter is organized as follows: Section 2 first presents the PN fundamentals that are necessary for the modelling and analysis of the considered RAS structure and behavior, and subsequently it proceeds to the systematic characterization of this RAS class through a series of definitions and assumptions. Section 3 develops the main structural results of this work, by establishing that for RAS with quasi-live, reversible and acyclic processes, non-liveness can be attributed to the development of deadly marked siphons in the modified reachability space of the RAS-modelling PN. It also indicates how all the currently existing results connecting liveness to empty or deadly marked siphons, can be obtained as special cases of this more general development. Moreover, the presented formal argument establishing the connection between non-liveness and deadly marked siphons provides also an intuitive explanation for it, since it reveals that, in the considered RAS class, non-liveness can be attributed to the formation of *total* deadlocks in the modified PN reachability space. Finally, Section 3 establishes that in the considered class of systems, liveness and reversibility are equivalent concepts, providing, thus, the formal link between the concept of PN liveness and the typical concerns of RAS deadlock avoidance theory. Section 4 overviews the MP-based sufficiency test for the non-existence of deadly marked siphons in the underlying modified reachability space, originally developed in [7], and it discusses how this test can support the synthesis of correct algebraic LES for any instance of the considered RAS class. Finally, Section 5 concludes the chapter, and identifies some additional research issues originating from the presented work.

9.2   The considered RAS class and its Petri net model

This section first overviews the Petri net (PN) related concepts that are necessary for the formal modelling of the considered RAS class and the analysis of its properties, and subsequently, it provides a detailed characterization of the PN structure modelling the considered resource allocation environments. Some excellent more extensive treatments of the PN modelling framework and the structural and behavioral analysis of PN models can be found in [17, 18].

9.2.1   Petri net preliminaries

A *marked Petri Net (PN)* is defined by a quadruple $\mathcal{N} = (P, T, W, M_0)$, where P is the set of *places*, T is the set of *transitions*, $W : (P \times T) \cup (T \times P) \to Z^+$

---

[4]This requirement can be relaxed under certain conditions; c.f. [15, 16] for details.

is the *flow relation*, and $M_0 : P \rightarrow Z^+$ is the net *initial marking*, assigning to each place $p \in P$, $M_0(p)$ *tokens*. In the special case that the flow relation W maps onto $\{0,1\}$, the Petri net is said to be *ordinary*. If only the restriction of W to $(P \times T)$ maps on $\{0,1\}$, the PN is said to be *PT-ordinary*. The set of input (resp., output) transitions of a place p is denoted by $^\bullet p$ (resp., $p^\bullet$). Similarly, the set of input (resp., output) places of a transition t is denoted by $^\bullet t$ (resp., $t^\bullet$). This notation is also generalized to any set of places or transitions, X, e.g. $^\bullet X = \bigcup_{x \in X} {}^\bullet x$. The ordered set $X = < x_1 \ldots x_n > \in (P \cup T)^*$ is a *path*, if and only if (iff) $x_{i+1} \in x_i^\bullet, i = 1, \ldots, n-1$. Furthermore, a path X is characterized as a *circuit* iff $x_1 \equiv x_n$. Finally, an ordinary PN such that (s.t.) $\forall t \in T$, $|t^\bullet| = |^\bullet t|$ $= 1$ (resp., $\forall p \in P$, $|p^\bullet| = |^\bullet p| = 1$), is characterized as a *state machine* (resp., *marked graph*).

Given a marking M, a transition t is *enabled* iff $\forall p \in {}^\bullet t$, $M(p) \geq W(p,t)$, and this is denoted by $M[t\rangle$. $t \in T$ is said to be *disabled* by $p \in {}^\bullet t$ at M iff $M(p) < W(p,t)$. Furthermore, a place $p \in P$ for which $\exists t \in p^\bullet$ s.t. $M(p) < W(p,t)$ is said to be a *disabling* place at M. Firing an enabled transition t results in a new marking M', which is obtained by removing $W(p,t)$ tokens from each place $p \in {}^\bullet t$, and placing $W(t,p')$ tokens in each place $p' \in t^\bullet$. The set of markings reachable from M_0 through any fireable sequence of transitions is denoted by $R(\mathcal{N}, M_0)$. A marked PN $\mathcal{N}$ with initial marking M_0 is said to be *bounded* iff all markings $M \in R(\mathcal{N}, M_0)$ are bounded, while $\mathcal{N}$ is said to be *structurally bounded* iff it is bounded for any initial marking M_0. $\mathcal{N}$ is said to be *reversible* iff $\forall M \in R(\mathcal{N}, M_0)$, $M_0 \in R(\mathcal{N}, M)$.

In case that a marked PN is *pure* (i.e., $\forall(x,y) \in (P \times T) \cup (T \times P)$, $W(x,y) > 0 \Rightarrow W(y,x) = 0$), the flow relation can be represented by the *flow matrix* $\Theta = \Theta^+ - \Theta^-$ where $\Theta^+[p,t] = W(t,p)$ and $\Theta^-[p,t] = W(p,t)$. A *p-semiflow* y is a $|P|$-dimensional vector satisfying $y^T \Theta = 0$ and $y \geq 0$, and a *t-semiflow* x is a $|T|$-dimensional vector satisfying $\Theta x = 0$ and $x \geq 0$. A p-semiflow y (t-semiflow x, resp.) is said to be *minimal* iff $\not\exists$ a p-semiflow y' (t-semiflow x', resp.) such that $\|y'\| \subset \|y\|$ ($\|x'\| \subset \|x\|$, resp.), where $\|y\| = \{p \in P \mid y(p) > 0\}$ ($\|x\| = \{t \in T \mid x(t) > 0\}$, resp.).

Given a marked PN $\mathcal{N} = (P, T, W, M_0)$, a transition $t \in T$ is *live* iff $\forall M \in R(\mathcal{N}, M_0), \exists M' \in R(\mathcal{N}, M)$ s.t. $M'[t\rangle$, and $t \in T$ is *dead* at $M \in R(\mathcal{N}, M_0)$ iff $\not\exists$ marking $M' \in R(\mathcal{N}, M)$ s.t. $M'[t\rangle$. A marking $M \in R(\mathcal{N}, M_0)$ is a (total) *deadlock* iff $\forall t \in T$, t is dead. A marked PN $\mathcal{N}$ is *quasi-live* iff $\forall t \in T, \exists M \in R(\mathcal{N}, M_0)$ s.t. $M[t\rangle$, it is *weakly live* iff $\forall M \in R(\mathcal{N}, M_0), \exists t \in T$ s.t. $M[t\rangle$, and it is *live* iff $\forall t \in T$, t is live. Of particular interest for the liveness analysis of marked PN is a structural element known as *siphon*, which is a set of places $S \subseteq P$ such that $^\bullet S \subseteq S^\bullet$. A siphon S is *minimal* iff $\not\exists$ a siphon S' s.t. $S' \subset S$. A siphon S is said to be *empty* at marking M iff $M(S) \equiv \sum_{p \in S} M(p) = 0$, and it is said to be *deadly marked* at marking M, iff $\forall t \in {}^\bullet S$, t is disabled by some $p \in S$ [7]. Obviously, empty siphons are deadly marked siphons. It is easy to see that, if S is a deadly marked siphon at some marking M, then (i) $\forall t \in {}^\bullet S$, t is a dead transition in M, and (ii) $\forall M' \in R(\mathcal{N}, M)$, S is deadly marked. Furthermore, it can be shown that if marking $M \in R(\mathcal{N}, M_0)$ is a total deadlock, then the set S of disabling places in M constitutes a deadly marked siphon [7]. This last result constitutes the generalization of a well-established relationship between total deadlocks and empty siphons in ordinary PN's [18].

Finally, given two PN's $\mathcal{N}_1 = (P_1, T_1, W_1, M_{01})$ and $\mathcal{N}_2 = (P_2, T_2, W_2, M_{02})$ with $T_1 \cap T_2 = \emptyset$ and $P_1 \cap P_2 = Q \neq \emptyset$ s.t. $\forall p \in Q$, $M_{01}(p) = M_{02}(p)$, the PN $\mathcal{N}$ resulting from the *merging* of the nets $\mathcal{N}_1$ and $\mathcal{N}_2$ *through the place set* Q, is defined by $\mathcal{N} = (P_1 \cup P_2, T_1 \cup T_2, W_1 \cup W_2, M_0)$ with $M_0(p) = M_{01}(p)$, $\forall p \in P_1 \backslash P_2$; $M_0(p) = M_{02}(p)$, $\forall p \in P_2 \backslash P_1$; $M_0(p) = M_{01}(p) = M_{02}(p)$, $\forall p \in P_1 \cap P_2$.

9.2.2 The considered RAS class and the associated PN model

For the purposes of the liveness analysis considered in this work, a *(sequential) resource allocation system (RAS)* is formally defined by a set of *resource types* $\mathcal{R} = \{R_l, l = 1, \ldots, m\}$, each of them available at some finite *capacity* $C_l \in Z^+$, and a set of *process types* $\mathcal{J} = \{J_j, j = 1, \ldots, n\}$, that execute sequentially, through a number of *tasks* or *stages*, $J_{jk}, k = 1, \ldots, \lambda_j$, and with each stage J_{jk} engaging a specific subset of the system resources for its execution. More specifically, it is assumed that a process instance advances to the execution of a certain stage, J_{jk}, only after it has secured the required resources, and upon its advancement, it releases the resources held for the execution of the previous stage $J_{j,k-1}$. Furthermore, the set of *tasks* or *stages*, $\{J_{jk}, k = 1, \ldots, \lambda_j\}$, corresponding to process type J_j, presents some additional structure that expresses the associated *process-defining logic* and characterizes the potential process *routings*. Typical structures involved in the definition of the process logic include linear, parallel, conditional and iterative structures, as well as more complex structures resulting from the nested combination of the basic ones. Most of the past research on RAS liveness and liveness-enforcing supervision has focused on simpler process structures that allow the modelling of simple linear process flows, potentially enhanced with some routing flexibility (e.g., [2, 19, 20, 21, 22, 7]).

This work does not make any explicit assumptions about the specific structure of the considered RAS processes, but it only requires that the involved process logic is "inherently consistent", and therefore, any non-liveness arising in the behavior of the resulting RAS and its associated PN model can be attributed to the (mis-)management of the allocation of the finite set of the system resources to the concurrently executing processes. A formal characterization of this notion of *"inherent process consistency"* is provided by the following definition of the considered *process subnet* and its assumed properties.

Definition 1 *For the purposes of this work, a* process (sub-)net *is a Petri net* $\mathcal{N}_P = (P, T, W, M_0)$ *such that:*

    i. $P = P_S \cup \{i, o\}$ with $P_S \neq \emptyset$;

    ii. $T = T_S \cup \{t_I, t_F, t^*\}$;

   iii. $i^\bullet = \{t_I\}$; $^\bullet i = \{t^*\}$;

   iv. $o^\bullet = \{t^*\}$; $^\bullet o = \{t_F\}$;

   v. $t_I^\bullet \subseteq P_S$; $^\bullet t_I = \{i\}$;

   vi. $t_F^\bullet = \{o\}$; $^\bullet t_F \subseteq P_S$;

   vii. $(t^*)^\bullet = \{i\}$; $^\bullet(t^*) = \{o\}$;

   viii. the underlying digraph is strongly connected;

   ix. $M_0(i) > 0 \ \wedge \ M_0(p) = 0, \ \forall p \in P \backslash \{i\}$;

   x. $\forall M \in R(\mathcal{N}_P, M_0), \ M(i) + M(o) = M_0(i) \Longrightarrow M(p) = 0, \ \forall p \in P_S$.

In the PN-based process representation introduced by Definition 1, process instances waiting to initiate processing are represented by tokens in place i, while the initiation of a process instance is modelled by the firing of transition t_I. Similarly, tokens in place o represent completed process instances, while the event of a process completion is modelled by the firing of transition t_F. Transition t^* allows the token re-circulation – i.e., the token transfer from place o to place i – in order to model *repetitive* process execution. Finally, the part of the net between transitions t_I and t_F that involves the process places P_S, models the sequential logic defining the considered process type, and, as it can be seen in Definition 1, it can be quite arbitrary. However, in order to capture the notion of the "inherent process consistency" introduced at the beginning of this sub-section, we further qualify the considered process sub-nets through the following two assumptions:

Assumption 1 *The process (sub-)nets considered in this work are assumed to be* quasi-live *for* $M_0(i) = 1$.

Assumption 2 *The process (sub-)nets considered in this work are assumed to be* reversible *for every initial marking M_0 that satisfies Condition (ix) of Definition 1.*

Assumption 1 stipulates that the every transition in the considered process sub-net models a meaningful event that can actually occur during the execution of some process instance, and therefore, it is not redundant. On the other hand, Assumption 2 essentially stipulates that, at any point in time, all *active* process instances can proceed to completion, and this completion can occur without the initiation of any additional process instances.[5] When taken together, Assumptions 1 and 2 imply also the *liveness* of the considered process nets; we state this result as a lemma, but we skip its proof, since it is a rather well-known result in the PN-research community.

---

[5]It is noticed, for completeness, that the requirement for process reversibility introduced by Assumption 2 when combined with Definition 1 and Assumption 1, subsumes the notion of process *soundness*, introduced in Workflow theory (c.f., [23, 24]) in order to characterize well-defined process (sub-)nets, for the case where only a single process instance re-circulates in the considered process net. However, Assumption 2 further stipulates that when more than one

Lemma 1 *Under Assumptions 1 and 2, the considered process nets are also* live.

Since the emphasis of this work is on the characterization and establishment of live resource allocation, the complete characterization of the class of process nets satisfying Assumptions 1 and 2 lies beyond its scope. We notice, however, that all the RAS classes for which there exist results connecting their non-liveness to the development of deadly marked / empty siphons, involve PN-based process models that satisfy the aforementioned assumptions.

Another assumption that is necessary for the development of the analytical results of the next section, is that the various process (sub-)nets are *acyclic*. This concept is defined as follows:

Assumption 3 *The process sub-nets considered in this work are assumed to be acyclic, i.e., the removal of transition t^* from them renders them acyclic digraphs.*

The modelling of the resource allocation associated with each process stage, $p \in P_S$, necessitates the augmentation of the process sub-net $\mathcal{N}_P$, defined above, with a set of *resource* places $P_R = \{r_l, \ l = 1, \ldots, m\}$, of initial marking $M_0(r_l) = C_l$, $i = 1, \ldots, m$, and with the corresponding flow sub-matrix, Θ_{P_R}, expressing the allocation and de-allocation of the various resources to the process instances as they advance through their processing stages. Notice that the interpretation of the role of transitions t^*, t_I and t_F implies that $(t^*)^\bullet \cap P_R = \,^\bullet(t^*) \cap P_R = (t_I)^\bullet \cap P_R = \,^\bullet(t_F) \cap P_R = \emptyset$. The resulting net will be called the *resource-augmented process (sub-)net* and it will be denoted by $\overline{\mathcal{N}_P}$. The *reusable* nature of the system resources is captured by the following assumption regarding the resource-augmented process net $\overline{\mathcal{N}_P}$:

Assumption 4 *Let $\overline{\mathcal{N}_P} = (P_S \cup \{i, o\} \cup P_R, T, W, M_0)$ denote a resource-augmented process (sub-)net. Then, $\forall l \in \{1, \ldots, |P_R|\}$, there exists a p-semiflow y_{r_l}, s.t.: (i) $y_{r_l}(r_l) = 1$; (ii) $y_{r_l}(r_j) = 0$, $\forall j \neq l$; (iii) $y_{r_l}(i) = y_{r_l}(o) = 0$; (iv) $\forall p \in P_S$, $y_{r_l}(p) =$ number of units from resource R_i required for the execution of stage p.*

While the p-semiflows introduced by Assumption 4 characterize the resource allocation taking place at each process stage and the conservative nature of the system resources, they do not reveal anything regarding the adequacy of the available resource set for supporting the execution of the various processing stages, under the sequencing constraints implied by the process-defining logic. This additional concern underlying the correct definition of the various RAS process-types

---

process instances have been activated, still they will always be able to complete, in spite of any additional effects arising from their interaction through the defining process logic. This requirement plays also an important role in the developments presented in [14]; specifically, in [14], the authors introduce the term *"strong reversibility"* in order to characterize the requirement expressed by Assumption 2 as an additional net property.

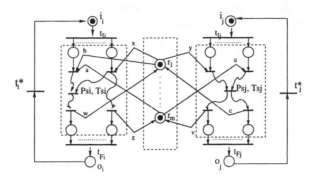

Figure 9.1: The process-resource net structure considered in this work

is captured by extending the requirement for *quasi-liveness* of the process net $\mathcal{N}_P$, introduced by Assumption 1, to the resource-augmented process net $\overline{\mathcal{N}_P}$:

Assumption 5 *The resource-augmented process (sub-)nets considered in this work are assumed to be* quasi-live *for* $M_0(i) = 1$ *and* $M_0(r_l) = C_l$, $\forall l \in \{1, \ldots, |P_R|\}$.

The complete PN-based model, $\mathcal{N} = (P, T, W, M_0)$, of any given instance from the considered RAS class is obtained by *merging* the resource-augmented process nets $\overline{\mathcal{N}_{P_j}} = (P_j, T_j, W_j, M_{0_j})$, $j = 1, \ldots, n$, modelling its constituent process types, through their common resource places. The resulting PN class is characterized as the class of *process-resource nets with quasi-live, reversible and acyclic process sub-nets*, and its basic structure is depicted in Figure 9.1. Let $P = \bigcup_j P_j$, $P_S = \bigcup_j P_{S_j}$; $I = \bigcup_j \{i_j\}$; $O = \bigcup_j \{o_j\}$. Then, $P = P_S \cup I \cup O \cup P_R$. Furthermore, the re-usable nature of the resource allocation taking place in the entire process-resource net is characterized by a p-semiflow y_{r_l} for each resource type R_l, $l = 1, \ldots, m$, defined by: (i) $y_{r_l}(r_l) = 1$; (ii) $y_{r_l}(r_j) = 0$, $\forall j \neq l$; (iii) $y_{r_l}(i_j) = y_{r_l}(o_j) = 0$, $\forall j$; (iv) $\forall p \in P_S$, $y_{r_l}(p) = y_{r_l}^{(j*)}(p)$, where $\overline{\mathcal{N}_{P_{j*}}}$ denotes the resource-augmented process sub-net containing place p, and $y_{r_l}^{(j*)}()$ denotes the corresponding p-semiflow for resource R_l. Finally, it is easy to see that Assumption 5 regarding the quasi-liveness of the constituent resource-augmented process sub-nets $\overline{\mathcal{N}_{P_j}}$ implies also the quasi-liveness of the entire process-resource net $\mathcal{N}$.

The next definition extends to the class of process-resource nets, considered in this work, the notion of the *modified* marking, originally introduced in [25, 7] for analyzing the liveness of a more restricted PN subclass, modelling the behavior of sequential RAS with multi-unit resource allocation per stage and routing flexibility.

Definition 2 *Given a process-resource net* $\mathcal{N} = (P_S \cup I \cup O \cup P_R, T, W, M_0)$ *and* $M \in R(\mathcal{N}, M_0)$, *the* modified marking $\overline{M}$ *is defined by*

$$\overline{M}(p) = \begin{cases} M(p) & \text{if } p \notin I \cup O \\ 0 & \text{otherwise} \end{cases} \tag{9.1}$$

Furthermore, the set of all modified markings *induced by the net reachable markings is defined by* $\overline{R(\mathcal{N}, M_0)} = \{\overline{M} \mid M \in R(\mathcal{N}, M_0)\}$

We conclude this section by noticing that, from a completely practical standpoint, the main requirement underlying the classical RAS deadlock avoidance theory, is that every process activated in the system will be able to run to completion, without getting entangled in a deadlock situation [26]. In the PN-modelling framework, this requirement is explicitly modelled by stipulating that the corresponding process-resource net is *reversible*. However, in the considered class of process-resource nets, reversibility is equivalent to liveness. This result is established in Section 3, and justifies, in terms of the more typical requirements of the RAS deadlock avoidance theory, the overall approach taken in this work.

9.3   Liveness analysis of process-resource nets with quasi-live, reversible and acyclic process sub-nets

The main result of this section links the non-liveness arising in the class of process-resource nets with quasi-live, reversible and acyclic process sub-nets,[6] to the development of a special type of deadly marked siphon in the net modified reachability space. It is also discussed how this new result encompasses and explains all existing similar results, pertaining to more restricted RAS classes. The last part of the section establishes that, for the considered class of process-resource nets, liveness and reversibility are equivalent concepts.

The result connecting the non-liveness arising in the class of process-resource nets with quasi-live, reversible and acyclic process sub-nets to the presence of deadly marked siphons is developed in a three-step argument, that further reveals the fundamental structures and mechanisms behind it. Hence, its derivation provides also the intuitive explanation requested in the opening discussion of this chapter. The first step in this development is established by the following lemma:

Lemma 2 *Consider a process-resource net* $\mathcal{N} = (P_S \cup I \cup O \cup P_R, T, W, M_0)$ *with quasi-live and reversible process sub-nets. If* $\exists M \in R(\mathcal{N}, M_0)$ *s.t.* $\exists$ *a process sub-net* $\mathcal{N}_{P_{j^*}}$ *with* $M(i_{j^*}) + M(o_{j^*}) \neq M_0(i_{j^*})$ *and* $\overline{M}$ *is a total deadlock, then* $\exists$ *siphon* S *s.t.*

---

[6]We clarify that in the subsequent development of this chapter, a process (sub-)net is characterized *quasi-live* if it satisfies Assumption 1 and the corresponding resource-augmented process sub-net satisfies Assumption 5, it is characterized *reversible* if it satisfies Assumption 2, and it is characterized *acyclic* if it satisfies Assumption 3.

   i. S is deadly marked at $\overline{M}$;

  ii. $S \cap P_R \neq \emptyset$;

iii. $\forall p \in S \cap P_R$, p is a disabling place at $\overline{M}$.

Proof: Let S denote the set of disabling places in modified marking $\overline{M}$. Since $\overline{M}$ is a total deadlock, $S^\bullet = T \supseteq {}^\bullet S$. Therefore, S is a siphon, while the definition of S implies also that it is deadly marked. This establishes part (i) in the above lemma.

To establish that $S \cap P_R \neq \emptyset$, consider the process sub-net $\mathcal{N}_{P_{j\bullet}}$. The fact that $M(i_{j\bullet}) + M(o_{j\bullet}) \neq M_0(i_{j\bullet})$ implies that there are active process instances in the sub-net $\mathcal{N}_{P_{j\bullet}}$. But then, Assumptions 2 and 1 imply that sub-net $\mathcal{N}_{P_{j\bullet}}$ remains live in spite of any token removal from places $i_{j\bullet}$ and $o_{j\bullet}$ requested by Definition 2. Hence, the occurrence of the system deadlock at $\overline{M}$ must involve insufficiently marked resource places.

Finally, part (iii) of Lemma 2 is an immediate consequence of the above definition of set S. $\diamond$

In the following, a deadly marked siphon S satisfying also the conditions (ii) and (iii) in Lemma 2, will be called a *resource-induced* deadly marked siphon. Lemma 2 essentially specializes the more general connection between total deadlocks and deadly marked siphons (c.f., Section 2.1), to the subclass of process-resource nets with quasi-live and reversible active processes. From a methodological standpoint, it provides a vehicle for connecting the liveness of resource allocation – and, in certain cases, even the quasi-liveness – taking place in process-resource nets, to resource-induced deadly marked siphons, as long as it can be established that the lack of (any of) these properties implies the existence a reachable marking M s.t. (i) there exists a process sub-net $\mathcal{N}_{P_{j\bullet}}$ with $M(i_{j\bullet}) + M(o_{j\bullet}) \neq M_0(i_{j\bullet})$ and (ii) the corresponding modified marking $\overline{M}$ is a total deadlock. The next lemma establishes that this is the case for the class of process-resource nets with quasi-live, reversible and acyclic process sub-nets.

Lemma 3 *Consider a process-resource net $\mathcal{N} = (P_S \cup I \cup O \cup P_R, T, W, M_0)$ with quasi-live, reversible and acyclic process sub-nets. If $\mathcal{N}$ is not live, then, $\exists M \in R(\mathcal{N}, M_0)$ s.t. (i) $\exists$ process sub-net $\mathcal{N}_{P_{j\bullet}}$ with $M(i_{j\bullet}) + M(o_{j\bullet}) \neq M_0(i_{j\bullet})$ and (ii) $\overline{M}$ is a total deadlock.*

Proof: Since $\mathcal{N}$ is not live, $\exists M' \in R(\mathcal{N}, M_0)$ and $t' \in T$ s.t. t' is dead in M'. We claim that $\exists M \in R(\mathcal{N}, M')$ s.t. (i) $\exists$ process sub-net $\mathcal{N}_{P_{j\bullet}}$ with $M(i_{j\bullet}) + M(o_{j\bullet}) \neq M_0(i_{j\bullet})$ and (ii) every transition $t \notin (I \cup O)^\bullet$ is disabled in M. Indeed, the acyclic structure of the process sub-nets $\mathcal{N}_{P_j}$, $j = 1, \ldots, n$, implies that every transition sequence σ s.t. $M'[\sigma\rangle$ and $\forall t \in \sigma$, $t \notin (I \cup O)^\bullet$, will be of finite length. Consider such a maximal transition sequence $\hat{\sigma}$ and let $M'[\hat{\sigma}\rangle M$. Then, at marking M there must exist a process sub-net $\mathcal{N}_{P_{j\bullet}}$ with $M(i_{j\bullet}) + M(o_{j\bullet}) \neq M_0(i_{j\bullet})$, since otherwise the initial marking M_0 is reachable from M, and then, the quasi-liveness of $\mathcal{N}$ implies that t' is not dead at M'. To see that $\overline{M}$ is a total deadlock for $\mathcal{N}$, simply notice that the specification of $\overline{M}$, by setting $\overline{M}(i_j) = \overline{M}(o_j) = 0$, $\forall j$, essentially disables all transitions $t \in (I \cup O)^\bullet$, that, by construction, are the only transitions potentially enabled in M. $\diamond$

The next theorem completes the aforementioned three-step development of the key result of this section, by stating and proving, by means of Lemmas 2 and 3, that in the class of process-resource nets with quasi-live, reversible and acyclic processes, there is a direct relationship between the RAS non-liveness and the presence of resource-induced deadly marked siphons in the modified reachability space of the RAS-modelling PN.

Theorem 1 *Let $\mathcal{N} = (P_S \cup I \cup O \cup P_R, T, W, M_0)$ be a process-resource net with quasi-live, reversible and acyclic processes. $\mathcal{N}$ is live if and only if the space of modified reachable markings, $\overline{R(\mathcal{N}, M_0)}$, contains no resource-induced deadly marked siphons.*

Proof: To show the necessity part, suppose that $\exists M \in R(\mathcal{N}, M_0)$ s.t. $\overline{M}$ contains a resource-induced deadly marked siphon S. Let $r \in S \cap P_R$ be one of the disabling resource places, and consider $t \in r^\bullet$ s.t. $\overline{M}(r) < W(r,t)$. The definition of deadly marked siphon implies that $\forall t' \in {}^\bullet r$, t' is dead in $R(\mathcal{N}, \overline{M})$. This remark, when combined with Definition 2 and Assumption 4, further imply that $\forall M' \in R(\mathcal{N}, M)$, $M'(r) \leq M(r)$, since the re-introduction of the tokens removed from places $p \in I \cup 0$ and their potential loading in the system, can only decrease the resource availabilities. Therefore, t is a dead transition at M, which contradicts the assumption of net liveness.

To show the sufficiency part, suppose that $\mathcal{N}$ is not live. Then, Lemma 3 implies that $\exists M \in R(\mathcal{N}, M_0)$ s.t. (i) $\exists$ process sub-net $\mathcal{N}_{P_{j^*}}$ with $M(i_{j^*}) + M(o_{j^*}) \neq M_0(i_{j^*})$, and (ii) $\overline{M}$ is a total deadlock. But then, Lemma 2 implies that $\overline{R(\mathcal{N}, M_0)}$ contains a resource-induced deadly marked siphon, which contradicts the working hypothesis. $\diamond$

The following corollary results immediately from Theorem 1; its original statement (and a formal proof) can be found in [25, 7].

Corollary 1 *Let $\mathcal{N} = (P_S \cup I \cup O \cup P_R, T, W, M_0)$ be a process-resource net where (i) the process sub-nets $\mathcal{N}_{P_j}$, $j = 1, \ldots, n$, are strongly connected state machines with each circuit containing the places i_j and o_j, and (ii) the resource-augmented process nets $\overline{\mathcal{N}_{P_j}}$ are quasi-live. Then, $\mathcal{N}$ is live if and only if the space of modified reachable markings, $\overline{R(\mathcal{N}, M_0)}$, contains no resource-induced deadly marked siphons.*

The next corollary specializes Theorem 1 to the sub-class of process-resource nets where the process sub-nets $\mathcal{N}_{P_j}$ are acyclic marked graphs. A stronger version of this result, that connects also the lack of quasi-liveness to the presence of resource-induced deadly marked siphons, is presented in [8].

Corollary 2 *Let* $\mathcal{N} = (P_S \cup I \cup O \cup P_R, T, W, M_0)$ *be a process-resource net where (i) the process sub-nets* $\mathcal{N}_{P_j}$, $j = 1, \ldots, n$, *are strongly connected marked graphs with each circuit containing the places* i_j *and* o_j, *and (ii) the resource-augmented process nets* $\overline{\mathcal{N}_{p_j}}$ *are quasi-live. Then,* $\mathcal{N}$ *is live if and only if the space of modified reachable markings,* $\overline{R(\mathcal{N}, M_0)}$, *contains no resource-induced deadly marked siphons.*

The next result states that for the case of *PT-ordinary* PN's, the problematic siphons interpreting the RAS non-liveness are, in fact, *empty* siphons, and they can also be identified in the *original* net reachability space $R(\mathcal{N}, M_0)$ (besides the modified reachability space $\overline{R(\mathcal{N}, M_0)}$).

Corollary 3 *Let* $\mathcal{N}$ $(P_S \cup I \cup O \cup P_R, T, W, M_0)$ *be a PT-ordinary process-resource net with quasi-live, reversible and acyclic process sub-nets.* $\mathcal{N}$ *is live if and only if the space of reachable markings,* $R(\mathcal{N}, M_0)$, *contains no empty siphons.*

Proof: According to Theorem 1, under the assumptions of Corollary 3, net $\mathcal{N}$ is non-live, iff there exists a marking $M \in R(\mathcal{N}, M_0)$, s.t. $M \neq M_0$ and its modified marking $\overline{M}$ contains a resource-induced deadly marked siphon, S. Furthermore, the development of the result of Theorem 1 (c.f., Lemmas 2 and 3) indicates that S is defined by the set of disabling places of a total deadlock contained in $\overline{M}$. Since every place $p \in S$ is a disabling place in $\overline{M}$, and net $\mathcal{N}$ is PT-ordinary, $\overline{M}(p) = 0$, $\forall p \in S$. Hence, S is an empty siphon in $\overline{M}$. It remains to be shown that the presence of the resource-induced empty siphon S in the modified marking $\overline{M}$ implies the presence of an empty siphon S' in the original marking M. For that, let $S' = \{r_i : r_i \in S\} \cup \{p \in P_S : M(p) = \overline{M}(p) = 0 \land \exists r_i \text{ s.t. } (r_i \in S \land y_{r_i}(p) > 0)\}$. Notice that $S' \neq \emptyset$, since S is a resource-induced empty siphon. We show that S' is a siphon (which is empty, by construction), by considering the next two main cases:

  Case I – $t \in {}^\bullet r_k$ **for some** $r_k \in S$: Then, $\exists q \in S$ s.t. $t \in q^\bullet$. If $q \in P_R$, then $q \in \{r_i : r_i \in S\} \subset S'$. On the other hand, if $q \notin P_R$, then $q \in P_S$, since $(q^\bullet)^\bullet \cap P_R \neq \emptyset$. Furthermore, $y_{r_k}(q) > 0$ and $M(q) = 0$ (since $q \in S$). Therefore, $q \in \{p \in P_S : M(p) = \overline{M}(p) = 0 \land \exists r_i \text{ s.t. } (r_i \in S \land y_{r_i}(p) > 0)\} \subset S'$. In both cases, $t \in (S')^\bullet$.

  Case II – $t \in {}^\bullet q$ **for some** $q \in P_S$ **with** $M(q) = \overline{M}(q) = 0 \land \exists r_k$ **s.t.** $(r_k \in S \land y_{r_k}(q) > 0)$: Then, if $\exists r_l$ s.t. $r_l \in S \land t \in r_l^\bullet$, $t \in \{r_i : r_i \in S\}^\bullet \subseteq (S')^\bullet$. Otherwise, $\exists q' \in (I \cup O \cup P_S) \cap {}^\bullet t$ with $\overline{M}(q') = 0$. Furthermore, since $y_{r_k}(q) > 0$ and, by the sub-case assumption, $\forall r_l \in {}^\bullet t$, $M(r_l) > 0$, it must be that $y_{r_k}(q') > 0$. But then, $t \in \{p \in P_S : M(p) = \overline{M}(p) = 0 \land \exists r_i \text{ s.t. } (r_i \in S \land y_{r_i}(p) > 0)\}^\bullet \subseteq (S')^\bullet$. $\diamond$

  Corollary 3 encompasses all the relevant results appearing in [2, 4, 11] and some of the results appearing in [5]. It also subsumes the general siphon-based characterization of liveness for the process-resource nets considered in [14], since that work considers ordinary Petri nets only. The next example demonstrates that

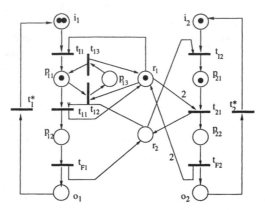

Figure 9.2: Example 1 – A case of RAS non-liveness which cannot be attributed to the development of resource-induced deadly marked siphons, due to enabled internal process cycles

for the case of process-resource nets where the process flows can present internal cycles, the structural concept of resource-induced deadly marked siphon might not be sufficient for interpreting the non-liveness of resource allocation in process-resource nets, even under the assumptions of quasi-live and reversible process sub-nets. The works of [15, 16] identify some special structure on the resource allocation requests, that allows the attribution of the net non-liveness to resource-induced deadly marked siphons, even for the case of process-resource nets with cyclic process routes. However, the complete characterization of the dynamics and the liveness-related properties of process-resource nets with cyclic process routes is an issue open to future investigation.

Example 1: Consider an RAS with two resource types, R_1 and R_2, available at 2 and 1 units, respectively, and two process types, J_1 and J_2. Process type J_1 involves three stages, J_{11}, J_{12} and J_{13}, with corresponding resource allocation requests $[1, 0]$, $[0, 1]$ and $[2, 0]$. Process type J_2 involves two stages, J_{21} and J_{22}, with corresponding resource allocation requests $[0, 1]$ and $[2, 0]$. The RAS-modelling process-resource net, $\mathcal{N}$, that expresses also the flow logic defining the possible process transitions among their stages, is depicted in Figure 9.2. In particular, Figure 9.2 depicts a marking $M \in R(\mathcal{N}, M_0)$, in which the two active processes are deadlocked (notice that transitions t_{11} and t_{21} are dead in the depicted marking M). Yet, the reader can verify that the corresponding modified marking $\overline{M}$, as well as all the modified markings $\overline{M'} \in R(\mathcal{N}, \overline{M})$, contain no resource-induced deadly marked siphon. This results from the fact that the deadlocked process in place p_{11} can circulate freely in the circuit $< p_{11}, t_{12}, p_{13}, t_{13} >$, and therefore, the RAS deadlock of the two processes does not translate to a total deadlock in

$\overline{R(\mathcal{N}, \overline{M})}$. ⋄

We conclude this section by formally stating and proving that in the considered class of process-resource nets, liveness and reversibility are equivalent concepts.

Theorem 2 *A process-resource net* $\mathcal{N} = (P_S \cup I \cup O \cup P_R, T, W, M_0)$ *with quasi-live, reversible and acyclic process sub-nets is reversible if and only if it is live.*

Proof: The necessity ("only-if") part of this theorem results immediately from Lemma 3, since otherwise $\exists M \in R(\mathcal{N}, M_0)$ s.t. $\exists$ process sub-net $\mathcal{N}_{P_{j\bullet}}$ with $M(i_{j\bullet}) + M(o_{j\bullet}) \neq M_0(i_{j\bullet})$, and $\overline{M}$ is a total deadlock. In order to establish the sufficiency ("if") part of the theorem, consider a marking $M \in R(\mathcal{N}, M_0)$ s.t. $M \neq M_0$. Then, if for every process sub-net $\mathcal{N}_{P_j}$ it holds that $M(i_j) + M(o_j) = M_0(i_j)$, it should be obvious from the structure of net $\mathcal{N}$ that $M_0 \in R(\mathcal{N}, M)$. Otherwise, using an argument similar to that in the proof of Lemma 3, one can construct a maximal-length firing sequence σ leading to a marking M' s.t. every transition $t \notin (I \cup O)^\bullet$ is disabled in M'. We claim that at M', $\forall$ process sub-net $\mathcal{N}_{P_j}$ it holds that $M'(i_j) + M'(o_j) = M_0(i_j)$, and therefore, $M_0 \in R(\mathcal{N}, M')$, which further implies that $M_0 \in R(\mathcal{N}, M)$. Indeed, by construction, $\overline{M'}$ is a total deadlock of $\mathcal{N}$, and if $\exists$ process sub-net $\mathcal{N}_{P_{j\bullet}}$ s.t. $M'(i_{j\bullet}) + M'(o_{j\bullet}) \neq M_0(i_{j\bullet})$, Lemma 2 implies that M' contains a resource-induced deadly marked siphon. But then, Theorem 1 implies that $\mathcal{N}$ is not live, which contradicts the working hypothesis. ⋄

9.4 Liveness verification and liveness-enforcing supervision for process-resource nets with quasi-live, reversible and acyclic process sub-nets

This section seeks to exploit the siphon-based characterization of non-liveness for process-resource nets with quasi-live, reversible and acyclic process sub-nets, in order to develop computational tools for assessing the liveness of any given instance of the considered PN sub-class, and if necessary, to synthesize a correct liveness-enforcing supervisor (LES). Hence, the first part of the section discusses a sufficiency test for the non-existence of resource-induced deadly marked siphons in the modified reachability space of any process-resource net, that was originally developed in [7]. The considered test extends relevant ideas presented in [4] regarding the detection of the development of empty siphons in ordinary Petri nets, and takes the form of a mathematical programming (MP) formulation, that is polynomially sized, in terms of variables and constraints, with respect to the underlying PN model. As a result, it is very practical from a computational standpoint. The second part of the section describes how the MP-based test discussed in the first part, can be integrated in a synthesis procedure that supports the design of *algebraic* LES for the considered class of process-resource nets.

Input: A marked PN $\mathcal{N} = (P, T, W, M_0)$ and a marking $M \in R(\mathcal{N}, M_0)$
Output: The maximal deadly marked siphon in M, S

1. $S := P$; $\mathcal{N}' := \mathcal{N}$

2. **while** $\exists\, t \in T$ such that t is fireable in the modified net $\mathcal{N}'$ **do**

   (a) Remove t from $\mathcal{N}'$

   (b) Remove $t^\bullet$ from $\mathcal{N}'$

   (c) $S := S \backslash t^\bullet$

   endwhile

3. **Return** S

Figure 9.3: An algorithm for computing the maximal deadly marked siphon in a given PN marking M

A mathematical programming-based sufficiency test for the liveness of process-resource nets with quasi-live, reversible and acyclic process sub-nets The starting point for the development of the considered MP-based sufficiency test for the liveness of process-resource nets with quasi-live, reversible and acyclic process sub-nets, is the observation that, given a marked PN $\mathcal{N} = (P, T, W, M_0)$ and a marking $M \in R(\mathcal{N}, M_0)$, the maximal deadly marked siphon S in M can be computed by the algorithm of Figure 9.3, originally developed in [7]. For the case of *structurally bounded* nets, the algorithm of Figure 9.3 can be converted to an IP formulation through the use of the *binary indicator* variables v_p, z_t and f_{tp}, respectively defined by the following conditions:

$$v_p = 1 \iff \text{place } p \text{ is removed by the algorithm,}$$
$$\forall p \in P$$
$$z_t = 1 \iff \text{transition } t \text{ is removed by the algorithm,}$$
$$\forall t \in T$$
$$f_{pt} = 1 \iff M(p) \geq W(p, t) \ \lor\ v_p = 1, \ \ \forall W(p, t) > 0$$

Furthermore, we let $SB(p)$ denote a structural bound for the markings of place $p \in P$. Then, the work of [7] establishes the following theorem:

Theorem 3 *Given a marking $M \in R(\mathcal{N}, M_0)$ of a structurally bounded PN $\mathcal{N} = (P, T, W, M_0)$, the maximal deadly marked siphon S contained in M is determined by:*

$$S = \{p \in P \mid v_p = 0\} \tag{9.2}$$

where v_p, $p \in P$, is obtained through the following IP formulation:

$$G(M) = \min \sum_{p \in P} v_p \tag{9.3}$$

s.t.

$$f_{pt} \geq \frac{M(p) - W(p,t) + 1}{SB(p)}, \quad \forall W(p,t) > 0 \tag{9.4}$$

$$f_{pt} \geq v_p, \quad \forall W(p,t) > 0 \tag{9.5}$$

$$z_t \geq \sum_{p \in {}^\bullet t} f_{pt} - |{}^\bullet t| + 1, \quad \forall t \in T \tag{9.6}$$

$$v_p \geq z_t, \quad \forall W(t,p) > 0 \tag{9.7}$$

$$v_p, z_t, f_{pt} \in \{0,1\}, \quad \forall p \in P, \forall t \in T \tag{9.8}$$

In order to understand the formulation of Theorem 3, notice that Equation 9.6 together with Equation 9.4 imply that all transitions z_t fireable in marking M will have $z_t = 1$. Furthermore, Equation 9.7 implies that all places $p \in t^\bullet$ for some t with $z_t = 1$ will have $v_p = 1$, which implements Step (2.b) in the algorithm of Figure 9.3. Similarly, Equation 9.5 combined with Equation 9.6 force $z_t = 1$ for all transitions t with $v_p = 1$, $\forall p \in {}^\bullet t$. Finally, the fact that no additional place p (resp., transition t) has $v_p = 1$ (resp., $z_t = 1$), is guaranteed by the specification of the objective function in the above formulation.

In case that net $\mathcal{N}$ is a process-resource net, the formulation of Theorem 3 can be restricted to the computation of the maximal *resource-induced* deadly marked siphon, through the introduction of the following two constraints [7]:

$$\sum_{r \in P_R} v_r \leq |P_R| - 1 \tag{9.9}$$

$$\sum_{t \in r^\bullet} f_{rt} - |r^\bullet| + 1 \leq v_r, \quad \forall r \in P_R \tag{9.10}$$

Specifically, Constraint 9.9 enforces that the identified siphon S must contain at least one resource place, while Constraint 9.10 requires that all resource places included in S must be disabling. The resulting necessary and sufficient condition for the non-existence of resource-induced deadly marked siphons in a given marking M of a process-resource net is as follows [7]:

Corollary 4 *A given marking M of a process-resource net $\mathcal{N}$ contains no resource-induced deadly marked siphons, if and only if the corresponding formulation of Equations 9.3–9.10 is infeasible.*

The test of Corollary 4 can be extended, in principle, to a test for the non-existence of resource-induced deadly marked siphons over the entire modified reachability space, $\overline{R(\mathcal{N}, M_0)}$, of a process-resource net $\mathcal{N} = (P, T, W, M_0)$, by: (i) substituting marking vector M in the IP formulation of Theorem 3 with the modified marking vector $\overline{M}$; (ii) introducing an additional set of variables, M, representing the net reachable markings; (iii) adding two sets of constraints, the first one linking variables M and $\overline{M}$ according to the logic of Equation 9.1, and the second one ensuring that the set of feasible values for the variable vector M is equivalent to the PN reachability space $R(\mathcal{N}, M_0)$. Unfortunately, however, any system of linear inequalities exactly characterizing the set $R(\mathcal{N}, M_0)$ is of exponential complexity with respect to the net size [27]. On the other hand, a superset of the reachability space $R(\mathcal{N}, M_0)$ is provided by the system *state equation* [18]:

$$M = M_0 + \Theta \bar{x} \tag{9.11}$$

$$M \geq 0, \ \bar{x} \in Z^+ \tag{9.12}$$

The above remarks give rise to a *sufficient* condition for the non-existence of resource-induced deadly marked siphons S in the entire space $\overline{R(\mathcal{N}, M_0)}$ of a given process-resource net $\mathcal{N}$. Furthermore, in the light of Theorem 1, this condition constitutes a *sufficient* condition for liveness of process-resource nets with quasi-live, reversible and acyclic process sub-nets.

Corollary 5 *Let* $\mathcal{N} = (P, T, W, M_0)$ *be a process-resource net with quasi-live, reversible and acyclic process sub-nets. If the mixed integer program defined by (i) Equations 9.3–9.10, where vector variable M is replaced by vector variable $\overline{M}$, (ii) Equations 9.11–9.12, and (iii) Equation 9.1, is infeasible, then $\mathcal{N}$ is live.*

Concluding this paragraph, we notice that for the case of PT-ordinary process-resource nets with quasi-live, reversible and acyclic process sub-nets, a similar but simpler, from a computational standpoint, liveness sufficiency test can be derived, based on the result of Corollary 3. We refer the reader to [4, 6] for a detailed discussion of the corresponding formulation.

Synthesizing correct algebraic LES for process-resource nets with quasi-live, reversible and acyclic process sub-nets Corollary 5 can provide also the basis for the development of a systematic methodology for the design of liveness-enforcing supervisors (LES) for process-resource nets with quasi-live, reversible and acyclic process sub-nets. This is the result of the fundamental stipulation that a LES for any given RAS is *correct* if and only if the controlled system behavior is *live*. Hence, to the extent that Corollary 5 constitutes a liveness criterion, it can provide a LES correctness verification tool, as long as the LES synthesis process is restricted in a way that the controlled system behavior can be modelled by a PN, $\mathcal{N}^c$, that remains in the class of process-resource nets with quasi-live, reversible and acyclic process sub-nets. This can be the case for a large class of RAS LES encountered in the literature, characterized as *algebraic* LES [26, 6]. Essentially, algebraic LES seek to restrict the concurrency supported by the underlying RAS, by setting explicit limits on the number of process instances that can execute simultaneously certain subsets of the RAS process stages. For implementation purposes, this idea is operationalized through the imposition of a set of linear inequalities

$$A \cdot M_S \leq \mathbf{b} \tag{9.13}$$

that must always be met by the projection M_S of marking M of the RAS-modelling PN to the subspace defined by its components corresponding to $p \in P_S$. The subset of $R(\mathcal{N}, M_0)$ that is reachable under the observation of Equation 9.13 constitutes the *LES-admissible* sub-space, $R^{LES}(\mathcal{N}, M_0)$. For a correct algebraic

LES, this sub-space must (i) contain the initial marking M_0, and (ii) be strongly connected.

From a representational standpoint, the constraint(s) expressed by Equation 9.13 can be modelled in the PN-modelling framework, through the theory of *control-place invariants*, presented in [28]. According to [28], each of the inequality constraints

$$\mathbf{a}_{[l,\cdot]} \cdot M_S \leq b_l \tag{9.14}$$

can be implemented on the net behavior by superimposing on the original net structure a *control* place w_l, connected to the rest of the network according to the flow matrix

$$\theta_{w_l} = -\mathbf{a}_{[l,\cdot]} \cdot \Theta_S \tag{9.15}$$

where Θ_S denotes the flow sub-matrix of the uncontrolled network $\mathcal{N} = (P, T, W, M_0)$ corresponding to places $p \in P_S$. The initial marking of place w_l is set to

$$M_0(w_l) = b_l \tag{9.16}$$

and the resulting controller imposes Constraint 9.14 on the system behavior by establishing the place invariant

$$\mathbf{a}_{[l,\cdot]} \cdot M_S + M(w_l) = b_l \tag{9.17}$$

Equation 9.17, when interpreted in the light of Assumption 4 of Section 2.2, implies that the control places w_l, implementing each of the constraints in the LES-defining Equation 9.13, essentially play the role of fictitious new resources in the dynamics of the net $\mathcal{N}^c$, that models the controlled system behavior. This observation further implies that the superimposition of an algebraic LES to a process-resource net with quasi-live, reversible and acyclic process sub-nets leads to a controlled net $\mathcal{N}^c$ that falls in to the class of process-resource nets that satisfy Assumptions 2 and 3. However, in order to ensure that the net $\mathcal{N}^c$ satisfies also Assumption 5 with respect to the extended "resource" set $P_R \cup P_W$, some additional restrictions must be imposed on the specification of the LES-defining Equation 9.13, which will ensure that the constituent process sub-nets remain quasi-live after the introduction of the control places. In that case, it is obvious that the liveness sufficiency condition of Corollary 5, applied on the controlled net $\mathcal{N}^c$, can function as a correctness verification tool for the considered supervisor.

Currently, we lack a complete theory that will address, in the broadest context of process-resource nets, the issue of synthesizing algebraic LES that preserve the quasi-liveness of the constituent RAS processes. An additional limitation of the currently available results is our inability to characterize, for a given process-resource net $\mathcal{N}$, the set of A matrices in Equation 9.13 that will lead, through Equation 9.15, to a controlled net $\mathcal{N}^c$ which is *structurally live* with respect to markings $M_0(w_l)$, $l = 1, \ldots, \dim(\mathbf{b})$. Sporadic results, providing algebraic LES classes that preserve the RAS quasi-liveness and are structurally live with respect to markings $M_0(w_l)$, $l = 1, \ldots, \dim(\mathbf{b})$, and that are appropriate for Single-Unit

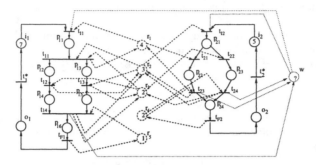

Figure 9.4: Example 2 – The considered process-resource net

and/or Conjunctive/Disjunctive RAS, can be found in [19, 29, 6, 7].[7] While the development of a complete methodology able to systematically synthesize (algebraic) LES for the class of process-resource nets considered in this work is an important and challenging problem open to further investigation, the results of Sections 9.3 and 9.4 can still enable the systematic verification of the correctness of algebraic LES that might have been heuristically developed for any given quasi-live, reversible and acyclic process-resource net. The following example demonstrates this capability.

Example 2: Consider the process-resource net depicted in Figure 9.4. As it can be seen from the figure, the underlying RAS consists of two processes, J_1 and J_2, and five resource types, $R_1, \ldots, R_5$. Process type J_1 has a flow represented by an acyclic marked graph, and it involves six tasks, $J_{11}, \ldots, J_{16}$, with corresponding resource requirements: $[1, 0, 0, 0, 0]$, $[0, 1, 0, 0, 0]$, $[0, 0, 1, 0, 0]$, $[0, 0, 1, 0, 0]$, $[0, 1, 0, 0, 0]$ and $[0, 0, 0, 0, 1]$. Process type J_2 has a flow represented by an acyclic state machine, and it involves four stages, $J_{21}, \ldots, J_{24}$, with corresponding resource requirements: $[0, 1, 0, 0, 0]$, $[1, 1, 0, 0, 0]$, $[0, 1, 1, 0, 0]$ and $[0, 0, 0, 1, 0]$. A closer inspection of the task/stage resource requirements for these two processes reveals that the only resources that could be entangled in a deadlock are R_1, R_2 and R_3. Therefore, the critical sections for J_1 and J_2 are respectively defined by the stage sets $\{J_{11}, J_{12}, J_{13}, J_{14}, J_{15}\}$ and $\{J_{21}, J_{22}, J_{23}\}$.

Our intention is to develop a LES for this net that will establish the liveness of the controlled net by restricting the number of process instances that can simultaneously execute in their critical sections identified above. Hence, the proposed supervisor constitutes a more refined implementation of the *"process-release"* control scheme, previously proposed in the literature,[8] to the particular process-resource net of Figure 9.4. The discussion of the previous paragraph sug-

---

[7] Also, some of the results presented in [30, 2, 20, 9, 10] can be recast in the same framework.

[8] c.f., for instance, the policy presented in [2] and some of the policies presented in [20]; however, the results developed in those works will encompass neither the non-ordinary structure of the process-resource net under consideration, nor the complexity of the involved process flows.

gests that, from an algebraic representational standpoint, the control logic of the considered LES can be expressed by a single linear inequality

$$\mathbf{a} \cdot M_S \le b \qquad (9.18)$$

where b defines the ceiling on the process concurrency imposed by the considered supervisor, and the elements of the (row) vector $\mathbf{a}$ are provided by a set of p-semiflows characterizing the control flow logic for the various process types in their critical sections. In the PN modeling framework, this LES is superimposed to the original process-resource net of Figure 9.4 through the introduction of a control place w, connected to the original process-resource net through the flow structure depicted in dotted lines in Figure 9.4.

Next we seek to determine the maximal marking for w that leads to live behavior for the (controlled) net structure of Figure 9.4, using the siphon-based liveness analysis developed in this work. For this, we first determine an upper bound to the maximal number of processes that can be executed simultaneously by the considered RAS. The reader can convince herself that, based on the resource capacities and the process flows annotated in Figure 9.4, an upper bound for the system concurrency w.r.t. job type J_1 (resp., J_2) is 7 (resp., 5) process instances. Then, using the MIP formulation of Corollary 5 in a binary search over the integer set $\{1, \ldots, 12\}$, reveals that the maximal marking for control place w leading to a correct algebraic LES – or equivalently, the maximal number of jobs that can be simultaneously loaded in the system without the possibility of running into any deadlocking problems – is 6. For completeness, we mention that the deadlock marking identified by the computerized solver when the MIP formulation of Corollary 5 was solved with $M_0(w) = 7$, was: $M(i_1) = 1$; $M(p_{11}) = 4$; $M(p_{12}) = M(p_{13}) = 2$; $M(i_2) = 4$; $M(p_{21}) = 1$; $M(r_4) = 2$; $M(r_5) = 1$; and zero for every other place. ◇

We conclude this section with some remarks on the potential of synthesizing a LES for any given process-resource net, based on the mechanism of process-release control and the structural test for liveness introduced in this section. It is easy to see that, if the process sub-nets of the original process-resource net $\mathcal{N}$ are quasi-live, reversible and acyclic, then the process sub-nets of the controlled net $\mathcal{N}^c$, resulting from the introduction of the control place $\{w\}$, are also reversible, acyclic and quasi-live with respect to the broader "resource" set $P_R \cup \{w\}$, *iff* $M_0(w) \ge 1$. However, $\mathcal{N}^c$ may *not* be structurally live with respect to place w. This effect results from the fact that process nets that contain synchronizing / merging transitions, might need additional control logic to ensure their liveness, even for the execution of a *single* process instance,[9] and exemplifies the extent and nature of the difficulties that must be addressed by any research effort seeking to systematically develop LES appropriate for the considered class of process-resource nets.

---

[9]Luckily, this effect did not appear in the case of Example 2, in spite of the presence of the synchronizing transition t_{14} in the process type J_1. In fact, the reader should convince herself that, because of the particular structure presented by process subnet between transitions t_{11} and t_{14}, J_1 will be live *iff* it is quasi-live, for *any* given resource availability.

9.5   Conclusions

The work presented in this chapter extended the currently existing results regarding the siphon-based characterization of (non-)liveness in sequential RAS. Specifically, it provided a unifying framework for interpreting all the relevant results currently existing in the literature, and even more importantly, it extended the theory applicability to broader RAS classes[10] and it revealed its limitations. It was shown that some key RAS properties that facilitate the interpretation of its non-liveness through the concept of resource-induced deadly marked siphon, are the quasi-liveness, reversibility and acyclicity of its constituent processes.

This finding further suggests that, for RAS with acyclic processes, live behavior can be established through a *two-stage decomposition* procedure, where the first stage seeks to establish inherently consistent – i.e., quasi-live and reversible–process behaviors, and the second stage seeks to develop, if necessary, a control policy, in the form of an (algebraic) LES, that will ensure the RAS liveness in its process enactment phase. In order to support the first stage of this decomposition, more work is necessary towards developing a more profound understanding of the emerging concepts of process quasi-liveness and reversibility, as defined by Assumptions 1, 2 and 5; some preliminary results in this direction can be found in [14]. An issue that needs further investigation in order to support the second stage of the aforementioned decomposition, is the identification – or even better, the development of a mechanism for the automated synthesis – of algebraic LES structures that are guaranteed to maintain the process quasi-liveness of the underlying RAS, and to be structurally live with respect to the marking of the associated control places, in the context of the broader RAS classes considered in this work. Prior experience with the development of similar algebraic LES for the more restricted classes of SU-RAS and CD-RAS can offer useful guidance in this task. Understanding and controlling the dynamics of RAS with internal process cycles is another issue that was shown to lie beyond the boundary of the theory developed in this work, and therefore, it stands open to further investigation. Finally, from an application standpoint, the successful implementation of such a research program will extend our capability towards the effective deployment and (re-)configuration of flexible automation in a broad scope of applications, ranging from automated (e.g., 300mm semiconductor) manufacturing, to driver-less urban mono-rail and railway systems, to web-based workflow management systems.

Acknowledgement

This work was partially supported by the Keck Foundation through the Keck Virtual Factory Lab of the School of Industrial & Systems Engineering at Georgia Institute of Technology.

---

[10]c.f. Example 2 in Section IV, where the addressed process-resource net does not belong to any of the RAS classes that have been studied in the literature.

Bibliography

[1] S. Reveliotis. Liveness enforcing supervision for sequential resource allocation systems: State of the art and open issues. In B. Caillaud, X. Xie, P. Darondeau, and L. Lavagno, editors, *Synthesis and Control of Discrete Event Systems*, pages 203–212. Kluwer Academic Publishers, 2002.

[2] J. Ezpeleta, J. M. Colom, and J. Martinez. A petri net based deadlock prevention policy for flexible manufacturing systems. *IEEE Trans. on R&A*, 11:173–184, 1995.

[3] S. A. Reveliotis, M. A. Lawley, and P. M. Ferreira. Polynomial complexity deadlock avoidance policies for sequential resource allocation systems. *IEEE Trans. on Automatic Control*, 42:1344–1357, 1997.

[4] F. Chu and X-L. Xie. Deadlock analysis of petri nets using siphons and mathematical programming. *IEEE Trans. on R&A*, 13:793–804, 1997.

[5] X. Xie and M. Jeng. Ercn-merged nets and their analysis using siphons. *IEEE Trans. on R&A*, 13:692–703, 1999.

[6] J. Park and S. Reveliotis. Algebraic synthesis of efficient deadlock avoidance policies for sequential resource allocation systems. *IEEE Trans. on R&A*, 16:190–195, 2000.

[7] J. Park and S. A. Reveliotis. Deadlock avoidance in sequential resource allocation systems with multiple resource acquisitions and flexible routings. *IEEE Trans. on Automatic Control*, 46:1572–1583, 2001.

[8] S. A. Reveliotis. Structural analysis of resource allocation systems with synchronization constraints. In *2003 IEEE International Conference on Robotics and Automation*, pages –. IEEE, 2003.

[9] K. Barkaoui and I. Ben Abdallah. Analysis of a resource allocation problem in fms using structure theory of petri nets. In *Proc. of the 1st Intl Workshop on Manufacturing and Petri Nets*, pages 1–15, 1996.

[10] K. Barkaoui, A. Chaoui, and B. Zouari. Supervisory control of discrete event systems based on structure theory of petri nets. In *Proc. of the IEEE Intl Conf. on Systems, Man and Cybernetics*, pages 3750–3755. IEEE, 1997.

[11] F. Tricas, F. Garcia-Valles, J. M. Colom, and J. Ezpeleta. A structural approach to the problem of deadlock prevention in processes with resources. In *Proceedings of the 4th Workshop on Discrete Event Systems*, pages 273–278. IEE, 1998.

[12] F. Tricas, J. M. Colom, and J. Ezpeleta. A solution to the problem of deadlock in concurrent systems using petri nets and integer linear programming. In *Proceedings of the 11th Eurpoean Simulation Symposium*, pages 542–546, 1999.

[13] M. P. Fanti, B. Maione, and T. Turchiano. Comparing digraph and petri net approaches to deadlock avoidance in fms modeling and performance analysis. *IEEE Trans. on Systems, Man and Cybernetics, Part B*, 30:783–798, 2000.

[14] M. Jeng, X. Xie, and M. Y. Peng. Process nets with resources for manufacturing modeling and their analysis. *IEEE Trans. on Robotics and Automation*, 18:875–889, 2002.

[15] J. Park. *Structural Analysis and Control of Resource Allocation Systems using Petri nets*. PhD thesis, Georgia Institute of Technology, Atlanta, GA, 2000.

[16] M. Jeng and X. Xie. Modeling and analysis of semiconductor manufacturing systems with degraded behaviors using petri nets and siphons. *IEEE Trans. on Robotics and Automation*, 17:576–588, 2001.

[17] T. Murata. Petri nets: Properties, analysis and applications. *Proceedings of the IEEE*, 77:541–580, 1989.

[18] J. Desel and J. Esparza. *Free Choice Petri Nets*. Cambridge Univerrsity Press, 1995.

[19] S. A. Reveliotis and P. M. Ferreira. Deadlock avoidance policies for automated manufacturing cells. *IEEE Trans. on Robotics & Automation*, 12:845–857, 1996.

[20] M. P. Fanti, B. Maione, S. Mascolo, and B. Turchiano. Event-based feedback control for deadlock avoidance in flexible production systems. *IEEE Trans. on Robotics and Automation*, 13:347–363, 1997.

[21] M. Lawley, S. Reveliotis, and P. Ferreira. The application and evaluation of banker's algorithm for deadlock-free buffer space allocation in flexible manufacturing systems. *Intl. Jrnl. of Flexible Manufacturing Systems*, 10:73–100, 1998.

[22] M. A. Lawley. Deadlock avoidance for production systems with flexible routing. *IEEE Trans. Robotics & Automation*, 15:497–509, 1999.

[23] W. Van der Aalst. Structural characterizations of sound workflow nets. Technical Report Computing Science Reports 96/23, Eindhoven University of Technology, 1996.

[24] W. Van der Aalst. Verification of workflow nets. In P. Azema and G. Balbo, editors, *Lecture Notes in Computer Science, Vol. 1248*, pages 407–426. Springer Verlag, 1997.

[25] J. Park and S. A. Reveliotis. A polynomial-complexity deadlock avoidance policy for sequential resource allocation systems with multiple resource acquisitions and flexible routings. In *Proc. of CDC 2000*. IEEE, 2000.

[26] S. A. Reveliotis, M. A. Lawley, and P. M. Ferreira. Structural control of large-scale flexibly automated manufacturing systems. In C. T. Leondes, editor, *The Design of Manufacturing Systems*, pages 4-1 – 4-34. CRC Press, 2001.

[27] M. Silva, E. Teruel, and J. M. Colom. Linear algebraic and linear programming techniques for the analysis of place/transition net systems. In W. Reisig and G. Rozenberg, editors, *Lecture Notes in Computer Science, Vol. 1491*, pages 309–373. Springer-Verlag, 1998.

[28] J. O. Moody and P. J. Antsaklis. *Supervisory Control of Discrete Event Systems using Petri nets*. Kluwer Academic Pub., Boston, MA, 1998.

[29] M. Lawley, S. Reveliotis, and P. Ferreira. A correct and scalable deadlock avoidance policy for flexible manufacturing systems. *IEEE Trans. on Robotics & Automation*, 14:796–809, 1998.

[30] Z. A. Banaszak and B. H. Krogh. Deadlock avoidance in flexible manufacturing systems with concurrently competing process flows. *IEEE Trans. on Robotics and Automation*, 6:724–734, 1990.

10

Elementary Siphons of Petri Nets for Efficient Deadlock Control in FMS

ZhiWu Li
Xidian University, Xi'an, China.

MengChu Zhou
New Jersey Institute of Technology, Newark, NJ, USA.

A variety of important Petri net (PN) based methods of preventing deadlocks arising in flexible manufacturing systems (FMS) are to add a monitor and related arcs for each possibly emptiable siphon such that no siphon can be emptied. Since the number of siphons grows in general exponentially with respect to a PN size, their disadvantages lie in that they have to add so many additional monitors to the net that the resulting net supervisor is too complex compared with the original one. This chapter explores the ways to minimize the number of monitors to be added when liveness enforcing PN supervisors are designed. Siphons in a PN are distinguished by elementary and redundant ones. This chapter proposes conditions under which a redundant siphon can be always marked by making its elementary siphons invariant-controlled. Based on the theory of elementary siphons, two novel deadlock prevention policies are developed. FMS examples are used to illustrate the proposed concepts and policies and show the significant advantages over the previous methods.

10.1   Introduction

An FMS is a computer-controlled configuration where different operations
can be executed. Generally it consists of various kinds of general-purpose
workstations, a palletized and programmable material handling system,
and other types of resources such as fixtures and buffers. To effectively
operate an FMS and meet its production objectives, the use of limited
resources among various competing jobs has to be carefully controlled or
coordinated. Since various jobs are concurrently processed and these jobs
have to share some common resources, deadlocks may occur in an FMS during its operation, which are undesirable phenomena in a highly automated
FMS. This chapter focuses on the deadlock problems in such FMS.

One way of dealing with deadlock problems is to model an FMS with
PNs. PNs [1] [24] [35] have a simple mathematical representation. Linear
matrix algebra can be used to make them particularly useful for the analysis
and design of discrete event systems including FMS.

To cope with deadlocks based on a PN formalism, a few approaches are
developed. The first one is called deadlock avoidance [31] [38] [9] [22] [16] [19]
[10] [11] [13]. When adopted, some constraints are imposed on the system
evolutions such that it is always possible to ensure that the processing of
each job can be finished.

The second one is the deadlock detection and recovery. It permits deadlock to occur and is able to detect it. Once detected, some recovery actions
can be manually or automatically taken [31] [23] [33] [34]. This approach is
suitable when deadlocks are rare in a system and a detection and recovery
procedure is in place.

The last one is called deadlock prevention approaches. Deadlock prevention is usually achieved either by effective system design [25] [23] [27] [26] [36]
or by using an off-line mechanism to control the requests for resources to
ensure that deadlocks never occur. Monitors or control places and related arcs are often used to achieve such purposes [10] [18] [17] [12] [37]
[29] [39][30] [7] [6][28].

To aim at finding a relationship between the behavior properties of
the net, such as liveness and boundedness, and its structure, captured in
graph theoretical or algebraic terms, the structure theory of PNs is widely
employed in these available deadlock prevention policies. The research of
Ezpeleta et al. [12] is usually considered to be the seminal work using
structure theory of PNs to design monitor-based PN supervisors for FMS,
which are deadlock-free. The method in [12] is simple and guarantees a
success. However, too many monitors and arcs have to be added, leading
to a much more complex PN supervisor than the originally built PN model.
Effective ways to obtain more permissive monitor-based PN supervisors are

the iterative methods [29] [7] [17]. However, a hard nut remains to crack that those methods will not work for complex or large PN structures. The real cause behind this seems very simple. There are often many siphons in a large-size PN as the iterations proceed. At every iterative step, monitors have to be added. Hence the number of siphons may likely spiral up, which finally becomes unmanageable as the iterations proceed. The shortcoming of the existing methods that need introduce successive monitors when the number of siphons is large motivates this particular research.

The theory of regions [32] [3] which can derive PNs from the automaton-based models has been an important method for supervisory control of discrete event systems [28] [30]. An optimal PN supervisor is obtained using the theory of regions in [28] and for the convenience of application-oriented PN researchers, [30] presents an interpretation for the theory of regions in the PN formalism. The most attractive advantage of this approach is that an optimal or maximally permissive liveness enforcing PN supervisor can be generally generated by adding monitors which are used to separate events from states. The major disadvantage is the much computational cost since we have to generate the reachability graph for a plant PN and many sets of inequalities have to be solved in order to separate some events from dangerous states.

The rest of this chapter is organized as follows. Section 10.2 reviews basic PN definitions and properties. Section 10.3 introduces the class of S^3PR PN models which our approaches target. The basics of the theory of regions are given in Section 10.4. Section 10.5 proposes the concepts of elementary and redundant siphons in PNs. Siphon control techniques based on the theory of elementary siphons are developed in Section 10.6. Two deadlock control policies are developed in Section 10.7 and 10.8, respectively. Section 10.9 introduces FMS examples to illustrate the proposed concepts and deadlock prevention policies. Discussions and concluding remarks are summarized in Section 10.10.

10.2 PN Preliminaries

A PN is a 3-tuple $N = (P, T, F)$ where P and T are finite, nonempty, and disjoint sets. P is the set of places and T is the set of transitions. $F \subseteq (P \times T) \cup (T \times P)$ is called flow relation or the set of directed arcs. The preset of a node $x \in P \cup T$ is defined as $^\bullet x = \{y \in P \cup T \mid (y, x) \in F\}$. The postset of a node $x \in P \cup T$ is defined as $x^\bullet = \{y \in P \cup T \mid (x, y) \in F\}$. The preset (postset) of a set is defined as the union of the presets (postsets) of its elements.

A marking of N is a mapping $M : P \to \mathbf{IN}$, where $\mathbf{IN} = \{0, 1, 2, \ldots\}$.

(N, M) is called a net system or a marked net. A transition $t \in T$ is enabled under M, in symbols $M[t\rangle$, if and only if $\forall p \in^{\bullet} t : M(p) > 0$ holds. If $M[t\rangle$ holds the transition t may fire, resulting in a new marking M', denoted by $M[t\rangle M'$, with $M'(p) = M(p) - 1$ if $p \in^{\bullet} t \backslash t^{\bullet}$; $M'(p) = M(p) + 1$ if $p \in t^{\bullet} \backslash^{\bullet} t$; and otherwise $M'(p) = M(p)$, for all $p \in P$. For net N, the set of all markings reachable from a marking M_0, in symbols $R(N, M_0)$, is the smallest set in which $M_0 \in R(N, M_0)$ and $M' \in R(N, M_0)$ if both $M \in R(N, M_0)$ and $\exists t : M[t\rangle M'$ hold. A transition $t \in T$ is live under M_0 if and only if $\forall M \in R(N, M_0)$, $\exists M' \in R(N, M) : M'[t\rangle$ holds. N is dead under M_0 if and only if $\neg \exists t \in T : M_0[t\rangle$ holds. (N, M_0) is deadlock-free if and only if $\forall M \in R(N, M_0)$, $\exists t \in T : M[t\rangle$ holds. (N, M_0) is live if and only if $\forall t \in T : t$ is live under M_0. A transition sequence $\sigma = t_1 t_2 \ldots t_n$ is said to be firable at marking M if there exist markings $M_1, M_2, \ldots, M_n$ such that $M[t_1\rangle M_1[t_2\rangle M_2 \ldots M_{n-1}[t_n\rangle M_n$ holds. (N, M_0) is bounded if and only if $\exists k \in \mathbf{N}$, $\forall M \in R(N, M_0)$, $\forall p \in P : M(p) \leq k$ holds, where $\mathbf{N} = \{1, 2, \ldots\}$. $N = (P, T, F)$ is pure if and only if $\neg \exists (x, y) \in (P \times T) \cup (T \times P) : (x, y) \in F \wedge (y, x) \in F$. We assume that in the following, all PNs are bounded and pure.

A P-vector is a column vector $I : P \to Z$ indexed by P and a T-vector is a column vector $J : T \to Z$ indexed by T, where Z is the set of integers. The incidence matrix of N is a matrix $[N] : P \times T \to Z$ indexed by P and T such that $[N](p, t) = -1$ if $p \in^{\bullet} t \backslash t^{\bullet}$; $[N](p, t) = 1$ if $p \in t^{\bullet} \backslash^{\bullet} t$; and otherwise $[N](p, t) = 0$ for all $p \in P$ and $t \in T$. We denote column vectors where every entry equals $0(1)$ by $\mathbf{0}(\mathbf{1})$. I^T and $[N]^T$ are the transposed versions of a vector I and a matrix $[N]$, respectively.

I is a P-invariant (place invariant) if and only if $I \neq 0$ and $I^T \cdot [N] = \mathbf{0}^T$ hold. P-invariant I is called a P-semiflow if its every entry is greater than or equal to zero. $\| I \| = \{p \in P \mid I(p) \neq 0\}$ is called the support of I. I is called a minimal P-invariant if $\| I \|$ is not a superset of the support of any P-invariant. $X \subseteq P \cup T$ generates the subnet $N_X = (P_X, T_X, F_X)$, where $P_X = P \cap X, T_X = T \cap X$, and F_X is the restriction of F to P_X and T_X. A string $x_1 \ldots \ldots x_n$ is called a path of N if and only if $\forall i \in \{1, 2, \ldots, n-1\} :$ $x_{i+1} \in x_i^{\bullet}$, where $\forall x \in \{x_1, \ldots, x_n\}, x \in P \cup T$. A simple path from x_1 to x_n, denoted by $SP(x_1, x_n)$, is a path whose nodes are all different. PN N is called a state machine if and only if $\forall t \in T, |^{\bullet} t| = |t^{\bullet}| = 1$.

A nonempty set $S \subseteq P$ is a siphon if and only if $^{\bullet}S \subseteq S^{\bullet}$ holds. A siphon is minimal if and only if there is no siphon contained in S as a proper subset. Unless otherwise stated, a siphon we talk about refers to a minimal one. Siphon S is said to be a strict minimal one if and only if S is minimal and $^{\bullet}S$ is a proper subset of $S^{\bullet}$. If siphon S is the support of a P-invariant and is initially marked, then it can never be emptied. $M(p)$ indicates the number of tokens on p under M. p is marked by M if and only if $M(p) > 0$. A subset $D \subseteq P$ is marked by M if and only if at least one place in D is marked by M. The sum of tokens on all places in D is denoted by $M(D)$, where $M(D) = \sum_{p \in D} M(p)$. An empty siphon with respect to a PN marking M is a siphon S such that $\sum_{p \in S} M(p) = 0$.

Let (N, M_0) be a net system with $N = (P, T, F)$, I be a P-invariant, and $S \subseteq P$ be a siphon of N. Siphon S is controlled by P-invariant I under M_0 if and only if $I^T \cdot M_0 > 0$ and $I(p) \leq 0$ for all $p \subset P \backslash S$ hold, or equivalently, $I^T \cdot M_0 > 0$ and $\{p \in P \mid I(p) > 0\} \subseteq S$. Such a siphon is also called an invariant-controlled siphon. S is said to be uncontrollable if $M_0(S) = 0$. S is said to be controllable if $M_0(S) > 0$. And S is said to be controlled if $\forall M \in R(N, M_0), M(S) > 0$.

Also the following facts are known. (1) If I is a P-invariant of N then $\forall M \in R(N, M_0) : I^T \cdot M = I^T \cdot M_0$. (2) Let $S \subseteq P$ be a siphon of N. If S is controlled by a P-invariant I under M_0, S cannot be emptied, i.e., $\forall M \in R(N, M_0) : S$ is marked under M. (3) A siphon S free of tokens at a marking remains token-free. Furthermore, all transitions connected to S are not live. (4) For any marking such that no transition is enabled, the set of empty places forms a siphon. (5) A PN is deadlock-free if no (minimal) siphon eventually becomes empty. (6) A pure PN is live and bounded if it is covered by P-invariants, the support of each P-invariant is initially marked, and no siphon is ever cleared of tokens [1].

10.3 S³PR PNs

A subclass of the ordinary and conservative PNs called System of Simple Sequential Processes with Resources (S³PR) is defined to model a class of FMS[12]. The proposed methods in this chapter target S³PR PNs.

Definition 10.1 *A Simple Sequential Process (S²P) is a PN $N = (P \cup \{p^0\}, T, F)$, where: 1) $P \neq \emptyset$ ($p \in P$ is called an operation place), $p^0 \notin P(p^0$ is called a process idle place); 2) N is a strongly connected state machine; and 3) every circuit of N contains place p^0.*

Definition 10.2 *A Simple Sequential Process with Resources (S²PR) is a PN $N = (P \cup \{p^0\} \cup P_R, T, F)$ such that 1) the subnet generated by $P \cup \{p^0\} \cup T$ is an S^2P; 2) $P_R \neq \emptyset (r \in P_R$ is called a resource or a resource place in a net formalism) and $(P \cup \{p^0\}) \cap P_R = \emptyset$; 3) $\forall p \in P, \forall t \in {}^\bullet p, \forall t' \in p^\bullet, \exists r_p \in P_R, {}^\bullet t \cap P_R = t'^\bullet \cap P_R = \{r_p\}$; and 4) the two following statements are verified: a) $\forall r \in P_R, {}^{\bullet\bullet} r \cap P = r^{\bullet\bullet} \cap P \neq \emptyset$ and b) $\forall r \in P_R, {}^\bullet r \cap r^\bullet = \emptyset$; 5) ${}^{\bullet\bullet}(p^0) \cap P_R = (p^0)^{\bullet\bullet} \cap P_R = \emptyset$.*

For $r \in P_R$, $H(r) = {}^{\bullet\bullet} r \cap P$, the operation places that use r, is called the set of holders of r. We will denote $H(r_1) \cup H(r_2) \cup \ldots \cup H(r_m)$ as

$\cup_{r \in \Re} H(r)$, where $\Re = \{r_1, r_2, \ldots, r_m\}$ is a set of resources.

Definition 10.3 *Let* $N = (P \cup \{p^0\} \cup P_R, T, F)$ *be an* $S^2 PR$. *An initial marking* M_0 *is called an acceptable initial marking for* N *if and only if:* 1) $M_0(p^0) \geq 1$; 2) $M_0(p) = 0, \forall p \in P$; *and* 3) $M_0(r) \geq 1, \forall r \in P_R$.

The couple (N, M_0) is called a (acceptable) marked $S^2 PR$. In the sequel, when we talk about a marked $S^2 PR$, $N = (P \cup \{p^0\} \cup P_R, T, F)$, we will refer to N with an acceptable marking and denote $P^0 = \{p^0\}$. We introduce now, recursively, the definition of a system of $S^2 PR$, that is called $S^3 PR$.

Definition 10.4 *A System of* $S^2 PR$, $S^3 PR$, *is defined recursively as follows:* 1) *An* $S^2 PR$ *is an* $S^3 PR$ 2) *Let* $N_i = (P_i \cup P_i^0 \cup P_{R_i}, T_i, F_i), i \in \{1, 2\}$, *be two* $S^3 PR$ *such that* $(P_1 \cup P_1^0) \cap (P_2 \cup P_2^0) = \emptyset, P_{R_1} \cap P_{R_2} = P_C \neq \emptyset$, *and* $T_1 \cap T_2 = \emptyset$ *(in which case we say that* N_1 *and* N_2 *are two composable* $S^3 PR$); *then, the net* $N = (P \cup P^0 \cup P_R, T, F)$ *resulting from the composition of* N_1 *and* N_2 *via* P_C *(denoted as* $N_1 \circ N_2$), *defined as follows:* 1) $P = P_1 \cup P_2$; 2) $P^0 = P_1^0 \cup P_2^0$; 3) $P_R = P_{R_1} \cup P_{R_2}$; 4) $T = T_1 \cup T_2$; *and* 5) $F = F_1 \cup F_2$, *is also an* $S^3 PR$.

A marking of an $S^3 PR$ is acceptable if and only if one of the two following statements is true: 1) (N, M_0) is an acceptably marked $S^3 PR$; 2) $N = N_1 \circ N_2$, such that (N_i, M_{0i}) is an acceptably marked $S^3 PR$ and a) $\forall i \in \{1, 2\}, \forall p \in P_i \cup P_i^0, M_0(p) = M_{0i}(p)$; b) $\forall i \in \{1, 2\}, \forall r \in P_{R_i} \backslash P_C$, $M_0(r) = M_{0i}(r)$; and c) $\forall r \in P_C, M_0(r) = max\{M_{01}(r), M_{02}(r)\}$. In the sequel, when talking about a marked $S^3 PR$ we refer to an $S^3 PR$ with an acceptable initial marking.

Definition 10.5 *Let* $N = \bigcirc_{i=1}^k N_i = (P \cup P^0 \cup P_R, T, F)$ *be an* $S^3 PR$ *and* S *be a strict minimal siphon in* N, *where* $S = S_P \cup S_R, S_R = S \cap P_R$, *and* $S_P = S \backslash S_R$. *Let* $[S] = (\cup_{r \in S_R} H(r)) \backslash S$. $[S]$ *is called the complementary set of siphon* S.

An $S^3 PR$ $N = \bigcirc_{i=1}^k N_i = (P \cup P^0 \cup P_R, T, F)$ has the following properties [12]: (1) $\forall i \in \{1, 2, \ldots, k\}, \forall r \in P_R, P_i \cup P_i^0$ and $H(r) \cup \{r\}$ are the supports of P-invariants. The support of any P-invariant of N is initially marked; (2) Let $S = S_P \cup S_R$ be a strict minimal siphon in N, where $S_R = \{r_1, r_2, \ldots, r_n\}$. Then $\forall p \in [S], \exists i \in \{1, 2, \ldots, n\}, p \in H(r_i)$ and $\forall j \in \{1, 2, \ldots, n\} \backslash \{i\}, p \notin H(r_j)$; (3) Given a strict minimal siphon S in N, $[S] \cup S$ is the support of a P-invariant of N; and (4) All strict minimal siphons are emptiable and controllable.

10.4   Theory of Regions

In this section, we illustrate the ideas underlying the theory of regions in a PN formalism and its application to deadlock prevention by a small manufacturing example.

Let us consider an FMS with two machine tools M1 and M2, each of which can process only one part at a time, and one robot, which can hold one part at a time. Parts enter the FMS through input/output buffers I1/O1 and I2/O2. The system can repeatedly produce two part-types J1 and J2. The production sequences are J1: M1→Robot→M2 and J2: M2→Robot→M1.

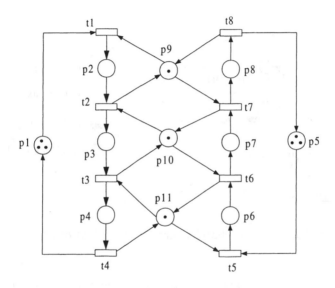

Figure 10.1. PN model (N_0, M_0) of an FMS.

The first step using the theory of regions for deadlock prevention is to model the FMS as a PN by taking into account the production sequences and manufacturing resources such as machine tools and robots in it. Figure 10.1 shows the PN model, denoted by (N_0, M_0), of the system. In Figure 10.1, tokens in p_1 and p_5 indicate the maximal number of parts of J1 and J2, which can be concurrently processed in the system, p_2, p_3, p_4, p_6, p_7, and p_8 represent the operations on J1 and J2 and p_9, p_{10}, and p_{11} denote the availability of M1, M2, and the robot, respectively.

The second step is to generate the reachability graph for the model. It is shown in Figure 10.2. In the reachability graph of a PN model, markings are generally categorized into four kinds in the sense of deadlock control: deadlock, bad, dangerous, and good markings. A deadlock one means a dead system state which has no successive markings. A bad one is the one that must *inevitably* reach a deadlock one. A dangerous one can *possibly* reach a bad or deadlock one depending on supervisory control. Good markings are the ones except deadlock, bad, and dangerous ones. In Figure 10.2, M_{13} and M_{14} are deadlock and M_4, M_8, and M_9 are bad ones. While M_1, M_2, M_3, M_5, M_6, and M_{11} are dangerous ones. All the other markings are hence good ones. The set of good and dangerous markings in $R(N_0, M_0)$, denoted by $R_L(N_0, M_0)$, should constitute the legal behavior if a supervisory controller is properly designed.

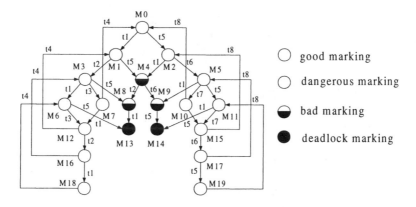

Figure 10.2. The reachability graph $R(N_0, M_0)$ of (N_0, M_0).

The third step is to find all state/event separation instances in the reachability graph. A state/event separation instance is with the form of (M, t), where M is a dangerous state (marking), and t is an(a) event (transition) whose occurrence (firing) results in marking $M[t\rangle$ which is a bad or deadlock one. Actually we can call state/event separation instances marking/transition separation instances using PN terminology. In Figure 10.2 they are (M_1, t_5), (M_2, t_1), (M_3, t_5), (M_5, t_1), (M_6, t_5), and (M_{11}, t_1).

The last step is to design a monitor and then add it to the original PN for each marking/transition separation instance (M, t) such that t is disabled at M. Before a monitor p_m is properly added to implement the marking/transition separation instance (M, t), we have to find the initial number of tokens in p_m, say $M_0(p_m)$, and the incidence relationships between the monitor and all the transitions in the net, $C(p_m, T)$. Let $x = M_0(p_m), x_1 = C(p_m, t_1), x_2 = C(p_m, t_2), \ldots$ in the sequel.

Note that it shall be ensured that the addition of p_m does not exclude the markings in $R_L(N_0, M_0)$, which implies that p_m has to satisfy the following reachability condition (10.1) and equation (10.2).

$$M(p_m) = M_0(p_m) + C(p_m, \bullet)\overrightarrow{\Gamma}_M \geq 0, \forall M \in R_L(N_0, M_0) \qquad (10.1)$$

where $C(p_m, \bullet)$ denotes the vector with its elements being $C(p_m, t_1)$, $C(p_m, t_2)$, ..., Γ_M is any non-oriented path in $R_L(N_0, M_0)$ from M_0 to M, and $\overrightarrow{\Gamma}_M$ is the counting vector of the path Γ_M, which denotes the algebraic sum of all occurrences of transitions in Γ_M.

Consider any non-oriented cycle γ in $R_L(N_0, M_0)$. Applying the state equation to the nodes in γ and summing them up give the following cycle equation.

$$\sum_{t \in T} C(p, t) \bullet \overrightarrow{\gamma}[t] = 0, \forall \gamma \in S \qquad (10.2)$$

where $\overrightarrow{\gamma}[t]$ denotes the algebraic sum of all occurrences of t in γ and S is the set of non-oriented cycles of the reachability graph with legal behavior $R_L(N_0, M_0)$. $\overrightarrow{\gamma}$ is called the counting vector of γ. Accordingly, $\overrightarrow{\Gamma}_M$ can be called the counting vector of Γ_M.

Second, the addition of p_m necessarily forbids the firing of t for marking/transition separation instance (M, t). That is to say, $M(p_m) + C(p_m, t) \leq -1$. Thanks to $M(p_m) = M_0(p_m) + C(p_m, \bullet)\overrightarrow{\Gamma}_M$, where Γ_M is any non-oriented path in $R_L(N_0, M_0)$ from M_0 to M, we have the marking/transition separation equation as follows.

$$M_0(p_m) + C(p_m, \bullet)\overrightarrow{\Gamma}_M + C(p_m, t) \leq -1 \qquad (10.3)$$

Next we illustrate the methods using the example. First let us consider (M_1, t_5). Suppose that a monitor p_{m1} is employed to achieve this purpose. Hence we have the following reachability condition equations (10.4)–(10.18), cycle equations (10.19)–(10.20) owing to the fact that there are two basic circuits in the reachability graph in Figure 10.2, and marking/transition separation equation (10.21). Note that $M_0(p_{m1}) \geq 0$ is trivial and for simplicity, let $x = M_0(p_{m1})$ and $x_i = C(p_{m1}, t_i)$, where $i \in \{1, 2, \ldots, 8\}$.

$$x \geq 0 \qquad (10.4)$$
$$x + x_1 \geq 0 \qquad (10.5)$$
$$x + x_1 + x_2 \geq 0 \qquad (10.6)$$

$$x + x_1 + x_2 + x_1 \geq 0 \qquad (10.7)$$
$$x + x_1 + x_2 + x_3 \geq 0 \qquad (10.8)$$
$$x + x_1 + x_2 + x_3 + x_1 \geq 0 \qquad (10.9)$$
$$x + x_1 + x_2 + x_3 + x_1 + x_2 \geq 0 \qquad (10.10)$$
$$x + x_1 + x_2 + x_3 + x_1 + x_2 + x_1 \geq 0 \qquad (10.11)$$
$$x + x_5 \geq 0 \qquad (10.12)$$
$$x + x_5 + x_6 \geq 0 \qquad (10.13)$$
$$x + x_5 + x_6 + x_5 \geq 0 \qquad (10.14)$$
$$x + x_5 + x_6 + x_7 \geq 0 \qquad (10.15)$$
$$x + x_5 + x_6 + x_7 + x_5 \geq 0 \qquad (10.16)$$
$$x + x_5 + x_6 + x_7 + x_5 + x_6 \geq 0 \qquad (10.17)$$
$$x + x_5 + x_6 + x_7 + x_5 + x_6 + x_5 \geq 0 \qquad (10.18)$$
$$x_1 + x_2 + x_3 + x_4 = 0 \qquad (10.19)$$
$$x_5 + x_6 + x_7 + x_8 = 0 \qquad (10.20)$$
$$x + x_1 + x_5 \leq -1 \qquad (10.21)$$

Solving inequalities (10.4)–(10.21), one can get $x = 1, x_1 = -1, x_2 = 1, x_5 = -1, x_6 = 1$, and $x_3 = x_4 = x_7 = x_8 = 0$. Hence monitor p_{m1} is accordingly added, shown in Figure 10.3, to the original PN.

Now we deal with marking/transition separation instance (M_2, t_1). It is obvious to see that the reachability and cycle equations for all marking/transition separation instances are the same, i.e., (10.4)–(10.20), in this example. When we deal with a new marking/transition separation instance, what we shall do is to replace (10.21) with the corresponding separation equation. The separation equation for (M_2, t_1) happens to be (10.21) as well. Hence we can say that p_{m1} has implemented (M_2, t_1). Similarly, we can get monitor p_{m2} which implements (M_3, t_5) and (M_6, t_5) and monitor p_{m3} which implements (M_5, t_1) and (M_{11}, t_1). Consequently, the resultant monitor-based controller with three monitors and related arcs is live, as shown in Figure 10.3.

Note that although the number of monitors to add is theoretically at most equal to, practically much smaller than, the number of marking/transition separation instances in the reachability graph of a PN, the number of the sets of inequalities that we have to solve is actually equal to that of marking/transition separation instances since we do not know whether a monitor can implement two or more marking/transition separation instances until all the sets of inequalities have already been solved.

For example, there are 20 reachable markings in Figure 10.2, where two of them are deadlock markings and six are dangerous markings and hence

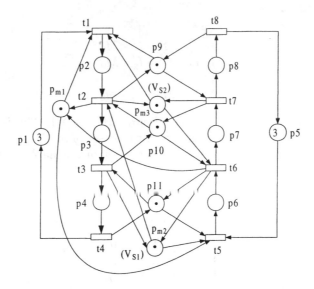

Figure 10.3. A monitor-based PN controller which is live.

there are six marking/transition separation instances in this example. We know that three monitors actually implement these six marking/transition separation instances only after we have solved six sets of inequalities. This is the major disadvantage of the method. In this chapter, we will explore some methods to alleviate the computation burden at this step.

10.5 Elementary Siphons in PNs

10.5.1 Nominal Siphons

Definition 10.6 *Let* (N, M_0) *be a net system and* S *be a siphon of* N. *S is called a nominal siphon if* $\forall M \in R(N, M_0), M(S) > 0$.

Obviously, a nominal siphon can always be marked. To avoid explicit state enumeration, an effective way to find nominal siphons in a net system is integer programming technique. Let (N, M_0) be a net system and $I_1, I_2, \ldots, I_m$ $(m \in \mathbf{N})$ be its minimal P-semiflows. By solving the following integer programming problem,

$$min\{M(S)\}$$
$$\text{subject to}$$

$$\begin{cases} I_1^T \cdot M = I_1^T \cdot M_0 \\ I_2^T \cdot M = I_2^T \cdot M_0 \\ \cdots\cdots \\ I_m^T \cdot M = I_m^T \cdot M_0 \end{cases}$$

we can see that S is a nominal siphon if $min\{M(S)\} \geq 1$. This is a sufficient condition for the non-emptiness of S since the set of markings derived from P-semiflows is generally a superset of the set of reachable markings in a PN system. It is known that the general integer programming problems are NP-complete. The determination of a nominal siphon can be transformed into the problem of solving a set of inequalities. If the following set of inequalities has no solution, S is hence a nominal siphon.

$$\begin{cases} \sum_{p\in S} M(p) \leq 0 \\ I_1^T \cdot M = I_1^T \cdot M_0 \\ I_2^T \cdot M = I_2^T \cdot M_0 \\ \cdots\cdots \\ I_m^T \cdot M = I_m^T \cdot M_0 \end{cases}$$

By Lenstra's algorithm [2], for each fixed natural number n, there exists a polynomial algorithm which finds an integral solution for a given rational system $Ax \leq b$, in n variables or decides that no such solution exists, where A is a matrix and b is a column vector.

10.5.2 Equivalent Siphons

In this subsection, we define equivalent siphons. Different numbers of tokens initially marked at equivalent siphons lead to the concepts of poor and rich siphons.

Definition 10.7 *Let $S \subseteq P$ be a subset of places of PN $N = (P,T,F)$. P-vector λ_S is called the characteristic P-vector of S if and only if $\forall p \in S : \lambda_S(p)=1$; otherwise $\lambda_S(p) = 0$.*

Definition 10.8 *η_S is called the characteristic T-vector of S if $\eta_S^T = \lambda_S^T \bullet [N]$.*

Definition 10.9 *Let S_1 and S_2 be two siphons in a net. S_1 and S_2 are said to be equivalent, denoted by $S_1 \cong S_2$, if $\eta_{S_1} = \eta_{S_2}$ holds.*

Definition 10.10 *Let Π be the set of siphons in a net N. $\langle S \rangle \subseteq \Pi$ is called a set of equivalent siphons if (1) $\forall S', S'' \in \langle S \rangle, \eta_{S'} = \eta_{S''}$ and (2) $\forall S' \in \langle S \rangle, \forall S'' \in \Pi\backslash\langle S \rangle, \eta_{S'} \neq \eta_{S''}$.*

Definition 10.11 *S is said to be a poor siphon in net system (N, M_0) if $\neg \exists S' \in \langle S \rangle$ such that $M_0(S') < M_0(S)$ holds.*

Corollary 10.1 *Let S and S' be two poor siphons in a net system (N, M_0). Then we have $M_0(S) = M_0(S')$.*

Definition 10.12 *In net system (N, M_0), $S' \in \langle S \rangle$ is called a rich siphon if S' is not a poor one in $\langle S \rangle$.*

Corollary 10.2 *Let S be a rich siphon in (N, M_0). Then S is a nominal one.*

Proof: Since S is a rich siphon, there necessarily exists a siphon $S' \in \Pi$ such that both $\eta_{S'} = \eta_S$ and $M_0(S) > M_0(S')$ hold. Hence the firing of any transition removes the same number of tokens from S and S'. For marking $M \in R(N, M_0), M(S') = 0$, we have $M(S) > 0$ due to $M_0(S) > M_0(S')$. At marking M, no transition which can remove tokens from S is enabled again since S' is emptied. Hence the least number of tokens staying at S is $M_0(S) - M_0(S') > 0$. This leads to the truth of this corollary. $\square$

10.5.3 Elementary and Redundant Siphons

In this subsection, we present the formal definitions of elementary and redundant siphons in a PN.

Definition 10.13 *Let Π be the set of siphons in a net N. $\forall S \in \Pi$, if $\neg \exists S_1, S_2, \ldots$, and $S_n \in \Pi (n \in \mathbf{N}, n \geq 2)$ such that $\eta_S = a_1 \cdot \eta_{S_1} + a_2 \cdot \eta_{S_2} + \ldots + a_n \cdot \eta_{S_n}$ holds, where $a_1, a_2, \ldots, a_n \in \mathbf{N}$, then S is called an elementary siphon of N.*

Definition 10.14 *Let Π_E be the set of elementary siphons in a net N. $S \in \Pi$ is called a strict redundant siphon if $\exists S_1, S_2, \ldots$, and $S_n \in \Pi_E$ and $a_1, a_2, \ldots$, and $a_n \in \mathbf{N}$ such that $\eta_S = a_1 \cdot \eta_{S_1} + a_2 \cdot \eta_{S_2} + \ldots + a_n \cdot \eta_{S_n}$ holds.*

Definition 10.15 *Let S be a siphon in a net N. S is called a slack redundant siphon if $\exists S_1, S_2, \ldots, S_n, S_{n+1}, \ldots$, and $S_{n+m} \in \Pi_E$ and $a_1, a_2, \ldots, a_n, a_{n+1}, \ldots$, and $a_{n+m} \in \mathbf{N}$ such that $\eta_S = (a_1 \cdot \eta_{S_1} + a_2 \cdot \eta_{S_2} + \ldots + a_n \cdot \eta_{S_n}) - (a_{n+1} \cdot \eta_{S_{n+1}} + a_{n+2} \cdot \eta_{S_{n+2}} + \ldots + a_{n+m} \cdot \eta_{S_{n+m}})$ holds.*

Let (N, M_0) be a net system and S be a redundant siphon of N. Suppose we have $\eta_S = (a_1 \cdot \eta_{S_1} + a_2 \cdot \eta_{S_2} + \ldots + a_n \cdot \eta_{S_n}) - (a_{n+1} \cdot \eta_{S_{n+1}} + a_{n+2} \cdot \eta_{S_{n+2}} + \ldots + a_{n+m} \cdot \eta_{S_{n+m}})$. Let $\Gamma^+(S) = a_1 \cdot \eta_{S_1} + a_2 \cdot \eta_{S_2} + \ldots + a_n \cdot \eta_{S_n}$ and $\Gamma^-(S) = a_{n+1} \cdot \eta_{S_{n+1}} + a_{n+2} \cdot \eta_{S_{n+2}} + \ldots + a_{n+m} \cdot \eta_{S_{n+m}}$. Hence, we have $\eta_S = \Gamma^+(S) - \Gamma^-(S)$. Obviously, $\Gamma^-(S) = 0$ if S is a strict redundant siphon.

If S is a (strict or slack) redundant siphon with respect to elementary siphons S_1, S_2, ..., and S_n, we may say that S_1, S_2, ..., and S_n are the elementary siphons of S. In the following, the set of redundant siphons in a net is denoted by Π_R. Obviously, one can get $\Pi = \Pi_E \cup \Pi_R$.

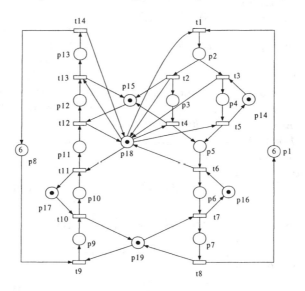

Figure 10.4. A PN system.

By the characteristic T-vector of a siphon and Definition 10.14 and 10.15, we can see that the change of token count in a redundant siphon is strongly related to the token flow of its elementary siphons. For example, S is a redundant siphon with respect to elementary siphons S_1 and S_2 in some net system (N, M_0) that has four transitions t_1, t_2, t_3, and t_4, where $\eta_S = (-1, -1, 1, 1)^T$, $\eta_{S_1} = (-1, 0, 0, 1)^T$, and $\eta_{S_2} = (0, -1, 1, 0)^T$. Obviously, we have $\eta_S = \eta_{S_1} + \eta_{S_2}$. It is clear that firing t_1 decreases tokens in S_1 and S and firing t_2 decreases tokens in S_2 and S. Let $M_0(S) = m$, $M_0(S_1) = m_1$, and $M_0(S_2) = m_2$. Suppose we can find a way to guarantee that (1) the maximal difference between the number of times that t_1 fires and the number of times that t_4 fires is $m_1 - 1$, which ensures that S_1 cannot be cleared of tokens and (2) the maximal difference between the number of times that t_2 fires and the number of times that t_3 fires is $m_2 - 1$, which ensures that S_2 cannot be cleared of tokens. If $m > m_1 - 1 + m_2 - 1$ holds as well, obviously redundant siphon S can never become unmarked.

In other words, redundant siphon S will always be marked provided that S_1 and S_2 are guaranteed to be marked. In Section 6, we will present the formal conditions under which a redundant siphon can never be emptied by controlling its elementary siphons not to be emptied.

10.5.4 The Number of Elementary Siphons in Nets

Definition 10.16 *Let $N = (P, T, F)$ be a net with $\mid P \mid = m, \mid T \mid = n$ and we assume N has k siphons, $S_1, S_2, \ldots S_k, m, n, k \in \mathbf{N}$. Let $\lambda_{S_i}(\eta_{S_i})$ be the characteristic $P(T)$-vector of siphon $S_i, i \in \{1, 2, \ldots, k\}$. We define $[\lambda]_{k \times m} = [\lambda_{S_1} \mid \lambda_{S_2} \mid \ldots \mid \lambda_{S_k}]^T$ and $[\eta]_{k \times n} = [\lambda]_{k \times m} \times [N]_{m \times n} = [\eta_{S_1} \mid \eta_{S_2} \mid \ldots \eta_{S_k}]^T$. $[\lambda]([\eta])$ is called the characteristic $P(T)$-vector matrix of the siphons in N.*

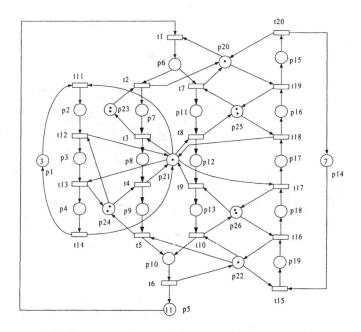

Figure 10.5. A PN system.

Theorem 10.1 *The number of elementary siphons in a net N is equal to the rank of $[\eta]$ and is bounded by the number of transitions.*

Proof: Assume that N has k siphons and k' elementary siphons. Note that $k \geq k'$ because the set of elementary siphons in a net is a subset of the set of siphons. When there is no redundant siphon in a net, we have $k = k'$. Otherwise, there are $k - k'$ redundant siphons in N. By Definitions 10.14 and 10.15, $\eta_{S_i}(i = k' + 1, k' + 2, \ldots, k)$ can be linearly represented by $\eta_{S_j}(j = 1, 2, \ldots, k')$. According to the definition of the rank of a matrix, we have that the rank of $[\eta]_{k \times n}$ is k'. Since $k' \leq \min k, n$, $k' \leq |T|$. $\square$

Table 10.1. Monitors added to the Figure 10.5

No.	preset	postset	No.	preset	postset
p_{27}	t_{10}, t_{16}	t_9, t_{15}	p_{30}	t_9, t_{17}	t_8, t_{16}
p_{28}	$t_5, t_{10}, t_{13}, t_{17}$	t_3, t_8, t_{11}, t_{15}	p_{31}	t_3, t_8, t_{19}	t_1, t_{17}
p_{29}	t_4, t_{13}	t_3, t_{11}	p_{32}	t_8, t_{18}	t_7, t_{17}

Table 10.2. Monitors added to the Figure 10.5

No.	preset	postset	No.	preset	postset
p_{27}	t_{10}, t_{16}	t_9, t_{15}	p_{36}	t_9, t_{18}	t_7, t_{16}
p_{28}	t_8, t_{18}	t_7, t_{17}	p_{37}	t_3, t_9, t_{19}	t_1, t_{16}
p_{29}	t_3, t_8, t_{19}	t_1, t_{17}	p_{38}	t_4, t_9, t_{13}, t_{17}	t_3, t_8, t_{11}, t_{16}
p_{30}	t_4, t_{13}	t_3, t_{11}	p_{39}	t_4, t_9, t_{13}, t_{18}	t_3, t_7, t_{11}, t_{16}
p_{31}	t_9, t_{17}	t_8, t_{16}	p_{40}	t_4, t_9, t_{13}, t_{19}	t_1, t_{11}, t_{16}
p_{32}	$t_5, t_{10}, t_{13}, t_{17}$	t_3, t_8, t_{11}, t_{15}	p_{41}	t_{10}, t_{18}	t_7, t_{15}
p_{33}	t_{10}, t_{17}	t_8, t_{15}	p_{42}	t_3, t_{10}, t_{19}	t_1, t_{15}
p_{34}	t_4, t_8, t_{13}, t_{18}	t_3, t_7, t_{11}, t_{17}	p_{43}	$t_5, t_{10}, t_{13}, t_{18}$	t_3, t_7, t_{11}, t_{15}
p_{35}	t_4, t_8, t_{13}, t_{19}	t_1, t_{11}, t_{17}	p_{44}	$t_5, t_{10}, t_{13}, t_{19}$	t_1, t_{11}, t_{15}

It is well known that the number of siphons is exponential with respect to the number of places in a net. This holds true for (strict) minimal siphons but at a slower pace. From the above theorem, we can see that the number of elementary siphons is limited by the number of transitions in a net. Table 10.3 shows the number of various types of siphons in four selected nets Figure 10.4, Figure 10.5, Figure 10.5a, and Figure 10.5b, where $\mathcal{N}_S$, $\mathcal{N}_{SM}$, $\mathcal{N}_R$, and $\mathcal{N}_D$ denote the number of siphons, strict minimal, redundant, and elementary ones, respectively, and Figures 10.5a and 10.5b represent the nets obtained by adding the monitors given in Table 10.1 and 10.2 to the PNs shown in Figure 10.5, respectively. Here only strict minimal siphons are distinguished by elementary and redundant ones since the supports of all P-semiflows in these net systems are initially marked.

Table 10.3. The number of various types of siphons in four PNs.

PNs	$|T|$	$\mathcal{N}_S$	$\mathcal{N}_{SM}$	$\mathcal{N}_R$	$\mathcal{N}_E$
Figure 10.4	14	13	5	2	3
Figure 10.5	20	28	18	12	6
Figure 10.5a	20	130	114	102	12
Figure 10.5b	20	1961	1933	1920	13

The case study shows that with the exponential increase in the number of siphons and minimal ones in PNs and the number of elementary siphons is clearly less than that of transitions. From the viewpoint of preventing deadlocks in a PN, this is of significance since we can see from the next section that elementary siphons can be employed to make redundant siphons controlled. That means that a large number of siphons can be always marked by making only a small number of siphons controlled.

10.6 Siphon Control Approaches

This section mainly focuses on the development of general conditions under which a redundant siphon can always be marked when its elementary siphons are invariant-controlled.

10.6.1 Siphon Control

Corollary 10.3 *Let S' and S'' be two poor siphons in $\langle S \rangle$. S' is controlled if S'' is controlled.*

Proof: Assume that S' and S'' are two poor siphons in a net system (N, M_0), $N=(P, T, F)$. Therefore, they have the identical characteristic T-vectors and the same number of initial tokens. $\forall t \in T$, the number of tokens removed from S' is identical to that from S'' if t fires. The controllability of S' means that the least number of tokens in S' is greater than 0. Hence, the least number of tokens staying at S'' is greater than 0. S'' is therefore controlled. $\square$

Proposition 10.1 *Let $(N, M_0), N = (P, T, F)$, be a net system, $S = \{p_x, \ldots, p_y\} \subseteq P$ be a siphon, and $\bar{S} = \{p_\alpha, \ldots, p_\beta\}$ be a subset of P, where $\{\alpha, \ldots, \beta\} \subseteq \{1, 2, \ldots, |P|\}$, $\{x, \ldots, y\} \subseteq \{1, 2, \ldots, |P|\}$, and $\{\alpha, \ldots, \beta\} \cap \{x, \ldots, y\} = \emptyset$. Add a monitor V_S to N and the new*

net system is denoted by (N', M_0') *such that* $I = (0, \ldots, 0, 1_{p_x}, \ldots, 1_{p_y},$
$0, \ldots, 0, -b_{p_\alpha}, \ldots, -b_{p_\beta}, 0, \ldots, 0, -1_{V_S})^T$ *is a P-invariant of* N', *where*
$\forall i \in \{\alpha, \ldots, \beta\}, b_{p_i} \in \mathbf{N}; \forall p \in P, M_0'(p) = M_0(p)$. *S is controlled if*
$M_0'(S) > \sum_{i \in \{\alpha, \ldots, \beta\}} b_{p_i} \cdot M_0'(p_i) + M_0'(V_S)$ *holds.*

Proof: This proposition is trivial since both $\{p \mid I(p) > 0\} \subseteq S$ and
$I \cdot M_0 = M_0(S) - \sum_{i \in \{\alpha, \ldots, \beta\}} b_{p_i} \cdot M_0(p_i) - M_0'(V_S) > 0$ hold. $\square$

    Let L_{V_S} be the row vector due to the addition of monitor V_S. Hence
we have $[N'] = [[N]^T \mid L_{V_S}^T]^T$. Let $I' = (0, \ldots, 0, 1_{p_x}, \ldots, 1_{p_y}, 0, \ldots,$
$0, -b_{p_\alpha}, \ldots, -b_{p_\beta}, 0, \ldots, 0, 0_{V_S})^T$ and $I'' = (0, \ldots, 0, 0_{p_x}, \ldots, 0_{p_y}, 0, \ldots,$
$0, 0_{p_\alpha}, \ldots, 0_{p_\beta}, 0, \ldots, 0, 1_{V_S})^T$. Clearly, $I = I' - I''$. $I^T \cdot [N'] = I'^T \cdot [N'] -$
$I''^T \cdot [N'] = I'^T \cdot [N'] - L_{V_S} = \mathbf{0}^T$. Let $\hat{I} = (0, \ldots, 0, 1_{p_x}, \ldots, 1_{p_y}, 0, \ldots,$
$0, -b_{p_\alpha}, \ldots, -b_{p_\beta}, 0, \ldots, 0)^T$. We have $I'^T \cdot [N'] = \hat{I}^T \cdot [N]$, which leads to
$L_{V_S} = \hat{I}^T \cdot [N]$.

Proposition 10.2 *Let* $S = \{p_i, p_j, \ldots, p_k\}$ *be a siphon of a net system*
(N_0, M_0), *where* $N_0 = (P_0, T_0, F_0)$. *Add a control place* V_S *to* N_0 *to make*
P-vector $I = (0, \ldots, 1_{p_i}, \ldots, 1_{p_j}, \ldots, 1_{p_k}, \ldots, 0, -1_{V_S})^T$ *be a P-invariant*
of the new net system (N_1, M_1), *where* $\forall p \in S, I(p) = 1; \forall p \in P_0 \backslash S,$
$I(p) = 0; I(V_S) = -1; \forall p \in P_0, M_1(p) = M_0(p)$. *Let* $M_1(V_S) = M_0(S) - \xi_S$,
where $1 \leq \xi_S < M_0(S)$. *Then S is invariant-controlled.*

    Proof: It is true from Proposition 10.1. $\square$
    ξ_S is called the control depth variable of S. The larger ξ_S is, the more
behavior of the modelled system will be restricted. That in PN formalism
means that more reachable states will be forbidden. Therefore, let the
siphon control depth variable be 1 whenever possible.

Theorem 10.2 *Let* $(N, M_0), N = (P, T, F)$, *be a net system and S be*
a strict redundant siphon of N. *Let* $S_1, S_2, \ldots$ *and* S_n *be the elementary*
siphons of S and we have $\eta_S = a_1 \cdot \eta_{S_1} + a_2 \cdot \eta_{S_2} + \ldots + a_n \cdot \eta_{S_n}$. *S is invariant-*
controlled if (1) $\forall i \in \{1, 2, \ldots, n\}, I_i = (0, \ldots, 0, 1_{p_{x_i}}, \ldots, 1_{p_{y_i}}, -b_{p_{\alpha_i}}, \ldots,$
$-b_{p_{\beta_i}}, 0, \ldots, 0)^T$ *is a P-invariant of* N *and* (2)$M_0(S) > \sum_{u \in \{\alpha_1, \ldots, \beta_1\}} a_1 \cdot$
$b_{p_u} \cdot M_0(p_u) + \sum_{u \in \{\alpha_2, \ldots, \beta_2\}} a_2 \cdot b_{p_u} \cdot M_0(p_u) + \ldots + \sum_{u \in \{\alpha_n, \ldots, \beta_n\}} a_n \cdot$
$b_{p_u} \cdot M_0(p_u)$, *where* $\forall i \in \{1, 2, \ldots, n\}, S_i = \{p_{x_i}, \ldots, p_{y_i}\}, \{\alpha_i, \ldots, \beta_i\} \subseteq$
$\{1, 2, \ldots, \mid P \mid\}, \forall u \in \{\alpha_i, \ldots, \beta_i\}, b_{p_u} \in \mathbf{N}$.

    Proof: $\forall i \in \{1, 2, \ldots, n\}$, we have $S_i = \{p_{x_i}, \ldots, p_{y_i}\}$ and $I_i = (0, \ldots,$
$0, 1_{p_{x_i}}, \ldots, 1_{p_{y_i}}, 0, \ldots, 0, -b_{p_{\alpha_i}}, \ldots, -b_{p_{\beta_i}}, 0, \ldots, 0)^T$. Let $I_i = \lambda_{S_i} + \tilde{I}_i$,
where $\lambda_{S_i} = (0, \ldots, 0, 1_{p_{x_i}}, \ldots, 1_{p_{y_i}}, 0, \ldots, 0)^T$ and $\tilde{I}_i = (0, \ldots, 0, -b_{p_{\alpha_i}},$
$\ldots, -b_{p_{\beta_i}}, 0, \ldots, 0)^T$. Let $\hat{I}_i = a_i \cdot I_i$. Then $\forall i \in \{1, 2, \ldots, n\}, \hat{I}_i$ is a

P-invariant of N since I_i is a P-invariant of N. Let $I = \lambda_S + a_1 \cdot \tilde{I}_1 + a_2 \cdot \tilde{I}_2 + \ldots + a_n \cdot \tilde{I}_n$. We claim that I is a P-invariant of N.

$$I^T \cdot [N] = \lambda_S^T \cdot [N] + a_1 \cdot \tilde{I}_1^T \cdot [N] + a_2 \cdot \tilde{I}_2^T \cdot [N] + \ldots + a_n \cdot \tilde{I}_n^T \cdot [N] =$$
$$\eta_S^T + a_1 \cdot \tilde{I}_1^T \cdot [N] + a_2 \cdot \tilde{I}_2^T \cdot [N] + \ldots + a_n \cdot \tilde{I}_n^T \cdot [N] = a_1 \cdot \eta_{S_1}^T + a_2 \cdot \eta_{S_2}^T + \ldots +$$
$$a_n \cdot \eta_{S_n}^T + a_1 \cdot \tilde{I}_1^T \cdot [N] + a_2 \cdot \tilde{I}_2^T \cdot [N] + \ldots + a_n \cdot \tilde{I}_n^T \cdot [N] = (a_1 \cdot \lambda_{S_1}^T \cdot [N] + a_1 \cdot$$
$$\tilde{I}_1^T \cdot [N]) + (a_2 \cdot \lambda_{S_2}^T \cdot [N] + a_2 \cdot \tilde{I}_2^T \cdot [N]) + \ldots + (a_n \cdot \lambda_{S_n}^T \cdot [N] + a_n \cdot \tilde{I}_n^T \cdot [N]) =$$
$$a_1 \cdot (\lambda_{S_1}^T + \tilde{I}_1^T) \cdot [N] + a_2 \cdot (\lambda_{S_2}^T + \tilde{I}_2^T) \cdot [N] + \ldots + a_n \cdot (\lambda_{S_n}^T + \tilde{I}_n^T) \cdot [N] =$$
$$\sum_{i=1}^n \hat{I}_i^T \cdot [N] = \mathbf{0}^T. \text{ Hence } I \text{ is a } P\text{-invariant of } N.$$

Note that $\{p \mid I(p) > 0\} = S$ and $\forall M \in R(N, M_0)$, $I^T \cdot M = I^T \cdot M_0 = M_0(S)$ ($\sum_{u \in \{\alpha_1,\ldots,\beta_1\}} a_1 \cdot b_{p_u} \cdot M_0(p_u) + \sum_{u \in \{\alpha_2,\ldots,\beta_2\}} a_2 \cdot b_{p_u} \cdot M_0(p_u) + \ldots + \sum_{u \in \{\alpha_n,\ldots,\beta_n\}} a_n \cdot b_{p_u} \cdot M_0(p_u))$. It is clear to see that $I^T \cdot M > 0$. Therefore, S is an invariant-controlled siphon. $\square$

Theorem 10.3 *Let* $(N, M_0), N = (P, T, F)$, *be a net system and* S *be a slack redundant siphon of* N. *Let* $S_1, S_2, \ldots, S_n, S_{n+1}, S_{n+2}, \ldots,$ $S_{n+m} (n \geq 2, m \geq 1)$ *be the elementary siphons of* S *and we have* $\eta_S = (a_1 \cdot \eta_{S_1} + a_2 \cdot \eta_{S_2} + \ldots + a_n \cdot \eta_{S_n}) - (a_{n+1} \cdot \eta_{S_{n+1}} + a_{n+2} \cdot \eta_{S_{n+2}} + \ldots + a_{n+m} \cdot \eta_{S_{n+m}})$. S *is controlled if* (1) $\forall i \in \{1, 2, \ldots, n\}$, $I_i = (0, \ldots, 0, 1_{p_{x_i}}, \ldots, 1_{p_{y_i}}, 0, \ldots, 0, -b_{p_{\alpha_i}}, \ldots, -b_{p_{\beta_i}}, 0, \ldots, 0)^T$ *is a* P-*invariant of* N *and* (2)$M_0(S) > \sum_{u \in \{\alpha_1,\ldots,\beta_1\}} a_1 \cdot b_{p_u} \cdot M_0(p_u) + \sum_{u \in \{\alpha_2,\ldots,\beta_2\}} a_2 \cdot b_{p_u} \cdot M_0(p_u) + \ldots + \sum_{u \in \{\alpha_n,\ldots,\beta_n\}} a_n \cdot b_{p_u} \cdot M_0(p_u)$, *where* $\forall i \in \{1, 2, \ldots, n\}, S_i = \{p_{x_i}, \ldots, p_{y_i}\}, \{\alpha_i, \ldots, \beta_i\} \subseteq \{1, 2, \ldots, \mid P \mid\}, \forall u \in \{\alpha_i, \ldots, \beta_i\}, b_{p_u} \in \mathbf{N}$.

Proof: $\forall i \in \{1, 2, \ldots, n\}$, the maximal number of tokens removed from S_i is $\sum_{u \in \{\alpha_i,\ldots,\beta_i\}} a_i \cdot b_{p_u} \cdot M_0(p_u)$. Therefore, the maximal number of tokens removed form $S_1, S_2, \ldots,$ and S_n is $\sum_{u \in \{\alpha_1,\ldots,\beta_1\}} a_1 \cdot b_{p_u} \cdot M_0(p_u) + \sum_{u \in \{\alpha_2,\ldots,\beta_2\}} a_2 \cdot b_{p_u} \cdot M_0(p_u) + \ldots + \sum_{u \in \{\alpha_n,\ldots,\beta_n\}} a_n \cdot b_{p_u} \cdot M_0(p_u)$.

Due to $\eta_S = (a_1 \cdot \eta_{S_1} + a_2 \cdot \eta_{S_2} + \ldots + a_n \cdot \eta_{S+n}) - (a_{n+1} \cdot \eta_{S_{n+1}} + a_{n+2} \cdot \eta_{S_{n+2}} + \ldots + a_{n+m} \cdot \eta_{S_{n+m}})$, we have $\eta_S + a_{n+1} \cdot \eta_{S_{n+1}} + a_{n+2} \cdot \eta_{S_{n+2}} + \ldots + a_{n+m} \cdot \eta_{S_{n+m}} = a_1 \cdot \eta_{S_1} + a_2 \cdot \eta_{S_2} + \ldots + a_n \cdot \eta_{S+n}$.

$\forall t \in T$, let ω denote the sum of the number of tokens removed from S_1, $S_2, \ldots,$ and S_n after firing transition t. Obviously, the sum of the number of tokens removed from $S, S_{n+1}, S_{n+2}, \ldots,$ and S_{n+m} is also ω. We consider the worst case that the tokens in S are only removed when tokens in $S_1, S_2, \ldots,$ and S_n are removed. Hence if $M_0(S) > \sum_{u \in \{\alpha_1,\ldots,\beta_1\}} a_1 \cdot b_{p_u} \cdot M_0(p_u) + \sum_{u \in \{\alpha_2,\ldots,\beta_2\}} a_2 \cdot b_{p_u} \cdot M_0(p_u) + \ldots + \sum_{u \in \{\alpha_n,\ldots,\beta_n\}} a_n \cdot b_{p_u} \cdot M_0(p_u)$ holds, S can never be emptied. $\square$

Theorem 10.2(10.3) shows that under some conditions a redundant siphon is controlled. Therefore, $\forall i \in \{1, 2, \ldots, n\}$, when elementary siphon S_i is controlled by P-invariant $I_i = (0, \ldots, 0, 1_{p_{x_i}}, \ldots, 1_{p_{y_i}}, 0, \ldots, 0,$

$-b_{p_{\alpha_i}}, \ldots, -b_{p_{\beta_i}}, 0, \ldots, 0)^T$ and the conditions (1) and (2), stated in Theorem 10.2(10.3), hold, we can conclude that a redundant siphon S is successfully controlled by making its elementary siphons invariant-controlled. As we have already known, the number of elementary siphons is limited by the number of transitions. Hence Theorem 10.2(10.3) provides an effective way to control a large number of siphons by controlling a small number of siphons. Note that Theorem 10.2 and 10.3 are the sufficient conditions for the controllability of strict and slack redundant siphons, respectively. Theorem 10.3 is rather conservative. That means that in many cases a slack redundant siphon is controlled even if the conditions in Theorem 10.3 are not met.

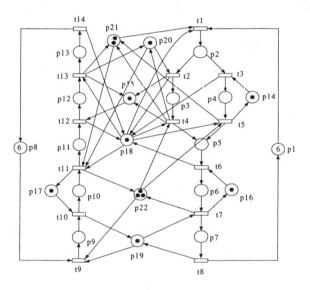

Figure 10.6. A PN system.

Examples. The PN system (N, M_0) shown in Figure 10.6 is employed to illustrate the concepts and techniques proposed above. There are 15 strict minimal siphons in Figure 10.6, which are $S_1=\{p_2, p_5, p_{13}, p_{15}, p_{18}\}$, $S_2=\{p_5, p_{13}, p_{14}, p_{15}, p_{18}\}$, $S_3=\{p_2, p_7, p_{11}, p_{13}, p_{16}, p_{17}, p_{18}, p_{19}\}$, $S_4=\{p_5, p_6, p_{11}, p_{12}, p_{21}, p_{22}\}$, $S_5=\{p_5, p_{11}, p_{13}, p_{14}, p_{18}, p_{20}\}$, $S_6=\{p_7, p_{13}, p_{14}, p_{15}, p_{16}, p_{17}, p_{18}, p_{19}\}$, $S_7=\{p_2, p_7, p_{13}, p_{15}, p_{16}, p_{17}, p_{18}, p_{19}\}$, $S_8=\{p_7, p_{12}, p_{15}, p_{17}, p_{19}, p_{21}, p_{22}\}$, $S_9=\{p_7, p_{11}, p_{12}, p_{17}, p_{19}, p_{21}, p_{22}\}$, $S_{10}=\{p_7, p_{11}, p_{13}, p_{14}, p_{16}, p_{17}, p_{18}, p_{19}, p_{20}\}$, $S_{11}=\{p_5, p_6, p_{12}, p_{15}, p_{21}, p_{22}\}$, $S_{12}=\{p_7, p_{12}, p_{15}, p_{17}, p_{19}, p_{20}, p_{22}\}$, $S_{13}=\{p_7, p_{11}, p_{12}, p_{17}, p_{19}, p_{20}, p_{22}\}$, $S_{14}=\{p_5, p_6, p_{12}, p_{15}, p_{20}, p_{22}\}$, and $S_{15}=\{p_5, p_6, p_{11}, p_{12}, p_{20}, p_{22}\}$.

By integer programming, it is easy to verify that $S_{15} = \{p_5, p_6, p_{11}, p_{12}, p_{20}, p_{22}\}$ is a nominal siphon since $min\{\sum_{p \in S_{15}} M(p) \mid M \in R(N, M_0)\} = 1$. Also, S_6, S_7, S_{10}, S_{11}, and S_{14} are nominal ones.

The characteristic T-vector matrix of strict minimal siphons of the net is as follows. The ith row corresponds to the ith strict minimal siphon. We have $\eta_{S_2} = \eta_{S_5} = (-1, 0, 0, 1, 1, 0, 0, 0, 0, 0, -1, 0, 1, 0)^T$ and $\eta_{S_6} = \eta_{S_{10}} = (-1, 0, 0, 0, 0, 0, 1, 0, -1, 0, 0, 0, 1, 0)^T$. Hence we have that $S_2 \cong S_5$ and $S_6 \cong S_{10}$. There are 13 sets of equivalent strict minimal siphons, which are $\langle S_1 \rangle = \{S_1\}$, $\langle S_2 \rangle = \{S_2, S_5\}$, $\langle S_3 \rangle = \{S_3\}$, $\langle S_4 \rangle = \{S_4\}$, $\langle S_6 \rangle = \{S_6, S_{10}\}$, $\langle S_7 \rangle = \{S_7\}$, $\langle S_8 \rangle = \{S_8\}$, $\langle S_9 \rangle = \{S_9\}$, $\langle S_{11} \rangle = \{S_{11}\}$, $\langle S_{12} \rangle = \{S_{12}\}$, $\langle S_{13} \rangle = \{S_{13}\}$, $\langle S_{14} \rangle = \{S_{14}\}$, and $\langle S_{15} \rangle = \{S_{15}\}$.

It is easy to see that $M_0(S_2) = M_0(S_5) = 3$ and $M_0(S_6) = M_0(S_{10}) = 6$. Hence we say that S_2 and S_5 are poor siphons. S_6 and S_{10} come to the same thing. There is no rich siphon in $\langle S_2 \rangle$ and $\langle S_6 \rangle$. In Figure 10.5a, $S = \{p_{12}, p_{17}, p_{30}, p_{32}\}$ and $S' = \{p_6, p_7, p_{12}, p_{16}, p_{17}, p_{30}, p_{31}\}$ are two strict minimal siphons with the same characteristic T-vectors. However, the numbers of tokens initially marked in S and S' are 4 and 7, respectively. Therefore, S is a poor siphon and S' is a rich one.

There are five elementary siphons in the net, which are S_1, S_2, S_3, S_4, and S_5. It can easily be seen that $\eta_{S_6} = \eta_{S_2} + \eta_{S_3}$, $\eta_{S_7} = \eta_{S_1} + \eta_{S_3}$, $\eta_{S_8} = \eta_{S_1} + \eta_{S_3} + \eta_{S_4}$, $\eta_{S_9} = \eta_{S_3} + \eta_{S_4}$, $\eta_{S_{10}} = \eta_{S_2} + \eta_{S_3}$, $\eta_{S_{11}} = \eta_{S_1} + \eta_{S_4}$, $\eta_{S_{12}} = 2 \cdot \eta_{S_1} - \eta_{S_2} + \eta_{S_3} + \eta_{S_4}$, $\eta_{S_{13}} = \eta_{S_1} - \eta_{S_2} + \eta_{S_3} + \eta_{S_4}$, $\eta_{S_{14}} = 2 \cdot \eta_{S_1} - \eta_{S_2} + \eta_{S_4}$, and $\eta_{S_{15}} = \eta_{S_1} - \eta_{S_2} + \eta_{S_4}$. Hence we can say that S_6, S_7, S_8, S_9, S_{10}, and S_{11} are strict redundant siphons. And S_{12}, S_{13}, S_{14} and S_{15} are slack redundant siphons.

Let $I_1 = (0, 1, 0, 0, 1, 0, 0, 0, 0, 0, 0, 0, 1, 0, 1, 0, 0, 1, 0, -1, 0, 0)^T$. We have $I_1^T \cdot [N] = \mathbf{0}^T$, $\{p \mid I_1(p) > 0\} \subseteq S_1$, and $I_1^T \cdot M_0 = M_0(p_2) + M_0(p_5) + M_0(p_{13}) + M_0(p_{15}) + M_0(p_{18}) - M_0(p_{20}) = 1 > 0$. Then S_1 is invariant-controlled. Let $I_2 = (0, 0, 0, 0, 1, 0, 0, 0, 0, 0, 0, 0, 1, 1, 1, 0, 0, 1, 0, 0, -1, 0)^T$ and $I_3 = (0, 1, 0, 0, 0, 0, 1, 0, 0, 0, 1, 0, 1, 0, 0, 1, 1, 1, 1, 0, 0, -1)^T$. We have $I_2^T \cdot [N] = \mathbf{0}^T$, $I_3^T \cdot [N] = \mathbf{0}^T$, $\{p \mid I_2(p) > 0\} \subseteq S_2$, $\{p \mid I_3(p) > 0\} \subseteq S_3$, $I_2^T \cdot M_0 = M_0(p_5) + M_0(p_{13}) + M_0(p_{14}) + M_0(p_{15}) + M_0(p_{18}) - M_0(p_{21}) = 1 > 0$, and $I_3^T \cdot M_0 = M_0(p_2) + M_0(p_7) + M_0(p_{11}) + M_0(p_{13}) + M_0(p_{16}) + M_0(p_{17}) + M_0(p_{18}) + M_0(p_{19}) - M_0(p_{22}) = 4 - 3 > 0$. Therefore, both S_2 and S_3 are invariant-controlled siphons. Next we check the controllability of redundant siphons S_6 and S_7. Note that $\eta_{S_6} = \eta_{S_2} + \eta_{S_3}$, S_2 is controlled by I_2, $\{p \mid I_2(p) < 0\} = \{p_{21}\}$, S_3 is controlled by I_3, $\{p \mid I_3(p) < 0\} = \{p_{22}\}$, and $M_0(S_6) > M_0(p_{21}) + M_0(p_{22})$. By Theorem 10.2, S_6 is invariant-controlled. Similarly, we can verify S_7 is invariant-controlled as well.

$$[\eta] = \begin{bmatrix}
0 & -1 & 0 & 0 & 1 & 0 & 0 & 0 & 0 & 0 & -1 & 0 & 1 & 0 \\
-1 & 0 & 0 & 1 & 1 & 0 & 0 & 0 & 0 & 0 & -1 & 0 & 1 & 0 \\
0 & 0 & 0 & -1 & -1 & 0 & 1 & 0 & -1 & 0 & 1 & 0 & 0 & 0 \\
-1 & 0 & 0 & 1 & 1 & 0 & 0 & 0 & -1 & 0 & 1 & 0 & 0 & 0 \\
-1 & 0 & 0 & 1 & 1 & 0 & 0 & 0 & 0 & 0 & -1 & 0 & 1 & 0 \\
-1 & 0 & 0 & 0 & 0 & 0 & 1 & 0 & -1 & 0 & 0 & 0 & 1 & 0 \\
0 & -1 & 0 & -1 & 0 & 0 & 1 & 0 & -1 & 0 & 0 & 0 & 1 & 0 \\
-1 & -1 & 0 & 0 & 1 & 0 & 1 & 0 & -2 & 0 & 1 & 0 & 1 & 0 \\
-1 & 0 & 0 & 0 & 0 & 0 & 1 & 0 & -2 & 0 & 2 & 0 & 0 & 0 \\
-1 & 0 & 0 & 0 & 0 & 0 & 1 & 0 & -1 & 0 & 0 & 0 & 1 & 0 \\
-1 & -1 & 0 & 1 & 2 & 0 & 0 & 0 & -1 & 0 & 0 & 0 & 1 & 0 \\
0 & -2 & 0 & -1 & 1 & 0 & 1 & 0 & -2 & 0 & 1 & 0 & 1 & 0 \\
0 & -1 & 0 & -1 & 0 & 0 & 1 & 0 & -2 & 0 & 2 & 0 & 0 & 0 \\
0 & -2 & 0 & 0 & 2 & 0 & 0 & 0 & -1 & 0 & 0 & 0 & 1 & 0 \\
0 & -1 & 0 & 0 & 1 & 0 & 0 & 0 & -1 & 0 & 1 & 0 & 0 & 0
\end{bmatrix}$$

Now let us suppose that the marked net shown in Figure 10.4 is the plant model of some system. $S_1=\{p_2, p_5, p_{13}, p_{15}, p_{18}\}$, $S_2=\{p_5, p_{13}, p_{14}, p_{15}, p_{18}\}$, $S_3=\{p_2, p_7, p_{11}, p_{13}, p_{16}, p_{17}, p_{18}, p_{19}\}$, $S_6=\{p_7, p_{13}, p_{14}, p_{15}, p_{16}, p_{17}, p_{18}, p_{19}\}$, $S_7=\{p_2, p_7, p_{13}, p_{15}, p_{16}, p_{17}, p_{18}, p_{19}\}$ are its strict minimal siphons, and S_1, S_2, and S_3 are elementary ones. Each of the five siphons is emptiable. By Proposition 10.2, three monitors p_{20}, p_{21}, and p_{22} are added to the net system such that S_1, S_2, and S_3 are invariant-controlled by I_1, I_2, and I_3, respectively. The resultant net system is the one shown in Figure 10.6. We can see that redundant siphons S_6 and S_7 are controlled due to the addition of monitors p_{20}, p_{21}, and p_{22}. That means that a redundant siphon can be marked by making its elementary siphons invariant-controlled. Next section will see an application of this approach.

10.6.2 Siphon Control and Optimality

One criterion that is usually accepted as a measure of the quality of a dead-lock control policy is its "permissivity": the more states in the supervisor, the better the control policy is. The sequel shows the relationship between state permissivity and siphon control depth variables in a marked S^3PR.

Definition 10.17 *Let (N_0, M_0), $N_0 = (P, T, F)$, be a marked S^3PR. $S \in \Pi$ is said to be optimally controlled if the least number of tokens in S is 1.*

An optimally controlled siphon makes significant sense for the deadlock prevention since such a siphon neither contributes to the deadlocks, nor excludes dangerous and good markings.

Proposition 10.3 *Let* (N_0, M_0) *be an* S^3PR *net system.* $\forall S \in \Pi_E$, *a monitor* V_S *is added by Proposition 10.2. S is optimally controlled if* $\xi_S = 1$.

Proof: Let (N_1, M_1) denote the augmented net system of (N_0, M_0). For $S \in \Pi_E$, we have $M_1(S) = M_0(S)$. By Proposition 10.2, $\xi_S = 1$ means that $M_1(V_S) = M_1(S) - \xi_S = M_1(S) - 1 = M_0(S) - 1$. Hence the least number of tokens staying at S is 1. $\square$

Corollary 10.4 *Let* (N_0, M_0) *be an* S^3PR *net system and S be a strict redundant siphon with respect to* $S_1, S_2, \ldots,$ *and* S_n. *By Proposition 10.2, add* n *monitors to* N_0 *such that* $\forall i \in \{1, 2, \ldots, n\}$, S_i *is invariant-controlled. S is optimally invariant-controlled if* $M_0(S) = \Sigma_{i=1}^n (a_i \bullet M_0(S_i)) - \Sigma_{i=1}^n (a_i \bullet \xi_{S_i}) + 1$.

Proof: Assume that n monitors $V_{S_1}, V_{S_2}, \ldots,$ and V_{S_n} are added to (N_0, M_0) resulting in the augmented net system (N_1, M_1). As we have already known $\forall i \in \{1, 2, \ldots, n\}, M_1(V_{S_i}) = M_0(S_i) - \xi_{S_i}$. Let $\eta_S = a_1 \bullet \eta_{S_1} + a_2 \bullet \eta_{S_2} + \ldots + a_n \bullet \eta_{S_n}$. In accordance with the proof of Theorem 10.2, $(\lambda_S^T, -a_1, -a_2, \ldots, -a_n)^T$ is a P-invariant of N_1. That means that the maximal number of tokens flowing from S is $\Sigma_{i=1}^n (a_i \bullet M_1(V_{S_i})) = \Sigma_{i=1}^n (a_i \bullet M_0(S_i)) - \Sigma_{i=1}^n (a_i \bullet \xi_{S_i})$. We can conclude that the minimal number of tokens staying at S is 1 at any reachable marking in $R(N_1, M_1)$ if $M_0(S_0) = \Sigma_{i=1}^n (a_i \bullet M_0(S_i)) - \Sigma_{i=1}^n (a_i \bullet \xi_{S_i}) + 1$ is true. Consequently, siphon S is optimally invariant-controlled. $\square$

Corollary 10.5 *Let* (N_0, M_0) *be a net system and S be a slack redundant siphon with respect to* $S_1, S_2, \ldots,$ *and* S_{n+m}. *By Proposition 10.2, add* $n + m$ *monitors to* N_0 *such that* $\forall i \in \{1, 2, \ldots, n+m\}, S_i$ *is invariant-controlled. S is optimally invariant-controlled if* $M_0(S) = \Sigma_{i=1}^n (a_i \bullet M_0(S_i)) - \Sigma_{i=1}^n (a_i \bullet \xi_{S_i}) + 1$ *holds.*

From the above corollaries, it is obvious that a redundant siphon can be optimally invariant-controlled in a marked S³PR even if its elementary siphons are not optimally invariant-controlled. In case that a redundant siphon is not optimally invariant-controlled due to the optimal control of its elementary siphons, a monitor can be added to make the redundant siphon optimally invariant-controlled. In fact, in order to make all siphons optimally invariant-controlled, it is possible for us to add more monitors than the method of controlling redundant siphons only by elementary siphons.

As shown in Figure 10.3, we add two monitors V_{S_1} and V_{S_2} to make S_1 and S_2 invariant-controlled, respectively. Also we know that redundant siphon S_3 is invariant-controlled. Meanwhile, we can see that S_3 is optimally invariant-controlled since $M_0(S_3) = M_0(S_1) + M_0(S_2) - \xi_{S_1} - \xi_{S_2} + 1$, where $\xi_{S_1} = \xi_{S_2} = 1$.

As we have mentioned, the deadlock in an S^3PR is caused by the empty siphons. Next proposition shows that after adding monitors to an S^3PR to make all strict minimal siphons invariant-controlled, the number of deadlock markings in the augmented net system is less than that of the original net model.

Proposition 10.4 *Let (N_0, M_0) be a marked S^3PR. Suppose that n monitors are added such that all strict minimal siphons in N_0 are (optimally) invariant-controlled. The augmented net system is denoted as (N_1, M_1). The number of deadlock markings in $R(N_1, M_1)$ is less than that in $R(N_0, M_0)$.*

Proof: Note that the reachability graph of a marked S^3PR is finite and the existence of deadlock markings in the reachability graph of a marked S^3PR is due to unmarked siphons.

Let $P = \{p_1, p_2, \ldots, p_{|P|}\}$ and P_1 be the set of places of net N_0 and N_1, respectively. Clearly, we have $P_1 = P \cup \{p_{m_1}, p_{m_2}, \ldots, p_{m_n}\}$, where p_{m_i} is the ith monitor, $i \in \{1, 2, \ldots, n\}$. Due to the fact that $\forall i \in \{1, 2, \ldots, n\}, p_{m_i}$ is added to make a strict minimal siphon controlled, the addition of p_{m_i} is a constraint and restriction for the evolution of net system (N_0, M_0) and hence the markings at which S_i is unmarked are necessarily eliminated. That is to say, $\forall (M(p_1), M(p_2), \ldots, M(p_{|P|}), M(p_{m_1}), M(p_{m_2}), \ldots, M(p_{m_n}))^T \in R(N_1, M_1)$, we definitely have $(M(p_1), M(p_2), \ldots, M(p_{|P|}))^T \in R(N_0, M_0)$. As a result, the reachability graph of (N_1, M_1) is a subgraph of that of (N_0, M_0). Some dead and bad markings are eliminated due to the addition of the monitors. This proposition obviously holds. $\square$

This proposition suggests that after strict minimal siphons in the original PN are optimally invariant-controlled by adding monitors, the number of marking/transition separation instances in the resulting PN is reduced. As we will see later, we develop a deadlock prevention policy for S^3PR, which consists of two stages. At the first stage, each strict minimal siphon is optimally controlled by adding a monitor. If the resultant PN contains deadlocks, the theory of regions is then applied. Since the resultant PN has a small number of marking/transition separation instances, this approach lowers the computation cost when designing the liveness enforcing PN supervisor using the theory of regions.

10.7 Deadlock Control Policy–I

First, we propose an approach to the control of strict minimal siphons in an S³PR. Note that a siphon that is the support of a P-invariant in a marked S³PR is initially marked and hence can never be emptied.

Let (N, M_0) be a marked S³PR, $N = \bigcirc_{i=1}^{k} N_i = (P \cup P^0 \cup P_R, T, F)$, let $S = \{p_x, \ldots, p_y\}$ be a strict minimal siphon of N, and let $\mathcal{D}_S = \{p_\alpha, \ldots, p_\beta\} = \bigcup_{p \in [S]} \{p' \mid p \in P_i, i \in \{1, 2, \ldots, k\}, \forall SP(p_i^0, p), p' \in (SP(p_i^0, p) \cap P) \setminus [S]\}$, where $\{x, \ldots, y\} \cup \{\alpha, \ldots, \beta\} \subseteq \{1, 2, \ldots, \mid P \cup P^0 \cup P_R \mid\}$. Clearly, $\mathcal{D}_S \cap [S] = \mathcal{D}_S \cap S = S \cap [S] = \emptyset$.

By Proposition 10.1, add a monitor V_S to (N, M_0) such that $I_S = (0, \ldots, 0, \underbrace{1_{p_x}, \ldots, 1_{p_y}}_{S = \{p_x, \ldots, p_y\}}, 0, \ldots, 0, \underbrace{1_{p_\alpha}, \ldots, 1_{p_\beta}}_{\{p_\alpha, \ldots, p_\beta\} = \mathcal{D}_S}, 0, \ldots, 0, \underbrace{1_{V_S}}_{V_S})^T$ be a P-invariant of the augmented net system. The new net system is denoted by (N', M_0'), where $N' = (P \cup P^0 \cup P_R \cup \{V_S\}, T, F')$ and $M_0'(V_S) = M_0(S) - \xi_S, \xi_S \geq 1$.

Since $\{p \mid I_S(p) > 0\} \subseteq S, \forall p \in \mathcal{D}_S, M_0'(p) = M_0(p) = 0$, and $I_S^T \cdot M_0' = M_0'(S) - M_0'(V_S) = \xi_S > 0$, S is invariant-controlled. The major feature of this siphon control approach is that, as stated in [12], no (new) control-induced siphon is produced by the addition of the monitor since $\forall i \in \{1, 2, \ldots, k\}$, if $[S] \cap P_i \neq \emptyset$, then $\forall t \in p_i^{0\bullet}, (V_S, t) \in F'$.

Corollary 10.6 $\mathcal{D}_S \cup \{V_S\} \cup [S]$ *is the support of a P-semiflow of N'.*

Proof: It is easy to verify that $I = (0, \ldots, 0, \underbrace{1_{p_x}, \ldots, 1_{p_y}}_{S = \{p_x, \ldots, p_y\}}, 0, \ldots,$
$0, \underbrace{1_{p_u}, \ldots, 1_{p_v}}_{[S] = \{p_u, \ldots, p_v\}}, 0, \ldots, 0)^T$ and $I' = (0, \ldots, 0, \underbrace{1_{p_x}, \ldots, 1_{p_y}}_{S = \{p_x, \ldots, p_y\}}, 0, \ldots, 0,$
$\underbrace{-1_{p_\alpha}, \ldots, -1_{p_\beta}}_{\{p_\alpha, \ldots, p_\beta\} = \mathcal{D}_S}, 0, \ldots, 0, \underbrace{-1_{V_S}}_{V_S})^T$ are P-invariants of N'.

Let $I'' = I - I'$. Then $I'' = (0, \ldots, 0, \underbrace{1_{p_u}, \ldots, 1_{p_v}}_{[S] = \{p_u, \ldots, p_v\}}, 0, \ldots, 0, \underbrace{1_{p_\alpha}, \ldots, 1_{p_\beta}}_{\{p_\alpha, \ldots, p_\beta\} = \mathcal{D}_S},$
$0, \ldots, 0, \underbrace{1_{V_S}}_{V_S})^T$ is a P-semiflow of N'. Clearly, $\mathcal{D}_S \cup \{V_S\} \cup [S]$ is the support of I''. $\square$

Corollary 10.7 (N', M_0') *is covered by P-invariants and all P-invariants are initially marked.*

Proof: It is known that (N, M_0) is covered by P-invariants and all P-invariants are initially marked. By Corollary 10.6, V_S is an element of the support of a P-invariant of N' and $M_0'(V_S) > 0$. Therefore, (N', M_0') is covered by P-invariants and all P-invariants are initially marked. $\square$

Corollary 10.8 N' *is an ordinary and pure net.*

Corollary 10.9 *Let* $(N, M_0), N = (P \cup P^0 \cup P_R, T, F)$, *be a marked* S^3PR *and* S *be a redundant siphon with* $\Gamma^+(S) = a_1 \cdot \eta_{S_1} + \ldots + a_n \cdot \eta_{S_n}$, *where* $\{S_1, \ldots, S_n\} \subseteq \Pi_E$. *Add* n *monitors* $V_{S_1}, \ldots, V_{S_n}$ *to* N, *the new net system is denoted by* (N', M_0'), *such that* $S_1, \ldots, S_n$ *are invariant-controlled by* P-invariants $I_1, \ldots, I_n$ *of* N', *respectively, where* $\forall i \in \{1, 2, \ldots, n\}, \{p \mid I_i(p) = 1\} = S_i; \forall p \in \mathcal{D}_{S_i} \cup \{V_{S_i}\}, I(p) = -1; \forall p \notin \mathcal{D}_{S_i} \cup \{V_{S_i}\} \cup S_i, I(p) = 0;$ $N' = (P \cup P^0 \cup P_R \cup \{V_{S_1}, \ldots, V_{S_n}\}, T, F'); \forall p \in P \cup P^0 \cup P_R, M_0'(p) = M_0(p); \forall i \in \{1, 2, \ldots, n\}$, *let* $M_0'(V_{S_i}) = M_0(S_i) - \xi_{S_i}$. S *is controlled if* $M_0(S) > \sum_{i=1}^n a_i \cdot M_0(S_i) - \sum_{i=1}^n a_i \cdot \xi_{S_i}$ *holds.*

Proof: $\forall i \in \{1, 2, \ldots, n\}, \forall p \in \mathcal{D}_{S_i}, M_0'(p) = 0$. By Theorem 10.2 or 10.3, S is controlled if $M_0(S) > a_1 \cdot M_0'(V_{S_1}) + \ldots + a_n \cdot M_0'(V_{S_n})$ holds. Due to $M_0'(V_{S_i}) = M_0(S_i) - \xi_{S_i}$, it is true that S is controlled if $M_0(S) > \sum_{i=1}^n a_i \cdot M_0(S_i) - \sum_{i=1}^n a_i \cdot \xi_{S_i}$ holds. $\square$

Corollary 10.10 *Let* $(N, M_0), N = (P \cup P^0 \cup P_R, T, F)$, *be a marked* S^3PR. $\forall S \in \Pi_E$, *a monitor* V_S *is added to* N *and the extended net system is denoted as* (N', M_0'). $\forall p \in P \cup P^0 \cup P_R, M_0'(p) = M_0(p)$. $\forall i \in \{1, \ldots, |\Pi_E|\}, M_0'(V_{S_i}) = M_0(S_i) - \xi_{S_i}$, *where* $\xi_{S_i} \geq 1$. *Then* (N', M_0') *is live if no siphon can be emptied.*

Proof: This corollary is trivial due to the fact that a pure PN is live and bounded if it is covered by P-invariants, all P-invariants are initially marked, and no siphon is ever cleared of tokens. $\square$

The siphon control approach here is almost identical to that developed by [12], in which multiple definitions, concepts, lemmas or theorems are proposed. Based on the P-invariant method for siphon control, this chapter presents the siphon control policy in a very concise and readily comprehensible way.

Next, to save space, we informally propose a deadlock prevention algorithm based on the siphon control technique for S³PR.

Deadlock Prevention Policy–I

Step 1. Compute the set of elementary siphons;

Step 2. Add a monitor for each elementary siphon and let the siphon control depth variable be one;

Step 3. Check the controllability of redundant siphons by Corollary 10.9;

Step 4. If the controllability of a redundant siphon cannot be decided by Corollary 10.9, integer programming technique is used to verify whether it is a nominal siphon. If not, increase the related siphon control depth variables and make it controlled.

Remarks: The important motivation of this deadlock prevention policy is to use elementary siphon to make redundant siphons controlled. This way we utilize at most $| T |$ monitors to make a large number of siphons controlled. Thus, a structurally simple PN supervisor can be developed. However, whether or not a redundant siphon in an S^3PR, or in more general PNs, can be always controlled by adjusting the control depth variables of its elementary siphons remains open.

10.8   Deadlock Control Policy–II

In this section we will propose our second deadlock prevention policy based on elementary siphons and the theory of regions. The deadlock control algorithm consists of two stages: siphon control in terms of elementary siphons and deadlock control using the theory of regions. As we can see, our siphon control approach can ensure every strict minimal siphon in an S^3PR is optimally controlled. We present this two-stage algorithm as follows, where the original S^3PR net model is denoted as (N_0, M_0).

Deadlock Prevention Policy–II

Step 1. Compute Π in N_0.
Step 2. **if** $\Pi = \emptyset$ **then** go to Step 16
  endif.
Step 3. Find Π_E and let $\Pi_E = \{S_i | i=1, 2, \ldots, n\}$.
Step 4. Find Π_R and let $\Pi_R = \{RS_j | j=1, 2, \ldots, m\}$.
Step 5. $i := 1$.
Step 6. Let $\xi_{S_i} = 1$ and add V_{S_i} for S_i by **Proposition 10.2**; $i := i+1$.
Step 7. **If** $i = n+1$ **then** go to Step 8
  else go to Step 6
  endif.
Step 8. $j := 0$.
Step 9. $j := j+1$.
  if $j = m+1$ **then** go to Step 11.
Step 10. Check the control optimality of RS_j.
  If RS_j is optimally controlled **then** go to Step 9
  else add V_{RS_j} to make RS_j optimally controlled; go to Step 9
  endif.
  /* Denote the new net with additional monitors by (N_1, M_1). */
Step 11. Generate the reachability graph $R(N_1, M_1)$ for PN (N_1, M_1).

Step 12. Generate the legal behavior $R_L(N_1, M_1)$ from $R(N_1, M_1)$. And find the set of marking/transition separation instances $MTS = \{(M, t) \mid (M, t)$ is a marking/transition separation instance$\}$.
    /* MON denotes the set of monitors that will be added. */
Step 13. $MON := \emptyset$.
Step 14. **If** $MTS = \emptyset$ **then** go to Step 16
        else $\forall (M, t) \in MTS$, design a monitor p_m such that p_m
          implements (M, t); $MTS := MTS - \{(M, t)\}$.
        endif
Step 15. **If** $\nexists p_{m\prime} \in MON$ such that $M_0(p_m) = M_0(p_{m\prime})$
        and $C(p_m, \bullet) = C(p_{m\prime}, \bullet)$
        then add p_m to (N_1, M_1); $MON := MON \cup \{p_m\}$
        else go to Step 14.
        endif
Step 16. over.

   To better understand this algorithm, we finish the small example in Figure 10.1. As we have seen, there are two elementary siphons S_1 and S_2 and two monitors V_{S_1} and V_{S_2} can be used to make all strict minimal siphons S_1, S_2 and S_3 optimally invariant-controlled. Note that the new net system has new strict minimal siphons and deadlocks due to the addition of these monitors. After this stage, we use the theory of regions to implement the deadlock prevention. The reachability graph of the PN with V_{S_1} and V_{S_2} has 16 reachable markings among which only one is deadlock marking and two are dangerous markings. Hence, we have only two marking/transition separation instances. A monitor p_{m_1} can be used to implement the two marking/transition separation instances, as shown in Figure 10.3. Thus the net system in Figure 10.3 is live.

   From this small example, we can see that after the elementary siphons have been controlled, the number of separation instances is to some extent reduced which alleviates the computational burden at the second stage. The example in the next section can further show the advantage of this approach.

Remarks: The ideas underlying this policy are based on the following facts. First of all, too many sets of inequalities have to be solved due to a large number of marking/transition separation instances in the original PN model if the theory of regions is alone employed. It is known that integer programming technique is usually employed to solve the sets of inequalities, which is theoretically time-consuming since the general integer programming problems are NP-complete. Although Lenstra's algorithm [2] shows that for each fixed natural number n, there exists a polynomial algorithm which can find an integral solution for a given rational system

$Ax \leq b$, in n variable or decide that no such solution exists, where A is a matrix and b is a column vector. However, the problem is that the existence of a polynomial time algorithm and the fact that we can definitely find such an algorithm are two entirely different things. Moreover, we do not think it is feasible that we engage in mental drudgery to design an elaborate polynomial algorithm for the solution to every set of inequalities. Note that without the siphon control stage, the number of sets of inequalities to be solved is much larger even in a moderate scale system when only using the theory of regions.

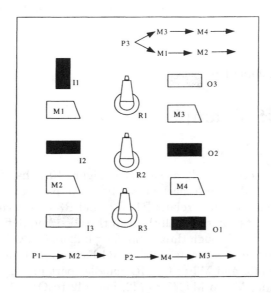

Figure 10.7. The layout of an FMS cell.

Second, although the number of siphons grows exponentially with respect to the number of elements in a PN [14] [21] and this is true for strict minimal siphons but in a slower pace, the number of elementary siphons is limited by the number of transitions. Note that siphons are a kind of structural objects of PNs, which depend on only net structures. While, the state space of a given net system greatly varies as initial markings fluctuate. Importantly, ad hoc techniques can be used to solve the minimal siphons in some special classes of PNs. Furthermore, the number of deadlock and dangerous markings greatly decreases after elementary siphons are controlled by adding monitors to the original PN model. This hence leads to the fact that the number of marking/transition separation instances, in the second stage of our approach, is considerably reduced. As we will see, there are 16 deadlock and 77 dangerous markings in the PN model in Figure 10.4, where 77 marking/transition separation instances have to be dealt with. However, after only three monitors are added, which are used to make three elementary siphons controlled, the number of deadlock and dangerous markings comes to one and five, respectively, where only eight separation instances remain.

The major shortcoming of this approach is the state explosion problem when we target a large PN model owing to the need of generating the whole reachability graph for the system, which is as a matter of fact the inherent characteristics of the theory of regions because it is a method to derive PNs from the existing automaton-based models. Therefore, a naturally arising issue is, based on the idea of the theory of regions, to derive liveness-enforcing PN supervisors from other more condensed net representation such as net unfolding [20].

10.9   FMS Examples

10.9.1   FMS Example I

A flexible manufacturing cell, as shown in Figure 10.7, has four machines M1, M2, M3, and M4. Each machine can hold two parts at the same time. Also the cell contains three robots R1, R2, and R3 and each of them can hold one part. Parts enter the cell through three loading buffers I1, I2, and I3, and leave the cell through three unloading buffers O1, O2, and O3. The robots deal with the movements of parts. R1 handles part movements from I3 to M1, I3 to M3, and M3 to O2. R2 handles part movements from M1 to M2, M4 to M3, M3 to M4, I1 to M2, and M2 to O1. R3 handles part movements from I2 to M4, M4 to O3, and M2 to O3. Three part types P1, P2, and P3 are produced. The PN model of the system, which is an S^3PR, is shown in Figure 10.5. In this net system, p_1, p_5, and p_{14} are idle places. p_2, p_3, p_4, p_6, p_7, p_8, p_9, p_{10}, p_{11}, p_{12}, p_{13}, p_{15}, p_{16}, p_{17}, p_{18}, p_{19} are operation places. p_{20}, p_{21}, p_{22}, p_{23}, p_{24}, p_{25}, p_{26} denote R1, R2, R3, M1, M2, M3, and M4, respectively.

The strict minimal siphons in Figure 10.5 are given in Table 10.4, where the redundant siphons are marked by *. Monitors V_{S_1}, V_{S_4}, $V_{S_{10}}$, $V_{S_{16}}$, $V_{S_{17}}$, and $V_{S_{18}}$ are added for elementary siphons S_1, S_4, S_{10}, S_{16}, S_{17} and S_{18}, respectively, by the method stated in subsection 10.7, where $\xi_{S_1} = \xi_{S_4} = \xi_{S_{10}} = \xi_{S_{16}} = \xi_{S_{17}} = \xi_{S_{18}} = 1$. For example, $S_1 = \{p_{10}, p_{18}, p_{22}, p_{26}\}$. We have $[S_1] = \{p_{13}, p_{19}\}$, $SP(p_5, p_{13}) = \{p_6, p_{11}, p_{12}, p_{13}\}$, and $SP(p_{14}, p_{19}) = \{p_{19}\}$. Hence $\mathcal{D}_{S_1} = (\{p_6, p_{11}, p_{12}, p_{13}\}\backslash[S_1])\cup(\{p_{19}\}\backslash[S_1]) = \{p_6, p_{11}, p_{12}\}$. Monitor V_{S_1} and its incidence relationship with transitions are shown in Figure 10.8, where $M_0'(V_{S_1}) = M_0(S_1) - \xi_{S_1} = 2$. Accordingly, monitors

Table 10.4. Strict minimal siphons in the net shown in Figure 10.5

siphon	place	$M_0(S)$
S_1	$p_{10}, p_{18}, p_{22}, p_{26}$	3
S_2^*	$p_4, p_{10}, p_{15}, p_{20}, p_{21}, p_{22}, p_{23}, p_{24}, p_{25}, p_{26}$	11
S_3^*	$p_4, p_{10}, p_{16}, p_{21}, p_{22}, p_{24}, p_{25}, p_{26}$	8
S_4	$p_4, p_{10}, p_{17}, p_{21}, p_{22}, p_{24}, p_{26}$	6
S_5^*	$p_4, p_9, p_{13}, p_{15}, p_{20}, p_{21}, p_{23}, p_{24}, p_{25}, p_{26}$	10
S_6^*	$p_4, p_9, p_{13}, p_{16}, p_{21}, p_{24}, p_{25}, p_{26}$	7
S_7	$p_4, p_9, p_{13}, p_{17}, p_{21}, p_{24}, p_{26}$	5
S_8	$p_4, p_9, p_{12}, p_{15}, p_{20}, p_{21}, p_{23}, p_{24}, p_{25}$	8
S_9^*	$p_4, p_9, p_{12}, p_{16}, p_{21}, p_{24}, p_{25}$	5
S_{10}	$p_4, p_9, p_{12}, p_{17}, p_{21}, p_{24}$	3
S_{11}^*	$p_2, p_4, p_8, p_{10}, p_{15}, p_{20}, p_{21}, p_{22}, p_{23}, p_{25}, p_{26}$	9
S_{12}^*	$p_2, p_4, p_8, p_{13}, p_{15}, p_{20}, p_{21}, p_{23}, p_{25}, p_{26}$	8
S_{13}^*	$p_2, p_4, p_8, p_{10}, p_{16}, p_{21}, p_{22}, p_{25}, p_{26}$	6
S_{14}^*	$p_2, p_4, p_8, p_{13}, p_{16}, p_{21}, p_{25}, p_{26}$	5
S_{15}^*	$p_2, p_4, p_8, p_{10}, p_{17}, p_{21}, p_{22}, p_{26}$	4
S_{16}	$p_2, p_4, p_8, p_{13}, p_{17}, p_{21}, p_{26}$	3
S_{17}	$p_2, p_4, p_8, p_{12}, p_{15}, p_{20}, p_{21}, p_{23}, p_{25}$	6
S_{18}	$p_2, p_4, p_8, p_{12}, p_{16}, p_{21}, p_{25}$	3

Table 10.5. Relationships between redundant and elementary siphons

η relationship	initial marking relationships
$\eta_2 = \eta_4 + \eta_{17}$	$M_0(S_2) > M_0(S_4) + M_0(S_{17})\text{-}2$
$\eta_3 = \eta_4 + \eta_{18}$	$M_0(S_3) > M_0(S_4) + M_0(S_{18})\text{-}2$
$\eta_5 = \eta_{10} + \eta_{16} + \eta_{17}$	$M_0(S_5) > M_0(S_{10}) + M_0(S_{16}) + M_0(S_{17})\text{-}3$
$\eta_6 = \eta_{10} + \eta_{16} + \eta_{18}$	$M_0(S_6) > M_0(S_{10}) + M_0(S_{16}) + M_0(S_{18})\text{-}3$
$\eta_7 = \eta_{10} + \eta_{16}$	$M_0(S_7) > M_0(S_{10}) + M_0(S_{16})\text{-}2$
$\eta_8 = \eta_{10} + \eta_{17}$	$M_0(S_8) > M_0(S_{10}) + M_0(S_{17})\text{-}2$
$\eta_9 = \eta_{10} + \eta_{18}$	$M_0(S_9) > M_0(S_{10}) + M_0(S_{18})\text{-}2$
$\eta_{11} = \eta_1 + \eta_{16} + \eta_{17}$	$M_0(S_{11}) = M_0(S_1) + M_0(S_{16}) + M_0(S_{17})\text{-}3$
$\eta_{12} = \eta_{16} + \eta_{17}$	$M_0(S_{12}) > M_0(S_{16}) + M_0(S_{17})\text{-}2$
$\eta_{13} = \eta_1 + \eta_{16} + \eta_{18}$	$M_0(S_{13}) = M_0(S_1) + M_0(S_{16}) + M_0(S_{18})\text{-}3$
$\eta_{14} = \eta_{16} + \eta_{18}$	$M_0(S_{14}) > M_0(S_{16}) + M_0(S_{18})\text{-}2$
$\eta_{15} = \eta_1 + \eta_{16}$	$M_0(S_{15}) = M_0(S_1) + M_0(S_{16})\text{-}2$

V_{S_4}, $V_{S_{10}}$, $V_{S_{16}}$, $V_{S_{17}}$, and $V_{S_{18}}$ are added, as shown in Figure 10.8.

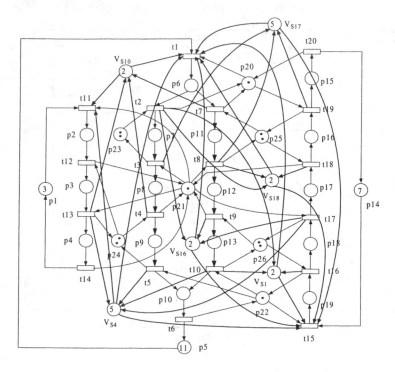

Figure 10.8. The liveness enforcing PN supervisor.

Now we check the controllability of redundant siphons. By Corollary 10.9 and Table 10.5, we can see that S_2, S_3, S_5, S_6, S_7, S_8, S_9, S_{12}, and S_{14} are controlled. The controllability of S_{11}, S_{13}, and S_{15} is undecidable by Corollary 10.9. Note that $\forall S \in \{S_{11}, S_{13}, S_{15}\}, \Gamma^+(S)$ contains $\eta_{S_{16}}$. By letting $\xi_{S_{16}} = 2$, the three equalities in the right column of Table 10.5 can be transformed into inequalities and hence S_{11}, S_{13}, and S_{15} become invariant-controlled. However, to have more permissive behavior in the supervisor, we shall try to make the number of siphons with their control depth variables being unit as large as possible. By integer programming, it is easy to verify that S_{11}, S_{13}, and S_{15} are nominal siphons. Therefore, we can say that every strict minimal siphon in Figure 10.8 is invariant-controlled and no siphon can be emptied. Consequently, the PN supervisor is live by adding only six control places and 32 arcs. In [12], 18 control places and 106 arcs are added, which makes the liveness enforcing PN supervisor three times more complex than that of ours. Both PN supervisors have the same number of reachable states, 6287.

10.9.2 FMS Example–II

In order to compare the results with the previous work, we use a manufacturing example investigated in [28] where deadlock prevention is addressed by the theory of regions alone.

The FMS, along with its production sequences as shown in Figure 10.9, consists of two robots, namely R1 and R2, each of which can hold one part at a time, and four machine tools, namely M1, M2, M3, and M4, each of them can process only one part at a time. For loading and unloading the system, there are two loading buffers I1 and I2, and two unloading buffers O1 and O2. Two part-types are considered in this FMS. The PN model for this system is shown in Figure 10.4, which is an S^3PR.

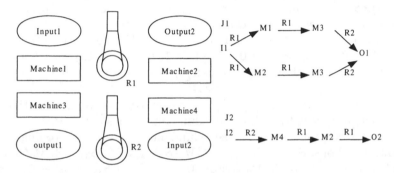

Figure 10.9. An FMS layout and its production sequences.

Initially, it is assumed that there are no parts in the system. The PN model has 19 places and 14 transitions. Places $p_9, p_{10}, p_{11}, p_{12},$ and p_{13} represent the operations of R2, M4, R1, M2 and R1, respectively, for production sequence of the part-type J2. The number of tokens in p_8 is six, representing the number of concurrent activities that can at most take place for J2. Similarly, places p_2, p_3, p_4, p_5, p_6 and p_7 represent the operations of R1, M2 or M1, R1, M3 and R2, respectively, for the production sequence of the part-type J1. The number of tokens in p_1 is six which represents that the number of concurrent activities that can at most take place for J1. Places $p_{17}, p_{15}, p_{18}, p_{19}, p_{14},$ and p_{16} denote the manufacturing resources M4, M2, R1, R2, M1, and M3. Initial markings of places $p_{17}, p_{15}, p_{18}, p_{19}, p_{14},$ and p_{16} are all one, as each machine tool or robot can only process or hold one part at a time. The PN system is denoted as (N_0, M_0).

Note that in the PN in Figure 10.4 there are 282 reachable markings and 16 of them are deadlock ones. There are also 61 bad markings which inevitably lead to deadlock ones. Hence a maximally permissive monitor-based liveness enforcing PN supervisor shall have 205 reachable markings. It is easy to see that there are 77 (16+61) dangerous markings. This example happens to have 77 markings/transition separation instances as well. Note that in some cases the number of marking/transition separation instances is greater than that of dangerous markings. Obviously, we have to solve 77 sets of inequalities to prevent deadlocks in this example if the theory of regions is alone applied.

Let us examine our deadlock prevention algorithm by this example. First of all, we compute the strict minimal siphons in the PN model of this FMS. There are five strict minimal siphons, namely $S_1=\{p_2, p_5, p_{13}, p_{15}, p_{18}\}$, $S_2=\{p_5, p_{13}, p_{14}, p_{15}, p_{18}\}$, $S_3=\{p_2, p_7, p_{11}, p_{13}, p_{16}, p_{17}, p_{18}, p_{19}\}$, $S_4 = \{p_7, p_{13}, p_{14}, p_{15}, p_{16}, p_{17}, p_{18}, p_{19}\}$, and $S_5 = \{p_2, p_7, p_{13}, p_{15}, p_{16}, p_{17}, p_{18}, p_{19}\}$. The characteristic T-vectors of them are $\eta_{S_1} = (0, -1, 0, 0, 1, 0, 0, 0, 0, \ 0, \ -1, \ 0, \ 1, \ 0)^T$, $\eta_{S_2}=(-1, 0, 0, 1, 1, 0, 0, 0, 0, \ 0, \ -1, \ 0, \ 1, \ 0)^T$, $\eta_{S_3} = (0, 0, 0, -1, -1, 0, \ 1, \ 0, \ -1, \ 0, \ 1, \ 0, 0, 0)^T$, $\eta_{S_4} = (-1, 0, 0, 0, 0, 0, 1, 0, -1, 0, 0, 0, 1, 0)^T$, and $\eta_{S_5}=(0, -1, 0, -1, 0, 0, 1, 0, -1, 0, 0, 0, 1, 0)^T$.

It is easy to verify that $\eta_{S_4} = \eta_{S_2} + \eta_{S_3}$ and $\eta_{S_5} = \eta_{S_1} + \eta_{S_3}$. Hence, strict minimal siphons S_4 and S_5 are redundant siphons in this PN. Next we will check the controllability of these redundant siphons by controlling their elementary siphons. Since $M_0(S_1) = 2, M_0(S_2) = 3, M_0(S_3) = 4, M_0(S_4) = 6$, and $M_0(S_5) = 5$, both $M_0(S_4) > M_0(S_2) + M_0(S_3) - \xi_{S_2} - \xi_{S_3}$ and $M_0(S_5) > M_0(S_1) + M_0(S_3) - \xi_{S_1} - \xi_{S_3}$ hold when $\xi_{S_1} = \xi_{S_2} = \xi_{S_3} = 1$. Consequently, both S_4 and S_5 are controlled if three monitors V_{S_1}, V_{S_2}, and V_{S_3} are added, where $M_0(V_{S_1}) = 1, M_0(V_{S_2}) = 2$, and $M_0(V_{S_3}) = 3$, to the PN model in Figure 10.4. Furthermore, it is easy to verify that S_1, S_2, S_3, S_4, and S_5 are all optimally invariant-controlled. We denote the new PN system as (N_1, M_1). The incidence relationships between the three additional monitors and transitions are listed in Table 10.6.

Now the theory of regions is utilized to design monitors to prevent deadlocks for (N_1, M_1). There are 210 reachable markings, denoted by $M_1, \ldots, M_{210}$, in $R(N_1, M_1)$ and only one of them is deadlock marking, $M_{57}=(2, 0, 1, 1, 0, 1, 0, 3, 1, 1, 0, 0, 0, 0, 0, 0, 0, 1, 0, 0, 0, 0)^T$. Also there are 5 dangerous markings and 8 marking/transition separation instances, which are (M_{43}, t_9), (M_{44}, t_9), (M_{49}, t_9), (M_{48}, t_9), (M_{47}, t_9), (M_{53}, t_4), (M_{59}, t_1), and (M_{74}, t_2), where

$$M_{43} = (2, 1, 0, 1, 0, 1, 0, 4, 0, 1, 0, 0, 0, 0, 1, 0, 0, 0, 1, 1, 0, 1)^T,$$
$$M_{44} = (2, 0, 1, 1, 0, 1, 0, 4, 0, 1, 0, 0, 0, 0, 0, 0, 0, 1, 1, 0, 0, 1)^T,$$

$M_{49} = (2, 1, 1, 0, 0, 1, 0, 4, 0, 1, 0, 0, 0, 1, 0, 0, 0, 0, 1, 0, 0, 1)^T$,
$M_{48} = (3, 0, 1, 0, 0, 1, 0, 4, 0, 1, 0, 0, 0, 1, 0, 0, 0, 1, 1, 0, 1, 1)^T$,
$M_{47} = (3, 0, 1, 0, 1, 0, 0, 4, 0, 1, 0, 0, 0, 1, 0, 1, 0, 0, 1, 0, 1, 1)^T$,
$M_{53} = (3, 0, 1, 1, 0, 0, 0, 3, 1, 1, 0, 0, 0, 0, 0, 1, 0, 1, 0, 0, 0, 1)^T$,
$M_{59} = (3, 0, 0, 1, 0, 1, 0, 3, 1, 1, 0, 0, 0, 0, 1, 0, 0, 1, 0, 1, 1, 0)^T$, and
$M_{74} = (3, 1, 0, 0, 0, 1, 0, 3, 1, 1, 0, 0, 0, 1, 1, 0, 0, 0, 0, 1, 1, 0)^T$.

By solving eight sets of inequalities determined by the above marking/tranition separation instances, one can find that three monitors, namely V_{S_4}, V_{S_5}, and V_{S_6} as shown in Table 1, have to be added to implement these separation instances. The final monitor-based PN supervisory controller, denoted by (N_2, M_2), is thus obtained, which is live. The number of markings in the reachability graph of (N_2, M_2) is 205. That is to say, this supervisory controller is maximally permissive. Hence, by adding six monitors, deadlock prevention is implemented for this example. However, in [28], the theory of regions is alone used, where 77 sets of inequalities have to be solved, and the resultant liveness enforcing PN supervisor is also maximally permissive but with nine additional monitors.

Table 10.6. The monitors added and their incidence relationships

monitor	$M_0(\bullet)$	preset	postset
$V_{S_1}(p_{20})$	1	t_5, t_{13}	t_2, t_{11}
$V_{S_2}(p_{21})$	2	t_4, t_5, t_{13}	t_1, t_{11}
$V_{S_3}(p_{22})$	3	t_7, t_{11}	t_4, t_5, t_9
V_{S_4}	3	t_6, t_{11}	t_2, t_4, t_9
V_{S_5}	3	t_5, t_7, t_{11}	t_2, t_6, t_9
V_{S_6}	4	t_2, t_4, t_7, t_{11}	t_1, t_6, t_9

10.10   Conclusion and Discussion

The deadlock in a PN usually results from empty siphons. A siphon in a net system can never become empty if either it contains a marked trap or it is invariant-controlled. Whether a siphon contains a marked trap is decided by the plant model. Therefore, for an emptiable siphon, an effective way to prevent the siphon from being unmarked is to make it invariant-controlled. This is usually achieved by adding a monitor to the original PN model.

The most important result of this chapter is the concept of elementary siphons, a special class of siphons. This chapter shows that the concept of elementary siphons make better use of the structure information of a PN, which is very useful in designing liveness enforcing PN supervisors when the deadlocks in a plant PN model result from empty siphons.

This chapter explores ways to minimize the number of new additional places. We distinguish siphons in a PN by redundant and elementary ones and develop conditions under which a redundant siphon can be always marked when its elementary siphons are invariant-controlled. Based on elementary siphons and the theory of regions, two deadlock prevention policies are developed. This chapter shows their significant advantages over the existing approaches.

A naturally arising problem is, based on the theory of elementary siphons, to develop novel deadlock prevention and avoidance policies and extend this theory to generalized PNs.

Bibliography

[1] A. A. Desrocher and R. Y. AI-Jaar, "Applications of Petri Nets in Manufacturing Systems: Modeling, Control, and Performance Analysis", IEEE Press, 1995.

[2] A. Schrijver, "Theory of Linear and Integer Programming," John Wiley & Sons, NY, 1998.

[3] E. Badouel and P. Darondeau, "Theory of Regions," *Lecture Notes in Computer Science, Lectures on Petri Net I: Basic Models*, vol.1491, W. Reisig and G. Rozenberg (Eds.), Advances in Petri Nets, pp.529-586, 1998.

[4] E. Yamalidou, J. O. Moody, and P. J. Antsaklis, "Feedback Control of Petri Nets Based on Place Invariants," *Automatica*, vol.32, no.1, pp.15-28, 1994.

[5] F. Chu and X. L. Xie, "Deadlock Analysis of Petri Nets Using Siphons and Mathematical Programming," *IEEE Trans. Robot. and Automat.*, vol.13, no.6, pp.793-840, 1997.

[6] F. Tricas, "Deadlock Analysis, Prevention and Avoidance in Sequential Resource Allocation Systems," *Doctoral disserataion*, Departamento de Informática e Ingeniería de Sistemas, Universidad de Zaragoza, Spain, 2003.

[7] F. Tricas, F. G. Valles, J. M. Colom and J. Ezpeleta, "An Iterative Method for Deadlock Prevention in FMSs," *Discrete Event Systems: Analysis and Control, the Proceedings of 5th Workshop on Discrete Event Systems*, R. Boel and G.Stremersch (Eds.), Kluwer Academic Publishers, Ghent, Belgium, pp.139-148, August, 2000.

[8] F. Tricas, F. Garacía Vallés, J. M. Colom, and J. Ezpeleta, "A Partial Approach to the Problem of Deadlocks in Processes with Resources,"

Research Report, Departamento de Informática e Ingeniería de Sistemas, Universidad de Zaragoza, Spain, GISI-RR-97-05, 1998.

[9] F. S. Hsien and S. C. Chang,"Dispatching-driven Deadlock Avoidance Controller Synthesis for Flexible Manufacturing Systems," *IEEE Trans. Robot. and Automat.*, vol.10, no.2, pp. 196-209, 1994.

[10] I. B. Abdallah and H. A. ElMaraghy, "Deadlock Prevention and Avoidance in FMS: A Petri Net Based Approach," *International Journal of Manufacturing Technology*, vol.14, no.4, pp.704-715, 1998.

[11] J. Ezpeleta, F. Tricas, F. García-Vallés, and J. Colom, "A Banker's Solution for Deadlock Avoidance in FMS with Flexible Routing and Multisource States," *IEEE Trans. Robot. and Automat.*, vol.18, no.4, pp.621-625, 2002.

[12] J. Ezpeleta, J. M. Colom, and J. Martinez, "A Petri Net Based Deadlock Prevention Policy for Flexible Manufacturing Systems," *IEEE Trans. Robot. and Automat.*, vol.11, no.2, pp.173-184, 1995.

[13] J. Ezpeleta and L. Recalde, "A Deadlock Avoidance Approach for Non-Sequential Resource Allocation Systems," *IEEE Tran. Systems, Man, and Cybernetics, Speical Issue on Deadlock Resolution in Computer-Integrated Systems*, vol. 34, no. 1, 2004.

[14] J. Ezpeleta, J. M. Couvreur, and M. Silva, "A New Technique for Finding a Generating Family of Siphons, Traps, and St-Components: Application to Colored Petri Nets," *Advances in Petri Nets 1993, Lecture Notes on Computer Science*, no.674, G. Rozenberg, Ed., New York: Springer-Verlag, pp.126-147, 1993.

[15] J. O. Moody and P. J. Antsaklis, "Supervisory Control of Discrete Event Systems Using Petri Nets," Kluwer Academic Publishers, 1998.

[16] J. Park, "Deadlock Avoidance in Sequential Resource Allocation Systems with Multiple Resource Acquisitions and Flexible Routings," *IEEE Trans. Robot. and Automat.*, vol.46, no.10, pp. 1572-1583, 2001.

[17] K. Barkaoui, A. Chaoui, and B.Zouari, "Supervisory Control of Discrete Event Systems Based on Structure Theory of Petri Nets," *Proceedings of IEEE International Conference on Systems, Man, and Cybernetics*, pp.3750 -3755, 1997.

[18] K. Barkaoui and I. B. Abdallah, "A Deadlock Prevention Method for a Class of FMS," *Proceedings of IEEE International Conference on Systems, Man, and Cybernetics*, pp.4119-4124, 1995.

[19] K. Barkaoui and I. B. Abdallah, "An Efficient Deadlock Avoidance Control Policy in FMS Using Structural Analysis of Petri Nets," *Proceedings of the IEEE International Conference on System, Man, and Cybernetics*, San Antonio, Texas, U.S.A, pp.525-530, 1994.

[20] K. L. McMillan, "A technique for state space search based on unfolding," *Formal Methods in System Design*, vol.6, no.1, pp. 45-65, 1995.

[21] K. Lautenbach, "Linear Algebraic Calculation of Deadlocks and Traps," *In Concurrency and Nets*, Voss Genrich and Rozenberg, Ed., New York: Springer-Verlag, pp.315-336, 1987.

[22] K. Y. Xing, B. S. Hu, and H. X. Chen, "Deadlock Avoidance Policy for Petri-net Modelling of Flexible Manufacturing Systems with Shared Resources," *IEEE Trans. Automatic Control.*, vol. 42, no.2, pp. 289-295, 1996.

[23] M. C. Zhou and F. DiCesare, "Petri Net Synthesis for Discrete Event Control of Manufacturing Systems," Kluwer Academic Publishers, 1993.

[24] M. C. Zhou and K. Venkatesh, " Modelling, Simulation and Control of Flexible Manufacturing Systems: A Petri Net Approach," World Scientific, Singapore, 1998.

[25] M. C. Zhou and F. DiCesare, " Parallel and Sequential Mutual Exclusions for Petri Net Modelling for Manufacturing Systems," *IEEE Trans. Robot. and Automat.*, vol.7, no.4, pp.515-527, 1991.

[26] M. D. Jeng, X. L. Xie, and M. Y.Peng "Process Nets with Resources for Manufacturing Modelling and their Analysis," *IEEE Trans. on Robot. and Automat.*, vol.18, no.6, pp.875-889, 2002.

[27] M. D. Jeng and X.L. Xie, "Analysis of Modularly Composed Nets by Siphons," *IEEE Trans. on Systems, Man and Cybernetics, part A*, vol.29, no.4, pp. 399-405, 1999.

[28] M. Uzam, "An Optimal Deadlock Prevention Policy for Flexible Manufacturing Systems Using Petri Net Models with Resources and the Theory of Regions," *International Journal of Advanced Manufacturing Systems*, vol.19, pp.192-208, 2002.

[29] M. V. Iordache, J. O. Moody, and P. J. Antsaklis, "Synthesis of Deadlock Prevention Supervisors Using Petri Nets," *IEEE Trans. Robot. and Automat.*, vol.18, no.1, pp.59-68, 2002.

[30] A. Ghaffari, N. Nidhal, and X. L. Xie, "Design of a Live and Maximally Permissive Petri Net Controller Using the Theory of Regions," *IEEE Trans. Robot. and Automat.*, vol.19, no.1, pp.137-142, 2002.

[31] N. Viswanadham, Y. Narahari, and T. Johnson, " Deadlock Prevention and Deadlock Avoidance in Flexible Manufacturing Systems Using Petri Net Models," *IEEE Trans. Robot. and Automat.*, vol.6, no.6, pp.713-723, 1990.

[32] P. Darondeau, "Region Based Synthesis of P/T-nets and Its Potential Applications," *in Proceedings of the 20th International Conference on Application and Theory of Petri Nets*, Springer-Verlag, LNCS, vol.1825, pp.16-23, 2000.

[33] R. A. Wysk, N. S. Yang, and S. Joshi, "Detection of Deadlocks in Flexible Manufacturing Systems," *IEEE Trans. Robot. and Automat.*, vol.7, no.6, pp.853-859, 1991.

[34] T. K. Kumaran, W. Chang, H. Chao et al, "A structural approach for deadlock detection and, avoidance, and resolution in felxible manufacturing systems," *International Journal of Production Research*, vol.32, no.10, pp.2361-2379, 1994.

[35] T. Murata, "Petri Nets: Properties, Analysis, and Application", *in Proceedings of the IEEE*, vol.77, no.4, pp.541-580, 1989.

[36] X. L. Xie and M. D. Jeng, "ERCN-Merged Nets and Their Analysis Using Siphons," *IEEE Trans. Robot. and Automat.*, vol.15, no.4, pp.692-703, 1999.

[37] Y. S. Huang, M. D. Jeng, X. L. Xie, and S. L. Chung, "Deadlock Prevention Policy Based on Petri nets and Siphons," *International Journal of Production Research*, vol.39, no.3, pp.283-305, 2001.

[38] Z. Banaszak and B. H. Krogh, "Deadlock Avoidance in Flexible Manufacturing Systems with Concurrently Competing Process Flows," *IEEE Trans. Robot. and Automat.*, vol.6, no.6, pp. 720-734, 1990.

[39] Z. W. Li and M. C. Zhou, "Elementary Siphons of Petri Nets and their Application to Deadlock Prevention in Flexible Manufacturing Systems," *IEEE Trans. on System, Man, and Cybernetics, Part A: Systems and Humans, Special Issue on Deadlock Resolution in Computer Integrated Systems*, vol. 34, no. 1, 2004.

11

Resource-Oriented Petri Nets in Deadlock Prevention and Avoidance

Naiqi Wu
Guangdong University of Technology, Guangzhou, P. R. China.

MengChu Zhou
New Jersey Institute of Technology, Newark, NJ, USA.

11.1 INTRODUCTION

In response to global market competition, a well-recognized way is for a manufacturer to adopt agile automated manufacturing systems (AMS). An AMS is composed of versatile machines and an automated material handling system (MHS), and is controlled by a computer. The MHS is composed of robots and/or automated guided vehicles (AGV). The AGVs form an AGV system. AMSs are characterized by the ability to process multiple part types simultaneously. The parts are manufactured by routing material through the machines according to the prescribed sequence of operations for each part type. The multiple parts move from buffers to machines, machines to buffers, or buffers to buffers concurrently, competing for the finite set of resources in the system such as machines, the material handling system, tools and buffers. It is a great challenge to operate such systems effectively. It is important that the flexibility of the AMS is exploited sufficiently. This requires effective application of control and management techniques and theories to model and analyze the behavior of the systems [1].

Petri nets (PN) are widely used to model AMS to deal with deadlock problems. In earlier studies, PN models were used to prove the existence or absence of deadlocks [2-5]. These studies did not handle the deadlock control issue. One way

349

to control deadlock is to synthesize a live and bounded PN [6-10] because a live PN is deadlock-free. This is a static way to control deadlock, called deadlock prevention. The second way to control deadlock is called deadlock detection and recovery. By this technique, deadlock is detected based on the model, then a recovery strategy is applied [11] as it does in computer systems [12]. The third way is deadlock avoidance. This is a dynamic way to control deadlock and deadlock is avoided by allocating the limited resources based on the state of the system [10, 13-20].

There are two types of deadlocks in the operations in AMS. The first type is caused by the competition by parts for such manufacturing resources as machines, buffers and MHS. It occurs during the part processing. The second type is due to the competition for nodes and lanes by AGVs when multiple AGVs are used in MHS. All the mentioned studies addressed the first type of deadlock in AMS but not the second one. When there are several AGVs in AMS, some serious problems may arise in managing them, e.g., blocking, conflict, deadlock, and collision [21-25]. This chapter focuses on the deadlock avoidance problem for both types of deadlocks in AMSs by using colored resource-oriented Petri nets (CROPN) [26-30].

11.2 RESOURCE-ORIENTED PETRI NET (ROPN)

11.2.1 Finite Capacity Petri Net

A finite capacity PN [31] is a particular kind of directed graph, PN = (P, T, I, O, M, K) where

1. $P = \{p_1, p_2, ..., p_m\}$ is a finite set of places,
2. $T = \{t_1, t_2, ..., t_n\}$ is a finite set of transitions, $P \cup T \neq \varnothing, P \cap T = \varnothing$,
3. $I : P \times T \rightarrow N$ is an input function,
4. $O: P \times T \rightarrow N$ is an output function where $N=\{0, 1, 2, ...\}$,
5. $M: P \rightarrow N$ is a marking representing the numbers of tokens in places with M_0 denoting the initial marking, and
6. $K: P \rightarrow \{1, 2, 3, ...\}$ is a capacity function where $K(p)$ represents the number of tokens that place p can hold.

(P, T, I, O) defines the structure of a PN. We use $\cdot t$ ($\cdot p$) to denote the set of input places of transition t (the set of input transitions of place p) and $t\cdot$ ($p\cdot$) the set of output places of t (the set of output transitions of p).

Definition 11.1: A transition $t \in T$ in a finite capacity PN = (P, T, I, O, M_0, K) with marking M is said to be enabled if

$$M(p) \geq I(p, t), \forall p \in P \tag{11.1}$$

and

$$K(p) \geq M(p) - I(p, t) + O(p, t) \tag{11.2}$$

Firing an enabled transition $t \in T$ at M changes M into M' according to

$$M'(p) = M(p) - I(p, t) + O(p, t) \qquad (11.3)$$

A sequence of transition firings yield a sequence of markings. M is said to be reachable from M_0 if there exists a sequence of transition firings that transform M_0 to M. The set of all possible markings reachable from M_0 is denoted by $R(M_0)$. The set of all possible transition firing sequence from M_0 is $L(M_0)$.

11.2.2 Modeling Resources

The resources relative to deadlock in AMSs include machines, buffers, robots or AGVs, and zones and lanes in an AGV system. Often, buffers are associated with machines. Thus, when there are buffers for a machine, we can model the machine and its associated buffers as a primitive with multiple capacity. Here, we first present the PN models for the resources.

It is assumed that no part visits the same machine more than one time consecutively. If a machine has a buffer (input or output buffer), then the ROPN models the primitive by two places x and y connected by a transition t. This model is shown in Figure 11.1. Place x is for the input buffer if the machine has an input buffer and y for the machine. If the machine has an output buffer, then x is for the machine and y is for the buffer. The capacity of the places represents the number of parts that can be held by the buffer or machine. A token in a place means that there is a part in the buffer or on the machine. Transition t connecting these two places represents the operation process of loading (unloading) a part onto the machine (buffer). The multiple input transitions of place x in Figure 11.1 represent the sharing of the machine primitive. The multiple output transitions of place y represent multiple output routes. For the sake of simplicity, we often write $\{u_i\}$ for $\{x_i, t_i, y_i\}$, or u_i denotes the primitive of resources corresponding to machine i.

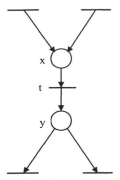

Figure 11.1. The PN model for the machine primitive.

If a machine has no input and output buffers, the machine becomes a single-capacity resource. Because only one AGV is allowed to enter a zone in an AGV system, a zone in an AGV system is treated as a single-capacity resource. Often, in a semiconductor manufacturing system, the devices for processing wafers are single capacity as well. A robot and an AGV are also single capacity resources. A single-capacity resource in AMS can be modeled by a single place, as shown in Figure 11.2. Note that $t_i(I)$ and $t_j(O)$, i, j=1, 2, ..., n represent the transfer of a part from and to another primitive, respectively.

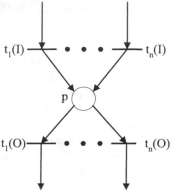

Figure 11.2. The PN model for single capacity resource.

11.2.3 Modeling the Manufacturing Processes

We can model production processes by using the PN models of resources. Without the loss of generality, we assume that the machines in the system have an input buffer with finite capacity. At the same time, routing flexibility is considered. Let Q denote the set of types of parts to be produced in the system. The operation sequence for a part type is prescribed, and some operations may be processed by alterative machines due to the routing flexibility. When an operation requires machine i to process, the resources required for the operation correspond to primitive i in our model. Assume that the number of operations of part type $q \in Q$ is L_q and let $A_q = \{A_q(1), A_q(2), ..., A_q(L_q)\}$ denote the required sequence to produce the part type, where $A_q(i) \neq \varnothing$ is a set of primitives corresponding to the alterative machines for operation i. For instance, if $A_q = \{u_1, u_2, (u_3, u_1)\}$, then operation 1 (2) requires machine 1 (2) to process, and operation 3 can be performed by either machine 3 or 1. We call $(a_q(i), a_q(i+1))$ a primitive pair from $A_q(i)$ and $A_q(i+1)$ if $a_q(i) \in A_q(i)$ and $a_q(i+1) \in A_q(i+1)$. In the primitive pair, $a_q(i)$ is the upstream primitive of $a_q(i+1)$ that is called downstream one of $a_q(i)$. To model the production process of a part type is to add a transition between each primitive pair from $A_q(i)$ and $A_q(i+1)$ for i = 1, 2, ..., L_q - 1, respectively, such that the transition is the output transition of an upstream primitive and the input transition of a downstream one. Finally an input (output) transition is added to each primitive $a_q(1) \in A_q(1)$ $(a_q(L_q) \in A_q(L_q))$. These transitions are connected through a place p_0 representing the load/unload station. Therefore, to complete the modeling of the system, we first choose a part type arbitrarily, say q_1, and carry out the above procedure. Then we choose q_2 and do the same, but this time if u_i and u_{i+1} are the primitive pair for q_2 and there is already a transition connecting these two primitives, then we do not add any new transition to connect them. Carrying out this procedure for all other part types, we obtain the so-called ROPN because we address the resources and each resource corresponds o only one place in the model.

Let n_{qi} denote the number of parts for part type q_i and $n = \sum_{q_i \in Q} n_{q_i}$. Without the

loss of generality, we let $M_0(p_0) = n$ and $M_0(p_i) = 0$ if $i \neq 0$, as the initial marking. This implies that initially all the parts to be processed are in the load/unload station.

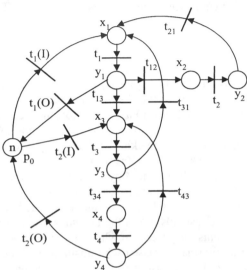

Figure 11.3. The ROPN for a system.

The ROPN for a system containing four machines and three types of parts is shown in Figure 11.3 and the operation sequences of the three types of parts are: $A_1 = \{u_1, u_3, (u_4, u_1)\}$, $A_2 = \{u_3, u_1, (\{u_3, u_4\}, \{u_2, u_1\})\}$ and $A_3 = \{u_3, u_4, u_3, u_1\}$. The type-1 parts can be released into the system from p_0 to u_1 by going through $t_1(I)$. The third operation can be processed by machine 1 or 4, or the parts can go from y_3 to x_1 or x_4 through t_{31} or t_{34}. When a part is completed by machine 1 (machine 4), it goes back to p_0 through $t_1(O)$ ($t_2(O)$). The flow of the other part types is modeled similarly by the ROPN in Figure 11.3. It should be pointed out that according to the operation sequences, there are four operations for a type-2 part. The third operation can be processed by machine 3 or 2. If it is processed by machine 3, the fourth operation should be processed by machine 4. If it is processed by machine 2, the fourth operation should be processed by machine 1.

Structurally, an ROPN is a state machine PN, a subclass of free choice PN. Thus it is simple and suitable for our analysis. In a free choice PN, a token in a place enables all the output transitions of that place, or any one of the output transitions can be chosen to fire. In ROPN, however, a token in a place does not enable all the output transitions of that place. For example, in Figure 11.3 a token representing part type 1 in place y_3 enables both transitions t_{31} and t_{34}, but a token representing part type 3 in that place enables only t_{31}. This implies that when a token is in a place only some of the output transitions of that place can be chosen to fire, this is the difference between the ROPN and free choice PN. To model this characteristic we introduce colors into the ROPN, and the ROPN becomes a CROPN.

A colored PN (CPN) is the extension of a regular PN. In a CPN there is a set of colors associated with each place $p \in P$ and transition $t \in T$, and a transition can fire with respect to each of its colors [32-33].

Let $C(p)$ and $C(t)$ denote the sets of colors associated with place $p \in P$, and transition $t \in T$, $|\bullet|$ denote the cardinality of a set, where $C(p_i) = \{a_{i1}, a_{i2}, ..., a_{zi}\}$, $zi = |C(p_i)|$, $i = 1, 2, ..., m$, $C(t_j) = \{b_{j1}, b_{j2}, ..., b_{wj}\}$, $wj = |C(t_j)|$, $j = 1, 2, ..., n$. Then $I(p,t): C(p) \times C(t) \to N$ and $O(p,t): C(p) \times C(t) \to N$ are the input and output functions, respectively, and $M(p): C(p) \to N$ is the marking of CPN.

Let $I(p_i, t_j)(a_{ih}, b_{jk})$ and $O(p_i, t_j)(a_{ih}, b_{jk})$ denote the weight of arc (p_i, t_j) and (t_j, p_i) with respect to (a_{ih}, b_{jk}), respectively. Then a transition $t_j \in T$ is said to be enabled with respect to color b_{jk} in marking M if and only if for any $p_i \in P$, $a_{ih} \in C(p_i)$

$$M(p_i)(a_{ih}) \geq I(p_i, t_j)(a_{ih}, b_{jk}) \qquad (11.4)$$

The marking M' reached from M by firing t_j with respect to color b_{jk} is

$$M'(p_i)(a_{ih}) = M(p_i)(a_{ih}) + O(p_i, t_j)(a_{ih}, b_{jk}) - I(p_i, t_j)(a_{ih}, b_{jk}) \qquad (11.5)$$

Based on the concept of CPN, we define the colors in our CROPN. First we define the colors for transitions. From the last subsection, we know that a transition in ROPN represents the process in which a part is moved from a buffer (machine) to another buffer (machine), so each transition needs only one color.

Definition 11.2: Define $C(t_i) = \{b_i\}$ as the only color of transition $t_i \in T$. If a token in place p enables p's output transitions $\{t_1, ..., t_k\}$, it has color $\{b_1, ..., b_k\}$. If $p^\bullet = \{t_1, ..., t_i\}$, p's token color set is $\{t_1, ..., t_i\}$.

This color is used to identify a transition. In other words, $b_i \neq b_j$ if $i \neq j$. Based on Definition 11.2 we can then define token colors. We use $M(p)(b_i)$ to denote the number of tokens with color b_i in p in marking M. Because of the routing flexibility, a token in p may enable more than one transition simultaneously. A token of color $\{b_1, ..., b_k\}$ in p can be used to fire any transition in $\{t_1, ..., t_k\}$, while a token of b_j can fire only t_j.

Note that with the above definition we do not distinguish part types. We only want to know which output transition is enabled when a token is in a place. This is because a token may represent a different stage of a part in the same place. For instance, in Figure 11.3, when a type-1 part is in y_1 with its first operation completed, it enables t_{13}. When the same part is in y_1 with its third operation completed, it enables $t_1(O)$. Therefore, the above color definition describes the essential characteristics of part flows in AMS.

11.2.4 Modeling the Process of Material Handling

In AMS, a material handling system (MHS) is often composed of robots and/or AGVs used to deliver materials. Consider the operation process of moving a part from a buffer to another buffer by an MHS. This process can be divided into three steps: first the MHS picks a part up, then moves it to a destination buffer, and finally unloads it there. This process is often modeled by three events in a PN mode as shown in Figure 11.4(a). Modeling this detail seems unnecessary from the deadlock avoidance viewpoint. In fact, these three steps are closely related and cannot be divided. When the MHS picks up a part, it can do nothing else except moving it to the destination and then unloading it. Hence, this process can be thought of as a single event and can be modeled by a single transition in a PN in Figure 11.4(b).

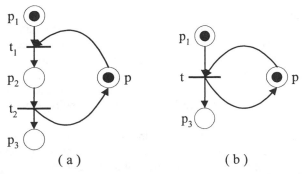

(a)   (b)

Figure 11.4. The PN models for the process of material handling.

Now we consider the CROPN introduced in the previous section. The process that a part goes from a machine to another is modeled by a transition in the CROPN which connects the two machine primitives through the place representing the machine of the upstream primitive and the input place of the downstream primitive. The process that a part goes from the load/unload station (a machine) to a machine (load/unload station) is also modeled by a transition that connects the place p_0 and the machine primitive. In other words, these processes are modeled by one event in the CROPN. Thus, the events modeled by such transitions exactly match the operation process of the MHS moving a part from a buffer to another. Therefore, to model an MHS process in CROPN, we add a place with a token to represent the MHS availability, a transition t to represent the MHS process, and an input arc and an output arc between p and t, as shown in Figure 11.4(b). Clearly, p and t modeling the MHS process form a self-loop. Note that for this PN model the transition enabling and firing rule given by Definition 11.1 is still applicable with no change for the CROPN.

11.3 DEADLOCK AVOIDANCE IN THE MANUFACTURING PROCESS

Now we can discuss the problem of deadlock avoidance in a manufacturing process by using the PN model developed in the last section.

11.3.1 Existence of Deadlock

Before we discuss the policy of avoiding deadlocks in a manufacturing process, we analyze the structural characteristics of CROPN. In a PN each place (transition) can be regarded as a node. A PN is said to be strongly connected if and only if there is a directed path from any node to any other node. A PN is called a state machine if each transition $t \in T$ has exactly one input place and exactly one output place. Observing the ROPN we know that structurally a ROPN is a strongly connected state machine PN, a class of free choice PN. It is also a finite capacity PN. All the places other than p_0 (without the loss of generality, we assume that p_0 has infinite capacity) have finite capacity. Hence, the enabling and firing rules are given by (11.1) and (11.2). In ROPN when a token is in a place, if (11.1) is satisfied for transition t, we say that t is process-enabled, or, without confusion, that the token enables t. When (11.2) is satisfied for t, t is resource-enabled. Because of the exclusive use of a resource in AMS, each of the arc weights in an ROPN is 1. It should also be noticed that there is at most one transition connecting two primitives in the ROPN.

Because of the strong connectedness of an ROPN, it contains a number of circuits. The production process circuit in is a special class of circuits which plays an important role in analyzing the liveness of an ROPN.

Definition 11.3: A circuit in an ROPN is called a production process circuit (PPC) if place p_0 representing the load/unload station is not a member of the set of places on the circuit.

We use C to denote a PPC in ROPN. Because of the routing complexity in AMSs, there may be many PPCs in an ROPN, but only some of PPCs in an ROPN need to be identified.

Definition 11.4: A PPC C in an ROPN is said to be an elementary PPC if it goes from one node through a series of nodes back to this node such that no node is repeated. Otherwise C is nonelementary.

Lemma 11.1: A nonelementary PPC in an ROPN is composed of several elementary PPCs.

Proof: Consider a sequence of places on a nonelementary PPC along the direction of the circuit. Assume that the sequence is $S = \{p_1, p_2, ..., p_i, p_{i+1}, ..., p_n\}$ such that $p_1 = p_{i+1}$ and p_{i+1} is the first repeated place. This sequence can be divided into two subsequences $\{p_1, ..., p_i\}$ and $\{p_{i+1}, ..., p_n\}$. Obviously, the first subsequence of places forms an elementary PPC. The second subsequence forms another PPC, surely it may not be an elementary one. If it is not an elementary PPC, change the starting place such that the sequence has the same characteristic as S.

Then do the same as before. By repeating this procedure, a number of elementary PPCs can be obtained. This proves the lemma. □

Lemma 11.1 implies that only the elementary PPCs in ROPN need to be considered. Thereafter, when we mention a PPC, we refer to an elementary PPC.

In an ROPN, the number of places on a PPC C must be equal to the number of transitions on C and the input place of a transition on C must also be on C. Let $P(C) = \{p_1, ..., p_k\}$ and $T(C) = \{t_1, ..., t_k\}$ be the sets of places and transitions on C with $p_i \in {}^\bullet t_i$, $i=1, 2, ...k$, respectively. We use $M(p_i(C))(b_i)$, with b_i being the color of t_i, to denote the number of tokens in p_i which enable t_i. Because these tokens enable only t_i, after firing t_i these tokens remain in C. Hence, they are called the cycling tokens of C. Other tokens in p_i can leave C after firing the transitions other than t_i, which are named the possible leaving tokens of C. For example, in Figure 11.3, the token representing part type 1 in place y_1 is a cycling token of $C = \{u_1, t_{13}, u_3, t_{31}\}$, since it enables only t_{13} that is on C. The token for the same part type in place y_3 enables both t_{31} and t_{34}, and it can leave C by firing t_{34}. Hence, it is not a cycling token, but a possible leaving token of C.

Definition 11.5: In CROPN define $M(C) = \sum M(p_i(C))(b_i)$, $p_i \in C$ as the number of cycling tokens of PPC C in marking M.

We will see the important role played by expression $M(C)$ in our discussion. In the CROPN, the interaction of PPCs complicates the problem of liveness of the net. We discuss the interactive PPC subnet as follows.

Definition 11.6: In ROPN a subnet formed by a number of PPCs is said to be an interactive PPC subnet, if every PPC in the subnet has common places and transitions with at least one other PPC in the subnet and the subnet is strongly connected.

We will call interactive PPC subnet interactive subnet for short. Because place p_0 is not on any PPC, it is not in any interactive subnet either. We denote an interactive subnet formed by n PPCs by C^n, where n stands for the number of PPCs that form the subnet. Let $P(C^n)$ be the set of places in C^n. For place $p_i \in C^n$, let $T_i = \{t_1, t_2, ..., t_j\}$ denote the set of output transitions of place p_i that are in subnet C^n. If the transitions enabled by a token in $p_i \in C^n$ are all in T_i, then after firing any such transition, the token remains in C^n. Such a token is a cycling one of C^n. If the transitions enabled by a token in p_i contain a transition that is not in T_i, then this token is not necessarily a cycling token of C^n because it is possible for it to leave C^n when a transition fires. Let $M(p_i)(C^n)$ be the number of cycling tokens of C^n in p_i. The number of cycling tokens in C^n is defined as follows.

Definition 11.7: In a CROPN define $M(C^n) = \sum M(p_i)(C^n)$, $p_i \in C^n$, as the number of cycling tokens in subnet C^n in marking M.

Up until now we have developed a CROPN model for AMS. It fully describes the characteristic of concurrent resource contention and part flows with routing flexibility. Yet it has a simple structure, i.e., a state machine PN graphically. Deadlock in a manufacturing process is a circular wait situation. In this situation a set of parts or jobs wait for never-to-be-released resources.

Definition 11.8: Assume that there are tokens in a CROPN, then deadlock occurs in a CROPN if there exists a transition set T_d in $M \in R(M_0)$ such that every transition in T_d is process-enabled but none is resource-enabled.

In a PN, if it is possible for deadlocks to occur, we say that there exist potential deadlocks in the PN. With CROPN the existence of potential deadlocks in an AMS can easily be analyzed because a PPC in CROPN models a possible circular wait situation. Deadlocks in an AMS are strongly related to nonliveness of the PN model of the system. Let $L(M)$ denote the set of all possible firing sequences from M in a PN with marking M, then the liveness of a PN can be defined as follows:

Definition 11.9 [31]: A PN with initial marking M_0 is said to be live if, no matter what marking $M \in R(M_0)$ is reached, it is ultimately possible to fire any transition of the net by progressing through some further firing sequence.

The relationship between liveness and deadlock is discussed as follows.

Lemma 11.2 [31]: An infinite capacity state machine with initial marking M_0 is live if and only if the net is strongly connected and M_0 has at least one token.

It is known from the previous subsection that a CROPN is a strongly connected state machine. We assume that there are always tokens in ROPN, or there are parts in an AMS to be processed. Otherwise it is not meaningful. Therefore, it is the finiteness of capacity in a CROPN that causes deadlock. This implies that the buffers and machines are two key resources in deadlock control.

Let $K(C_i) = \sum K(p_j)$, $p_j \in P(C_i)$, denote the capacity of PPC C_i. To see the deadlock situation, let us observe Figure 11.3 which has three PPCs: $C_1 = \{u_1, t_{13}, u_3, t_{31}\}$, $C_2 = \{u_1, t_{12}, u_2, t_{21}\}$ and $C_3 = \{u_3, t_{34}, u_4, t_{43}\}$. Since y_i, $i = 1, ..., 4$, represents a machine, its capacity is 1. Assume that a marking M is reached such that C_1 is full of tokens, the token in y_1 is part type 1 that enables only t_{13} and the token in y_3 is part type 3 with the third operation just completed that enables only t_{31}. Then no transitions on C_1 can fire any more and a deadlock occurs at C_1. $M(C_1) = K(C_1)$. In fact, this time the overall system is disabled, and no transition can fire after limited time. By this observation, the following results about the relationship of deadlocks and liveness in CROPN are obvious:

Lemma 11.3: If an ROPN is not live, then there exist PPCs in the net.

Lemma 11.4: The following two statements are equivalent:

1) An ROPN is not live.

2) An ROPN is not deadlock-free.

Lemmas 11.3 and 11.4 show that if deadlocks occur in a CROPN, then they occur in its PPCs. Hence, to control deadlocks in AMS is to control deadlocks in the PPCs in CROPN.

Theorem 11.1: The necessary condition for the existence of potential deadlocks in a CROPN is that there exists at least one PPC C such that $M_0(p_0) \geq K(C)$.

Proof: It is clear and thus omitted.   □

This theorem indicates that if the number of active parts in a system is greater than or equal to the capacity of some PPCs, then there is potential deadlock in the system. This chapter assumes that the potential deadlocks exist in the considered system, or there are enough active parts in the system to cause deadlocks.

11.3.2 The Deadlock Avoidance Policy

Before discussing the deadlock-free conditions and control policy, we first present some definitions and notations.

Definition 11.10: A transition t in a CROPN is said to be controlled if its firing is determined by a control policy when t is both process and resource-enabled according to the enabling rules of CROPN.

Therefore, a control policy for the CROPN is a restrictive policy. It determines if each controlled transition can fire by observing the state of the net even if the transition is process and resource-enabled. When a controlled transition t can fire according to a control policy, t is control-enabled under this control policy.

Definition 3.9: A CROPN is said to be a controlled CROPN if at least one transition in the net can be controlled.

According to Definitions 3.8 and 3.9, it is known that a controlled transition in a controlled CROPN is enabled only when it is process-, resource- and control-enabled. The CROPN considered here is not live. Our goal is to control the CROPN by a restrictive policy so that the CROPN becomes live. Under a control policy, the set of reachable markings is changed, as denoted by $R_c(M_0)$.

A transition in a PN is live if it can fire at least once in some firing sequence for every marking M reachable from M_0 [31].

Definition 11.12: A PPC C in a CROPN is said to be live if every transition in C is live.

We know that the PPCs in CROPN contribute to the occurrence of deadlock in AMS. Therefore, to avoid deadlock, a policy must control the number of tokens in all PPCs in a CROPN. PPCs are overlapping with each other and a number of interactive subnets are formed.

Definition 11.13: A transition t is said to be an output (input) transition of an interactive subnet C^n if t is not in C^n and the input (output) place of t is in C^n.

It is the firing of the input and output transitions of C^n that changes the number of tokens in C^n. An interactive subnet C^n may have more than one output (input) transition. We let $T_O(C^n)$ ($T_I(C^n)$) denote the set of the output (input) transitions of C^n. When we discuss the deadlock avoidance problem for an interactive subnet, we assume that every $t \in T_O(C^n)$ is resource-enabled and later we will show every such transition is live when all the interactive subnets are live under control. Similarly, we use $T_O(C)$ and $T_I(C)$ to denote the set of the output and input transitions of the subnet formed by C, respectively.

Definition 11.14: Define $S'(C_i) = \sum(K(p_j) - M(p_j))$, $p_j \in P(C_i)$, and $S(C_i) = K(C_i) - M(C_i)$ as the number of spaces and the number of currently potential spaces available in PPC C_i in marking M.

In the following sections, we discuss the control problem in different interactive subnets. In this section we assume that there are tokens in a subnet considered and let $M(L(C))$ denote the number of possible leaving tokens of PPC C in marking M.

A. Case One: Subnet Formed by One PPC

This is the special case of an interactive subnet formed by only one PPC. Figure 5 shows such a subnet. The ROPN in Figure 11.5 describes the concurrent contention for resources by two types of parts with sequences $A_1 = \{u_1, u_2, u_3, (u_4, u_2)\}$ and $A_2 = \{u_3, u_2\}$. In the net there is a PPC $C = \{u_2, t_{23}, u_3, t_{32}\}$. We use C to denote the subnet formed by C.

Definition 11.15: A circuit in a PN is said to be finite if the number of places and the number of transitions on the circuit are all finite.

It is clear that any PPC in a CROPN has a finite number of places and transitions, because the resources in an AMS are limited. We call such PPC a finite one. For the subnet C we have the following result.

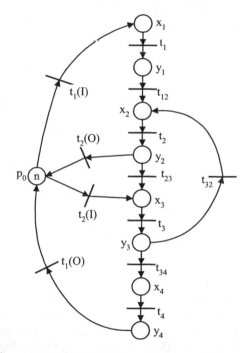

Figure 11.5. The CROPN contains one PPC.

Theorem 11.2: A subnet formed by a PPC C in a CROPN is live if and only if for any marking $M \in R_c(M_0)$,

$$S(C) \geq 1. \tag{11.6}$$

Proof: It is clear and omitted. $\square$

Similar to the concept of enabling a transition in CROPN, we can discuss the enabling of a PPC C. C in marking M is said to be potential process-enabled if for every $t_i \in C$, once $M(p_i) = K(p_i)$, then $M(p_i)(b_i) \geq 1$, or some tokens in p_i enable transitions in $T_O(C^n)$, where p_i is t_i's input place and b_i is t_i's color. It should be noted that when p_i is full of tokens, or $M(p_i) = K(p_i)$, the condition guarantees that t_i is process-enabled and a token in p_i enabling a transition $t \in T_O(C^n)$ can be seen as a potential space. If $S'(C) > 0$ and/or there are tokens in C which enable transitions in $T_O(C^n)$, then C is to be potential resource-enabled.

Definition 11.16: A PPC C in a CROPN is said to be enabled if C is both potential process-enabled and potential resource-enabled.

From the discussion above, we know that there are spaces in an enabled PPC C or some spaces will move into it after some possible leaving tokens leave it. Once there are spaces in an enabled PPC, the transitions on it can fire one by one. Thus, tokens and spaces can move into the PPC. In a subnet formed by a PPC C all the possible leaving tokens must enable the transitions in $T_O(C)$, so we have the following corollary.

Corollary 11.1: If the condition in (11.6) is satisfied for a subnet formed by a PPC C, then C is an enabled PPC.

B. Case Two: Interactive Subnet Formed by Two PPCs

In this section we discuss the deadlock control problem for an interactive subnet formed by two PPCs, a subnet more complex than the one discussed in the last section. C^2 denotes an interactive subnet formed by two PPCs. Figure 11.6 shows an example of C^2.

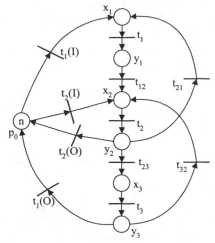

Figure 11.6. CROPN containing a subnet formed by two PPCs

From Figure 11.6, we try to explain why C^2 may not be live even if (11.6) is satisfied for both PPCs in C^2. The CROPN contains two PPCs: $C_1 = \{u_1, t_{12}, u_2, t_{21}\}$ and $C_2 = \{u_2, t_{23}, u_3, t_{32}\}$. When all the places in the subnet are full of tokens, and the token in place y_1 enables t_{12}, the token in y_2 enables both t_{23} and t_{21}, the token in y_3 enables t_{32}, so $S(C_1) = 1$ and $S(C_2) = 1$. But no transitions in the subnet can fire, or it is not live. In this state, there is no space in the subnet and no token in the subnet enables $t_1(O)$ or $t_2(O)$, i.e., neither PPC is potential resource-enabled. This implies that there is no enabled PPC in the subnet. This concludes that the condition given in Theorem 11.2 is not adequate to make C^2 deadlock-free. We must find more conditions under which C^2 is live.

The two PPCs in a C^2 have common places (shared resources) and transitions. These common places are connected by the common transitions and form a common place chain. It can be observed that the first (last) place on the common place chain has two input (output) transitions belonging to different PPCs. We call these input (output) transitions as intercircuit input (output) transitions (IIT and IOT). Let t_{iik} denote an IIT external to PPC C_k and t_{iok} denote an IOT on C_k.

Assume that C^2 has two PPCs C_1 and C_2, P_{12} is the set of their common places, and p_r is the last place in their common place chain. Let $M(E(C^n))$ denote the number of enabled PPCs in C^n in marking M.

Lemma 11.5: If $M(E(C^2)) \geq 1$ in an interactive subnet C^2 in marking M, then $S(C_i) \geq 1$, for both $i = 1$ and 2.

Proof: It is sufficient to show that the lemma holds when $M(E(C^2)) = 1$. We assume that C_1 is enabled, then t_{io1}, the IOT on C_1, must be process-enabled. This implies that it is one of the cases: (1) place p_r is empty; (2) the token in p_r enables t_{io1} and a transition in $T_O(C^2)$; (3) the token enables both t_{io1} and t_{io2}; (4) the token enables only a transition in $T_O(C^2)$; and (5) the token enables only t_{io1}. In the first four cases $S(C_i) \geq 1$ holds for both $i = 1$ and 2, or the lemma holds. In the last case $S(C_2) \geq 1$ holds and to make PPC C_1 enabled, there must be at least one space in C_1 or there is at least one token in C_1 which enables a transition in $T_O(C^2)$. This implies that $S(C_1) \geq 1$ also holds. $\square$

From the above discussion, we derive the following result.

Theorem 11.3: An interactive subnet C^2 in a CROPN is live if and only if $M(E(C^2)) \geq 1$ in any marking $M \in R_c(M_0)$.

Proof: *Necessity*. We show that if the condition given in the theorem does not hold, or $M(E(C^2)) = 0$, then C^2 is not live. By assumption there are tokens in the subnet, so when $M(E(C^2)) = 0$ place p_r must be full or $M(p_r) = K(p_r)$, otherwise both PPCs are enabled. If the token in p_r enables both t_{io1} and t_{io2}, then both PPCs in C^2 are potential process-enabled. This time $M(E(C^2)) = 0$ implies that all the places in C^2 are full and no token enables a transition in $T_O(C^2)$, so in any firing sequence in the CROPN no space can move into the subnet. Therefore, all the transitions in C^2 are process-enabled, but none is resource-enabled, and thus C^2 is not live. If the token in p_r enables only one of the IOTs, say t_{io1}, then C_1 is potential process-enabled. By $M(E(C^2)) = 0$, C_1 must not be potential resource-enabled, or there is no space in C_1 and no token in C_1 enables a transition in $T_O(C^2)$. Therefore, C_1 is deadlocked, and the subnet is not live.

Sufficiency. By assumption there are tokens in C^2. If there is only one space in C^2 and this space is in a place in the common place chain, no token in C^2 enables a transition in $T_O(C^2)$. This space can move into the first place of the common place chain by firing the transitions on the chain one by one. This time place p_r is full. If the token in p_r enables only one of IOTs, say t_{io1} on C_1, then C_1 is enabled, so the transitions on C_1 can fire one by one. The first transition to fire is t_{ii2}, the IIT on C_1. After the firing of t_{ii2}, the space moves into the input place of t_{ii2} which is on C_1. The space then moves into the output place of t_{io1} in some time so that t_{io1} is process and resource-enabled and can fire. The firing of t_{io1} moves the space into the common place chain again. If the space is in the first place of the common place chain and the token in p_r enables both t_{io1} and t_{io2}, then both PPCs are enabled, or $M(E(C^2)) = 2$, so the transitions on one PPC, C_1 or C_2, can fire one by one. Thus one of IITs, t_{ii1} or t_{ii2}, can be selected to fire. If t_{ii1} is selected, then the space moves into C_2. In some time the space can move into the output place of t_{io2} and then moves into the common place chain again with the firing of t_{io2}. Therefore, in both cases the subnet is live.

Now we assume the only space is not in a place on the common place chain. If the token in place p_r enables only one IOT, say t_{io1}, then by $M(E(C^2)) \geq 1$ the space must be in C_1. From the above discussion, we know that the subnet is live. If the token in p_r enables both t_{io1} and t_{io2}, then the space can be in any PPC and the subnet is still live. Clearly, if there are two or more spaces in the subnet and the condition in the theorem holds, the subnet is live.

When there is no space available in the subnet, there must be some tokens that enable transitions in $T_O(C^2)$. If the token in p_r enables only one IOT, say t_{io1}, then to make $M(E(C^2)) \geq 1$, there must be a token in C_1 which enables transition $t \in T_O(C^2)$. By assumption t is resource-enabled, after its firing, a space moves into C_1, so the subnet is live. If the token in p_r enables both t_{io1} and t_{io2}, there must be a token in the subnet that enables $t \in T_O(C^2)$, but the token can be in any a PPC, and the subnet is still live. □

It is known from the discussion above that in an interactive subnet only the transitions on the enabled PPCs can fire immediately. Therefore, the firing order of the IITs is very important to the liveness of an interactive subnet. The IITs on the enabled PPCs should fire first, though other IITs may be process- and resource-enabled at the same time. After the firing of the transitions on the enabled PPCs, the IOT on another PPC may become process-enabled and the PPC becomes enabled. In other words, the PPCs in the subnet become enabled one by one.

C. Case Three: Interactive Subnet Formed by Multiple PPCs

An interactive subnet formed by multiple PPCs is much more complex than C^2. In a C^n ($n>2$), the common places can be shared by the PPCs in a complex way and a number of common place chains can be formed. There may be many IOTs on a PPC. In C^n, the condition $M(E(C^n)) \geq 1$ does not guarantee that $S(C_i) \geq 1$ for every PPC C_i. This can be seen in Figure 11.3. If all the places except x_3 are full of tokens, the token in y_1 enables only t_{12} and the token in y_3 enables both t_{31} and t_{34}, then both $C_2 = \{u_1, t_{13}, u_3, t_{31}\}$ and $C_3 = \{u_3, t_{34}, u_4, t_{43}\}$ are potential resource-enabled and C_3 is potential process-enabled. Thus C_3 is enabled, or $M(E(C^n)) \geq 1$. But it is easy to verify that $S(C_1) = 0$ where $C_1 = \{u_1, t_{12}, u_2, t_{21}\}$.

Because of the complexity of the PPC interaction in C^n, we define and discuss two particular classes of interactive subnets.

Definition 11.17: Let C_1, C_2, ..., and C_k be k PPCs in C^n. If C_1 and C_2 have a common place chain P_1, C_2 and C_3 have P_2, ..., and C_{k-1} and C_k have P_{k-1}, and $P_i \cap P_j = \varnothing$, these k PPCs form a PPC chain. If C_1 and C_k of a PPC chain formed by C_1, C_2, ..., and C_k have common places, they form a PPC ring.

Lemma 11.6: In C^n without a PPC ring in a CROPN, there exists at least one PPC that is potential process-enabled in any reachable marking M.

Proof: To show the lemma, it is sufficient to show that there exists at least one PPC C in the subnet such that the IOTs on that PPC are all process-enabled. By assumption there are tokens in the subnet. Hence, if every t_i in the IOTs on a C is process-enabled when $M(p_i) = K(p_i)$, with p_i being the input place of t_i, then the lemma holds. First, we show this by assuming that a token in a place enables only one of the output transitions of that place.

If all the n PPCs in the subnet have common places with the same place chain, then there is only one IOT on each PPC and the token in p_r enables one transition, which is the only IOT on a PPC. Therefore the lemma holds.

If n PPCs form a PPC chain, we can check these PPCs beginning with C_1 of the chain. If the only IOT on C_1 is process-enabled, then the lemma is true. If it is not, then we check C_2. If the IOT on C_2 is the output transition of P_2 and is process-enabled, then the lemma is true. Otherwise we check C_3, and so on. If the IOT on C_{n-1}, which is the output transition of P_{n-2}, and the IOT on C_{n-1}, which is the output transition of P_{n-1}, are both process-enabled, then the lemma holds. Otherwise the only IOT on C_n is process-enabled.

If C has common places with several PPCs with different place chains, then the net must be a star form, or a PPC that has common places with C is the end PPC of a PPC chain. If all IOTs on C are process-enabled, then the lemma holds. If one of the IOTs on C, say t, is not process-enabled, then t is the output transition of a common place chain of C and another PPC, and assume that the place chain is P_1, the common place chain of C and C_1. Let CH be the PPC chain with C_1 being the end PPC. Surely there must be at least one PPC C_2, which is on the PPC chain CH such that all IOTs on C_2 are process-enabled.

Any interactive subnet without a PPC ring can be composed of the subnets discussed above; therefore, the lemma holds for the case that a token enables only one transition. When a token can enable more than one transition, more transitions are process-enabled. Hence, the lemma still holds. □

The following lemma shows that the conclusion given in Lemma 11.6 still holds when an interactive subnet contains PPC rings.

Lemma 11.7: If an interactive subnet C^n contains a PPC ring in a CROPN, there exists at least one PPC that is potential process-enabled in any reachable marking M.

Proof: We can show the lemma similarly to the proof of Lemma 11.6, or show that there exists at least one PPC on which the IOTs are all process-enabled when each token in the subnet enables only one transition. Assume that k PPCs C_1, C_2, ..., and C_k form a PPC ring, and all the places in this ring are full and for every PPC C_i, i = 1, 2, ..., k, $M(L(C_i)) = 1$ since, otherwise, there exists at least one PPC C in these k PPCs such that the IOTs on C are all process-enabled. We also assume that p_{rh} is the last place of the common place chain P_h of C_h and C_{h+1}, p_{rk} is the last place of P_k of C_k and C_1, and the token in p_{r1} enables t_1 on C_1. To satisfy the assumption that $M(L(C_i)) = 1$, i = 1, 2, ..., k, the token in p_{r2} must enable t_2 on C_2, ..., and the token in p_{rk} must enable t_k on C_k. In this case there must be a path from t_1 to P_k, thus to t_k, a path from t_k to t_{k-1}, ..., and a path from t_2 to t_1. Transitions t_1, t_2, ..., and t_k are the IOTs on the PPC C composed of these paths. Hence, all the IOTs on C are process-enabled. Obviously, this still holds when a token enables more than one transition. Therefore, the proof is completed. □

Figure 11.7 shows a subnet containing a PPC ring, the three PPCs $C_1 = \{u_1,$ $t_{12}, u_2, t_{23}, u_3, t_{34}, u_4, t_{41}\}$, $C_2 = \{u_3, t_{35}, u_5, t_{56}, u_6, t_{67}, u_7, t_{73}\}$ and $C_3 = \{u_6, t_{69}, u_9, t_{91},$ $u_1, t_{18}, u_8, t_{86}\}$ form a PPC ring. If t_{34}, t_{18} and t_{67} are process-enabled, then all the IOTs on PPC C = $\{t_{34}, u_4, t_{41}, u_1, t_{18}, u_8, t_{86}, u_6, t_{67}, u_7, t_{73}, u_3\}$ are process-enabled.

From Lemmas 11.6 and 11.7 we have immediately the following corollary.

Corollary 11.2: For any interactive subnet C^n in a CROPN, there exists at least one potential process-enabled PPC in any marking M.

A potential process-enabled PPC becomes enabled if it is also potential resource-enabled. It follows from Corollary 11.2 that there can be enabled PPCs in an interactive subnet C^n in a CROPN if there are enough spaces in it. Based on this observation, now we can present the necessary and sufficient conditions of deadlock-free operation for an interactive subnet C^n.

Theorem 11.4: An interactive subnet in a CROPN is live if and only if in any marking $M \in R_c(M_0)$ reachable from M_0,

$$S(C_i) \geq 1, \quad \text{for every } C_i \qquad (11.7)$$

and $M(E(C^n)) \geq 1$ (11.8)

Proof: *Necessity*. If there exists a PPC C in the subnet such that S(C) =S'(C) + M(L(C)) = 0 in marking M, then there is no space available in C and there is no possible leaving token of C. This implies every transition including IOTs on C is process-enabled, but none on C is resource-enabled. Furthermore, in this situation, every transition on C can become resource-enabled only when a space occupied by another token on C is released. This is impossible and C is deadlocked, or the subnet is not live.

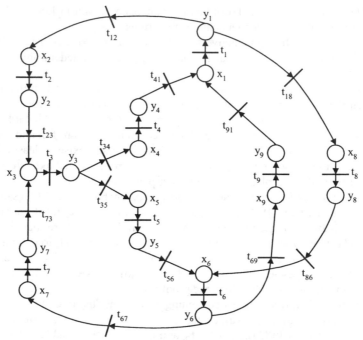

Figure 11.7. Subnet containing a PPC ring.

If $M(E(C^n)) = 0$, then there is no enabled PPC in the subnet. By assumption there are tokens in the subnet. Hence, there exists at least one potential process-enabled PPC in the subnet. By $M(E(C^n)) = 0$, all the potential process-enabled PPCs in the subnet are not potential resource-enabled. Therefore, there is no space available in any of these PPCs and no token in any of these PPCs enables a transition in $T_O(C^n)$. This implies that no space can move into any of these PPCs and the transitions on these PPCs cannot fire. Obviously, the transitions on the PPCs that are not potential process-enabled cannot fire either. Thus C^n is not live.

Sufficiency. It is sufficient to show that the theorem is true when $S(C_i) = 1$ for every C_i in the subnet and $M(E(C^n)) = 1$. When $M(E(C^n)) = 1$, a PPC in the subnet, say C_1, is enabled. The other n - 1 PPCs in the subnet are not enabled. For a non-enabled PPC C_i, when $S(C_i) = 1$ there is no space and no token to enable a transition in $T_O(C^n)$, but there is a possible leaving token. By the definition of an enabled PPC, every IOT on C_1 is process-enabled, or the token in the input place of the IOT enables a transition in $T_O(C^n)$, or the input place is empty. We assume, without the loss of generality, that all the IOTs on C_1 are process-enabled. Therefore, the transitions on C_1 can fire sequentially. Finally, the space moves into a common place chain shared by C_1 with some other PPCs and the token in a p_r does not enable the IOT on C_1, instead it enables an IOT on another PPC, say C_2. Because the space is in the common place chain, C_2 becomes enabled. This time the transitions on C_2 can fire, then another PPC becomes enabled. For any non-enabled PPC C_i, assume that the possible leaving token is in p. Place p must be the last one of a common place chain and the IOT t on C_i is the output transition of p. When one IOT enabled by the token in p fires, a new token can move into p and t on C_i can be process-enabled. Meanwhile, the space is in the common place chain shared by C_i with other PPCs, and thus C_i is enabled. In other words, all the PPCs in C^n can become enabled sequentially and all the transitions can fire. This means the subnet is live. □

From the Proof of Theorem 11.4, we know that to make an interactive subnet live, there must be some spaces in the subnet. The problem is how many spaces are necessary and where these spaces should be in a marking M. Theorem 11.4 provides such conditions.

We can observe that in M if the token in every p_r, the last place of a common place chain, enables all output transitions of p_r, then all IOTs in the subnet are process-enabled. Hence, all the PPCs in the subnet are potential process-enabled and $S(C_i) \geq 1$ for every C_i. Similar to $S(C)$, we use $S(C^n) = K(C^n) - M(C^n)$ to denote the spaces potentially available in C^n in M. From Theorem 11.4, we have:

Corollary 11.3: In an interactive subnet C^n, if all the IOTs are process-enabled in marking M, the subnet is live if and only if

$$S(C^n) \geq 1 \tag{11.9}$$

Corollary 11.3 indicates that in this situation only one space is required to make the subnet live and this space can be in any PPC. It is the extreme case that a token in a place enables all the output transitions of the place, or an operation in AMS can be processed by all machines. This indicates that the routing flexibility can reduce the possibility of the deadlock occurrence in some way. In fact, if any operation can be processed by any machine in AMS, we can schedule the system such that all the parts go in the same direction, leading to no deadlock.

Because the original CROPN is not live, to make it live, some transitions in the net cannot fire spontaneously and a control policy is necessary to restrict the firing of some transitions according to the marking reached. From the Proof of Theorem 11.4, we know that to make the subnet live, the firing order of some transitions must be carefully controlled so that no matter what marking is reached the conditions given in (11.7) and (11.8) are always satisfied.

Definition 11.18: A PPC in a CROPN is an entering PPC of transition t, if t is not, but its output place is on the PPC.

We call t the input transition of the PPC. It may have more than one entering PPC. Let $C_{en}(t)$ denote the set of t's entering PPCs. We have the following result for the deadlock control law for C^n.

Theorem 11.5: An interactive subnet C^n in a CROPN is deadlock-free if and only if any transition $t \in T_l(C^n)$ and any IIT in the subnet is fired only when $S(C_i) \geq 2$ for every $C_i \in C_{en}(t)$ and $M'(E(C^n)) \geq 1$, where M' is the marking reached from M by firing t.

Proof: Necessity follows from Theorem 11.4.

Sufficiency. If the control law given in the theorem is applied, then the firing of any $t \in T_I(C^n)$ or any IIT guarantees that the conditions given in (11.7) and (11.8) be satisfied. Thus, from Theorem 11.4, such firing guarantees the liveness of the subnet. Notice that no firing of other transitions can move tokens and spaces from or into a PPC in the subnet. Hence, the firing of other transitions does not impact the liveness of the subnet. Therefore, the proof is completed. □

The control law given by Theorem 11.5 is a restrictive policy. By controlling the transition firing order. It restricts the firing of the transitions in $T_I(C^n)$ and the IITs in the subnet such that they can fire only in some markings. By this control law, only $T_I(C^n)$ and IITs should be controlled, and the other transitions can fire spontaneously. Notice that this control law is necessary and sufficient for deadlock-free operation in AMS. Hence, it permits as many active parts as possible in AMS while deadlock is totally avoided. In scheduling an AMS, two things should to be avoided. One is deadlock and the other is starvation. Avoiding starvation requires that there are as many parts as possible in the system. Thus, when this control law is embedded into a real-time scheduler, it provides a good opportunity to avoid starvation or to improve resource utilization while avoiding deadlocks.

11.3.3 Liveness of Overall System

The control law presented above is for subnets in CROPN. We will show that if every subnet in the CROPN is controlled by this law, then the overall controlled CROPN is live.

When we discuss the deadlock avoidance problem for interactive subnets, we assume that the transitions in $T_O(C^n)$ are resource-enabled. It can be observed that a transition t in $T_O(C^n)$ is either an input transition of another interactive subnet in the CROPN or an input transition of place p_0. An input transition of place p_0 is always resource-enabled. Hence, to show the liveness of CROPN is to show that all the input transitions of all the interactive subnets in it are live. We assume that there are k interactive subnets, $C^n(1)$, $C^n(2)$, ..., and $C^n(k)$. First we present the following lemma.

Lemma 11.8: Assume that a CROPN is formed by k subnets, $C^n(1)$, $C^n(2)$, ..., and $C^n(k)$, and is under control by the law given in Theorem 11.5. If a subnet $C^n(i)$ is replaced by a place $p^n(i)$ with $K(p^n(i)) = K(C^n(i))$ and $T_I(C^n(i))$ and $T_O(C^n(i))$ are the set of input and output transitions, respectively, then the liveness of the net does not change.

Proof: The control law given Theorem 11.5 guarantees the liveness of the subnet C^n assuming the transitions in $T_O(C^n)$ are resource-enabled. Hence we need to show that the liveness of the transitions that are not in C^n is not changed. These transitions are in $T_I(C^n)$ and $T_O(C^n)$. From Theorem 11.5, we know that for each C^n the controlled transitions are in $T_I(C^n)$ and IITs. By controlling the IITs, we control the token distribution within a subnet, so it does not impact the liveness of transitions not in the subnet. By controlling transitions in $T_I(C^n)$, we restrict the number of tokens in the subnet. With $K(p^n(i)) = K(C^n(i))$, when $M(p^n(i)) = K(p^n(i))$ no transition in $T_I(p^n(i))$ can fire due to the control law. Each part in a subnet can be completed and leaves the subnet by firing one of the transitions in $T_O(C^n)$. A token in $p^n(i)$ enabling a transition in $T_O(C^n(i))$ represents this process. Therefore, when a subnet $C^n(i)$ is replaced by $p^n(i)$, the overall net structure is not changed and the enabling of transitions in $T_I(C^n(i))$ and $T_O(C^n(i))$ is not changed either. $\square$

The resulting net from Lemma 11.8 is called a simplified CROPN. In a simplified net, the key point is that no transition in $T_O(C^n(i))$ which is not resource-enabled in the original CROPN is made resource-enabled. Therefore, if the simplified CROPN is live, then a transition in $T_O(C^n)$ in the original CROPN will be resource-enabled in some time, or the assumption that the transitions in $T_O(C^n)$ is resource-enabled is justified. A simplified CROPN containing six subnets is shown in Figure 11.8.

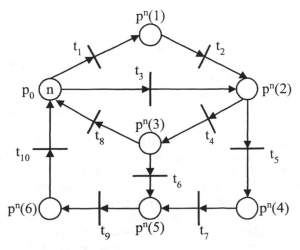

Figure 11.8. A simplified CROPN.

By observing the simplified CROPN, we have immediately the following Lemma.

Lemma 11.9: In a simplified CROPN place p_0 representing the load/unload station is a common place of all circuits in the net.

For the liveness of the simplified CROPN, we have the following lemma.

Lemma 11.10: The simplified CROPN is live.

Proof: We only need to show that when each place $p^n(i)$ has tokens there is no dead transition, for this state represents that each subnet C^n is waiting for a transition in $T_O(C^n)$ to fire so that the other transitions in the subnet can fire. In this state, there is a circuit C, such that the output transition t_i of $p^n(i)$ on C is process-enabled for any i. Assume that the input transition of p_0 on C is t_1 and the input place of t_1 is $p^n(1)$, then t_1 is process and resource-enabled and can fire. After the firing of t_1, the other transitions on C can fire one by one. Then we can fire the transitions in another circuit. By doing so, any transition in the simplified CROPN can fire again no matter what marking is reached, or the net is live. □

From Lemma 11.10, the following result is obvious.

Theorem 11.6: A CROPN is live if and only if it is controlled by the control law given in Theorem 11.5.

It is seen that if each subnet is live then the tokens in the system can flow from a subnet to another, then to place p_0. Thus, the key is to make each subnet live as we have done.

11.3.4 An Illustrative Example ·

Consider the CROPN in Figure 11.3. It contains three PPCs: $C_1 = \{u_1, t_{12}, u_2, t_{21}\}$, $C_2 = \{u_1, t_{13}, u_3, t_{31}\}$ and $C_3 = \{u_3, t_{34}, u_4, t_{43}\}$. These three PPCs form an interactive subnet C^3 and the input transition set of this interactive subnet is $T_I(C^3) = \{t_1(I), t_2(I)\}$. In the initial marking M_0 there are n tokens (parts) in place p_0 and the other places in the net are all empty.

We assume, without the loss of generality, that all the places other than p_0 have capacity of 1. According to the control law given in Theorem 11.5, at the initial marking M_0, both transitions $t_1(I)$ and $t_2(I)$ are process-, resource- and control-enabled and can fire. If, after the firing of some transitions, only place x_3 is empty, all the other places are full, the token in y_3 represents a type-1 part, the token in y_1 represents a type-2 part (operation 2 just completed) and enables both t_{12} and t_{13}, and the token in y_4 represents a type-3 part, then $t_1(I)$ is not resource- and control-enabled, and $t_2(I)$ is not control-enabled although it is process- and resource-enabled. Thus, in this marking, neither cannot fire to avoid deadlock. In this marking, both C_2 and C_3 are enabled. Hence, t_{13} or t_{43} can be selected to fire. If, however, the token in y_4 represents a type-1 part and enables $t_2(O)$, an output transition of the subnet, then $t_2(I)$ is control-enabled and can fire. In some time, the parts can be completed and leave the subnet, and then $t_1(I)$ and $t_2(I)$ can fire again.

From the example we can see that deadlock in a CROPN can be totally avoided if the control law given in Theorem 11.5 is used in real-time. By observing the state of the system, the control law controls the holding order of resources by the jobs/parts that compete for the resources.

11.4 AVOIDING DEADLOCK AND REDUCING STARVATION AND BLOCKING

The deadlock avoidance policy presented above is a maximally permissive control policy. Such policy allows releasing as many parts as possible into AMS. A new question arises whether it is an optimal policy in terms of production rate. We will show that it may not be under many practical environments. Thus, a new deadlock avoidance policy is developed to improve the performance.

11.4.1 A Simple Example

A simple example is taken to show that a maximally permissive deadlock avoidance policy can lead to undesired blocking situations in AMS. This motivates the study of a new control policy for efficient operation of AMS.

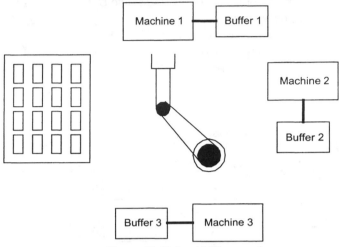

Figure 11.9. An AMS example.

Table 11.1. Operation sequences and processing time.

Operations / Part types	Operation 1		Operation 2		Operation 3	
	Machine	Time(h)	Machine	Time(h)	Machine	Time(h)
C	M_1	1.5	M_2	1	M_1	1.5
D	M_2	1	M_3	3	M_2	1

The AMS shown in Figure 11.9 contains three machines (M_{1-3}) and a robot as an MHS. Machines M_{1-3} have buffers B_{1-3} with capacity 1, 2, and 2, respectively. The capacity of a load/unload station can be considered as unlimited. The raw parts are delivered to the machines for processing from the load/unload station, and come back to the load/unload station after completed. Consider two types of jobs/parts, C and D, both having three operations. The sequences and processing times of these operations are shown in Table 11.1 where "h" means hours.

According to the processing times in Table 11.1, if the number of parts for either type is the same (assume that each part type has 10 parts to be processed), then the workload for each machine is also the same. In other words, this is a reasonable production plan. Now consider how the processing is carried out. Denote the load/unload station by L/U. According to the control law presented in the last section, the events that occur at time 0 to 5 are shown as follows where "processed" means that a machine completes an operation. Note that the subscript j in C_j and D_j is used to indicate the j-th part of C and D, respectively.

1. Time 0: C_1 in L/U $\to$ M_1, and D_1 in L/U $\to$ M_2;
2. Time 1: D_1 on M_2 (processed) $\to$ B_2 $\to$ M_3 and D_2 in L/U $\to$ M_2;
3. Time 1.5: C_1 on M_1 (processed) $\to$ B_1 and C_2 in L/U $\to$ M_1;
4. Time 2: D_2 on M_2 (processed) $\to$ B_2 and C_1 in B_1 $\to$ M_2;
5. Time 3: C_2 on M_1 (processed) $\to$ B_1, C_3 in L/U $\to$ M_1, C_1 on M_2 (processed) $\to$ B_2, and D_3 in L/U $\to$ M_2;
6. Time 4: D_1 on M_3 (processed) $\to$ B_3, D_2 in B_2 $\to$ M_3, D_3 on M_2 (completed) $\to$ B_2, and C_2 in B_1 $\to$ M_2;
7. Time 4.5: C_3 on M_1 (processed) $\to$ B_1 and C_4 in L/U $\to$ M_1;
8. Time 5: C_2 on M_2 is processed, but it cannot be unloaded.

Table 11.2. The state of resource assignment.

M/B	K	T0	T1	T1.5	T2	T3	T4	T4.5	T5
M_1	1	□C_1	□C_1	□C_2	□C_2	□C_3	□C_3	□C_4	□C_4
B_1	1			□C_1		□C_2		□C_3	□C_3
M_2	1	◆D_1	◆D_2	◆D_2	□C_1	◆D_3	□C_2	□C_2	□C_2
B_2	2				◆D_2	◆D_2□ C_1	◆D_3□C_1	◆D_3□C_1	◆D_3□C_1
M_3	1		◆D_1	◆D_1	◆D_1	◆D_1	◆D_2	◆D_2	◆D_2
B_3	2						◆D_1	◆D_1	◆D_1

Table 11.2 shows the resource assignment at different times where symbols □ and ◆ denote jobs C and D, respectively. It should be noted that a machine can process only one part at a time. In other words, each machine's capacity is one. From Table 11.2 we know that at time 5, only buffer 3 has an open space. All the other resources in AMS are occupied by jobs. According to the necessary and sufficient conditions presented in the last section, at this time the system does not have deadlock. But the part just completed at M_2 cannot be unloaded and delivered to B_2, i.e., it is "blocked." It is easy to verify that at time 6, the part completed on M_1 is also blocked. In fact, the part at M_2 can be unloaded into B_2 only after the part at M_3 is completed at time 7. This means that the blocking lasts for 2 hours.

It is known that if the deadlock avoidance policy is too conservative, the number of active parts allowed to be in a system may be too small, leading some machines into starvation, which results in lower resource utilization and productivity. This motivates one to find a maximally permissive control policy for deadlock avoidance to reduce starvation. But, from the above example, we know that when the number of active parts in the system is too large (although there is no deadlock), blocking may occur, affecting the resource utilization and productivity. Therefore, a good deadlock avoidance policy should take not only starvation, but also blocking into consideration, and make trade-offs between them. Fortunately, the deadlock boundary identified by the control policy presented above can be used to derive a control policy that keeps the state of the system close to the boundary, but not at the boundary. Thus it controls an AMS to achieve high productivity by reducing unnecessary starvation and blocking.

11.4.2 A Relaxed Control Policy

Consider the control policy derived from the necessary and sufficient condition for deadlock avoidance. It requires that there be at least one leaving token in every PPC. A leaving token in a PPC is not necessary to leave the PPC immediately even though the operation is completed. It may stay there and it takes a space in the PPC for some time. Although the system is not deadlocked, it is blocked for some time because there is no space to move the tokens in the PPC. Hence, if every PPC in CROPN keeps a space in any marking M reached from the initial marking, less blocking may happen, and at the same time it is not too conservative. In other words, by doing so, we keep a liveness margin for the system. The problem is whether such a control policy makes the interactive subnets in CROPN live. We will show that this is true as follows.

Denote the capacity of PPC C_i by $K(C_i)$. Let

$$S(C_i) = \sum_{p \in C_i} (K(p) - M(p))$$

be the number of free spaces available in C_i, and $S(p_i) = K(p_i) - M(p_i)$ the free spaces in p_i in marking M. Similarly, we use $S(C^n)$ to denote the free spaces in an interactive subnet C^n. In the following discussion, we assume that there are tokens in the interactive subnets, implying that there are parts to be processed.

Because of the existence of common places in C^n, when a free space is in one of the common places, this space is shared by all PPCs. To make C^n deadlock-free and reduce the blocking possibility, it may be better to keep a free space for each PPC in the subnet. A free space in a common chain can be allocated to any PPC that shares the common chain, but to one and only one PPC. Once it is allocated, it is called a nonshared space.

Definition 11.19: *L-condition* holds for PPC C and marking M if and only if there is at least one nonshared free space available in C at M.

Theorem 11.7: An interactive subnet C^n composed of n PPCs in a CROPN is live if L-condition holds for any marking $M \in R_c(M_0)$ and any PPC in C^n.

Proof: First we consider C^1 (or C), the case with n = 1. If $T_I(C) = \varnothing$ and $T_O(C) = \varnothing$, C is called an isolated PPC. Due to a finite number of nodes in a CROPN, C has a finite number of nodes. Obviously, an isolated PPC is live if the L-condition holds.

If $T_I(C) \neq \varnothing$ and $T_O(C) \neq \varnothing$, and assume that S(C) = 1 or the L-condition holds. In a marking M, if $T_O(C)$ is not enabled, then we can treat it as an isolated PPC, or C is not deadlocked. When $T_O(C)$ is enabled in a marking M, we can fire $T_O(C)$ and one token is removed from C, or L-condition still holds. Given the nature of manufacturing systems, in some time all the tokens can be removed from C in this way. When S(C) > 1 after some tokens are removed from C, we can fire

$T_I(C)$ to move some tokens into C, but control the times of firing $T_I(C)$ so that L-condition is not violated. Thus, if L-condition holds, C^1 is live.

Now we show that C^n is live with n being an arbitrary finite positive integer if L-condition holds. Assume that C_i is a PPC in C^n, let $P_{ns}(C_i) \subset P(C_i)$ be the set of places on C_i that are not shared with other PPCs, and $P_s(C_i) \subset P(C_i)$ be the set of places on C_i that are shared with other PPCs. Further we let p_h (p_r) denote the first (last) place on the common place chain. Assume that there are n free spaces in C^n or $S(C^n) = n$ and L-condition holds. If there are tokens in a common chain and $t_{io1} \subset T_{iok}$ on C_1 is enabled in marking M, then we can treat C_1 as an isolated PPC, and firing any transition on C_1 keeps L-condition satisfied. If the free space allocated to C_1 is in $P_s(C_1)$ and t_{io1} is not enabled, this time the input transition of p_h on C_1 can fire and the L-condition still holds. If there is no token in a common chain, then let C_D be the set of PPCs whose free spaces are in the common chain, where $D = \{1, 2, ..., k\}$ is an index set. We only need to forbid the firing of transitions t_{iik} with $k \in D$ that are associated with the common chain, and the other t_{iik} associated with the chain and in C_D can fire. Thus, some tokens can move to the common chain. If there are more than n free spaces in C^n, we only need to ensure that each PPC has a free space and the remaining free spaces can be used by any PPC; or we can fire some transitions $t \in T_I(C^n)$ and move some tokens into C^n. In this way, C^n is live.

When some transitions in $T_O(C^n)$ are enabled, we can fire them and some tokens are removed from C^n, this time $S(C^n) > n$. In some time, all the tokens in C^n can be removed from C^n and the transitions in $T_I(C^n)$ can fire. Therefore, in all the cases, C^n is live.   □

From Theorem 11.7, we know that to make an interactive subnet C^n in CROPN live, we have to control the number of tokens in the subnet and the firing order of its IITs. In the following discussion, we define the control policy called *L-policy* where C^n is composed of n PPCs in CROPN.

Definition 11.20: *L-policy* for C^n is a control policy under which 1) L-condition holds for any C in C^n after t's firing if $t \in T_I(C^n)$ is selected to fire; and 2) L-condition holds for any C in subnet C^{n-1} of C^n after an IIT's firing if it is external to C^{n-1} and selected to fire.

Theorem 11.8: An interactive subnet C^n in CROPN is live under L-policy.

According to Theorem 11.8, for C^n to be live, the transitions that need to be controlled are those in $T_I(C^n)$ and IITs. In fact, controlling the transitions in $T_I(C^n)$ controls the number of parts released to C^n. Controlling the IITs decides the holding order of a free resource when multiple parts compete for one resource in the sense of deadlock avoidance.

From Theorem 11.7, each PPC in an interactive subnet requires a nonshared space. Then, how many PPCs can a subnet formed by h machine primitives have, and how many free spaces are required? It can be shown that the number of possible PPCs is $c(h) = \sum_{k=2}^{h} h(h-1)\cdots(h-k+1)/k$. It is independent of the jobs and how they route. Let P(h) denote the set of places in such a subnet, and |P(h)| be the number of places in P(h). Then c(h)>|P(h)|, when h > 3. Thus, the number of free spaces required to make the subnet live may be greater than the capacity of the subnet if $K(p) = 1$ for every $p \in P$.

By Theorem 11.7, when a new PPC is added into C^n, one more space is required to guarantee the liveness of the resulting subnet. However, it may be the case that the resulting subnet is live even if no free space is added. The concept of independent and dependent PPC is proposed to characterize these two cases. In fact, only an independent PPC needs a nonshared free space.

Definition 11.21: Assume that C^k is composed of k PPCs in C^n with n > k. Let V_b be the set of the k PPCs in C^k and V_d the set of the other n - k PPCs in C^n. Suppose that C^n is live when L-policy for C^k applies. Then, all PPCs in V_d are said to be *dependent* on the PPCs in V_b.

The dependence of PPCs is closely related to the connection of places. If a place in a CROPN has two or more input transitions, we say that a *merger* is formed. If a place has two or more output transitions, then a *choice* is formed. The interaction of PPCs in an interactive subnet forms the mergers and choices. The mergers and choices divide the connected places into a number of segments that are called place chains, denoted by CH. Given a PPC and the places p_1, p_2, ..., p_i, p_{i+1}, ..., and p_k on it, suppose that p_{i+1}, ..., and p_k are the only common places shared by another PPC. Then two place chains are p_1- p_i and p_{i+1}- p_k. Clearly, the common places of two PPCs form one place chain, e.g., x_2y_2 in Figure 11.11 (a). If p_1, p_2, ..., p_i, p_{i+1}, ..., and p_k are the common places of C_1 and C_2, and p_{i+1}, ..., p_k are the common places of C_1, C_2 and C_3, then we have two different chains: $CH_1 = p_1$-p_i and $CH_2 = p_{i+1}$-p_k. We have the following theorem for an interactive subnet with dependent PPCs.

Theorem 11.9: In a subnet C^{n+r}, r (>0) PPCs are dependent on the other n (>0) PPCs that form C^n without r dependent PPCs if there are n + 1 place chains in the subnet C^{n+r} and each PPC contains at least two place chains.

Proof: It is sufficient to show that C^{n+r} is live when there are only n spaces in it. Distribute these n spaces such that each chain has one space for arbitrary n chains. Because each PPC contains at least two chains and only one chain has no space, we assert that each PPC has one nonshared space in every subnet C^n that contains all the places. Since each PPC contains at least two chains, no chain in the subnet forms a circuit. Thus, each transition of the output transitions of the last place p_r on a chain is an input transition of the first place p_h on another chain. The transitions on the chains are not controlled, so they can fire spontaneously. Therefore, a space in a chain can move into the first place p_h on the chain automatically. Consider the chain that has no space and denote it by CH_1. Assume that there are transitions of IITs in the output transitions of the last place p_r on CH_1 and one of them, say t, is process-enabled. It is sure that the output place p (the first place on another place chain) of t has a space, or it is resource-enabled. Meanwhile all PPCs that contain p have at least two free spaces because there are at least two spaces in every PPC that does not contain chain CH_1. Assume that this place is on

CH_2. Then fire t to move a space from CH_2 to CH_1. If there is no transition of IITs in the output transitions of the last place on CH_1 or no such transition is process-enabled, then there must be a transition that is not an IIT and is process-enabled. This transition can fire spontaneously, allowing a space to move to chain CH_1 from the next chain. It is clear that the condition guaranteeing a live subnet is unchanged after the firing of a transition under L-policy for C^n. In this way every transition can fire no matter what marking $M \in R_c(M_0)$ is reached, or C^{n+r} is live. $\square$

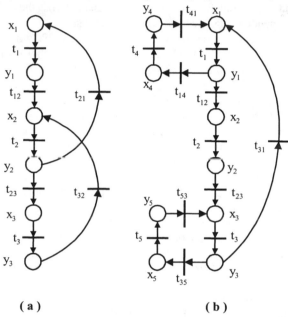

(a)   (b)

Figure 11.11. Interactive subnets in CROPN.

To make C^{n+r} live, each PPC in C^n must have at least one nonshared free space and meanwhile each dependent PPC must share at least one space with those n PPCs in C^n. This implies that to control an interactive subnet with dependent PPCs, L-policy should be applied to the subnet composed of the independent PPCs such that every dependent PPC shares at least one space with an independent PPC. Definition 11.21 and Theorem 11.9 present a criterion to identify dependent ones in an interactive subnet.

Since C^2 always contains three place chains, two PPCs in it are always independent of each other. For example, in Figure 11.11(b) the three place chains are: $CH_1 = \{x_1, t_1, y_1\} = u_1$, $CH_2 = \{x_2, t_2, y_2\} = u_2$ and $CH_3 = \{x_3, t_3, y_3\} = u_3$. A single PPC interactive subnet has only one place chain.

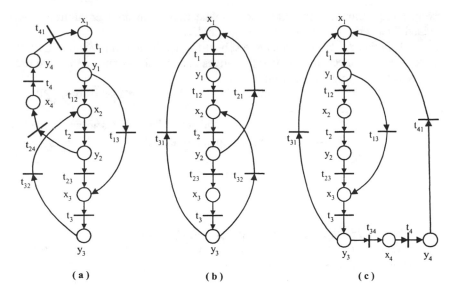

Figure 11.12. Subnets with a dependent PPC.

Figure 11.12 shows three examples of interactive subnets with a dependent PPC. In Figure 11.12(a) let $V_b = \{C_1, C_2\}$, $C_1 = \{u_1, t_{12}, u_2, t_{24}, u_4, t_{41}\}$, $C_2 = \{u_2, t_{23}, u_3, t_{32}\}$, $C = \{u_1, t_{13}, u_3, t_{32}, u_2, t_{24}, u_4, t_{41}\}$, and three place chains are: $CH_1 = \{u_4, t_{41}, u_1\}$, $CH_2 = \{u_2\}$ and $CH_3 = \{u_3\}$. For Figure 11.12(b) let $V_b = \{C_1, C_2\}$, $C_1 = \{u_1, t_{12}, u_2, t_{21}\}$, $C_2 = \{u_2, t_{23}, u_3, t_{32}\}$, $C = \{u_1, t_{12}, u_2, t_{23}, u_3, t_{31}\}$, and three place chains are: $CH_1 = \{u_1\}$, $CH_2 = \{u_2\}$ and $CH_3 = \{u_3\}$. In Figure 11.12(c), let $V_b = \{C_1, C_2, C_3\}$, $C_1 = \{u_1, t_{12}, u_2, t_{23}, u_3, t_{34}, u_4, t_{41}\}$, $C_2 = \{u_1, t_{13}, u_3, t_{31}\}$ and $C_3 = \{u_1, t_{12}, u_2, t_{23}, u_3, t_{31}\}$, $C = \{u_1, t_{13}, u_3, t_{34}, u_4, t_{41}\}$, and four place chains are: $CH_1 = \{u_1\}$, $CH_2 = \{u_2\}$, $CH_3 = \{u_3\}$ and $CH_4 = \{u_4\}$. In these three subnets every PPC contains at least two place chains. Therefore, for all the three cases, the conditions in Theorem 11.9 are satisfied, and thus C is dependent on the others.

Now consider three examples shown in Figure 11.13. In Figures 11.13(a) and (b), there are three PPCs and four place chains and every PPC contains at least two place chains. In Figure 11.13(c) there are three PPCs and two place chains. But $C_1 = \{u_1, t_{12}, u_2, t_{21}\}$ and $C_2 = \{u_3, t_{34}, u_4, t_{43}\}$ each contains only one chain. Hence there is no dependent PPC in any of these cases. In fact, in Figure 11.13(c), C_1 and C_2 cannot form an interactive subnet C^2 although all three PPCs form C^3.

Note that non-elementary PPCs must be dependent on the elementary PPCs in C^n. Besides, an elementary one may be a dependent one, e.g., C in Figure 11.12.

Up until now we have presented the dependency of PPCs in an interactive subnet. The question is how many independent PPCs an interactive subnet formed by h primitives can have. The following study of completely connected C^n answers the question and provides the absolute maximum number of free spaces needed for a general interactive subnet to stay live.

Definition 11.22: An interactive subnet formed by h primitives in a CROPN is completely connected if any two primitives u_i and u_j are connected by two transitions, t_{ij} from u_i to u_j, and t_{ji} from u_j to u_i.

Let $V(C^n)$ be the set of all the PPCs in C^n. We define a set of basic PPCs in an interactive subnet as follows.

Definition 4.5: A set V_b of PPCs is the set of basic PPCs in an interactive subnet C^n if any PPC $C \in V(C^n) - V_b$ is dependent on V_b, and no PPC in V_b is dependent on the others in V_b.

Denote by G_h a completely connected interactive subnet formed by h primitives in CROPN. G_3 is shown in Figure 11.14. Its five elementary PPCs are: $C_1 = \{u_1, t_{12}, u_2, t_{21}\}$, $C_2 = \{u_2, t_{23}, u_3, t_{32}\}$, $C_3 = \{u_1, t_{13}, u_3, t_{31}\}$, $C_4 = \{u_1, t_{13}, u_3, t_{32}, u_2, t_{21}\}$ and $C_5 = \{u_1, t_{12}, u_2, t_{23}, u_3, t_{31}\}$. Let $V_b = \{C_1, C_2\}$ and $|V_b|=2$ for G_3.

Theorem 11.10: In G_h, let $C_1 = \{u_1, t_{12}, u_2, t_{21}\}$, $C_2 = \{u_2, t_{23}, u_3, t_{32}\}$, ..., $C_{h-1} = \{u_{h-1}, t_{h-1, h}, u_h, t_{h, h-1}\}$, and $V_b = \{C_1, C_2, ..., C_{h-1}\}$. V_b is a basic set of PPCs in a completely connected subnet G_h in a CROPN.

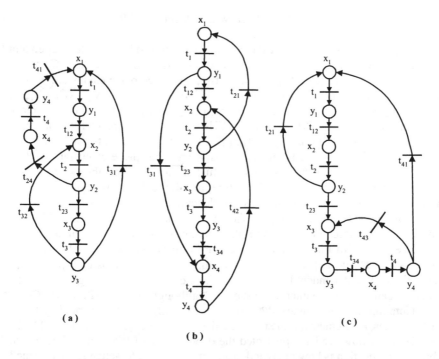

(a)

(b)

(c)

Figure 11.13. Subnets without dependent PPC.

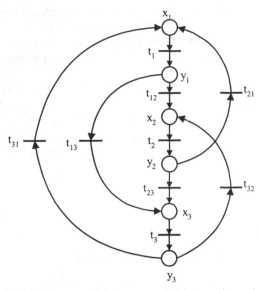

Figure 11.14. The completely connected interactive subnet G_3.

Proof: It is clear that PPCs in V_b are not dependent on each other. Let $F(G_h)$ = $H(u_1) + H(u_2) + ... + H(u_h)$, and C^{h-1} be composed of the PPCs in V_b. If $F(G_h) = h$ - 1, then the condition in Theorem 11.7 is satisfied for C^{h-1}. Assume that $H(u_h) = 0$ and $F(u_i) = 1$, $i = 1, 2, ..., h-1$, then according to Theorem 11.8, one of the output transitions t_{hi} ($i = 1, 2, ..., n-1$) of u_h can fire, for there are two spaces in every two-primitive PPC which does not contain u_h. Assume that t_{hk} is fired. Then there is at least one space in each primitive except u_k, and thus every output transition of u_k is enabled by the control policy (or control enabled). In this way, at any time, there are at least $h-1$ spaces distributed in at least $h-1$ primitives. Thus, there exists at least one primitive whose output transitions are enabled by the control policy. Any one of the enabled transitions can be chosen to fire. By choosing a different enabled transition to fire, we choose a different primitive whose output transitions are to be enabled in the next step. Therefore, every transition can fire in finite steps no matter what marking is reached, and this process can repeat endlessly. This means that G_h is live. Therefore, V_b is a basic set of PPCs in G_h. □

The theorem implies that all other PPCs in G_h are dependent on V_b. G_h has the highest number of PPCs among all interactive subnets in a CROPN formed by h primitives, and $|V_b| = h-1$. By Theorem 11.10, it needs $h-1$ free spaces to make G_h live. Therefore, it needs no more than $h-1$ free spaces to make a live interactive subnet involving h primitives. Each primitive contains two places. Thus an interactive subnet formed by h primitives has $2h$ places and its capacity is at least $2h$. Therefore, we can have at least $2h-(h-1) =h+1$ tokens representing parts in it. This shows that L-policy causes no deadlock and can allow sufficient parts in AMS for high productivity. G_h contains h place chains and each place chain is formed by a machine primitive. Then, we have the following corollary:

Corollary 11.4: For an AMS composed of h primitives (machines), if at any time there are $h - 1$ free spaces that are distributed in $h - 1$ different primitives, the system is deadlock-free.

In the existing techniques for deadlock avoidance, e.g., [17], the part types to be processed and their routes (with routing flexibility or not) should be known in advance, and thus a deterministic model can be built. By Corollary 11.4, to make the system live, it is not necessary to have such information and the part types and their routes can be changed on-line. Furthermore, using Corollary 11.4 no circuits need to be identified.

It should be pointed out that although we discuss the deadlock avoidance policy by assuming that there is a buffer for each machine, or the resources have multiple capacity, the control policy is a correct deadlock avoidance control policy for the systems with single-capacity resources.

11.4.3 Complexity in Applying the Control Law

The presented policy tells the controller what states should be avoided by disabling some transitions. To implement it, we need to build the model and identify the PPCs if the jobs/parts and their routes are known (if these are not known, we can use the control policy presented by Corollary 11.4 and no PPCs need to be identified). Although this is not trivial, it can be done off-line. After the PPCs are identified, for the teal-time control we need only to check the free spaces in the PPCs. The next question is how many PPCs one needs to check in real-time for a subnet formed by h primitives.

We analyze the complexity by considering the completely connected interactive subnet G_h. In G_h any two primitives (machines) u_i and u_j with i, j= 1, $\cdots$, h and $i \neq j$ form a PPC, denoted by C_{ij}. Let $V_H = \{C_{ij}\}$ be the set of all such PPCs. For example, in G_3 shown in Figure 11.14, there are five elementary PPCs: $C_{12} = \{u_1, t_{12}, u_2, t_{21}\}$, $C_{23} = \{u_2, t_{23}, u_3, t_{32}\}$, $C_{13} = \{u_1, t_{13}, u_3, t_{31}\}$, $C_4 = \{u_1, t_{13}, u_3, t_{32}, u_2, t_{21}\}$ and $C_5 = \{u_1, t_{12}, u_2, t_{23}, u_3, t_{31}\}$, and $V_H = \{C_{12}, C_{23}, C_{13}\}$. It is easy to observe that $P(C_{12}) \cup P(C_{23}) \cup \cdots \cup P(C_{h1}) = P(G_h)$ and $T(C_{12}) \cup T(C_{23}) \cup \cdots \cup T(C_{h1}) = T(G_h)$. This means that the set of places (transitions) in V_H contains all the places (transitions) in G_h. By applying the control law presented above, if we check all the PPCs in V_H then we guarantee that all the transitions in V_H are live, or G_h is live. Thus, we only need to check the PPCs in V_H instead of all the elementary PPCs in G_h in applying the control law. In fact, in G_h, if every PPC in V_b has a nonshared space and every PPC in $V_H - V_b$ has a shared space, then all other PPCs in G_h have a shared space. This is why we need to check only the PPCs in V_H. The number of PPCs in V_H is $|V_H| = \dfrac{h(h-1)}{2}$, or the computational complexity is $o(h^2)$ in real-time control. Notice that G_h has the highest number of PPCs in an interactive subnet formed by h primitives and the complexity of implementing this control law is from the number of PPCs to be checked. Hence, we only need to trace the V_b and V_H and at most $|V_H|$ PPCs need to be checked in real-time in any subnet formed by h primitives. Therefore, the complexity is $o(h^2)$ in applying the proposed control law, although the number of PPCs in a subnet formed by h primitives is exponential with respect to h.

11.4.4 Performance Improvement through Examples

So far, we have shown deadlock-free operation of an AMS under the L-policy, but not its performance improvement. In this section we show the performance improvement by the proposed control policy through two examples.

Example 11.1. The system is shown in Section 11.4.1. It is shown that the L-policy completely eliminates the blocking, ending with 11-hour cycle time. Under the maximally permissive policy, blocking can occur if a C-part is loaded at time 4.5, leading to 13-hour cycle time. The throughput improvement using L-policy is more than 15%.

Example 11.2. The system below has four machines and needs to deal with flexible routes. Products, routes, and average operation hours in the parentheses are as follows:

Product A:
Route 1: m1 (8), m3 (10), m4 (6), or
Route 2: m1 (8), m3 (10), m1 (8)
Product B:
Route 1: m3 (5), m1 (12), m3 (6), m4 (15), or
Route 2: m3 (5), m1 (12), m2 (18), m1 (3)
Product C: m3 (5), m4 (10), m3 (5)

The uniform distribution [0.9x, 1.1x] is assumed where x is the average operation time shown above. We tested both random and shortest-processing-time-first dispatching rules under the maximally permissive policy and L-policy. A number of randomly selected part mixes were tested. The smallest one has part types A, B and C, each having 100 parts. The largest set has 2000 parts of A, 1000 of B and 1000 of C. The results of the system throughput, blocking and starvation of Machine 3 are shown in Figure 11.15 for L-policy and the maximally permissive policy. All the cases show that the L-policy outperforms the maximally permissive policy on the average more than 10% in throughput. Similar throughput gains were obtained when we randomized all the operation times and sequences. With the L-policy, all machines are significantly less likely to be blocked (around 10%), but there is a small increase in starvation (3%).

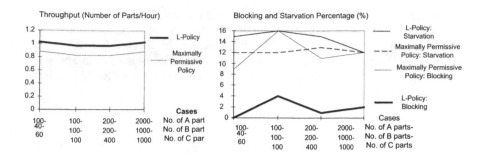

Figure 11.15.   System throughput, Machine 3's blocking and starvation under two policies.

11.5 DEADLOCK AVOIDANCE IN MANUFACTURING PROCESS WITH SHARED MHS

In the last two sections, we have discussed deadlock avoidance policy in manufacturing processes without considering MHS. However, if MHS is a shared resource in these processes, deadlock may occur due to the competition for the MHS. In this section, we will show that if the process of the material handling is properly modeled and the control policies presented in the last two sections are applied, then deadlock will be avoided.

11.5.1 Deadlock Situations

First we show the deadlock situations in the manufacturing processes with MHS considered. Consider the PN models for manufacturing processes shown in Figure 11.16. The material handling process by an MHS is modeled as shown in Figure 11.4. While p represents a robot or an AGV, a token in p_1 or p_2 represents the robot or AGV delivering a part from a machine (buffer) to another. We assume, without the loss of generality, that all the places except p_0 can hold only one part at a time. In Figure 11.16(a), there is no PPC. Hence, if we do not consider the material handling process, there is no deadlock at all. In the marking shown in Figure 11.16, the MHS is delivering a part from y_1 to x_2. At the same time, x_2 is full and the MHS can be released only when the part in y_2 is removed. However, the part in y_2 can be removed only when the MHS is released. Thus, the system is deadlocked because of the competition for the MHS.

In Figure 11.16(b), there is a PPC $C = \{x_1, t_2, y_1, t_3, x_2, t_4, y_2, t_5, p_2, t_8\}$. Hence, potential deadlocks exist. In PPC C, p_2 models if the MHS is busy. It cannot be treated as a space in C even though p_2 is empty. In the marking shown in Figure 11.16(b), we assume that the part in y_2 should be delivered to x_1 for further processing while x_1 is empty. Thus C is not in a deadlock state if the MHS is not taken into consideration. However, the MHS is delivering a part from p_0 to x_1. In this state, if the part in p_1 is loaded to x_1, C is deadlocked. If not, the MHS cannot be released. Thus, the system is also deadlocked.

By this observation, it is not sufficient to guarantee deadlock-free operation in manufacturing processes by the control policies presented in the last two sections if the MHS is considered. However, by properly modeling the material handling process, the manufacturing process is indeed deadlock-free if the policies presented in the last two sections are applied.

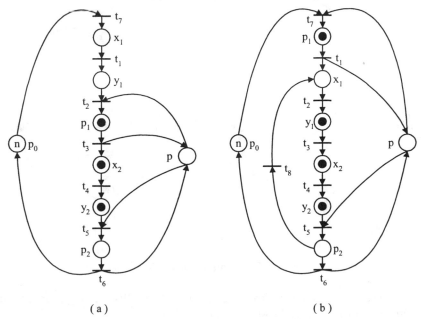

(a)   (b)

Figure 11.16. Deadlock situations with MHS considered.

11.5.2 Deadlock Avoidance with Shared MHS

Consider the deadlock situation shown in Figure 11.16(a), the key point is that transition t_3 is not resource-enabled. This means that to avoid deadlock, the MHS cannot pick the part in y_1 up. However, with the PN model shown in Figure 11.16(a), only if there is a token in y_1 and the MHS is free (a token in p), transition t_2 is process and resource-enabled. This implies that t_2 can fire and a deadlock occurs. The situation shown in Figure 11.16(b) is similar.

To avoid the deadlocks caused by shared MHS, one may develop a new control policy. Instead of doing so, we attempt to improve the modeling of the material handling process by taking the advantage of deadlock avoidance policies presented in Sections 11.3 and 11.4. We use the model for the material handling process presented in Section 11.2.4 and this model is added to the CROPN for a

manufacturing process. To do that is to add a place p representing the MHS, with
a token in it and the number of arcs into the CROPN such that p and some transitions in the CROPN form a number of self-loops. By doing so, the resultant PN is
called augmented CROPN (ACROPN). Because there is no self-loop in the
CROPN, all the self-loops in an ACROPN are associated with p. The ACROPNs
are obtained from Figure 11.16 by changing the model of material handling process, as shown in Figure 11.17. We will show that an ACROPN is live if it is controlled by one of the control policies presented before.

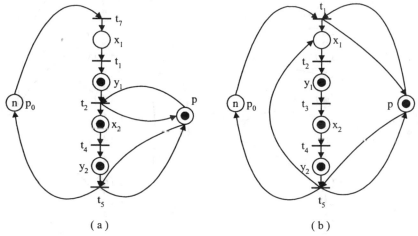

(a)   (b)

Figure 11.17. The augmented CROPNs.

Lemma 11.11: If the original CROPN of an ACROPN is a single circuit and
this circuit is not a PPC, the ACROPN is always live.

Proof: By assumption the circuit in the original CROPN is not a PPC.
Hence, place p_0 is on the circuit, and this place is never to be full. We first show
that the net is live when there is only one self-loop associated with place p assuming that transition t is on the self-loop.

To show the liveness of the net is to show that all the transitions in the net
can fire again no matter what marking is reached. Note that in a circuit if one transition can fire again in a marking then all the transitions on the circuit can fire
again in some way. Now we show that t on the circuit can fire again in any reachable marking. To do so, it only needs to show that in any marking, t can fire after a
sequence of firings of other transitions. Assume that places $p_1 = {}^\bullet t$ and $p_2 = t^\bullet$ are
the input and output places of t in the original CROPN, respectively. Then in any
marking t is in one of the following states: (1) there is a token in p_1 and p_2 is
empty; (2) p_1 is empty and p_2 is full; (3) both p_1 and p_2 are full; (4) both p_1 and p_2
are empty. In state 1, t can fire immediately because there is always a token in p,
unless t is in firing. In state 2, we can start from p_2 and go in the direction of the

circuit and check the state of each place on the path. We can find some places which have spaces available because p_0 is never full. Assume that the first place found with a space available is p_3, then the input transition t_1 of p_3 can fire and this makes the input place of t_1 empty. Therefore, after a number of firings of transitions, p_2 will become empty. Similarly, if we start from p_1 and go in the opposite direction of the circuit, we will find a place with a token. Therefore, after several firings of transitions, this token will go into p_1. Hence, t goes into state 1. In states 3 and 4 p_2 can be made empty and p_1 can be made full in a similar way, or state 1 can be reached from both states. Thus, we have shown that the net is live.

Now we show that the net is live when there are multiple self-loops, or p has several self-loops with several transitions on the circuit. Let T_r denote the set of these transitions. If $t \in T_r$ is enabled in the original CROPN, then t can fire in the ACROPN because there is a token in p. If several transitions, say a transition set $T_1 \subset T_r$, are enabled in the original CROPN simultaneously, then one of these transition, say t_1, can be chosen to fire. After firing t_1, a token goes back into p, and then another one in T_1 can be chosen to fire. By doing so, all the transitions in T_1 can fire one by one. This implies that once a transition is enabled in the original CROPN, the transition can fire sooner or later in the ACROPN. Therefore, any transition on the circuit can be made enabled in the original CROPN in any marking M after a sequence of firings of transitions in the ACROPN. This means that the net is live. □

It follows from Section 11.3 that if there is no PPC in a CROPN, a transition can fire when it is both process- and resource-enabled. By Lemma 11.11, no more condition is needed to avoid deadlock in ACROPN.

Theorem 11.11: If there is no PPC in the original CROPN of an augmented CROPN, the augmented CROPN is always live.

Proof: By assumption there is no PPC in the original CROPN of the augmented CROPN. The original CROPN must be formed by several parallel circuits with place p_0 as their common place. If the self-loops of p connect p with only one of the circuits, then it follows from Lemma 11.11 that the net is live. Now we show that the net is live when the self-loops of p connect p with k (k > 1) circuits. Let T_r denote the set of transitions which are on the self-loops with $T_1 \subset T_r$, $T_2 \subset T_r$, ..., and $T_k \subset T_r$ on circuits C_1, C_2, ..., and C_k, respectively. If several transitions in T_r, say two transitions $t_1 \in T_1$ and $t_2 \in T_2$, are enabled in the original CROPN, then t_1 on C_1 can be chosen to fire first, for there is a token in p. After t_1's firing, the token in p before its firing comes back into p. This time t_2 on C_2 can fire. This means that once the transitions in T_r are enabled in the original CROPN, they can fire one by one, no matter which circuit they are on. Because place p_0 is on all the circuits, in any marking M every transition can be made enabled in the original CROPN after a sequence of transition firing. Hence, the net is live. □

Theorem 11.11 means that an ACROPN is live if the original CROPN is free of PPC. We next show that an ACROPN with PPCs is live if it is under control by one of the policies presented in Sections 11.3 and 11.4.

Theorem 11.12: If the original CROPN of an ACROPN is an interactive subnet, the ACROPN is live if ACROPN is controlled by one of the deadlock avoidance policies presented in Sections 11.3 and 11.4.

Proof: It follows from the discussion in Sections 11.3 and 11.4 that if the original CROPN of an ACROPN is an interactive subnet and is controlled by one of the deadlock avoidance policies presented in Sections 11.3 and 11.4, then each transition in the subnet can fire again in any reachable marking. We say a transition is enabled in the original subnet if the transition can fire under the control of the applied policy. When a transition that is not on any self-loops of p is enabled in the sense of control policy in the original subnet and needs to fire, this transition can fire immediately in the ACROPN. If a transition that is on a self-loop of p is enabled in the original subnet and needs to fire, and at the same time the token in p is not being used for firing other transitions, the transition can be chosen to fire immediately by allocating the token in p to this transition first. When a transition is enabled in the original subnet and the token in p is being used by another transition, the transition can fire when the token comes back into p and becomes available. Such firings have no effect on the distribution of tokens in the original CROPN, or do not cause additional deadlocks. Hence, the ACROPN is live. □

As shown in Section 11.3, if every interactive subnet under control is live, then the overall system is live. Thus, from Theorem 11.12, an ACROPN is live if it is controlled by one of the deadlock avoidance policies presented in Sections 11.3 and 11.4.

11.6 DEADLOCK AVOIDANCE IN AGV SYSTEMS WITH UNI-DIRECTIONAL PATHS

As pointed out previously, we have two types of deadlocks in operating AMS. One is caused by the competition by parts for such manufacturing resources as machines, buffers and MHS. It occurs during the part processing. The other type is due to the competition for nodes and lanes by AGVs when multiple AGVs are used in MHS. In Sections 11.3, 11.4 and 11.5, we present deadlock avoidance policies for the manufacturing processes by using the CROPN. Now we discuss the deadlock avoidance problem in AGV systems by using CROPN.

In a manufacturing process, to improve the productivity and resource utilization, it is desired to have as many parts as possible in a system. However, the more parts are in AMS, the more likely the system is deadlocked. The parts need to be delivered from a station to another by MHS. Often, only a few AGVs are available in an AGV system mainly due to their high cost and easily satisfied transportation demand. The total number of AGVs likely remains constant. On the other hand, the following three differences lead to a more challenging deadlock control problem for AGVs:

1.   All AGVs always stay in the system. Parts in AMS are assumed to enter and depart the system after their completion. It is feasible to release only

a part to the system for processing, but it is infeasible to let only one AGV stay in the system if there are multiple AGVs. For example, applying the policies proposed in [34] to some AGV systems may allow only one AGV in such a system, making them infeasible.

2. While the route of each part type in AMS is often known in advance, the routes of an AGV frequently change based on real-time transportation requests. Hence, the policies obtained for handling the first type of deadlock requiring known routes become difficult to apply because of, primarily, their computational requirements, e.g., [13, 18, 26].

3. Finally, in AGV systems a lane and a node may hold one and only one AGV. This leads to a single-capacity resource system, invalidating many elegant deadlock policies that require multiple capacity resources, e.g., [13, 18].

Therefore, effective policies for avoiding deadlocks in AGV systems are necessary; and some work has been done [21-25, 35, 36]. Here we present a new approach.

11.6.1 Modeling AGV Systems with Unidirectional Paths by CROPN

The most widely used technique for vehicle management of AGV systems is zone control. Guided paths are divided into several disjoint zones. A zone can accommodate only one AGV at a time. Thus, an AGV system is a single-capacity system. Each zone (or node) can be treated as a resource with capacity 1 and can be modeled by the PN model shown in Figure 11.2.

An AGV system is composed of AGVs and built paths. Often, a zone contains a workstation or an intersection. Thus, we may refer to a zone as a node. There are lanes between workstations (intersections) and they form the paths. The configuration of an AGV system is determined by the configuration of the paths. Since the lanes are built in advance and cannot be changed often, the configuration of an AGV system is relatively static. In an AGV system with unidirectional paths, an AGV can go in the given direction on any lane, in other words, for any lane the direction is determined in advance. An AGV system with unidirectional paths adapted from [36] is shown in Figure 11.18. This AGV system contains six workstations, four intersections and four AGVs. It is divided into 10 zones, each containing a workstation or an intersection.

In modeling the manufacturing processes of parts, the CROPN is obtained by modeling the part flows based on the known part routes. In an AGV system, the routes of AGVs change dynamically, but the configuration of the system cannot be changed. Thus, we can obtain the CROPN for the AGV system with unidirectional paths by modeling the zones (nodes) as places and the directed lanes as transitions. In this way, the CROPN for the AGV system shown in Figure 11.18 can be obtained as shown in Figure 11.19.

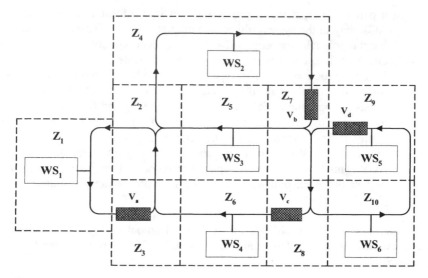

Figure 11.18. The configuration of an AGV system with unidirectional paths.

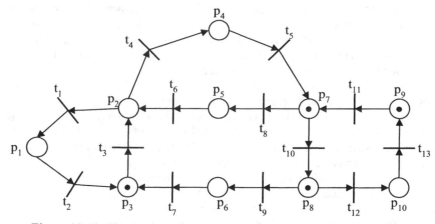

Figure 11.19. The CROPN for an AGV system with unidirectional paths.

With the structure of the obtained CROPN, it is easy to model the routes of AGVs in the system. When an AGV is assigned a mission to fulfill, it starts from a zone, goes through a number of zones, and finally reaches its destination according to the paths in the CROPN. Thus, through the token colors in the CROPN, the routes of AGVs are well modeled.

11.6.2 Deadlock Avoidance Policy

In manufacturing processes, when a part is competed and removed from the system, it does not affect the processing of other parts in the system. However, when an AGV gets to its destination and a mission is completed, the AGV may stay here and block other AGVs. To avoid this situation, we assume that when an AGV gets to its destination, it can be asked to travel to another zone if necessary.

In manufacturing processes, it is reasonable to assume that at the beginning there is no part in the system. In an AGV system we cannot take the AGVs out of the system. Thus, it is important that the system is initially live. In an AGV system, the location and route for an AGV change dynamically. Thus, the terminal state of one mission affects the initial state of the next mission. Here, we focus on the deadlock avoidance policy and we always assume that the system is initially live. To make the CROPN for an AGV system live, some necessary condition must be satisfied.

Lemma 11.12: Let K(P) denote the number of places (the number of zones) in the CROPN model. If the CROPN model for the AGV system is initially live in marking M_0, the number of tokens (the number of AGVs in the system) must be less than K(P).

The condition given in Lemma 11.12 is a necessary condition to make the CROPN of an AGV system live. In fact, it is always satisfied. Often, only a few AGVs are available in an AGV system mainly due to their high cost and easily satisfied transportation demand.

As discussed before, the circuits in a CROPN play a key role in generating deadlock. In the CROPN of manufacturing processes, only PPCs can be deadlocked since place p_0 has the infinite capacity. In the CROPN of an AGV system, every place represents a single-capacity resource. Thus, every circuit may be a potential deadlock source. The deadlock avoidance policy presented in Section 11.4 can be applied in single-capacity system. Hence, we have:

Theorem 11.13: The CROPN for an AGV system with unidirectional paths is live if every circuit C_i in it has at least one nonshared space in any marking M.

In general, the number of AGVs in the system is much less than the number of zones because of the easily satisfied transportation demand. Furthermore, because of the high cost and space required, the lanes are very limited. Thus, often there are no enough AGVs to occupy all the zones in two circuits, and there is no dependent circuit. Therefore, we can apply the deadlock avoidance policy presented in Section 11.4 in the simplest way as stated in Theorem 11.13.

As a simple example, we use the simple PN shown in Figure 11.20 to show how this policy is applied to the single-capacity system. It is shown that the maximally permissive control policy is computationally intractable for a single-capacity system [37]. In Figure 11.20, if there is only one free space, the system may be deadlocked. For example, suppose that only place p_2 is empty (the two circuits share the only free space) and the token in p_4 needs to go to p_3. When t_4 fires, the token in p_2 enables t_3, resulting in a deadlock. This state is identified in

[17] as the so-called second-level deadlock. However, by applying the presented policy, two free spaces are required. As shown in Figure 11.20, we can first fire t_2 and t_5. Then the token in p_4 can finally reach p_3 by firing t_1, t_4 and t_3. It is the requirement for no sharing of an empty space among circuits that makes the token in p_2 in Figure 11.20 able to go to any circuit in the net, guaranteeing a live net.

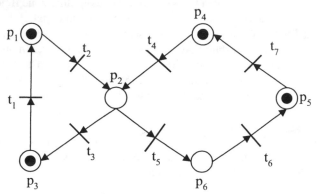

Figure 11.20. A simple CROPN formed by single capacity resources.

11.6.3 Computational Complexity

The AGV deadlock control problem is an NP-hard problem as pointed out in [36]. Hence, it is meaningful to analyze the complexity of the control law used here. From discussion above, we know that we need only to observe the state of the system on-line, calculate $S(C_i)$ for every C_i, and control the transitions in $T_l(C_i)$ through a one-step look-ahead policy.

The main difficulty in implementing the control law is the identification of the circuits in a PN model for an AGV system. However, this can be done off-line, since the configuration of an AGV system is known in advance and will not change often. Of course, theoretically the number of circuits may be exponential to the number of zones, but we do not need to identify and calculate $S(C_i)$ for all the circuits; we need to do that only for the elementary circuits. Furthermore, an AGV can travel only on the built paths, and the guided paths are very limited due to the high cost and space. Hence, in general, the number of circuits in a real AGV system is limited. Thus, it is expected that for a real AGV system, the number of circuits underlying its physical configuration and the number of circuits to be controlled will not be too large. For example, in the PN model shown in Figure 11.19, four circuits are identified: $C_1 = \{p_1, t_2, p_3, t_3, p_2, t_1, p_1\}$, $C_2 = \{p_7, t_{10}, p_8, t_{12}, p_{10}, t_{13}, p_9, t_{11}, p_7\}$, $C_3 = \{p_2, t_4, p_4, t_5, p_7, t_8, p_5, t_6, p_2\}$, and $C_4 = \{p_2, t_4, p_4, t_5, p_7, t_{10}, p_8, t_9, p_6, t_7, p_3, t_3, p_2\}$. In fact, the problem can be simplified further. According to the control law presented in the last subsection, we have the following result.

Theorem 11.14: A deadlock can occur in circuit C_i, only if the capacity of C_i, $K(C_i)$, is less than or equal to the number of AGVs in the system.

Theorem 11.14 presents the necessary condition for deadlock to occur. Thus, it is only necessary to identify the circuits that meet the condition given by Theorem 11.14 and control (calculate $S(C_i)$) only these circuits. For example, as shown in Figure 11.19, these circuits are C_1, C_2 and C_3, and only transitions t_3, t_6, t_7, t_5 and t_{11} need to be controlled. Considering the limited number of AGVs, there will be a limited number of circuits that satisfy the condition given in Theorem 11.14. In conclusion, it is expected that the proposed control algorithm will be implementable in real-time in many practical AGV configurations.

11.7 DEADLOCK AVOIDANCE IN AGV SYSTEMS WITH BIDIREC-TIONAL PATHS

Compared with an AGV system with unidirectional paths, the system with bidirectional paths is more efficient and cost-effective as pointed out in [38] but more complex to manage. In unidirectional systems, the resources to be competed for by AGVs are only the zones. In bidirectional systems, the resources to be competed for include both zones and lanes. This makes the conflict and deadlock avoidance in such systems more complicated.

11.7.1 Modeling the AGV System with Bidirectional Paths by CROPN

In an AGV system with unidirectional paths discussed in Section 11.6, we model a zone (node) by a place, and a lane by a transition. Notice that a transition models only one direction. However, in a bidirectional path system, an AGV can travel on a lane in both directions. Thus, we model a lane (a path between two adjacent nodes) by two transitions with different directions as shown in Figure 11.21. A token representing an AGV can flow from p_1 to p_2 by firing t_1 or p_2 to p_1 by firing t_2, implying that the lane is assigned to an AGV from p_1 to p_2 or p_2 to p_1. Note that when p_1 and p_2 are both marked, none of the transitions is enabled according to the enabling condition (11.2), thereby avoiding any collision on the lane. If a lane is one-way, e.g., from p_1 to p_2 only, then only t_1 is needed to model the lane.

In an AGV system with unidirectional paths, the direction in which an AGV travels on a lane is determined in advance. Hence, we can model the system by a static CROPN. In contrast, in an AGV system with bidirectional paths, an AGV can travel on the lanes in any direction, depending on the real-time routing. Thus, we can only model the system by CROPN dynamically. Each time AGVs are assigned new missions to fulfill and their routes are determined, a CROPN is configured as done in Section 11.3 to describe the AGV flow.

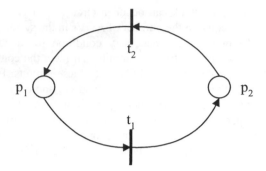

Figure 11.21. The PN model for a bidirectional lane between two nodes.

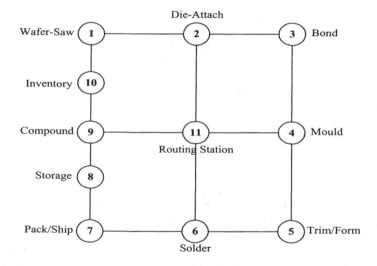

Figure 11.22. An AGV system configuration in semiconductor manufacturing.

The configuration of an AGV system in semiconductor manufacturing adapted from [39] is shown in Figure 11.22. Assume that two AGVs V_1 and V_2 are initially in nodes 8 and 10, respectively. For their next missions to be fulfilled, the routes are V_1: $8 \rightarrow 7 \rightarrow 6 \rightarrow 11 \rightarrow 2 \rightarrow 1$ and V_2: $10 \rightarrow 9 \rightarrow 11 \rightarrow 4 \rightarrow 5 \rightarrow 6 \rightarrow 7$, respectively. With these routes, we can obtain the CROPN as shown in Figure 11.23. Observing the CROPN in Figure 11.23, we call $C = \{p_{11}, t_{11. 4}, p_4, t_{45}, p_5, t_{56}, p_6, t_{6. 11}, p_{11}\}$ a circuit and $Y = \{p_6, t_{67}, p_7, t_{76}, p_6\}$ a cycle. A "cycle" as denoted by Y, is a special "circuit" modeling a bidirectional lane between two nodes as shown in Figure 11.21.

Compared with the CROPN for an AGV system with unidirectional paths, the CROPN for a system with bidirectional paths contains both circuits and cycles. This complicates the deadlock avoidance problem. We will discuss the deadlock avoidance problem for these two situations, respectively.

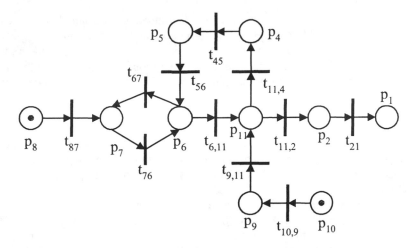

Figure 11.23. A CROPN for the AGV system with bidirectional paths.

11.7.2 Deadlock Avoidance in Cycle-Free CROPN

If the CROPN for an AGV system with bidirectional paths is cycle-free, then the CROPN is not different from the one for an AGV system with unidirectional paths. Thus, the deadlock avoidance policy presented in Section 11.4 or by Theorem 11.13 can be directly applied here.

It should be pointed out that because of the configuration of an AGV system, the CROPN for a system with unidirectional paths presented in Section 11.6 must be strongly connected. Thus, when an AGV reaches its destination, it can travel to another zone to block no other AGVs. However, a CROPN for an AGV system with bi-directional paths may not be strongly connected. Nonetheless, because of its configuration, a CROPN for an AGV system with bidirectional paths can be expanded based on the configuration so that it becomes a strongly connected one. This way, the deadlock avoidance policy presented in Section 11.4 or by Theorem 11.13 can be still applied.

11.7.3 Deadlock Avoidance in CROPN with Cycles Only

In an AGV system, the conflict and deadlock caused by bidirectional paths are more difficult to avoid. When two AGVs travel on the same path and in the opposite directions, cycles are formed in the CROPN of an AGV system. Cycles are the important source of conflicts and deadlocks. When two AGVs are in a cycle they compete for both nodes and lanes. This section discusses the problem of deadlock avoidance in the cycles in a CROPN.

A. Single Cycle

A single cycle is formed by two AGVs competing for a lane between two adjacent nodes. One AGV travels in one direction, and the other in the opposite direction. The CROPN shown in Figure 11.23 contains a cycle $Y = \{p_6, t_{67}, p_7, t_{76}, p_6\}$. If both AGVs take the same lane, a collision (conflict) occurs. If both enter the nodes (both p_6 and p_7 have a token in the cycle Y in Figure 11.23), a deadlock occurs. Thus, we have the following result.

Lemma 11.13: A single cycle formed by routings of two AGVs in a CROPN is deadlock-free if and only if there is at most one token in it in any marking M.

Proof: Necessity: If the condition in the lemma is not satisfied, then places p_1 and p_2 in the cycle shown in Figure 11.21 are all occupied by tokens. The token in p_1 is waiting to enter p_2 and the token in p_2 is waiting to enter p_1. This is a circular wait or a deadlock.

Sufficiency: If the condition is satisfied, there is at most one token in the cycle shown in Figure 11.21. Assume that there is a token in p_1 and p_2 is empty. Then t_1 can fire and the token in p_1 enters p_2 and then leaves the cycle. After that, a token can enter p_2 and t_2 can fire. Thus, no deadlock occurs in the cycle. □

Clearly, if there is no deadlock in a single cycle, two AGVs never occupy the two adjacent nodes in the cycle simultaneously. Thus, the conflict of using the lane never occurs.

B. Cycle Chain

A single cycle is the simplest case that causes conflict and deadlock. If there are multiple cycles distributed in the CROPN separately, then we can treat each cycle as a single cycle separately. However, the cycles may appear in a serial way.

Definition 11.23: In a CROPN of an AGV system, if p_1 and p_2 form a cycle, p_2 and p_3 form a cycle, ..., and p_{n-1} and p_n form a cycle (n>2), these n places form a cycle chain.

A cycle chain example is shown in Figure 11.24. It is formed by the AGV routings $V_1: p_8 \to p_2 \to p_3 \to p_4 \to p_5 \to p_{10}$ and $V_2: p_{11} \to p_5 \to p_4 \to p_3 \to p_2 \to p_1 \to p_7$. Let $Y_1 = \{p_2, t_{23}, p_3, t_{32}, p_2\}$, $Y_2 = \{p_3, t_{34}, p_4, t_{43}, p_3\}$, and $Y_3 = \{p_4, t_{45}, p_5, t_{54}, p_4\}$. The situation in a cycle chain is different from that in a single cycle. Consider the firing process in Figure 11.24. Firing t_{82} leads the token standing for V_1 in p_8 to p_2. Firing $t_{11,5}$ leads the token standing for V_2 to p_5. Now although either one of cycles Y_1 and Y_3 has only one token, deadlock is inevitable. To progress, t_{23} and t_{34}, t_{54} and t_{43}, or t_{23} and t_{54} may fire, leading to two tokens in cycle Y_3, Y_1 or Y_2 and deadlock.

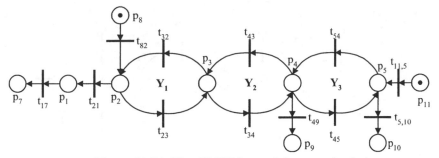

Figure 11.24. The CROPN containing a cycle chain.

It should be pointed out that a number of cycles form a cycle chain if there exist two AGVs that go through all the cycles in different directions. For example in Figure 11.24, if there are three AGVs with routes $p_8 \rightarrow p_2 \rightarrow p_3 \rightarrow p_4 \rightarrow p_9$, $p_3 \rightarrow p_4 \rightarrow p_5 \rightarrow p_{10}$, and $p_{11} \rightarrow p_5 \rightarrow p_4 \rightarrow p_3 \rightarrow p_2 \rightarrow p_1 \rightarrow p_7$, then Y_1 and Y_2 form a cycle chain, and Y_2 and Y_3 form another cycle chain.

Lemma 11.14: In a CROPN of an AGV system, if there is a cycle chain formed by the routes of two AGVs, the chain is deadlock-free iff there is at most one token in it in any marking M.

Proof: Necessity: If the condition is not satisfied, we assume that there are two tokens in the cycle chain. Because the two tokens go in opposite directions, after firing some transitions, they will enter a single cycle, resulting in a deadlock.

Sufficiency: If the condition is satisfied, we assume that there is one token in the cycle chain, then the token can go from one cycle to the next cycle in the cycle chain in the prespecified direction, and finally leaves the cycle chain. After that, the other token can enter and goes through the cycle chain. Thus, there is no deadlock. □

A cycle chain may be formed by routes of more than two AGVs. Assume that there is another AGV V_3 with route $p_6 \rightarrow p_1 \rightarrow p_2 \rightarrow p_3 \rightarrow p_4 \rightarrow p_9$. Then two cycle chains $H_1 = \{Y_1, Y_2, Y_3\}$ and $H_2 = \{Y_4, Y_1\}$, as shown in Figure 11.25, are formed by the routes of these three AGVs, where $Y_1 = \{p_2, t_{23}, p_3, t_{32}, p_2\}$, $Y_2 = \{p_3, t_{34}, p_4, t_{43}, p_3\}$, $Y_3 = \{p_4, t_{45}, p_5, t_{54}, p_4\}$ and $Y_4 = \{p_1, t_{12}, p_2, t_{21}, p_1\}$.

As circuits do, cycle chains can also interact with each other as a result of multiple AGV routes. The cycle chains formed by more than two AGVs may have overlaps. For example, in Figure 11.25, H_1 and H_2 have overlap Y_1.

Definition 11.24: A subnet of CROPN for an AGV system is called an interactive cycle chain if it is formed by two or more cycle chains and each of the chains has overlap with at least one of the other chains. It is called a cycle chain subnet for short and denoted by w.

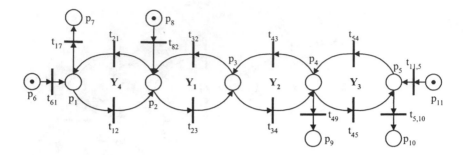

Figure 11.25. A cycle chain formed by routes of three AGVs.

The net shown in Figure 11.25 is an interactive cycle chain subnet. Assume that n cycle chains H_1, H_2, $\cdots$, and H_n form w that has m overlap segments D_1, D_2, $\cdots$, and D_m. Let $F_{Di}(w) = \{V_{fDi}, V_{bDi}, V_{cDi}; D_i\}$ and $F_{Hi}(w) = \{V_{fHi}, V_{bHi}, V_{cHi}; H_i\}$, where V_f is the set of AGVs that travel forward on D_i or H_i, V_b is the set of AGVs that travel backward on D_i or H_i, and V_c is the set of AGVs that cross D_i or H_i. It should be noticed that all the V_f and V_b for D_i and H_i are consistent in w.

Definition 11.25: Let

$$\delta(F_\bullet(w)) = \begin{cases} 1, \text{ if } Card(V_f) > 0 \text{ and } Card(V_b) > 0 \\ \\ 0, \text{ otherwise} \end{cases} \tag{11.10}$$

where $\bullet$ stands for a cycle chain H or overlap segment D in w. If $\delta(F_\bullet(w)) = 0$ in the current marking M, H or D is said to be conflict-free.

Further we let $g(w) = \sum_{i=1}^{n} \delta(F_{Hi}(w)) + \sum_{i=1}^{m} \delta(F_{Di}(w))$. We assume, without the loss of generality, that there is no same cycle chain in w, or $H_i \neq H_j$, if $i \neq j$. Then we have the following result.

Theorem 11.15: A subnet of cycle chains formed by n cycle chains in a CROPN of an AGV system is deadlock-free iff the following condition holds in any marking M.

$$g(w) = \tag{11.11}$$

Proof: The "only if" part is obvious and omitted.

Now we show the "if" part. Assume that H_1 and H_2 have overlap with D_1 as the common segment. If there is no token in D_1 in marking M, then $V_{fD1} = V_{fH1} \cup V_{fH2}$ and $V_{bD1} = V_{bH1} \cup V_{bH2}$, and condition (11.11) requires that the tokens in H_1 and H_2 must go in the same direction, respectively. Let B_1 and B_2 be the sets of tokens belonging to H_1 and H_2, respectively. If all the tokens in B_1 and B_2 go in the same direction, it is obvious that there is no deadlock. If the tokens in B_1 go in one direction and the ones in B_2 go in the other, we let the tokens in B_1 (or B_2) go through the subnet first, then the tokens in B_2 (or B_1) next, guaranteeing no deadlock. If, however, there are tokens in D_1 in M, then from (11.11) these tokens must go in the same direction. If all these tokens belong to one cycle chain, say H_1, then all the tokens in H_1 must go in the same direction as those in D_1 according to (11.11). This time the tokens of H_1 can go through the subnet first, and the tokens in H_2 can go next, for the direction in which they go is the same. If there are tokens in D_1, some of which belong to H_1 and the others to H_2, all the tokens in H_1 and H_2 must go in the same direction according to (11.11), or the subnet is live. When there are two or more overlap segments we can show that the subnet is live similarly.

If $H_1 \subset H_2$ in w, we can treat H_1 as the overlap segment of H_1 and H_2, and the subnet is live if (11.11) is met.

If there are tokens of V_c that cross the cycle chains in w in marking M, then they can be made to go first, generating no effect on the liveness of the subnet. In summary, the subnet is live if condition (11.11) is satisfied. □

In a two-AGV system, only cycle chains may create deadlock. Notice that for cycle chains Lemmas 11.13 and 11.14 are the special cases of Theorem 11.15. Thus we can use Condition (11.11) in Theorem 11.15 to avoid deadlock and conflict in all cycle chains.

A cycle chain can also be formed by the route of a single AGV. In fact, if an AGV goes to some nodes and comes back by the same path (with the opposite direction), a cycle chain is formed. By using the results presented in Theorem 11.15, no conflict or deadlock occurs in such a cycle chain since no other AGV enters it.

Definition 11.26: Transition t is said to be the input transition of cycle chain H if $t \notin H$ but $t^{\bullet} \in H$.

Let $T_I(H) \subset T$ denote the set of input transitions of H. To avoid deadlock and conflict in cycle chains is to control the firings of transitions in $T_I(H_i)$ such that condition (11.11) is always satisfied. Because the condition is necessary and sufficient, it is the least restrictive control law. It is easy to calculate g(w) and thus the policy is simple to implement.

C. Algorithm To Identify Cycle Chains

Consider that a CROPN is constructed dynamically in real-time. The following algorithm first finds cycles and then cycle chain subnets.

Algorithm 11.1:
1. Set CYCLES = $\emptyset$, and T'=T;
2. While T'$\neq\emptyset$,
    2.1. Select any $t \in T'$ and T'=T'-{t}
    2.2. If there is $r \in T'$ such that $r^{\bullet} = {}^{\bullet}t$ and ${}^{\bullet}r = t^{\bullet}$, then $Y_{tr}=\{{}^{\bullet}t, t, t^{\bullet}, r, {}^{\bullet}t\}$, T'=T'-{r}, and CYCLES=CYCLES$\cup Y_{tr}$.
3. Let U= UU= $\emptyset$ where U and UU represent sets of single cycles and cycle chain subnets, respectively.
4. While CYCLES$\neq\emptyset$, select Y={p, t, q, r}$\in$CYCLES and let Q={p, q}, H= {Y}, and CYCLES = CYCLES -{Y}.

4.1. While Q≠∅, select any u∈Q, find all X⊂CYCLES such that ∀Y'={p', t', q', r', p'}∈X, u∈Y'. If X≠∅, let Q=Q∪ $\underset{Y'∈C'}{\bigcup}$ Y'∩P.-

{u}, CYCLES = CYCLES – X, and H = H∪X;

4.2. If H={Y}, U= U∪{Y}; otherwise UU=UU∪{H}.

The algorithm's outcome is the set of all single cycles (U) and all cycle chain subnets (UU) in CROPN. Let $N_t = |T|$ be the number of transitions in it and $N_c = |CYCLES|$ be the number of cycles found. This algorithm's complexity is $o(N_t^2 + N_c^2) = o(N_t^2)$ since $N_c \le N_t/2$ (the number of bidirectional lanes).

11.7.4 Deadlock Avoidance in the CROPN

We have discussed how to avoid deadlocks and conflicts in circuits and cycle chains. In a CROPN of an AGV system, if there is no interaction between circuits and cycle chains, we can control the system by using the control laws presented in the last two sections to control circuits and cycle chains, respectively. However, the circuits and cycle chains may interact with each other. This makes the problem more complicated. Based on the results obtained in the last two sections, we present a rule to avoid deadlocks when the circuits and cycle chains interact with each other in a CROPN.

A subnet with interaction of a circuit and cycle chain is shown in Figure 11.26. This subnet contains the cycle chain made of places p_{1-5} and a circuit C = $\{p_2, t_{2,12}, p_{12}, t_{12,4}, p_4, t_{43}, p_3, t_{32}, p_2\}$. Places p_{2-4} are on both the cycle chain and C.

Let us consider condition (11.11). By this condition, a shared path can be used only in one direction. It requires switching from one direction to another appropriately. In switching from one direction to another, we allow AGVs to go in one direction at a time.

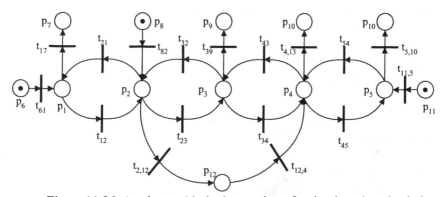

Figure 11.26. A subnet with the interaction of a circuit and cycle chain.

Definition 11.26: A shared path or direction is active in a CROPN if it is selected to allow AGVs to pass. All transitions along this direction are active. A circuit containing active transitions is also called an active circuit.

In Figure 11.26, if the direction from p_5 to p_1 is selected or active (i.e., some AGVs will occupy the places at some time if no deadlock occurs), then t_{54}, t_{43}, t_{32}, and t_{21} are active. When there exists interaction between a circuit and a cycle chain as shown in Figure 11.26, a part of the circuit must form a cycle chain. Because a cycle chain is composed of two directions, only the places and transitions on one direction can be on the circuit. For example, in Figure 11.26 only t_{43} and t_{32} on the cycle chain are on circuit C. Thus, only if the direction from p_5 to p_1 is active will circuit C play a role and is "activated." Hence, if the direction from p_5 to p_1 is active, so is C. On the other hand, if the direction from p_1 to p_5 is active, t_{12}, t_{23}, t_{34} and t_{45} are so but C is not. Circular wait in a circuit may occur only when it is active. Hence, we can state the result as follows.

Theorem 11.16: A subnet in a CROPN of an AGV system with interaction of circuits and cycle chains is deadlock-free if the following conditions hold in any marking M:

1) The conditions given in Theorem 11.13 and (11.11) hold, if the circuits are active and

2) The condition (11.11) holds, if the circuits are not active.

Proof: It follows from Theorem 11.13 and Theorem 11.15 directly. □

Because a circuit will never be deadlocked in a two-AGV system, we do not need to consider the deadlocks in circuits. However, if there are multiple AGVs and the AGV assignments are made to generate cycle chains and circuits, the result given in Theorem 11.13 needs to be applied to solve the problem.

In a CROPN for an AGV system, if neither circuits nor cycles exist, transitions can fire spontaneously. If in some part there are only circuits or cycle chains, the results presented in Theorems 11.13 and 11.15 can be applied, respectively. If the structure with interaction of circuits and cycle chains exists in some part, Theorem 11.16 needs to be applied. In this way, the overall CROPN is live.

It should be pointed out that when the number of circuits and cycles grows, the interaction between the circuits and cycle chains may theoretically be very complex. The computation required to identify the interaction between the circuits and cycle chains may be overwhelming, and the process has, in general cases, the exponential time complexity. Further studies in reducing it by allowing only certain structures in a system are needed. Yet, for AGV systems in practice, the number of AGVs is very limited, and owing to their fixed configurations, the number of circuits whose place count is smaller or equal to AGV count, as well as cycle chains is also limited. Since the proposed control law is a one step look-ahead control policy based on all those circuits and cycle chains, it can be applied to many practical AGV systems, and all AGV systems reported so far in the literature to the authors' knowledge.

11.7.5 Examples

We use some examples to show the application of the proposed approach to the AGV system in Figure 11.22. Two typical requests and assignments of AGVs are given below:

Case 1. V_1: $8 \rightarrow 7 \rightarrow 6 \rightarrow 11 \rightarrow 2 \rightarrow 1 \rightarrow 10$
            V_2: $10 \rightarrow 9 \rightarrow 11 \rightarrow 4 \rightarrow 11 \rightarrow 9$
Case 2. V_1: $10 \rightarrow 1 \rightarrow 2 \rightarrow 3 \rightarrow 4 \rightarrow 11 \rightarrow 9$
            V_2: $9 \rightarrow 11 \rightarrow 4 \rightarrow 5 \rightarrow 6 \rightarrow 7 \rightarrow 8$

The CROPN for Case 1 is shown in Figure 11.27. There are two cycles $Y_1 = \{p_4, t_{4,11}, p_{11}, t_{11,4}, p_4\}$ and $Y_2 = \{p_{11}, t_{11,9}, p_9, t_{9,11}, p_{11}\}$. These two cycles form a cycle chain. However, it is easy to see that the cycle chain is due to the route of the same AGV V_2. Thus, there will be no conflict and deadlock in it. In fact, even if transition $t_{10,9}$ fires first and the token representing V_2 enters into place p_9 in the cycle chain, t_{87}, t_{76} and $t_{6,11}$ can still fire and the token in p_8 (representing V_1) can enter p_{11}. Then we can fire $t_{11,2}$ and the token leaves p_{11} for p_2. If the token representing V_2 is in p_{11}, then $t_{6,11}$ cannot fire according to the transition enabling and firing rule. There is a circuit, but it cannot create the deadlock condition given in Theorem 11.7. Therefore, both AGVs can reach the destination with no deadlock.

The CROPN for Case 2 is shown in Figure 11.28. There are also two cycles $Y_1 = \{p_4, t_{4,11}, p_{11}, t_{11,4}, p_4\}$ and $Y_2 = \{p_{11}, t_{11,9}, p_9, t_{9,11}, p_{11}\}$ and no circuit. These two cycles form a cycle chain H. H is due to the routes of V_1 and V_2. Thus transition firings have to follow the control law specified in Theorem 11.15 to avoid deadlock. Theorem 11.15 requires that g(H) ˜. Since V_2 is already in H, we have to limit another token to enter H. This leads to the below transition firing order. Transitions $t_{10,1}$, t_{12} and t_{23} can fire any time. Transition t_{34} can fire only after $t_{9,11}$, $t_{11,4}$ and t_{45} fire. This way no conflict and deadlock will occur and it is clear that it is the least restrictive control. Both cases require no CROPN expansion.

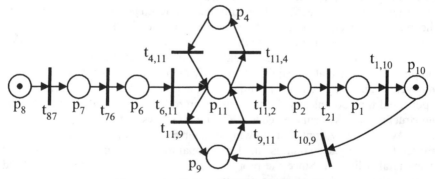

Figure 11.27. The CROPN for Case 1.

The two examples above show the cases with only two AGVs. This is because the discussed semiconductor manufacturing plant requires only two AGVs.

To show the power of the control policy presented here, we assume four AGVs in it and their initial locations as shown in Figure 11.29. The routes of the AGVs are $V_1: 10 \rightarrow 1 \rightarrow 2 \rightarrow 3 \rightarrow 4 \rightarrow 11 \rightarrow 6 \rightarrow 7 \rightarrow 8$, $V_2: 8 \rightarrow 9 \rightarrow 10 \rightarrow 1 \rightarrow 2 \rightarrow 11 \rightarrow 6 \rightarrow 7$, $V_3: 3 \rightarrow 4 \rightarrow 11 \rightarrow 9 \rightarrow 10 \rightarrow 1$, and $V_4: 5 \rightarrow 6 \rightarrow 11 \rightarrow 2$. It is easy to observe that only AGV V_4 has a free path to reach its destination. But when it reaches node 2, it blocks other vehicles. Thus, there is no simple way to control it.

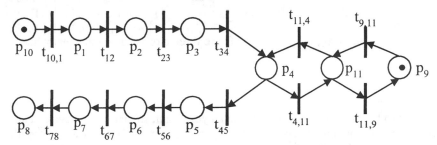

Figure 11.28. The CROPN for Case 2.

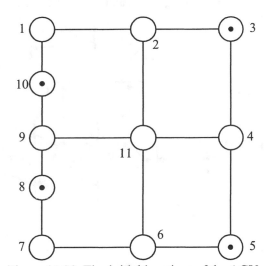

Figure 11.29. The initial locations of the AGVs.

The CROPN for this example is shown in Figure 11.30. It is possible that some AGVs may be blocked if some AGVs reach their destinations and stay there. For example, if V_3 reaches its destination first and stays there, V_2 is blocked. Although for this example the AGV movement process exists so that such situations do not occur, the control policy presented here avoids deadlock but not such situations. However, by adding transition t_{45} (feasible according to the system configuration), the CROPN becomes a strongly connected one. Thus, no matter what the firing order of the transitions is, provided the control policy is obeyed, all the AGVs can reach their destinations at least once. Originally there are five circuits: $C_1 = \{p_8, t_{89}, p_9, t_{9,10}, p_{10}, t_{10,1}, p_1, t_{12}, p_2, t_{23}, p_3, t_{34}, p_4, t_{4,11}, p_{11}, t_{11,6}, p_6, t_{67}, p_7, t_{78}, p_8\}$, $C_2 = \{p_8, t_{89}, p_9, t_{9,10}, p_{10}, t_{10,1}, p_1, t_{12}, p_2, t_{2,11}, p_{11}, t_{11,6}, p_6, t_{67}, p_7, t_{78}, p_8\}$, $C_3 = \{p_2, t_{23}, p_3, t_{34}, p_4, t_{4,11}, p_{11}, t_{11,2}, p_2\}$, $C_4 = \{p_9, t_{9,10}, p_{10}, t_{10,1}, p_1, t_{12}, p_2, t_{23}, p_3, t_{34}, p_4, t_{4,11}, p_{11}, t_{11,9}, p_9\}$ and $C_5 = \{p_9, t_{9,10}, p_{10}, t_{10,1}, p_1, t_{12}, p_2, t_{2,11}, p_{11}, t_{11,9}, p_9\}$. With the addition of transition t_{45}, three more circuits are added. They are $C_6 = \{p_2, t_{23}, p_3, t_{34}, p_4, t_{45}, p_5, t_{56}, p_6, t_{6,11}, p_{11}, t_{11,2}, p_2\}$, $C_7 = \{p_9, t_{9,10}, p_{10}, t_{10,1}, p_1, t_{12}, p_2, t_{23}, p_3, t_{34}, p_4, t_{45}, p_5, t_{56}, p_6, t_{6,11}, p_{11}, t_{11,9}, p_9\}$ and $C_8 = \{p_8, t_{89}, p_9, t_{9,10}, p_{10}, t_{10,1}, p_1, t_{12}, p_2, t_{23}, p_3, t_{34}, p_4, t_{45}, p_5, t_{56}, p_6, t_{67}, p_7, t_{78}, p_8\}$. These three circuits guarantee that when an AGV reaches its destination, it can be controlled to go to any other node to let other AGVs go through. There are also two cycles: $Y_1 = \{p_2, t_{2,11}, p_{11}, t_{11,2}, p_2\}$ and $Y_2 = \{p_{11}, t_{11,6}, p_6, t_{6,11}, p_6\}$. These two cycles form two cycle chains: $H_1 = \{Y_1, Y_2\}$ from the routes of V_2 and V_4, and $H_2 = \{Y_2\}$ from the routes of V_1 and V_4. These two cycle chains are interactive, forming a cycle chain subnet w. The cycle chains and the circuits are also interactive. Among the circuits, only C_3 meets the condition that the number of places is less than or equal to the number of AGVs. In fact, if we fire $t_{89}, t_{10,1}, t_{9,10}, t_{12}, t_{10,1}, t_{34}, t_{23}, t_{12}, t_{56}$, and $t_{6,11}$, C_3 will be deadlocked.

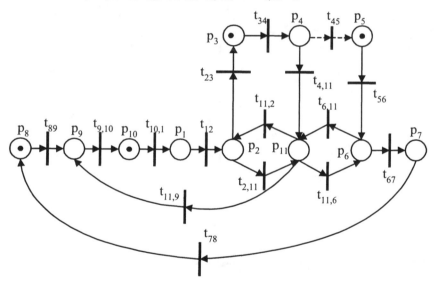

Figure 11.30. The CROPN for the system in Figure 11.29.

Because both circuits and cycle chains exist and are interactive, Theorem 11.16 should be applied to control the system. To avoid deadlock, we need to keep $S(C_3) > 0$ and $g(w) = 0$ all the time. According to the control law, first we can fire $t_{89}, t_{10,1}, t_{9,10}, t_{12}, t_{10,1}, t_{34}, t_{23}$, and t_{12} so that V_1 moves to p_3, V_2 moves to p_2 and V_3 moves to p_4. As a result, there are three tokens in C_3 (one space available) and the direction $p_2 \rightarrow p_{11} \rightarrow p_6$ is active, so V_4 is forbidden to enter p_6. Then by firing $t_{4,11}$, $t_{11,9}$, $t_{9,10}$, and $t_{10,1}$ V_3 reaches its destination. By this time, C_3 will not be dead-locked, we only need to avoid deadlock in the cycle chain. After that we can fire t_{34}, $t_{4,11}$, $t_{11,6}$, $t_{2,11}$, t_{67}, $t_{11,6}$, and t_{78} and V_1 and V_2 reach their destinations. Now the direction $p_2 \rightarrow p_{11} \rightarrow p_6$ is freed, so finally we fire t_{67}, t_{56}, $t_{6,11}$ and $t_{11,2}$ and V_4 gets to its destination. It should be noticed that in the above transition process both V_1 and V_2 are in the cycle chain subnet w at a time, but since g(w) = 0 holds, thus no deadlock is generated. Although there are five circuits, only one of them, i.e., C_3, needs to be identified to carry out this control law.

11.8 CONCLUDING REMARKS

Automated manufacturing systems (AMS) exhibit by complex discrete event system characteristics that are difficult to analyze and control. Because Petri nets can describe the concurrency, choice, mutual exclusion, and synchronization in the system, they are widely used to model AMS.

In modeling AMS by Petri nets, one mainly uses process-oriented modeling method in, e.g. [3]-[8]. Motivated by the need to solve the deadlock avoidance problems, this chapter presents another important method based on resource viewpoints, i.e., resource-oriented modeling method. This method generates resource-oriented Petri net models and colored resource-oriented Petri net models [26]-[30]. Their applications to deadlock problems in AMS and AGV systems are comprehensively discussed.

The future work includes

1. Theoretical exploration of the CROPN in terms of the commonly used concepts in ordinary Petri nets, e.g., siphons, elementary siphons, P- and T-invariants, and their meanings and applications [31]-[33] [39][40];
2. Extension of the modeling methods and models to flexible assembly systems where part/component flow, base component flow, and assembly operations can all contribute to deadlock [41][42];
3. Comparison studies between process- and resource oriented modeling methods and resultant models. Such studies will allow engineers to select the models fit to their particular application needs.
4. Investigation of a CROPN as a plant model for better supervisory controller de-sign.

REFERENCES

1. S. B. Joshi, E. G. Mettala, J. S. Smith, and R. A. Wysk, "Formal models for control of flexible manufacturing cells: Physical and system models," *IEEE Transactions on Robotics and Automation*, vol. 11, 558-570, 1995.
2. H. Alla, P. Ladet, J. Martinez, and M. Silva, "Modeling and validation of complex systems by colored Petri nets: application to a flexible manufactur-ing system," In *Advanced in Petri Nets 1984*, G. Rozenberg, H. Genrich, and G. Roucairol (ed.), Springer-Verlag, pp. 15-31, vol. 188, 1985.

3. Y. Narahari and N. Viswanadham, "A Petri net approach to modeling and analysis of AMS," *Annals of Operations Research*, vol. 3, pp. 449-472, 1985.
4. C. L. Beck and B. H. Krogh, "Models for simulation and discrete control of manufacturing systems," in *Proc. Int. Conf. Robotics & Automat.*, April 1986, pp. 305-310.
5. M. Kamath and N. Viswanadham, "Application of Petri net based model in the modeling and analysis of flexible manufacturing systems," in *Proc. 1986 IEEE Conf. Robotics Automat.*, April 1986, pp. 312-316.
6. M. Zhou and F. DiCesare, "A Petri net design method for automated manufacturing systems with shared resources," in *Proc. 1990 IEEE Conf. Robotics Automat.*, 1990, pp. 526-531.
7. M. Zhou and F. DiCesare, "Parallel and sequential mutual exclusions for Petri net modeling of manufacturing systems with shared resources," *IEEE Trans. on Robotics & Aut.*, 7(4), 515-527, 1991.
8. M. Zhou, F. DiCesare, and A. Desrochers, "A hybrid methodology for synthesis of Petri nets for manufacturing systems", *IEEE Trans. on Robotics and Automation*, vol. 18, no. 3, 350-361, 1992.
9. J. Ezpeleta, J. M. Colom, and J. Martinez, "A Petri net based deadlock prevention policy for flexible manufacturing systems," *IEEE Trans. on Robotics and Automation*, vol. 11, no. 2, 173-184, 1995.
10. N. Viswanadham, Y. Narahari, and T. L. Johnson, "Deadlock prevention and deadlock avoidance in flexible manufacturing systems using Petri net models," *IEEE Trans. on Robotics and Automation*, vol. 6, no. 6, 713-723, 1990.
11. R. A. Wysk, N. S. Yang, and S. Joshi, "Detection of deadlocks in flexible manufacturing cells," *IEEE Trans. on Robotics and Automation*, vol. 7, no. 6, 853-859, 1991.
12. T. Murata, B. Shenker, and S. M. Shatz, "Detection of ada static deadlocks using Petri net invariants," *IEEE Transactions on Software Engineering*, vol. 15, no. 3, 1989.
13. Z. A. Banaszak and B. H. Krogh, "Deadlock avoidance in flexible manufacturing systems with concurrently competing process flows," *IEEE Trans. on Robotics and Automation*, 6(6), 724-734, 1990.
14. F. Hsieh and S. Chang, "Dispatching-driven deadlock avoidance controller synthesis for flexible manufacturing systems,"*IEEE Trans. on Robotics and Automation*, vol. 10, no. 2, 196-209, 1994.
15. C. O. Kim and S. S. Kim, "An effective real-time deadlock-free control for automated manufacturing systems," *International Journal of Production Research*, vol. 35, no. 6, 1545-1560, 1997.
16. S. A. Revelotis and P. M. Ferreira, "Deadlock avoidance policies for automated manufacturing cells," *IEEE Trans. on Robotics and Automation*, vol. 12, no. 6, 845-857, 1996.
17. M. P. Fanti, B. Maione, S. Mascolo, and B. Turchiano, "Event-based feedback control for deadlock avoidance in flexible production systems," *IEEE Trans. Robotics Automat.*, Vol. 13, 347-363, 1997.

18. K. Y. Xing, B. S. Hu, and H. X. Chen, "Deadlock avoidance policy for Petri net modeling of flexible manufacturing systems with shared resources," *IEEE Trans. on Automatic Control*, 41(2), 289-295, 1996.
19. M. Lawley, S. Reveliotis and P. Ferreira, "A correct and scalable deadlock avoidance policy for flexible manufacturing systems," *IEEE Trans. Robotics Automat.*, Vol. 14, 796-809, Oct. 1998.
20. E. Roszkowska and J. Jentink, "Minimal restrictive deadlock avoidance in AMS," In *Proc. of The Second European Control Conf. ECC '93*, Groningen, Holland, volume 2, pages 530-534, 1993.
21. G. A. Koff, "Automatic guided vehicle: application, control, and planning," *Material Flows*, vol. 4, 3-16, 1987.
22. J. Malmbog, "A model for the design of zone-control automated guided vehicle systems," *International Journal of Production Research*, vol. 28, 1741-1758, 1990.
23. C. W. Kim and J. M. A. Tanchoco, "Conflict-free shortest bi-directional AGV routing," *International Journal of Production Research*, vol. 29, 2377-2391, 1991.
24. L. Zeng, H.-P. Wang, and S. Jin, "Conflict detection of automated guided vehicles: a Petri net approach," *International Journal of Production Research*, vol. 29, 865-879, 1991.
25. S. A. Reveliotis, "Conflict resolution in AGV systems," *IIE Trans.*, vol. 32, no. 7, 647-659. 2000.
26. N. Wu, "Necessary and sufficient conditions for deadlock-free operation in flexible manufacturing systems using a colored Petri net model," *IEEE Trans. On Systems, Man, and Cybernetics*, Part C, vol. 29, no. 2, 192-204, 1999.
27. N. Wu, "Avoiding deadlocks in automated manufacturing systems with shared resources," *Proceedings of 1997 IEEE International Conference on Robotics and Automation*, Albuquerque, USA, April, vol. 3, 2427-2432, 1997.
28. N. Wu and M. C. Zhou, "Resource-oriented Petri nets for deadlock avoidance in automated manufacturing," in *Proceedings of 2000 IEEE International Conference on Robotics and Automation* 3377-3382, 2000.
29. N. Wu and M. C. Zhou, "Resource-oriented Petri nets in deadlock avoidance of AGV systems," in *Proceedings of 2001 IEEE International Conference on Robotics and Automation*, 64-69, 2001.
30. N. Wu and M. C. Zhou, "Avoiding deadlock and reducing starvation and blocking in automated manufacturing systems based on a Petri net model," *IEEE Trans. on Robotics and Automation*, 17(5), 658-669, October 2001.
31. T. Murata, "Petri nets: properties, analysis, and application," *Proc. of the IEEE*, vol. 77, 541-579, 1989.
32. K. Jensen, "Coloured Petri nets and the invariant method," *Theoretical Computer Science*, vol. 14, 317-336, 1984.

33. N. Viswanadham and Y. Narahari, "Coloured Petri net models for automated manufacturing systems," in *Proc. 1987 Conf. Robotics and Automat.*, 1987, 1985-1990.

34. A. Lawley, "Deadlock avoidance for production systems with flexible routing zone-control automated guided vehicle systems," *International Journal of Production Research*, vol. 33, 3249-3265, 1995.

35. M.-S. Yeh and W.-C. Yeh, "Deadlock prediction and avoidance for zone-control AGVS," *International Journal of Production Research*, vol. 36, no. 10, 2879-2889, 1998.

36. S. A. Reveliotis, M. Lawley, and P. Ferreira, "Polynomial complexity deadlock avoidance policies for sequential resource allocation systems," *IEEE Transactions on Automatic Control*, vol. 42, 1344-1357, 1997.

37. P. J. Egbelu and J. M. A. Tanchoco, "Potential for bidirectional guided-path for automated vehicles based systems," *International Journal of Production Research*, vol. 24, no. 5, 1075-1097, 1986.

38. G. Hammond, *AGVS at Work*, Springer-Verlag, New York, 1986.

39. Z. Li and M. C. Zhou, "Elementary Siphons of Petri Nets and Their Applications to Deadlock Prevention in Flexible Manufacturing Systems," *IEEE Trans. on Systems, Man, and Cybernetics,* 34(1), 38-51, Jan. 2004.

40. M. C.Zhou and K. Venkatesh, *Modeling, Simulation and Control of Flexible Manufacturing Systems: A Petri Net Approach*. World Scientific, Singapore, 1998.

41. E. Roszkowska, "Supervisory control for deadlock avoidance in compound processes," *IEEE Transactions on Systems, Man, & Cybernetics*, Part A, vol. 34, no. 1, 52-64, 2004.

42. F.-S. Hsieh, "Fault-tolerant deadlock avoidance algorithm for assembly processes," *IEEE Transactions on Systems, Man, & Cybernetics*, Part A, vol. 34, no. 1, 65-79, 2004

12

The Effect of Modeling and Control Techniques on the Management of Deadlocks in FMS

Luca Ferrarini and Luigi Piroddi

Politecnico di Milano, Dipartimento di Elettronica e Informazione, Milano, Italy.

Modeling assumptions and techniques can have a great impact on the deadlock problem. This chapter shows how the use of appropriate model design methods can yield more compact models and reduce the number of deadlock states, thus simplifying both the analysis and search for deadlocks and the deadlock prevention/avoidance. Also, when it finally comes to applying deadlock avoidance algorithms, there is no practical aid for the designer in choosing the most appropriate method for the problem at hand. A basis for a comparative performance analysis of these algorithms is proposed here. Their application to a simulated flexible manufacturing system (FMS) example is studied in detail for the purpose of algorithm evaluation and comparison.

12.1. INTRODUCTION

FMS's are automated, multi-product systems, where any system resource can be shared by more operations of the same or different production sequences. Among the problems that can affect the performance of an FMS, there is that of *deadlocks* [1, 15, 21, 22, 26]. In a deadlock state, in order to complete the routing of a subset of products, a subset of resources is requested, but cannot be used because it is blocked by the same subset of products. The more complex the interaction between products and resources in an automated system, the higher the probability that it gets into a critical block. Even if deadlocks may involve only a sub-

set of the resources of an FMS, they represent highly disadvantageous and potentially dangerous situations that cause system performance to decrease seriously,
both in terms of total products processed and global processing time.

In the literature, the deadlock problem has been widely studied and many
algorithms have been proposed to deal with it. These can be grouped in the following categories: *deadlock detection/recovery* [25], *deadlock prevention* [5, 17,
18, 24, 28], and *deadlock avoidance* [1, 9, 10, 14, 16, 22, 27] methods. Deadlock
recovery methods allow the occurrence of deadlocks and specify procedures to
recover the correct process functioning. In deadlock prevention methods, the system model is modified off-line so that the resulting controlled model turns out to
be deadlock-free. Deadlock avoidance algorithms check the system flow on-line to
see that the system does not fall in a deadlock state. Both prevention and avoidance approaches finally amount to setting up a suitable control policy to regulate
the shared resource allocation in the system.

Regardless of the type of approach chosen, the elimination of deadlocks is a
complex activity for the following reasons:
- The number of discrete states of a logic system easily grows to thousands and
  more for even little more than trivial examples; even if there are algorithms
  that can find deadlock states within the state space in polynomial time, the
  computation of the whole state space can be prohibitive for those models that
  are compact and comfortable for modeling and design, such as Petri nets
  (PNs);
- The correspondence between *model* deadlocks and *system* deadlocks is not
  always one-to-one, and depends on many modeling assumptions; actually, a
  clear standardized and structured design methodology which yields models
  that are not intrinsically prone to deadlocks has not been defined yet; examples
  of the effects of different design approaches with respect to the deadlock
  problem are given in Section 12.2;
- The correct implementation of real-time deadlock avoidance policies may result in algorithms requiring uncommon programming and engineering skills;
  the maintenance of such algorithms may turn out to be complex and costly in
  real industrial settings, where the process under control is subject to frequent
  modifications.

Clearly, a pragmatic approach must be adopted to deal with the deadlock
problem, in order to obtain reliable and applicable solutions for an industrial context. In this view, various design guidelines can be defined at different levels of the
design process, from the modeling phase, to the deadlock prevention design, or in
the setup of an on-line deadlock avoidance policy.

The modeling approach adopted in the control system development is crucial for the complexity of the deadlock problem, and model reduction techniques may significantly simplify and reduce the deadlock problem.

The model can be completed either by simple modifications of the resource allocation mechanism, suggested in the modeling phase to eliminate obvious deadlocks, or by nontrivial additional constraints derived by means of deadlock prevention algorithms. Notice that there are cases in which the application of a deadlock prevention algorithm actually results in a pure modification of the resource allocation mechanism (anticipated allocation or postponed release).

If the system is still subject to potential deadlocks after the model design, a deadlock avoidance algorithm can be enforced. In this case, the designer must decide which one of the many available techniques can be the most suitable for global performance improvement. In this respect, the effort to achieve a complete elimination of deadlock occurrences in an FMS may prove to be non-cost-effective [15, 24], in view of the following observations:

- The system may be subject to frequent changes or updating, e.g., to account for different system operation conditions and needs of production changes, so that the anti-deadlock control policy (and consequently the control software) may require a corresponding flexibility and adaptation;
- The system may be subject to frequent machine or buffer breakdowns or may need manual intervention, so that avoiding *all* deadlocks does not significantly improve the performance;
- Anti-deadlock algorithms are necessary when the full saturation of the usage of some of the system (critical) resources is imposed, which may not always be a sound idea in a real system, where unpredictable events may occur;
- The design of anti-deadlock control schemes is typically performed on the basis of a previous analysis performed on a logical model of the system; however, the latter is in fact *timed*, so that the deadlock states we wish to avoid may be extremely rare or even impossible due to the constraints imposed on the flow of the system by the task timings; more in general, it is not trivial to evaluate the rate of occurrence of specific deadlocks in a given FMS and state their real influence on the system's functioning.

For these reasons, "partial" deadlock avoidance control policies, i.e., control policies that avoid most but not all the deadlocks of a system, are also often used in the FMS context.

Few efforts have been made so far to assess in a methodical way the real performance of the various types of deadlock avoidance algorithms, especially in timed models (see, e.g., [3, 6, 14, 15, 21]). In the second part of the chapter we address the problem of evaluating the performance of different deadlock avoidance algorithms, in terms of the structural modifications and the enhancements of production performance they confer to typical FMS. The objective here is to put the basis for a more formal, integrated study of deadlock avoidance and performance analysis problems, and to build up a structured framework for the evaluation and comparison of different control strategies, designed to be effectively integrated within a computer-aided environment.

Different deadlock avoidance control algorithms, both "partial" and "total," among the most common in the literature, have been considered. The problem is discussed here for both untimed and timed models, and for models both with and without deadlock avoidance control policies. In addition, some indices are proposed to assess the structural properties of FMS with respect to deadlock occurrence and their performance. Such indices should be used in the design phase in order to realize the real effectiveness of complex deadlock avoidance control algorithms. Notice that, in the case of "partial" deadlock avoidance control policies, deadlock recovery can obviously be enforced as a final remedy, but will not be addressed in this chapter.

The chapter is organized as follows. The role of modeling assumptions and techniques with regard to the deadlock problem is discussed in Section 12.2. The basis for a comparative performance analysis of deadlock avoidance algorithms is established in Section 12.3. A comparison between these algorithms is then performed in Section 12.4, by means of a simulated FMS example. Finally, some conclusions are drawn.

12.2. DEALING WITH DEADLOCKS IN THE MODEL DESIGN PHASE: BASIC GUIDELINES

The design methodology employed in the development of the logic control functions has a significant impact on the deadlock problem, in that it influences the difficulty with which deadlock states are found and avoided. In detail, the following subsections focus on such issues as operation and resource aggregation, duplication of operations, multiple resource booking policies, deadlock prevention algorithms and modularization.

The PN formalism will be adopted in the following (see, e.g., [19]) for modeling and analysis purposes. A PN is a bipartite graph, where nodes are classified either as *places* or *transitions*, and directed arcs connect places to transitions and transitions to places. Places are endowed with integer variables called *tokens*, or *place markings*. In the PN context, a system deadlock is associated to a group of transitions permanently disabled. This property is studied by means of a particular structure called *siphon*. A *siphon* is a set S of places such that $\bullet S \subseteq S\bullet$, where $\bullet S$ (*pre-set* of S) is the set of input transitions for the places in S, while $S\bullet$ (*post-set* of S) is the set of output transitions for the places in S. Many siphon properties are documented in the literature. In particular, an unmarked siphon S remains unmarked, which implies that the transitions in $S\bullet$ are dead, and if no minimal siphon eventually becomes empty, then there is at least one enabled transition at any reachable marking [19].

12.2.1. Operation and Resource Aggregation

The model design phase is the result of a complex compromise between two conflicting objectives, namely accuracy and simplicity. The more accurate the model, the richer its description capability and its detail in representing the system behavior. However, model accuracy is paid in terms of complexity, with respect to size, structure and topology. Complexity is a critical issue in the analysis of discrete event models, especially with regard to the deadlock problem, since the number of siphons in a PN increases exponentially with size. This calls for suitable exploiting of hierarchy and modularity in control design, such that deadlock analysis is confined in a specific portion of the control system which models all the possible sources of deadlock at the lowest possible level of detail. In particular, such model must synthetically represent the allocation of shared resources, and all further details should be modeled separately. In this respect, techniques for the aggregation of operations and the aggregation of resources can help in simplifying the model to the necessary detail. These model simplifications may be grouped as follows:
1. Model reductions that do not modify the resource allocation mechanism,
2. Model reductions that modify the resource allocation mechanism.

The first category of model simplifications do not modify the number and type of circular waits among resources represented by the model, though the PN reduction decreases the number of siphons, thus making deadlock analysis easier. These model simplifications are particularly useful when the natural modeling phase tends to include redundant operations or resources in the model, by a one-to-one translation of the physical system in the model. For example, a long sequence of actions performed on a single resource is equivalent to a single aggregated operation from the point of view of solving the deadlock problem. Similarly, multiple resources used by an operation need not be modeled separately.

On the other hand, model simplifications of the second type imply a modification of the actual model behavior, besides a model reduction. Constraints are implemented which simplify the resource allocation mechanism and therefore reduce the causes and number of actual model deadlocks. These model simplifications can be exploited to avoid known deadlock configurations by means of simple local design actions, which do not require a full analysis of the model topology and behavior.

More in detail, the following operation and resource aggregation techniques can be considered, with reference to systems with unitary capacity resources:

1a. *Aggregation of parallel resources*
Consider an operation O1 using two resources (R1 and R2) in parallel, represented in Figure 12.1 by places p_{O1}, p_{R1}, p_{R2}, respectively. This is the case, for example, of transporting tasks in batch processes, which use many (possibly shared) valves and pipes to establish a path connection between two tanks [11, 23].

An equivalent model can be obtained by grouping together R1 and R2 in a single logical resource R12. Notice, in fact, that the marking of place p_{O1} is constrained in the same way in both models of Figure 12.1. Clearly, if R1 and/or R2 are shared with other operations, the appropriate mutual exclusion constraints must also be represented in the model.

This simple model modification reduces the number of siphons in the PN model. In fact, if there exists a siphon $S' = \{p_{R1}, P\}$, where P is a suitable set of net places, then there exists also another siphon $S'' = \{p_{R2}, P\}$, since $\bullet p_{R1} = \bullet p_{R2}$, and $p_{R1} \bullet = p_{R2} \bullet$. These two siphons are not independent, since S' cannot be unmarked without unmarking S'' as well. The reduced model has a single siphon instead, $S = \{p_{R12}, P\}$, which is unmarked when S' and S'' are unmarked in the original net. Therefore, both S' and S'' can be easily controlled by designing the deadlock prevention control for S.

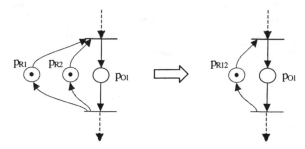

Figure 12.1. Operation and resource aggregation: case 1a.

1b. *Aggregation of parallel operations*
Consider a resource R1 employed by two operations (O1 and O2) in parallel represented in Figure 12.2 by places p_{R1}, p_{O1}, p_{O2}, respectively. This is the case, for example, of a pneumatic circuit with one electrovalve (to open/close the circuit) and two different pistons, which perform different operations (e.g., stamping and printing). Then, an equivalent model can be obtained by grouping together O1 and O2 in a single logical operation O12. Notice in

fact that places p_{O1} and p_{O2} are either both marked or both unmarked, at any time, and that, when places p_{O1} and p_{O2} are marked (unmarked), then place p_{O12} is marked (unmarked).

Similarly to case 1a, this simple model modification reduces the number of siphons in the PN model: if there exists a siphon $S' = \{p_{O1}, P\}$, where P is a suitable set of net places, then there exists also another siphon $S'' = \{p_{O2}, P\}$, since $\bullet p_{O1} = \bullet p_{O2}$, and $p_{O1}\bullet = p_{O2}\bullet$. S' and S'' are not independent, since they always get unmarked together. The reduced model has a single siphon instead, $S = \{p_{O12}, P\}$, which is unmarked when S' and S'' are unmarked in the original net. Therefore, both S' and S'' can be easily controlled by designing the deadlock prevention control for S.

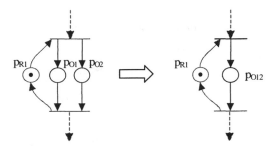

Figure 12.2. Operation and resource aggregation: case 1b.

1c. *Aggregation of sequential operations*
Consider a sequence of two operations (O1 and O2) employing a single resource R1 (Figure 12.3).

This is the case, for example, of a manipulator that first makes a move operation followed by a grasp one. Then, an equivalent model can be obtained by grouping together O1 and O2 in a single logical operation O12. This simple model modification reduces the size of siphons in the PN model. Every siphon S of the original net which contains p_{O2} contains also p_{O1}; on the contrary, in the reduced model S will contain only p_{O12}.

Let us now consider model reductions that modify the resource allocation mechanism.

2a. *Aggregation of sequential resources*
Consider two operations O1 and O2 using two resources R1 and R2, respectively, and suppose that O1 and O2 are two operations in sequence. In Figure 12.4 these are represented by places p_{O1}, p_{O2}, p_{R1}, p_{R2}.

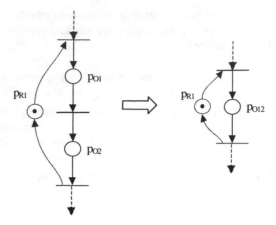

Figure 12.3. Operation and resource aggregation: case 1c.

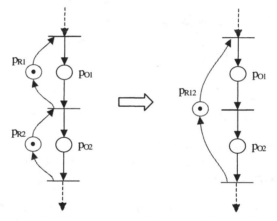

Figure 12.4. Operation and resource aggregation: case 2a.

This aggregation consists of the definition of a unique logical resource, p_{R12}, with unitary capacity, which is allocated before the first operation and released after the second one. Clearly, place p_{R12} represents resources R1 and R2. This means that before the simplification R1 is released at the end of O1, while after the simplification R1 is released only at the end of O2. Thus, the resource R1 has been occupied longer than needed (release postponed). Similarly, before the simplification R2 is allocated at the start of O2, while after the simplification R2 is allocated already at the start of O1. Thus, even the resource R2 has been occupied longer than needed (allocation anticipated).

Thus, the resource allocation mechanism is changed by the presented modification. In particular, since a resource is allocated in advance (R2) and another (R1) is released later than needed, the resource allocation mechanism is transformed into a more stringent one, which implies not only a reduction of possible behaviors but also a reduction of deadlock situations. In addition, the concurrent execution of O1 and O2 is no longer allowed.

If the further simplification shown in Figure 12.3 (serial operation aggregation) is enforced, then the model reduces from 4 to 2 places only, with a clear reduction of the complexity of the siphon search problem.

2b. *Aggregation of sequential operations with individual resources*
Similarly to case 2a (Figure 12.4), another simplification is the aggregation of the sequenced operations into one (Figure 12.5). The result is also similar: a resource is allocated in advance (R2) and another (R1) is released later than needed.

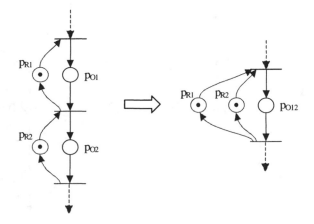

Figure 12.5. Operation and resource aggregation: case 2b.

2c. *Aggregation of asynchronous join/split operations*
Consider two resources R1 and R2 used by two operations O1 and O2 in parallel and, in sequence with them, by a third one (O3). Such a model is very common since it corresponds to the assembly of parts in manufacturing, and to the concurrent transfer of fluids into a unique tank in batch systems. In the latter case, the resources R1 and R2 collectively represent the sink tank T and operations can correspond to "unload tank 1 to tank T" (O1), "unload tank 2 to tank T" (O2), "mix the content of T" (O3), as explained in [12].

The modeling of such behaviors is given in the left-hand part of Figure 12.6, where resources p_{R1} and p_{R2} are allocated independently and used by operations O1 and O2 (modeled with places p_{O1}, p_{O2}), but released at the same time. The simplification shown consists in the representation of the two concurrent operations as one logical operation, modeled with place p_{O12}, which now would require the allocation and release of the two resources at the same time. Applying the transformation 1a, one obtains the model shown in the right-hand part of Figure 12.6, where the two resources have also been aggregated in a unique logical resource R12.

In the simplified model, the allocation of resources R1 and R2 is forcedly simultaneous and is only possible when all the operations preceding O1 and O2 have been completed. This in general reduces the number of possible deadlocks, since the cases when only one operation out of the two (O1 and O2) is involved in a deadlock are avoided by construction.

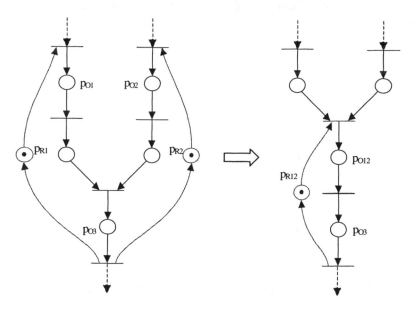

Figure 12.6. Operation and resource aggregation: case 2c.

12.2.2. Duplication of Operations

Inappropriate modeling assumptions may result in the presence of structural deadlocks in the model not corresponding to any system deadlock. Suppose, for example, that two recipes are executed in an FMS or batch plant. In the i-th recipe, i = 1, 2, operations Oi1 and Oi2, which use resources R1 and R2, respectively, can be executed in whatever order; when both have been completed, operation Oi3 can be performed and only afterwards are the resources released. Suppose, in addition, that operations O12 and O22 in fact perform the same operation on the same raw materials to yield an identical semi-finished product which is used by both recipes. For example, the first recipe may represent an assembly process of two subparts A and B, and the second one an assembly of B and C. The resource R1 represents a robot manipulator transporting subparts A or C to the assembly station. Similarly, robot R2 transports B subparts for both recipes. Operations Oi3 are the assembly operations.

A possible representation of these recipes is shown in Figure 12.7, where b_{Oij} and e_{Oij} represent the begin and end events associated to operation Oij. With such a modeling approach, identical operations performed in different recipes are distinguished and represented separately (by means of different places and transitions).

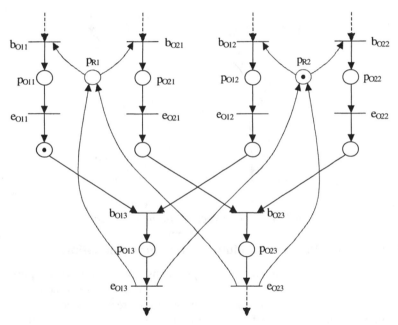

Figure 12.7. A redundant modeling approach generating logical deadlocks.

Clearly, if in the state represented in Figure 12.7 resource R2 is assigned to operation O12 the system can proceed correctly, whereas if operation O22 is activated a deadlock state is reached. However, the material produced by operations O12 and O22 is identical, so that in the real problem the first recipe could in fact be successfully completed using the "physical" outcome of operation O12. Therefore, the deadlock must be interpreted not as a physical blocking of the system, but as a design error resulting from the adopted modeling approach which duplicates identical operations if performed by different recipes.

A correct modeling approach that avoids the duplication of the two identical operations is shown in Figure 12.8. This time no "fictitious" deadlocks are generated in the model.

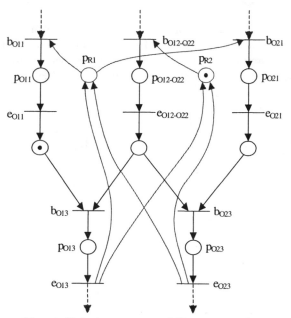

Figure 12.8. A correct modeling approach.

12.2.3. Booking Policies for Multiple Resource Allocation

One of the most intricate control problems regarding resource allocation concerns operations that need multiple resources and that share some of them. In this case, the allocation system must ensure that all the resources needed for a specific operation are available before executing it. A possible way to implement this task is by means of a booking mechanism. When an operation is requested, the necessary resources are asynchronously reserved for it as they become available, and the operation is actually executed when all the resources have been booked. When an operation books a resource, it acquires a priority with respect to all other operations requiring the same resource. This approach is quite common in the technical literature (see, e.g., [23]). Although appealing and quite intuitive, the booking policy for dealing with multiple resource allocation has several drawbacks:

1. *Model complexity* – the operation model is more detailed, since it must include both the resource booking and the operation execution; individual booking events are also required for each resource and for each operation;
2. *Inefficient resource usage* – booked resources are unavailable for other operations, but remain idle until the operation is actually executed;
3. *Booking deadlocks* – in addition to the possible deadlocks due to circular waits of the resources *used* by operations, deadlocks may be introduced in the form of circular waits of the resources *booked* by operations.

Consider for example the two operations O1 and O2, which both require the same two resources R1 and R2. Figure 12.9 represents a possible implementation of the booking mechanism described above for these resources. Four types of events are used: b_{Oi} (begin of operation Oi, which actually activates the resource booking), b_{Ri} (booking of resource Ri), x_{Oi} (begin of execution of operation Oi), e_{Oi} (end of operation Oi and resource release). When an operation Oi is requested (event b_{Oi}), the associated transition is fired and the individual resource booking transitions (events b_{Ri}) are enabled. Only when both b_{R1} and b_{R2} have been fired (in any order) is the actual operation started by firing the transition labeled x_{Oi}. Finally, all the resources are released at the end of the operation (e_{Oi}).

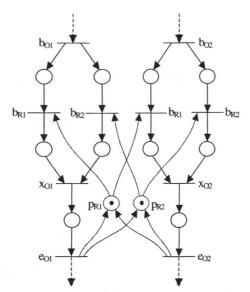

Figure 12.9. Asynchronous resource booking model.

The PN model of Figure 12.9 may end in a state where both operations have booked only one resource (e.g., R1 is booked by O1 and R2 by O2). In this case, a circular wait actually occurs, in which R1 and R2 are both booked but unused, both operations are unable to start and the process is deadlocked.

The obvious alternative to the asynchronous booking mechanism is the *simultaneous* resource allocation model shown in Figure 12.10. This simpler model is less detailed and flexible, but it has no deadlocks related to individual resource booking.

Interestingly enough, should a maximally permissive deadlock prevention method be used to avoid the booking deadlocks in the model of Figure 12.9, the asynchronous booking of R1 and R2 would be still allowed, but when one of the two is booked by an operation, the only admissible event is the booking of the other resource by the same operation. This implies that the operation activation is actually the same as in the model of Figure 12.10 (with the two operations in mutual exclusion), though the resource that has been booked first remains idle until the booking is completed.

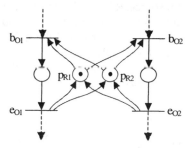

Figure 12.10. Simultaneous resource allocation model.

In summary, an asynchronous booking policy cannot change the actual resource allocation constraints for the execution of operations, and only establishes a priority between operations using shared resources. From the point of view of the deadlock problem, it is then more convenient to adopt a simpler simultaneous resource allocation model, and confine the fulfillment of the priority requirements, if any, to the control code implementation.

12.2.4. Correcting the Model with Deadlock Prevention Algorithms

The use of deadlock prevention algorithms can be envisaged as the last "modeling" phase, specially designed to correct the model in order to guarantee that it is deadlock-free. In the PN modeling context, most of these methods are based on the neutralization of potentially dangerous siphon structures, typically by means of the P-invariant approach [18, 28], i.e., by adding suitably connected control places to the PN which introduce new P-invariants in the model to prevent the siphons from getting empty of tokens. Unfortunately, deadlock prevention algorithms become cumbersome or even practically inapplicable when the complexity of the model increases, as well as the number of deadlock states, since:

1. The computation of siphons is by no means a trivial task, and
2. The control algorithm introduces constraints to the PN flow, which may even add new unwanted siphons to the model.

A possible and practical way to deal with this situation is to drastically reduce the number of deadlocks by means of heuristic local prevention methods. In fact, deadlocks that involve a limited number of resources and that, therefore, are confined to a small portion of the PN are not infrequent in complex systems. By eliminating these deadlocks, only the few global deadlocks should remain in the model. Notice that most deadlock prevention algorithms introduce control places imposing constraints to the process flow and resource allocation, which can be interpreted as additional fictitious resource places. In many cases, the combination of the real and fictitious resources really amounts to a control policy which re-allocates the real resources in a more restrictive way. Based on such motivations, heuristic local prevention methods can be developed which operate directly by re-allocating the real resources.

Consider the simple PN model shown in Figure 12.11. This can represent, e.g., a simple 3-operation FMS with 2 resources, where a machine (R2) performs a processing operation on a product part (O2). The machine is served by a robot manipulator (R1), both for loading (O1) and unloading operations (O3).

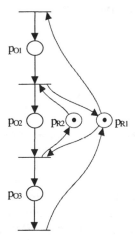

Figure 12.11. PN model of a non-deadlock-free FMS.

A minimal siphon $S = \{p_{O3}, p_{R1}, p_{R2}\}$ can be easily spotted in the system. To prevent the siphon from getting unmarked and causing deadlock in the system, a control place (p_{SC}) can be added with the P-invariant approach as in Figure 12.12. In the resulting PN, place p_{R2} turns out to be redundant with respect to the process flow, since the P-invariant approach has introduced a more restrictive constraint with respect to that imposed by p_{R2}. To see this, observe that the following constraints (P-invariants) apply on the net marking of the uncontrolled system (Figure 12.11): $m(p_{O2}) + m(p_{R2}) = 1$, and $m(p_{O1}) + m(p_{O3}) + m(p_{R1}) = 1$. The new P-invariant introduced to control siphon S forces the marking constraint: $m(p_{O1}) + m(p_{O2}) + m(p_{SC}) = 1$.

Clearly, the same result obtained by this supervisory control method can also be achieved by simply anticipating the acquisition of resource R2 at the onset of operation O1 (Figure 12.13).

Notice also that the interpretation of such a more restrictive allocation of p_{R2} is simple: before using the manipulator R1 to load the machine R2 make sure that the latter is available.

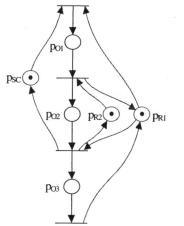

Figure 12.12. Controlled PN model of the FMS.

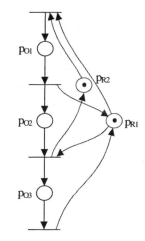

Figure 12.13. PN model of the FMS with reallocation of the machine resource.

More in general, simple resource reallocation yields a sub-optimal, non-maximally permissive, but local, extremely simple control solution. Notice that a solution to the deadlock problem in an FMS can always be found on the basis of the reallocation of shared resources. In the worst case one can allocate all the needed resources at the beginning of every production sequence.

12.2.5. Modularization

In general, deadlocks depend on nontrivial interactions between different portions of the overall system model. For this reason, it is not possible to find them by local inspection of the model, though this would be very convenient from a computational point of view. However, the use of appropriate modular and hierarchical approaches can help in reducing the complexity of the deadlock problem, both in the analysis and the control phases.

Deadlocks mainly arise from circular wait conditions between shared resources. These could be too many in the system under consideration to allow an easy solution of the deadlock problem. However, a subset of the system deadlocks may be found by analyzing a submodel in which only some of the system's shared resources are actually represented as shared resources in the model, and the other ones are represented as dedicated resources. The submodel can be extremely reduced with respect to the complete model, since operations performed on dedicated resources can be trivialized in the deadlock analysis. Nevertheless, it still can represent all the deadlock conditions of the complete model which involve a circular wait between the resources represented as shared in the submodel.

To see this, consider for example the FMS model of Figure 12.14, where two products are realized by means of two sequences of 3 operations (O_{ij}, where $i = 1, 2$ is the product type and $j = 1, 2, 3$ is the operation order in the product routing), using 3 resources (R1, R2, R3) in reverse order.

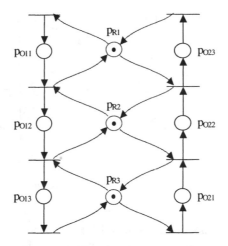

Figure 12.14. Modularization.

If we are interested in the deadlocks related to the subset {R1, R3} of the shared resources, we can resort to the modified model where R2 is represented as a dedicated resource (Figure 12.15). Both models can deadlock when R1 is occupied by operation O11 and R3 by operation O21.

Furthermore, for the purpose of deadlock analysis, operations O12 and O22 can be discarded from the model, since they are not directly responsible for the deadlock. This results in the simplified model of Figure 12.16. This is the simplest submodel still capable of representing the deadlock involving R1 and R3.

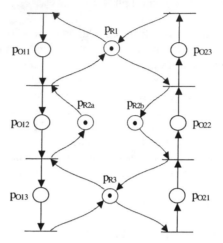

Figure 12.15. Modified FMS model where R2 is represented as unshared.

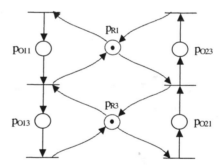

Figure 12.16. Simplified FMS model.

There surely exists at least a deadlock in the original model directly corresponding to each deadlock of the submodel. For example, the PN of Figure 12.16 contains a minimal siphon $S' = \{p_{O13}, p_{O23}, p_{R1}, p_{R3}\}$, while the PN of Figure 12.14 has a minimal siphon $S = \{p_{O13}, p_{O23}, p_{R1}, p_{R2}, p_{R3}\} \supset S'$. This result can be exploited in two ways:

(a) Find S in the PN of Figure 12.14, by searching for siphons containing S';
(b) Design the deadlock prevention control for S' in the PN of Figure 12.16, and derive the corresponding deadlock prevention control for the PN of Figure 12.14.

By constructing a series of simple submodels with this rationale a significant part of the system deadlocks can be rapidly found and the correponding control actions designed. Obviously, this partialization approach cannot guarantee that all system deadlocks will be found, and a liveness check must still be performed on the overall model. However, the reachability space of the latter model will be greatly reduced by the deadlock prevention control actions already designed by means of the submodels, thus greatly simplifying this final step.

A similar *divide-et-impera* approach is adopted in [23], where the control of a batch process is obtained using several modules, dedicated to the correct allocation of different resources. In particular, a control module is designed for the prevention of the deadlocks concerning only transporting resources, while another one deals with the residual deadlocks and allocates the process resources.

12.3. DEADLOCK AVOIDANCE ALGORITHMS: A COMPARATIVE PERFORMANCE ANALYSIS

If, after the modeling phase the resulting controlled model is still subject to deadlocks, a deadlock avoidance method can be employed on-line to eliminate them. Many algorithms have been proposed in the literature for this purpose. However, it is not very clear on what grounds should the different algorithms be compared and how should the designer choose among the many available.

In this section, we address the problem of evaluating and comparing the performance of deadlock avoidance control policies applied to FMS. The problem is discussed for both untimed and timed models. In this respect, observe that the introduction of the time variable in FMS models does not force other deadlock configurations to occur with respect to the corresponding untimed model. Actually, the number of deadlocks may decrease due to the constraints imposed by operation timing. However, the analysis and simulation of timed models is often much more complex, even from a conceptual point of view. In the present work, we concentrate on the case of constant and known processing times.

In the following, the concept of *deadlock configuration* will be used to characterize univocally deadlocks in an FMS. A deadlock configuration is defined as the mapping of a minimal subset of operations on a minimal subset of resources, which represents the resource circular wait condition that causes the deadlock [22]. In other words, the deadlock configuration identifies the (minimal) portion of the FMS that is actually responsible for the deadlock. A more formal definition of deadlock configuration is given in [1, 22].

12.3.1. Deadlock Avoidance Algorithms

The deadlock avoidance algorithms considered in the following analysis are among the most common and best-known in the literature, and as such must be regarded as fairly representative of the many available. A brief description of the selected methods is given hereafter. More detailed references are given throughout this subsection.

12.3.1.1. "Partial" deadlock avoidance algorithms (PDA)

Many simple algorithms can be used to avoid some, but not all, deadlock configurations. We will refer to these as *"partial" deadlock avoidance algorithms.* By definition, these algorithms result in non-deadlock-free controlled systems. As an example, a simple deadlock avoidance algorithm will be considered, where a new product is allowed to enter the system only if all the resources needed in the job sequence are available at that time. Notice that such an algorithm is not deadlock-free, since it does not guarantee that the resources will also remain free for the same product in the successive steps.

12.3.1.2. Banker's algorithm [4, 13] (Bank)

In this model a product is moved to the next machine of its routing, only if, after its possible allocation, all the resources still needed by the product to complete its routing are available. This condition must be met in the worst case, i.e., when every product in the system simultaneously requires a resource to continue its routing.

12.3.1.3. Banaszak and Krogh's algorithm [1, 2] (BK)

The job routes are divided into zones, each one in turn divided into two subzones: a subzone corresponding to operations using only unshared resources and the other one corresponding to operations using only shared resources. Unshared resources are considered always available for allocation. On the contrary, a product can enter a shared subzone if the capacity of the unshared subzone exceeds the number of products of the zone. In addition, a request for a generic shared resource is satisfied only if all the shared resources of the remainder of the zone are available at the time of the request.

12.3.1.4. Modified Banaszak and Krogh's algorithm (BK_m)

The modification here considered allows shared resources to be allocated if the remaining resources of the same zone are available or occupied by products of the same type.

12.3.1.5. Modified Lee-Lin's algorithm (LL_m)

The basic control algorithm has been described in [15] with reference to the deadlock avoidance problem for automated guided vehicle (AGV) systems. For any allocation request, the algorithm analyses the next required resource, say R1, on its route. If the resource R1 is not available, it is recursively checked to see if the product that is occupying R1 can be pushed forward on its routing, so that R1 can be set free. This recursive procedure, which "jumps" from one sequence to another, ends if any product can complete its routing, then the original allocation is performed, otherwise another allocation request is examined.

12.3.1.6. Forbidden-State algorithm (FS)

All deadlocks and those states inevitably leading to a deadlock (pre-deadlock states) are identified in the first place. For example, this can be done with a suitable inspection of the coverability tree. Second, the algorithm prevents any state transition if the next state is one of the before-mentioned ones. Notice that this method requires that all deadlocks are known. In [6, 7, 8] an innovative FS policy is described that solves this problem in polynomial time, avoiding an exhaustive search for all the system's states.

12.3.2. Modeling and Simulation Assumptions

We assume that each product type has a unique production sequence, and that this cannot change during the system evolution. A production sequence can be described as a sequence of operations (like machining, transportation, drilling, etc.), which exploit some resources. In the sequel, the following terminology will be employed: a *product* (a part or a unique part batch) is *processed* (machined, stored, moved) on a *resource* (a machine, a buffer, a transport device), to denote a generic state transition in the considered FMS. The following hypotheses, quite common in practice, are assumed:
(a) The system is conceived to work for a virtually unlimited input batch size (continuous production);
(b) The resources can have multiple capacity (more parts or products can be processed at a time);
(c) There is an infinite-capacity input queue (input store) and, similarly, an infinite-capacity output queue (output store).

In addition, for a given production sequence the following assumptions are made with respect to the resource allocation criteria:
(a) A generic operation is allowed to start only if the corresponding resource is available and can be concluded only if the resource for the next operation is available;
(b) If the resource for the next operation is *not* available, the resource for the current operation remains occupied (that is, there is no intermediate buffer, unless otherwise explicitly stated);
(c) The allocation of a resource for an operation and the release of the resource for the preceding operation are simultaneous.

In order to evaluate the performance of the various models and to compute the different indices, a well-known modeling and simulation package has been used (SIMAN [20]). The following characteristics will be assumed to hold for all models in simulation:

(a) There is a unique input queue for all products of all types; such a queue is managed with a FIFO policy;

(b) The type of products arriving at the input queue is chosen randomly; all product types have the same probability to arrive at the input queue;

(c) The choice of the next product to process in the system among those whose next resource is available is random among the products in the input queue and the buffer queues, with constant probability distribution function;

(d) The buffer queues are managed with a FIFO policy.

Moreover, in the timed models, an execution time is assigned to every operation (including, besides the actual processing time, machine loading and unloading times and set-up times).

A simulation run ends when no transition state can happen in the system. This is caused by one of the following reasons:

(a) All input products have been processed (all the queues, including the input one, are empty);

(b) A deadlock has occurred that involves all the shared resources of the system (all the shared resource queues are not empty);

(c) A deadlock has occurred that involves some of the shared resources of the system (the corresponding resource queues are not empty, while the input one is empty).

In order to distinguish the different causes and to determine the exact impact of a deadlock, a careful and nontrivial inspection of simulation results, system data and system indices has to be performed.

12.3.3. Deadlock Tendency and Performance Indices for Untimed Models

12.3.3.1. Structural indices

Systems subject to deadlocks can be more or less critical to control, depending on the number and type of the possible deadlock configurations and on the frequency of occurrence of such system states. Control effectiveness can be fully assessed if the number of avoided deadlocks and the relative importance of the avoided deadlock configurations are evaluated. Hence the need for structural indices, that specify in a quantitative way the tendency of a system (with or without control action) to fall in a deadlock state.

The *deadlock percentage* (DP) index shows how a system is subject to deadlocks by evaluating the percentage of simulation runs which end in a deadlock:

$$DP = \frac{N_{DL}}{N},$$

where N is the total number of simulation runs, and N_{DL} is the number of simulation runs that end in a deadlock state. A high value of the DP index clearly calls for a deadlock control solution or a redesign of the FMS. Though intuitive, it is not always easy to compute, owing to the fact that exact detection of deadlock states is not trivial. This is particularly true for predeadlock states and deadlock configurations that block only a part of the system.

Deadlock states lower the overall performance by partially or totally blocking product throughput. Thus, it is important to compute the number of products that pass through the whole system before a deadlock state is reached. The following normalized index evaluates the *product survival rate* (PSR):

$$PSR = \frac{\sum_{1}^{N} {}_i P_{out}(s_i)}{\sum_{1}^{N} {}_i P_{in}(s_i)},$$

where $P_{in}(s_i)$ and $P_{out}(s_i)$ are the total number of products given as input to the system in the i-th simulation run (s_i) and the total number of products that pass through the system in the i-th simulation run, respectively. This index computes indirectly the "damage" caused by deadlocks. If a deadlock is relatively rare or blocks only a section of the system, most of the incoming products will be able to complete their sequence of operations. Thus, index PSR accounts mostly for the effect of severe deadlocks. In batch processing, index PSR can also be used in the dimensioning of production batches, so as to minimize the occurrence of deadlocks.

Different deadlock configurations affect the system to different degrees. Thus, it is important to classify them in terms of frequency of occurrence and blocking capability. The *blocking capability* (BC_i) is measured by:

$$BC_i = NP_i,$$

where index i identifies the specific deadlock configuration, and NP_i is the number of products/resources involved in the i-th minimal deadlock configuration. If products of different types enter the system with equal probability, deadlock configurations with the same BC value are *a priori* equally likely to occur. Also, deadlock configurations that involve fewer products (lower value of index BC) can occur more easily, and hence more frequently. The BC index can range from a minimum value of 2 (which has the higher probability of occurrence) to a maximum value equal to the system capacity, i.e., the total number of available resource places.

The *frequency of occurrence* of a particular deadlock configuration is given by:

$$f_i = \frac{N_{DL,i}}{N_{DL}},$$

where index i identifies the specific deadlock configuration, and $N_{DL,i}$ is the number of simulation runs that end in a deadlock state associated with the i-th deadlock configuration. A measure of this type is helpful in determining the most dangerous deadlock configurations for a specific system, so that control algorithms can be designed to prevent at least these critical cases.

12.3.3.2. Indices for systems controlled with "partial" algorithms

Consider now "partial" deadlock avoidance algorithms. Since these algorithms result in non-deadlock-free controlled systems, a comparison analysis based on the structural indices presented in the previous section can be performed. This way, the effectiveness of a specific control algorithm can be assessed by measuring the variations of indices DP, PSR and f_i.

Some useful related indices can also be introduced as follows. For example, the *deadlock rejection percentage* (DRP):

$$DRP = \frac{DP_C}{DP_F},$$

where the index C or F refers to the controlled or free case, respectively, or the *deadlock configuration rejection percentage* (CRP):

$$CRP = \frac{NC_C}{NC_F},$$

where NC is the total number of deadlock configurations. Though useful in principle, the latter index is difficult to compute since, except from simple cases, an analytical search of all the deadlock configurations is computationally excessively demanding, and simulation cannot guarantee that all deadlock configurations are found. In practical cases an empirical version of the same index, based on a sufficient amount of simulation runs, can be considered acceptable enough. Note that (1–CRP) accounts for the residual deadlock configurations in the controlled system.

Since deadlock configurations have different importance, an algorithm comparison based on the CRP index can be misleading. It is not necessarily true that, if algorithm A avoids more deadlock configurations than algorithm B, then A is better than B. However, if algorithm A avoids all the deadlock configurations also avoided by algorithm B, plus some other configurations, then A dominates B.

It goes without saying that if DRP = CRP = 0, the control algorithm is to be considered *optimal* with respect to the deadlock avoidance problem.

12.3.3.3. Interference indices for control algorithms

A useful classification of control algorithms can be attempted in terms of their actual interference with the normal behavior of the system. Sophisticated algorithms impose many constraints on the system, which can be thought of as forbidden states. Particularly in the case of "total" deadlock avoidance algorithms, a structural comparison can be performed only on the basis of their level of inter-vention. In timed models unnecessary constraints will result in a degradation of performance, whereas only structural differences take place in untimed models.

A suitable indicator of the *Rigidity* (R) of a controlled system is given by:

$$R = \frac{\sum_{1}^{N} {}_i NF(s_i)}{N},$$

where $NF(s_i)$ is the number of forbidden operations in the i-th simulation run s_i. This index counts the times that the control algorithm prevents a product from accessing a new resource because an internal test has failed. Note that products may be blocked not only on resources, but also in the input queue. Index R strongly depends on the structural characteristics of the controlled system.

An index that is very useful in principle, but computationally expensive to evaluate, is the *unreachable states percentage* (USP), which measures the forbid-den states imposed by the control algorithm:

$$USP = \frac{NUS}{NRS},$$

where NUS is the number of system states that becomes unreachable when the control algorithm is applied, and NRS is the total number of reachable states of the uncontrolled system. The reachable states of a free or controlled system can be determined by constructing a suitable state transition tree. The nodes represent the reachable states.

12.3.4. Performance Evaluation for Timed Models

When timed models are considered, the structural indices proposed in Sec-tion 12.3.3 still apply, but they can be usefully completed by means of a perform-ance analysis. In general, the design objectives for an automated manufacturing system can be summarized in the following points:
(a) Reduction of the time the products take to pass through the system,
(b) WIP (*work in process*) limitation,
(c) Maximization of the saturation rate of the system.

These objectives translate directly into quantitative performance indices. For example, to account for the time the products take to pass through the system, one can use the *average flowtime* (the term flowtime defines the time taken by a product to pass through the entire system, and constitutes a fraction of the lead time of an order):

$$AF = \frac{\sum_{i}^{NP} F_i}{NP},$$

where F_i is the flowtime of the i-th product and NP is the total number of products.

Another possible index is the total *processing time* (PT) of a batch of NP products. Note that, since more products can be processed at the same time on different machines, PT is less than the sum of the individual flowtimes of the corresponding batch of products.

The WIP indicator is defined as:

$$WIP = \frac{1}{t_{fin} - t_{in}} \int_{t_{in}}^{t_{fin}} WIP(t) \, dt,$$

where WIP(t) is the number of products that are present in the system at time t, and t_{in} and t_{fin} are the time when the first product enters the system and the time when the last product exits the system, respectively.

The *system saturation coefficient* (SSC) is defined as follows:

$$SSC = \frac{1}{t_{fin} - t_{in}} \int_{t_{in}}^{t_{fin}} NWM(t) \, dt,$$

where t_{in} and t_{fin} are defined as previously and NWM(t) is the number of machines that are working at time t. Multiple machines must be counted with their multiplicity in parameter NWM(t). For example, a double machine contributes to NWM(t) with a value of:
- 0 if it is not processing any part;
- 1 if it is processing only 1 part in any of the two possible places;
- 2 if it is processing 1 part in each of the two possible places.

To use these standard indices meaningfully for our purposes, two benchmark situations are introduced:
1. *FMS with infinite capacity interoperational queues (IIQ)*: each machine is endowed with an infinite capacity buffer, where output products are temporarily stored, when the next machine for that product is busy. This model is by definition deadlock-free, even if many products may be queued in output buffers. In addition, it is optimal from the total processing times point of view for job shop systems. Thus, this "ideal" model can be taken as a reference when comparing different control algorithms.
2. *Original system controlled with the forbidden state (FS) algorithm*: this situation represents the optimal performance that can be achieved by a deadlock

avoidance control algorithm, since the FS algorithm forbids an operation if and only if it results or will inevitably result in a deadlock state.

12.4. COMPARISON ANALYSIS OF A SIMULATED FMS

12.4.1. Example 1: a 3-machine 3-product untimed model

A completely automated FMS station, which has been already studied in the literature [10, 21], is shown in Figure 12.17. The station is composed of:
* Three machines R1, R2 and R3 (R1 is double, i.e., it can process up to two products at a time),
* An input and an output cart,
* A robotic manipulator to load and unload machines.

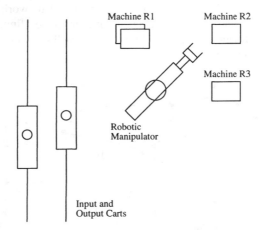

Figure 12.17. Completely automated FMS station.

The station produces three different products P1, P2 and P3. Each product requires three sequential operations on the three machines, according to the product routing listed in Table 12.1. Nine operations Oij are performed by the station, where i = 1, 2, 3 denotes the product type Pi, and j = 1, 2, 3 denotes the operation order.

In order to evaluate the occurrence of deadlocks, a simplified model can be considered, which includes the four machines only. The input and output carts and the robotic manipulator have been omitted in the following analysis, since it is assumed that their use and release are not subject to any structural constraint and consequently they do not introduce any causes of deadlocks. Typically, these resources are used only if their operation can be successfully completed (e.g. the robotic manipulator is called only when its destination is known to be available).

Product	Machine used by operation		
type (Pi)	Oi1	Oi2	Oi3
P1	R1	R2	R3
P2	R2	R1	R3
P3	R3	R2	R1

Table 12.1. Product routing on the three machines.

In the present section the untimed model of the FMS station is analyzed, to highlight structural properties of the system. The resulting untimed PN model is represented in Figure 12.18. This model is structured to work for an unlimited batch size. On the contrary, in the actual simulation model, finite batches are considered. In the following section, the timed model will be considered for performance evaluation purposes.

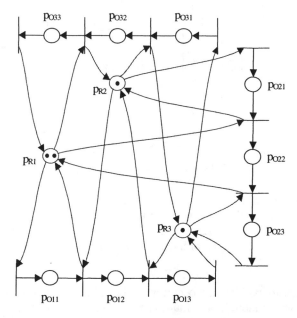

Figure 12.18. Untimed PN model of the FMS station.

The PN model of the FMS station has three minimal siphons:
$S1 = \{p_{O12}, p_{O22}, p_{O33}, p_{R1}, p_{R2}\}$,
$S2 = \{p_{O13}, p_{O21}, p_{O23}, p_{O32}, p_{R2}, p_{R3}\}$,
$S3 = \{p_{O13}, p_{O23}, p_{O33}, p_{R1}, p_{R2}, p_{R3}\}$.

The corresponding seven possible deadlock configurations are shown in Table 12.2. The first column displays the deadlock configuration identifier, whereas the three following columns list the blocked operations in the deadlock state for each machine. Only the operations directly involved in the deadlock configuration are shown. In the last column the empty siphons corresponding to the deadlock configuration are reported.

12.4.1.1. Structural indices

To assess the influence of these deadlock states, the structural indices DP, PSR, BC_i and f_i of the FMS have been estimated by simulation with SIMAN. For each index, a large number of simulation runs have been executed to achieve statistical significance (the 95% confidence interval must be less than 10% of the average), and the average of the data is taken as an estimate of the real value. In each simulation a batch of 100 products, chosen with a uniform random distribution among the three available product types, are processed.

Deadlock identifier	Blocked operations on machines			Empty siphons
	R1	R2	R3	
A	O11, O11	O21	-	S1
B	O11, O11	O32	-	S1
C	O11, O22	O32	O31	S3
D	O11, O22	O21	O31	S3
E	-	O12	O31	S2
F	O22, O22	O21	O31	S3
G	O22, O22	O32	O31	S3

Table 12.2. Deadlock configurations of the FMS station.

The aggregate indices DP and PSR display the following values:
DP = 1,
PSR = 0.04.

Due to the particular structure of the FMS, where all resources are shared, every simulation run terminated in a deadlock state, as shown by index DP. In addition, the deadlock takes place very soon, since very few products complete the job sequence. The number of completed products ranges from 0 to 30 with an average of 4 (index PSR).

With such a low PSR index, it may not be advisable to reduce the batch size to 4 units, in order to avoid deadlocks. On the contrary, this is a case where a well-designed control algorithm can noticeably increase the performance. Therefore, it is convenient to examine the other indices, which distinguish each deadlock configuration.

$BC_A = 3$, $BC_B = 3$, $BC_C = 4$, $BC_D = 4$, $BC_E = 2$, $BC_F = 4$, $BC_G = 4$,

$f_A = 0.187$, $f_B = 0.098$, $f_C = 0.043$, $f_D = 0.085$, $f_E = 0.536$, $f_F = 0.035$, $f_G = 0.016$,

where the subscript refers to the specific deadlock configuration.

Note that in this case, despite the differences in the BC value, all deadlock configurations are equally damaging. Whatever deadlock configuration is reached, after a few state transitions the system is completely blocked, basically because all machines are involved in the completion of the job sequence of any of the three product types. However, the frequencies of occurrence are extremely different. Deadlock configurations with lower BC_i have a higher frequency of occurrence f_i, e.g., configuration E which involves only two products occurs more than 50% of the times. This fact is to be taken into account in control system design.

12.4.1.2. Analysis of a "partial" deadlock avoidance control algorithm

The behavior of the FMS controlled with the PDA control algorithm (see Section 12.3.1) is discussed hereafter.

The new DP and PSR values are:

DP = 0.837 (DPR = 0.837/1 = 0.837),

PSR = 42.7.

Even if the DPR index is not particularly good, the average number of completed products has significantly increased. However, the standard deviation of this estimate (which is also computed by SIMAN) is very high (33.9). This means that setting up a batch process based on the value of index PSR, in the hope that the occurrence of deadlocks might be significantly reduced, can still yield unacceptable performance. For example, if the same process is simulated with a batch size of 40, the PSR decreases to a value of 27.7, while the DP index is equal to 0.5.

Resuming the analysis of the 100 batch size case, it is interesting to examine the behavior of the control algorithm with respect to the seven possible deadlock configurations. Simulation results show that all the deadlock configurations but one are avoided (CRP = 6/7 = 0.857). However, the surviving deadlock configuration is actually the worst (configuration E), which explains the still unsatisfactory results.

12.4.1.3. Analysis of "total" deadlock avoidance control algorithms

The FMS has also been analyzed in combination with the "total" deadlock avoidance control algorithms introduced in Section 12.2. The performance of these algorithms has been classified in terms of index R which counts the number of the operations forbidden by the control algorithms (Table 12.3).

Not surprisingly, the FS algorithm imposes the smallest number of constraints to the dynamics of the system. Only the LL_m algorithm is close to this performance, while all the other algorithms strongly limit the system evolution, imposing many unnecessary constraints.

	R
Bank	195
BK	173
BK_m	120
LL_m	28.2
FS	25.7

Table 12.3. Rigidity of the FMS controlled with "total" deadlock avoidance control algorithms.

12.4.2. Example 2: a 3-machine 3-product timed model

In this section a timed version of the same FMS used in the previous example is considered. Constant processing times are assumed for every couple product-machine as shown in Table 12.4.

	M1	M2	M3
P1	50	30	20
P2	55	40	25
P3	42	25	27

Table 12.4. Processing times for system S2.

Loading and unloading times of input and output carts are neglected, while the wait time of the unloaded products in the input queue is taken into account in the computation of the performance indices. In addition, robotic manipulator transfer times are considered much smaller than processing times, and therefore omitted. In any case, as already noticed, the presence of these components does not introduce new constraints in the deadlock analysis. Finally an infinite capacity queue is assumed at the system input.

The introduction of processing times heavily influences the evolution of the system. Some states may be unreachable and in general all reachable states are reached with frequencies that are different from those of the untimed model. With respect to the deadlock problem, this means that the frequencies of occurrence of the deadlock configurations will be different from the untimed case (some of the deadlock configurations may even be naturally avoided). In particular, we obtain:
$f_A = 0.108$, $f_B = 0.036$, $f_C = 0.047$, $f_D = 0.105$, $f_E = 0.65$, $f_F = 0.029$, $f_G = 0.025$.

It is no longer true that deadlock configurations with lower BC_i have a higher frequency of occurrence f_i. For example, configuration D occurs nearly as frequently as A, and more frequently than B. In addition, the frequency of occurrence of the E configuration has noticeably increased. This is the reason why the PDA algorithm performs worse than in the untimed case:
DP = 0.987 (DPR = 0.987/1 = 0.987),
PSR = 19.7.

In the following Table 12.5 the results of a full performance analysis on the timed FMS are shown. The system has been controlled with the "total" deadlock avoidance control algorithms described in Section 12.2. All the simulations have been executed with an input frequency of one product every 40 seconds. To give more significance to the comparison, the performance indices have been computed also for the two benchmarks, i.e., the FMS controlled with the forbidden state (FS) algorithm and the FMS modified with infinite interoperational queues (IIQ). Notice that all the indices yield the same ordering with respect to algorithm performance. As in Example 1, the LL_m control algorithm yields a performance comparable to that of the benchmark FS, while Bank, BK and BK_m display largely worse performance. The abstract IIQ model gives the best performance. The LL_m algorithm is the only one to impose a number of constraints comparable to the FS algorithm.

More insight on control algorithms and performance indices can be gained by studying the system behavior with varying *input time intervals* (ITI) between successive arrivals of input products of any type. ITIs have been chosen in the range [10 sec., 100 sec.], so that the system's capabilities are tested to the limit. The lower bound can be explained as follows: in the hypothesis that the input product type distribution is uniform, a product of type Pi enters the system every 30 sec. (on average), and this is close to the mean processing time of Pi on machine Rj (see Table 12.4). Further lowering this bound would only result in products being queued at the input. The upper bound of 100 sec., on the other hand, is close to the maximum routing (110 sec.). Using an ITI value higher than 110 would result in a single product being serviced at a time.

	AF	PT	WIP	SSC	R
Bank	2536	8888	28.5	1.15	145
BK	1180	6214	19	1.65	141
BK_m	595	4993	11.9	2.05	84.7
LL_m	342	4509	7.55	2.27	12.7
FS	339	4502	7.49	2.28	11.9
IIQ	119	4075	2.93	2.51	0

Table 12.5. Performance analysis on the timed FMS.

Figure 12.19 shows the performance indices evaluated with different values of ITI. All diagrams of the four performance indices show monotone behavior, which allows for an easy tailoring of the performance. The ordering of the control algorithms does not vary with ITI or the performance index, but the four indices convey different information. AF and WIP yields similar results for an ITI value higher than 40, while at high input frequency AF has a wider spread of values than WIP. At low ITI values the machines are nearly saturated and products are queued at the input. The WIP index sums the number of products in the machines to the number of products in the input queues, and the latter number dominates at low ITI values. Note also that this second number is almost independent of the control algorithms and this explains the low scattering of WIP values. On the other hand, the AF index measures both wait times in the input queue and processing times. While the former are almost equal for any product type and control algorithm, the latter strongly depend on the control policy. This is why at low ITI values AF displays a wide spread of values.

The plots of PT and SSC indices convey analogous information. Each control algorithm saturates the performance of the system at different ITI values, with significantly different results. Given the control algorithm this diagram can be used to find the optimal ITI value.

Finally, it can be noticed that all control algorithms have similar behavior at low input frequency (the uncontrolled system does not even reach deadlock states). The quality of a control algorithm can be evaluated by checking the range of ITI values in which its behavior resembles the optimal performance of the FS algorithm. The smarter the algorithm, the wider the range. The Banker algorithm is nearly as good as FS only in [80, 100], while BK performance is optimal in [60,

100]. The LL_m algorithm yields maximum performance in the whole range, while BK_m takes the second place, due to little performance losses at low ITI values.

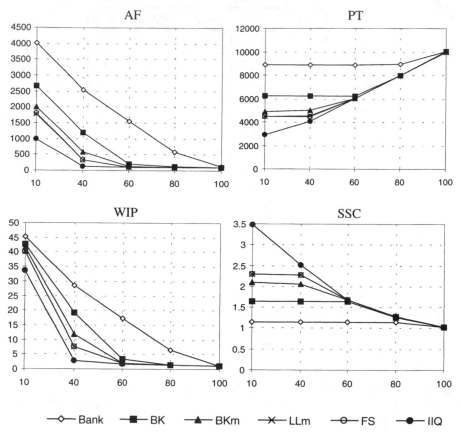

Figure 12.19. Performance indices vs. input time intervals.

CONCLUSIONS

Modeling assumptions and techniques in the design of a logic control system for an FMS have a great effect with regard to the deadlock problem. In particular, different modeling assumptions may result in models with different deadlock situations. Also, modular and hierarchical approaches may be conveniently employed to separate the deadlock problem in smaller subproblems, thus simplifying its solution. The usage of heuristic local deadlock prevention methods, e.g., based on the reallocation of the system's critical resources, is envisaged as an alternative to classical deadlock prevention algorithms, which become impractical to use with models of great size or complexity, such as are frequently encountered in normal industrial applications.

Deadlocks can also be dealt with after the modeling phase, applying deadlock avoidance algorithms on-line. However, it is difficult for the control designer to choose the most appropriate method among the many available. In the chapter, a formal basis for the structural and performance comparison of deadlock avoidance algorithms is established. Through the definition of suitable indices and reference models, and of suitable analysis and simulation approaches, it is shown how it is possible to design appropriate control schemes tailored to specific purposes.

REFERENCES

[1] Banaszak, Z., and Krogh, B.H., "Deadlock Avoidance in Flexible Manufacturing Systems with Concurrently Competing Process Flows", IEEE Transactions on Robotics and Automation, Vol. 6, no. 6, pp. 724-734, 1990.

[2] Banaszak, Z., and Roszkowska, E., "Deadlock avoidance in pipeline concurrent processes", Foundations of Control (Podstawy Sterowania), Vol. 18, pp. 3-17, 1988.

[3] Barkaoui, K., Chaoui, A., and Benamara, R., " The performance of alternative strategies for dealing with deadlocks in FMS", 6th International Conference on Emerging Technologies and Factory Automation Proceedings, ETFA '97, pp. 281-286, 1997.

[4] Dijkstra, E.W., "Co-operating sequential processes", in Programming Languages, F. Genuys (ed.), New York, Academic Press, pp. 43-112, 1968.

[5] Epzeleta, J., Colom, J.-M., and Martinez, J., "A PN Based Deadlock Prevention Policy for Flexible Manufacturing Systems", IEEE Transactions on Robotics and Automation, Vol. 11, no. 2, p. 173, 1995.

[6] Fanti, M.P., Maione, B., Mascolo, S., and Turchiano, B., "Performance of Deadlock Avoidance Algorithms in Flexible Manufacturing Systems", Journal of Manufacturing Systems, Vol. 15, no. 3, pp. 164-178, 1996.

[7] Fanti, M.P., Maione, B., and Turchiano, B., "Digraph-Theoretic Approach for Deadlock Detection and Recovery in Flexible Production Systems", Studies in Informatics and Control, Vol. 5, no. 4, pp. 373-383, 1996.

[8] Fanti, M.P., Maione, B., Mascolo, S., and Turchiano, B., "Event-Based Feedback Control for Deadlock Avoidance in Flexible Production Sys-

tems", IEEE Transactions on Robotics and Automation, Vol. 13, no. 3, pp. 347-363, June 1997.

[9]   Ferrarini, L., and Araki, M., "On Deadlock Occurrence in Manufacturing Systems", Proceedings of the INRIA/IEEE Conference on Emerging Technology and Factory Automation (ETFA '95), Paris, France, Vol. 3, pp. 141-152, October 1995.

[10] Ferrarini, L., and Maroni, M., "Deadlock Avoidance Control For Manufacturing Systems With Multiple Capacity Resources", International Journal of Advanced Manufacturing Technology, Special Issue on PNs and Manufacturing Systems, Vol. 16, no. 1, August 1998.

[11] Ferrarini, L., and Piroddi, L., "Modeling and control of transporting systems in batch processes with multiple aggregated resources", ISIC 2001, IEEE Int. Symposium on Intelligent Control, pp. 258-263, Mexico City, Mexico, 5-7 September, 2001.

[12] Ferrarini, L., and Piroddi, L., "Modular design and implementation of a logic control system for a batch process", *Computers and Chemical Engineering*, Vol. 27, no. 7, pp. 983-996, 2003.

[13] Hauschildt, D., and Valk, R., "Safe states in banker like resouce allocation problems", in Advances in PNs, Vol. 222, W. Brauer (ed.), Springer Verlag, pp. 253-277, 1985.

[14] Hsieh, F.-S., and Chang, S.-C., "Dispatching-Driven Deadlock Avoidance Controller Synthesis for Flexible Manufacturing Systems", IEEE Transactions on Robotics and Automation, Vol. 10, no. 2, p. 196, 1994.

[15] Lee, D.Y., and DiCesare, F., "Scheduling Flexible Manufacturing Systems Using PNs and Heuristic Search", IEEE Transactions on Robotics and Automation, Vol. 10, no.2, p. 123, 1994.

[16] Lee, C.C., and Lin, J.T., "Deadlock Prediction and Avoidance Based on PNs for Zone-Control Automated Guided Vehicle Systems", International Journal of Production Research, Vol. 33, no. 12, p. 3249, 1995.

[17] Minoura, T., and Ding, C., "A Deadlock Prevention Method for a sequence Controller for Manufacturing Control", International Journal of Robotics and Automation, Vol. 6, no. 3, p. 149, 1991.

[18] Moody, J.O., Yamalidou, K., Lemmon, M.D., and Antsaklis, P.J. "Feedback Control of PNs based on place invariants", Proceedings of the 33rd IEEE Conf. on Decision and Control, Vol. 3, pp. 3104-3109, Lake Buena Vista, FL, 1994.

[19] Murata, T., "PNs: properties, analysis and application", *Proceedings of the IEEE*, Vol. 77, no. 4, pp. 541-580, 1989.

[20] Pegden, D., "Introduction to SIMAN 3.0", Reference Manual, July 1985.

[21] Ramaswamy, S.E., and Joshi, S.B., "Deadlock-Free Schedules for Automated Manufacturing Workstations", IEEE Transactions on Robotics and Automation, Vol. 12, no. 3, p. 391, 1996.

[22] Reveliotis, S.A., and Ferreira, P.M., "Deadlock Avoidance Policies for Automated Manufacturing Cells", IEEE Transactions on Robotics and Automation, Vol. 12, no. 6, pp. 845-857, Dec. 1996.

[23] Tittus, M., and Lennartson, B., "Hierarchical Supervisory Control for Batch Processes," IEEE Trans. on Control System Technology, Vol. 7, no. 5, pp. 542-554, 1999.

[24] Viswanadham, N., Narahari, Y., and Johnson, T.L., "Deadlock Prevention and Deadlock Avoidance in Flexible Manufacturing Systems Using PN Models", IEEE Transactions on Robotics and Automation, Vol. 6, no. 6, p. 713, 1990.

[25] Wysk, R.A., Yang, N.-S., and Joshi, S.B., "Resolution of Deadlocks in Flexible Manufacturing Systems: Avoidance and Recovery Approaches", Journal of Manufacturing Systems, Vol. 13, no. 2, p. 128, 1994.

[26] Xie, X., "Deadlock-free Dispatching Control of Manufacturing Systems using PNs", Proceedings of the 13th IFAC World Congress, San Francisco, p. 507, 1996.

[27] Xing, K.-Y., Hu, B.-S., and Chen, H.-X., "Deadlock Avoidance Policy for Petri-Net Modeling of Flexible Manufacturing Systems with Shared Resources", IEEE Transactions on Automatic Control, Vol. 41, no. 2, p. 289, 1996.

[28] Yamalidou, K., Moody, J.O., Lemmon, M.D., and Antsaklis, P.J. "Feedback Control of PNs based on place invariants", Automatica, Vol. 32, no. 1, pp. 15-28, 1996.

APPENDIX: SELECTED NOTATION

AF	Average flowtime
BC	Blocking capability
Bank	Banker algorithm
BK	Banaszak-Krogh algorithm
BK_m	Modified Banaszak-Krogh algorithm
DP	Deadlock percentage
DRP	Deadlock rejection percentage
f_i	Frequency of occurrence of a deadlock configuration
FS	Forbidden state algorithm
IIQ	Infinite interoperational queues model
ITI	Input time interval
LL_m	Modified Lee-Lin algorithm
PSR	Product survival rate
PT	Total processing time of a batch of NP products
SSC	System saturation coefficient
WIP	Work in process

13

Deadlock Characterization and Resolution in Interconnection Networks

Timothy Mark Pinkston
University of Southern California, Los Angeles, CA, USA.

This chapter describes three important classes of deadlocking behavior that can occur in interconnection networks used in computer systems and discusses various techniques that can be used to handle them. Network attributes and phenomena that influence the formation of network deadlocks are identified. Ways in which a network's susceptibility to deadlock can be reduced are presented. Advantages and disadvantages of various proposed approaches are highlighted, and practical usage of certain techniques in experimental and commercial systems is also given.

13.1 INTRODUCTION

High-performance interconnection networks comprise the communication backbone in digital systems at several system levels. At the higher system levels, local-area networks (LANs) [1] are used in clusters of PCs, networks of workstations and other distributed processing systems which serve as cost/performance-effective alternatives to tightly-coupled massively parallel processing systems. System-area networks (SANs) [2] are used for interconnecting processors, memories, and I/O devices in systems with the primary goal of increasing reliability in the presence of link/router failures (often at the expense of duplicating physical resources). Storage-area networks (STANs) [3] are used to increase performance and reliability of large disk arrays by offering access to stored data by processors through multiple paths, thus providing continued service in the presence of processor failure. Internet protocol router fabric (IPRF) networks [4] are used within IP routers to handle IP traffic at high (multigigabit) sustained line rates. Server I/O (SIO) and interprocessor communication (IPC) networks [5,6] are used to overcome many of the scalability limitations of multichip bus-based systems, allowing high-speed interconnections between memory controllers and I/O devices, direct access to disk from LAN adapters, and concurrent communication between processors, memories and I/O devices in multiprocessors. Likewise, at lower levels, networks-on-chip (NOCs) [7–9] are used to overcome many of the performance limitations of bus-based systems at the chip level.

Parallel computing and communication systems built from the above networks require high-performance communication services with high reliability, availability and dependability—collectively, high robustness. The performance of the interconnection network is measured, in part, by packet delivery time from source to destination (i.e., latency) and by the number of packets delivered per unit time (i.e., throughput). In essence, a high-performance network allows the maximum number of packets to make forward progress to their destinations in minimal time, preferably along shortest paths to preserve network bandwidth. Likewise, the reliability, availability and dependability of a network equally impact the overall "goodness" quality of a system. These attributes are measured, in part, by the network's ability to remain up and running at near normal levels even when events occur which change its configuration, possibly due to changes in users' needs and/or system state. Such reconfiguration events may include, for example, hot-swapping of components, failure or addition of links/nodes, activation or deactivation of hosts/routers, etc., in a LAN environment depicted in Figure 13.1. Irrespective of the system, all of the above mentioned attributes have significant importance with the emergence of bandwidth-hungry applications such as high-definition video/audio-on-demand processing, distributed on-line transaction processing, database/decision support systems, grid and Internet applications. Such applications impose a great demand on the communication subsystem not only to be of high performance but also to be highly robust.

In the past, research concentrated on improving topological aspects of interconnection networks, but in recent years, research efforts have focused on improving the router as the primary means of increasing network performance. This includes efforts in such diverse areas as improving router switching, scheduling, injection limitation, flow control, and the routing algorithm. Among these, some of the more significant contributions have arisen from the notion of virtual cut-through switching [10], congestion control [11,12], virtual channel flow control [13,14], virtual output queuing [15] and adaptive routing [16–18]. Figure 13.2 shows a simple router model which allows the implementation of many of these techniques. Virtual cut-through switching allows pipelined transmission of packets across multiple routers and links without occupying multiple routers/links when a

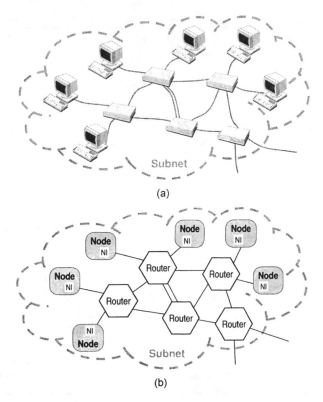

Figure 13.1. An illustration of a switched-LAN subnetwork: (a) its actual components, and (b) a high-level conceptual model of the network components, where NI is the network interface.

packet blocks, which is the case with wormhole switching [19]. Congestion control limits the number of packets injected into the network when the network load is considered to be too high (e.g., nearing saturation). This reduces the chances of the network becoming overly congested and saturated. Virtual channels and virtual output queuing mitigate head-of-line blocking of packets temporarily stored in channels (i.e., edge and/or central queues) during transmission. They provide logically independent multiple communication paths to packets multiplexed across each network link and/or the router crossbar. Adaptive routing increases the degree of flexibility in routing allowed by packets as they traverse the network to their destinations. This allows packets the option of choosing between multiple paths in the network according to prevailing blockage conditions.

Because network resources are finite and, ultimately, are contended for, structural hazards on those resources are inevitable which delay or prevent packet

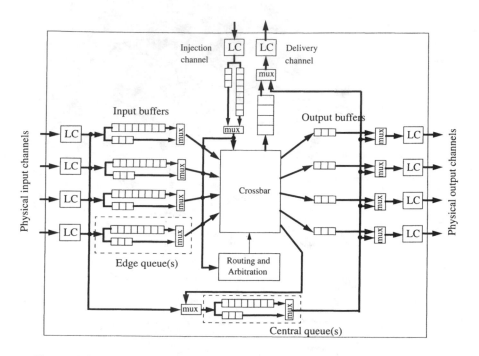

Figure 13.2. A simple model of a generic network router. Each physical channel may have one or more virtual channels associated with it, implemented as edge queue(s). Central queue(s) may also accept flits and be assigned physical channel bandwidth. Flow over the channels is controlled by link controllers (LCs), and multiplexed access (mux) to the internal crossbar ports and other shared resources of the router is determined by the routing and arbitration unit. (From Ref. 18 ©2003 IEEE.)

transmission in the network. This occurs even in networks that feature advanced router architectures. Such hazards cause packets to block which, eventually, can lead to network congestion and, possibly, *deadlock*. One of the more critical problems to be addressed in order to achieve high network performance and robustness is that of efficiently handling deadlock anomalies. Deadlock occurs when there is a circular hold-and-wait dependency relation on network resources by in-flight packets such that progress in routing those packets is indefinitely inhibited. That is, packets would block in the network forever unless some action to resolve the deadlock situation were taken. This phenomenon can result in the entire network (and system) coming to a complete stand-still, consequently degrading system reliability, availability, and dependability considerably. Thus, it is vitally important to guard against deadlock in such a way as not to impose overly restrictive measures that under-utilize network resources.

Deadlocks in interconnection networks are classified into three basic categories, depending on the circumstances under which they form. *Routing-induced deadlocks* are those caused by interactions and dependencies created within the network—between network endpoints—by the routing function which prevents packets from reaching their destinations. The routing function supplies the possible paths packets are allowed to take in the network to reach their destinations from their current locations. *Message-induced deadlocks* (also called protocol-induced deadlocks) are those caused by interactions and dependencies created at the network endpoints among different message types (i.e., requests, replies, etc.), which prevent packets from sinking upon arrival at their destinations. *Reconfiguration-induced deadlocks* are those caused by the interactions and dependencies created through time (dynamically) in a network that undergoes reconfiguration, which prevents packets from reaching their destinations due to being routed under the influence of multiple active routing functions. This can occur even if each of those routing functions is independently deadlock-free under static conditions. Note that we exclude from our deadlock categorization indefinite blocking situations which appear to be deadlocked but really are not, such as those arising from network disconnectivity, i.e., fault-induced indefinite blocking [20]. Such blocking situations are excluded from those termed as deadlock since, in fact, no cyclic hold-and-wait dependency relation on network resources exists.

Given this brief introduction, the remainder of this chapter is organized as follows. The next section describes ways in which deadlocks in interconnection networks can be depicted. This is followed by a section that presents the basic approaches for handling interconnection network deadlocks. While each of these approaches are applicable to all three forms of deadlock, specific examples for each class of deadlock are given. This chapter ends with a few concluding remarks, some bibliographic notes, acknowledgements, and references.

13.2   DEPICTING DEADLOCKS IN INTERCONNECTION NETWORKS

There are a number of different ways in which a network's deadlocking properties can be depicted. Two of the more common ways are to use channel dependency graphs (CDGs) or channel waiting (or wait-for) graphs (CWG). Both are directed graphs in which the vertices represent the channels (either physical or virtual) of the interconnection network. However, the arcs or edges between two channels (c_i, c_j) in CDGs denote a possible channel dependency from c_i to c_j allowed by the routing function whereas in CWGs they denote the next channel c_j reserved and being waited for by a packet in c_i. Thus, CDGs are static and depict all possible channel dependencies allowed by a routing function (whether currently used or not); CWGs are dynamic and represent actual resource allocations and requests existing in a network at a given instance in time. It follows that the CWG provides a critical subset of allowed dependencies represented by a network's CDG.

Channel dependency graphs and channel wait-for graphs can be used to depict the deadlocking properties of a network simply by noting the existence and make-up of cycles that may be present. If no cycles are present, there can be no deadlock as cycles are a necessary condition for deadlock, but they are not sufficient for deadlock to occur. If cycles are present in either of the graphs, the potential for deadlock exists, but whether or not deadlock actually exists for a given configuration of packets must be determined by examining the "reach" of dependencies involved in the cyclic relation. No deadlock exists as long as the reach of dependencies extends beyond the scope of cyclically related resources.

More formally, the *reachable set* of a vertex in a CWG is the set of vertices comprising all paths starting from that vertex. If the reachable set is larger than the set of vertices involved in the cycle, a way of escape for packets involved in the cyclic dependency is provided. If, however, the reachable set of all vertices in the cycle is the set itself, there would be no way of escape. A set of vertices that has this property is referred to as a *deadlock set*, and it forms a *knot* [21,22]. A knot comprises the set of resources involved in cyclic dependency for which there is no alternative reachable resource that can be used to escape from deadlock. As a result, once all resources comprising the knot become full, deadlock abounds. Below, the circumstances under which the three classes of deadlock form and how deadlocks may be depicted using CDGs and CWGs are presented.

13.2.1 Routing-Induced Deadlocks

As noted to earlier, the routing function is responsible for supplying at least one output channel or delivery channel to a packet arriving on a given input channel or injection channel at each router. The aggregation of these routing-induced channel dependence relations for all possible packet configurations of a network is captured by the network's CDG. Accordingly, each channel used by a packet has a dependence relation on the next channel(s) supplied by the routing function, creating a chain or path of dependencies captured by the CWG. As such, routing-induced dependencies take into account only those dependencies on channel and queue resources shown in Figure 13.2; specifically, injection and delivery channels, edge queues, and/or central queues. Interactions occurring at network endpoints are excluded from this set, meaning that packets are assumed always to sink upon reaching their destinations. If knotted cycles appear along a fully occupied set of these resources, *routing-induced deadlock* is said to form.

The likelihood of routing-induced deadlock occurring is largely influenced by three key interrelated factors: the *routing freedom* of the routing algorithm, the number of *blocked packets* within the network, and the number of *resource dependency cycles* as depicted in the channel wait-for graph [22]. Routing freedom corresponds to the number of routing options available to a packet being routed at a given node within the network. Routing freedom is reflected in the CWG by the fan-out of vertices, which can be location dependent for packets en route in the network: smaller fan-out than that which is maximally allowed by the routing function may be the result if adaptivity is exhausted. Blocked packets are those packets in the network that cannot acquire any of the alternative channels required to make progress at a given point in time due to those channels being fully occupied by other packets. Correlated packet blocking can result in wait-for dependency cycles on resources, possibly leading to deadlock.

On the one hand, routing freedom can considerably increase the potential number of cycles that can form once packets block, i.e., at network saturation. This is due to the compounding effects of routing freedom with the number of network hops experienced by packets and the number of blocked packets in the network. For example, given an average distance of h hops each allowing a routing freedom of F channel options at each router, the theoretical upper bound on routing freedom of a packet from source to destination is F^h (i.e., routing a packet diagonally over an n-dimensional space), whereas blocking opportunity is only h. This upper bound on routing freedom may not be reached if F decreases as hops are taken (i.e., routing a packet minimally over the periphery of an n-dimensional space). Given a total of B blocked packets each with a routing freedom of F, the theoretical upper bound on the number of unique cycles which can form is F^B. This upper bound may not be reached due to limitations on possible topological connections allowed. Nevertheless, as the number of blocked packets increases due to an exhaustion of routing freedom and/or the network reaching saturation, the potential for cycle formation increases considerably, which can increase the probability of deadlock.

On the other hand, routing freedom has an opposite and more influential effect on deadlock probability than it does on the creation of cycles. As routing freedom is increased, the number of blocked packets decreases substantially. More importantly, the degree of correlation required among blocked packets to form a knot also increases substantially. This greatly decreases the likelihood of the occurrence of deadlock. Given enough routing freedom, this correlation factor offsets the opposing effect on deadlock probability caused by the potential increase in the number of cycles. Networks with minimal routing freedom may not offset the opposing effects as there may exist a one-to-one correspondence between cycles and deadlocks, e.g., single-cycle deadlocks. However, networks with greater routing freedom may offset the opposing effects as a large number of cycles can exist without deadlock formation, e.g., cyclic non-deadlocks.

Consider, for example, the 2×4 torus network shown in the left-hand side of Figure 13.3. If the network's routing function supplies all possible channels along minimal paths to packets' destinations from their current positions (i.e., adaptive minimal routing is used), the CDG shown on the right-hand side of the figure is formed. Clearly, cycles exist in this graph, indicating that deadlock may be possible for some configurations of packets routing in the network. The CWG (shown in the middle) for packet configuration p_1, p_2, and p_3 routing in this network depict the critical subset of allowed dependencies "alive" in the network, assuming wormhole switching. The channels currently occupied (possibly only partially)

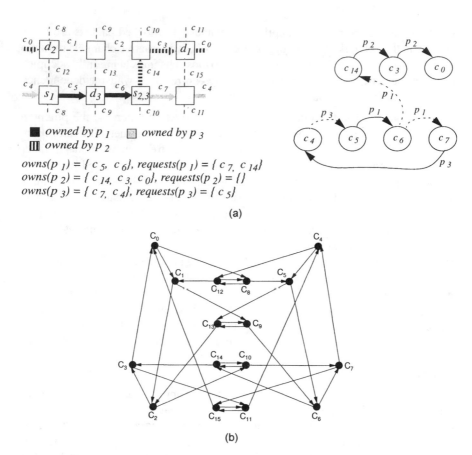

(a)

(b)

Figure 13.3. (a) The network graph and channel wait-for graph, and (b) the channel dependency graph. These are for packets routed adaptively within a 2×4 torus network (the links on the periphery are wrap-around links). Although cycles exist in the CWG and CDG, this packet configuration is not deadlocked.

by packet p_i are represented by the set $owns(p_i)$ shown as solid arcs and channels supplied by the routing function for the packet to continue routing is represented by the set $requests(p_i)$ shown as dotted arcs. The added routing freedom given by adaptive minimal routing is reflected in the request set for some blocked packets having a cardinality greater than one (i.e., $|requests(p_1)| = 2$). As shown, a cycle for this packet configuration exists consisting of the set of vertices $\{c_4, c_5, c_6, c_7\}$. However, there is no deadlock as the reach of dependencies extends beyond the set of resources involved in this cycle of dependency.

This cyclic non-deadlock situation is easily verified by examining the reachable set for each vertex. The reachable set for vertex c_{14} is $\{c_3, c_0\}$; for c_3 is $\{c_0\}$;

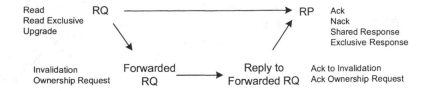

Figure 13.4. Ordering among message types allowed by a typical cache coherence protocol, where RQ and RP are request and reply message types, respectively, and arrows indicate a message dependency from one message type to another.

for c_0 is $\{\}$; and for vertices c_4, c_5, c_6 and c_7 which are involved in the cycle, the reachable set is $\{c_4, c_5, c_6, c_7, c_{14}, c_3, c_0\}$. Clearly, the reachable set is larger than the set of vertices involved in the cycle, thus providing a way of escape for packets involved in the cyclic dependency. If, however, the destination for p_1 were in the bottom row instead of the top row of the same column, the reachable set of all vertices in the cycle would be identical to the set itself, i.e., $\{c_4, c_5, c_6, c_7\}$, as there would be no escape through channel c_{14} for packet p_1. Given packet p_1's current position relative to the new destination, routing freedom is decreased as the routing function supplies only channel c_7. In essence, all packets involved in the cycle have exhausted their adaptivity. This resource set, therefore, comprises a deadlock set on which a knot forms—which, in this case, is composed of only a single cycle. Adaptive routing functions typically have knots composed of a large number of cycles in most cases, i.e., multicycle deadlocks. No matter the case, routing-induced deadlock occurs once all channels comprising the deadlock set become fully occupied. The occurrence of such deadlocks, however, have been shown to be very rare and may never occur in practice when multiple virtual channels are used with maximum routing freedom [22,23].

13.2.2 Message-Induced Deadlocks

The exchange of various types of messages is pervasive in computer systems in which interconnection networks are employed. Many message types—as defined by the communication protocol of the system—may be used to complete data-interchange transactions. For instance, cache coherence protocols may permit data transactions to be composed of certain combinations of *request, forwarded-request, reply-to-forwarded-request*, and *reply* message types, as shown in Figure 13.4. At any given end-node in the system, there can be a coupling between the two message types: the generation of one message type, e.g., the reply message generated by the destination, is directly coupled to the reception of another message type, e.g., the request message received by the destination. As the coupling between message types is transferred to network resources due to the finiteness of resources along the

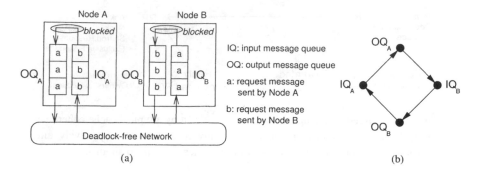

Figure 13.5. (a) A simple example of message-induced deadlock occurring between two nodes connected by a network free of routing-induced deadlock. (b) The corresponding dependency graph for resources at network endpoints, where dependencies form a cyclic (and knotted) wait-for relationship.

message path inside each node (at network endpoints), additional dependencies on network resources are created, referred to as *message or protocol dependencies*.

A distinct class of message dependency is created for each pair of message types for which a direct coupling exists and is transferred to network resources. Each combination may present different kinds of message dependencies and a corresponding *message dependency chain*, which is a series of message types used to complete a transaction on network resources. Since message dependencies may prevent messages from sinking at their destinations, they must be added to the complete set of resource dependencies. If knotted cycles form along a set of resources when resources at the network endpoints are also taken into account, a type of deadlock called *message-induced or protocol-induced deadlock* forms once all resources comprising the knot become full.

A message dependency chain represents an ordered list of message dependencies allowed by the communication protocol. We define the partial order relation "$\prec$" between two message types m_1 and m_2 by the following: $m_1 \prec m_2$ if and only if m_2 can be generated by a node receiving m_1 for some data transaction. Message type m_2 is said to be *subordinate* to m_1, and all message types subordinate to m_2 are also subordinate to m_1. The final message type at the end of the message dependency chain is said to be a *terminating* message type. The number of message types allowed within a message dependency chain is referred to as the *chain length*. For example, if the system defines only two message types, *request* and *reply*, for all data transactions and the message types establish the dependency relation *request* $\prec$ *reply*, then the chain length is two.

Consider the following example of queue resource sharing at network endpoints by messages of two different types (*request* $\prec$ *reply*), shown in Figure 13.5. Depicted in the figure is a simple message-induced deadlock represented by a

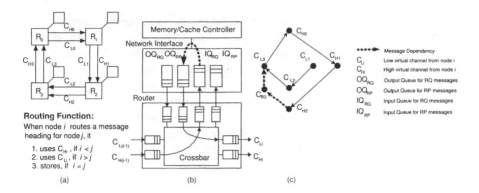

Figure 13.6. (a) A four node system interconnected by a unidirectional ring network using two virtual channels to avoid routing deadlocks, as described in Section 13.3.1. (b) Message dependencies occurring inside network interfaces. (c) The corresponding resource dependency graph consisting of network channels (i.e., C_{Hj} and C_{Lj}) and queue resources at Node $R3$ (i.e., C_{R3}). (From Ref. 61 ©2003 IEEE.)

resource dependency graph in which two nodes, Node A and Node B, are each sending request messages to one another and expecting to receive reply messages over a network free from routing-induced deadlock. Each node's network interface has an output message queue and an input message queue, which are used to buffer messages of any type being injected into or received from the network. If no buffer space is available in the output queue, no message in the input queue that generates a subordinate message type is serviced. Otherwise, the message generated by the serviced message would cause overflow in the output queue or indefinitely stall the network interface from servicing other messages. These are situations which are avoided to ensure correct execution. If the arrival rate of request messages exceeds the consumption rate, a backlog starts to form at the input message queue IQ_A at Node A. After a while, the backlog propagates backward in the direction of message injection at the output message queue OQ_B at Node B. The backlog eventually reaches the input message queue IQ_B at Node B, and, further, to the output message queue OQ_A at Node A. At this point, a deadlock forms as no buffer space can be freed for reply messages needed by both nodes to continue execution.

Consider next how the sharing of channel resources *between* network endpoints (i.e., within the network) among messages of two different types (*request* ≺ *reply*) can cause message-induced deadlocks. Shown in Figure 13.6 is a simple four node system interconnected by a unidirectional ring network consisting of two virtual channels used in such a way as to avoid routing-induced deadlock between network endpoints (refer to Section 13.3.1 to understand the routing function given in Figure 13.6(a)). A processor-memory node is connected to each router via the node's network interface which transmits and receives messages to/from the network through its output and input queues, respectively. Figure 13.6(b) depicts the message dependency that can occur at the network endpoint. The channel dependency graph for the routing algorithm is shown as solid arcs in Figure 13.6(c) and is cycle-free between endpoints. However, when node $R1$ sends a request message to $R3$ which responds back to the request by sending a reply message to $R1$, a message dependency from C_{H2} to C_{L3} exists in the network (shown as dotted arcs in the figure for node $R3$ only) through the network interface channel represented by C_{R3} at $R3$. This completes the cycle in the channel dependency graph, making message-induced deadlocks possible.

13.2.3   Reconfiguration-Induced Deadlocks

When a change in network topology or routing arises through time, it may be necessary to reconfigure the routing function in order to remap and/or reconnect routing paths between nodes in the system. Reconfiguring a network's routing function can cause additional dependencies among network resources both during and after the reconfiguration process that are not independently allowed by either the old or new routing functions. The paths of channels occupied by some undelivered packets routed with the old routing function (i.e., their *configuration*) could be illegal under the new routing function. As a result, two adjacent units of such packets (called *flits*[1]) could be stored in two different channels—one allowed only by the old routing function and the other allowed only by the new routing function. This can create a set of residual dependencies, referred to as *ghost dependencies* [24], that must be taken into account in the total set of resource dependencies when determining the network's deadlock properties. Ghost dependencies can interact with dependencies allowed by the new routing function to close dependency cycles on resources used to escape from deadlock, causing *reconfiguration-induced deadlock*.

Figure 13.7 illustrates how ghost dependencies brought on by undelivered packets in a wormhole network undergoing reconfiguration can cause reconfiguration-induced deadlock. The arrows in the figures indicate the up directions assigned to the links for up*/down* routing [25], a routing technique that is free from routing-induced deadlocks (see Section 13.3.1). Up*/down* routing allows packets to follow any path leading to their destination which is comprised only of zero or more up links followed by zero or more down links. This avoids cycles from forming, which makes the routing algorithm deadlock-free in the case of no reconfiguration. In the example shown, the network undergoes reconfiguration in response to the old root node being removed. Link directions are altered for some links in order for a new root node to be established for the new up*/down* routing function. Reconfiguration-induced deadlock may be caused by the ghost

---

[1] A *flit* is the smallest unit of a packet on which flow control is performed. The flit size can be less than the packet size when wormhole switching is used; it is equal to the packet size when virtual cut-through switching is used.

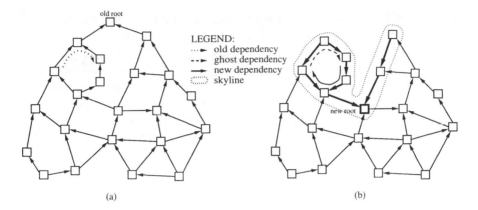

Figure 13.7. (a) Reconfiguration of a network that uses Up*/Down* Routing which is free from routing-induced deadlock (see Section 13.3.1). In it, packets route toward their destinations over paths consisting of zero or more "up" links followed by zero or more "down" links. The "up" direction for each link in the figure is indicated by the direction of the arrowheads (and is also implied by the relative vertical positions of the nodes). In (b), the old root node is removed, which triggers a new root node to be discovered within the skyline of the network (enclosed by dotted lines), where the thicker lines indicate links which reverse their directions after reconfiguration completes. Ghost dependencies (dashed arc) carried from the old routing function can form a dependency cycle with new dependencies (solid arc) from the new routing function, thus creating the potential for deadlock.

dependency between channels, shown as a dashed arc. This dependency is not among the normal dependencies allowed by the new routing function, yet it persists even after reconfiguration is completed if a packet that was routed using the old routing function remains in the network and holds resources that were supplied by the old routing function. Its existence closes the channel dependency cycle as shown, preventing escape from deadlock once all affected resources become fully occupied.

13.3 APPROACHES FOR HANDLING DEADLOCKS

Approaches for handling deadlock in interconnection networks are mainly based either on applying restrictions to avoid them (i.e., avoidance-based) or on lifting restrictions but supplying nominal resources to detect and resolve them (i.e., recovery-based). A third approach is based on reserving all needed resources prior to transmission. This way, deadlock is altogether prevented as no blockage of any kind is encountered. However, since this strategy is typically used only in legacy circuit switched networks, it will not be discussed further in this chapter as we focus on techniques for packet switched networks.

From an implementation point of view, the primary distinction between avoidance and recovery approaches lies in the tradeoff made between increasing the routing freedom and reducing the potential for deadlock formation. Routing freedom can be increased by adding physical channels, i.e., increasing the number of alternative paths *available across* different directions and dimensions of the network by using bidirectional and high-degree (rich) topologies. It can also be increased by adding more virtual channels per physical channel, i.e., increasing the number of logical routing options *available within* each dimension/link. Increasing the adaptivity of the routing function also increases routing freedom as the number of routing options *allowed within and across* each dimension is increased. However, as previously discussed in Section 13.2.1, increasing the routing freedom increases the potential number of cycles and, likewise, affects the probability of knot formation. Hence, the advantages of techniques based either on deadlock avoidance or deadlock recovery depend on how infrequently deadlocks might occur if routing freedom is maximized and how efficiently packets can be routed through the network if routing freedom is restricted such that deadlocks are completely avoided.

Let us first consider deadlock avoidance approaches. The simplest way of avoiding deadlock is to disallow the appearance of cycles in the network's CDG [19]. As cyclic resource dependency is necessary for deadlock, the lack of cycles precludes deadlock. We can think of this as deadlock avoidance in the *strict sense* since the phenomena that precipitate deadlock, i.e., cyclic dependencies, cannot exist anywhere in the network. An alternative way of avoiding deadlock is to allow cycles in the network's CDG but to enforce routing restrictions only on a subset of network resources used to escape deadlock such that all dependencies on those resources (as given by an *extended* CDG) are acyclic [16]. This is the situation in which the "reach" of all possible cyclic dependencies are guaranteed at all times to extend outside the scope of cyclically related resources. We can think of this as deadlock avoidance in the *wide sense* since cyclic dependencies which precipitate deadlock at certain points in the network are prevented from escalating into knotted dependencies due to the constant availability of escape resources network-wide. Yet a third alternative for avoiding deadlock in the *weak sense* is to allow cycles in the network's CDG and extended CDG, and even to allow knots to form, but to require at least some subset of escape resources (i.e., those in the extended CDG) to be large enough such that they never become fully occupied [26]. This guarantees that packets along knotted resources eventually are able to make forward progress, albeit slowly.

Deadlock recovery approaches, on the other hand, require correct detection and resolution of all potential deadlocks that may occur in a network. Precisely detecting the occurrence of a potential deadlock situation in interconnection networks requires an excessive amount of distributed resources controlled under a complex management mechanism. To reduce costs, less accurate heuristic techniques that detect all true potential deadlock situations but, consequently, also some occasional false ones are typically used, such as time-out or flow-control based mechanisms [27]. Once detected, deadlock can be resolved either in the wide sense or in the weak sense.

The simplest way of resolving potential deadlock is to remove from the network one or more packets in the deadlock set [20], i.e., by killing and later re-injecting it for subsequent delivery after some random delay. We can think of this as *regressive* deadlock recovery since the abort-and-retry process, in effect, makes packets regress back to their source in order to resolve deadlock. Alternatively, deadlock can be resolved by ensuring that at least one packet in the deadlock set no longer waits only for resources occupied by other packets in the aggregation of all deadlock sets in the network [20]. This can be done either *deflectively* or *progressively*, depending upon whether recovering packets make progress toward their destination or are simply deflected out of the potential deadlock situation obliviously with regard to their ultimate destination.

Below, some well-known as well as some recently proposed approaches for handling the three types of deadlocks that can occur in interconnection networks are described. As mechanisms for handling each is discussed separately, it is assumed that other mechanisms are in place to sufficiently handle the other two types of deadlocks, i.e., using the avoidance or recovery techniques discussed in the other sections given below.

13.3.1 Handling Routing-Induced Deadlocks

A. *Routing-Induced Deadlock Avoidance in the Strict Sense*

Prior to the past decade, routing-induced deadlock was handled primarily by avoiding it in the strict sense. Cyclic-wait situations were completely avoided by imposing severe restrictions on the order in which all network channel queues were allocated to packets. Techniques for accomplishing this can be classified as being *path-based*, *queue-based*, or some *hybrid* combination of the two. Queue-based techniques may be subdivided into *channel-based* schemes and *buffer-based* schemes. The idea behind path-based schemes is to avoid cyclic-wait dependencies on resources by restricting the possible paths packets can take from source to destination, as supplied by the routing function. By prohibiting certain turns in routing while maintaining network connectivity, it is possible to eliminate some critical resource dependencies that might otherwise close dependency cycles. This effectively leads to some total ordering being imposed on the use of network resources. Similarly, queue-based schemes accomplish the same by restricting the possible queues (virtual channels for channel-based schemes or queue buffers for buffer-based schemes) used by packets to their destinations, as supplied by the routing function.

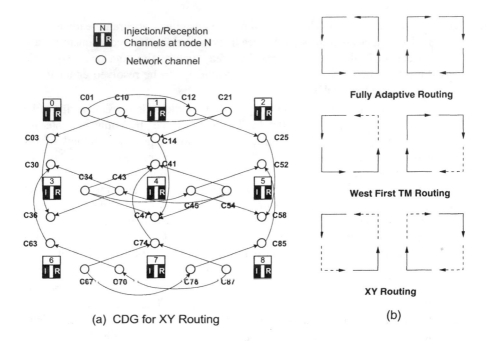

(a) CDG for XY Routing   (b)

Figure 13.8. (a) A 3×3 bidirectional mesh network with its corresponding acyclic CDG shown for XY dimension-order routing (i.e., channel Cij is the channel from node i to node j). (b) Inter-dimensional turns allowed for routing functions with higher (top) to lower (bottom) routing freedom, where dashed arcs indicate turns disallowed by the routing function.

A number of path-based schemes have been proposed and many implemented in multiprocessor, network-based, and supercomputer systems. Dimension-Order Routing (DOR), used in the Cray T3D [28] and SGI Origin 2000 [29] for example, constrains packets to *deterministically route* minimally to their destinations in network dimension order. Figure 13.8(a) shows the network and channel dependency graph for XY dimension-order routing on a 3×3 mesh, where packets must reach their X dimension coordinates first before routing in the Y dimension. DOR is similar except that routing freedom along the two directions of each dimension is increased. Turn Model (TM) Routing [30], used in the Rapid Reconfigurable Router (RCube) [31], prohibits the minimum number of turns needed to prevent inter-dimensional cycles in an n-dimensional mesh in order to further increase routing freedom. This is $n(n-1)$ or a quarter of the possible turns instead of half the turns for DOR, as shown in Figure 13.8(b). West-first Turn Model routing, for example, requires all packets to be routed non-adaptively west first before being routed adaptively in other directions. Although the Turn Model increases routing freedom, its applicability is limited primarily to mesh networks. Up*/Down* Routing, used in Autonet [25] and Myrinet [1] for example, is generally applicable to arbitrary network topologies. As shown in Figure 13.7, each link is assigned a direction, and packets route toward their destinations over paths consisting of zero or more "up" links followed by zero or more "down" links. This forces an ordering on network resources such that turn dependencies from "down" links to "up" links are prohibited, thus disallowing cycles to be completed in the network's CDG.

Path-based schemes have the advantage of not requiring virtual channels to strictly avoid deadlock. However, their routing flexibility (i.e., routing freedom) is sacrificed and, more importantly, these schemes may not always provide a complete deadlock-free solution for networks with wrap-around links, like rings and tori, unless some network links (i.e., the wrap-around links) go unused. This is demonstrated for the ring network shown in Figure 13.9(a), where its corresponding cyclic CDG is shown in Figure 13.9(b). Queue-based schemes can effectively deal with network topologies that inherently have cycles since they decouple the allocation of queue resources (virtual channels or buffers) from the use of physical links by packets. Buffer-based schemes, such as structured buffer pools [32,33] used in legacy packet switched networks, place packets into buffer classes associated with the number of hops left to reach their destinations. This requires $D + 1$ distinct buffer classes[2], where D is the network diameter which is the maximum number of hops (or distance) between any two nodes along a minimal path in the system.

Channel-based schemes which use virtual channels such as [19,34,35] allow the number of required queue resources to be independent of the network diameter. As shown in Figure 13.9(c) and (d) (and alluded to earlier in Figure 13.6) for a four node unidirectional ring network, each physical channel can be associated with two virtual channels—a high channel and a low channel—and an ordering on the use of those virtual channels can be imposed explicitly by the routing function. For example, in the figure, physical channel c_0 from router 0 to router 1 is associated with virtual channels c_{H0} (high) and c_{L0} (low). The routing function supplies the high channel c_{Hi} to a packet at router i destined to node j if $i < j$; or it supplies the low channel c_{Li} if $i > j$; otherwise, it delivers the packet to the node associated with router i. Thus, deadlock is strictly avoided with the use of just two virtual channels per physical channel independent of network diameter, but only one of those channels is supplied to packets at any given point in the network. That is, there is an upper bound on routing freedom and network capacity of only 50% utilization of virtual channel resources.

Pure channel-based schemes that do not restrict the allowable paths packets can take in routing to their destinations, i.e., those that allow *fully adaptive routing*

---

[2]This number can be halved using a *negative hop* scheme in which adjacent nodes are partitioned into distinct positive and negative subsets (i.e., via graph coloring), and packets are placed into a buffer of class j if it has traveled exactly j negative hops.

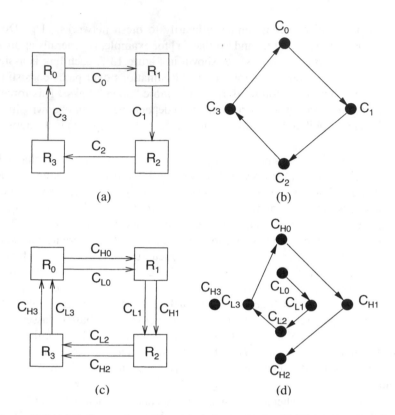

Figure 13.9. (a) A four node unidirectional ring network and (b) its corresponding cyclic CDG for unrestricted routing. (c) The same four node unidirectional ring network with two virtual channels per physical channel and (d) its corresponding acyclic CDG for a routing function which enforces an ordering on the use of the virtual channels.

illustrated at the top of Figure 13.8(b), such as Linder and Harden's scheme [34], consequently require an exponential growth[3] in the number of virtual channels needed to prevent cycles in the CDG. This growth can increase the implementation complexity of the router considerably. Even with such a large number of virtual channels, these schemes allow only a small subset of those resources to be usable by each packet as virtual channels are grouped into ordered levels and classes. This has motivated the development of hybrid schemes that are based partially on both path and channel restrictions. Hybrid path/channel schemes are prevalent in systems which strictly avoid reconfiguration-induced deadlock, including the

---

[3]This growth is based on network dimensionality, i.e., $2^{n-1}(n+1)$ virtual channels per physical channel are required, where n is the number of network dimensions.

SGI Spider [36], and Intel Cavallino [37] to name a few. As an example, Planar Adaptive Routing (PAR) [35] is a *partially adaptive routing* scheme that strictly avoids deadlock using a combination of both path and channel restrictions. This scheme requires three virtual channels per physical channel in n-dimensional mesh networks and six in torus networks, of which only one can be used in each of the allowed dimensions by packets routing in the network. Deadlock is avoided in the strict sense by restricting the possibility of routing adaptively to, at most, two dimensions at a time and by ordering the traversal of adaptive planes taken by packets. Although routing freedom is increased over a purely deterministic path-based scheme like DOR, it is still very much limited as some idle channels along minimal paths in the $n - 2$ other dimensions of the network (i.e., those not in the current adaptive plane) are automatically excluded from use by blocked packets since they lie outside of the adaptive plane.

B. Routing-Induced Deadlock Avoidance in the Wide Sense

Routing freedom can be increased considerably while still guarding against routing-induced deadlock using routing schemes based on avoiding deadlock in the wide sense. This has been the technique of choice for most systems implemented within the past decade and continues to be popular since network resources are used much more efficiently. The most well-known and widely used scheme is Duato's Protocol [16]. It is a hybrid path/channel-based scheme that has seen widespread use in research and commercial systems, including the MIT Reliable Router [38], Cray T3E [39], Alpha 21364 [40], and IBM BlueGene/L supercomputer [41]. The idea behind this scheme is to allow unrestricted fully adaptive routing on the majority of network virtual channels while providing a way of escape from deadlock on a connected minimal subset of virtual channels.

Virtual channels are divided into two classes or sets: one susceptible to cyclic dependencies, i.e., those on which fully adaptive routing is permitted, and the other free from cyclic dependencies, i.e., those on which escape routing (usually deterministic) is performed. The escape channel set can be made deadlock-free by using any of the strict deadlock avoidance techniques described previously on them. Deadlock is avoided in the wide sense as no restrictions are placed on the adaptive channels. This can lead to dependency cycles forming on them. When packets block (possibly cyclically) on adaptive channels, they may use escape channels which are always supplied by the routing function. A packet can either stay on the set of escape channels until it reaches its destination or it can come back to adaptive channels, depending on which switching technique is used (i.e., wormhole or virtual cut-through, respectively) [17]. The existence of a coherent and connected escape path which has no cycles in its extended channel dependency graph is sufficient to avoid deadlock in the wide sense.

A number of schemes similar to Duato's Protocol based on avoiding deadlock in the wide sense have also been proposed in the past decade, but with slight differences. The more interesting are the *-channels [42], Schwiebert and

Jayasimha's algorithm [43], and the Dynamic Routing Algorithm by Dally and Aoki [44]. As an example, deadlocks are avoided in the wide sense by the Dynamic Routing Algorithm by not allowing cycles in the packet wait-for graph instead of the channel wait-for graph. In this hybrid path/channel-based scheme, each packet keeps track of the number of network dimension reversals it makes. Similar to Duato's Protocol, a packet is routed adaptively on any channel in the adaptive class until blocked with all supplied output channels being used but, in this case, by packets with equal or lower values of dimension reversals. Upon this condition, the packet is forced onto the deadlock-free deterministic class of channels and must remain there until routed to its destination. A packet's dimension reversals relative to other packets at a given router ultimately places an upper bound on adaptivity, and the deterministic channel class ultimately becomes a performance bottleneck.

Hybrid path/channel-based routing schemes which avoid deadlock in the wide sense may have the advantage of requiring only a few additional resources (in the form of virtual channels) over that required by pure path-based schemes which avoid deadlock in the strict sense, but they still have some inefficiencies. Although all virtual channels in the adaptive set are supplied to packets, typically only one of the virtual channels composing the escape set is supplied to packets at each router. Restrictions on escape virtual channels consequently cap the routing freedom of such schemes below the upper bound provided by *true fully adaptive routing*, where full adaptivity is maintained across all physical link dimensions of a network topology as well as across all virtual channels within a given link dimension, without restriction. For example, if three virtual channels were implemented in a torus network, these schemes could use only one virtual channel for fully adaptive routing and only one is supplied for escape routing whereas all three could be used by a true fully adaptive routing scheme. Likewise, if only two virtual channels were implemented, fully adaptive routing would not be permitted on either channel by these schemes, but it would be permitted on both with a true fully adaptive scheme. Consequently, it may be very inefficient to allow fully adaptive routing on only a subset of the total number of virtual channels, particularly if knotted dependencies which can lead to deadlock occur very infrequently, as is shown to be the case typically [22,23].

C.   Routing-Induced Deadlock Avoidance in the Weak Sense

Routing freedom can be increased further by using routing schemes which avoid deadlock in the weak sense by never allowing knotted resources to become fully occupied. These are typically hybrid path/queue-based schemes which operate on the principles of deflection and/or injection limitation. To better understand these principles, consider closely what takes place when packets make forward movement in the network. Each time a packet moves forward, an empty buffer in a queue associated with the next router port along the path is consumed by the head of the packet. Likewise, an occupied buffer associated with a prior router port is released by the tail of the packet. Assuming that the unit of an empty buffer space is defined as a *bubble* [26], each forward movement of a packet in one direction is equivalent to the backward propagation of a bubble in the opposite direction. Thus, the movement of packets in a network can be characterized simply by considering the availability of bubbles in resources needed by packets and how those bubbles flow through those network resources: the more bubbles flowing within needed network resources, the greater the number of packets that can make forward progress.

All of the techniques mentioned in Section 13.1 in some way affect the availability and/or flow of bubbles in the network. Virtual cut-through switching defines the granularity of bubbles to be the size of a packet. Network throttling or injection limitation regulates the number of bubbles that flow out of the network (or network dimensions) to keep the number of bubbles available within the network (or network queues) above some threshold. Virtual channel flow control confines bubbles to flow within logical networks so that bubble movement within different logical networks can be independent of one another, subject to the channel scheduling algorithm. Likewise, virtual output queuing confines bubbles to flow within separate network dimensions. Techniques for avoiding routing-induced deadlock in the strict or wide sense as discussed in Sections A. and B. restrict bubble flow such that all bubbles in the network always flow through some defined subset (or entire set) of network resources in some total or partial order. Given the above facilities to manipulate bubbles and their displacement, the real challenge essentially becomes how to apply the fewest restrictions on bubble flow so as to always maintain deadlock freedom, thus avoiding deadlock in the weak sense.

Increasing the routing freedom relaxes restrictions on packet movement, which allows bubbles to flow more freely among network resources, but some restrictions must still be enforced to ensure deadlock freedom. The idea behind techniques designed to avoid deadlock in the weak sense is to allow complete freedom of forward packet movement without regard for avoiding cyclic or knotted dependencies. The resulting flexibility in routing options provided by true fully adaptive routing on a multitude of network resources (i.e., virtual channels, virtual output queues, etc.) reduces the probability that correlated resource dependencies form in the first place, as discussed in Section 13.2.1.

In the rare case that knotted dependencies do form on a set of queues, deadlock can be avoided by *limiting injection* into that set by resources external to them once some threshold on their occupancy is reached. This concept is illustrated in Figure 13.10 for the case of a threshold equal to one buffer space less than the maximum aggregate queue capacity along the cycle (Figure 13.10(a)). Such a cycle could arise from inter-dimensional turns or from routing along a ring (or wrap-around links in a torus network). Once this state is detected as being reached, packet $E1$ is denied access to Queue 4 as shown in Figure 13.10(b); otherwise, knotted resources would become fully occupied as shown in Figure 13.10(c). While intuitive and straightforward to conceive of in theory, verifying the existence of a

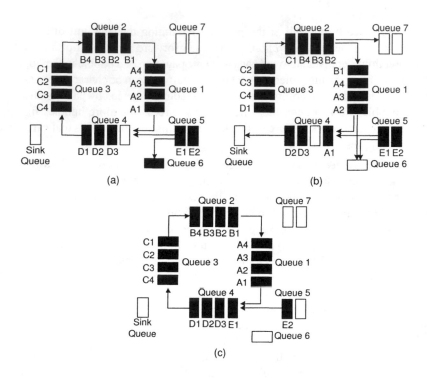

Figure 13.10. Importance of controlling bubble flow in one of possibly many logical (virtual channel) networks with adaptive routing. Only queue resources and dependencies on them by packets are shown. (a) Packets A1 and E1 compete for a bubble in Queue 4, the only one in the knotted dependency cycle consisting of Queues 1–4. Bubbles in other queues are not available; that is, they are not supplied by the routing function for A1, B1, and D1, shown as arcs. When available, a bubble in Queue 6 can be used by packet E1. (b) If the bubble is allocated to A1, deadlock is prevented as the knot keeps the bubble. Assuming the bubble traverses the cycle, new head packets establish a different dependency pattern, making other bubbles available, i.e., packet D2 sinks; A2 and B2 have additional routing options; and E1 can use the bubble in Queue 6. (c) If allocated to E1, the bubble exits the cycle, causing knotted resources to become fully occupied and deadlock to ensue.

single bubble within all possible knots may be difficult to implement in practice. One possible mechanism for identifying cycles nearing full occupancy is described in Section D..

An example of a scheme based partially on this technique is the hybrid path/channel-based Adaptive Bubble Routing scheme [26]. Injection limitation is used to implement the escape routing function in the weak sense *within each dimension* of a torus network, thus requiring only one virtual channel for escape routing instead of two. However, escape routing across dimensions is still implemented using dimension order routing, thus disallowing the formation of inter-dimensional knots. Because of this, this scheme places some restrictions on routing freedom, which keeps it from being true fully adaptive. This scheme can, therefore, be said to be hybrid in another respect: it avoids deadlock in the wide sense for inter-dimensional escape routes and avoids deadlock in the weak sense for intra-dimensional escape routes. Although packet injection and flow into each network dimensional ring is allowed, in theory, if as few as only two free buffers exist *along the ring*, gathering the global status information needed to enforce this condition may be costly to implement in practice (the pinging mechanism described in Section D. may facilitate this). As a simplification, the decision to inject packets into dimensional rings could be made locally by requiring that at least two free buffers exist in the appropriate escape queue *at each router* in the network, as is implemented in the IBM BlueGene/L supercomputer [41].

An alternative way of avoiding routing-induced deadlock in the weak sense is to allow the full network capacity always to be supplied to packets via controlled deflection of packets out of cyclic or knotted dependencies, consequently through misrouting. That is, there is always at least one packet in each knot that is supplied some nonminimal path to reach its destination as long as the input degree (# of ports) of each router is equal to the output degree. This is done through *deflection rerouting*. Since injection and delivery ports are included in the input/output degree of a router, nonminimal paths could include delivery into attached nodes that are not the ultimate destination of a packet, as is done in the In-Transit Buffer scheme [45] and Hot Potato Routing [46]. This would be the case for packet $D1$ in Figure 13.10(c) if it were deflected into the sink queue. Alternatively, packet $B1$ could be deflected into Queue 7, which also happens not to be along a minimal path but does have several bubbles (empty queue buffers) available to route packets. A technique similar to this is used in the hybrid path/queue-based true fully adaptive Chaotic Routing scheme [47] implemented in the ChaosLAN [48]. The availability of bubbles is regulated using a packet exchange protocol, which allows a packet from router i to be deflected to router j as long as router i has queue space to receive a packet from router j. This ensures that bubbles are always available for deflecting packets between neighboring routers.

With both techniques, some bubble(s) are always available to any set of network resources on which a path of cyclic or knotted dependencies can form, thus averting routing-induced deadlock. All blocked packets along resource dependency chains or cycles are able to shift forward by at least one buffer position within queues by consuming bubbles. This operation may not immediately remove packets from cyclic or knotted dependencies, but it does reduce the probability of sustaining those dependency relations. This is because new routing candidates arising from the shift may supply bubbles to those packets involved. That is, after the shift, some packets reaching the head of the queues which now become eligible for routing may then be able to use alternative resources or sink at their destination, as illustrated in Figure 13.10(b). This decreases the coupling among packets involved in dependency relations on congested resources. In effect, this provides a way for packets to disperse out of those areas, which is the main advantages of maximizing routing freedom.

Some of the disadvantages of these techniques, however, are that they are applicable only to virtual cut-through networks, not wormhole networks. Also, limiting injection into some resources prevents the network's full capacity from being utilized, and it could cause some packets never to be granted access to needed resources—a situation commonly referred to as *starvation*. For example, in Figure 13.10(a), packet $E1$ might remain indefinitely in the network waiting endlessly on Queue 4 and Queue 6 resources if packets in Queue 1 are always granted bubbles which may appear in those queues and other packets are continuously injected into the cycle at other queues. Moreover, nonminimal routing can wastefully consume scarce network bandwidth on each deflection, causing the network to saturate earlier. Unless controlled, deflection routing might also result in packets continuing to bounce around in the network indefinitely, never reaching their destinations—a situation commonly referred to as *livelock*. Many of these problems can be mitigated with some of the recovery-based routing approaches discussed below.

D. Routing-Induced Deadlock Recovery

Deadlock recovery routing approaches aim to optimize routing performance in the absence of deadlock. This is achieved by allowing unrestricted, true fully-adaptive routing on all physical and virtual channels and efficiently handling impending deadlock if it occurs using minimal resources. This is in contrast to deadlock avoidance routing schemes which typically devote a greater number of physical or virtual channel resources for avoiding improbable deadlock situations. In avoidance-based schemes, a set of escape resources are always supplied by the routing function whereas nominal resources (if any) are supplied in recovery-based schemes and only when potential deadlock situations are detected. Another distinguishing factor is that physical resources (i.e., link bandwidth) may be deallocated from normal packets in some progressive recovery-based schemes whereas no such deallocation occurs in any of the avoidance based schemes. In general, the viability of recovering from routing-induced deadlock depends critically on the recovery overhead, which is determined by the frequency with which deadlock is detected and, as importantly, the costs associated with resolving deadlock.

Regressive recovery routing schemes kill at least one packet detected as participating in potential deadlock so as to create a bubble(s) along knotted resources, as described in Section C. earlier. For example, in Figure 13.10(c), if packet $E1$ were killed, the unfilled cycle shown in Figure 13.10(a) (with $E1$ removed from Queue 5 and $E2$ put in its place) would come about, which resolves the deadlock. Aggressively killing more than just one packet in the cycle (i.e., all the packets at the end of Queues 1–4) reduces the probability of subsequent potential deadlocks occurring that involve those packets remaining in the cycle. In order for the source node that generated a killed packet to know it must re-inject the killed packet, some form of a "tether" must trace the packet's progress back to its source. This can be done in wormhole networks by using packet padding flits as is done in the Compressionless Router [49] or, in general, by using a combination of end-to-end acknowledgements and timeouts implemented by control signals of a higher network protocol layer. The additional latency, bandwidth overhead and control complexity needed to implement the killing and re-injection process increase cost and reduce network performance.

Proposed deflective recovery routing schemes operate on the same principle as deflective avoidance-based schemes described in the previous section once potential deadlock is detected, but with one major distinction: bubbles are not guaranteed always to be available at all neighboring routers. Instead, bubble movement in the network can be made to be stochastic (i.e., random) due to bubbles being subjected to causal motion: bubbles are allocated randomly to normal packets when multiple packets compete to consume them at each router. In addition to this, any bubble in the vicinity of a router participating in the knotted set of resources gets "sucked in" since potentially deadlocked packets that are to be deflected have priority over normal packets. With this, bubbles are guaranteed to propagate randomly to needed areas in the network and be used by packets in need of deflection eventually (in finite time) to resolve deadlock. This kind of guarantee on the arrival of bubbles to potentially deadlocked packets can be thought of as the dual case of the probabilistic guarantee on the arrival of packets to their destinations provided by the Chaos Router for resolving livelock. Hole-based routing [50] is one proposed deflective recovery routing scheme which follows this approach. Software-based Recovery [51] is a deflective recovery scheme that is less dependent on stochastic bubble movement within the network and more dependent on the deterministic availability of bubbles at network endpoints (e.g., like the In-Transit Buffer scheme). Although deflective recovery routing lifts certain requirements on packet exchanges between neighboring routers, it suffers from the other disadvantages common to deflective avoidance-based schemes mentioned previously.

In contrast to regressive and deflective recovery, progressive deadlock recovery is based on the idea of providing access to a connected, deadlock-free recovery path through which an eligible packet is progressively routed out of the knotted cyclic dependency to resolve deadlock. The deadlock-free recovery path need not be implemented using physical paths or virtual channels (edge queues) devoted specifically for this purpose. Instead, a special *deadlock buffer* central to each router and accessible from all neighboring routers can be used as a "floating" internal channel shared by all physical dimensions of a router to accomplish the same. Such a deadlock buffer is shown in Figure 13.2 as the central queue. The size of the buffer depends on the switching technique used, i.e., flit-sized for

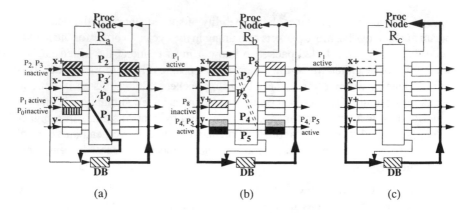

Figure 13.11. Dynamic recovery path formation and progressive deadlock resolution in *Disha*. Packet P_1 at router R_a recovers by routing through a recovery lane consisting of deadlock buffers (DBs) at R_a, R_b, and finally R_c which is its destination node. P_1 preempts physical channel bandwidth from P_8, suspending normal packet routing until deadlock is recovered. (From Ref. 56 ©2003 IEEE.)

wormhole switching and packet-sized for virtual cut-through switching. Deadlock buffers can be used to progressively resolve routing-induced deadlock either in the wide sense or in the weak sense, as explained below.

A well-known progressive recovery technique is *Disha* [52] used in the *WARRP* router [53]. In forming an escape recovery path system wide, deadlock buffers are used to route eligible packets minimally to their destinations. Packets in deadlock buffers preempt packets in normal resources so that network bandwidth is dynamically allocated for resolving deadlock if it occurs on rare occasions. As the tail of a recovering packet passes, network bandwidth is reallocated to the pre-empted packets. The recovery path is made deadlock-free by enforcing mutually exclusive access to it (i.e., *Disha Sequential* [52]) or by structuring routing on it to enforce some total ordering on resources such that cyclic dependencies are prohibited (i.e., *Disha Concurrent* [54]). One way of enforcing mutual exclusion is to use a circulating token which visits all routers in a predetermined cyclic path and is captured by a router participating in a potential deadlock [55]. The router progressively routes a recovering packet over a preempted output physical channel while having the corresponding control line set to indicate that this packet should be directed to the deadlock buffer at the next router in sequence, as illustrated in Figure 13.11. A new token is released by the destination node once the packet header is received. As there exists at least one packet in each deadlock that can fairly gain access to and route progressively on the recovery path which is connected and deadlock-free, this routing scheme safely recovers

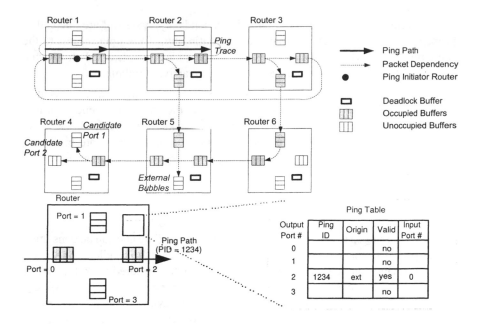

Figure 13.12. Illustration of packet dependency and ping movement for detecting congestion (top). Possible organization of router ping table for recording path reservation information (bottom).

from all deadlock [56]. Thus, we can think of the Disha scheme as using deadlock buffers to progressively resolve routing-induced deadlock in the wide sense.

The *Ping and Bubble* scheme is a more recently proposed progressive recovery technique [57]. The idea behind this scheme is to correctly trace all cyclic dependencies on network resources *in real time* and to dynamically supply a bubble to those resources and force it to traverse the entire cycle. Small control packets called "pings" are used to globally probe only those resources suspected of participating in potential deadlock once detected as possibly occurring. This works as follows. A ping is generated by a router for a given input port when certain deadlock precipitating conditions are detected, e.g., due to its buffer being occupied for longer than some threshold amount of time or some other criteria. It is then sent through one of the output ports requested by the packet at the head of that input port queue in order to probe the network for possible cyclic dependency. When a ping arrives at a neighboring router port, it is further propagated if the deadlock precipitating conditions are met there as well, and that router port queue is added to a path or *trace* of such dependent resources. This is illustrated in Figure 13.12 for an example scenario. In addition, a reservation is made in a ping table at that router so that any arriving bubble will be allocated to the pinged port. The ping table allows for precise control over bubble movement so that bubbles remain within resources along the dependency cycle and are coerced to propagate backward along the trace path. Continuing, if the ping returns to the same router port which initiated it, a cycle of dependency is detected on which a set of resources have reserved the allocation of an arriving bubble.

Along with the pinging mechanism, the special deadlock buffer is used to temporarily "shelter" a culprit packet at the head of the input port queue identified as closing a dependency cycle. This removes the packet from the deadlock cycle, creating an "escape" bubble in that queue which starts to propagate backward along the ping trace. As at most one router (the one with the highest ranking ping) detects each cycle and all non-overlapping cycles are detected, a bubble is guaranteed to be made available to resources along the cycle. Also, since bubble movement is totally controlled by the ping table entries in other routers along the detected cyclic trace path, the escape bubble generated by sheltering the culprit packet is guaranteed to arrive back at that router in finite time and can be consumed by the packet in the special deadlock buffer. This frees the deadlock buffer for future use. Once the returned bubble is allocated to the sheltered packet, all other packets along the dependency cycle will have already been shifted progressively forward by at least one position, possibly breaking the cycle. In the unlikely event that the same cycle recurs due to no change in the dependency relation among new routing candidates at the head of the queues, the procedure repeats. As packets are routed along minimal paths, at least one packet will eventually reach its destination in finite time even if the dependency relation persists until then. Thus, we can think of the Ping and Bubble scheme as using deadlock buffers to progressively resolve routing-induced deadlock in the weak sense.

Operation of the Ping and Bubble scheme is illustrated using the simplistic example given in Figure 13.10(c). Assuming that a potential deadlock is detected by packets at the head of Queue 1 and Queue 5. A ping is generated by the router for either Queue 1 or Queue 5 (assume both are associated with the same router) and transmitted to Queue 4 in the neighboring router. Subsequently, the ping is transmitted to Queue 3, then Queue 2, and returns back to Queue 1 following the path supplied by the routing function for the packets at the head of those fully occupied queues. No matter whether the ping was generated by Queue 1 or Queue 5, Queue 1 is the one identified as closing a cycle of resource dependencies, like the cyclic path shown in Figure 13.12. Alternatively, other pings could simultaneously have been generated by the other queues in the cycle. If not squashed by an outranking ping generated by a different queue that alone would detect the cycle, those pings would follow the same cyclic path and return to their initiating router—identifying one of those other queues as closing the dependency cycle.

Preliminary results show that substantial performance gains are possible. As shown in Figure 13.13, the proposed Ping and Bubble scheme can sustain near maximum throughput even under heavily loaded network conditions, yielding twice the throughput that can be sustained by Duato's Protocol and Disha. All

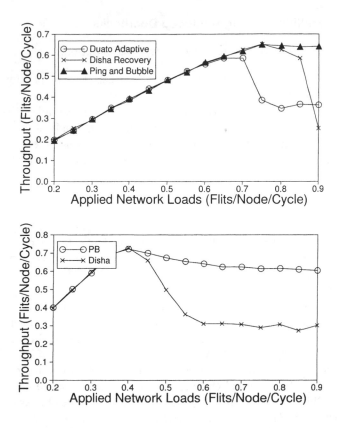

Figure 13.13. Network throughput for an 8×8 bidirectional torus with 4 virtual channels for the proposed Ping and Bubble scheme compared to Disha Sequential and Duato's Protocol (top) and Ping and Bubble (PB) compared to Disha for a network with an increased bristling factor of 2, i.e., two injecting nodes attached to each router in the network (bottom).

the while, routing-induced deadlock is effectively resolved. In addition to the increased routing freedom it has over Duato's Protocol, the main reason for the Ping and Bubble scheme's improved performance is that escape bubbles are made more accessible to packets needing them most under saturated network conditions (i.e., packets involved in cyclic dependencies). With Duato's Protocol and Disha, the escape and recovery paths can become a performance bottleneck; there is no such bottleneck with the Ping and Bubble scheme.

13.3.2   Handling Message-Induced Deadlocks

A.   *Message-Induced Deadlock Avoidance Techniques*

Message-induced deadlock can be avoided in the weak sense by providing enough buffer space in each node's network interface queues to hold at least as many messages as can be supplied, as is done in [58,59], for example. Even though knotted dependencies on a set of resources may exist, deadlock never actually occurs as the set never becomes fully occupied. This guarantees that packets can sink at their destinations eventually. Although simple to implement, this technique is not very scalable since the size of the network interface queues grows as $O(P \times M)$ messages, where P is the number of processor nodes and M is the number of outstanding messages allowed by each node in the system.

At the opposite extreme, message-induced deadlock can be avoided in the strict sense by providing logically independent communication networks for each message type (implemented as either physical or virtual channels) and restricting the use of those networks based on message type, as is done in [28,37,39,40], for example. The partial ordering on message dependencies defined by the communication protocol is transferred to the logical networks such that the usage of network resources is acyclic. This restriction on routing freedom guarantees that no deadlock can form due to message dependencies. Figures 13.14 illustrates this for the four node ring system shown previously in Figure 13.6 and 13.9(c), but this time with four virtual channels per physical channel. With two logical networks each consisting of two virtual channels to avoid routing-induced deadlocks (see Section A.), this network is able to avoid message-induced deadlocks for message dependency chains of length two, i.e., *request* ≺ *reply*, but no greater.

For message-induced deadlock handling techniques based on enforcing routing restrictions, the size of network resources does not influence deadlock properties, making such techniques more scalable. Because of this, these are the more commonly used, but they still suffer the cost disadvantage of requiring at least as many logical networks as the length of the message dependency chain. Such partitioning of network resources not only increases network cost but also decreases potential resource utilization and overall performance, particularly when message dependencies are abundant and resources (i.e., virtual channels) are scarce. For example, the Alpha 21364 processor/router chip [40] used in AlphaServer systems requires seven logically separated networks to avoid message-induced deadlocks on seven message types. For six of these, two virtual channels are required to escape from routing-induced deadlocks in a torus network and an additional one is used for adaptive routing. Therefore, of the 19 total virtual channels implemented, at most only two can be used at any given time by any given message type. This is a severe limitation on routing freedom.

In general, routing freedom at any given point in the network is limited to $(1 + (C/L - E_r))$ of the C virtual channels on a link, where L is the message dependency chain length, E_r is the minimum number of virtual channels required

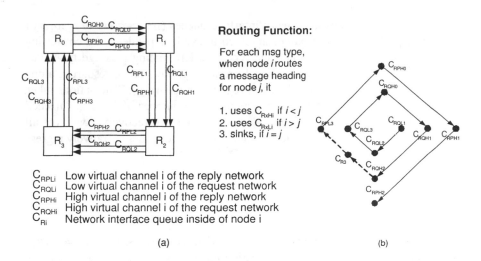

Routing Function:

For each msg type, when node *i* routes a message heading for node *j*, it

1. uses C_{RxHi} if $i < j$
2. uses C_{RxLi} if $i > j$
3. sinks, if $i = j$

C_{RPLi} Low virtual channel i of the reply network
C_{RQLi} Low virtual channel i of the request network
C_{RPHi} High virtual channel i of the reply network
C_{RQHi} High virtual channel i of the request network
C_{Ri} Network interface queue inside of node i

(a)

(b)

Figure 13.14. (a) Separation of request and reply networks avoids cyclic dependencies in the channel dependency graph shown in (b), but it reduces channel utilization. Shown in (b) is the case in which R1 is the requester and R3 is the responder. (From Ref. 61 ©2003 IEEE.)

to escape from routing-induced deadlock for a given network, $E_m = L \times E_r$ is the minimum number of virtual channels required to escape from message-induced deadlock for a given network, and $C \geq E_m$. Routing freedom can be increased if message-induced deadlock is, instead, avoided in the wide sense by allowing all channels other than the minimum number required to escape from message-induced deadlock to be shared amongst all message types, as proposed in [60]. That is, cycles among message-dependent resources are allowed as long as it is always possible to reach some set of escape resources on which no cyclic message dependencies can exist. With this technique, the upper limit on virtual channel availability is increased to $(1 + (C - E_m))$. Nevertheless, restrictions enforced on escape channels due to only one channel being supplied by the routing function out of the E_m channels acts to limit the overall potential performance.

B. Message-Induced Deadlock Recovery Techniques

Evidently, the main disadvantage of avoiding deadlock by disallowing cyclic dependencies on escape resources is the number of partitioned logical networks required. It is possible to reduce the number of partitions by allowing different message types to use the same logical network and removing message(s) from cyclic dependencies only when a potential deadlock situation is detected. Since a detection mechanism and recovery action are required to resolve the potential deadlock situation, this technique for handling message-induced deadlock is said to be based on deadlock recovery. Detected deadlocks can be resolved by killing and later re-injecting packets in network interface queues (i.e., *regressive recovery*), deflecting packets out of resources involved in cyclic dependency by converting them from a nonterminating message type to a terminating message type (i.e., *deflective recovery*), or by progressively routing packets using resources along a path that is guaranteed to sink (i.e., *progressive recovery*). The actions taken by regressive and deflective recovery increase the number of messages needed to complete each data transaction, whereas progressive recovery does not; all packets make progress toward their destinations and never degeneratively regress or deflect.

The differences between the above techniques are illustrated using an example cache coherence protocol that could be used in a multiprocessor system which permits generic message dependency chains shown in Figure 13.15(b). In this protocol, an original request message ($m_1 = ORQ$) arriving at some home node is forwarded to the owner or sharers as a forwarded-request message ($m_3 = FRQ$) before being responded to by a terminating reply message ($m_4 = TRP$) if the home node is unable to fulfill the request. Thus, the length of the message dependency chain for data transactions can be two ($ORQ \prec TRP$) or three ($ORQ \prec FRQ \prec TRP$), depending upon where the requested data is located. Message-induced deadlocks can be avoided in the strict sense by partitioning resources into three separate logical networks, one for each of these message types. However, to reduce the number of logical networks to two, both ORQ and FRQ messages may be allowed to use the same *request network* and TRP messages can use a separate *reply network*. Since message-induced deadlocks can now potentially form on the request network, they must be resolved once detected.

Consider first how resolution might be done with a deflective recovery scheme such as the one used in the SGI Origin 2000 multiprocessor [29], shown in Figure 13.15(a). If a potential deadlock situation is detected at a home node, the node takes ORQ messages that would generate FRQ messages from the head of the input request queue and deflects back to the requesters "backoff" reply message types ($m_2 = BRP$). These messages contain owner or sharer information that allows the requester to generate FRQ message(s) directly to the intended target(s) without further intervention from the home node. They are additional messages needed to carry out the data transaction. That is, with this protocol, the $ORQ \prec FRQ \prec TRP$ message dependency chain is converted into a $ORQ \prec BRP \prec FRQ \prec TRP$ chain when potential message-induced deadlock is detected. Although the message dependency chain length is increased during recovery, the number of logical networks implemented need not increase; it remains at two. In order for this to happen, the system allows BRP messages to use the same reply network as TRP messages and avoids message-induced deadlock in the weak sense on the reply network by dynamically reserving (preallocating) sufficient space in the incoming reply queue of the requester in order to be able to sink responses for all outstanding ORQ messages. This reservation is made before ORQ messages enter the network.

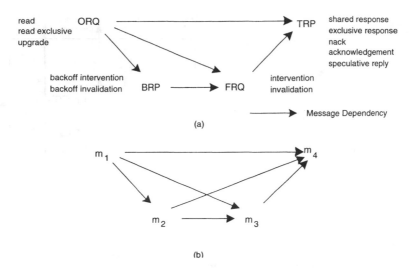

Figure 13.15. (a) The ordering among message types (shown in uppercase) and message subtypes (shown in lowercase) in the Origin 2000. Note that BRP occurs only if a message-induced deadlock is detected, otherwise the maximum chain length is three. (b) The ordering among message types (m_i) for a generic cache coherence protocol with four message types. (From Ref. 61 ©2003 IEEE.)

By relaxing restrictions in the way in which network resources are used, resources can be utilized more efficiently and provide increased network performance. However, as potential deadlock situations mainly occur when the system nears a saturated state, resolving potential deadlock situations by increasing the number of messages required to complete data transactions only exacerbates the problem. Progressive recovery techniques resolve potential deadlock situations more efficiently by using the same number of messages as are required to avoid deadlock. One such recently proposed technique is derived from the *Disha* technique described in Section D..

The proposed technique, referred to as *mDisha* [61], extends the notion of *Disha-Sequential* recovery paths existing only between network endpoints to one that includes network endpoints as well, as shown in Figure 13.16. Hence, the circulating token must also visit all network interfaces attached to each router node, and a deadlock buffer (referred to as a deadlock message buffer or DMB) must also be provided in each network interface. The size of the DMB is determined by the minimum unit of information on which end-to-end error detection/protection (i.e., ECC, checksum) is performed. Typically, this is at the packet level, requiring these deadlock buffers to be at least packet-sized. This is also the minimum size of the network interface input and output queues; however, larger input/output queues would typically be used to increase performance. All network resources

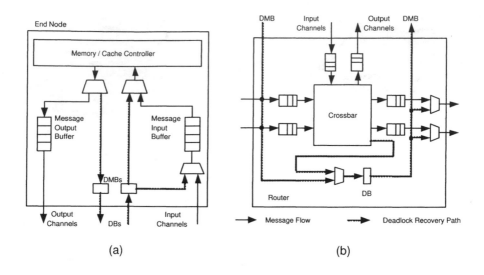

Figure 13.16. Network interface and router architecture for *mDisha* progressive recovery of message-induced deadlock. (From Ref. 61 ©2003 IEEE.)

can be completely shared, independent of the message types. Relaxing resource allocation and routing restrictions in this way maximizes the utilization of resources while allowing for all potential message-induced deadlocks to be recovered once detected as long as the same token is reused to recover all subordinate messages along a given message dependency chain until one of them sinks. The progressive recovery process is guaranteed to terminate since each message dependency chain is acyclic and has a terminating message type. However, like its *Disha-Sequential* predecessor, limitations of this scheme are its single point-of-failure due to the token mechanism and the sequential nature of recovery, which should not be a problem since the frequency of message-induced deadlocks typically is low. However, it is necessary to have a reliable token management mechanism, i.e., one that can be transmitted as an in-band control packet multiplexed with data packets over network channels. This way, the path taken by the token can be logical and, thus, reconfigurable for increased reliability.

13.3.3   Handling Reconfiguration-Induced Deadlocks

Traditional approaches for reconfiguring a network's routing function are based either on avoiding deadlocks in the strict sense or on regressively recovering from them. Both approaches rely mainly on dropping packets. Static reconfiguration techniques, for example, consist of first stopping and flushing *all* user traffic from the network before commencing and completing network-wide reconfiguration [3,

25,62]. Network flushing is typically done by actively *discarding* all nondelivered packets not yet reaching their destination nodes. In addition to this, the injection of packets into the network is halted during the entire reconfiguration process until it completes. This allows the routing function to be updated from old to new in one atomic action from the point-of-view of user packets, leading to the notion of *static* reconfiguration. As no packets are in the network at the time that the new routing function becomes active, no reconfiguration-induced cycles can form, thus strictly avoiding deadlocks. Alternatively, dynamic reconfiguration techniques allow reconfiguration to commence while user packets remain in the network and continue to be injected into the network. Reconfiguration-induced deadlock arising from dynamic interactions between packets routed by old and new routing functions during and after *dynamic* reconfiguration can be resolved regressively by reactively discarding packets in the event that buffers become full [1,3,63]. This simple approach is most applicable to systems implementing soft link-level flow control in which buffer overflow is solved through packet dropping, such as in wide-area networks. However, it is less applicable to systems that implement hard link-level flow control in which packet flow is regulated by means other than packet dropping, which is the case for most multiprocessor interconnects (including SIO, IPC, and NOCs), IPRF technologies, and many switched LAN/SAN/STAN technologies.

With both the strict avoidance and the regressive recovery-based approaches, a considerable number of packets may be dropped, possibly requiring upper layer protocols to be invoked and system state to be rolled back to ensure correct execution. This exacerbates the problem of providing real-time and quality-of-service support needed by some applications which have limited tolerance for recurring performance drop-offs. Moreover, disallowing packet injection during the reconfiguration process further degrades performance. For example, the transmission of video streams in a high-definition video-on-demand server would be halted during reconfiguration, leading to frozen frames for an undesirable, perhaps unacceptable, period of time. Similarly, when an interconnection network is used as the switch fabric within IPRFs [4], typically no packet dropping is allowed within a router. And since these switch fabrics are designed to operate close to their saturation point, the number of dropped packets using such degenerative approaches could be excessively high.

While no networking technology can guarantee that all packets will reach their destinations under all conditions, packet dropping should be the exception rather than the rule. Much research is currently being done on designing dynamic reconfiguration techniques implemented with hard link-level flow that do not halt the injection of user packets into the network nor rely on dropping user packets from the network before, during, or after the reconfiguration process. Such schemes aim to minimize restrictions on packet injection and delivery throughout the reconfiguration process. In addition, they aim to exploit the fact that reconfigurations often require only a few paths in the network to be changed (i.e., only those within the skyline [64], as shown in Figure 13.7), thus affecting only a few packets and router switches. A few such techniques have recently been proposed based on avoiding reconfiguration-induced deadlock in the wide sense. Deadlock is avoided by enforcing some total ordering on the usage of escape resources and remains consistent when taking into account the interactions of both the old and new routing functions. This is done by some form of logical separation of resources used to escape from deadlock by packets experiencing old and new routing functions and is accompanied by some form of step-wise or partial update of the routing function.

A. Reconfiguration-Induced Deadlock Avoidance in the Wide Sense

The basic idea behind techniques based on avoiding reconfiguration-induced dead-lock in the wide sense is the following: it is possible to consider the reconfiguration of a routing function as a change from an old routing function R_{old} to a new one R_{new} in a sequence of k steps ($R_{old} = R_0 \to R_1 \to \ldots \to R_k - R_{new}$) that can be completed and k associated conditions ($cond_1, \ldots, cond_k$) that can be fulfilled. Every step contains one or more updates to the routing function in the previous step. At each router, multiple updates within each step may be carried out in any order (or it can be assumed that all updates complete in one atomic action), but steps are sequentialized so that in updating the routing function from R_{i-1} to R_i, $step_i$ cannot start before $step_{i-1}$ completes and condition $cond_i$ is fulfilled. Network-wide, however, the completion of steps is not necessarily synchronized unless specified by a condition. So, it is possible for $step_i$ to be completed at a router before $step_{i-1}$ is completed at another router if condition $cond_i$ does not require synchronization. The conditions are usually related to packets in the network; they determine in what ways the dependencies allowed by routing functions of previous and current steps can interact with the dependencies allowed by routing functions of current and future steps. That is, conditions are used to "filter out" unwanted ghost dependencies on resources that may cause deadlock. For example, if at some step, $step_i$: $R_{i-1} \to R_i$, the condition specifies that some set of network resources is required to be empty before the start of that step, then the old dependencies (in particular, ghost dependencies) allowed by all previous routing functions before R_i on those resources can simply be ignored. Therefore, it is possible to define a series of reconfiguration steps that impose a minimum set of conditions to eliminate harmful ghost dependencies—those which could result in permanent deadlock. If the final step in the series of reconfiguration steps can be reached and provides a routing subfunction that is connected and deadlock-free over an escape set of resources taking into account all remaining ghost and normal dependencies from previous and current steps, the reconfiguration protocol is provably deadlock-free [24].

One recently proposed dynamic reconfiguration scheme is the Partial Progressive Reconfiguration (PPR) scheme [65]. The PPR scheme systematically performs sequences of partial updates to routing tables which implement the routing function, progressively removing old and adding new entries until all routing tables are completely updated to the new routing function. This is done by sequentially moving *root* nodes (i.e., nodes that only have links with up ends connected to them, as shown in Figure 13.7) and *break* nodes (i.e., nodes that have two or more links with only down ends connected to them, as shown in Figure 13.7) one router position at a time to their final positions by partially updating entries in the routing tables along the path. To avoid deadlock, each switch must synchronize with some of its neighbors after each partial update of a break node movement in order to ensure that no dependency cycles form along escape resources. The existence of the break node is what guarantees that cycles cannot be completed, i.e., they act to break the cycle. The required synchronizing steps on break node partial updates increases implementation complexity, and some link changes on the escape set of resources may render some packets unroutable. Unroutable packets are those that reach a point in the network for which no legal route is supplied. These packets must be discarded in order to avoid permanent blocking that results in reconfiguration-induced deadlock.

Another set of recently proposed dynamic reconfiguration schemes is the *Double Scheme* [24], which avoids reconfiguration-induced deadlocks in the wide sense by *spatially* separating resource allocations that may permanently close dependency cycles along escape paths[4]. The most straightforward way of accomplishing deadlock-free spatial separation is simply to double the number of resources used by a routing algorithm to escape from deadlock and to allow dependencies only from one set to the other but not from both at any given time. This can be implemented by using two distinct sets of physical or virtual channels: one set is used by the current routing function (*old* with respect to the next reconfiguration) to escape deadlock and the other set is used by the next routing function (*new* with respect to the next reconfiguration) to escape deadlock. Consistent with Duato's Protocol, an escape routing subfunction is defined on each set of channels in such a way as to be connected and deadlock-free for its corresponding network, i.e., the old network before reconfiguration or the new one afterwards. Of the four varieties of the *Double Scheme* mentioned in [24], we discuss only the *Enhanced Basic Double Scheme* below.

B.   The Enhanced Basic Double Scheme

The *Enhanced Basic Double Scheme* requires two sets of network channels for escape routing. The routing function is composed of three routing subfunctions: $R = R_I \circ R_{E_1} \circ R_{E_2}$, where R_{E_1} and R_{E_2} are two escape routing subfunctions defined on E_1 and E_2 channel sets, respectively, and R_I is the injection routing

---

[4]As an alternative to spatial separation of resource allocations, the *Single Scheme* [66] enforces *temporal* separation only on the one set of escape resources (as opposed to strict avoidance static schemes which enforce temporal separation on all resources, including non-escape resources).

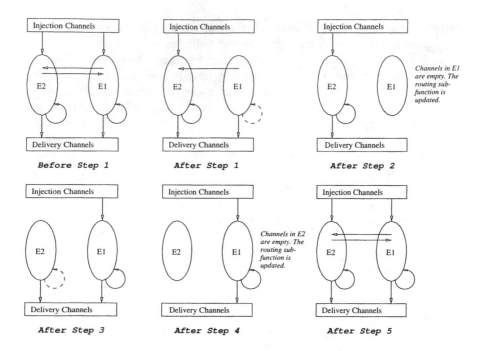

Figure 13.17. Illustration of the possible channel allocations occurring in the network for the *Enhanced Basic Double Scheme*. The dashed arc signifies that packets in a given escape set may continue to use those resources to drain from the network.

subfunction. Before and after reconfiguration, the routing function allows packets to route using both escape channel sets interchangeably. That is, the duplicate set of escape resources are always fully and efficiently used outside of reconfiguration, allowing no performance degradation to be suffered during normal network operation. During reconfiguration, however, packets are restricted to using only the escape channel set into which the packet is injected. This allows the routing subfunction defined on one set to be reconfigured while packets continue to be injected into the other set. Once the routing subfunctions defined on both sets are reconfigured, this restriction is relaxed. The five-step dynamic reconfiguration protocol implemented at each router is detailed below, and possible channel allocations resulting from it are illustrated in Figure 13.17.

THE ENHANCED BASIC DOUBLE SCHEME

Condition 1: A topology change is detected at the router or a reconfiguration notification is received.

Step 1: The routing function is changed ($R_{old} = R_0 \rightarrow R_1$) locally at the router such that R_I supplies only E_2 channels; R_{E_2} supplies only E_2 and delivery channels; and R_{E_1} and R_{E_2} are modified to discard only those packets encountering disconnectivity (if any).

Condition 2: All packets are drained from E_1 channels, and all new topology/routing information is acquired.

Step 2: The routing function is changed ($R_1 \rightarrow R_2$) locally at the router such that R_{E_1} is updated to supply only E_1 and delivery channels for the new escape routing subfunction. R_{E_2} continues to supply only E_2 and delivery channels, and it continues to discard only those packets encountering disconnectivity (if any).

Condition 3: All routers neighboring the router complete Step 2.

Step 3: The routing function is changed ($R_2 \rightarrow R_3$) locally at the router such that R_I supplies only E_1 channels.

Condition 4: All packets in E_2 channels that can route through the router are drained.

Step 4: The routing function is changed ($R_3 \rightarrow R_4$) locally at the router such that R_{E_2} is updated to supply E_1, E_2, and delivery channels for the new escape routing subfunction.

Condition 5: All routers neighboring the router complete Step 4.

Step 5: The routing function is changed ($R_4 \rightarrow R_5 = R_{new}$) locally at the router such that R_I supplies E_1 and E_2 channels. Also, R_{E_1} is modified to supply E_2 channels in addition to E_1 and delivery channels for the new escape routing subfunction.

Reconfiguration is completed once all routers complete this step.

Like all of the *Double Schemes*, the *Enhanced Basic Double Scheme* is based on the notion that an *empty* set of escape channels becomes available on which deadlock-free routing for the new network can take place, but it requires double the minimum number of resources as compared to static reconfiguration. Its advantage, however, is its lack of need to flush the entire network in order to nullify the effects of potentially harmful ghost dependencies. Instead, only a select subset of channels need to be drained. Packets do not need to be discarded in order to accomplish this drainage. All packets not encountering fault-induced disconnectivity are allowed to route normally in the network until draining at their destinations. That is, no reconfiguration-induced packet dropping is necessary (as may be the case with PPR) as no packets become unroutable on account of the reconfiguration algorithm. As injection of new packets into the network is allowed to continue during each reconfiguration step, the reconfiguration process is dynamic. Furthermore, as all future steps are reachable from each reconfiguration step and the routing function in the last step is deadlock-free, the dynamic reconfiguration protocol is provably deadlock-free.

13.4 CONCLUSION

Three important classes of deadlock in interconnection networks have been described in this chapter. Routing-induced deadlock has traditionally been the most widely studied of the three, but message-induced deadlock and reconfiguration-induced deadlock have equally devastating effects on system performance and robustness. Common to all three classes is the property of packets holding onto a set of network resources in a cyclic manner while waiting endlessly for some resource(s) within that set to become available. Unless somehow avoided or resolved once it occurs in the interconnection network subsystem, deadlock has the potential to bring an entire computer system down to a screeching halt

Also presented in this chapter are a number of interesting techniques for handling all three classes of interconnection network deadlocks. The techniques presented are based either on deadlock avoidance or on deadlock recovery. Deadlock can be avoided in the strict sense, in the wide sense, in the weak sense, or by a combination of these approaches. What distinguishes one approach from another mainly has to do with the allowed degree of routing freedom and the possible manifestations of resource dependencies: the more routing freedom allowed, the more complex the resource dependencies are that can be manifested. The same two factors also distinguish deadlock avoidance approaches from deadlock recovery approaches. By allowing maximum routing freedom on normal network resources, knotted dependencies on fully occupied resources can form, from which there is no way of escape. The outcome of this is deadlock which must be recovered from. Deadlocks can be resolved regressively, deflectively, or progressively, depending on how deadlock resolving resources are supplied to recovering packets.

Since the same blocking property is inherent to all deadlocks, fundamental aspects of most deadlock handling approaches are universally applicable to all classes. Even though this may be the case, some approaches may be better suited to handle certain deadlock classes and less suited to handle others. This largely depends on the requirements of the applications running on the system and on system resources. In terms of design complexity, the best strategy is to have a unified solution that can synergistically handle all forms of deadlock efficiently. From a practical point-of-view, solutions that are not based on probabilistic events or have no single points-of-failure are more easily verifiable and dependable. For these and perhaps other reasons, techniques based mainly on avoiding deadlock in the strict or wide sense typically are the solutions of choice for interconnection networks implemented in commercial systems. Other proposed solutions, while intriguing, have largely been relegated to experimental systems up to this point with a few exceptions. However, as trends in design philosophy continue to advance toward that of designing more efficient systems capable of recovering from rare anomalous behavior including deadlock, approaches based on deadlock recovery may someday gain greater prominence.

13.5 Bibliographic Notes

This chapter touches only on the tip of the iceberg of the compendium of concepts and techniques proposed in the literature for handling deadlocks in interconnection networks. Much of what is discussed here can be understood in much greater detail by reading the original papers that introduce and analyze these techniques. Quantitative comparisons can then be made to better help one arrive at the best deadlock handling technique for his/her particular interconnection network subsystem. In addition to reviewing the journal references cited in this chapter and listed below, the interested reader is also encouraged to seek out other texts that treat this subject well. These would include a recent text by Duato, Yalamanchili and Ni entitled, *Interconnection Networks: An Engineering Approach*, and a new text by Dally and Towles entitled, *Principles and Practices of Interconnection Networks*, both published by Morgan-Kaufmann Publishers.

13.6 Acknowledgements

Many of the original ideas presented in this chapter have come about through the collaborative efforts of many of my former graduate student researchers and other research colleagues. I acknowledge the overall contributions made by all current and former members of the *SMART* Interconnects group at USC and, in particular, specific contributions made by the following individuals: Wai Hong Ho, Ruoming Pang, Dr. Yongho Song, Anjan Venkatramani, and Dr. Sugath Warnakulasuriya. I also owe special thanks to Professor José Duato for his participation in some of the research projects that have contributed to the contents of this chapter and for his helpful review comments.

References

1. N.J. Boden, D. Cohen, R.E. Felderman, A.E. Dulawik, C.L. Seitz, J. Seizovic, and W. Su. Myrinet-A gigabit per second local area network. In *IEEE Micro*, pages 29–36. IEEE Computer Society, February 1995.

2. R. Horst. ServerNet deadlock avoidance and fractahedral topologies. In *Proceedings of the International Parallel Processing Symposium*, pages 275–280. IEEE Computer Society, April 1996.

3. K. Malavalli, et al. Fibre Channel Switch Fabric-2 (FC-SW-2). *NCITS 321-200x T11/Project 1305-D/Rev 4.3 Specification*, pages 57–74, March 2000.

4. W. Dally, P. Carvey, and L. Dennison. The Avici Terabit Switch/Router. In *Proceedings of the Hot Interconnects VI Symposium*, pages 41–50, August 1998.

5. F. Petrini, W.C. Feng, A. Hoisie, S. Coll, and E. Frachtenberg. The Quadrics Network: High-Performance Clustering Technology. *IEEE Micro*, 22(1):2–13, January-February 2002.

6. T.M. Pinkston, A.F. Benner, M. Krause, I.M. Robinson, and T. Sterling. InfiniBand: The "De Facto" Future Standard for System and Local Area Networks or Just a Scalable Replacement for PCI Buses? *Cluster Computing*, 6(2):95–104, April 2003.

7. W. Dally and B. Towles. Route Packets, Not Wires: On-Chip Interconnection Networks. In *Proceedings of the Design Automation Conference (DAC)*, pages 684–689. ACM, June 2001.

8. M.B. Taylor, W. Lee, S. Amarasinghe, and A. Agarwal. Scalar Operand Networks: On-Chip Interconnect for ILP in Partitioned Architectures. In *Proceedings of the 9th International Symposium on High-Performance Computer Architecture*, pages 341–353. IEEE Computer Society Press, February 2003.

9. W.H. Ho and T.M. Pinkston. A Methodology for Designing Efficient On-Chip Interconnects on Well-Behaved Communication Patterns. In *Proceedings of the 9th International Symposium on High-Performance Computer Architecture*, pages 377–388. IEEE Computer Society Press, February 2003.

10. P. Kermani and L. Kleinrock. Virtual cut-through: A new computer communication switching technique. *Computer Networks*, pages 267–286, 1979.

11. E. Baydal, P. Lopez, and J. Duato. A Simple and Efficient Mechanism to Prevent Saturation in Wormhole Networks. In *Proceedings of the 14th International Parallel and Distributed Processing Symposium*, pages 617–622, 2000.

12. M. Thottethodi, A.R. Lebeck, and S.S. Mukherjee. Self-Tuned Congestion Control for Multiprocessor Networks. In *Proceedings of the 7th International Symposium on High Performance Computer Architecture*, January 2001.

13. W. Dally. Virtual Channel Flow Control. *IEEE Transactions on Parallel and Distributed Systems*, 3(2):194–205, March 1992.

14. L.-S. Peh and W. Dally. Flit-Reservation Flow Control. In *Proceedings of the 6th International Symposium on High Performance Computer Architecture*, pages 73–84. IEEE Computer Society Press, January 2000.

15. Y. Tamir and G. Frazier. Dynamically-Allocated Multi-Queue Buffers for VLSI Communication Switches. *IEEE Transactions on Computers*, 41(6):725–734, June 1992.

16. J. Duato. A New Theory of Deadlock-free Adaptive Routing in Wormhole Networks. *IEEE Transactions on Parallel and Distributed Systems*, 4(12):1320–1331, December 1993.

17. J. Duato. A Necessary and Sufficient Condition for Deadlock-free Adaptive Routing in Wormhole Networks. *IEEE Transactions on Parallel and Distributed Systems*, 6(10):1055–1067, October 1995.

18. J. Duato and T.M. Pinkston. A General Theory for Deadlock-Free Adaptive Routing Using a Mixed Set of Resources. *IEEE Transactions on Parallel and Distributed Systems*, 12(12):1219–1235, December 2001.

19. W. Dally and C. Seitz. Deadlock-free Message Routing in Multiprocessor Interconnection Networks. *IEEE Transactions on Computers*, 36(5):547–553, May 1987.

20. S. Warnakulasuriya and T.M. Pinkston. A Formal Model of Message Blocking and Deadlock Resolution in Interconnection Networks. *IEEE Transactions on Parallel and Distributed Systems*, 11(2):212–229, March 2000.

21. R.C. Holt. Some Deadlock Properties on Computer Systems. *ACM Computer Surveys*, 4(3):179–196, September 1972.

22. S. Warnakulasuriya and T.M. Pinkston. Characterization of Deadlocks in *k*-ary *n*-cube Networks. *IEEE Transactions on Parallel and Distributed Systems*, 10(9):904–921, September 1999.

23. S. Warnakulasuriya and T.M. Pinkston. Characterization of Deadlocks in Irregular Networks. *Journal of Parallel and Distributed Computing*, 62(1):61–84, January 2002.

24. T.M. Pinkston, R. Pang, and J. Duato. Deadlock-Free Dynamic Reconfiguration Schemes for Increased Network Dependability. *IEEE Transactions on Parallel and Distributed Systems*, 14(8):780–794, August 2003.

25. M.D. Schroeder et al. Autonet: A High-Speed, Self-Configuring Local Area Network Using Point-to-Point Links. *IEEE Journal on Selected Areas in Communication*, 9(8):1318–1335, October 1991.

26. V. Puente, R. Beivide, J.A. Gregorio, J.M. Prellezo, J. Duato, and C. Izu. Adaptive bubble router: A design to improve performance in torus networks. In *Proceedings of the 28th International Conference on Parallel Processing (28th ICPP'99)*, Aizu-Wakamatsu, Fukushima, Japan, September 1999. University of Aizu.

27. J.M. Martinez, P. Lopez, and J. Duato. FC3D: Flow Control Based Distributed Deadlock Detection Mechanism for True Fully Adaptive Routing in Wormhole Networks. *IEEE Transactions on Parallel and Distributed Systems*, 14(8):765–779, August 2003.

28. S. Scott and G. Thorson. Optimized Routing in the Cray T3D. In *Proceedings of the Workshop on Parallel Computer Routing and Communication*, pages 281–294, May 1994.

29. J. Laudon and D. Lenoski. The SGI Origin: A ccNUMA Highly Scalable Server. In *Proceedings of the 24th International Symposium on Computer Architecture*, pages 241–251. IEEE Computer Society, June 1997.

30. L. Ni and C. Glass. The Turn Model for Adaptive Routing. In *Proceedings of the 19th Symposium on Computer Architecture*, pages 278–287. IEEE Computer Society, May 1992.

31. B. Zerrouk, V. Reibaldi, F. Potter, A. Greiner, and A. Derieux. RCube: A Gigabit Serial Links Low Latency Adaptive Router. In *Proceedings of the Symposium on Hot Interconnects IV*, pages 13–17. IEEE Computer Society, August 1996.

32. K.D. Gunther. Prevention of Deadlocks in Packet-switched Data Transport Systems. *IEEE Transactions on Communications*, (4):512–524, April 1981.

33. D. Gunther. A DAG-Based Algorithm for Prevention of Store-and-Forward Deadlock in Packet Networks. *IEEE Transactions on Computers*, (10):709–715, October 1981.

34. D. Linder and J. Harden. An Adaptive and Fault Tolerant Wormhole Routing Strategy for k-ary n-cubes. *IEEE Transactions on Computers*, 40(1):2–12, January 1991.

35. A.A. Chien and J.H. Kim. Planar-Adaptive Routing: Low-Cost Adaptive Networks for Multiprocessors. In *Proceedings of the 19th International Symposium on Computer Architecture*, pages 268–277. IEEE Computer Society, May 1992.

36. M. Galles. Spider: A High Speed Network Interconnect. In *Proceedings of the Symposium on Hot Interconnects IV*, pages 141–146. IEEE Computer Society, August 1996.

37. J. Carbonaro. Cavallino: The Teraflops Router and NIC. In *Proceedings of the Symposium on Hot Interconnects IV*, pages 157–160. IEEE Computer Society, August 1996.

38. W. Dally, L. Dennison, D. Harris, K. Kan, and T. Zanthopoulos. Architecture and Implementation of the Reliable Router. In *Proceedings of the Hot Interconnects II Symposium*, August 1994.

39. S.L. Scott and G.M. Thorson. The Cray T3E Network: Adaptive Routing in a High Performance 3D Torus. In *Proceedings of the Symposium on Hot Interconnects IV*, pages 147–156. IEEE Computer Society, August 1996.

40. S.S. Mukherjee, P. Bannon, S. Lang, A. Spink, and D. Webb. The Alpha 21364 Network Architecture. In *Symposium on High Performance Interconnects (HOT Interconnects 9)*, pages 113–117. IEEE Computer Society Press, August 2001.

41. W. Barrett et al. An Overview of the Blue-Gene/L Supercomputer. In *Proceedings of the 2002 ACM/IEEE Conference on Supercomputing, CD ROM*, November 2002.

42. L. Gravano, G. Pifarre, P. Berman, and J. Sanz. Adaptive Deadlock- and Livelock-Free Routing With all Minimal Paths in Torus Networks. *IEEE Transactions on Parallel and Distributed Systems*, 5(12):1233–1251, December 1994.

43. L. Schwiebert and D.N. Jayasimha. A Necessary and Sufficient Condition for Deadlock-free Wormhole Routing. *Journal of Parallel and Distributed Computing*, 32(1):103–117, January 1996.

44. W. Dally and H. Aoki. Deadlock-free Adaptive Routing in Multicomputer Networks using Virtual Channels. *IEEE Transactions on Parallel and Distributed Systems*, 4(4):466–475, April 1993.

45. J. Flich, P. Lopez, M.P. Malumbres, and J. Duato. Boosting the Performance of Myrinet Networks. *IEEE Transactions on Parallel and Distributed Systems*, 13(7):693–709, July 2002.

46. A.G. Greenberg and B. Hajek. Deflection Routing in Hypercube Networks. *IEEE Transactions on Communications*, COM-40(6):1070–1081, June 1992.

47. S. Konstantinidou and L. Snyder. Chaos Router: Architecture and Performance. In *Proceedings of the 18th International Symposium on Computer Architecture*, pages 212–221. IEEE Computer Society, May 1991.

48. N. McKenzie, K. Bolding, C. Ebeling, and L. Snyder. ChaosLAN: Design and Implementation of a Gigabit LAN Using Chaotic Routing. In *Proceedings of the 2nd PCRCW*, pages 211–223. Springer-Verlag, June 1997.

49. J. Kim, Z. Liu, and A. Chien. Compressionless Routing: A Framework for Adaptive and Fault-tolerant Routing. *IEEE Transactions on Parallel and Distributed Systems*, 8(3):229–244, March 1997.

50. M. Coli and P. Palazzari. An Adaptive Deadlock and Livelock Free Routing Algorithm. In *3rd Euromicro Workshop on Parallel and Distributed Processing*, pages 288–295. San Remo, Italy, January 1995.

51. J.M. Martinez, P. Lopez, J. Duato, and T.M. Pinkston. Software-based Deadlock Recovery for True Fully Adaptive Routing in Wormhole Networks. In *Proceeding of the 1997 International Conference on Parallel Processing*, pages 182–189. IEEE Computer Society, August 1997.

52. K.V. Anjan and T.M. Pinkston. An Efficient, Fully Adaptive Deadlock Recovery Scheme: *DISHA*. In *Proceedings of the 22nd International Symposium on Computer Architecture*, pages 201–210. IEEE Computer Society, June 1995.

53. T.M. Pinkston, Y. Choi, and M. Raksapatcharawong. Architecture and Optoelectronic Implementation of the WARRP Router. In *Proceedings of the 5th Symposium on Hot Interconnects*, pages 181–189. IEEE Computer Society, August 1997.

54. K.V. Anjan, T.M. Pinkston, and J. Duato. Generalized Theory for Deadlock-Free Adaptive Wormhole Routing and its Application to Disha Concurrent. In *Proceedings of the 10th International Parallel Processing Symposium*, pages 815–821. IEEE Computer Society, April 1996.

55. K.V. Anjan and T.M. Pinkston. *DISHA*: A Deadlock Recovery Scheme for Fully Adaptive Routing. In *Proceedings of the 9th International Parallel Processing Symposium*, pages 537–543. IEEE Computer Society, April 1995.

56. T.M. Pinkston. Flexible and Efficient Routing Based on Progressive Deadlock Recovery. *IEEE Transactions on Computers*, 48(7):649–669, July 1999.

57. Y.H. Song and T.M. Pinkston. A New Mechanism for Congestion and Deadlock Resolution. In *The 2002 International Conference on Parallel Processing*, pages 81–90. IEEE Computer Society, August 2002.

58. C.B. Stunkel et al. The SP2 high-performance switch. *IBM Systems Journal*, 34(2):185–204, 1995.

59. A. Agarwal, R. Bianchini, D. Chaiken, K. Johnson, D. Kranz, J. Kubiatowicz, B-H. Lim, K. Mackenzie, and D. Yeung. The MIT alewife machine: Architecture and performance. In *Proc. of the 22nd Annual Int'l Symp. on Computer Architecture (ISCA'95)*, pages 2–13, June 1995.

60. J.F. Martinez, J. Torrellas, and J. Duato. Improving the Performance of Bristled CC-NUMA Systems Using Virtual Channels and Adaptivity. In *Proceedings of 13th International Conference on Supercomputing*, June 1999.

61. Y.H. Song and T.M. Pinkston. A Progressive Approach to Handling Message-Dependent Deadlock in Parallel Computer Systems. *IEEE Transactions on Parallel and Distributed Systems*, 14(3):259–275, March 2003.

62. D. Teodosiu, J. Baxter, K. Govil, J. Chapin, M. Rosenblum, and M. Horowitz. Hardware Fault Containment in Scalable Shared-Memory Multiprocessors. In *Proceedings of the 24th International Symposium on Computer Architecture*, pages 73–84. IEEE Computer Society Press, June 1997.

63. *InfiniBand^{TM} Architecture Specification Volume 1*. InfiniBand Trade Association, October 24, 2000.

64. O. Lysne and J. Duato. Fast Dynamic Reconfiguration in Irregular Networks. In *The 2000 International Conference on Parallel Processing*, pages 449–458. IEEE Computer Society, August 2000.

65. F.J. Quiles, J.L. Sanchez, R. Casado, A. Bermudez and J. Duato. A protocol for deadlock-free dynamic reconfiguration in high-speed local area networks. *Special Issue on Dependable Network Computing. IEEE Transactions on Parallel and Distributed Systems*, 12(2):115–132, February 2001.

66. R. Pang, T.M. Pinkston and J. Duato. Dynamic Reconfiguration of Networks with Distributed Routing: The Single Scheme. In *Proceedings of the International Conference on Parallel and Distributed Processing Techniques and Applications (PDPTA)*, pages 2042–2048, June 2001.

14

Deadlock Models for a Multi-Service Medium Access Protocol Employing a Slotted Aloha or Q-ary Tree Based Signaling Channel

Milosh Vladimir Ivanovich[1]
Telstra Research Laboratories, Melbourne, Australia.

14.1 INTRODUCTION

Medium access control (MAC) protocols for many contemporary wireline and wireless networks, both in the narrow- and broadband domains, often use a collision-based capacity request signalling channel. Prime examples are cable modem hybrid fibre/coaxial (HFC) networks [1], wireless ATM (WATM) [2], as well as the general packet radio service (GPRS) [3]. This signalling channel typically relies on either the slotted aloha [4] or splitting algorithm [5] multi-access principles.

In this chapter, we study in detail the performance of a p-persistence slotted aloha contention resolution algorithm (CRA) [6], subject to extreme inter-station correlation, by means of a discrete-time Markov chain analysis. We also spend some time in examining by simulation, the performance of both (i) a simple binary

---

[1] This work was performed during the author's Ph.D. candidature at the Faculty of Information Technology, Monash University, Australia, and is in no way associated with the author's current employer.

tree CRA called blocked access protocol (BAP) [7], and (ii) a modified free-access Q-ary stack algorithm called msSTART (multi-slot stack random access algorithm) [8]. msSTART is included to provide an idea of splitting algorithm baseline performance, while msSTART was proposed for use in the IEEE 802.14 HFC standard [9]. The performance of the three types of CRA BAP is discussed and contrasted, under what the IEEE 802.14 working group has termed the "disaster scenario," where the entire station population simultaneously requests capacity after a neighbourhood-wide power failure, for example.

Of great interest to the MAC protocol engineer is the protocol's resiliency to conditions potentially leading to a disaster scenario, often termed deadlock. Such an event must be avoided, through both preemptive and dynamically adaptive measures, since it usually means that congestion collapse of the signalling, and hence data channels, has taken place and stations' access delay has exceeded practically usable levels. We analyze a practically significant disaster scenario deadlock model and study the effect of channel error probability, signalling traffic load, and the contention resolution algorithm used. Key behaviors of each of the CRAs are identified, with the finding that it is the collision rate and not channel errors more strongly govern throughput performance.

The msSTART is shown to provide superior throughput performance and better guarantees of non-case sensitive performance, regardless of medium (fixed/wireless), than its simpler binary tree and slotted aloha CRA counterparts. Of the three signalling capacity allocation schemes considered, the full CMS sharing (FCS) scheme employing multiple CMSs per upstream super-slot extends the msSTART CRA's usable load region the furthest, and with a significant dimensioning saving (33%) over the slotted aloha (p-persistence) CRA under identical circumstances.

The important issue of MAC-layer signalling traffic prioritization is studied in detail, and three schemes for providing this functionality are identified and evaluated: (i) CCS_M, (ii) CCS_S, and (iii) hybrid CCS_S / FCS. We find that the usefulness of any given signalling capacity allocation scheme is clearly dependent on the CRA it is trying to "assist" – a case in point being the far more prominent deadlock resilience improvement in slotted aloha (p-persistence) than msSTART, under CCS_M.

In summary, this chapter conveys to the MAC protocol designer the important message that the final choice of framing structure, CRA and SCA scheme must not be made in isolation, but always within the guidelines of the stated system objectives and with the aim of ensuring optimum performance level, including consideration of our topic at hand – deadlock resilience.

14.2 THE PRINCIPLE OF COLLISION-BASED RESERVATION CHANNELS

A crucial challenge in the field of MAC protocol research in the areas of wireless and broadband access mediums is to design a protocol able to cope efficiently with the multiplicity of traffic types that such networks will be expected to carry, while still offering stable operation under all arrival distributions. Expected traffic types in these systems include constant bit rate (CBR), variable bBit rate (VBR), available bit rate (ABR) and signalling for resource reservation [10], [11], [12], [13]. Previous studies have shown that guaranteed and semi-guaranteed traffic falling under the CBR/VBR/ABR umbrella is optimally carried using *reserved* channels or portions of a channel, at the data link layer [14], [15]. The alternatives would usually involve sending very small packets of user data without separate signalling, and experiencing collisions within the actual traffic channel – an approach shown in [14], [15] to be less efficient than one based on reservation.

Having decided to implement a system using a reservation-based paradigm for our packet data traffic, we need to consider the aspect of signalling the user terminal state: how does the system know when and how much individual stations have to transmit, and hence how much resources to reserve for each one? If the stations were all co-located in an ideal single server queue (SSQ) environment, where the resource scheduler (see below) had instantaneous knowledge of each station's state, the need for signalling traffic would be eliminated. However, the stations in today's wireless and wireline networks are spread over wide ranging distances, and furthermore it is not practically possible to implement a system where a central controller would always have full instantaneous knowledge of station state, without some degree of signalling. There needs to be a separate signalling channel in order to coordinate "reservation activity." This raises the question of how multiple access should be regulated on such a channel, and research has shown that the signalling traffic (used to reserve resources for packet data traffic) is most efficiently carried using a random access method [14], [16], [17] giving a clear context for the study at hand.

Three contemporary protocols designed with the *"random access signalling /reserved data" philosophy* in mind are:

- The wireless ATM MAC protocol [2], [18], [19],
- The MAC protocol defined in the IEEE 802.14 standard for hybrid fibre/coax networks [9], [20], [21] and
- The MAC protocol associated with the general packet radio service (GPRS) [3].

All these protocols are based on a central controller (located at the head-end in HFC and at the base station controller in WATM/GPRS networks), and significantly for this study of deadlock analysis, all employ the concept of collision-based reservation channels. Naturally, implementation differences exist between these diverse systems, but from the point of view of a network user with data to transmit, the generic paradigm adopted by all the MAC protocols we are considering, as alluded to above, relies on two phases:

1. ***Contention resolution***, where the station competes with other stations by using a collision-prone *signalling channel*, in order to attempt to reserve capacity on a *data channel*.
2. ***Reservation-based transmission***, where the station has been reserved its own allocation of bandwidth and transfers data in a collision-free manner.

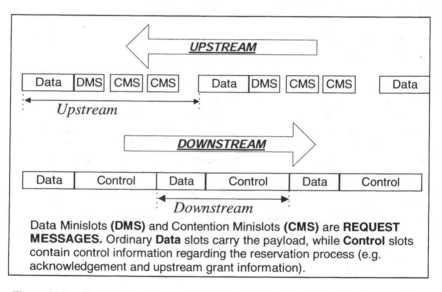

Figure 14.1.   Slot structure of a generic MAC protocol with collision-based reservation.

Reservation requests are sent using two types of signalling, in the station-to-controller (upstream) direction: contention minislots (CMS), which may be thought of as out-of-band signalling and data minislots (DMS), interpreted as in-band signalling [9], [11], [20], [21], [22]. Figure 14.1 illustrates that the (multiple) CMSs are parts of the upstream MAC-layer frame into which any station can send its signalling, while the (single) DMS is attached to the reserved data transmission part of the frame, and is thus accessible only to the currently transmitting station, as a means to signal that station's need for further reserved bandwidth. As a result, no collisions occur in DMSs.

The user data is transmitted, based on the capacity allocated by the controller, collision-free. A scheduling algorithm, which is implementation specific and not part of relevant MAC protocol standards, regulates the capacity allocations which the controller decides upon for individual stations.

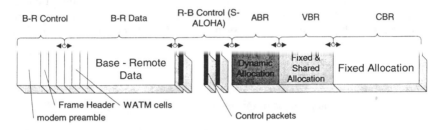

Figure 14.2. Schematic representation of a proposed wireless ATM frame structure [2].

An example of a specific WATM frame structure proposal is pictured in Figure 14.2, [2] :

- The downlink (base to remote, or B-R) subframe is transmitted at the start of the TDMA frame, and contains the preamble, frame header, wireless network control signals and user data payload.
- The uplink subframe consists of the uplink control region for remote to base (R-B) control information transmission, followed by allocated ABR, VBR and CBR data slots in positions assigned by the MAC protocol.

Note that this particular frame structure proposal envisages time division duplexing (TDD), so that data from the upstream and downstream directions uses the same channel, but is separated in time. The total overhead from frame headers and preamble makes the maximum utilization of the channel before consideration of retransmission, modulation constellation and forward error correction as low as 75%.

The MAC design principles, framing structure and controller's scheduling algorithms are not our focus here. Instead, in this chapter, we will study the contention resolution phase of two commonly used CRAs, subject to extreme inter-station correlation, in order to ascertain conditions leading to MAC protocol deadlock. That is, how far the protocols may be pushed (in terms of station arrival rates and profiles), before they become unusable, and what mitigation techniques are possible.

14.3 CONTENTION RESOLUTION ALGORITHMS (CRA)

Many factors in the design of a MAC protocol have a direct impact on the collision probability experienced within the access network. An example is the provision of multiple CMSs in a reservation-based MAC protocol (Figure 14.1), where we essentially divide the potential collision set into the number of CMS signalling channels available. However, once a collision has already occurred, we wish to define efficient retransmission rules, which will hopefully yield a resolution of the collision in as short an interval as possible. The set of such rules is called the CRA, and is the topic of this section.

CRAs may be categorized into two different random access philosophies, each belonging to a distinct family of algorithms: (i) the *individualism* of the aloha family and (ii) the *collective operation* of the splitting algorithm family [9].

Take as an example three CRA variants, all belonging to the slotted aloha (sub)family of aloha algorithms: uniformly distributed retransmission period, p-persistence, and truncated binary exponential back-off [4]. Each of these CRAs is a slightly different "flavor" of slotted aloha, but they all nonetheless share the same random access *philosophy of individualism*. This philosophy is one where the network stations should only be interested in the outcome of their own transmissions, with this outcome being conveyed to them via positive acknowledgements, also known as feedback. Therefore, a typical slotted aloha station need only monitor the channel immediately after its transmission. Being based on the individualism philosophy, this applies to all CRAs of the aloha family, with the exception of Ethernet [23] where carrier sensing is used and the channel is also monitored <u>before</u> transmission.

The other major random access philosophy is that of *collective operation* and is associated with the *splitting* family of algorithms. The guiding principle here is that of a collective effort by all stations registered on the system to continuously monitor the feedback information provided by the central controller node, and update their state accordingly. Note that there are some variants of this family of CRAs, where only <u>active</u> stations need to monitor the feedback information (i.e., those currently participating in a collision or not yet allowed to participate but wanting to transmit data). In either type of system, all (re)transmission decisions are taken based on the current feedback and state information. Two main categories of splitting algorithms exist:

- *Tree-search*-also known as <u>blocked-access</u> splitting algorithms since new packets are not allowed into the system while a collision resolution is under way. Further subdivision of these algorithms is possible, according to the <u>first transmission</u> rule used. This rule controls when and how the blocked stations are first allowed to transmit in the system.

- *Stack* also known as <u>free-access</u> splitting algorithms since new packets are permitted to enter the system during an ongoing collision resolution.

In general, both splitting and slotted aloha families may be further classified based on the feedback they require for operation. Feedback, and other important CRA classifiers applicable to both the slotted aloha and splitting algorithm families, are thoroughly explained below (excerpts from [9], [24]):

- **Sensing** refers to the way in which the CRA imposes the algorithm rules to the user population. A system referred to as a *full sensing* (FS) CRA enforces rules and restrictions on all users, even if they are not currently involved in the contention process. In such a case, all stations need to continually be monitoring the reverse control path. An example of FS CRAs are all blocked-access (tree) algorithms, since a new station is restricted to transmitting only in certain time intervals. A *limited sensing* (LS) CRA, however, only requires those stations that are currently participating in unresolved collisions to process the central controller feedback information. Free-access (stack) algorithms are an example of LS CRAs, in that all new arrivals immediately join the collision resolution process, without any signalling or restrictions. LS has two major advantages over FS: a significant saving in station computation power and better **robustness** (as qualitatively graded in Table 14.1) to loss of information from the head-end. The latter point refers to the fact that in FS, because the users do not rely on their own local states, they are totally dependent on communicated global state "updates." In the presence of errors on the downstream channel, the loss of this global state picture would cause a deadlock situation due to the loss of synchronization (until a centralized recovery scheme took hold of the system problems).

- A CRA's **feedback** parameter describes the number of states that can be determined by a user from reading central controller feedback on the channel. Algorithms requiring three states (collision, success, idle) are those with *ternary feedback*, while algorithms where only the collision and success states are required, are known as *binary feedback* CRAs. Although the former type of scheme achieves greater throughput, in some access network types such as wireless environments, it is not possible to implement it. Note that although less common, there are algorithms that allow more than three states of feedback, thus allowing the colliding user to deduce exact numbers of collision participants, and take an appropriate course of action, as dictated by the CRA in use.

- The **maximum stable throughput** of a scheme is the theoretical maximum value of arrival rate for which the system's departure rate is the same (i.e., for which the system remains stable). Another definition is that it is the maximum proportion of time during which the channel is used to make successful transmissions.

- The **contention resolution interval (CRI)** is the time period during which (i) collisions occur, followed by (ii) retransmissions and ultimately (iii) overall contention resolution. The CRA has as its chief task to define exactly the rules of retransmission during this interval. When this interval has some predetermined maximum duration, it is said to be *bounded*. Tree-search splitting algorithms have the advantage of bounded CRIs; for all slotted aloha algorithms, it is not possible to identify such distinct intervals, so it is said that they have unbounded CRIs.

- CRA **stability** is used to describe whether the algorithm causes the system to become unable to cope at extreme loads, with the surge of request traffic. That is, if the *average access delay per packet is still finite* at a given arrival rate, the CRA is considered stable at that arrival rate. If the CRA is considered unstable, a secondary mechanism is required for acceptable system performance. Good examples of this secondary mechanism are a station's own load control mechanism, or, the addition of a second, usually collision free, signalling channel (an example is the piggybacked data request (DMS) used in many proposed MAC protocols, and illustrated previously in Figure 14.1).

- Ability to operate in a **DPD** (difference in propagation delay) environment states whether the CRA can operate as part of a system where differences in propagation delay are tolerated. This has an impact on CRA complexity, and the examples of DPD systems include HFC networks, while wireless and wireline LANs are systems with negligible DPD.

Characteristic ⇨ CRA ⇩	Sensing	Feed- back	Max. Stable T'put	Bounded CRI	Robustness	DPD
Unstabilized Slotted Aloha (p-persistence)	Limited	Binary	0	NO	Excellent	YES
Static Binary Tree-search [5]	Full	Binary	0.346	YES	Poor	NO
Stack *(n=2)*	Full	Binary	0.360	YES	Poor	NO
Stabilized Slotted Aloha (p-persistence)	Full or Limited	Binary or Ternary	0.368	NO	Excellent	YES
Stack *(n=3)*	Limited	Binary	0.402	NO	Good	NO
Dynamic Tree-search [5]	Full	Ternary	0.429	YES	Poor	NO

Table 14.1. The most well-known CRA types.

Table 14.1 is a combined reproduction of Table 1 in [9], and Table 3 in [24], and summarizes key performance and operational characteristics of six common CRA types.

Another important aspect of CRA performance, and one which is our particular topic of interest in this chapter, is CRA resiliency in the face of extreme stress scenarios.

One such scenario is the simultaneous arrival of a large number of packets into a previously empty system. Of interest in this case, is the average number of slots it will take to clear (i.e., successfully transmit) all the packets, under the assumption that no new packet enters the system. Table 14.2, reproduced from [9], shows the average time to clear a batch of 2000 packets under the circumstances just described, for some of the well-known CRAs we have discussed previously.

Note that the quantity α may be thought of as the average contribution of each station, to the overall CRI length in upstream super-slots, L_N. It is interesting to see that the ideal stabilized slotted aloha CRA is a very close second to the static binary tree-search algorithm. Interestingly in [9] it is stated that the *ideal* stabilized slotted aloha is also <u>non-implementable</u> (in [4] it is explained that all stabilization schemes are only estimation-based and cannot guarantee peak theoretical throughput 100% of the time).

Contention Resolution Algorithm	Avg. Time to Clear $N = 2000$ packets (in slots)	$\alpha = L_N / N$
Dynamic Tree-search (Ternary feedback)	$\approx 5,328$	≈ 2.664
Ideal Stabilized Slotted Aloha (p-persistence)	$\approx 5,436$	≈ 2.718
Stack *(n=3)* (Binary feedback)	$\approx 5,462$	≈ 2.731
Static Binary Tree-search (Binary feedback)	$\approx 5,770$	≈ 2.885
Implementable Stabilized Slotted Aloha (p-persistence)	$\approx 6,400$	≈ 3.2
Unstabilized Slotted Aloha (p-persistence)	>10,000	>5

Table 14.2. Performance of selected CRAs under stress conditions [9].

We note that the practically implementable stable slotted aloha CRA comes a distant second to last. This type of CRA stress testing is our focus in the next section, and serves as a foundation for our suite of deadlock models, based on the CRAs used in two separate multi-service MAC protocols. These are: (a) Slotted aloha (p-persistence) used in fair centralized priority reservation (F-CPR) [10] and (b) a modified free-access Q-ary stack used in the msSTART [8].

14.4 MODELLING CONTENTION RESOLUTION ALGORITHM DEAD-LOCK

Of great interest to the MAC protocol engineer is the protocol's resiliency to conditions potentially leading to a disaster scenario, often termed *deadlock*. Such an event must be avoided, through both preemptive and dynamically adaptive measures, since it usually means that congestion collapse of the signalling, and hence data, channels has taken place and stations' access delay has exceeded practically usable levels. We now present two analytic models dealing with deadlock, where the time to resolve collisions approaches infinity (or a large enough value to be equivalent to infinity for practical systems). Three algorithms are investigated. In each case we use the basic deadlock model (BDM) first described in [7], [10] which focuses on the performance of the CRA under extreme traffic patterns in order to determine the worst case and give a useful performance measure of the underlying stability of the CRA scheme:

1. *An analytic* deadlock model is derived for a *p-persistence slotted aloha CRA*, as used in the F-CPR protocol [10]. New packets are retransmitted with fixed or adapted probability in a slot following initial contention. This method is used in the R-B control region of a proposal for a WATM MAC [2], [18]. The basic p-persistence scheme is simple to implement, however variants with higher performance such as estimators for adaptive optimization of p create significant extra control complexity.

2. Deadlock is modeled by *simulation* for a simple *blocked-access binary tree CRA protocol (BAP)* [5]. New packets arriving are transmitted in the first slot after all previous conflicts are resolved, so that packets are blocked at their transmitters until the current CRI terminates. This requires each station to monitor channel feedback such that they can keep track of when each CRI ends. This is a significant disadvantage since stations are not allowed to be turned off in the absence of packets to transmit.

3. *Simulation* is also used to model deadlock for an evolved version of a free access *Q-ary stack splitting algorithm called msSTART* [8]. msSTART is an evolution of the unblocked stack algorithm: an easy way to implement high-efficiency, free-access, robust, stable CRA optimized to operate in an environment where the number of available CMSs (and method of accessing them) could be changed dynamically. Its congestion-related unsteady operation threshold (see Section 14.4.2) is significantly higher than that of the basic unblocked stack algorithm as a result of the temporary blocking of new arrivals until the start of the next block (note: *not* the start of the next CRI [8]). The algorithm can be easily interleaved and requires only binary feedback for operation.

Regardless of the CRA used, the main assumption of the BDM is that in most circumstances, the worst case is obtained under extreme inter-station correlation. That is, when *all* stations in the system generate *periodic* and *simultaneous* signalling request "storms" [9], [10], [21]. For this reason, instead of the well-known Poisson request arrival process typically used to model signalling or data packet arrivals on slotted aloha-like channels, we adopt an arrival process where all N stations in a population signal simultaneously into one CMS at a particular point in time. The BDM studied here enhances a similar model investigated in [21], due to its analytic instead of simulation-based framework, and because it includes signalling channel errors. Additionally, as part of the BDM, a range of signalling capacity allocation schemes, as discussed in Section 14.5, is also modelled.

A principal motivation for the development of deadlock models, is what has been coined as the "disaster scenario" within deliberations of the IEEE 802.14 committee [9], [21], where it is assumed that the totality of stations in an HFC fibre serving area neighborhood (say, 2000) are all simultaneously powered-up (for example, after a power failure) and transmit a single packet in the same upstream CMS. Note that the particular attention we pay to modelling and exploring this particular type of deadlock scenario is warranted because, as described in [10], the piggybacked reservation feature of most HFC and wireless MACs (take for example F-CPR), will ensure relatively "uneventful" and efficient operation of both the signalling and data channel under most normal conditions. The bottleneck, point of interest, then becomes the set of scenarios where it is impossible to use this piggybacked reservation feature and the entire station population burdens the signalling channel directly. Modelling such a situation permits mitigation measures through choice of the optimal CRA and signalling capacity allocation techniques, thus enhancing the deadlock resiliency of a multi-service MAC protocol.

14.4.1 Slotted Aloha (p-persistence) BDM: Assumptions, Definitions and Analysis

In analyses of the classical slotted aloha multi-access approach [4], [6] it has often been stated that the assumption of arrivals modeled by a Poisson process, is somewhat inappropriate for real traffic and it is mainly used to enable analytic tractability. Additionally, real HFC and wireless networks are prone to errors from noise, and interference, making the perfect reception assumption in the classical slotted aloha analysis very idealized.

Table 14.3 compares and contrasts the assumption sets of our basic deadlock model for slotted aloha, with the classical slotted aloha analysis presented in [4]. The station population in our model (N) is finite, so the notoriously unstable nature of the slotted aloha family of multi-access algorithms is not a factor by itself (since slotted aloha is theoretically stable for a finite population).

However, the concepts of *theoretical* and *practical* stability are worlds apart, and this paradigm forms a major part of our investigation of the deadlock models we study. In presenting the analytic model for p-persistence slotted aloha under the BDM, the interested reader is referred to [6] where the authors go beyond the basic deadlock model, and define and compare a number of such variants for a multi-service medium access protocol employing a slotted ALOHA signaling channel.

Classical Slotted Aloha Assumption	Applicability to Deadlock Model
Slotted System	✓
Poisson Arrivals	✗ (Instead we use periodic arrivals of a batch of capacity requests, N).
Collision or Perfect Reception	✗ (Instead, we assume channel errors are possible, and quantify with probability P_{err}).
Immediate Feedback	✓
Retransmission of Collisions	✓
No Buffering / Infinite Set of Nodes	✓ and ✗

Table 14.3. Similarities between classical slotted aloha and basic deadlock model (BDM).

Allowing N to be the number of active stations, then all of the N stations request capacity, each for a single-cell message, all at the same time, at the beginning of the CRI, which is measured in number of CMSs. As stated earlier (see Figure 14.1 and 14.2), in modelling the signalling channel we assume that time is divided into fixed-length intervals. In order to justify this assumption in the context of an HFC or WATM MAC protocol, we note that each of these fixed-length intervals represents one CMS minislot. In practice, depending on the number of CMSs associated with each upstream data slot, there may or may not be variable-length gaps between consecutive CMSs. This means that, by using the notion of the number of CMSs elapsed, we are measuring time nonlinearly for systems with $M>1$ CMS. However, due to the cyclic nature of this nonlinear relationship in a practical MAC protocol, we can assume linearity in our discrete-time model.

At time $t = 0$, a batch of size N arrives. Let $P(j, t)$ be the probability of having j contending requests at the end of time interval t, ($t = 1, 2, ...$) and $j = 1, 2, ..., N$. We also define $P(0, t)$ as the probability of having no contending requests at time t, for the first time. In other words, $P(0, t)$ is the probability that the CRI length, denoted by ϕ is exactly equal to t upstream CMSs. Since all N stations try to access a CMS during the first time interval, and they all collide, we shall still have N outstanding requests at the end of the first interval. Hence, $P(N, 1) = 1$ and $P(j, 1)=0$ for all $j=0, 1,..., N-1$.

Following the p-persistence algorithm, after the first time interval all N stations try to access with probability p, but any given CMS also has the possibility of suffering a random error (which causes the transmission to fail) and we assume that, during each CMS, errors are independent so the error process is one with geometrically distributed inter-occurrence times (parameter P_{err}). The probability of a successful transmission is therefore given by

$$(1 - P_{err}) \cdot Np(1-p)^{N-1} \quad \cdots (1)$$

In general, when we have j stations contending for transmission, the probability of successful transmission (i.e., a reduction of one in the number of requests "waiting" for resolution) will be given by

$$P_S(j) = (1 - P_{err}) \cdot jp(1-p)^{j-1} \quad \cdots (2)$$

On the other hand, the failure outcome when j stations are contending is defined as the event when the number of outstanding requests does not decrease by one. The probability of failure is given by

$$P_F(j) = (1 - jp(1-p)^{j-1}) + P_{err} \cdot jp(1-p)^{j-1} = 1 - P_s(j) \quad \cdots (3)$$

The case $j = N$ is an upper bound on the system occupancy and hence a special boundary condition exists: $P(N, 2) = P_F(N)$, $P(N, 3) = P_F(N)^2$, $P(N, 4) = P_F(N)^3$, and in general, $P(N, t) = P_F(N)^{t-1}$. The general case arises when $j = 1, 2, \ldots, N-1$, and the state j could have been entered from a higher state, or remained unchanged from the previous timeslot

$$P(j,t) = P(j+1, t-1) \cdot P_S(j+1) + P(j, t-1) \cdot P_F(j) \quad \cdots (4)$$

Finally, the probability of zero outstanding requests at time t is given by

$$P(0,t) = p \cdot P(1, t-1) \cdot (1 - P_{err}) \quad \cdots (5)$$

The model we have described has a bounded state-space, and for any given state j, the probability of an increase in state is zero. It is therefore trivial to show that the *absorption probability of such a system must be unity* [25]. This rather intuitive result suggests that, as expected, the mean CRI duration T_C will always be finite, regardless of our choice of model parameters. Employing the "summation of steps" technique from [25], we obtain the analytical expression for the mean CRI duration in CMSs, given an initial state $j = N$,

$$T_C = \sum_{j=1}^{N} \frac{1}{P_S(j)} \quad \cdots (6a)$$

The model described is a discrete-time pure death process, with no possibility of increase from any state j. This explains the very simple form of Equation

(6a)-it is merely a sum of the average sojourn times in each of the states the system descends down through, from $j=N$ to $j=1$. A slightly more useful method of obtaining T_C is numerical recursion. A numerical recursive solution of the set of Equations (2)-(4) will yield the probabilities $P(0,t)$, $(t=1, 2, 3, \dots)$ from which T_C is obtained, in CMSs,

$$T_C = E[\phi] = \sum_{t=1}^{\infty} t \cdot P(0,t) \ \dots (6b)$$

Note that in all our numerical solutions, we use the termination condition: $t \cdot P(0, t) < 10^{-9}$. The method of numerical recursive solution of the model's state transition equations is extremely useful because it yields the series of exact system occupancy probability distributions, from timeslots 1 through to ∞ (in theory). This then allows other important statistics to be calculated, such as the entire discrete probability density function for ϕ, not just its mean value, T_C. However, if we were solely interested in calculating the mean CRI length, T_C, adopting an analytical solution approach would have been quicker and simpler.

Having determined T_C, we now know the maximum achievable throughput of our basic deadlock model: it is merely the ratio of N request messages to the T_C CMSs it takes to clear them from the contention state (assuming an upstream super-slot structure with only $M=1$ CMS per data slot). Let us define this ratio as L_{crit}, signifying *critical load*. This load is considered critical because if the N requests arrive with a period less than T_C, the arrival rate exceeds the system's service rate, and the system becomes *unsteady*, with the number of outstanding requests increasing toward infinity.

Note we do not say *unstable* because we have already proved <u>analytically that T_C is always finite</u>; in this sense unsteady signifies an uncontrolled increase in the number of backlogged requests, so that T_C, although theoretically finite, becomes so large that for practical purposes it tends to infinity. This last point clearly illustrates the definition of a system which is **practically unstable**, yet **theoretically stable**, in the described deadlock scenario.

In situations where L_{crit} is very small (such as it tends toward some arbitrary threshold of practical instability), it may be desired to increase it by some other means. This is where *signalling capacity allocation schemes* play a role. Such schemes describe how to allocate and manage multiple CMSs per upstream data slot, and three new such schemes are proposed in Section 14.5.

14.4.2 Splitting Algorithm BDM for BAP and msSTART: Assumptions, Definitions and Simulation Framework

In defining our deadlock model for the BAP and msSTART CRAs, we make the following key assumptions:

1. Time is slotted (as per diagram in Figure 14.1);

2. One user group is interrogated in each set of Q concurrent related slots in a resolution node – we do not segment the resolution process; Q is also commonly referred to as the *"splitting parameter"*;

3. There is immediate feedback of collision or no collision, but the action taken in any slot of a group of Q concurrent related slots cannot depend on the contents of other slots within the same group. We do not take advantage of efficiency gains available as a result of tree collapse made available by ternary feedback; and

4. There is retransmission of collisions and no buffering.

As is the case with our slotted aloha BDM, the principal difference between our study and other Q-ary tree analyses is that we do not assume Poisson arrivals. Instead we again model the correlated arrivals by having each of the N stations in the population transmit periodic batches of capacity requests to the central controller. Concerning performance, the focus is once again upon the mean, T_C, and the pdf of the CRI length, $f_\phi(x)$, rather than on an individual user's signalling delay.

The BAP is perhaps the simplest of all the splitting algorithms, and the interested reader is directed to [5] for the basic algorithm. Here we turn our attention to the more interesting and complex msSTART CRA, which as mentioned earlier, represents an evolution of the Q-ary free-access family of "stack" splitting algorithms. In such CRAs, after a collision each transmitter flips a "Q-sided coin" with values $1, 2, \ldots, Q$ (we assume that the Q-sided coins are fair). This splits the set of contending transmitters into Q subsets and to each of these subsets an index is assigned indicating the number of the "Q sided coin" that was "flipped."

If N is the number of active stations, then all N stations request capacity for a single cell message at the same point of the beginning of the CRI. As discussed in Section 14.4.1, from a signaling contention perspective this extreme correlation is the worst case scenario. The aim is to derive the mean CRI duration, measured in the number of CMSs (ϕ), and denoted $T_C = E[\phi]$, as before (Equation (6b)).

msSTART is an example of a more advanced CRA that was considered for use in the IEEE 802.14 standard. This CRA is often analyzed as a pointer to a stack [8] and the msSTART counter-update algorithm is given below (loop until CRI is complete):

When an inactive station becomes active, initialize $COUNT = random\{0, \ldots, M-1\}$ where M is the number of CMSs for the current upstream data slot ("contention block");

If *(COUNT < M)* then

      Station transmits in CMS number *COUNT*;

      Upon receiving feedback information:

      If *(did not collide)* then

          Done;

      Elseif *(collide)*

          Set: $COUNT \leftarrow Q * col\{COUNT\} + random\{0, \ldots, Q\text{-}1\}$;

Elseif *(COUNT > M − 1)* then

      Station does not transmit in current block;

      Upon receiving feedback information:

          Set: $COUNT \leftarrow Q * col\{M\} + COUNT - M$;

Table 14.4 . msSTART counter-update algorithm.

    col{M} is the number of collisions during an upstream data slot with M CMSs (i.e., the "contention block"), returned to each station as feedback information. T_C is approximated for the msSTART algorithm using a computer simulation written in C++ [7], designed to mimic the operation of the MAC layer of a multi-service HFC or wireless network, and providing utilization, delay and stability statistics for a range of system specifications. Input traffic characteristics, CRA type, CMS number and type per frame as well as error distribution and probability can all be controlled by the user, giving flexibility to study the deadlock performance of a number of different CRAs. An additional benefit of the simulation was the validation of analytic results derived in Section 14.4.1 for the p-persistence slotted aloha CRA.

14.5 SIGNALLING CAPACITY ALLOCATION (SCA) SCHEMES

Apart from selection of an optimal CRA, other methods of deadlock mitigation exist and one of these is employing a signalling capacity allocation scheme. We now consider three such schemes to allocate and manage access to CMS signaling minislots. In addition to deadlock mitigation, use of signalling capacity allocation schemes over and above the basic CRA is motivated by the desire to enable MAC-layer traffic differentiation and prioritization. Namely, there are proposals in the areas of multi-service wireless networks and HFC networks for MAC-layer priority schemes in order to provide QoS to users with real-time data such as voice, video and interactive services [3], [8], [11], [22]. This would allow mapping of IP-layer QoS classes, being used by IntServ of DiffServ classified IP traffic, to approximately equivalent MAC QoS classes.

The simplest scheme we present here is full CMS sharing with multiple (M) CMSs per data slot (FCS). All arriving signalling requests are able to access *any* CMS, hence the term "full CMS sharing." This is basically a pure signalling capacity expansion scheme, with an expansion factor of M. Here the critical load definition given in Section 14.4.1 is slightly augmented :

$$L^{FCS}{}_{crit} = \frac{MN}{T_C(CRA, N, (p), P_{err})} \quad \dots \quad (7)$$

This defines the critical load $L^{FCS}{}_{crit}$ as the ratio of work arriving in a batch, namely N and the average time in upstream super-slots (containing a data and M associated CMSs during which the resolution of these N requests is completed). Note that there are M CMSs per super-slot, so the average time in super-slots is $T_C(CRA, N, (p), P_{err})/M$. In the expression for T_C the CRA and P_{err} parameters highlight the fact that the critical load, as defined in Equation (7), is a performance measure applicable to any CRA, and always dependent on the signalling channel error rate. The p-persistence parameter is only applicable to our specific p-persistence slotted aloha BDM, and is thus shown in parentheses.

Under the second scheme, the N stations are subdivided into M groups, so that each group must access a different CMS associated with the data slot. Concerning implementation, the station counts passing CMSs and is allowed to access every M^{th} CMS, which occurs once per data slot since we have M CMSs for every one data slot. Unlike the first scheme, where all signalling traffic could transmit in any CMS, in this scheme the effective load accessing any CMS is reduced to N/M. This scheme is denoted by the term cyclic CMS sharing with multiple CMSs per data slot (or CCS_M for short), and has a critical load of

$$L^{CCS-M}{}_{crit} = \frac{N}{T_C(CRA, (N/M), (p), P_{err})} \quad \dots \quad (8)$$

Finally, the third scheme, which is similar to the multi-CMS cyclic sharing, is its *single-CMS* variant (CCS_S for short). Using only one CMS per data slot, if we divide the N stations into k groups, whereby each group may only access every k^{th} CMS, we obtain a critical load of

$$L^{CCS\_S}{}_{crit} = \frac{N}{k \cdot T_C(CRA, (N/k), (p), P_{err})} \quad \dots (9)$$

Note that if single-CMS cyclic sharing is used, $M=1$ but there is an additional fifth factor : the number of separate contention resolution groups, k. This scheme most closely corresponds to the separate collision resolution for different priorities of traffic. Stations initially transmit in slots exactly matching their priority level so the head-end knows that all stations participating in a particular collision are of the same priority level. Requests only collide with other requests of the same priority preventing other priorities from interfering with them.

One of the extensions to the basic deadlock model presented in [6] is the novel binomial deadlock model (BIN) which considers the situation where there are L stations in total, but initially, of these, only N transmit simultaneously. The remaining $L - N$ stations are generating background traffic. The limited population of stations $L - N$ experience a state-dependent probability of an additional arrival during a timeslot. Since our focus in this chapter is on protocol deadlock (that is, performance of all-station "signalling storms" as would occur immediately following serious failures like neighborhood-wide power outages), we limit the results section only to the most relevant model : the BDM.

However, a noteworthy observation from the point of view of analytic modelling, is that for the BAP CRA case, the BIN model may be approximated by the BDM where the number of simultaneously transmitting stations is determined as the expected number of arrivals during the average CRI plus the N simultaneously transmitting stations. Namely, BAP dictates that those of the $L - N$ who receive requests during the current CRI must wait until the resolution of the current batch. They then send their new packet in the first slot following the resolution of *all* collisions that had occurred previously to the arrival of the signalling request. This behavior makes the BAP algorithm amenable to analytic study with this BIN / BDM deadlock model combination.

14.6 RESULTS AND DISCUSSION

We first concentrate on the p-persistence slotted aloha CRA in Section 14.6.1, by considering the impact of various system parameters on the signalling channel performance as modelled by the BDM. We explore additional techniques for alleviating deadlock problems, by way of either enhancing or more efficiently utilizing the signalling channel capacity using the three SCA schemes defined in Section 14.5.

The focus of Section 14.6.2 shifts to the deadlock behavior of two splitting CRAs under study: BAP and msSTART. Here we also compare and contrast the performance of these algorithms and p-persistence slotted aloha, under deadlock conditions. We also present results detailing the impact of the SCA schemes on the splitting algorithm performance, and discuss implications for SCA-based MAC-layer prioritization of packet data traffic.

14.6.1 Slotted Aloha (p-persistence) and Associated SCA Schemes

Numerical results are presented here for the basic deadlock model in the context of p-persistence slotted aloha, as used in the F-CPR MAC protocol [10]. The aim is to study the effect on F-CPR protocol resiliency, of (i) the persistence probability parameter p, (ii) the number of CMSs M, per upstream super-slot for the basic FCS signalling capacity allocation scheme, (iii) the probability of CMS errors, P_{err} and (iv) the number of separate contention resolution groups, k, under the CCS_S signalling capacity allocation scheme. In addition to this, we also compare between the FCS and CCS_M schemes, to determine whether full or partial resource sharing is more efficient if the number of allocated CMSs is kept identical.

We begin by observing the behavior of the critical load as a function of the number of stations for different values of p, without considering the presence of signalling channel errors ($P_{err} = 0$ in Figure 14.3). We are initially unconcerned with the particular signalling capacity allocation scheme being implemented, so we use the simplest and *default* scheme: the Full CMS sharing scheme, with only one CMS minislot (i.e., FCS with $M=1$). In the ensuing figures and discussion, note that unless we are focusing on the performance of some specific signalling scheme, this default FCS scheme is assumed. The batch size (N contending stations) dimensions are "number of ATM cells" because the F-CPR belongs to an ATM-centric family of MAC protocols and it is assumed that the CMSs / DMSs are the size of one atomic ATM cell. It follows that for the purposes of our modelling there is a one-to-one mapping between the number of competing stations in the batch and the number of cells sent as part of the batch (each station signals with a single ATM cell).

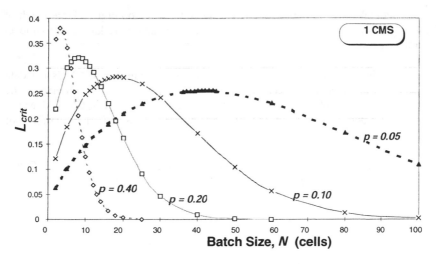

Figure 14.3. Finding an optimum batch size for a given *p*, FCS (*M*=1) scheme.

As shown in Figure 14.3, aggressive p-persistence (large values of the parameter *p*) allows a greater critical load (*L*_{*crit*}) when the batch size (the number of simultaneously contending stations) is small. On the other hand, a low level of *p* (e.g. *p*=0.05) which provides reasonable protection against deadlock (notice that 50 contending stations can achieve utilization of 0.25, avoiding deadlock), achieves quite a low L_{crit} for a small number of contending stations. Nevertheless, the reader is reminded that in a scenario where a small number of simultaneously contending stations are heavily loaded, a "piggybacked" DMS is more likely to be used and higher overall signalling throughput can be achieved, due to the reduced pressure on the contention-based signalling channel.

These results suggest that where it is impossible to vary *p* in *real-time* system operation, a relatively high level of *p* should be used, given the presence of the DMS contention-free minislots. The issue of stability is an interesting one in this setting. Recall that if the assumptions of this model were slightly augmented, to apply to an infinite population generating Poisson arrivals, we would have instability for any nonzero arrival rate. However, the arrivals are <u>not Poisson;</u> they are simultaneous batches of *N* requests. Also, there is <u>no infinite pool of stations,</u> rather, just *N* stations.

Hence, we have a system where the mean CRI length is theoretically finite but can, under certain conditions, be so large that it is for all practical purposes infinite. A practically infinite T_C leads to a near-zero throughput level. From Figure 14.3 we see that this undesirable scenario can happen when the fixed value of *p* is far from its optimal value (shown in Figure 14.5): if *p* is too low, a small batch will take unnecessarily long to be cleared; if p is too high, a large batch of messages will result in repeated collisions that maintain the backlog at a high level for a long time.

In Figure 14.4 we demonstrate the effect of the number of CMSs per data slot for the FCS scheme (once again ignoring the probability of CMS error). The important message of Figure 14.4 is that increasing the number of CMSs does not provide the desired protection against deadlock for the case of a large number of contending stations.

The reader is reminded of the cost of increasing the number of CMSs. Given the various protocol overheads for HFC systems (as a specific example [10]), increasing the number of CMSs from 1 to 3, would add another 10% of signalling overhead and decrease the "actual user data" throughput capability of an HFC system. Although the exact numbers may be different depending on frame format, a similar outcome would be observed in a WATM system.

Indeed, this method will triple the critical load (L_{crit}) for any number of stations and may provide efficient operation and protection against deadlock, but only for a relatively small number of contending stations, as seen in Figure 14.4. When the number of contending stations is large, and the critical load approaches zero (and hence the system approaches deadlock), tripling the critical load is shown not to be beneficial.

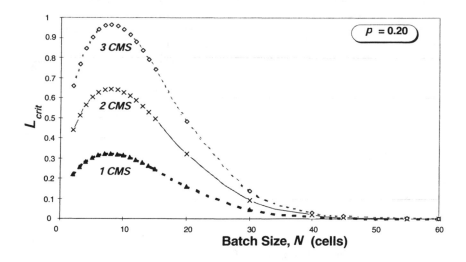

Figure 14.4. Effect of number of CMSs-FCS (M=1,2 and 3) scheme.

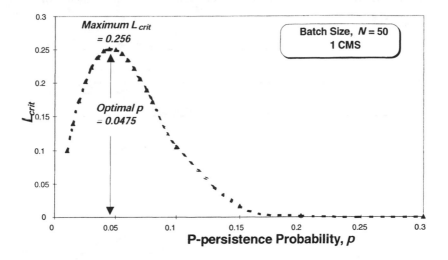

Figure 14.5. Optimizing the p-persistence algorithm-FCS (*M*=1) scheme.

In Figure 14.5 (with $P_{err} = 0$ once again), we demonstrate that the parameter *p* not only has a significant effect on the critical load (and on the resiliency of the protocol), but that it can be optimized for maximum load, for each combination of other parameters. A well-known fact is that the optimal value of the p-persistence algorithm is $1/n$, if the system currently has *n* contending stations [26], since this value maximizes the probability of a successful contention resolution (see Equation (2)).

However, as the collisions are resolved from an initial batch of *N*, the outstanding number *n* decreases in such a way that the system spends some amount of time in each of the states {n=*N*, n=*N*-1, n=*N*-2 ... , n=1}, prior to final absorption into state n=0. This is why, as explained in [21], the optimal *p* for the contention resolution of *N* initial backlogged requests is not 1/*N*, but would be bounded by the inequality $1/N < p_{opt} < 1$. This inequality for p_{opt} is clearly illustrated in Figure 14.5. A different way of looking at the inequality is provided in Figure 14.3. For a given fixed value of *p*, the optimal *N* is always larger than 1/*p* (i.e., the previous inequality is reversed, so that $N_{opt} > 1/p$).

We now turn to look at the effect of the presence of errors on our signalling channel. These typically manifest themselves as data corruption due to noise and signal interference, as mentioned earlier. The graphs in Figure 14.6 highlight the fact that the critical signalling load is largely unaffected by the presence of CMS errors.

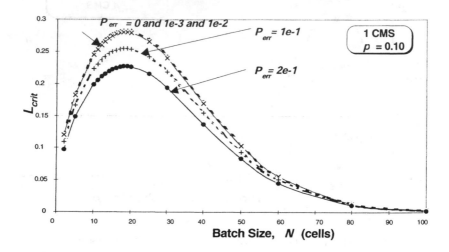

Figure 14.6. CMS error sensitivity for the slotted aloha (p-persistence) CRA-FCS (M=1), p=0.1.

At CMS error levels of 10^{-2} or less, the critical load versus batch size behavior is identical to that of error-free systems, as can be seen from the graph. Note that even an unrealistically high CMS error level of 0.2 causes only a marginal ($\approx$15%) worst-case decrease in the critical signalling load level (when $N = 20$).

Let us now turn to another of the three SCA schemes: multi-CMS cyclic CMS sharing, or CCS_M. This can be thought of as "circuit switching" and it involves more complexity at the station than its FCS counterpart. In particular, with CCS_M, we need the ability for the central controller node to randomly assign the stations to subgroups; these groups then use only one of the multiple CMSs available. However, the added complexity notwithstanding, Figure 14.7 shows that the CCS_M scheme yields better performance than FCS since the critical load (L_{crit}) is maintained at a significantly higher level for a larger number of contending stations under identical system conditions.

Below a certain threshold when the batch size is relatively small (approximately $N = 13$ in the graph), collisions upon retries are less likely to happen and so it is more efficient to implement full CMS sharing ("packet switching") and not to waste CMS slots, by cyclically reserving them in TDM-like fashion. As Figure

14.7 illustrates, it is clear that both of these observations apply not only to error-free systems, but also to those with severe (0.2) CMS error rates.

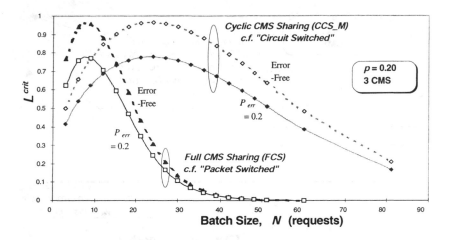

Figure 14.7. Cyclic (CCS_M) vs. full (FCS) CMS sharing with M=3 CMS minislots, with and without CMS errors.

With regards to CMS error-sensitivity, note from Figure 14.7 that even an extreme CMS error level of P_{err}=0.2 causes, for both schemes, a maximum decrease in L_{crit} of only about 18%, which is of little impact since a data link layer error level of one minislot lost in every five will be extremely unlikely to be observed and tolerated in practice, and also since it is a worst-case figure for the range of N values studied. For example, there are other points in the graph where the error-free and errored FCS scheme curves converge to the same line ($N > 35$). A final point to note from Figure 14.7 is that the introduction of errors does not change the shapes of the curves, or the conclusions drawn earlier about the better overall performance of the cyclic multi-CMS sharing scheme.

In Figure 14.8 we demonstrate the effect of the number of groups k on the critical load for the CCS_S scheme. The synchronous mode of access implicit in this scheme, has similarities with time division multiplexing (TDM) systems. It is therefore quite sensible to also think of k as the *TDM cycle length*. Although there is only one CMS per upstream super-slot, the access to this CMS is regulated in a TDM-like cyclic manner, so that each station is assigned membership to a group that has a certain position in the cycle (say $TDM_{position}$), and is allowed to access a CMS only at that position and every k (i.e., cycle length) timeslots (notice that k is both the period length and the number of groups). That is, access is allowed at time T, *only if*

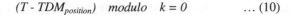

$$(T - TDM_{position}) \quad modulo \quad k = 0 \qquad \dots (10)$$

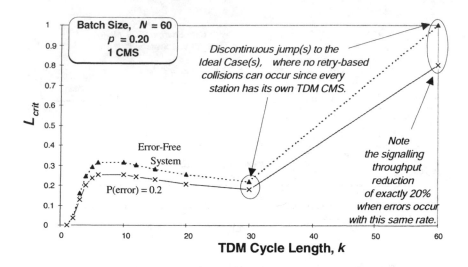

Figure 14.8. Cyclic single-CMS sharing (with and without errors)-TDM-based access to CMSs.

More complexity would be required within the MAC protocol, both at the stations and central controller, in order to implement this scheme. Also, the dead-lock resilience is achieved only for a narrow range of TDM cycle lengths (approximately $7 < k < 15$ CMSs, for system parameters used) because past a certain threshold value of k (15 in this case), the increase in the introduced "cyclic delay" starts to outweigh any shrinkage in T_C.

The TDM technique implicit within CCS_S is good for the alleviation of signalling congestion created by the extreme inter-station correlation (i.e., large batches of simultaneous arrivals) which we are studying. However, under normal conditions (when the reservation requests are not generated just by single-cell user message traffic, which in turn is not deterministically arriving in simultaneous batches any more), one can see that such a TDM technique introduces an amount of unnecessary increase in the average access delay. Hence, a trade-off between cost and benefit exists, the balance of which depends strongly on the traffic profile. This kind of scheme would only be truly practical if there was a simple way of dynamically adjusting k.

As with the previous two figures exploring the error-sensitivity of signalling performance, Figure 14.8 illustrates the relatively small effect of the presence of errors in the CMS signalling channel, where we once again see no more than an 18% worst-case drop in maximum achievable signalling throughput (L_{crit}), even when the CMS error rate is 0.2.

Also of interest in this graph, is the 20% difference in L_{crit} which may be observed between the very last pair of points, when $k = 60$. While the dotted curve, representing the error-free case, shows an L_{crit} of exactly one (collision-free operation for 60 stations, each with their own CMS, and a cycle time of $k=60$), the solid curve L_{crit} drops to 0.8, with the error level at 0.2.

We now account for this special case: the CMS minislots are segmented in a TDM-like fashion, and since $N = k = 60$ there can never be any interference between the request arrivals which would cause a collision. The only outcome to require a retry (for any given slot, and <u>independent</u> of other slots) is an errored CMS. Recalling that the probability of a CMS error is denoted by P_{err}, we find that the time to successfully clear a single request is <u>geometrically distributed</u> with an average value of $1/(1-P_{err})$ CMSs. However, as each station is only afforded one CMS per cycle of k CMSs, the "real time" that passes is $1/(1-P_{err})$ cycles, or in other words $k/(1-P_{err})$ CMSs. We have, not one, but $N=k$ users, and due to the TDM-like nature of each of these k users, they all proceed in parallel with the same (independent, identically distributed) geometric "successful transmission" process. Therefore, the mean time to clear *all* $N=k$ slots is given by $k/(1-P_{err})$, giving a critical load of $N/\{k/(1-P_{err})\}= 1-P_{err} = 0.8$, for $N=k$, as seen in Figure 14.8.

14.6.2 Splitting Algorithms (BAP and msSTART) and Associated SCA Schemes

We start this section by verifying the analytic BDM results against the computer simulation of the slotted aloha p-persistence CRA, for the F-CPR protocol under study. In Figure 14.3 the analytic results are shown. This is compared with Figure 14.9 containing the simulated approximation.

The results from the two methods of evaluation of L_{crit} are very closely aligned and thus verify our analytic model. We use the analytic model in the following figures depicting the p-persistence slotted aloha CRA, and we continue to use simulation approximations for the less analytically tractable, evolved free-access Q-ary stack CRA (msSTART). Note that all results are for $Q = 3$, unless otherwise stated.

It is the variability of L_{crit} with N, at all values of p, that motivates a comparative study between the simple slotted aloha and other CRAs. To this end, Figure 14.10 compares network performance after failure for four schemes in line with the basic deadlock model we have developed: (1) fixed p-persistence slotted aloha with moderate p; (2) an implementable adaptive p-persistence slotted aloha CRA using a pseudo-Bayesian estimator; (3) a binary (blocked-access) tree CRA, and (4) msSTART. The method used in (2) was introduced in 1985 by Rivest for stabilizing the conventional slotted aloha algorithms and seeks to estimate the number of backlogged requests [26].

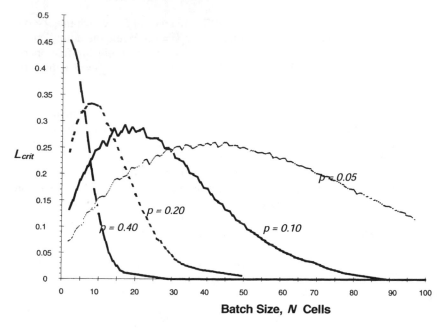

Figure 14.9. Simulated BDM performance for the p-persistence slotted aloha CRA.

It can achieve a stable maximum throughput of e^{-1} under Poisson arrivals. Note, however, that the method requires all the stations to use the same retransmission probability and since the arrival rate is not known, this must also be estimated, causing increased control complexity in the wireless system. Such complexity is to be avoided because errors in the multicast of the estimated value of p from the central controller to the stations can cause cumulative errors and hence non-optimal performance. Moreover, the requirement that the stations monitor the channel to determine the current value of p they should use to "flip the coin" to transmit is wasteful of power.

By giving insights into the CRA performance under the aforementioned disaster scenario, Figure 14.10 gives an indication of overall MAC protocol deadlock resiliency performance in the uplink, for the 4 CRAs depicted. The p-persistence adaptive algorithm gives reduced sensitivity to the number of contending stations in the system (N), and yields greater L_{crit} values than the fixed-p CRA, over most of the graph range. As the size of our simultaneously contending batch of stations tends to one, the adaptive p-persistence CRA exceeds its theoretical L_{crit} limit of e^{-1}, as when loaded by Poisson traffic.

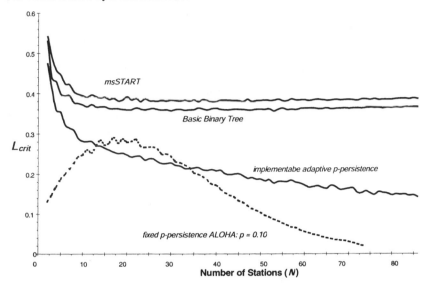

Figure 14.10. Comparison of simulated results for 4 selected CRAs.

The reader is reminded that the theoretical maximum stable throughput e^{-1} is the limiting value only in the case of Poisson arrivals being generated by an infinite number of sources [26]. As discussed earlier in this chapter, the simultaneously arriving batch of N stations is a very different traffic scenario, and hence yields the different L_{crit} limit we observe in the graph (tending toward $L_{crit} = 1$ for batch size $N=1$, with perfect backlog estimation and p parameter adaptation).

Of utmost interest in Figure 14.10 is the superior performance of msSTART and its relative insensitivity to N. The binary tree algorithm also exhibits better L_{crit} values than either of the slotted aloha algorithms, along with an improved insensitivity to N. Importantly, msSTART and the binary tree CRAs do not require any of the additional control complexity involved in estimating the optimal p. Stations either do not require updates from the central controller of the optimal retransmission probability, at the beginning of each upstream super-slot.

Figure 14.11 demonstrates the effect of varying the number of CMSs per upstream super-slot using the full sharing CMS (FCS) scheme for both p-persistence slotted aloha and msSTART. It has already been explained in Section 14.6.1 that increasing the number of CMSs increases the "survivability" of the system in disaster scenarios; doubling the number of CMSs has the effect of doubling L_{crit} for any number of stations, for both CRAs considered in Figure 14.11.

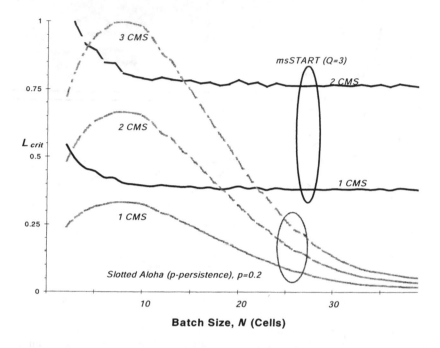

Figure 14.11. Effect of the number of CMSs for the full CMS sharing (FCS) scheme as applied to the slotted aloha (p-persistence) and msSTART CRAs.

On the down side however, increasing the number of CMSs further reduces the maximum utilization of the MAC protocol by decreasing the actual user data throughput capability (more of each frame is devoted to signalling, less to data carriage). Unlike the slotted aloha CRA, msSTART exhibits significant additional stability for any number of contending stations. This finding confirms that the combination of using multiple CMSs and the FCS signalling capacity allocation scheme significantly increases the deadlock robustness of a MAC protocol based on the msSTART CRA–something in direct contrast to our observations for a MAC protocol based on a p-persistence slotted aloha CRA.

We now compare the effect of errors on both the slotted aloha (p-persistence) CRA, Figure 14.6, and msSTART CRA, Figure 14.12. Both CRAs are quite insensitive to reasonable levels of noise in the wireless channel. Error probabilities as high as 0.1 give only marginal (15%) reductions in signaling channel performance. In both cases, the effect of errors on the system is small since the CRAs cannot distinguish between collision and error.

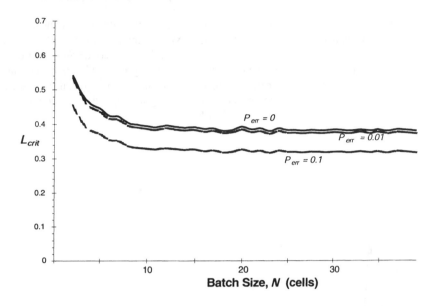

Figure 14.12. CMS error sensitivity for the msSTART FCS scheme (single CMS, $Q = 3$).

In the case of msSTART's Q-ary stack, errors are only significant when they occur in a slot in which there would otherwise have been a successful transmission. In this situation, the performance penalty is an additional node in the stack that would have been absent without the error. This corresponds to an additional Q slots for the resolution of the stack.

For p-persistence slotted aloha, an error is also only significant in the instance that there would otherwise have been a successful transmission. In this case the performance penalty is an additional q slots where q is directly proportional to the probability of collision with another station on a repeat transmission attempt.

14.6.3 MAC-layer Traffic Prioritization

Cyclic CMS sharing with multiple CMSs per data slot (CCS_M) is considered next, with the critical load achievable for the msSTART and slotted aloha (p-persistence) CRAs pictured in Figure 14.13, as a function of the initial batch size, N. The CCS_M signalling capacity allocation scheme requires increased control complexity compared to its fully shared counterpart (FCS), because the central controller must assign the stations to subgroups. However, this added complexity may not be an issue in situations where explicit MAC-layer prioritization of traffic is required, and station classification into subgroups is a system requirement.

In Figure 14.13 we see that the p-persistence slotted aloha CRA shows significant additional stability as a result of CCS_M implementation. Namely, L_{crit} is maintained at a higher level for a larger number of contending stations. MsSTART, on the other hand, is not greatly affected by CCS_M, due to its relative insensitivity to the number of stations in a contention group (recall the results shown in Figure 14.10). L_{crit} improvements are marginal regardless of the number of CMSs used, and only become tangible when N is exceedingly small (i.e. $N < 5$). For $N < 5$ the L_{crit} gains correspond to the increased probability of each station being assigned a different CMS for transmission and hence avoiding the need for any contention resolution whatsoever.

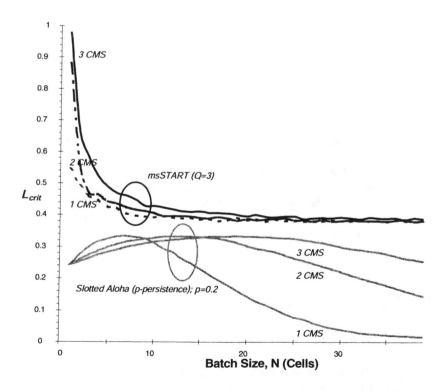

Figure 14.13. CCS_M scheme for signalling capacity allocation. Effect of the number of CMSs used with the msSTART and slotted aloha (p-persistence) CRAs.

The excellent performance of the msSTART / CCS_M pair of schemes for small N raises the important paradigm of ***MAC-layer traffic prioritization.***

To implement an effective priority access mechanism for an HFC or WATM MAC, it is necessary to use a combination of two methods. The first method entails the central controller using a preemptive scheduler when allocating bandwidth to stations with different priorities [10], [11], [24]. Some proposed multi-service MAC protocol structures seek to merely add a queue identifier (QI) field in the CMS to indicate traffic priority level. The central controller then uses the QI as a priority scheduling parameter for stations. This proposal, on its own, is insufficient, because during signalling contention all stations are treated equally without regard for their QI-indicated priority. Thus the newcomers can easily be blocked for extended periods of time, and particularly during signalling "storms" which would occur in the disaster scenarios which we are modelling here. This may result in unacceptably large delays for high priority stations. The fundamental issue is that a high priority station cannot rely **_only_** on preemptive scheduling at the central controller to receive low access delays. What is required in the multi-service MAC protocol design is *a method of giving higher priority stations immediate access to the channel* so that bandwidth can be speedily allocated.

This is where the second method of MAC-layer prioritization comes in. The MAC protocol should explicitly regulate collisions so that high-priority stations are able to transmit bandwidth requests without interference from lower priorities. Two of the three signalling capacity allocation (SCA) schemes presented, CCS_M and CCS_S, are able to regulate collisions in this fashion, and we now look at each in turn.

Let us firstly focus on the CCS_M scheme, the performance of which is highlighted in Figure 14.13. Traffic segmentation can be implemented by choosing the station subgroups in an unbalanced fashion, such that very few high-priority stations use a very lightly loaded CMS and achieve a proportionally higher fractional L_{crit} than the low-priority stations assigned to a "crowded" CMS. The already documented insensitivity of the msSTART L_{crit} to the number of stations N (Figure 14.10) means that in combination with the CCS_M scheme, this splitting algorithm can be used to effectively prioritize traffic. The low-priority stations will continue to enjoy a high and deadlock-resilient level of signalling throughput, while the high-priority stations will attain a greater relative degree of L_{crit} by virtue of a less crowded shared resource and hence a briefer contention resolution interval.

These observations are significant because they illustrate the CCS_M scheme's dual usefulness, for two very different families of CRA: (a) through an increased critical load limit, CCS_M achieves generic MAC protocol stabilization

in disaster scenarios, and for widely ranging numbers of contending stations; and
(b) by requiring the segmenting of the initial contending station population into
subgroups, the CCS_M scheme enables the MAC protocol to more easily offer the
ability to provide differentiated MAC-layer signalling performance (signalling
traffic prioritization), than its FCS counterpart (which treats all stations equally).
This is clearly illustrated in Figure 14.13. However, the beneficial "stabilizing"
effect of CCS_M, as described in (a), is far less pronounced if the msSTART CRA
is used in place of the slotted aloha (p-persistence) CRA. Clearly there is a dependency of the usefulness of any given signalling capacity allocation scheme, on
the CRA it is trying to "assist."

The second scheme that is able to explicitly regulate collisions in order to
provide signalling traffic prioritization is CCS_S, and we now study its behavior
in this context. In order to compare with the CCS_S slotted aloha (p-persistence)
L_{crit}, as shown in Figure 14.8, Figure 14.14 plots the effect of varying the TDM
cycle length, k, on the CCS_S msSTART critical load performance.

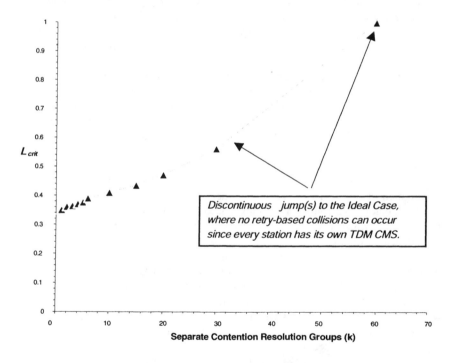

Figure 14.14 : Simulating msSTART ($Q=3$) performance using cyclic CMS sharing with a
single CMS (CCS_S), with variable TDM cycle length, k.

We take the example of a population of 60 stations, and assume the usual ternary stack ($Q=3$) for msSTART and $p=0.2$ as the p-persistence parameter. As explained earlier, the stations transmit only in the group to which they are assigned membership, meaning the ability to only access every k^{th} CMS. Although we assume that stations are distributed in equal numbers throughout the TDM cycle ($k_1 \ldots k_{60}$), it is important to note that in a realistic priority scheme, station population would be weighted toward the TDM cycle CMSs which correspond to the lower priority groups.

Figure 14.8 and previous Section 14.6.1 results illustrate the fact that the slotted aloha (p-persistence) / CCS_S combination shows very limited promise as a method by which to implement priority and also avoid deadlock for a large number of contending stations ($N=60$). The first problematic issue is that the deadlock resilience is achieved only for a narrow range of TDM cycle lengths (approximately $7 < k < 15$ CMSs, for system parameters used). Second, it was found that this resilience was heavily dependent on the uniform distribution of the 60 stations over the k TDM cycle positions, which is not the way in which a MAC protocol signalling traffic priority scheme would be implemented. In direct contrast to this, Figure 14.14 shows that the msSTART provides significantly superior performance over all k. The monotonically increasing L_{crit} curve results from the decrease in T_C offsetting the increased "cyclic delay" for greater k. Additionally, the simulation has shown that msSTART is virtually immune to the distribution of the N contending stations over the k TDM cycle positions.

A third, hybrid, way of implementing priority is the awarding of different numbers of FCS-based CMSs to each of the k separate TDM cycle positions (which in effect represent contention resolution groups). This would entail running the CCS_S scheme "globally," by imposing a TDM-like cycle for each priority group, but then within each group, "locally" employing the FCS scheme with a priority-dependent number of CMSs (high-priority groups obviously being assigned more CMSs). The net effect would be smaller user access delays at the MAC level, and greater MAC protocol stability, for higher priority traffic. In all of the foregoing discussions, and regardless of the type of CRA used with the CCS_S scheme, the reader's attention is drawn toward the overarching need for small values of k. Large values of k introduce unacceptable individual user access delay despite the additional stability of the system.

To conclude, the overall messages to the MAC protocol designer are clear:

(i) A more complex CRA has been shown to deliver significantly higher stability and signalling throughput, requiring lesser dimensioning for "deadlock resilience," but at the expense of increased system implementation complexity.

and

(ii) The final choice of framing structure, CRA and SCA scheme must **not be made in isolation**, but always within the guidelines of the stated system objectives and with the aim of ensuring optimum performance level, including consideration of our topic at hand: deadlock resilience. A practical example might be that an msSTART-based MAC designed to purely extend the deadlock resiliency for best effort data traffic as far as possible, would best be suited to using a signalling capacity allocation scheme like FCS. On the other hand, a similar MAC, which had as its stated objective the provision of differential data traffic priority levels, would need to use a scheme such as CCS_M or CCS_S, for the reasons just discussed.

REFERENCES

[1] C. Bisdikian, K. Maruyama, D. Seidman and D. N. Serpanos, "Cable Access Beyond the Hype: On Residential Broadband Data Services over HFC Networks", *IEEE Comm. Mag.*, vol. 34, no. 11, pp. 128-135, November 1996.

[2] D. Raychaudhuri et al., "WATMnet: A prototype wireless ATM system for multimedia personal communication", *IEEE J. Select. Areas Commun.*, vol. 15, pp. 83-94, Jan. 1997.

[3] ETSI TS 101 351 V6.7.0 (2000-03), "Digital cellular telecommunications system (Phase 2+) (GSM); General Packet Radio Service (GPRS); Mobile Station - Serving GPRS Support Node (MS-SGSN) Logical Link Control (LLC) layer specification", GSM 04.64 version 6.7.0, Release 1997.

[4] B. Bertsekas and R. Gallager, *Data Networks*, 2nd Edition, Prentice-Hall, Upper Saddle River, NJ, 1992.

[5] J. I. Capetanakis, "Tree Algorithm for Packet Broadcasting Channel", *IEEE Trans. Inform. Theory*, vol. IT.25, pp. 505-515, September 1979.

[6] M. Ivanovich, M. Zukerman and F. Cameron, "A Study of Deadlock Models for a Multi-Service Medium Access Protocol Employing a Slotted Aloha Signalling Channel", *IEEE/ACM Transactions on Networking*, vol. 8, no. 6, pp. 800-811, December 2000.

[7] F. Cameron, M. Zukerman, M. Ivanovich, S. Saravanabavananthan and R.Hewawasam, "A Deadlock Model For A Multi-Service Medium Access Protocol Employing Multi-Slot N-Ary Stack Algorithm (msSTART)", *Proc. IEEE wmATM'99*, San Francisco, June 1999.

[8] C. Bisdikian, "Performance Analysis of the Multislot N-ary Stack Random Access Algorithm (msSTART)", IEEE 802.14 Working Group Document No. 802.14-96/117, May 1996.

[9] C. Bisdikian, "A review of random access algorithms", *IEEE 802.14 Working Group Document No. 802.14-96/019*, January 1996.

[10] M. Ivanovich, "Teletraffic Modelling, Analysis and Synthesis of a Generic Broadband Multi-service Access Protocol", Doctoral Dissertation, Monash University, Melbourne, Australia, April 1998.

[11] B. T. Doshi et al., "A Broadband Multiple Access Protocol for STM, ATM, and Variable Length Data Services on Hybrid Fiber-Coax Networks", *IEEE 802.14 Working Group Document No. 802.14-96/222*, September 1996.

[12] ATM Forum af-tm-0121.000, "Traffic Management 4.1", July 1999.

[13] ATM Forum af-tm-95-0177, "Congestion Control and Traffic Management in ATM Networks: Recent Advances and a Survey", August 1995.

[14] S. Jangi and L. Merakos, "Performance Analysis of Reservation Random Access Protocols for Wireless Access Network," *IEEE Trans. Comm.*, vol. 42, no. 2/3/4, pp. 1223-1234, Feb./March/April 1994.

[15] D. Goodman, R. Valenzuela, K. Gayliard and B. Ramamurthi, "Packet Reservation Multiple Access for Local Wireless Communications," *IEEE Trans. Comm.*, vol. 37, no. 8, pp. 885-890, August 1989.

[16] M. Yuang and P. Tien, "Multiple Access Control with Intelligent Bandwidth Allocation for Wireless ATM Networks," *IEEE J. Select. Areas Comm.*, vol. 18, no. 9, pp. 1658-1669, Sept. 2000.

[17] L. Lenzini, M. Luise and R. Reggiannini, "CRDA: A Collision Resolution and Dynamic Allocation MAC Protocol to Integrate Date and Voice in Wireless Networks," *IEEE J. Select. Areas Comm.*, vol. 19, no. 6, pp. 1153-1163, June 2001.

[18] H. Xie, P. Narasimhan, R. Yuan and D. Raychaudhuri, "Data link control protocol for wireless ATM access channels", *Proc. ICUPC*, pp. 753-757, Tokyo, Japan, Nov. 1995.

[19] N. Passas, S. Paskalis, S. Vali and L. Merakos, "`Quality-of-Service-Oriented Medium Access Control for Wireless ATM Networks,'" *IEEE Comm. Mag.*, vol. 35, no. 11, pp. 42-50,Nov. 1997,.

[20] C. Bisdikian, B. McNeil, R. Norman and R. Zeisz, "MLAP: A MAC access protocol for the HFC 802.14 network", *IEEE Comm. Mag.*, vol. 34, no. 3, pp. 114-121, March 1996.

[21] D. Sala, D. Hartman and J.O. Limb, "Comparison of Algorithms for Station Registration on Power-up in an HFC Network", *IEEE 802.14 Working Group Document No. 802.14-96/012*, January 1996.

[22] J.O. Limb and D. Sala, "An Access Protocol to Support Multimedia Traffic over Hybrid Fibre-Coax Systems", *Proc. 2nd International Workshop in Community Networking*, pp. 35-40, Princeton, July, 1995.

[23] L. Kleinrock and F. A. Tobagi, "Packet Switching in Radio Channels: Part I - Carrier Sense Multiple Access Modes and Their Throughput-Delay Characteristics", *IEEE Trans. Comm.*, 23, no. 12, pp. 1400-1416, December 1975.

[24] D. Sala, "MAC Protocols for Multimedia Data over HFC Architecture", *Georgia Tech Technical report GIT-CC-95-48*, October 1995.

[25] S. Karlin and H. M. Taylor, A First Course in Stochastic Processes, 2nd Ed, Chapter 4, pp. 117-166, Academic Press, London, 1975.

[26] R. L. Rivest, "Network Control by Bayessian Broadcast", *MIT Report no. LCS-TM-285*, Massachussets Institute of Technology, Laboratory for Computer Science, Cambridge, MA, 1985.

15

Deadlock-Free TCP Over High-Speed Internet

Rocky K. C. Chang
The Hong Kong Polytechnic University, Kowloon (Hong Kong).

Ho Y. Chan
University of Southern California, Los Angeles, CA, USA.

Adam W. Yeung
Cisco Systems Inc., San Jose, CA, USA.

In this paper, we consider TCP throughput deadlock problems caused by an interplay between the Nagle algorithm, delayed acknowledgment algorithm, and several implementation details. For some combinations of send and receive buffers, a TCP sender cannot send more segments due to the Nagle algorithm and, at the same time, a TCP receiver cannot acknowledge more segments received due to the delayed acknowledgment algorithm. The outcome is a deadlock, which can only be resolved by the receiver's timer. Although the deadlock can take place in any types of networks, it is generally more difficult to ensure deadlock-free connections on high-speed networks. Moreover, the impact is much more significant on high-speed networks, and the deadlock renders the connection practically unusable. Several straightforward solutions, such as turning off the Nagle algorithm and acknowledging every segment, have been proposed; however, they reintroduce the same problems that they were initially designed for. In this paper we propose an adaptive acknowledgment algorithm (A^3) to eliminate throughput deadlocks on the receiver side while preserving the original intent of employing the Nagle algorithm and delayed acknowledgment. An A^3-receiver uses the same delayed acknowledgment as before, but with an additional component to adaptively compute the acknowledgment threshold, which is adjusted according to the maximum amount of segments sent by the sender. By adapting to the sender's state, an A^3-receiver can avoid deadlocks when there is no network congestion. To further adapt to possible network congestion, A^3-receivers are enhanced by incorporating a slow-start-like algorithm to adjust the acknowledgment threshold when network congestion is suspected. The resulting algorithm is referred to as congestion-sensitive A^3 (CSA^3). Extensive simulation experiments have confirmed the effectiveness of both A^3 and CSA^3.

15.1 INTRODUCTION

Transport control protocol (TCP) continues to dominate Internet traffic by providing end-to-end reliability, flow control, and congestion control services to a number of very popular application and session protocols, such as HTTP, FTP, TELNET, SSL, etc. Being designed as a generic transport protocol back in the mid-1980s, the TCP performance has to keep up with rapid advances in the underlying networking technologies and new application requirements. One area of TCP performance degradation is brought by new data-link technologies' characteristics, such as long delay-bandwidth-product of satellite links [1-3], channel asymmetry of cable modem networks [4], and high error rates of wireless links [5]. Each of these issues affects the growth of TCP sending window size in different ways, but the results are the same: the TCP's throughput is severely limited with respect to the available bandwidth between end hosts.

On the other hand, implementation issues are equally, if not more, important in affecting TCP performance, e.g., [6-8]. The performance of a network protocol realization is particularly important for TCP because TCP is currently defined by implementations rather by formal protocol specifications [7]. In this paper, we consider TCP throughput deadlock problems that are caused mainly by an interplay between the Nagle algorithm, delayed acknowledgment algorithm, and various TCP implementation issues. The Nagle algorithm and delayed acknowledgment algorithm were in fact designed to address the "small-packet problem," which significantly reduces network throughput as a result of sending small-sized data (say 1 byte) in one IP datagram (usually 40 bytes) instead of a full segment. The small-packet problem is also referred to as a silly window syndrome (SWS) problem [9]. The Nagle algorithm is a sender-side SWS avoidance solution, which prevents a sender from sending small segments when there are outstanding segments to be acknowledged [10]. A TCP segment is considered small if it is less than the sender-side maximum segment size (MSS); therefore, a nonMSS-sized segment is considered small. The delayed acknowledgment algorithm, on the other hand, is a receiver-side SWS avoidance solution, which prevents a receiver from acknowledging small segments [11].

A throughput deadlock rises when a pair of TCP sender and receiver gets into a circular-wait situation. That is, the sender cannot send more segments due to

Nagle algorithm, while the receiver cannot send acknowledgments due to the delayed acknowledgment algorithm. Although the deadlock state is finally escaped by the firing of a coarse-spaced delayed acknowledgment timer, the resulting TCP throughput is so low that the connection is practically not usable. A necessary condition for getting into the deadlock situation is that a TCP sender sends nonMSS-sized segments. When the amount of outstanding segments is not enough to trigger an immediate acknowledgment from the receiver, a throughput deadlock will occur. However, there are different factors responsible for the sending of nonMSS-sized segments. For example,

1. An application data may consist of an odd number of MSS-sized segments with a nonMSS-sized final segment. In this case, the receiver may not be able to promptly acknowledge the last MSS-sized segment due to the delayed acknowledgment algorithm. At the same time, the sender is unable to send the nonMSS-sized final segment due to Nagle algorithm. The resulting throughput degradation was reported in the context of persistent HTTP connections [12].
2. Even if the application data size does not fall into scenario (1), nonMSS-sized segments may still be generated as a result of *buffer tearing*, in which an application data is usually broken up into a number of nonMSS-sized segments when copied to the write buffers used by TCP. This is because the write buffer sizes are usually not multiples of MSS.
3. Other OS implementation issues, such as the send-receiver buffer size combinations, data copying rules, and order of actions when receiving acknowledgments, can cause the sender to send nonMSS-sized segments. Throughout degradation as a result of these issues was reported by Moldeklev and Gunningberg [14], and Comer and Lin [15].

The three scenarios discussed above involve the application, socket, and TCP layers. Moreover, all three factors could cause throughput deadlocks on low-speed networks as well as high-speed networks. However, the impact is more noticeable in high-speed, end-to-end connections, e.g., client and server on a 100-Mbps LAN. Furthermore, it is more difficult to guarantee deadlock-free TCP connection in high-speed networks, because the MSS value is usually very high on those networks. Hence, we consider the deadlock problems mainly for high-speed TCP connections. Although the speed of an end-to-end connection is generally not high today, this TCP deadlock problem is expected to have a more significant impact as the effort of deploying TCP/IP on top of many high-speed networks, such as ATM, WDM, and broadband satellites, accelerates.

In terms of resolving throughput deadlocks, Mogul and Minshall [13] proposed an improved implementation of the Nagle algorithm to overcome the first two scenarios of deadlocks. However, they did not address the third scenario. Moldeklev and Gunningberg, on the other hand, proposed several straightforward solutions to solving the deadlock problems arising from the third scenario, such as disabling the Nagle algorithm and acknowledging every segment [14]. These solutions can guarantee deadlock-free connections, but they will clearly reintroduce the SWS problem. Murayama and Yamaguchi [16] proposed to use new TCP flags to implement "No Delayed ACK" and "Force Delayed ACK" options. But this proposal also requires new TCP implementations on all systems, which is unlikely to happen.

In this paper we propose an adaptive approach to avoid SWS on the receiver side, referred to A^3. An A^3-receiver is the same as a typical TCP receiver except for an additional component that "adaptively" determines when to send acknowledgments based on the information gathered on the sender. In other words, throughput deadlocks are avoided on the receiver, instead of the sender side. The A^3 also does not distinguish the exact causes for throughput deadlocks, and it is therefore designed to handle all three scenarios of deadlocks.

The rest of this paper is organized as follows: In Section 15.2, we first describe necessary background information on the socket buffer management, the Nagle algorithm, and delayed acknowledgment algorithm. We then describe the throughput deadlock problem in more details. In Section 15.3, we introduce the A^3 and show that it eliminates all classes of deadlocks in the absence of network congestion. In Section 15.4, we explain why throughput deadlocks still occur to the A^3 in the presence of network congestion. Subsequently, we introduce Congestion-Sensitive A^3 (CSA^3), and show that the CSA^3 is able to ensure deadlock-free TCP connections even in a congested network environment. Finally, we conclude this paper with future work in Section 15.5.

15.2 THE TCP THROUGHPUT DEADLOCK PROBLEM

15.2.1 Unix Socket Layer

The networking codes in most BSD-based Unix kernels are organized into three layers: socket, protocol, and interface [17]. The socket layer is a protocol-independent interface to the protocol-dependent layer below while the latter two layers implement specific network protocol suites and device drivers for data-link technologies.

Data transfer between the application and protocol layers largely relies on memory buffers. An efficient memory management scheme called *mbufs* (memory buffers) was first introduced in BSD 4.3 and later adopted by SunOS 4.x. The mbufs scheme provides fixed and variable size memory allocation that improves efficiency by reducing physical data replication within the kernel memory space. The mbufs memory is allocated during system initialization and is part of the permanent kernel memory that always resides in the physical memory. There are two types of mbufs: small (or plain) and cluster. The plain mbufs are 128 bytes long with 112 bytes data storage which form a cluster of mbufs when an external page (1024 bytes from mbufs memory pool) is attached to the existing plain mbufs. The cluster mbufs' data is stored exclusively in the external page to facilitate pointer referencing.

In SunOS 4.1.3 bulk data transfer, data will be added in the form of multiple 1024-byte cluster mbufs when the send buffer and user data are larger than or equal to 512 bytes. Figure 15.1 illustrates the data copy routine in the socket layer. One important thing to note from the figure is that as soon as the send buffer collects 4096 bytes of data, it will send them out to the TCP output for delivery, without waiting for more application data. This data copy mechanism, as we will see later, turns out to be an important implementation issue that is partially responsible for TCP throughout deadlock.

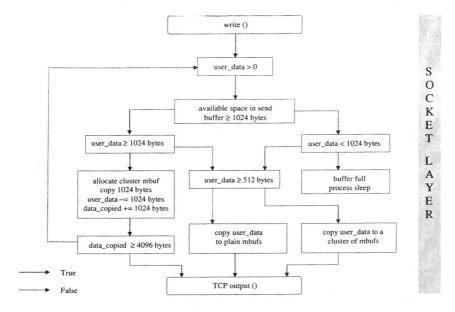

Figure 15.1. Socket layer data copy rules in BSD.

15.2.2 Nagle algorithm and delayed acknowledgment algorithm

Figure 15.2 shows the Nagle algorithm implemented in SunOS 4.x. When there is no outstanding unacknowledged data or the Nagle algorithm is off, the sender can send a segment of any size as long as it is permitted by the usable window size. Otherwise, the unsent data needs to wait in the send buffer if the data unsent is less than both MSS and half of the maximum usable window size. In this case, the sender waits either for more data delivered from the socket layer or for acknowledgments.

The delayed acknowledgment strategy, on the other hand, delays sending acknowledgments until they can be piggybacked onto either a data segment or a window update packet. For example, in the SunOS implementation, a separate window update with a piggybacked acknowledgment will be sent if the window can slide more than either (a) 35% of the receive buffer size or (b) two MSSes of the size. Even if both conditions are not met, a delayed acknowledgment timer allows sending 1 acknowledgment every 200 ms.

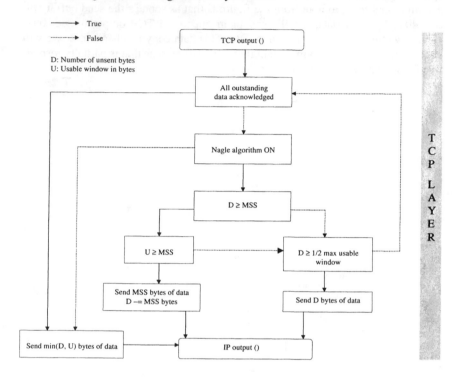

Figure 15.2. The Nagle algorithm.

15.2.3 An Experimental Setup

Unlike the ATM network setup used in [14], in this section we demonstrate that the throughput experiments can be performed in a single workstation (running SunOS 4.1.3 in our case). To allow communication between a sending process and a receiving process, both running in the same machine, we make use of the loop-back interface as a logical data link between them. Therefore, the kernel performs complete data processing in SunOS 4.1.3's transport and network layers, and the loopback driver redirects packets sent to the receiving process back to an appropriate input queue. It turns out that changing the loopback driver's MTU is not a trivial task. Our solution is to perform a "software hijack" by putting a loopback MTU adjustment request (a few lines of code) in *tcp_trace.c*, a debug function that can be initiated via *SO_DEBUG* socket option at the socket level. We also wrote a socket program *lperf* to measure SunOS 4.1.3 memory-to-memory TCP throughput. The program uses BSD socket interface to perform inter-process communication. Upon execution, the program forks a receiver process to collect all sender data via the loopback routine. The sender transmits a continuous data stream, and the established TCP connection would not terminate until the sender finishes sending data.

$\frac{R}{S}$	4 KB	8 KB	16 KB	24 KB	32 KB	40 KB	48 KB	52 KB
4 KB	23.49	31.61	0.16	0.16	0.16	0.161	0.16	0.16
8 KB	28.33	30.28	0.16	0.16	0.16	0.16	0.16	0.16
16 KB	27.89	34.97	36.24	0.49	0.53	0.47	0.47	0.47
24 KB	27.19	35.42	34.81	41.15	40.83	40.50	0.53	0.53
32 KB	27.63	34.63	35.41	39.60	39.58	38.92	38.46	38.50
40 KB	26.58	34.63	34.97	38.81	39.73	39.39	39.57	38.73
48 KB	27.35	34.50	34.55	38.21	39.61	39.31	39.47	39.09
52 KB	27.01	34.23	34.07	38.35	39.29	39.23	38.89	40.27

Class I deadlocks

Class II deadlocks

Class III deadlocks

Table 15.1. Throughput measurements for a TCP connection with an MSS of 9148 bytes (in Mbps).

The throughput measurements are based on two timestamps generated from the *gettimeofday* system call. The start time is taken at the instant when the sender makes the *write* system call, and the end time is taken at the instant when the sender completes the data transmission. The TCP throughput is computed by dividing the total amount of application data sent by the difference between the two timestamps. In Table 15.1, we present the throughput measurements with the MSS set to 9148 bytes. Each data is an average value computed from 10 independent experiments. All measurements assume zero connection setup time, no packet losses, and a bulk data transfer. Moreover, there is a delay of 180 seconds between experiments in order to alleviate the CPU loading. As shown in the table, throughput deadlocks occur in the shaded region, which are contributed from three different sources, as will be explained next.

15.2.4 Three Classes of Throughput Deadlocks

As explained in Section 15.1, all throughput deadlocks are resulted from a circular-wait condition between a TCP sender and a TCP receiver. Moldeklev and Gunningberg classified the causes for the throughput deadlock into (I) deadlocks predictable from the acknowledgment strategy, (II) deadlocks caused by the socket copy rule and the Nagle algorithm, and (III) deadlocks caused by the timer acknowledgment and the Nagle algorithm [3]. To summarize, class I deadlock occurs if Equation (1) is satisfied, and classes II and III deadlocks occur if Equation (2) is satisfied.

$$S < \min\{2\,\text{MSS}, 0.35\,R\}. \tag{1}$$
$$S < \min\{3\,\text{MSS}, 0.35\,R + \text{MSS}\}, \tag{2}$$

where S and R are the send socket buffer size and receive socket buffer size, respectively.

Equation (1) represents a sufficient deadlock condition for which a maximum sized segment sent by the sender cannot trigger acknowledgments from the receiver. Thus, this type of deadlock depends only on the socket buffer size combination, but not on other implementation issues, such as data copying rules.

Even when Equation (1) does not hold, class II and III deadlocks could still occur according to Equation (2), and these two classes, unlike the first one, depend also on other implementation details. Moreover, the exact causes for classes II and III deadlocks are subtly different. In class II deadlocks, a sender may immediately push out a nonMSS-sized segment of size d because of the data copying rule, thus leaving $S - d$ for buffering new data in the send buffer. As a result, sufficient conditions for deadlocks are given by (i) $S - d < \text{MSS}$ and (ii) $d < \min\{2\,\text{MSS}, 0.35\,R\}$. The Nagle algorithm and condition (i) prevent the sender from sending more segments. The delayed acknowledgment strategy and condition (ii), on the other hand, prevent the receiver from acknowledging immediately. $S/R = 8\,\text{KB}/16\,\text{KB}$ and $16\,\text{KB}/40\,\text{KB}$ are examples of this class of deadlocks (see Table 15.1).

Class II deadlocks could not occur in $S/R = 16\,\text{KB}/24\,\text{KB}$, $16\,\text{KB}/32\,\text{KB}$, $24\,\text{KB}/48\,\text{KB}$, and $24\,\text{KB}/52\,\text{KB}$, because the sender has enough buffer space to compose an MSS-sized segment. However, class III deadlocks could still occur to them when a sender receives a timer-triggered acknowledgment from the receiver. To be specific, let d be the amount of outstanding segments sent by the sender at a certain time. After that, the sender receives a timer-triggered acknowledgment, which generally could acknowledge any amount of the outstanding segments, and let $a \le d$ be the amount of segments acknowledged by the timer-triggered acknowledgment. Similar to class II deadlocks, sufficient conditions for deadlocks are given by (i) $S - (d - a) < \text{MSS}$, (ii) $d - a < \min\{2\,\text{MSS}, 0.35\,R\}$. These two conditions are again reduced to Equation (2).

Based on Equation (2), a straightforward solution to avoiding throughput deadlocks is to choose an S/R that violates Equation (2). That is, a static approach is to set the send socket buffer to 3 MSS, regardless of the receive socket buffer size. For 10/100-Mbps Ethernet, for example, only 4380 bytes of socket memory to meet the requirement. However, this requirement becomes more demanding in the ATM networks with MSS equal to 9148 bytes, where a sender needs to reserve more than 27 KB of buffer memory for a single TCP connection. When the sender maintains a large number of concurrent connections, the memory allocated to the TCP communication would be too enormous to support. Further, this solution is still dependent on the network speed, and the buffer requirement becomes more stringent as the Internet's speed continues to increase.

Another method of violating Equation (2) is to let the sender obtain receive socket buffer information, but this requires additional support from the TCP protocol. Yet another obvious solution is to turn off the Nagle algorithm on the sender side and to explicitly acknowledge every segment received, i.e., without delayed acknowledgment. This solution will clearly reintroduce the small-segment problems that the Nagle algorithm and the delayed acknowledgment strategy were originally designed to solve. To sum up, the inadequacies of these solutions motivate us to examine better solutions to eliminate the deadlock problems, to be discussed next.

15.3 AN ADAPTIVE ACKNOWLEDGMENT ALGORITHM (A^3)

We have identified three important requirements for any solution to the deadlock problem. First, the solution must cater to heterogeneous receivers, which may or may not implement the new solution. Second, an implementation of the solution must involve only a minimal change in the coding. Third, the solution must be adaptive to the network size and the amount of socket buffers available. All three requirements above ensure that the solution is compatible with the current TCP and is immediately deployable. Moreover, the requirements imply that the solution is scalable to the rapid development of the Internet in the future. Based on these requirements, we expect that the new algorithm is a receiver-side SWS avoidance algorithm and the sender-side SWS avoidance algorithm should remain unchanged. In other words, the receiver is solely responsible for ensuring deadlock-free operations, and it only assumes that the sender transmission behavior is governed by a window-based flow control mechanism.

Based on the design requirements, we propose a new A^3 that determines when to send acknowledgments based on the sender's behavior. A key quantity maintained by an A^3-receiver is referred to as *maximum unacknowledged data size* (MUDS) in terms of bytes, which is defined to be the maximum amount of data continuously sent by the sender when the receiver is not acknowledging. When deadlocks do not occur and there is no network congestion, the MUDS is upper bounded by $\min\{S, R\}$. In general, the MUDS' exact value depends on the buffer sizes, data copying rule, and other implementation issues. For example, the MUDS is given by MSS + 4 KB for MSS + 4 KB $\leq S <$ min{3 MSS, 0.35 R + MSS} (class II deadlocks). Given an MUDS estimate, an A^3-receiver sends an acknowledgment whenever the segments received reach or exceed 35% of the estimated

MUDS. Thus, an A^3-receiver no longer relies on the receiver's actual buffer size and the actual value of the MSS, and it is able to adapt to various network MTUs and different combinations of send and receive buffer sizes. Moreover, it is clear that the new acknowledgment algorithm removes all three classes of deadlocks by having the receiver promptly send back acknowledgments.

One approach to estimating the MUDS is to perform "samplings" periodically by an A^3-receiver. During a sampling, the receiver keeps track of the amount of segments received, and it will not acknowledge any segments. Based on the sampling information, an A^3-receiver estimates the sender's MUDS. Thus, an A^3-receiver alternates between sampling periods and nonsampling periods.

The packet samplings incur overheads and delay, because acknowledgments will not be sent during these periods. Thus, controlling the length of the sampling periods and the frequency of performing samplings are major factors influencing the A^3's performance. For this purpose, an A^3-receiver is equipped with the following timer, counter, and thresholds. We also show in Figure 15.3 an A^3-receiver's state transition diagram during sampling periods.

- Sampling period timer (SP_timer): A timer to control the length of a sampling period
- Sampling period threshold (SP_t): A value (in time units) used in conjunction with the SP_timer to control the length of a sampling period
- Inter-sampling period counter (ISP_counter): A counter to control the inter-sampling period
- Inter-sampling period threshold (ISP_t): A value (in number of packets) used in conjunction with the ISP_counter to control the inter-sampling period

15.3.1 Inter-Sampling Period Control and Sampling Initialization

The value of ISP_t determines the time interval between two consecutive samplings and it is set according to the following algorithm, where $MUDS_{current}$ and $MUDS_{previous}$ are the current and previous estimates of the MUDS, respectively.

> *if ($MUDS_{previous}$ does not exist)*
>   *ISP_t = 10;*
> *else {*
>   *if ($|MUDS_{current} - MUDS_{previous}| < MSS$) {*
>   *ISP_t = 3 ISP_t;*
>   *the acknowledgment threshold remains unchanged;*
>   *} else {*
>   *ISP_t = 10;*
>   *if ($MUDS_{current} > MUDS_{previous}$)*
>   *the acknowledgment threshold = 0.35 $MUDS_{current}$;*
>   *}*
> *}*

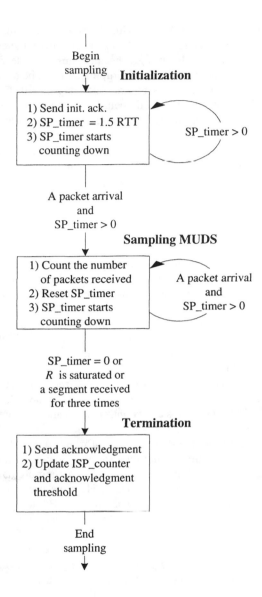

Figure 15.3. An A^3-receiver's state diagram during a sampling period.

The ISP_t is set to a constant (10 in the algorithm) as soon as a TCP connection is established, and the ISP_counter is initialized to ISP_t and begins to count down, i.e., the counter is decremented whenever a packet is received. A packet sampling starts when the ISP_counter's value drops to zero. At the end of a packet sampling, the counter may be reset to ISP_t again. However, the counter is tripled if $MUDS_{current}$ is "close" to $MUDS_{previous}$ because this is a clear indication that $MUDS_{current}$ is accurate and the number of samplings should be decreased.

At the beginning of a packet sampling, the receiver will first send a maximum window update with an acknowledgment for all the segments received in the buffer. The acknowledgment and window update therefore allow the sender to transfer the maximum amount of data permitted by the sender-side SWS avoidance mechanism. At the same time, the SP_timer is initialized to 1.5 RTT (round-trip time) and the timer starts counting down. This initialization allows adequate time to receive the packets in transit and the packets sent upon receiving the receiver's first acknowledgment. Once a sampling is started, the receiver is prohibited from further acknowledging the incoming data until the sampling period ends.

15.3.2 Sampling Period Control

A TCP sender may dispatch an arbitrary amount of segments bounded by the sender-side flow control mechanism and the send buffer size. The receiver carefully records the amount of data received, and discards retransmissions. The sampling procedure terminates when (1) the receive buffer is saturated (or close to saturation) or (2) a single segment is received three times in a row (this is a strong indication of timeout or packet lost). Otherwise, the sampling will continue until (3) the connection has been inactive for a certain period of time, i.e., when the SP_timer becomes zero.

We have mentioned that the SP_timer is initialized to 1.5 RTT when a connection is established. The SP_timer is reset to the threshold SP_t whenever a packet is received. The timer then starts counting down and the receiver terminates the sampling period when the timer reaches zero. The choice of the threshold SP_t is important. Having a large threshold value will result in a performance penalty since no acknowledgments are sent during a sampling period. On the other hand, having a small value may result in terminating the sampling prematurely and, as a result, the receiver underestimates the MUDS. Here we use inter-packet arrival time (IPAT) to determine the threshold by setting the SP_t to 1.3 IPAT. In other words, the receiver concludes that the sender has sent a maximum amount of segment permitted by the sender-side SWS avoidance mechanism if there are no other packet arrivals after a period of 1.3 IPAT. To do so, the receiver continuously measures the IPAT for the incoming packets. For every five packets received, the receiver discards the maximum and minimum IPAT samples and takes the average of the remaining three values as the current IPAT estimate. The IPAT clearly depends on the transmission delay, sender packetization delay, and other factors. By computing the IPAT for every five packets, we are hoping to obtain the most updated estimate for the packet interarrival pattern.

One exception to resetting the SP_timer to 1.3 IPAT upon receiving a packet is when the remaining time in the timer upon a packet arrival is larger than 1.3

IPAT. This will occur if a transit packet arrives at the receiver shortly after the initialization of a packet sampling. If the SP_timer is immediately reset to 1.3 IPAT in this case, the packet sampling may terminate prematurely since the first acknowledgment sent by the receiver at the initialization stage may not arrive at the sender in time. Therefore, the A^3 ensures that the sampling period is at least 1.5 RTT.

The following summarizes the algorithm of updating the SP_timer when a packet is received.

if (SP_timer > 1.3 IPAT upon a packet arrival)

   SP_timer continues to count down;

else

   SP_timer = 1.3 IPAT and the timer starts counting down.

15.3.3 Computing the Thresholds

During and at the end of a sampling period, an A^3-receiver is required to update the ISP_t, SP_t, and the acknowledgment threshold. The updates for the ISP_t and SP_t have already been discussed in the previous two sections. As for the acknowledgment threshold, a sender's actual MUDS normally does not change significantly in the congestion avoidance phase. Thus, we only update the MUDS estimate when it is increased. To follow the delayed acknowledgment algorithm in the SunOS, we set the acknowledgment threshold to 35% of the MUDS estimate, as shown in the algorithm in Section 15.3.1.

15.3.4 Performance Evaluation

To compare the performance of an A^3-receiver with that of a typical TCP receiver equipped with the delayed acknowledgment algorithm, we simulate a TCP connection with an MSS of 9148 bytes. Each endpoint in the simulator is a 4.3 BSD Unix terminal, which observes the essential 4.3 BSD socket mechanism, including the data copying rules and TCP segment buffering. Our simulated TCP channel takes no time to establish a connection, and the packet loss is assumed negligible. The TCP performance is measured through a *ftp* session from a sender to a receiver. The throughput is computed by the total amount of data transferred by the total transmission time. The experiments cover 8×8 send-receive buffer size combinations ranging from 4 KB to 52 KB, and each individual experiment is a continuous (back to back) transmission of 10-MB data. Every throughput measurement reported in Table 15.2 is an average of 25 independent runs.

Our simulation results show that the A^3 has successfully reclaimed the TCP performance in the original deadlock regions. Additionally, the adaptive acknowledgment threshold improves the performance in other nondeadlock areas. This is due to an earlier response from the receiver when the A^3 is used, which results in a more efficient pipelining of the data from the sender. On the other hand, there is a marginal performance penalty caused by the A^3's operational overheads for small receivers, e.g., $R = 4, 8$ KB. Consider $S/R = 16$ KB/4 KB, the receiver acknowledgment threshold is 1.4 KB, and the sender maximum usable window size is 4 KB. This suggests that a single data segment (4 KB) from the sender is enough to trigger a receiver acknowledgment from either acknowledgment algorithm. Unfortunately, an A^3-receiver requires more time to compute the IPAT, sampling threshold, and acknowledgment threshold, and these additional overheads introduce performance degradation, as shown in the lower left triangular regions in Table 15.2, where the send buffer is relatively large when compared with the receive buffer.

R S	4 KB (1)	(2)	(3)	8 KB (1)	(2)	(3)	16 KB (1)	(2)	(3)	24 KB (1)	(2)	(3)
4 KB	20	20	21	20	20	21	6	20	20	6	20	20
8 KB	21	20	20	25	20	20	6	25	25	6	25	26
16 KB	21	20	20	41	41	41	55	50	50	19	50	50
24 KB	21	20	20	41	40	40	79	80	80	74	87	89
32 KB	20	20	21	41	40	40	81	80	82	80	89	95
40 KB	20	20	21	41	40	41	81	80	80	99	98	103
48 KB	20	20	20	41	40	42	81	80	81	99	99	102
52 KB	21	20	21	41	40	41	82	80	80	100	98	98

R S	32 KB (1)	(2)	(3)	40 KB (1)	(2)	(3)	48 KB (1)	(2)	(3)	52 KB (1)	(2)	(3)
4 KB	6	20	20	6	20	21	6	20	20	6	20	21
8 KB	6	25	25	6	25	26	6	25	25	6	25	26
16 KB	19	50	50	19	50	50	19	50	50	19	50	50
24 KB	73	87	88	74	87	87	26	87	88	26	87	87
32 KB	89	94	106	89	98	107	94	102	115	94	99	118
40 KB	99	99	103	141	134	137	111	139	144	111	137	146
48 KB	100	104	102	151	150	159	160	161	170	143	161	168
52 KB	100	99	105	152	152	160	162	168	165	171	162	170

(1) Delayed acknowledgment algorithm
(2) The A^3 according to Section 15.3
(3) The A^3 with a fewer number of samplings
Shaded region: Deadlock region for the delayed acknowledgment algorithm

Table 15.2. Throughputs of a TCP connection with an MSS of 9148 bytes (in KB per simulation second).

A possible way to further improving the A^3's throughput performance is therefore to reduce the number of samplings required for computing the MUDS.

There are two ways to achieve that: (1) increase the inter-sampling period and (2) decrease each sampling period. In Table 15.2, we also present simulation results for a modified A^3 in which ISP_t = 3 ISP_t is changed to ISP_t = 4 ISP_t under the if-statement, and ISP_t = 10 is changed to ISP_t = 0.5 ISP_t under the else statement in the algorithm presented in Section 15.3.1. Although the number of samplings decreases significantly (not shown in the table), the throughput improvement is not significant. In the original A^3, the overhead incurred from additional samplings is compensated by a gain in throughput. In the modified A^3, a loss of gain in throughput by not sampling as frequently is compensated by reducing the sampling overhead.

15.4 EFFECT OF NETWORK CONGESTION ON THE A^3

The A^3 was designed without network congestion in mind. In this section, we show and explain why the A^3 fails to ensure throughput deadlock-free when a TCP connection experiences network congestion. Then we propose an enhancement to the A^3, referred to as congestion-sensitive A^3 (CSA^3), to ensure deadlock-free even in the presence of network congestion.

It is well known that a TCP sender detects possible network congestion either by receiving three duplicate acknowledgments (fast retransmission) or by retransmission timeouts. In either case, the sender retransmits the oldest segment that has not been acknowledged. At the same time, the sender also adjusts its congestion window size. In the former case, the sender exercises fast recovery in which the congestion window is reduced to only half of the current value. In the latter, the window size is reset to one MSS. Both cases effectively reduce the sender's sending rate, and consequently the A^3-receiver's MUDS estimate overestimates the actual value. Therefore, the receiver may not be able to receive enough data to trigger acknowledgment, and throughput deadlock recurs.

S \ R	4 KB	8 KB	16 KB	24 KB	32 KB	40 KB	48 KB	52 KB
4 KB								
8 KB	Deadlock-free region							
16 KB				Deadlock-prone region I				
24 KB								
32 KB								
40 KB								
48 KB					Deadlock-prone region II			
52 KB								

Table 15.3. A classification of send-receive buffer combinations for an MSS of 9148 bytes for A^3-receivers.

15.4.1 A Classification of Operating Regions

Before introducing the CSA^3, it is convenient to divide the 64 send-receive buffer combination into three regions assuming that the MSS is 9148 bytes, as shown in Table 15.3. In the deadlock-free region, throughput deadlocks will not occur to TCP connections equipped with A^3-receivers in the presence of network congestion and we postpone the explanation to the next section. On the other hand, throughput deadlocks recur in the two deadlock-prone regions when there is network congestion. The throughput degradation is more serious in the deadlock-prone region II than that in the deadlock-prone region I.

A. Deadlock-Free Region

Figure 15.4 shows the throughput for a scenario in the deadlock-free region (S/R = 4 KB/4 KB). Network congestions of short durations are injected into the simulation at several time instants. The two curves, with and without congestion, are overlapped before the network congestion first occurred at around 500 seconds, and when the time is more than 2000 seconds. Between the two times, very small throughput drops are noted in the curve indicated by "A^3 under congestion" because the dropped segments need to be retransmitted. Other scenarios in this region, though not shown here, actually exhibit very similar behavior as Figure 15.4. Specific points about this set of experiments are as follows.

When the send buffers are small (4 KB and 8 KB), the sender's MUDS obviously cannot be very large. In fact, owing to the data copying rule, the sender always pushes out a 4-KB segment, and the next segment, if any, can be sent out only after receiving an acknowledgment from the receiver. As a result, the network congestion only causes the sender to time out and to retransmit the dropped segments (therefore the drops in the throughput), but it will not affect the MUDS value. Therefore, the receiver can promptly send back acknowledgments for any segments received, and no deadlocks occur.

When the send buffers are large enough ($\geq$ 16 KB), the send buffer allows the sender to send more than one segment at a time. However, since the receive buffers are small in this region (4 KB and 8 KB), the sender's usable window is limited by the receive buffer size, which is advertised to the sender in the TCP segments. Thus, the sender's MUDS is also given by 4 KB. Similar to the small send-buffer cases, network congestion will only delay the recipient of the dropped segments, but will not affect the MUDS estimates. As a result, no deadlocks occur.

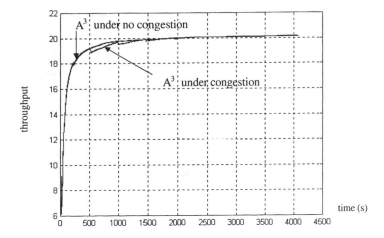

Figure 15.4. Throughput of a 4-KB sender with a 4-KB A^3-receiver.

B. Deadlock-Prone Region II

Figure 15.5 shows a scenario belonging to the deadlock-prone region II. The upper curve corresponds to the no-congestion case. Therefore, the throughput increases steadily as the window size continues to increase. However, congestions are injected into the simulation for the lower curve at three different times. Whenever congestion occurs, the throughput drops significantly, because the A^3-receiver has over-estimated the MUDS. When the sender times out due to congestion, the sender resets its congestion window size to one MSS. Therefore, without knowing the time-out event, the A^3-receiver continues to use the MUDS estimate, which is obtained before congestion, for computing the acknowledgment threshold. As a result, a deadlock recurs and the A^3-receiver acknowledges segments upon timing out its delayed acknowledgment timer. After updating the MUDS based on the new samplings, the A^3-receiver is again able to avoid deadlocks, and the throughput subsequently increases.

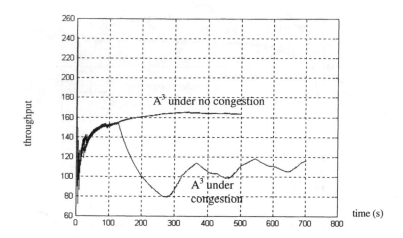

Figure 15.5. Throughput of a 52-KB sender with a 52-KB A^3-receiver.

C. Deadlock-Prone Region I

Figure 15.6 shows a scenario belonging to the deadlock-prone region I. Similar to the region II, throughput drops are observed in both scenarios. However, the magnitudes of the throughput degradation are not as significant and the throughput can also be recovered relatively quickly. Although the buffer sizes are much smaller than those in region II, the over-estimations of the MUDS are significant enough that deadlocks recur in this region.

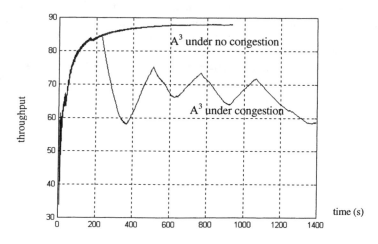

Figure 15.6. Throughput of a 24-KB sender with a 24-KB A^3-receiver.

15.4.2 Congestion-Sensitive A³ (CSA³)

A straightforward approach to resolving the congestion problem is to reset the MUDS and to perform samplings all over again to find the new value whenever congestion is detected. However, the main disadvantage of this approach is that deadlock still exists before the sampling is completed. As a result, the sampling needs to run for a long time, and therefore the overhead incurred would be very significant. Because of that, our approach proposed here is to enhance the A³ so that the enhanced A³ is able to react to network congestion.

A. A Slow-Start-Like Algorithm for Updating the MUDS

A CSA³-receiver is now required to infer network congestion based on the information received, and to reduce its MUDS estimate based on a procedure very similar to TCP senders' slow-start and congestion avoidance algorithms. Specifically, whenever a CSA³-receiver suspects network congestion based on the information to be discussed in the latter part of this section, it remembers MUDS/2 in a variable *r_ssthresh* and resets MUDS to one MSS. One exception to this is when the current MUDS is smaller than MSS, and this is possible when either the send buffer or receive buffer is smaller than MSS, such as those cases in the deadlock-free region. In other words, this MUDS updating procedure does not apply to the scenarios in the deadlock-free region.

After resetting MUDS to one MSS, the CSA³-receiver doubles MUDS for every nonduplicate acknowledgment sent out. This phase corresponds to the sender's slow-start phase. When the MUDS finally reaches or exceeds *r_ssthresh*, it is further increased linearly, which is similar to senders' congestion avoidance phase. When the MUDS is finally increased to the old value before congestion, the CSA³-receiver continues to update the MUDS in the same way as for an A³-receiver.

The MUDS updating algorithm upon detecting congestion is summarized below.

$r\_ssthresh = MUDS / 2;$
while (*a new acknowledgment sent out by the receiver*) {
    if ($MUDS \leq r\_ssthresh$)
        $MUDS = MUDS * 2;$
    else {
        $MUDS += MSS * (MSS / MUDS);$
        if ($MUDS \geq r\_ssthresh * 2$) *exit;*
    }
}

There are altogether three conditions that would trigger a CSA³-receiver to update its MUDS estimate according to the algorithm above:

1. When a router experiences short-term congestion, it drops a small number of segments. As a result, it is very likely that a CSA³-receiver is able to receive three duplicate acknowledgments, and it will perform fast retransmit and fast

recovery. Moreover, it will update its MUDS estimate according to the slow-start-like algorithm.

2. When a router experiences serious congestion, it drops a large number of segments. As a result, a CSA^3-receiver may not be able to receive enough duplicate acknowledgments to perform fast retransmit and fast recovery. Therefore, the sender will finally time out and retransmit lost segments. This also suggests that a CSA^3-receiver needs to time out its MUDS estimate after a certain inactivity period. Upon time out, it performs the same slow-start-like algorithm to update the MUDS.

3. Besides dropping segments, congested routers may also drop acknowledgments on the reverse path. As a result, the sender will eventually time out and retransmit lost segments, and a CSA^3-receiver may receive duplicate data segments. Therefore, the CSA^3-receiver also performs the slow-start-like algorithm when it receives duplicate segments.

B. Performance Evaluation of the CSA^3

In Figures 15.7-15.9, we present simulation results to compare the throughput performance of the A^3 and CSA^3 in the presence of network congestion. Since the A^3's throughput is minimally affected by congestion in the deadlock-free region, as shown in Figure 15.4, we only consider the two deadlock-prone regions in this section. The simulation settings are the same as those in Section 15.4.1. Network congestions occur at several time instants, and the TCP sender retransmits lost segments upon timeout.

Among all three scenarios (one in region I and two in region II), the improvement in throughput is most significant in the deadlock-prone region II when the CSA^3 is employed. Since both send and receive buffers are large in this region, the MUDS value can be quite high when there is no congestion. Therefore, the CSA^3's receiver also keeps a large MUDS estimate. When network congestion occurs, the sender resets the congestion window to one MSS. Both the CSA^3-receiver and A^3-receiver are unable to promptly acknowledge new segments due to the over-estimation of the sender's MUDS, thus resulting in throughput drops in both cases. However, the CSA^3-receiver is able to recover from throughput drop much faster than the A^3-receiver, because the former promptly reduces the MUDS estimate and therefore can send a new acknowledgment much earlier than the A^3-receiver can. In TCP, the sender's congestion window size increases based on a self-clocking acknowledgment mechanism. The faster new acknowledgments are received, the faster the window is opened up. As a result, the CSA^3-receiver can recover from the throughput loss quickly, as shown in Figure 15.7.

The throughput behaviors shown in Figure 15.8 and 15.9 for region I, on the other hand, are quite similar. The CSA^3 attains similar throughput as the A^3 at the beginning, but the former again responds to and recovers from network congestion much faster than the A^3. In this region, the MUDS estimate may or may not be large enough to cause deadlocks. Apparently, when the first congestion occurs, the CSA^3 receiver is unable to detect the network congestion; therefore, there is no throughput gain by using the CSA^3. However, in the latter congestion the CSA^3 receiver is able to detect congestion and to respond to it promptly. This shows that the CSA^3 does not impose any penalty on the throughput performance even though it occasionally fails to detect congestion.

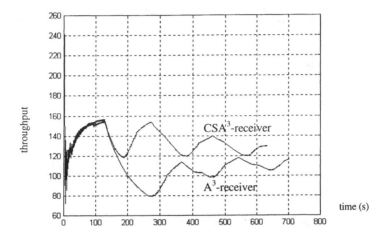

Figure 15.7. Throughput of a 52-KB sender with a 52-KB A^3/CSA^3-receiver under congestion.

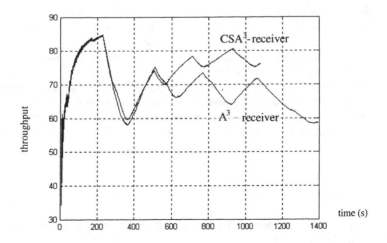

Figure 15.8. Throughput of a 24-KB sender with a 24-KB A^3/CSA^3-receiver under congestion.

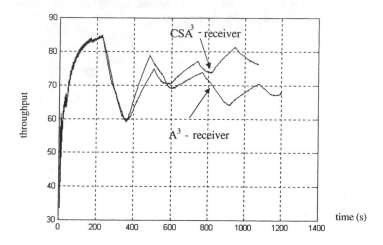

Figure 15.9. Throughput of a 24-KB sender with a 48-KB A^3/CSA^3-receiver under congestion.

15.5 CONCLUSIONS AND FUTURE WORK

In this paper we have presented the TCP throughput deadlock problems in high-speed networks. This problem becomes very serious as the end-to-end network speed continues to increase. We have proposed the A^3 and CSA^3 to overcome this problem. We have shown by simulations that they have successfully reclaimed all deadlock regions for noncongested networks and congested networks, respectively. Currently, we are implementing them in Linux systems and we will put them in field tests. Another important area to study concerns fairness between the CSA^3 receivers and nonCSA^3 receivers. It remains to be seen whether the new acknowledgment algorithms impose any unfairness toward those that do not implement them.

Acknowledgment

This work is partially supported by The Hong Kong Polytechnic University Research Grant G-S909.

REFERENCES

[1] N. Ghani and S. Dixit, "TCP/IP Enhancements for Satellite Networks," *IEEE Commun. Mag.*, pp. 64-72, July 1999.

[2] C. Charalambous, V. Frost, and J. Evans, "Performance Evaluation of TCP Extensions on ATM Over High Bandwidth Delay Product Networks," *IEEE Commun. Mag.*, pp. 57-63, July 1999.

[3] C. Partridge and T. Shepard, "TCP/IP Performance Over Satellite Links," *IEEE Network Mag.*, pp. 44-49, Sept/Oct. 1997.

[4] H. Balakrishnan and V. Padmanabhan, "How Network Asymmetry Affects TCP," *IEEE Commun. Mag.*, vol. 39, no. 4, pp. 60-67, Apr. 2001.

[5] G. Xylomenos, G. Polyzos, P. Mahonen, and M. Saaranen, "TCP Performance Issues Over Wireless Links," *IEEE Commun. Mag.*, vol. 39, no. 4, pp. 52-59, Apr. 2001.

[6] C. Papadopoulos and G. Parulkar, "Experimental Evaluation of SUNOS IPC and TCP/IP Protocol Implementation," *IEEE/ACM Trans. Networking*, pp. 199-216, April, 1993.

[7] V. Paxson, "Automated Packet Trace Analysis of TCP Implementations," *Proc. ACM SIGCOMM*, pp. 167-179, 1997.

[8] J. Semke, J. Mahdavi, and M. Mathis, "Automatic TCP Buffer Tuning," *Proc. ACM SIGCOMM*, pp. 315-323, 1998.

[9] D. Clark, "Window and Acknowledgment Strategy in TCP," *RFC 813*, July 1982.

[10] J. Nagle, "Congestion Control on TCP/IP Internetworks," *RFC 896*, Jan. 1984.

[11] R. Braden, "Requirements for Internet Hosts—Communication Layers," *RFC 1122*, Oct. 1989.

[12] J. Heidemann, "Performance Interactions Between P-HTTP and TCP Implementations," *ACM Computer Communication Review*, vol. 27, no. 2, pp. 65-73, Apr. 1997.

[13] J. Mogul and G. Minshall, "Rethinking the TCP Nagle Algorithm," *ACM Computer Communication Review*, vol. 31, no. 1, pp. 6-20, Jan. 2001.

[14] K. Moldeklev and P. Gunningberg, "How a Large ATM MTU Causes Deadlocks in TCP Data Transfers," *IEEE/ACM Trans. Networking*, vol. 3., no. 4., pp. 409-422, Aug. 1995.

[15] D. Comer and J. Lin, "TCP Buffering and Performance over an ATM Network," *Internetworking: Research and Experience*, vol. 6, pp. 1-13, May 1995.

[16] Y. Murayama and S. Yamaguchi, "A Proposal for a Solution of the TCP Short-Term Deadlock Problem," *Proc. 12th Intl. Conf. Information Networking*, pp. 269-274, 1998.

[17] G. Wright and W. Stevens, *TCP/IP Illustrated*, vol. 2, Addison-Wesley, 1995.

16

Deadlock Resolution in Large-Scale Internet Computing

Jonghun Park
Seoul National University, Korea

Abstract – The Internet has revolutionized the way computing is carried out by providing a new medium of information highway. For instance, with the emerging Internet computing infrastructures such as grid, peer-to-peer, and web services, it has become possible to deploy applications that support various Internet-wide collaborations. Yet, as Internet computing is becoming popular, it also presents a number of new challenges in coordinating resource usage. In particular, the resource allocation protocol that provides clear directives on the acquisition of shared resources, is complicated by the inherent characteristics of Internet computing, such as (i) the large-scale application deployment, (ii) the need for co-allocation of distributed resources that span multiple administrative domains, (iii) the lack of means for exchanging information between the independent Internet applications, and finally (iv) the availability of functionally redundant resources. The implication is that the resource allocation method must be decentralized, scalable, and most importantly it should be able to allocate the required resources with minimum time and cost. Recognizing the need for a systematic approach to the resource allocation for large-scale Internet computing, in this chapter we seek to promote the Internet resource allocation theory by presenting a new scalable resource allocation protocol that can address the characteristics of current Internet computing practices. The proposed protocol is free from deadlock and livelock, and seeks to effectively exploit the available alternative resource co-allocation schemes. Experimental results demonstrate that the proposed protocol yields a significant performance improvement over the existing deadlock prevention protocol.

16.1   An Overview of the Resource Allocation Problem in Internet Computing

Distributed computing has been popular within local area networks for many years, and it took a major leap by adopting the Internet and supporting open standards. The last decade has witnessed tremendous popularity of computing infrastructures that aim to support various kinds of Internet-wide collaborations through seamlessly harnessing appropriate Internet resources. Computational grids, federations of geographically distributed heterogeneous hardware resources, have emerged as a means for delivering computational power to applications in the same manner as electrical energy is distributed to appliances through national power grids [1]. Such grid environments are being actively used to construct sophisticated, performance-sensitive applications in such areas as supercomputer-enhanced instrumentation, distributed supercomputing, and tele-immersive environments [1, 2].

At the same time, the emerging paradigms of distributed computing technologies like peer-to-peer (P2P) computing [3], distributed object computing [4], and Internet mobile agents [5], have also opened up a possibility of building Internet-scale information infrastructures, not only allowing resource sharing among the peers but also enabling on-demand, multi-institutional virtual organizations to be dynamically deployed on the Internet [6]. More recently, with the advent of Web services [7], it has become much easier than ever to develop a component-based application in the open distributed environment of the Internet. The Web services are building blocks for creating highly distributed systems, allowing any applications to be integrated as long as they are Internet-enabled. One of the Web services' contributions is that it removes the distinction between traditional software development and Internet application development [8]. It is anticipated that many of existing services in diverse areas such as metacomputing, e-commerce, and entertainment will be turned into the Web services, which will result in the market of Internet service grid [9].

The resulting computational models that use geographically distributed Internet resources, are collectively referred to as Internet computing, and it is increasingly likely that more and more applications will be deployed on a variety of Internet resources. Yet, as Internet computing is becoming pervasive, it also presents a number of new challenges in coordinating resource usage. The need for coordination arises mainly due to the fact that the resources are shared while at the same time they are available only in a finite number of units. Therefore, it is necessary to have an explicit resource allocation policy that provides clear directives on the equitable distribution of scarce resources. Some allocation rules, while being satisfactory on a standalone basis, often fail when interaction among the applications is considered. In particular, the problem of allocating Internet resources is complicated by the following characteristics that do not typically arise in other situations: First, the resources on the Internet are inherently heterogeneous. They can be hardware resources such as CPU cycles, memory, network

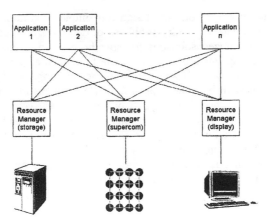

Figure 16.1: An Internet resource co-allocation example in scientific computing.

bandwidth, storage space, sensors, and visualization devices, or more broadly, software entities such as databases, libraries, applications, components, and Web services, all connected and available through the Internet. Second, the resources are subject to dynamic availability due to the unexpected failure, upgrade, and network breakdown, and also exhibiting dynamically varying performance due to the unpredictable resource access pattern and latency of today's Internet.

On the other hand, the Internet applications that use the resources are increasingly deployed in large scale, and they are built by the run-time integration of distributed resources that may span multiple administrative domains, implying that the application behavior may not be known to the resource managers priori, and also that a single resource allocation policy cannot be enforced to all the participating resource managers. Furthermore, the Internet applications often have resource co-allocation requirements that can be satisfied only by acquiring multiple resources simultaneously at several sites [10]. Correct execution of such applications may sometimes also require an end-to-end provision of high quality of service (QoS), which can be achieved through proper allocation of corresponding resources. For instance, in scientific computing, an application for interactive data analysis may require simultaneous access to a storage system holding data, a supercomputer for analysis, and a display device for interaction, with each resource providing a certain level of QoS in terms of storage capacity, processor speed, and the number of bits per pixel, respectively [11]. Figure 16.1 depicts the situation in which more than one such application exists and each resource is managed by an independent administrative domain.

Accordingly, the problem of resource allocation in the context of the Internet computing characterized above has recently received increased attention [10, 12, 11, 13]. However, as will be discussed in detail in Section 16.2.1, most existing work has focused primarily on the design and implementation of architectures, ignoring correctness and scalability problems of the resource allocation, or on the development of customized solutions for specific problem domains (e.g., multimedia) without paying much attention to the fundamental aspects. As a result, there has been little theoretical work done on the development of generic resource allocation methods with broader applicability that can ensure logical correctness as well as high performance. The logical correctness in the context of resource allocation refers to *eventuality*, i.e., the method should guarantee that the required resource can be allocated eventually. To this end, it is essential that the logically correct method should guarantee the freedom from deadlock and livelock. Specifically, a deadlock will arise if the method results in the resource allocation state where a set of concurrently active Internet applications are permanently blocked due to the fact that each application in the set is allocated and holds resource(s) requested by some other application in the set [14]. On the other hand, a livelock will happen in the process of resource allocation if the method allows a situation in which applications allocate and de-allocate resources repetitively without any progress, failing to guarantee that all the required resources will be eventually allocated.

As a motivational example of the deadlock problem arising in the Internet resource co allocation, we consider the grid applications for which processors need to be pooled from multiple remote sites. The resources can be allocated only by the request from an application to an appropriate remote site. Suppose that application α_1, requiring 2 processors from site 1 (represented by resource type R_1) and 3 processors from site 2 (represented by R_2) for its execution, has already allocated 2 units of R_1. Also suppose that another application, α_2, requires 1 unit of R_1 and 2 units of R_2. We further assume that only 2 and 3 processors are available at site 1 and 2, respectively. Figure 16.2(a) shows the resource allocation graph (RAG) [15] of the considered state. In the RAG representation, circle nodes are applications and square nodes are resources, and edges of the graph depict allocations or pending requests. A pending request is represented by an edge directed from the application node to the requested resource node, whereas resource allocation is represented by an edge directed from the node of a resource to the node of the application assigned. Furthermore, a positive integer is associated with each edge to represent how many units are requested or allocated. Finally, an integral vector at each application node indicates its resource requirement, and an integer at each resource node represents its capacity.

From the RAG shown in Figure 16.2(a), two applications, α_1 and α_2, would get into a deadlock if α_2 makes a request to R_2 before α_1, and the site 2 grants the allocation to α_2 accordingly. That is, after this allocation, α_1 (α_2, respectively) will indefinitely wait for the resource held by α_2 (α_1, respectively). The resulting deadlock state is depicted in Figure 16.2(b).

Having discussed the requirements for the resource allocation methods to be logically correct, we proceed to discuss the performance and QoS aspects pertaining to Internet resource allocation. Any logically correct method can be evaluated

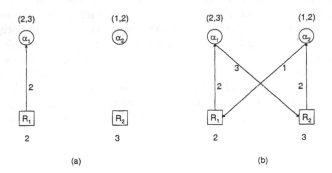

Figure 16.2: A simple deadlock arising in Internet resource co-allocation.

based on its performance, and ideally, the resource allocation method with the maximum performance would allow the acquisition of required resources with the smallest possible delay. However, in the Internet computing environment, difficulties arise when seeking to develop such methods due to the following reasons: First, any logically correct method will require some control on the applications' resource allocation behavior, because, otherwise, uncontrolled resource allocations may result in deadlock or livelock. That is, for the sake of deadlock and livelock freedom, some performance degradation may be unavoidable in the presence of control. This brings up the issue of designing flexible resource allocation methods that are logically correct as well as minimally restrictive so that the applications implementing the method do not suffer from long waiting for their required resources to be allocated.

Second, the existence of multiple redundant or functionally equivalent resources with varying QoS characteristics, introduces the problem of effectively utilizing the available alternatives as well as the resource selection subject to a desired QoS level. Given the diversity of dimensions defining the QoS of resources, including the continuous measures such as reliability, availability, and latency, and discrete measures such as types of CPU and instrumentation devices, the resource selection problem is concerned with determining the set of resources out of many possible configurations satisfying the specified set of QoS measures, with minimum possible cost. Third, in the open, dynamic, and uncertain environment of the Internet, the applications are not able to be fully aware of other applications' resource allocation behavior and status, nor the current and future availability of resources. This further necessitates a decentralized approach to solving the problem of designing high performance resource allocation methods.

Finally, current trends indicate that future complex Internet applications will be developed by composing the components (i.e., resources) distributed on the Internet [16, 13], and that more and more Internet components will be exposed through the Internet services such as Web services [17]. The lifetime of such applications may span from seconds to years [18]. For instance, there are many different projects currently ongoing from government, academia, and industry that provide Internet services in distributed environments, and it will be possible to deploy various types of applications (e.g., monitoring, forecasting) by use of those services [19]. Consequently, many of future Internet applications will require multiple components to be dynamically allocated and de-allocated over the life cycle of the applications in order to deal with various contingencies such as (i) application initialization and termination, (ii) the unexpected performance degradation or failure of the remote components, and (iii) the need for sequential resource allocation, arising when an application is composed of a series of components communicating over the Internet [20].

From the above discussion, it is clear that a new approach is needed to address all the characteristics of current Internet computing, and that it should also be realistic enough to be used in many real world Internet computing applications. With this motivation, this chapter seeks to promote the Internet resource allocation theory by presenting a scalable, decentralized resource co-allocation protocol for large-scale Internet computing. In particular, the proposed protocol will be logically correct as well as highly flexible, so that it can address today's Internet computing practices characterized by large scale, heterogeneity, abundance of redundant resources, site autonomy, and dynamic resource availability. It is anticipated that the proposed decentralized resource co-allocation protocol will be widely demanded not only by the applications themselves but also by the resource brokers as dependability requirements of Internet resource allocation become more stringent.

The rest of this chapter is organized as follows: Section 16.2 is devoted to the current state of the art in Internet computing infrastructures and deadlock-free resource allocation methods. Section 16.3 presents a formal model for analyzing deadlocks arising in Internet resource allocation and then provides preliminary results necessary for the subsequent development. Section 16.4 presents the main result of the chapter, a deadlock and livelock free protocol for Internet resource co-allocation. In Section 16.5, the performance of the proposed protocol is demonstrated via simulation experimentation. Finally Section 16.6 concludes the chapter and provides some discussion on potential future research.

16.2   Current State of the Art

16.2.1   Internet Computing Infrastructures

The infrastructures for supporting the sharing of Internet resources are now pervasive. In particular, grid computing is becoming increasingly popular, and currently there are a number of ongoing projects worldwide that seek to build various grid computing infrastructures and services. While Globus [1] and Legion [21] are two major pioneering efforts to build a world-wide virtual supercomputing structure, there are also many other grid-centered projects that are targeted to support more application-specific areas such as data grids (e.g., CERN DataGrid [22]), meta-computing (e.g., Condor [23], SETI@Home [24]), and desktop supercomputing (e.g., MetaNEOS [25], NetSolve [26]).

In the grid computing environment, a wide variety of heterogeneous computational resources are logically aggregated and presented as a single coherent resource to the user. Typically a user interacts with grid information services that discover and acquire the resources, and subsequently map tasks to resources, deploy the applications, and finally provide results to the user. In many cases, grid applications require the co-allocation of multiple resources, potentially managed by different administrative domains with diverse policies in widely distributed locations. As a consequence, resource management has been one of the central components for the successful deployment of such computing infrastructure. The basic function of the resource management system is to accept requests for resources from users and assign specific resources to the request from the pool of grid resources for which the user has access permission [27]. There are a number of resource management systems proposed and implemented, including AppLes [28], GRAM [10], and Condor-G [29]. Nevertheless, most past work has been primarily concerned with the development of architecture and/or application-specific prototype for the grid resource management, without specifically addressing the logical correctness and performance problems arising when a large number of multi-resources are co-allocated across the independent resource managers or even across the different grid resource management systems.

On the other hand, the emerging distributed computing technologies have also made it possible to share the objects scattered on the Internet. An object represents and encapsulates a resource that it uses to provide services to other objects. The objects that provide services, in turn, might rely on services provided by other objects. Some representative commercial platforms include Jini [30] and CORBA [31], and there are also many other distributed computing middleware prototypes developed under various contexts in research communities (e.g., [32, 33]).

In this paradigm, it is possible to set up a global object network that connects a large number of distributed objects that represent people, devices, software, or services, enabling many interesting applications like virtual organizations, personal networks, and collaborative problem solving environment, to be deployed over the wide-area network. For example, as indicated in [32], a virtual task force team that handles a national crisis may need to be dynamically formed by drawing members from different organizations, while, at the same time, some of the team members may also need to belong to other teams. Setting up a virtual team essentially involves the resource co-allocation problem, and this can be efficiently materialized by appropriately allocating the objects representing the correspond-

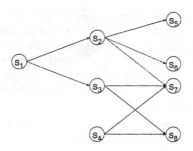

Figure 16.3: An example of dynamic service composition.

ing people. Hence, object (i.e., resource) sharing is one of the key characteristics of the applications built on top of the Internet-wide distributed computing infrastructures.

However, as the global object network is created and changed dynamically, sharing relationships among the objects can also vary over time in terms of the resources involved and the participating applications. Accordingly, the dynamic nature of sharing relationships requires mechanisms for discovering, locating, and allocating multiple resources efficiently and effectively. A similar problem can also be identified in other, more sophisticated Internet computing infrastructures for supporting Internet mobile agents [34], coordination-based systems [35], and peer-to-peer computing [3]. For instance, for an Internet mobile agent to be able to migrate itself (or clone children agents) from one host to another, it is necessary to allocate the destination hosts before the migration (or cloning) starts, since the number of agents that can be accommodated by a single host is finite.

Finally, component-based software development is increasingly drawing much attention in the software engineering community [36], and there is a growing consensus that the development of future Internet applications will be greatly facilitated by the use of the high level abstraction and encapsulation provided by the component-based design patterns. In particular, the recent advent of Web services has opened up the possibility of constructing a large-scale service grid by allowing an application to be composed from distributed Web services. The Web services are self-contained, modular applications that can be described, published, located, and invoked over the Web. A Web service provider can create and deploy a Web service, and define its structure and contents in WSDL [7]. The service can be registered in UDDI registries [7] that enable developers to publish their Web services, and to search for services offered by others.

More specifically, Web services may be *simple* or *composite* [37]. Composite services consist of a number of other simple or composite services. That is, Web services may have a recursive structure in that they can be composed of other published Web services while in turn they are also considered to be component services themselves [38]. In this regard, we refer to the services that are used by a composite service as *components*. Hence, with this emerging computing paradigm, it is possible to deploy a value-added service by use of a large number of other Web services as its resources, resulting in the Web of Web services that can be characterized as time-dependent sharing relationships. The co-allocation requirements of composite services can be represented as a Web service flow graph (WSFG) [39] whose nodes represent simple or composite Web services. In the WSFG, an edge directed from service s_i to s_j indicates that s_i uses s_j as its component. In order to accommodate the existence of more than one co-allocation scheme, the WSFG can be extended by representing different component co-allocation schemes of a composite service as different arc patterns originating from it. Figure 16.3 shows an example WSFG for dynamic service composition. In this example, services s_7 and s_8 are components of s_3 which, in turn, is a potential component of s_1 since s_1 can be instantiated by use of either s_2 or s_3. Likewise, service s_2 can be instantiated by composing either s_5 or s_6 and s_7.

We envision that future Internet application developers will draw lots of resources from Web services, and they will view the Web as a dynamic component library that is persistently available. At the same time, as the high-performance network is becoming omnipresent, users have come to expect delivered application performance in the Internet computing environment. For instance, it will be a common practice that the future applications will use the Web services not only to retrieve information but also to cohesively harness computing resources for remote computation, process migration, and sharing of devices such as storage and sensors [1]. Therefore, from all of the aforementioned Internet computing infrastructures, it is clear that there is an emerging need for an effective and efficient solution to the problem of end-to-end, dynamic resource co-allocation, and yet, there is few work that has addressed the logical correctness and performance issues arising during the resource allocation.

16.2.2   Deadlock-Free Resource Allocation

During the last decade there has been a surge of analytical and algorithmic results in various problem contexts that can provide the basis for the development of a deadlock-free resource allocation method sought in this chapter. Some of the key insights that can be cited, are (i) the formal modeling of the structure and dynamics of the resource allocation problems through the abstract notion of sequential resource allocation systems (RAS) [40, 41], (ii) the analytical characterization of the underlying RAS deadlock problems and synthesis of deadlock prevention/avoidance policies by means of the Finite State Automata (FSA) [42] and Petri Net (PN) [43] frameworks [44, 45, 14], and (iii) the emergence of generalized algorithmic methods for detecting, preventing, or resolving resource deadlocks in distributed systems [15, 46, 47].

Of particular interest to the problem context in this chapter is the RAS abstraction that is characterized by a finite set of concurrent processes contesting for a finite set of shared resources. Specifically, in the RAS, each resource type is defined by its finite capacity that may not be known to the processes and that can be possibly varying over time, while each process has an associated resource acquisition plan, i.e., a set of all the possible sequences of resource acquisitions that the process can take in order to complete successfully. Hence, each element in the sequence, called process stage, represents a state defined by a specific resource acquisition requirement. It follows that the detailed assumptions underlying the resource acquisition behavior give rise to RAS of different behavioral patterns and complexity [48]. The class of RAS that can be used as an effective model for the dynamics of multi-resource allocation from a set of multiple alternatives, has been characterized as CD (Conjunctive/Disjunctive)-RAS [14], which allows co-allocation of arbitrary units and types of resources (conjunctivity) as well as non-deterministic choice of resource allocations due to the existence of alternative resource sets (disjunctivity). Hence this RAS class can serve as a base model for analyzing the resource allocation behavior of the Internet computing.

Having discussed the importance of the RAS as a formal model for the application's behavior of multi-resource allocation in Internet computing, we proceed to identify relevant approaches for resolving deadlock problems in the considered problem context by reviewing various alternatives proposed in the literature. We focus on the deadlock problems in the distributed systems, and exclude any frameworks based on centralized algorithms such as Banker's [49] as they are not applicable to our problem context. In principle, there are two strategies for handling deadlocks in a distributed system, namely deadlock prevention/avoidance and deadlock detection and resolution [49]. The prevention/avoidance method guarantees that any process in the resource allocation system will never get into a deadlock state, whereas in the detection and resolution method, all resource requests are granted without checking any possibility of deadlock, and once a deadlock is detected, it is recovered by aborting one or more deadlocked processes. It is well known that the prevention scheme is more suitable for the situations in which deadlocks occur frequently, and resources are heavily utilized [50]. One of the major disadvantages of distributed deadlock detection and resolution is that a large amount of information must be exchanged between processes in order to detect and resolve deadlocks. It has been shown that the overhead of running deadlock detection algorithms when deadlocks do not exist is a substantial component of the total overhead and it tends to dominate the total overhead [51].

In order to address the characteristics of Internet computing mentioned in Section 16.1, the deadlock detection and recovery methods that require message passing among the applications for resolving resource deadlocks [15, 52] are not appropriate for our purpose. This is not only because the detection and resolution methods do not scale well to a very large number of resources and applications, but also because the applications in the considered problem context may not even know the existence of other applications that are sharing Internet resources with them if they are started and managed by different, independent organizations. For the same reason, the approaches that need a single central entity for deadlock management will not be satisfactory either. For instance, the widely used techniques for distributed deadlock prevention such as those based on the globally synchronized clock to provide a unique system wide process identifier [53] or the atomic multicast to provide a global order for the multicast messages [54], will hardly work in the Internet computing environment. As a consequence, we need a *decentralized deadlock prevention* approach that does not require communication between the applications to collect global or neighboring information.

We note that the deadlock could be prevented if we do not allow the applications to hold resources while they are waiting for other resources to become allocated. For instance, there will be no deadlock if each application repetitively multicasts its resource allocation requests until all the required resources are co-allocated simultaneously. However, livelock is inevitable in this case, and it will occur more frequently as the number of concurrently running applications and the number of resources co-allocated grow [55]. It is also well known that we can prevent the deadlock if we define a global linear ordering of all the resources and require each application to secure its resources one by one in increasing order according to this ordering [56]. We refer to this method as ODP^2 (Order-based Deadlock Prevention Protocol) in this chapter. An approach based on ODP^2 for co-allocating Grid resources is suggested in [11]. Although correct, ODP^2 does not provide an efficient solution to our problem. With ODP^2, applications are susceptible to long waits and congestion as reported in [32]. Furthermore, it fails to take into consideration the availability of alternative resource co-allocation schemes that are inherent in Internet computing.

Similar problems that address the deadlock prevention in distributed resource allocation have been considered in [57, 58]. However, the resource co-allocation problem considered herein is different from them in the following ways: First, in this chapter, Internet applications are assumed to be dynamically created and destroyed by independent users, and therefore the resource requirements of the applications are not known in advance. Second, as mentioned above, we're interested in the protocols that do not require communication between the applications. Finally, in contrast to the approaches in [57, 58], the variety of possible alternative co-allocation schemes needs to be considered and utilized to achieve fast resource allocation.

In the next section, we present a safety-based characterization of each application's resource allocation states only by use of application's local information, which provides the basis for the subsequent development of decentralized resource co-allocation protocol in Section 16.4.

16.3 Deadlock Analysis in Internet Resource Co-Allocation

As illustrated in the previous example in Section 16.1, the considered model of the multi-resource allocation in the Internet computing can be sequential. That is, we consider a general case in which applications may need to make more than one request to secure all the required resources. In fact, as indicated in [59], the popularity of hierarchical resource management architecture for resource acquisitions may enforce that even a single reservation may be subdivided and applied to multiple sequential resource allocations. Furthermore, we allow the non-deterministic choice among the possible resource allocation alternatives to model the existence of redundant or functionally equivalent resources on the Internet. Hence, the resulting model can be characterized as a sequential multi-resource allocation with choices.

We use the RAS abstraction to model the Internet resource co-allocation problem. We introduce a new class of RAS, to be called SD (Single-step Distributed)-RAS, which consists of a set of *Internet resource types*, $\mathcal{R} = \{R_1, \ldots, R_M\}$, with *finite capacity*, and a set of *Internet applications*, $\mathcal{A} = \{\alpha_1, \ldots, \alpha_N\}$, with respective *goal states*, denoted by $\mathcal{G}_{\alpha_k}$, $k = 1, \ldots, N$. It is not necessary to enumerate exact members in the sets of resources and applications as they will be dynamically changing. Furthermore, the capacity of a resource type may not be known to the applications and can possibly vary over time. Each resource type is assumed to be managed by an independent resource provider, requiring an application to make separate resource allocation requests to the corresponding resource providers when it needs to co-allocate more than one resource type. Specifically, an application uses two primitives, **request** and **cancel**, to request a positive amount of resources to be allocated to a remote resource provider, and to cancel the resources already allocated, respectively. We further assume that the message communication is reliable.

In the definition of SD-RAS, the goal states of each application specify the alternative resource co-allocation schemes available for applications. We refer to the number of resource types defined in a goal state as *co-allocation size*. The resource co-allocation requirement of an application can be satisfied if the resources defined in one of its goal states are successfully allocated. Once the resource allocation is complete, the allocated resources can be used for actual computation. For the sake of notational simplicity in the subsequent discussion, let α be an application in consideration. Upon creation, there is no resource allocated to α, and we denote this *initial state* by s_α^0. Subsequently, α may make a series of resource requests and/or cancellations until one of its goal states in $\mathcal{G}_\alpha$ is reached.

As a result, the resource allocation behavior of α in SD-RAS is defined as a finite state machine [42], $\mathcal{M}_\alpha$, which describes all the possible sequences of resource acquisitions α can take in order to fulfill its resource allocation requirement. Each state, s_α^i, $i = 0, 1, \ldots, L_\alpha$, in $\mathcal{M}_\alpha$ then represents a resource allocation state defined by a specific composition of allocated resources, where L_α is the number of states of $\mathcal{M}_\alpha$. Hence, it will be represented by use of a multiset notation, such as $s_\alpha^i = R_1 + 2R_2$, implying that one unit of resource type R_1 and two units of R_2 are co-allocated at state s_α^i. Furthermore, we use the notation $s_\alpha^i(R_j)$, $\forall R_j \in \mathcal{R}_\alpha$, to indicate how many units of resource type R_j are allocated at s_α^i, where $\mathcal{R}_\alpha$ is the set of resources that are elements of multisets in $\mathcal{G}_\alpha$. For example, if $\mathcal{G}_\alpha = \{2R_1 + R_3, 3R_2\}$, $\mathcal{R}_\alpha = \{R_1, R_2, R_3\}$. Note that it is not necessary for an

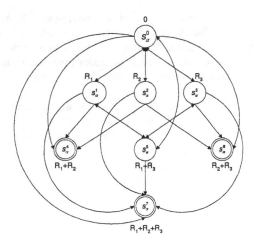

Figure 16.4: An example state trajectory for resource co-allocation.

application to reach exactly the same state as the one in the set of goal states in order to successfully co-allocate its required resources. As long as a state contains all the resources specified in some goal state, the state can be regarded as a goal state as well, since any surplus resources can be simply dropped out.

Example 1 Let us consider Internet application α that requires to co-allocate either $R_1 + R_2$ or $R_2 + R_3$. That is, $\mathcal{G}_\alpha = \{R_1 + R_2, R_2 + R_3\}$. The resulting finite state machine, $\mathcal{M}_\alpha$, is illustrated in Figure 16.4 where the goal states are depicted as double circles. As discussed above, the state $R_1 + R_2 + R_3$ is also a goal state, since R_1 or R_3 can be cancelled immediately after the co-allocation is complete. From s_α^0, there are several paths that can lead to the goal states. For example, if α requests one unit of R_1 and the result is successful, it will make a transition to state s_α^1. On the other hand, if α requests one unit of R_2 and one unit of R_3, but only the request for R_3 is granted, then this will result in state s_α^3. Hence, depending upon the resource availability and the specific resource allocation protocol used, α may need to go through the several resource allocation states until one of its co-allocation requirements is satisfied. Finally, note that all the transitions leading to the non-goal states are bi-directional, since α may de-allocate any of its currently allocated resources at any state. Therefore, the state machine is cyclic, which implies α may be involved in livelock without a proper resource allocation protocol. ⋄

As illustrated in Example 1, an application in SD-RAS may successfully co-allocate its required resources with a single step, which renders the name 'single-step'. Even in the case that an application needs to go through multiple states during its resource co-allocation process, it is not required for the application to take any specific sequence in order to reach a goal state. Hence, the underlying behavior of resource co-allocation in SD-RAS can be characterized as sequential resource allocation with choices. That is, SD-RAS takes into consideration the case in which (i) applications may need to make more than one state transition to secure all the required resources, and (ii) dynamic choice from the alternative resource co-allocation schemes is allowed.

Given the initial resource allocation state of an application and the set of its goal states, our objective is to develop a protocol that can ensure that every application can successfully co-allocate the resources specified by one of its goal states through a series of requests, while preventing the application from getting involved in deadlock or livelock during the allocation process. To this end, we use the idea of ordering resources. We assign an order, o_j, to each Internet resource, $R_j \in \mathcal{R}$, such that $\forall R_i, R_j \in \mathcal{R}$, $o_i \leq o_j$ or $o_i > o_j$. Since every Internet resource belongs to a networked host, an obvious total order of resources can be easily obtained from a lexicographical order induced by the unique identifier that is defined by concatenating resource's IP address with its unique local identifier.

From the example in Section 16.1, we have seen that some sequences of resource allocation may lead to a deadlock, and accordingly not every possible state of an application should be permitted in order to prevent the deadlock. For this purpose, we characterize an application's *local* resource allocation state as *safe* if it is possible for the application to successfully reach one of its goal states without getting into a deadlock, through further acquisition of resources from that state. Given application α, it is natural to assume that s_α^0 and all the states in $\mathcal{G}_\alpha$ are safe. The role of deadlock-free protocol is then to dictate the possible sequences of resource allocations for each application by deciding whether or not a specific local state is safe. As long as each application follows the sequence of safe states, the protocol will guarantee the eventuality of the resource allocation. Therefore, the problem of developing a deadlock-free resource co-allocation protocol essentially involves the safety test of local resource allocation states. The detail characterization of the state safety proposed in this chapter is given in the following definitions:

Definition 1. Let α be an Internet application in SD-RAS. A path of finite length in $\mathcal{M}_\alpha$, $< s_\alpha^{i_1}, \ldots, s_\alpha^{i_n} >$, such that $n > 1$ and $0 < i_l \leq L_\alpha, \forall l = 1, \ldots, n$, is said to be a *safe path* if (i) $s_\alpha^{i_n} \in \mathcal{G}_\alpha$, and (ii) $s_\alpha^{i_l}(R_j) \geq s_\alpha^{i_{l+1}}(R_j)$, $\forall l = 1, \ldots, n-1$, $\forall R_j \in \mathcal{R}_\alpha$ such that $o_j \geq \pi_\alpha^{i_l}$, where $\pi_\alpha^{i_l} = \min\{o_k \mid s_\alpha^{i_l}(R_k) > 0, R_k \in \mathcal{R}_\alpha\}$.

Definition 2. Given Internet application α of SD-RAS, its local resource allocation state, $s_\alpha^i \notin \mathcal{G}_\alpha$ such that $0 < i \leq L_\alpha$, is *safe* if there exists a safe path starting from s_α^i.

From the definition of the state safety and the structure of the underlying finite state machine representing the application's resource allocation behavior, we obtain the following proposition which lays a foundation for developing a scalable deadlock-free resource co-allocation protocol. A formal proof for this proposition is provided in [60].

Proposition 1. [60] For Internet application α of SD-RAS, its local resource allocation state, s_α^i, such that $0 < i \leq L_\alpha$ and $s_\alpha^i \notin \mathcal{G}_\alpha$, is *safe* if there exists a goal state $s_\alpha^j \in \mathcal{G}_\alpha$ such that $s_\alpha^i(R_k) \geq s_\alpha^j(R_k)$, $\forall R_k \in \mathcal{R}_\alpha$ satisfying $o_k \geq \pi_\alpha^i$.

Proposition 1 provides an effective and computationally efficient test of state safety. Essentially the safety characterization in Proposition 1 is based on the idea of ODP^2, since a resource cannot be allocated unless the resources of same or higher order are co-allocated. However, it effectively extends ODP^2 in the following ways: First, it can accommodate the resource co-allocation of arbitrary number of units from multiple resource types. Second, the availability of alternative resource co-allocation scheme is fully exploited since different goal states can be considered opportunistically during the resource co-allocation process. Finally, as will be shown in Section 16.4, it enables parallelization of resource requests to increase efficiency. We also remark that the test of state safety in Proposition 1 requires only the application's local information. Hence, it follows that the computational complexity of the test is invariant to the number of applications. The correctness of the safety characterization in Definition 2 is established in Section 16.4.

Example 2 To examine how the safety test works, let us consider Figure 16.2 again. From the definitions, $\mathcal{G}_{\alpha_1} = \{s_{\alpha_1}^g\}$ and $\mathcal{G}_{\alpha_2} = \{s_{\alpha_2}^g\}$ where $s_{\alpha_1}^g = 2R_1 + 3R_2$ and $s_{\alpha_2}^g = R_1 + 2R_2$. Suppose that the IP-based resource ordering results in $o_1 > o_2$. Starting from the initial state, application α_1's new state $s_{\alpha_1}^1 = 2R_1$ is safe, since there exists a goal state $s_{\alpha_1}^g$ that satisfies Proposition 1. Therefore such request is allowed. Note that, however, the request for 2 units of R_2 by α_2 is not allowed as it leads to state $s_{\alpha_2}^1 = 2R_2$, from which there is no goal state satisfying Proposition 1 (i.e., $\pi_{\alpha_2}^1 = o_2$, and for the goal state $s_{\alpha_2}^g$, the requirement that $s_{\alpha_2}^1(R_1) \geq s_{\alpha_2}^g(R_1)$ is violated.). The safety test mandates that α_2 should request R_1 or $R_1 + 2R_2$ first, but not $2R_2$, regardless of the behavior of α_1.

As another example, consider Figure 16.4 from Example 1, in which the application has more than one goal state. We arbitrarily assume $o_1 > o_3 > o_2$. It follows that state s_α^2 is not safe since there does not exist a goal state satisfying Proposition 1. For instance, for the goal state s_α^4 in Figure 16.4, we get $\pi_\alpha^2 = o_2$. That is, R_2 is the lowest ordered resource in s_α^2, and therefore it is required that $s_\alpha^2(R_1) \geq s_\alpha^4(R_1)$, $s_\alpha^2(R_2) \geq s_\alpha^4(R_2)$, and $s_\alpha^2(R_3) \geq s_\alpha^4(R_3)$, which, however, is not true due to the fact that $s_\alpha^2(R_1) = 0$ and $s_\alpha^4(R_1) = 1$. Note that the state machine is for illustration purpose only, and it does not have to be generated for testing the safety. $\diamond$

16.4 A Protocol for Deadlock and Livelock Free Internet Resource Co-Allocation

In this section, we present the main result of this chapter which is to be called ODP^3 *(Order-based Deadlock Prevention Protocol with Parallel requests)*. Based on the definition that the application's behavior in SD-RAS is represented as a finite state machine, an important question that must be addressed is how to select the next state. That is, at every state, if there is more than one next safe state to choose from, an application must make a choice so that the time to reach one of its goal states is minimized. This problem may be addressed by defining a value function and associating it with a resource allocation state to rank the next possible states. However, the evaluation of such a function will necessarily involve an identification of current state of Internet resources, which might result in a non-negligible overhead. Therefore, instead of taking a sequential approach to allocating resources, we adopt an idea that exploits parallelism.

As an example, let us consider Figure 16.4 again. At the initial state, the application may allocate either R_1 or R_3 depending on its choice. However, if we allow that resource allocation may be carried out concurrently, any parallel requests such as $R_1 \| R_2$[1] or $R_2 \| R_3$ can be made simultaneously through a multicast. In the extreme case, the application at its initial state might attempt to co-allocate all the resources defined in the goal states, which is $R_1 \| R_2 \| R_3$ in this particular example. Although this approach has a potential to reduce the time for resource co-allocation, one can identify a major drawback of this approach: The result of the individual resource allocation request will be a success or failure depending on the current availability of the resource. As a result, the probability of successful co-allocation with a single multicast will be decreasing as the size of parallel requests increases, and in general there is no guarantee that the required resources be co-allocated eventually.

Motivated by this, the proposed protocol seeks to take the best of both worlds: It takes advantage of concurrency by maximizing the number of parallel requests at every resource allocation state while ensuring to make a strict progress towards the application's goal states through gradually expanding the set of allocated resources. More specifically, given Internet application α, let $\mathcal{G}_\alpha = \{G_\alpha^1, G_\alpha^2, \ldots, G_\alpha^{n_\alpha}\}$ be the set of goal states of α and also let $\mathcal{R}_\alpha = \{R_1, R_2, \ldots, R_{m_\alpha}\}$ be the set of resource types defined in the multisets in $\mathcal{G}_\alpha$. For multiset S defined on $\{R_1, R_2, \ldots, R_{m_\alpha}\}$, we use the notation $S(R_i)$ to represent the number of occurrences of R_i in S, $i = 1, \ldots, m_\alpha$, and $\#(S)$ to represent the number of elements in S. That is, if $S = 3R_1 + 2R_2$, $S(R_1) = 3$, $S(R_2) = 2$, and $\#(S) = 5$. Furthermore, given two multisets, S_1 and S_2 defined on $\{R_1, R_2, \ldots, R_{m_\alpha}\}$, we define their union $S^+ = S_1 \uplus S_2$, and difference $S^- = S_1 \setminus S_2$ as follows:

$$S^+(R_i) = \begin{cases} \max\{S_1(R_i), S_2(R_i)\} & \text{if } R_i \in S_1 \text{ or } R_i \in S_2 \\ 0 & \text{otherwise} \end{cases}, i = 1, \ldots, m_\alpha$$

(16.1)

$$S^-(R_i) = \begin{cases} \max\{\{S_1(R_i) - S_2(R_i)\}, 0\} & \text{if } R_i \in S_1 \\ 0 & \text{otherwise} \end{cases}, i = 1, \ldots, m_\alpha \quad (16.2)$$

---

[1] $R_1 \| R_2$ represents that the application multicasts its requests in parallel to the respective resource providers managing R_1 and R_2.

For instance, if $S_1 = 3R_1 + 2R_2$ and $S_2 = 4R_2 + R_3$, then $S_1 \uplus S_2 = 3R_1 + 4R_2 + R_3$ and $S_1 \setminus S_2 = 3R_1$. Finally, multiset S_1 is said to *cover* S_2 if $S_2 \setminus S_1 = \emptyset$.

ODP^3 takes an optimistic approach, and it requires application α to start by multicasting parallel requests for all the resources and their respective allocation amount defined in $G_\alpha^+ = \uplus_{i=1}^{n_\alpha} G_\alpha^i$. We let Q_α be the multiset that maintains the resource types successfully allocated so far, and their respective allocation amount. Initially it is set to an empty set. After the results of the multicast of requests for resources are received, the resources that are successfully allocated are temporarily recorded in a multiset T_α. If any goal state in $\mathcal{G}_\alpha$ can be covered by the allocated resources in $Q_\alpha \uplus T_\alpha$, the procedure terminates. This can be tested by identifying if there exists $G_\alpha^i, i = 1, \ldots, n_\alpha$ such that $G_\alpha^i \setminus (Q_\alpha \uplus T_\alpha) = \emptyset$.

Otherwise, ODP^3 makes a progress toward the goal states by retaining some of the allocated resources according to the safety of the state represented by $Q_\alpha \uplus T_\alpha$. When $Q_\alpha \uplus T_\alpha$ is safe according to Proposition 1, it keeps all the resources defined in $Q_\alpha \uplus T_\alpha$, and advances the application's current resource allocation state Q_α to $Q_\alpha \uplus T_\alpha$. On the other hand, if $Q_\alpha \uplus T_\alpha$ is not safe, it is necessary to drop out some of the resources in T_α to make the state safe. It is interesting to note that α can always go back to a safe state by releasing all the resources in T_α. However, in order to achieve the livelock freedom, ODP^3 seeks to drop out as few resources as possible while it ensures the safety of the resulting state. For this purpose, we define *distance*, $d(Q_\alpha')$, of α's resource allocation state $Q_\alpha'(\subset Q_\alpha \uplus T_\alpha)$ with respect to $\mathcal{G}_\alpha$ as follows:

$$d(Q_\alpha') = \frac{\#(\uplus_{i=1}^{n_\alpha}(G_\alpha^i \setminus Q_\alpha'))}{n_\alpha} \tag{16.3}$$

The distance characterizes how far an application's resource allocation state is from its goal states on the average, and any two subsets of $Q_\alpha \uplus T_\alpha$ can be compared according to it. Therefore, the objective is to construct the subset Q_α^* of $Q_\alpha \uplus T_\alpha$ in such a way that Q_α^* is safe and minimizes the distance among all the proper subsets of $Q_\alpha \uplus T_\alpha$. Furthermore we require that $Q_\alpha \subseteq Q_\alpha^*$ to prevent livelock. Once Q_α^* is computed, the next step is to cancel all the surplus resources in T_α that are not selected in Q_α^*, and then set Q_α to Q_α^*. Subsequently, the procedure repeats for the remaining resources defined by $G_\alpha^+ \setminus Q_\alpha$ until one of the goal states in $\mathcal{G}_\alpha$ is reached. The pseudo code of the protocol for application α is summarized in Figure 16.5.

We note that the application's waiting time to receive all the responses to the multicast requests will be increasing as the number of concurrent requests increases, since the waiting time is equal to the maximum delay among the replies. This can be problematic when some resource providers undergo transient breakdown, resulting in no response for the requests for a long time. Hence, in practice, a timeout mechanism can be employed when constructing set T_α. Under the assumption that communication is reliable, a well-defined upperbound estimate for round-trip time (RTT) [61] will be useful for designing such a mechanism.

DONE $\leftarrow$ false; $Q_\alpha \leftarrow \emptyset$
while (!DONE) do
    $T_\alpha \leftarrow$ request $G_\alpha^+ \setminus Q_\alpha$
    if ($Q_\alpha \uplus T_\alpha$ can cover some state in $\mathcal{G}_\alpha$) then
        cancel $Q_\alpha \uplus T_\alpha \setminus G_\alpha^i$
        DONE $\leftarrow$ true
    else
        if (!safe($Q_\alpha \uplus T_\alpha$)) then
            compute Q_α^*
            cancel $T_\alpha \setminus Q_\alpha^*$
            $Q_\alpha \leftarrow Q_\alpha^*$
        else
            $Q_\alpha \leftarrow Q_\alpha \uplus T_\alpha$
endwhile

Figure 16.5: Order-based Deadlock Prevention Protocol with Parallel requests (ODP^3).

Example 3 Let us consider Internet application α with $\mathcal{G}_\alpha = \{G_\alpha^1, G_\alpha^2, G_\alpha^3\}$, where $G_\alpha^1 = 2R_1 + 2R_2$, $G_\alpha^2 = R_1 + 3R_3$, and $G_\alpha^3 = 3R_2 + 2R_4$. We arbitrarily assume $o_1 < o_2 < o_3 < o_4$. Q_α is initially set to $\emptyset$. According to ODP^3, α starts by multicasting the requests for the resources defined in $G_\alpha^+ = 2R_1 + 3R_2 + 3R_3 + 2R_4$. Suppose that only $T_\alpha = R_1 + 2R_2 + 2R_3 + 2R_4$ resources are allocated successfully as a result of multicasting the requests for G_α^+. Since there is no $G_\alpha^i, i = 1, 2, 3$ that satisfies $G_\alpha^i \setminus (Q_\alpha \uplus T_\alpha) = \emptyset$, and $Q_\alpha \uplus T_\alpha$ is not a safe state, the application needs to compute a safe state represented as $Q_\alpha^* (\subset Q_\alpha \uplus T_\alpha)$ that minimizes $d()$. Since the size of $Q_\alpha \uplus T_\alpha$ is small, we use an exhaustive search by testing the safety of all subsets of $Q_\alpha \uplus T_\alpha$, and we obtain the unique $Q_\alpha^* = 2R_2 + 2R_3 + 2R_4$, where $d(Q_\alpha^*) = \frac{2+2+1}{3} = \frac{5}{3}$. Consequently, α cancels the allocation of one unit of R_1, and Q_α is now set to Q_α^*. The process repeats subsequently. $\diamond$

Next, we establish the correctness of the proposed ODP^3 by showing that the Internet applications will be free from livelock and deadlock if they co-allocate the resources according to ODP^3. The starting point for the proof is the observation that when the Internet applications follow ODP^3, their resulting individual resource allocation behavior is restricted to an *acyclic* finite state machine with the property that the resource allocation amount is monotonically increasing in every path of the machine. We state this formally in the following proposition, proven in [60].

Proposition 2. [60] Consider an SD-RAS defined by $\mathcal{R}$ and $\mathcal{A}$ in which Internet applications co-allocate resources according to ODP^3. Let $\mathcal{M}_\alpha$ be the finite state machine that represents the resource allocation behavior of α ($\in \mathcal{A}$) under ODP^3. Then there does not exist a cycle in $\mathcal{M}_\alpha$. Furthermore, $s_\alpha^i(R_k) \leq s_\alpha^j(R_k), \forall R_k \in \mathcal{R}_\alpha, \forall i, j \ (i \neq j)$ such that $< s_\alpha^i, s_\alpha^j >$ is a direct path in $\mathcal{M}_\alpha$ and $o \leq i, j \leq L_\alpha$.

Since the existence of a cycle in the finite state machine representing an application's resource allocation behavior is a necessary condition for the livelock, we obtain the following result.

Theorem 1. The Internet applications that implement ODP^3 are free from livelock.

Therefore, given the set of Internet applications $\mathcal{A}$ of an SD-RAS, when the applications are controlled by ODP^3, they define a sub-class of SD-RAS, to be called MSD (Monotone, Single-step Distributed)-RAS, in which $\forall \alpha \in \mathcal{A}$, $\mathcal{M}_\alpha$ is restricted to an acyclic finite state machine and the resource allocation amount is subject to monotonically increasing along every path in $\mathcal{M}_\alpha$. Indeed it is easy to see that the class of MSD-RAS is a special case of the CD-RAS class, since, in CD-RAS, each application is associated with a predefined acyclic finite state machine that dictates all the possible sequences of resource acquisitions that the application can take for its successful completion. Accordingly, the subsumption relationship between two RAS classes follows from the fact that the resource allocation behavior of an application in MSD-RAS can be represented as an acyclic finite state machine.

Based on the fact that MSD-RAS is a special case of CD-RAS, in Proposition 3, we first give a formal characterization of deadlocks in MSD-RAS that can arise during the resource allocation of Internet applications implementing ODP^3. Proposition 3 is originally proved for the CD-RAS in [14] by means of Petri net, and it is an interpretation of the result in terms of the resource allocation in MSD-RAS. From Proposition 3, it follows that no further resource allocation is possible for all applications involved in a deadlock in MSD-RAS. Subsequently, we present a well-known result [52] that a cycle in RAG is a necessary condition for deadlocks in the resource allocation systems characterized as a CD-RAS. Hence, in Proposition 4, the result is stated in terms of MSD-RAS. Finally, the deadlock freedom of the applications that implement ODP^3 is stated in Theorem 2 of which the proof is provided in [60] by use of Proposition 3 and Proposition 4. Therefore, the correctness of ODP^3 follows from Theorem 1 and Theorem 2.

Proposition 3. Suppose that there exists a deadlock in MSD-RAS consisting of $\mathcal{R}$ and $\mathcal{A}$. Then, there exists a finite set of applications, $A \subseteq \mathcal{A}$ such that $\forall \alpha_i \in A$, α_i is permanently blocked due to the fact that any additional resource required for α_i to make further resource allocation is currently held by some $\alpha_j \in A$ such that $j \neq i$.

Proposition 4. Consider an MSD-RAS consisting of $\mathcal{R}$ and $\mathcal{A}$. Let s be a global resource allocation state of the MSD-RAS that is defined by the set $\{s_{\alpha_1}, \ldots, s_{\alpha_N}\}$. If there exists a set of deadlocked applications $A \subseteq \mathcal{A}$ at s, then (i) there exists a simple cycle $\mathcal{C}$ in the RAG representing s, and (ii) $\forall R_j \in \mathcal{R}_\mathcal{C}$, there is $\alpha_i \in A$ such that $s_{\alpha_i}(R_j) > 0$, where $\mathcal{R}_\mathcal{C}$ is the set of resource types contained in $\mathcal{C}$.

Theorem 2. [60] The Internet applications that implement ODP^3 are free from deadlock.

16.5   Experimental Results

In this section, we demonstrate the performance of ODP^3 by comparing it with ODP^2 introduced in Section 16.2.2. Two minor modifications are made to ODP^2 to address the problem characteristics considered in this chapter: First, when there is more than one goal state, ODP^2 selects one of them randomly. Second, application α under ODP^2 may hold the resources of type $R_j \in \mathcal{R}_\alpha$ only if the allocated amount of type R_j is greater than or equal to the required amount specified in the selected goal state.

We have implemented a simulation platform, named High-Performance Distributed Resource Allocation Simulator (HiDRAS), that can evaluate the performance of various protocols for distributed resource allocation. By use of HiDRAS, we can configure an RAS in terms of various parameters including the number of resource types along with their capacity, the maximum number of resource types and the amount of resources that each application may require, the resource usage time distribution, the applications' inter-arrival time distribution, and the maximum number of co-allocation schemes allowed for each application.

Another important parameter in the implementation of ODP^3 that can influence the performance of the protocol is the time between two successive multicasts when an application fails to co-allocate the resources that constitute one of its goal states. Obviously too sporadic retrials will result in increased waiting time of applications and low resource utilization. On the other hand, too frequent retrials will lead to a large volume of message communication between the applications and resource providers as well as increased resource contention, which in turn may lower the possibility of successful resource co-allocation. Hence, a trade-off must be considered when the retrial period is to be determined. A possible solution to this problem is to use a contention resolution mechanism such as backoff protocol [62], and we adopt a simple backoff function for the purpose of performance comparison. The actual determination of an optimal backoff function will depend upon the nature of Internet applications and resource providers as well as the characteristics of resource acquisition patterns, and is beyond the scope of this chapter.

We compare ODP^3 with ODP^2 for the case in which grid applications compete for the 10 different resource types that are geographically distributed. For each simulation run, the maximum capacity of each resource type is set to 20, the maximum possible co-allocation size for each application is 5, and the resource usage time is chosen to be a random value between 10 and 1000 seconds to reflect the diversity of grid applications. For our experiments, we assume that the delay for one way message delivery follows a uniform distribution with parameters $\frac{\overline{RTT}}{20}$ and $\frac{\overline{RTT}}{2}$, where $\overline{RTT}$ represents the estimated RTT upperbound for which we choose 2 seconds. We employ a uniform backoff function that determines the inter-retrial times to be $\delta \times \overline{RTT}$, where δ is a random sample from a uniform distribution with parameters 1 and 10. The same backoff function is used for ODP^2 and ODP^3.

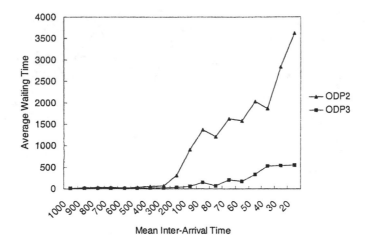

Figure 16.6: The impact of the inter-arrival time on the average waiting time.

We first experimentally compare ODP^3 with ODP^2 by examining the effect of varying the applications' arrival rates on the average waiting time. The waiting time of an application is measured by the time between its arrival and successful resource co-allocation. We used an exponential distribution to simulate the inter-arrival times of applications, and varied the mean inter-arrival time from 1000 to 20 seconds. The simulations were done 100 times for each case. In this experimentation, each application was allowed to have up to 5 different alternative co-allocation schemes. Figure 16.6 shows the average waiting time results obtained for ODP^2 and ODP^3. Comparing the plots in Figure 16.6 indicates that there is not much difference in the performance when the arrival rate is low since applications can easily find idle resources upon creation. However, ODP^3 achieves a significant improvement over ODP^2 when the contention for resources is not negligible. It is also interesting to note that the average waiting time of ODP^2 blows up quite quickly as the arrival rate increases.

Next, in order to investigate the effect of the available alternative co-allocation schemes, we conducted experiments in which the mean inter-arrival time was chosen to be 100 and the maximum number of co-allocation schemes allowed for each application was varied from 1 to 10. Figure 16.7 compares the average waiting time results for ODP^2 and ODP^3 for this experimentation. As the number of alternative co-allocation schemes increases, the average waiting time of ODP^3 decreases accordingly, while ODP^2 does not appear to benefit from this flexibility. The result indicates that ODP^3 performs significantly better than ODP^2 when there are available alternative co-allocation schemes, able to successfully utilize

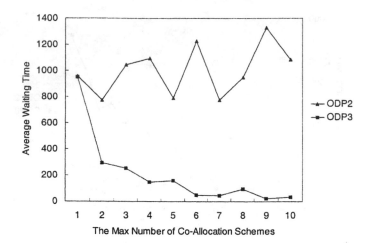

Figure 16.7: The impact of the number of co-allocation schemes on the average waiting time.

the flexibility of Internet resource allocation.

Finally, the effect of the co-allocation size on the average waiting time was examined through the experiments in which inter-arrival time was fixed to 100 and the maximum allowed co-allocation size for each application was changed from 1 to 8. The resulting performance is shown in Figure 16.8. As expected, the increased co-allocation size of applications leads to increased contention among applications for both protocols. However, the plots in Figure 16.8 show that the performance of ODP^3 is much less sensitive to the increase in the co-allocation size than that of ODP^2.

16.6   Discussion

This chapter provided a quick overview of resource allocation problems in Internet computing, and presented a scalable, decentralized resource co-allocation protocol that can facilitate the dependable deployment of Internet applications. The proposed protocol, named ODP^3, ensures deadlock and livelock freedom during the resource co-allocation process, while at the same time it takes advantage of parallelism in making resource allocation requests in order to achieve increased efficiency. Since each Internet application embedding ODP^3 only needs to use its own local information for the resource co-allocation to be deadlock and livelock free, it is expected that the proposed protocol can be effectively used when a large

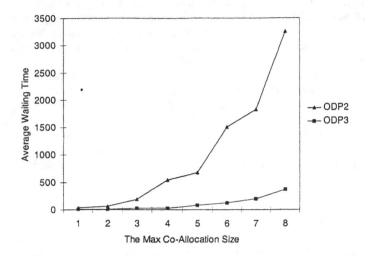

Figure 16.8: The impact of the co-allocation size on the average waiting time.

number of multi-resources are co-allocated across the independent, multiple resource management systems. Our experimental evaluation showed that (i) ODP^3 yields a significant improvement over the existing deadlock prevention protocol when the resource contention is not negligible, and (ii) it successfully utilizes the available alternative resource co-allocation schemes to increase performance.

Future research can be pursued along the various lines of directions for further enhancing the performance of ODP^3. First, an in-depth investigation is necessary to obtain an efficient backoff protocol to adaptively determine inter-retrial times of ODP^3 through conducting extensive simulation experiments. Second, assessing the impact of resource ordering on the applications' execution priority is an interesting separate research topic. Without the alternative resource co-allocation schemes, applications requiring most of their resources from high ordered resources are likely to have lower priority due to the increased contention for the high ordered resources. However, when there are available alternative co-allocation schemes, such limitation can be overcome since the resource orders for an application are more likely to be evenly distributed. Although ODP^3 takes advantage of the availability of alternative schemes as demonstrated in this chapter, we remark that the IP-based ordering scheme suggested in this chapter is just one possibility. Therefore, in some cases, the resource ordering itself can be assigned carefully to evenly distribute the orders. For instance, when there are two resource types, R_1 and R_2, that are equivalent, one can define an orthogonal ordering scheme such that o_1 becomes the lowest ordered resource and o_2 becomes the highest one.

Third, we remark that it is not possible to effectively enforce the priority of applications using ODP^3. ODP^3 is proposed for preventing deadlock and livelock. Nevertheless, by assigning appropriate resource ordering, we can increase the chance of realizing the given priority. For instance, if application α requires $R_1 + R_2$ and another application β requires $R_1 + R_3$, one can assign an order, $o_3 > o_1 > o_2$, so that α can allocate R_1 as soon as it becomes available whereas β is required to allocate R_3 before R_1. Under the assumption that all three resources are busy with the same probability, α will have a higher chance to be executed first.

Finally, another future work can be identified along the line of increasing the flexibility of the protocol through strengthening the safety test. Given two deadlock-free protocols, $\mathcal{P}_1$ and $\mathcal{P}_2$, $\mathcal{P}_1$ is said to be more flexible than $\mathcal{P}_2$ if all the safe states admitted by $\mathcal{P}_2$ are also admitted by $\mathcal{P}_1$ for all applications, and there are some states admitted by $\mathcal{P}_1$ that are not admitted by $\mathcal{P}_2$ for some applications. The key observation is that the safety test in Definition 2 is only a sufficient condition, and therefore there is a possibility to design other correct protocols that are based on different sufficient conditions for the safety. In some cases, the sets of admitted safe states may be different, and it is not possible to directly compare the flexibility of two different safety tests. Nevertheless, we can still obtain a more flexible protocol by use of the disjunction of results from the different safety tests. More specifically, it is established in [14] that, given multiple different, correct safety tests, a resource allocation state is safe if there exists a test of which the test result for the state is safe. Therefore, as we develop more and more correct safety tests, we will be able to obtain a more efficient resource allocation protocol.

Bibliography

[1] I. Foster and C. Kesselman. *The Grid: Blueprint for a New Computing Infrastructure*. Morgan Kaufman, 1998.

[2] G. Allen, T. Dramlitsch, I. Foster, N. Karonis, M. Ripeanu, E. Seidel, and B. Toonen. Supporting efficient execution in heterogeneous distributed computing environments with cactus and globus. In *Proceedings of the Supercomputing (SC-2001)*, 2001.

[3] D. Barkai. *Peer-To-Peer Computing: Technologies for Sharing and Collaborating on the Net*. Intel Press, 2001.

[4] C. McFall. An object infrastructure for internet middleware. *IEEE Internet Computing*, pages 46–51, March/April 1998.

[5] G. Cabri, L. Leonardi, and F. Zambonelli. Mobile-agent coordination models for internet applications. *IEEE Computer*, pages 82–89, Feb. 2000.

[6] I. Foster, C. Kesselman, and S. Tuecke. The anatomy of the grid: Enabling scalable virtual organizations. *International Journal of Supercomputer Applications*, 15(3), 2001.

[7] E. Newcomer. *Understanding Web Services*. Addison-Wesley, 2002.

[8] B. Meyer. .Net is coming. *IEEE Computer*, 34(8):92–97, 2001.

[9] J. B. Weissman and B-D. Lee. The service grid: Supporting scalable heterogeneous services in wide-area networks. In *Proceedings of the 2001 Symposium on Applications and the Internet (SAINT 2001)*, 2001.

[10] K. Czajkowski, I. Foster, N. Karonis, C. Kesselman, S. Martin, W. Smith, and S. Tuecke. A resource management architecture for metacomputing systems. In *Proceedings of the IPPS/SPDP '98 Workshop on Job Scheduling Strategies for Parallel Processing*, pages 62–82, 1998.

[11] I. Foster, C. Kesselman, C. Lee, B. Lindell, K. Nahrstedt, and A. Roy. A distributed resource management architecture that supports advance reservations and co-allocation. In *Proceedings of the International Workshop on Quality of Service*, 1999.

[12] K. Czajkowski, I. Foster, and C. Kesselman. Resource co-allocation in computational grids. In *Proceedings of the Eighth IEEE International Symposium on High Performance Distributed Computing (HPDC-8)*, pages 219–228, 1999.

[13] F. Berman, A. Chien, K. Cooper, J. Dongarra, I. Foster, L. Johnsson D. Gannon, K. Kennedy, C. Kesselman, J. Mellor-Crummey, D. Reed, L. Torczon, and R. Wolski. The GrADS project: Software support for high-level grid application development. *International Journal of High Performance Computing Applications*, 15(4):327–344, 2001.

[14] J. Park and S. Reveliotis. Deadlock avoidance in sequential resource allocation systems with multiple resource acquisitions and flexible routings. *IEEE Transactions on Automatic Control*, 46(10):1572–1583, 2001.

[15] M. Singhal. Deadlock detection in distributed systems. *IEEE Computer*, pages 37–48, November 1989.

[16] R. Bramley, K. Chiu, S. Diwan, D. Gannon, M. Govindaraju, N. Mukhi, B. Temko, and M. Yechuri. A component based services architecture for building distributed applications. In *Proceedings of the 9th IEEE International Symposium on High Performance Distributed Computing*, 2000.

[17] C. Vawter and E. Roman. J2EE vs. microsoft .NET: A comparison of building XML-based web services. Technical report, Sun Microsystems Inc., 2001.

[18] F. Manola. Technologies for a web object model. *IEEE Internet Computing*, pages 38–47, January/February 1999.

[19] W. Smith, D. Gunter, and D. Quesnel. A simple XML producer-consumer protocol. Technical Report GWD-Perf-8-2, Performance Working Group, Grid Working Document, 2001.

[20] J. B. Weissman. Scheduling multi-component applications in heterogeneous wide-area networks. In *Proceedings of the International Parallel and Distributed Processing Symposium (IPDPS)*, 2000.

[21] A. S. Grimshaw, W. A. Wulf, and the Legion team. The legion vision of a worldwide virtual computer. *Communications of the ACM*, 40(1):39–45, 1997.

[22] W. Hoschek, J. Jean-Martinez, A. Samar, H. Stockinger, and K. Stockinger. "data management in an international data grid project. In *Proceedings of the 1st IEEE/ACM International Workshop on Grid Computing*, 2000.

[23] T. Tannenbaum and M. Litzkow. The condor distributed processing system. *Dr. Dobbs Journal*, Feb. 1995.

[24] SETI@home. Search for extraterrestrial intelligence at home. http://setiathome.ssl.berkeley.edu/, 2002.

[25] S. J. Wright. Solving optimization problems on computational grids. Technical report, Argonne National Lab., 2000.

[26] H. Casanova and J. Dongarra. Netsolve: A network server for solving computational science problems. *International Journal of Supercomputer Applications and High Performance Computing*, 11(3):212–223, 1997.

[27] K. Krauter, R. Buyya, and M. Maheswaran. A taxonomy and survey of grid resource management systems. Technical Report TR-2000/18, University of Manitoba, 2000.

[28] F. Berman and R. Wolski. The apples project: A status report. In *Proceedings of the 8th NEC Research Symposium*, 1997.

[29] J. Frey, I. Foster, M. Livny, T. Tanenbaum, and S. Tuecke. Condor-g: A computation management agent for multi-institutional grids. Technical report, University of Wisconsin Madison, 2001.

[30] W. K. Edwards. *Core Jini*. Prentice Hall, 2nd edition, 2001.

[31] R. Ben-Naten. *CORBA: A Guide to the Common Object Request Broker Architecture*. McGraw Hill, 1995.

[32] K. M. Chandy. Caltech infospheres project overview: Information infrastructures for task forces. Technical report, California Institute of Technology, 1996.

[33] R. von Behren S. D. Gribble, M. Welsh. The Ninja architecture for robust internet-scale systems and services. *Computer Networks*, 35(4):473–497, 2001.

[34] D. Wong, N. Paciorek, and D. Moore. Java-based mobile agents. *Communications of the ACM*, 42(3), 1999.

[35] A. Omicini, F. Zambonelli, M. Klusch, and R. Tolksdorf, editors. *Coordination of Internet Agents: Models, Technologies, and Applications*. Springer, 2001.

[36] G. T. Heineman and W. T. Councill. *Component-Based Software Engineering*. Addison-Wesley, 2001.

[37] N. Sato, S. Saito, and K. Mitsui. Optimizing composite web services through parallelization of service invocations. In *Proceedings of the 6th International Enterprise Distributed Object Computing Conference*. IEEE, 2002.

[38] J. Yang and M. Papazoglou. Web component: A substrate for Web service reuse and composition. In *Proceedings of the International Conference on Advanced Information Systems Engineering (CAISE)*, 2002.

[39] D. A. Menascé. QoS issues in Web services. *IEEE Internet Computing*, pages 72–75, November/December 2002.

[40] S. A. Reveliotis, M. A. Lawley, and P. M. Ferreira. Polynomial complexity deadlock avoidance policies for sequential resource allocation systems. *IEEE Transactions on Automatic Control*, 42(10):1344–1357, 1997.

[41] J. Park and S. Reveliotis. Algebraic synthesis of efficient deadlock avoidance policies for sequential resource allocation systems. *IEEE Transactions on Robotics & Automation*, 16(2):190–195, 2000.

[42] D. C. Kozen. *Automata and Computability*. Springer Verlag, 1997.

[43] W. Reisig. *Petri Nets: An Introduction*. Springer-Verlag, 1985.

[44] F. Tricas, F. García-Vallés, J. M. Colom, and J. Ezpeleta. A structural approach to the problem of deadlock prevention in processes with resources. In *Proceedings of the 4th Workshop on Discrete Event Systems*, pages 273–278. IEE, 1998.

[45] J. O. Moody and P. J. Antsaklis. *Supervisory Control of Discrete Event Systems Using Petri Nets*. Kluwer Academic Publishers, 1998.

[46] A. D. Kshemkalyani and M. Singhal. Efficient detection and resolution of generalized distributed deadlocks. *IEEE Transactions on Software Engineering*, 20(1):43–54, 1994.

[47] J. R. G. de Mendívil, F. Fariña, J. R. Garitagoitia, and J. M. Bernabeu-Auban. A distributed deadlock resolution algorithm for the AND model. *IEEE Transactions on Parallel and Distributed Systems*, 10(5):433–447, 1999.

[48] J. Park and S. Reveliotis. Algebraic deadlock avoidance policies for conjunctive/disjunctive resource allocation systems. In *Proceedings of the IEEE International Conference on Robotics & Automation*, 2001.

[49] A. Silberschatz, P. Galvin, and G. Gagne. *Operating System Concepts*. John Wiley & Sons, 6th edition, 2001.

[50] S. S. Isloor and T. A. Marsland. The deadlock problem: An overview. *IEEE Computer*, 13:58–78, Sept. 1980.

[51] A. N. Choudhary. Cost of deadlock detection: A performance study. In *Proceedings of the IEEE Conference on Data Engineering*, 1990.

[52] A. D. Kshemkalyani and M. Singhal. Distributed detection of generalized deadlocks. In *Proceedings of the International Conference on Distributed Computing Systems*, 1997.

[53] F. Cristian. Probabilistic clock synchronization. *Distributed Computing*, 3:146–158, 1989.

[54] H. Garcia-Molina and A. Spauster. Ordered and reliable multicast communication. *ACM Transactions on Computer Systems*, 9(3):242–271, 1991.

[55] J. Jardine, Q. Snell, and M. Clement. Livelock avoidance for meta-schedulers. In *Proceedings of the 10th IEEE International Symposium on High Performance Distributed Computing*, 2001.

[56] M. Singhal and N. G. Shivaratri. *Advanced Concepts in Operating Systems: Distributed, Database, and Multiprocessor Operating Systems*. McGraw-Hill, 1994.

[57] N. A. Lynch. Upper bounds for static resource allocation in a distributed system. *Journal of Computer and System Sciences*, 23:254–278, 1981.

[58] I. Page, T. Jacob, and E. Chern. Fast algorithms for distributed resource allocation. *IEEE Transactions on Parallel and Distributed Systems*, 4(2):188–197, 1993.

[59] K. Czajkowski and V. Sander. Grid resource management protocol: Requirements. Technical Report SchedWD 12.1, GGF Scheduling Working Group, 2001.

[60] J. Park. A deadlock and livelock free protocol for decentralized internet resource co-allocation. *IEEE Transactions on Systems, Man, & Cybernetics*, 34(1):123 – 131, 2004.

[61] P. Karn and C. Partridge. Improving round-trip time estimates in reliable transport protocols. *ACM SIGCOMM Computer Communication Review*, 17(5):2–7, 1987.

[62] L. A. Goldberg and P. D. MacKenzie. Analysis of practical backoff protocols for contention resolution with multiple servers. In *Proceedings of the 7th Annual Symp. on Discrete Algorithms*, pages 554–563, 1996.

17

Models Used in Static Analysis for Deadlocks of Ada Tasking Programs

Mikko Tiusanen
Tampere University of Technology, Tampere, Finland.

Tadao Murata
University of Illinois at Chicago, IL, USA.

The advanced features of the programming language Ada at the time of its introduction included its tasking constructs. These gave software engineers the opportunity to structure a program into communicating entities, each of which has an independent thread of control. Together with this ability came the responsibility of avoiding tasking-related errors such as deadlocks. A specific problem in this case is coping with the nondeterminism introduced by the Ada tasking constructs. One of the suggested solutions to help meet this responsibility was to apply a suitable *static analysis* to the Ada tasking programs.

Static analysis of software aims at detecting erroneous or unwanted behavioral properties based on the *description* of the software, as opposed to the *execution* of it. Static analysis differs from simulation and testing in that it tries to explore the behavior of the system by analyzing whether some hazardous constructs or combinations of these are included, instead of comparing the runs of the system to the expected behavior. Rather than stating that an error was (not) found, it tries to state that evidence of an error is (not) present. This difference is not entirely clear cut, however, since some of the methods for static analysis do entail at least a kind of execution. *Symbolic execution* and *state space generation* are two examples of these borderline cases. The relative strength of the statements on errors depends strongly on the actual methods employed, both for analysis and for testing.

The typical static analysis techniques consist of some or all of the following steps:

- **Abstraction:** The software is scanned to extract features relevant to the particular kind of analysis. That is, a *model* enabling the further analysis is built of the software.
- **Preparation:** The model is preprocessed to be more usable during the actual analysis.
- **Analysis:** Some characteristics of the behavior of the model are extracted and demonstrated. In order for the analysis to be more efficient (focused), the characteristics of interest might be given prior to analysis. In some cases the characteristics to be verified are built into the analysis method by having each analysis tool only seek these specific ones.
- **Verification:** The characteristics of the model are related to those of the original software. The question here is whether the characteristics found are those of the original software, or only those of the model built.

Taylor [1] initiated the research on static analysis of Ada tasking programs, which has since then grown considerably, e.g., [2–10]. Most of the approaches use a form of *state space generation*, also called reachability analysis or exhaustive simulation, as a method of analysis. Very simply, the possible future behavior of the model, its state space, is made explicit. The explicit representation usually takes the form of a graph that has the set of possibly reachable states as nodes and an arc between two states when the other can be reached from the first without other intervening reachable states. The graph is sometimes called a *reachability graph* since a state of the model is reachable exactly when there is a directed path in the reachability graph to that state. The graph is then subjected to inspection or queries, e.g., formulae in Linear Temporal Logic, LTL [11], or Computation Tree Logic, CTL [12], that express that the graph exhibits a desired or undesired property. Deciding whether a formula is true or not of the reachability graph is called *model checking*, since if the formula is true, the graph is a model for the formula, see [13, p.48].

The attractiveness of the reachability graph generation lies in that it is a relatively complete characterization of the behavior of the model as long as the state space is finite. Therefore, many of the interesting questions about the behavior can be decided based on the graph. The practical difficulty involved, however, is that the state space of the model, even if finite, can be huge, much larger than can be generated in a reasonable time. A theoretical problem is that a program can conceivably have an infinite number of reachable states, which makes the reachability analysis inapplicable.

As we will see in Section 17.1, the latter problem can be solved with the age-old method of *abstracting from*, that is, ignoring, some aspects of the program when building the model.

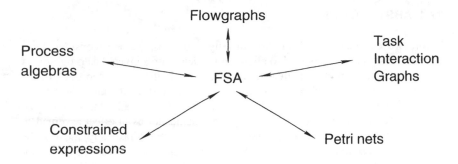

Figure 17.1. The equivalence of the models.

We shall discuss models for static analysis of Ada tasking programs as follows. First we will briefly discuss abstractions employed in the static analysis of Ada tasking programs in Section 17.1. Section 17.2 will describe a simple Ada tasking program example that will be used to portray the style each of the models uses to attack the problem. The models and an application of each of these to the example are then presented in the following sections. Section 17.7 will present a model that we will use to show the equivalence of all the other approaches on a fundamental level: the model is that of *finite state automata* (FSA[1]). We do *not* claim the model to be new, only that its relevance has not been explicitly recognized in this context in the past. Since the FSA are a well-known model, it will serve as an excellent vehicle in presenting the close connection between the other models. Specifically, we will show how each of the other models relates to FSA, as illustrated in Figure 17.1.

Last, we shall discuss some of the implications of the equivalence of the models. The FSA provide a bridge that allows the best of the results of each of the models to be transferred to benefit all. As an example, we shall mention some methods to improve upon the complexity of state space generation.

We will assume at least a rudimentary understanding of the tasking constructs of Ada. Any reasonable textbook on the language should, however, provide enough to make the discussion readable.

---

[1] The singular form of this is "finite state automaton", which we shall also abbreviate as FSA. Furthermore, we shall use the article "a" with the latter as if it had not been abbreviated.

17.1 ABSTRACTION

Before we consider models of Ada tasking programs, we will consider some common abstractions employed to elicit the models from a given Ada program. A major abstraction involved is that the models do not attempt to keep track of the values of the variables, even if these are relevant to the flow of control of the program. This is typical of static analysis in general. Specifically, the shared variables are commonly ignored, so that any communication is in effect assumed to occur using entry calls and **accept** statements. Even more drastically, most of the other statements are also ignored. Only the statements that represent either communication among tasks or choices relevant to these are represented explicitly. The former, called *synchronization actions* here, are fairly obvious, including the entry calls, **select** and **accept** statements; the latter, the *choice actions*, include **case** and **if** statements that contain statements of the former group. Any statement not in either of these two groups is abstracted away, except as a carrier of the flow of control. These are considered mere "padding" between the statements relevant to the static analysis. In effect, the ignored statements are assumed to terminate in finite time and to be correct in the sense of not disrupting the flow of control in any task.

Any choices, whether from **if, case, select,** or other statements, are usually modeled as being nondeterministic. In the context of state space generation this forces all the consequences of the alternatives to be explored. Sometimes this forces the exploration of some combinations of, say, two consecutive choices even if these might be contradictory in light of some ignored statements. A typical case of this occurs when an **if** or a **case** statement is used to determine which entry call to make, or maybe none at all. This will in many cases make the static analysis tool produce spurious error messages even if the choice of path based on the variable values excludes any erroneous behavior in all the relevant situations. It is usually also assumed that there are no Boolean guards in any branch of any **select** statement, since these depend in general on the values of variables and will have to be modeled as nondeterministic choices, generating an avalanche of potentially spurious messages. For similar reasons we choose not to consider conditional entry calls, nor **else** or **delay** alternatives in a **select** statement.

As a further consequence of ignoring the assignment statements, there will be no chance to keep track of the possible behavior of a program containing families of entries or dynamic creation of tasks, say, as members of arrays or records denoted by access types. Moreover, it is assumed that there are no subprograms containing synchronizing actions, since static analysis is not necessarily able to usefully track the behavior of, say, a collection of mutually recursive subprograms. This could be weakened to allow nonrecursive subprograms containing synchronizing actions, or even further, if the behavior of the subprograms as far as the synchronizing actions are concerned can be represented easily enough. This discussion is beyond the scope of this presentation, however. Likewise, the input queues of entries are not maintained during static analysis: this is sensible in many cases, though, since the order of insertion of the calls to the queue is nondeterministic. Similarly, the **count** attribute of the entries is usually ignored just as the variables are.

In essence, these abstractions attempt to include all possible behaviors at the cost of adding some that are not possible in the original program. Any tasks are usually also assumed to be activated simultaneously, though a later activation can be simulated using suitable new entries and calls to these [3].

One of the effects of the abstractions is to make a program have only a finite number of states. Since the values of the variables are ignored, the only relevant aspect of the state of a task is the location of the control, i.e., the value of an abstract program counter. As each task is obviously a finite piece of code, as it is assumed that there are a fixed number of tasks, and as recursion is not allowed, the abstracted program will have a finite number of states.

17.2 EXAMPLE

We will define each of the models and apply them to the well-known program of Helmbold and Luckham [14] describing an automated gas station:

> "An automated gas station consists of an Operator with a computer, a set of pumps, and a set of customers. Each Customer has unique identification (basically a credit card number called a Customer ID) and each pump has a unique number (called a pump ID). The Operator handles payments, and schedules the use of pumps, with the aid of the computer.
>
> A gas station may be specified informally as follows. Each Customer arrives at the gas station wanting a random amount of gas from a random pump. The Customer first goes to the Operator and Prepays for the pump he wants to use. Then the Customer goes to the pump and starts it. When the Customer is finished, he turns the pump off and collects his change from the Operator.
>
> The pumps have to be activated by the Operator before they can be used by the customers. Each time a pump is activated, it is given a limit (the Prepayment) on the amount of gas that can be pumped. When the pump is shut off, it reports the amount of gas dispensed to the Operator. The pump then waits until it is activated again.
>
> Whenever he [sic!] is ready, the Operator may either accept a Prepayment from a Customer, or receive a report from a pump. When a Prepayment is accepted, a record is entered in the computer showing the Prepayment, the Customer ID, and the pump ID. If the pump is not already in use, it is activated with the proper limit. When a pump reports a completed transaction, the current Prepayment record for that pump is retrieved from the computer. The charges are computed and any overpayment

is refunded to the Customer. If another Customer is waiting for the pump, it is reactivated with that Customer's Prepayment (retrieved from the computer)."

To make the Ada program more compact and perhaps easier to grasp we will use the abstract version presented in [6], given in Figures 17.2–17.4. This consists of the relevant tasking commands only and is further simplified by dropping the computer of the single Operator and assuming there is only one pump and one Customer.

```
task body Customer is -- statement 1
begin
  loop
    Operator.Prepay
    Pump.Start
    Pump.Finish
    accept Change
  end loop
end Customer
```

Figure 17.2. Abstract gas station program: Customer [6].

```
task body Pump is -- statement 10
begin
  loop
    accept Activate
    accept Start
    accept Finish do
      Operator.Charge
    end Finish
  end loop
end Pump
```

Figure 17.3. Abstract gas station program: Pump [6].

```
task body Operator is -- statement 20
begin
  loop
    select
      accept Prepay do
        Pump.Activate
      end Prepay
    or
      accept Charge do
        Customer.Change
      end Charge
    end select
  end loop
end Operator
```

Figure 17.4. Abstract gas station program: Operator [6].

Naturally, these simplifications also make the analysis much easier. As we will see, this program has a deadlock. It is also a very benign kind of deadlock, since it is unavoidable. A fairly short simulation of the program will also find the deadlock. Since the example is so simple, it does not display all the relevant aspects of the models. But it does give an idea of the style of each model, though any comparison among the models should be done more carefully than simply based on their performance in this particular example.

17.3 TASK FLOWGRAPHS

The task flowgraph model by Taylor [1] is one of the very first to be suggested for the purpose of static analysis of Ada tasking programs. In essence, it consists of the graphs describing the possible flow of control in each of a fixed collection of tasks (the *task flowgraphs*), and of a method of combining these to obtain a graph giving the possible flow of control of the whole set, the *concurrency graph*. A task flowgraph is obtained, e.g., by abstraction from the full flowgraph of the task produced by an Ada compiler. The following treatment summarizes [1].

Definition 17.3.1. *A* flowgraph *is a rooted, directed graph, that is, a 3-tuple* $G = \langle V; A, r \rangle$ *where*
- *V is a set of nodes (vertices) representing actions;*
- *$A \subseteq V^2$ is a binary relation on V, a set of (directed) arcs;*
- *$r \in V$ is the* root *of the graph, that is, there is a directed path from r to any vertex in V.*   □

A flowgraph is used in an obvious manner to represent the control flow of any task T by making
- a node correspond to a statement relevant to the static analysis to be executed next,
- an arc correspond to the possibility of a statement following another in accordance with the semantics of Ada, and
- the root be *task-begin(T)*, the first statement to be executed.

In some cases there is a need to represent a statement by more than one node, for example, **accept** statements and entry call statements, since these involve waiting for a rendezvous and then its completion. More specifically, an **accept** statement is represented in [1] by three nodes called awaiting-call, accept-engaged and accept-end, and an entry call by two nodes called call-pending and call-engaged.
The task flowgraphs produce a reachability graph as follows:

Definition 17.3.2. *Consider a program P consisting of some fixed number N of tasks with given disjoint flowgraphs $\{T_i = \langle V_i; A_i, r_i \rangle \mid 1 \le i \le N\}$. Let $\perp$ be a symbol not in the sets V_i. A* concurrency state *is an ordered N-tuple with its ith*

component from the set $V_i \cup \{\perp\}$. *That is, the set of conceivable concurrency states* C *is the Cartesian product*

$$\langle v_i \mid v_i \in V_i \cup \{\perp\} \wedge 1 \leq i \leq N\rangle.$$

The extra element $\perp$ *is used to denote that the task in question is inactive initially or finally.*   □

The successor relation on the concurrency states is defined based on the constituent sets of flowgraph arcs A_i and the semantics of Ada.

Definition 17.3.3. *The* immediate successor relation *on concurrency states, denoted by NEXT, is the relation strip(NEXT') where*

$$\langle c_1, \ldots, c_N\rangle \; NEXT' \; \langle c'_1, \ldots, c'_N\rangle$$

iff [2]

1. $c_i = c'_i$,
2. $c_i \; A_i^{+} \; c'_i$,
3. $c_i = \perp \wedge c'_i = task\text{-}begin(T_i)$, *or*
4. $c_i = task\text{-}end(T_i) \wedge c'_i = \perp$,

for all $1 \leq i \leq N$. *Here, strip(R) is the relation obtained from R by first making it irreflexive, that is, taking the largest irreflexive relation contained in R, and then removing all arcs that can be deduced by transitivity from the remaining arcs. Moreover, task-begin(T) and task-end(T) denote the* **begin** *and* **end** *statements of the task T, respectively.*

Any application of the cases 1–4 must adhere to the Ada semantics, in the choices of the c'_i from those possible, in the choice of the number of times A_i is repeated in case 2 (which should be the minimal number of steps consistent with the Ada semantics), and in the choices of which applications of case 2 cannot (or must) occur alone, that is, must (or must not) be synchronized with other arcs.   □

A relation R is irreflexive *iff* it satisfies $x R x$ for *no* value of x; it is transitive *iff* $x R z$ (the transitive arc) whenever $x R y$ and $y R z$ for some y. Above, A_i^{+} denotes the transitive closure of the relation A_i, that is, that there is a directed path from x to y of length one or more arcs in the task flowgraph T_i *iff* $x A_i^{+} y$.

---

[2] The word '*iff*' is read as 'if and only if'.

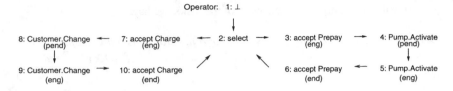

Figure 17.5. Flowgraph of Customer.

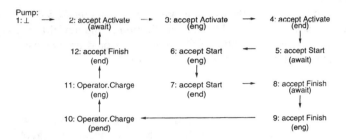

Figure 17.6. Flowgraph of Pump.

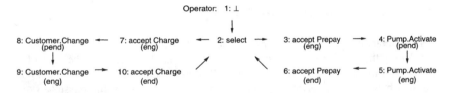

Figure 17.7. Flowgraph of Operator.

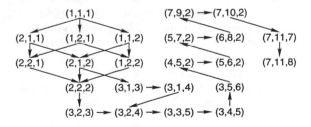

Figure 17.8. Concurrency graph of the example. The concurrency states consist of the states of Customer, Pump, and Operator, respectively.

Finally, to combine the behaviors of the tasks, we have

Definition 17.3.4. *The* concurrency graph *of a program P is a flowgraph* $\langle V; A, r \rangle$ *where* $r = \perp^N$, *the N-tuple of elements* $\perp$, $V = \{c \in C \mid \perp^N NEXT^* c\}$ *and* $A = NEXT \cap V^2$. □

Here $NEXT^*$ denotes the transitive and reflexive closure of the relation *NEXT*, that is, that there is a directed path of length zero or more from x to y in the concurrency graph *iff* $x NEXT^* y$.

The flowgraphs of the tasks of the example are given in Figures 17.5–17.7, and the concurrency graph is in Figure 17.8. This application of the model to the example is slightly better than a straightforward application would be. We have avoided generating additional states in the flowgraphs for the **loop** constructs. Also, we have merged the awaiting-call states with the **select** state for the **accept** statements immediately following the **select** or the **or** statements. The alternative would be to rely on the Ada semantics to force the move from **select** through the awaiting-call state to be a single arc in the concurrency graph. This would, however, make the connection between the task flowgraphs and the concurrency graph more difficult to understand.

17.4 TASK INTERACTION GRAPHS

A task interaction graph (TIG) aims at reducing the size of the reachability graph by reducing the number of nodes of the constituent task flowgraphs. The code of a task is partitioned into *task regions* that will then become the nodes of the TIG. The arcs between regions correspond to beginnings or ends of the possible synchronization actions. The following is summarizes [3].

Definition 17.4.1. *A task region of a given task T is a connected subgraph of the full flowgraph of T from a statement immediately following the task **begin** of T, an **accept** statement, or an entry call statement up to and including the **accept** statement, entry call statement, or task **end** of T, whichever is encountered next along a possible flow of control. We shall denote the set of regions of T by regions(T). The region that starts after the task **begin** of T is called the initial region and denoted init-region(T); a region that ends with the task **end** is called a final region and the set of these is denoted by final-regions(T).* □

Note that a task region can have many exiting statements due to the nondeterminism introduced either by **select** statements or by abstracting away the variables relevant to the flow of control.

Definition 17.4.2. *A task interaction graph (TIG) is a flowgraph where the task regions are the nodes and the arcs are the possible flow of control from region to region. In addition, the arcs going out of a region are labeled with the beginning or end of the interaction occurring next, i.e., an* **accept** *statement, entry call statement, or task* **end***:*

$$TIG(T) = \langle regions(T), nextreg(T), init\text{-}region(T), final\text{-}regions(T), labels(T), code(T) \rangle.$$

Here $nextreg(T) \subseteq (regions(T))^2$ is the next-region relation induced by the partition of the original flowgraph into regions, $code(T)$ gives the pseudocode associated with a particular region, and

$$labels : nextreg(T) \rightarrow \{S(x) \mid x \in X\} \cup \{E(x) \mid x \in X\}$$

is the arc labeling; by construction, the sets comprising the target of the function are disjoint. Here, $X = accepts(T) \cup calls(T) \cup taskends(T)$ is the set of relevant synchronization actions, where $accepts(T)$, $calls(T)$, and $taskends(T)$ are the instances of **accept***, entry call, and task terminating statements of task T, respectively, all sets assumed to be mutually disjoint.*   □

The pseudocode associated with a region consists of the Ada code comprising the region, together with $ENTER(x)$ and $EXIT(x,y)$ pseudo-statements that act as place holders for connections to other regions y through relevant synchronization actions x. We shall ignore the pseudocode assignment for now, but will discuss some of the consequences of its inclusion later.

The reachability graph of a program P consisting of the tasks T_i, $1 \leq i \leq N$, represented as the disjoint TIGs $\{TIG(T_i) \mid 1 \leq i \leq N\}$ is defined in an obvious manner:

Definition 17.4.3. *A task interaction concurrency state of the program P is an N-tuple $\langle v_i \in regions(T_i) \mid 1 \leq i \leq N \rangle$. The set of these is denoted by $TICS(P)$.*   □

Definition 17.4.4. *The immediate follower relation of task interaction concurrency states $NEXT \subseteq TICS(P)^2$ of P is defined by stating that $\langle v_1, ...,v_N \rangle$ NEXT $\langle v'_1, ..., v'_N \rangle$ iff there are i and j, $i \neq j$, with v_i $nextreg(T_i)$ v'_i and v_j $nextreg(T_j)$ v'_j such that the labels of the arcs match, and $v'_k = v_k$ for all other k, $1 \leq k \leq N$.*   □

The arc labels match *iff* one is the beginning (end) of a call to an entry and the other is the beginning (end, respectively) of an **accept** statement accepting the entry, or else the labels are equal. The latter case can be used to model, e.g., task termination or task activation by introducing new relevant synchronization actions.

Definition 17.4.5. *A task interaction concurrency graph (TICG) of a program P is a flowgraph $\langle V; A, r \rangle$ where $r = \langle init\text{-}region(T_i) \mid 1 \leq i \leq N \rangle$ is its root, $V = \{t \mid r\, NEXT^* t\}$ its set of vertices, and $A = NEXT \cap V^2$ its set of arcs.*   □

The above definition has a subtle error that causes it to miss deadlocks under certain circumstances. This has been noticed, e.g., by Damerla [15]. The error is that the choice actions have not been treated properly. On a high level, the problem is that the model ignores a distinction between so-called *internal* and *external* choice. Internal choice refers to decisions a task internally makes that affect its communication behavior. External choice refers to the joint decision of the tasks determining which communication takes place of those possible. This is one of the problems that *process algebras*, starting with CCS by Milner [16,17] have addressed in detail.

Here the problem surfaces in the case where a task executes, say, exactly one of a pair of **accept** statements based on an internal decision, say, the value of a local variable. The TICG would then allow either of these communications to take place, since the region would have both of these communication actions labeling an arc out of the region. This might lead to missing a deadlock in a case where there is no task calling the only entry that is actually available. That is, the model does not reflect the fact that it is not only up to the calling tasks to choose among the **accept** statements. In effect, the called task can *refuse* to accept the call, though it need not.

The cure for the problem is fairly obvious: a region should not contain choices. The choices should appear as arcs out of a region to other regions and these arcs should be labeled with a proper identification of the internal choice made, e.g., **if** and **else**, or even with λ, the empty string. Obviously, these arc labels should not match any label on other arcs, so as not to force them to synchronize. Please note that the choice involved in **select** statements with **accept** statements only **is** handled appropriately by the definitions.

The TIGs of the tasks of the example are given in Figures 17.9–17.11, and the TICG is in Figure 17.12. Since there are no internal choices involved in the example, its model is accurate up to the usual abstractions.

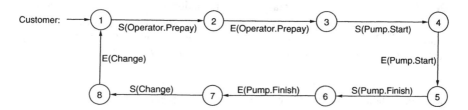

Figure 17.9. TIG of Customer.

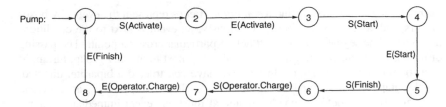

Figure 17.10. TIG of Pump.

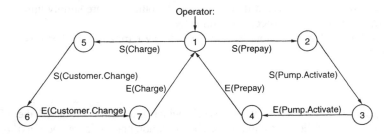

Figure 17.11. TIG of Operator.

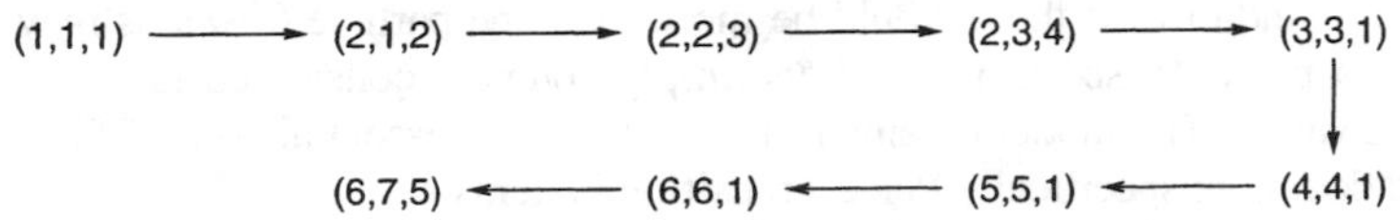

$$(1,1,1) \longrightarrow (2,1,2) \longrightarrow (2,2,3) \longrightarrow (2,3,4) \longrightarrow (3,3,1)$$

$$(6,7,5) \longleftarrow (6,6,1) \longleftarrow (5,5,1) \longleftarrow (4,4,1)$$

Figure 17.12. TICG of the example. The TICSs comprise the states of Customer, Pump, and Operator, respectively.

17.5 PETRI NETS

Petri nets (PNs) were invented by Carl Adam Petri and published in his Ph.D. thesis [18]. In a later paper [19] he discusses a possible motivation, which we will base the following introduction on. Consider a collection of world lines in a space-time continuum, say, a history of some of particles moving around and colliding with each other. The obvious interactions among the particles are represented by the world lines of two or more crossing at a point.

Now, group the points on these world lines so that a crossing point forms a group (equivalence class) on its own, and any line segment between some two crossings (or either end of a world line) without any other crossing point intervening forms another kind of group. Call any group of points of the first kind an *event* and any of the second kind a *condition*. Let us represent the events by boxes or bars, and conditions by circles. Obviously, an event is next to the conditions that have a line segment end or start at that particular crossing point. The passing of time gives a direction to this relation of being next to another group, turning it to a follower or *flow* relation. In fact, we have constructed a bipartite, directed, acyclic graph of groups and the flow relation. Moreover, there is at most one event immediately before a condition, and at most one event immediately after a condition.

Since this is a history of the particles, all the choices as to which interactions have taken place have already been fixed. The history is, however, *concurrent*: there are events that are not necessarily one before the other, but are simply unrelated to a large enough degree to occur concurrently.

Assume further that the history is the result of a system, a *physical* process, perhaps repetitive, perhaps containing choices, perhaps containing concurrent events. We could describe the system using the same kinds of primitives, say *transitions* and *places*, similarly interconnected. However, the flow relation need no longer be acyclic (to allow for repetitions), nor need the places have at most one predecessor (to allow for forgetting exactly which interaction produced the particle) or at most one follower (to allow for choices among possible interactions). Also, the system has a *state*, the distribution of the particles. The system would then produce the history much as the tire of a car leaves tracks in dirt, by "unfolding", with the current distribution of particles corresponding to the point of contact between the tire and dirt. If there would be more than one particle (*token* as they are called) in a place, these are most often simply counted, considered identical (though not always). The model obtained in this way is the essential core of PNs, sometimes called more specifically Place/Transition systems.

Since their conception, PNs and their variants have been used to model and analyze the behavior of a large variety of systems, such as computer, social, or economic. We hold that the appeal of the model stems from the basis in physics, since particles and their interactions are intuitively well understood ideas and easily identified almost anywhere. A token can model a person in a particular state of mind, a copy of a document in an office, or, as we shall see, the location of the control in a task.

There are many closely related formal definitions of PNs. We shall use the following. Let N be the set of natural numbers, with 0 as the least element.

Definition 17.5.1. *A Petri net N is a 5-tuple*

$$N = \langle P, T; F, W, M_0 \rangle$$

where
- *P is a finite set of places,*
- *T is a finite set of transitions,*
- *$F \subseteq (P \times T) \cup (T \times P)$ is a set of arcs, the* flow *relation,*

- $W : F \rightarrow (N \setminus \{0\})$ *is the* weight function *on the arcs, and*
- $M_0 : P \rightarrow N$ *is the* initial marking, *giving the initial distribution of tokens to places,*

such that the sets of places and transitions are disjoint, $P \cap T = \varnothing$, and there is at least one net element, $P \cup T \neq \varnothing$. The domain of the weight function W is usually extended to $(P \times T) \cup (T \times P)$ by setting $W(\langle x, y \rangle) = 0$ iff $\langle x, y \rangle \notin F$. Usually, either arc weight function is denoted simply as $W(x, y)$. Any function $M : P \rightarrow N$ is called a marking *of the net in question. The set of markings of a net with the places P is denoted by M_P. For any net element $x \in P \cup T$, the* preset *(input elements) of x is ${}^\bullet x = \{y \in P \cup T \mid y \, F \, x\}$ and the* postset *(output elements) of x is $x^\bullet = \{y \in P \cup T \mid x \, F \, y\}$. A net is called* simple *iff there are no net elements with identical presets and postsets.*   □

The definition of a post- or a preset of an element can obviously be extended to apply to a set of elements by taking the union of the post- or presets of the elements of the set, respectively. The behavior of a PN is defined as follows:

Definition 17.5.2. *A transition t of a Petri net $N = \langle P, T; F, W, M_0 \rangle$ is enabled at a marking $M : P \rightarrow N$ iff there are enough tokens on the input places:*

$$\forall p \in {}^\bullet t : M(p) \geq W(p, t).$$

This is denoted by M [t⟩. An enabled transition $t \in T$ may, but need not, occur (fire); if it does, it transforms the marking M to another M' that satisfies

$$\forall p \in P : M'(p) = M(p) + W(t, p) - W(p, t).$$

The relation that M' is obtained from M by firing transition t is denoted by M [t⟩ M'; this implies M [t⟩. We shall use M [⟩ M' to denote that there is a transition t such that M [t⟩ M'.   □

In effect, the firing of a transition removes tokens from the input and deposits tokens on the output places of the transition, as many as the arc weights require. For a simple net, if there is a transition t such that M [t⟩ M', it is *unique*.

Definition 17.5.3. *The* reachability graph *of a Petri net $\langle P, T; F, W, M_0 \rangle$ is the (labeled) flowgraph $\langle V, A; r \rangle$, where*

- $V = \{M \in M_P \mid M_0 \, []^* \, M\}$ *is the set of markings (finitely) reachable from the initial marking,*

- $A = \{\langle M, t, M' \rangle \mid M \in V \wedge M [t\rangle M' \}$ are the arcs labeled with the transition involved, and
- $r = M_0$. □

The subclass of PNs defined below is of considerable importance to static analysis of Ada tasking programs.

Definition 17.5.4. *A Petri net is called* safe *(1-bounded) iff there is at most one token in any place of the net in any reachable marking.* □

An approach to the translation of Ada tasking programs to PNs for the static analysis is described in depth in [6]. The translation rules are defined so that the resulting PN is safe. Those translation rules needed to translate the example are given in Figure 17.13. The translation of an **accept** statement produces the given subnet for each entry call statement to this entry in any other task, but all of these share the translation of the body S, if any. Note that this requires knowledge of which task possibly can call which entries. It is assumed that a name uniquely identifies a place over the whole net. Therefore, the names of the places sometimes need to be made unique across the whole translation of the Ada program, and sometimes not: these are achieved by appending suitable identifications, e.g., line numbers of the relevant Ada statements, to the names. In particular, the entry-ex places are appended with the names of both the calling and accepting statements. The application of the rules to the example is given in Figure 17.14. We have changed to numbers or removed most of the place and transition names and added some labels onto crucial places for convenience in interpreting the net and presenting the reachability graph. The reachability graph of the PN in Figure 17.14 is given in Figure 17.15.

Simply glancing at the relevant figures, it should be apparent that if the concurrency graph or the TICG of the example contain enough information to decide some interesting property, the given reachability graph of the PN contains redundancies. One reason for this is that there are many *intermediate* states in the PN model of each of the tasks, that is, states of the control flow of a task that are not relevant to the tasking behavior. An example of this can be seen in the translation of the **select** statements, which executes in three stages: (1) the **select** transition fires, (2) the appropriate **accept** is selected, and (3) only as a separate phase is the **accept** executed. When the reachability graph is then generated, the effect of the intermediate states is in a sense multiplied, since all the interleavings of the transitions of each task with those of the other tasks must be considered. Basically, the problem here is that of too fine *atomicity* of the transitions: something that intuitively is a single action, atomic, is broken up into consecutive transitions.

Another cause of the complexity of the reachability graph is that the PN model contains an initialization for every task. These are sequences of independent actions executing concurrently, causing all their interleavings to appear in the reachability graph, giving some $\Pi_i \ |\sigma_i|$ states where σ_i is the initialization sequence of task *i*. However, since the sequences are deterministic, uninterruptible, and have a local effect only, the states involved are of no interest. (Figure 17.12 shows a similar effect in a concurrency graph.)

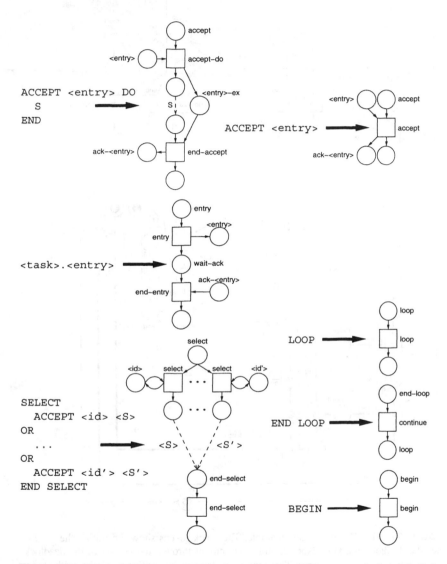

Figure 17.13. Translation rules to PNs for the example. The unnamed places are links to another translation. **select** assumes *S* and *S'* start with an **accept**.

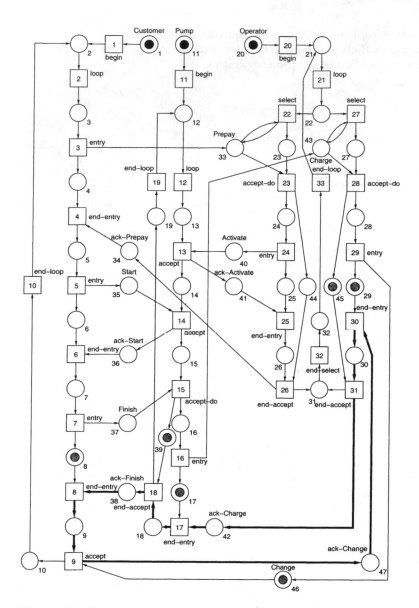

Figure 17.14. The PN of the example. The black tokens show the initial, the shaded ones the deadlock marking. Note the tokenless circuit through the postset of the deadlock places shown by the heavy lines. This represents the circular waiting condition with Customer waiting for Pump.Finish, Pump for Operator.Charge, and Operator for Customer.Change.

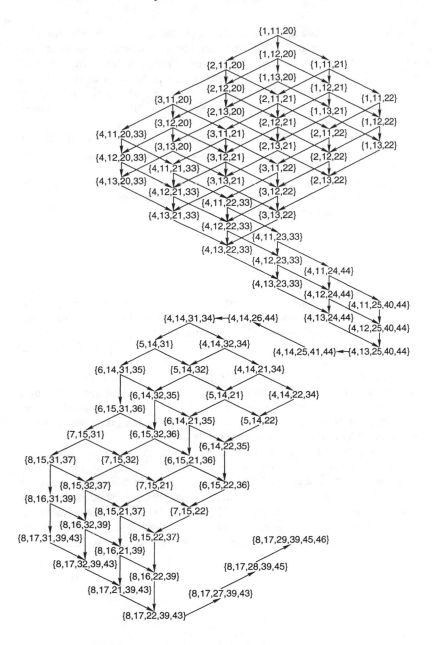

Figure 17.15. The reachability graph of the example without arc labels. The direction of an arrow represents the task, a transition of which should label the arc, whenever there are many transitions enabled. A marking is given as the set of places with one token.

Note that the translation rules do eliminate an intermediate state from the translation that is present in the TIGs as defined above: an **accept** statement without a body has no state for the rendezvous being in progress. Naturally, this small but not insignificant optimization can be performed in the other models also, as mentioned in [3]. Taylor et al [20] discuss even further elimination of states in this case, namely, that both the call and the accept can in this case each be modeled as single state transition.

It is a fairly simple matter to remove most of this redundancy [21]: the net can be transformed by
- removing the **loop** places and transitions,
- removing the **begin** places and transitions, and moving the token in the initial marking of any removed **begin** place to the output place of the corresponding **begin** transition,
- removing the **select** transition that merely tests whether a call is pending and merging the true output place of it with its input place, and
- removing **end** places (end-case, end-select, end-if, end-block, end-accept) and the associated transitions that have one input and output place.

After any removal, the remaining net must naturally be reconnected appropriately, if necessary. Note that removing the **begin** places and transitions also solves the problem of having the interleavings of the initialization sequences in the reachability graph. The resulting net model for the example is given in Figure 17.16 and its reachability graph in Figure 17.17.

For performance reasons, it might be beneficial to combine these transformations with the translation rules. This would, however, cause the translation rules to become more complex, making them harder to prove correct or justify otherwise. The labeling of the net elements can be used to make finding the points of application of each of the above rules trivial.

Shatz, Tu, Murata, and Duri [7] consider using PN *reductions* [22], both generally applicable rules and ones specifically chosen for the translations from Ada, to solve the particular problem of finding any possible deadlocks the system may have. These are transformations of the PN that preserve the deadlocks in its behavior while simplifying its structure. The application of the reductions to the PN of the example produces the PN in Figure 17.18, which has the reachability graph of Figure 17.19. Since this has a deadlock, the original net also has one.

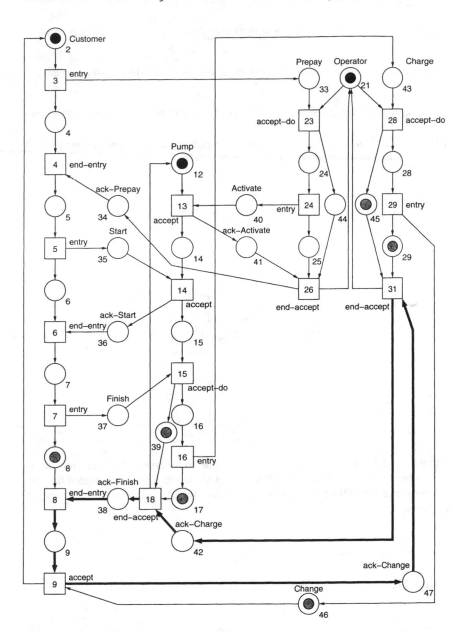

Figure 17.16. The simplified example net. The numbering of places and transitions refers to Figure 17.14. The black tokens show the initial, while the shaded tokens show the deadlock marking. Note the tokenless circuit (circular waiting condition) through the postset of the deadlock places shown by the heavy lines.

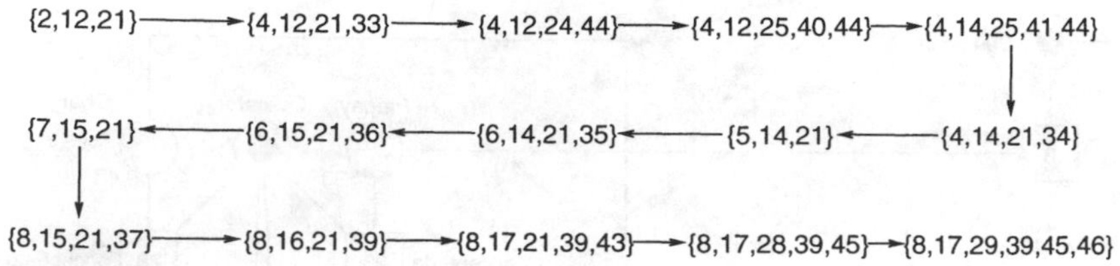

{2,12,21}
{4,12,21,33}
{4,12,24,44}
{4,12,25,40,44}
{4,14,25,41,44}
{7,15,21}
{6,15,21,36}
{6,14,21,35}
{5,14,21}
{4,14,21,34}
{8,15,21,37}
{8,16,21,39}
{8,17,21,39,43}
{8,17,28,39,45}
{8,17,29,39,45,46}

Figure 17.17. The reachability graph of the simplified example net without arc labels. A marking is represented as the set of places with one token.

2,3,8,9,10,12,
17,18,19,21,30,
31,32,33
33
22
23,24
13
40
9
46
4,5,6,7,13,14,
21,25,26,32,33
37
15,16,28,29

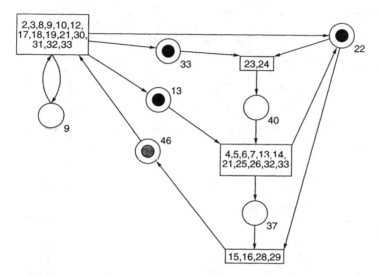

Figure 17.18. The reduced example net. The numbering of places and transitions refers to Figure 17.14. The black tokens show the initial, the shaded one the deadlock marking. Note that place 9 can never have a token, making its output transition dead.

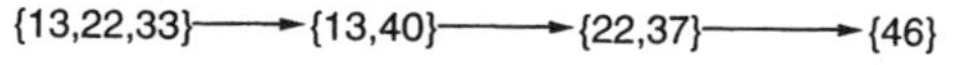

{13,22,33}
{13,40}
{22,37}
{46}

Figure 17.19. The reachability graph of the reduced example net.

17.6 CONSTRAINED EXPRESSIONS

Constrained expression models consist of *system expressions* and *constraints*. System expressions are regular expressions over an alphabet of events (actions, statement execution steps). Each of these denotes a regular *language*, i.e., a set of finite strings over the alphabet. In addition to the usual regular operators, system expressions and constraints can employ a binary infix operator "shuffle", denoted here by $\|$, to represent interleaving or merge of the two sets of sequences of events represented by the constituent expressions. That is, $E \| E'$ denotes the language of all the interleavings of the strings in the languages denoted by E and E'. An interleaving of two strings contains the elements of both so that they can be picked in order from the interleaving, but otherwise the order of elements in the result is not restricted. The length of the interleaving is the sum of the lengths of the constituents even if there are identical elements in the strings. Adding the shuffle operator does not extend the class of languages represented by such expressions beyond the regular sets. An expression using shuffle and the regular expression operators still denotes a regular language [23].

Based on the experience of the previous sections, it should be obvious that the possible control flow of a task can easily be represented as a regular expression over the instances of statements of the task. Any choices are represented by the union (choice, or) | of the relevant subexpressions; **loop**s are represented by the Kleene star, the transitive and reflexive closure of the concatenation operator, denoted by $(\ldots)^*$ or the transitive but not reflexive closure operator $(\ldots)^+$; sequencing is represented by concatenation. A program consisting of many tasks would then be a shuffle of all the task expressions.

However, this representation does not take the communication into consideration. The shuffle of the task expressions does not express in any way the fact that a calling task cannot proceed until the rendezvous has occurred, to give an obvious example. This aspect can be captured by the constraints, the other part of the constrained expression formalism. A constraint consists of an alphabet of events and an expression over this alphabet. This expression can employ yet another unary postfix operator, called the *dagger* $(\ldots)^{\dagger}$. This denotes the language of its argument shuffled any non-negative number of times with itself, a kind of reflexive and transitive closure of the shuffle just as Kleene star is for concatenation. It can be used to express constraints that involve any finite number of tasks. The dagger does not preserve regularity, that is, the language denoted by $L^{\dagger}$ need not be regular even if L is.

A major difference between the system expression and the constraints is in the interpretation of what languages these denote. The system expressions are interpreted to denote any *prefix* of any string in the language denoted by the system expression. A prefix of a string is any initial part (including the empty string and the string itself) of it. The constraints are interpreted as usual. A constraint is used to weed out "uninteresting" prefixes: any prefix, when *projected* onto the alphabet of the constraint, must be in the language denoted by the constraint in order to be considered. Projection of a string onto an alphabet means in this context that all the symbols of the string in question other than those in the alphabet, are deleted (ignored).

The prefixes of the language denoted by the shuffle of the system expressions represent intermediate, nonterminal, even nonsensical executions of the program, while the constraints force the prefixes to be *complete* in the sense of making up a rational whole. The constraints can in many cases be used to pick only those prefixes that are of interest to the analysis of the system, providing a simple method to focus the analysis. Constraints can also be used to enforce restrictions on communication, such as forcing certain events to occur sequentially, by letting the alphabet of a constraint straddle the alphabets of the relevant tasks. Also, some events can be denied of ever occurring in a viable prefix. We will see an example of how this is used in the case where a task has an explicit nonterminating **loop** and can never terminate normally. In most cases, some constraint templates (schemata) are chosen to remain the same for all the programs considered, providing for a separation of concerns, but this is not necessary.

A description of the event alphabet of our example is given in Figure 17.20. The task expressions for the tasks of the example are given in Figures 17.21–17.23. Note that the contents of the **loop** are iterated and followed by the possible error continuations. The non-event symbols are used to block further progress of a task beyond the symbol. This same method is also used to make explicit the chance of some task getting permanently blocked on an entry call or **accept**. Note also that the translations of the **accept** statements require knowledge of which tasks can call which entry.

The constraint templates for the example are given in Figure 17.24. The first template is used to enforce the behavior that the execution never proceeds beyond a non-event. This is achieved by making the alphabet of the first template the non-event of the given task. This corresponds to requiring that the *viable* prefixes (those in the language of the constraints) contain no non-events. The second constraints allow only prefixes that starve a task at most once; the third constraints allow only prefixes that starve the given task or then let it terminate. Together the latter two allow the shuffles of the executions that either starve or terminate all the tasks to be in the set of viable prefixes. The last two templates force the rendezvous' to occur appropriately, **accept**s without body resulting in all the four events occurring as a unit[3], and those with a body occurring in two steps. A prefix of a string in the language of the shuffle of the task expressions that satisfies the instantiated constraints is given in Figure 17.25.

---

[3] Constraints as described above cannot, in fact, force events to occur strictly as a unit. They merely make the prefixes of interest consist of sequences that have the required numbers of the events in the correct order. The events can still be interleaved arbitrarily with other events. However, the implementation described in [25] appears to have just this ability, since it uses products of FSA in the constraint elimination phase.

Symbol	Associated Event
call(T;T'.E)	Task T calls entry $T'.E$
starve_c(T;T'.E)	Task T starves trying to call on $T'.E$
resume(T;T'.E)	Task T resumes after rendezvous on $T'.E$
starve_r(T;T'.E)	Task T starves trying to resume from $T'.E$
beg_rend(T;T'.E)	Rendezvous between T and T' on $T'.E$ begins
end_rend(T;T'.E)	End of the rendezvous
starve_a(T.E)	Task T starves waiting for a call on $T.E$
comp(T)	Task T completes successfully
ne(T)	The non-event symbol for task T

Figure 17.20. The event alphabet of the constrained expressions of the example. These are modeled after a different example in [24].

[*call*(Customer;Operator.Prepay) *resume*(Customer;Operator.Prepay)
  call(Customer;Pump.Start) *resume*(Customer;Pump.Start)
  call(Customer;Pump.Finish) *resume*(Customer;Pump.Finish)
  beg_rend(Operator;Customer.Change)
  end_rend(Operator;Customer.Change)]*

[*ne*(Customer) *comp*(Customer)
  | *starve_c*(Customer;Operator.Prepay) *ne*(Customer)
  | *call*(Customer;Operator.Prepay)
    (*starve_c*(Customer;Operator.Prepay) *ne*(Customer)
    | *resume*(Customer;Operator.Prepay)
      (*starve_c*(Customer;Pump.Start) *ne*(Customer)
      | *call*(Customer;Pump.Start)
        (*starve_c*(Customer;Pump.Start) *ne*(Customer)
        | *resume*(Customer;Pump.Start)
          (*starve_c*(Customer;Pump.Finish) *ne*(Customer)
          | *call*(Customer;Pump.Finish)
            (*starve_c*(Customer;Pump.Finish) *ne*(Customer)
            | *resume*(Customer;Pump.Finish) *starve_a*(Customer.Change)
              ne(Customer))))))]

Figure 17.21. The task expression of Customer.

[*beg_rend*(Operator;Pump.Activate) *end_rend*(Operator;Pump.Activate)
  beg_rend(Customer;Pump.Start) *end_rend*(Customer;Pump.Start)
  beg_rend(Customer;Pump.Finish)
  call(Pump;Operator.Charge) *resume*(Pump;Operator.Charge)
  end_rend(Customer;Pump.Finish)]*

[*ne*(Pump) *comp*(Pump)
 | *starve_a*(Pump.Activate) *ne*(Pump)
 | *beg_rend*(Operator;Pump.Activate) *end_rend*(Operator;Pump.Activate)
   (*starve_a*(Pump.Start) *ne*(Pump)
   | *beg_rend*(Customer;Pump.Start) *end_rend*(Customer;Pump.Start)
    (*starve_a*(Pump.Finish) *ne*(Pump)
    | *beg_rend*(Customer;Pump.Finish)
      (*starve_c*(Pump;Operator.Charge) *ne*(Pump)
       call(Pump;Operator.Charge)
       starve_c(Pump;Operator.Charge) *ne*(Pump))))]

Figure 17.22. The task expression of Pump.

[*beg_rend*(Customer;Operator.Prepay)
  call(Operator;Pump.Activate) *resume*(Operator;Pump.Activate)
  end_rend(Customer;Operator.Prepay)

| *beg_rend*(Pump;Operator.Charge)
  call(Operator;Customer.Change) *resume*(Operator;Customer.Change)
  end_rend(Pump;Operator.Charge)]*

[*ne*(Operator) *comp*(Operator)

| *starve_a*(Operator.Prepay) *ne*(Operator)

| *beg_rend*(Customer;Operator.Prepay)
  (*starve_c*(Operator;Pump.Activate) *ne*(Operator)
  | *call*(Operator;Pump.Activate)
   starve_c(Operator;Pump.Activate) *ne*(Operator))

| *starve_a*(Operator.Charge) *ne*(Operator)

| *beg_rend*(Pump;Operator.Charge)
  (*starve_c*(Operator;Customer.Change) *ne*(Operator)
  | *call*(Operator;Customer.Change) *starve_c*(Operator;Customer.Change)
   ne(Operator))]

Figure 17.23. The task expression of Operator.

For each task T: λ.

For each entry $T'.E$ and task T that calls it:
$\lambda \mid starve_c(T;T'.E) \mid starve_r(T;T'.E) \mid starve_a(T'.E)$.

For each task T:
$\quad (\; \big\|_{T \text{ calls } T.E} starve_c(T;T'.E) \;)$
$\mid (\; \big\|_{T \text{ calls } T.E} starve_r(T;T'.E) \;)$
$\mid (\; \big\|_{T \text{ accepts } E} starve_a(T.E) \;)$
$\mid comp(T)$.

For each entry $T'.E$ and task T that calls it:
$[call(T;T'.E) \; beg\_rend(T,T'.E)$
$\mid end\_rend(T,T'.E) \; resume(T;T'.E)]^{*}$.

For each entry $T'.E$, all the **accept** statements of which contain no body, and task T that calls it: $[call(T;T'.E) \; beg\_rend(T,T'.E) \; end\_rend(T,T'.E) \; resume(T;T'.E)]^{*}$.

Figure 17.24. Constraint templates for the example. The alphabet is $\{ne(T)\}$ for instances of the first template, the sets of symbols appearing in the constraint for the others. $\big\|$ denotes choice among indexed alternatives.

$call$(Customer;Operator.Prepay) beg_rend(Customer;Operator.Prepay)
$\quad call$(Operator;Pump.Activate) beg_rend(Operator;Pump.Activate)
$\quad end\_rend$(Operator;Pump.Activate) $resume$(Operator;Pump.Activate)
end_rend(Customer;Operator.Prepay) $resume$(Customer;Operator.Prepay)
$call$(Customer;Pump.Start) beg_rend(Customer;Pump.Start)
end_rend(Customer;Pump.Start) $resume$(Customer;Pump.Start)
$call$(Customer;Pump.Finish) beg_rend(Customer;Pump.Finish)
$\quad call$(Pump;Operator.Charge) beg_rend(Pump;Operator.Charge)
$\quad starve_c$(Operator;Customer.Change) $starve_c$(Pump;Operator.Charge)
$\quad starve_c$(Customer;Pump.Finish)

Figure 17.25. A prefix of the example leading to starvation.

Research on constrained expressions has developed a very interesting new analysis method. This extracts an integer linear programming problem out of a model. This problem has no solution if there is no prefix to satisfy all the constraints. The solutions basically count the number of occurrences of each event in any viable prefix. If the integer linear programming problem has a solution, it must still be checked whether this corresponds to an actual viable prefix. Checking this amounts to state space generation where it is known exactly how many times each event is to take place, a problem often less complex than the original. We will not, however, illustrate the method further, but refer the reader to [25] for further details.

The constrained expression model is one of many related formalisms based on regular expressions such as COSY [26,27], which has also connections to labeled PNs [28], and path expressions [29]. We shall, however, consider these to be outside the scope of this chapter. For the interested reader, the paper by Avrunin et al. [24] contains further references.

17.7 CANONICAL MODEL: FSA

A finite state automaton (FSA; finite state machine) is a transition system with a finite number of possible states, finite (action) alphabet, a unique initial state, and a set of final states. We will discuss how each of the discussed models can be seen to describe each of the tasks they have been applied to as a FSA. Furthermore, we will show how combining the tasks to produce the reachability graph can be seen in terms of operations on FSA. We will first review some of the relevant definitions and theorems on FSA.

Definition 17.7.1. *A (nondeterministic)* finite state automaton *(with λ-moves) M is a 5-tuple $\langle V, \Sigma, \delta, r, \Omega \rangle$ where*
- *V is a finite set of states,*
- *Σ is a finite, non-empty set of symbols, the* alphabet,
- *$\delta : V \times (\Sigma \cup \{\lambda\}) \to 2^V$, where 2^V denotes the* powerset *(the set of subsets) of V, is a state transition function that maps a state and a symbol (or the empty string λ) to a collection of successor states,*
- *$r \in V$ is the* initial state, *and*
- *$\Omega \subseteq V$ is the set of final states.*   □

As stated, λ denotes here the empty string of symbols, not a member of any set of symbols. The state transition function δ can be extended to a function over strings of symbols from Σ, $\underline{\delta} : V \times \Sigma^* \to 2^V$. To do this, we need to be able to talk about all the states reachable from a given one using λ-moves only.

Definition 17.7.2. *Given a FSA $M = \langle V, \Sigma, \delta, r, \Omega \rangle$ the λ-closure of a state $v \in V$ is the set $E_M(v) = \{v' \in V \mid v R_\lambda^* v'\}$, where $R_\lambda = \{\langle v, v' \rangle \mid v' \in \delta(v, \lambda)\}$.*   □

Then the extension of δ can be done by letting $\underline{\delta}(q,\lambda) = E_M(q)$ and

$$\underline{\delta}(q,aw) = \bigcup_{q' \in E_M(q)} \bigcup_{q'' \in \delta(q',a)} \underline{\delta}(q'',w)$$

for any $a \in \Sigma$, $w \in \Sigma^*$. Furthermore, the transition function can be extended to a function over regular expressions over Σ, but we shall omit these details. Obviously, a FSA can be represented by a labeled directed graph with the states being the vertices and an arc labeled with $a \in \Sigma \cup \{\lambda\}$ from state, say, p to state q *iff*

$q \in \delta(p,a)$. We will assume without loss of generality that the graph is rooted at the initial state r (that is, there is a directed path from r to any state) since any states not reachable from r can simply be removed without affecting any of the following constructions in any relevant way.

There is a standard way a FSA is associated with a *language*, a subset of finite strings over the alphabet.

Definition 17.7.3. *The* language accepted by a FSA $M = \langle V, \Sigma, \delta, r, \Omega \rangle$ *is the set of strings* $L(M) = \{ w \in \Sigma^* \mid \underline{\delta}(r,w) \cap \Omega \neq \varnothing \}$. □

That is, a string is accepted *iff* there is a path in the graph from the initial state to some final state such that the arc labels spell out the string when concatenated in the order these appear on the path. (The empty string λ obviously contributes nothing when concatenated.) The set of strings accepted by the FSA is the language of the FSA.

We shall call a FSA that accepts the intersection of the languages of two given FSA a *semi-product* of the two FSA. There is a well-known construction for obtaining one particular semi-product for automata without λ-moves, see [30, p. 59–60]. For FSA with these moves we shall use the following:

Definition 17.7.4. *The* semi-product *of two given FSA, say,*

$$M' = \langle V', \Sigma', \delta', r', \Omega' \rangle$$

and

$$M'' = \langle V'', \Sigma'', \delta'', r'', \Omega'' \rangle$$

is the FSA

$$M = \langle V' \times V'', \Sigma' \cap \Sigma'', \delta, \langle r', r'' \rangle, \Omega' \times \Omega'' \rangle,$$

where

$$\delta(\langle v',v'' \rangle, a) = \{ \langle w',w'' \rangle \mid w' \in \underline{\delta}'(v',a) \wedge w'' \in \underline{\delta}''(v'',a) \}$$

for any $v' \in V'$, $v'' \in V''$, *and* $a \in (\Sigma' \cap \Sigma'') \cup \{\lambda\}$. *Again, without loss of generality we shall assume that any states of M not reachable from the initial state are removed. We shall use $M = M' * M''$ to denote that M is the semiproduct of M' and M'' obtained using the above construction.* □

Obviously, there are other definitions of semi-products that may have less states. The correctness of the construction is given by the

Theorem 17.7.1. *For any FSA M' and M'', $L(M' * M'') = L(M') \cap L(M'')$.*

Proof: Consider $M' = \langle V', \Sigma', \delta', r', \Omega' \rangle$, $M'' = \langle V'', \Sigma'', \delta'', r'', \Omega'' \rangle$, and $M = M' *$ M''. For any states $p' \in V'$ and $p'' \in V''$, if $q' \in \underline{\delta}'(p',a)$ and $q'' \in \underline{\delta}''(p'',a)$ for $a \in$ $(\Sigma' \cap \Sigma'') \cup \{\lambda\}$, then $\langle q',q'' \rangle \in \underline{\delta}(\langle p',p'' \rangle,a)$ by the definition of the transition function δ of the semi-product. Similarly, if $\langle q',q'' \rangle \in \underline{\delta}(\langle p',p'' \rangle,a)$, then there must be corresponding component paths in M' and M''. Therefore, there is a path from the initial state r to a final state in M labeled with a string, say w, exactly when there are corresponding paths labeled with w in each of the components. Since a state of the semi-product is final *iff* both the component states are final, this proves the theorem.   □

We shall attempt to use a semi-product to represent a program consisting of two tasks. The alphabets of the constituent FSA will represent the communications possible. This is intuitively appealing, since any task at most restricts the behavior of another by communicating with it. Any execution should be one allowed by *both* tasks. We shall use the empty string λ to label any arcs modeling nondeterministic choices or purely internal actions, if any. There are three problems, two simply solved ones and a tougher one, that we are faced with in order to achieve the goal. Let us treat the easier ones first.

Between tasks, an entry call is to match an **accept** statement, but in order for the tasks to be properly synchronized in a semi-product, the matching events constituting the call and **accept** should be represented by the same symbol. Renaming the symbols that represent the matching events just before applying the construction of a semi-product seems first sufficient to solve this. However, the task accepting calls must still be able to accept them from other tasks, if any, even after the renaming. Because of this and because the **accept** may have a body containing synchronization actions, a simple renaming is not enough. The symbol representing a particular **accept** statement, say a, must be substituted with a regular expression $(x_{b1a} | ... | x_{bna} | a)$ where each x_{bia} is an expression representing the rendezvous between the entry call b_i and a. For an **accept** statement with a body containing synchronization actions these must reflect the whole rendezvous. Specifically, there must be an initial symbol in x_{bia}, say s_{bia} representing the start of the rendezvous between b_i and a and a final symbol of the rendezvous, say e_{bia}, and these must be distinct from any other symbols. In a sense, s_{bia} corresponds to the "**accept**...**do**", and e_{bia} to the "**end accept**" in the program. Obviously, a corresponding substitution must occur for the entry call in the calling task, but there the expression need only be a choice among $s_{bia} e_{bia}$, the initial and final symbols concatenated, for all the **accept** statements a for the entry that b_i called. For an **accept** without body or with a body abstracted away the x_{bia} and a can each be a single symbol, which is also the symbol to be included in the substitution on the caller side. Both renaming and substitution map a regular language to a regular language [30, p. 60]. There is simple modification to the original FSA that makes it act as desired.

Note that, by the definition of a semi-product, no string containing a symbol in $(\Sigma' \cup \Sigma'') \setminus (\Sigma' \cap \Sigma'')$ can be accepted. However, in a program consisting of two tasks any action in the above set should be possible without any interference from the other task, since it is either internal or at least does not require synchronization with the other task. This can be solved by adding a *reflexive* arc, one that does not change the state even if taken, to each state of both of the FSA on any symbol solely in the alphabet of the other FSA. This makes the alphabets coincide and allows the semi-product to make moves local to one FSA without interference from the other FSA. The semi-product obtained from the above construction then recognizes the language such that the projection onto the original alphabet of the first FSA is the language of the first automaton, and simultaneously the same holds for the second FSA. Projection of a language has here the same meaning as with the constrained expressions.

The third problem, the hardest one, is that the equality of languages of two automata is not a sufficient criterion to distinguish between a program having a deadlock and one not having one. That is, even if two FSA recognize the same language, one may deadlock when the other does not. And usually at least the possibility of a deadlock is of interest in an Ada tasking program.

The last problem is closely related to the problem with the original definition of TICGs. The internal decisions are significant with respect to finding deadlocks, even if they are given using λ-moves, that is, moves that are not synchronization actions. But the language of the automaton is unaffected by these moves due to its definition, since there *exists* a way to recognize a string, though the string cannot be "forced" to be recognized.

We will return to this last problem later. For now, we will take the conservative approach of simply calling the FSA resulting from the construction outlined above, that is, substituting the communication actions, adding reflexive arcs, and applying the above construction for a semi-product, *the task product* of the two FSA. Simply by repeating the task product a finite number of times we can combine any number of FSA representing tasks to a FSA representing the program consisting of those tasks. Note that the task product is associative, that is, the order of application of the task product is irrelevant in the sense that the end results are isomorphic. This is based on the Cartesian product of the state sets being associative. We could also generalize the task product to $N \geq 2$ instead of 2 tasks and achieve basically the same construction. Usually, all the chances to communicate with any additional tasks through **accept** statements that were introduced using the substitution step must be removed from the end result. This is due to the program usually being considered *closed*, not subject to outside influence, at the time of analysis.

Note, however, that the order of application of the task products *is* significant from a computational point of view. If two independent tasks get combined, for example, the task product will in fact have as many reachable states as the Cartesian product of the state sets. This can be much more than the number of states in the final product, since a third FSA could restrict the behavior of both the combined FSA. This phenomenon is pointed out, e.g., in [31]. Moreover, keeping the **accept** statements open until the last step will usually result in larger intermediate task products than if the assumption about the program being closed is made early, see, e.g., [32].

Task Flowgraphs

A flowgraph is almost a FSA; only the arc labeling and the set of final states are missing. The arc labels can obviously be produced by inspecting the code of the task, since each arc is the result of executing a sequence of statements. Specifically, the empty sequence λ can be used to label nondeterministic choices internal to a task. The final states of the FSA could be the vertices of the flowgraph that correspond to successful termination of the task in question. Another choice, such as the one chosen for the system expression of the constrained expressions, would be to make all the states final so that the FSA would recognize the prefix language of the original. The choice between the two depends on how the final states of the flowgraphs are to be interpreted. Obviously, a FSA provides us with a flowgraph by just ignoring the irrelevant parts.

In order to compare the concurrency graph and the task product, the relevant parts of the semantics of Ada should be presented. For the sake of brevity, we shall refrain from even trying this. Subject to the correctness of the other models in that these also represent the behavior of Ada programs, the equivalences of the other models to FSA do, however, suggest that the concurrency graph is also closely related to the task product.

Task Interaction Graphs

Inclusion of the pseudocodes to a TIG causes the original Ada program to become a later recoverable part of the TIG. This means that anything that can be done to or with the original can also be done to or with the TIG after simply recovering the program and ignoring the rest. In effect, the abstractions common to the static analysis have not been applied, and TIGs are equivalent to the original program. However, ignoring the pseudocodes to a degree makes the TIGs equivalent to FSA, as we shall see.

Assume that the problem of TIGs ignoring choice statements has been solved as discussed above, by using λ to label the nondeterministic choices, but denying this from ever matching even itself. Then a region becomes a state of the FSA, final regions become final states, and the initial region becomes the initial state. The arc labels are simply the same, though differently formulated in the two models. Clearly, we can set

$$\delta(v,a) = \{ v' | v \; nextreg(T) \; v' \wedge [labels(T)] \; (v,v') = a \}$$

for any $a \in \{S(x) \mid x \in X\} \cup \{E(x) \mid x \in X\} \cup \{\lambda\}$ to get the transition function of a FSA out of a TIG. Recall that X is the set of relevant synchronization actions for the TIG.

The effect of matching the relevant synchronization actions can be achieved by suitably substituting these actions. This is basically the same substitution that was described when discussing the task product of FSA, though now the start and end symbols of an **accept** body are already in place. Then the task product of all the task FSA, with all the added choices for **accept** statements (introduced by substitution) removed and all the arc labels dropped, is the same as (isomorphic to) the TICG.

In Figures 17.26–17.28 we have given substituted versions of the FSA from the TIGs of the example, before the introduction of the reflexive arcs. We have used subscripting by the states of the caller and the callee before a synchronizing transition is made in order to make the symbols on arcs unique. In the example, this is redundant since there is exactly one call and one **accept** statement for any entry[4]. We have also made the substitutions assuming that the three tasks form a closed system, omitting the open **accept** statement representations. In order to more easily compare the task product in Figure 17.29 with the TICG, the former shown is that of all three tasks, computed in a single step, not in pairwise products: the substitution performed is that necessary for achieving this. If the product were obtained through pairwise task products, each of the states in Figure 17.29 would be of the forms $\langle x, \langle y, z \rangle \rangle$ or $\langle \langle x, y \rangle, z \rangle$ where x, y, and z are states of Customer, Pump, and Operator in some order that is fixed across the states and depends on the order that the pairwise products are applied. Any one of these forms is obviously isomorphic to the ones given in the figure. Comparing Figures 17.12 and 17.29, it is easy to note that the TICG and the product are the same after the arc labels of the product are dropped.

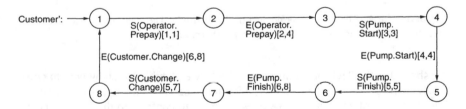

Figure 17.26. The FSA obtained from the TIG of Customer after substitution and assuming the collection of the tasks to be closed.

---

[4] For this to work in general, the states of all the FSA must be assumed to be pairwise disjoint. The uniqueness of the calls and **accepts** makes this assumption unnecessary in this case.

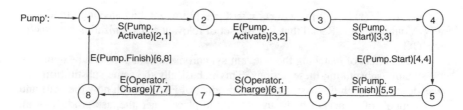

Figure 17.27. The FSA obtained from the TIG of Pump like that in Figure 17.26.

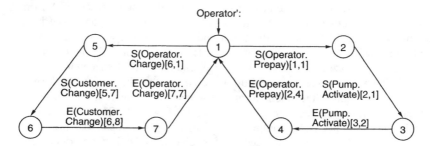

Figure 17.28. The FSA obtained from the TIG of Operator like that in Figure 17.26.

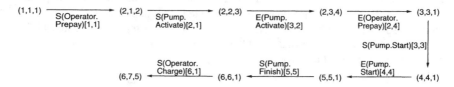

Figure 17.29. The closed task product of the example. The states of the product comprise the states of Customer, Pump, and Operator, respectively.

To show that the TIGs are equivalent to FSA, we should also show how to construct a TIG given a FSA. Obviously, this cannot be done directly, since the labeling of the arcs of an arbitrary FSA does not have to conform to the $S(x)$–$E(x)$ discipline that those of the TIG do. The FSA can, however, be modeled by an Ada program with one task that has **accept** statements only, all without a body and other tasks, one for each symbol in the alphabet of the FSA, that simply repeatedly call the entry corresponding to the symbol. The arcs labeled with λ in the FSA will become **case** or **if** statements with unknown branching conditions. The Ada program can then be abstracted to a collection of TIGs. If there are transitions with both λ and some other symbol out of any state, the Ada program needs to employ an **else** alternative in a **select** statement, which we have decided to ignore.

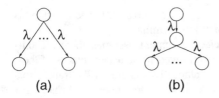

(a)   (b)

Figure 17.30. (a) A FSA. (b) A FSA possibly equivalent to that of Figure 17.30a.

Even then, if there are many λ transitions out of the state, the construction would require that any FSA containing a subgraph in Figure 17.30a is considered equivalent for the purposes of the analysis to a FSA where the subgraph is replaced with that in Figure 17.30b. For a FSA obtained from an Ada program using the abstractions described, these should not be problems, however. Note also that going through the Ada program described also gives pseudocode assignments necessary to obtain the TIGs.

Petri Nets

The reachability graph of the whole PN model of a program is a FSA without final states. As was the case with flowgraphs, final state information can be added to the PN models of the tasks and can then be used to recognize the final states in the reachability graph. The PNs of the individual tasks belong to the subclass of PNs known as *state machines* once any places needed for modeling the communication are removed. All the arcs of a state machine have weight one, and all the transitions have exactly one input and one output place. Any transition is then effectively an arc between these two places. The initial marking of each consists of exactly one token. These force the token representing the value of the program counter to be in a uniquely determined place, so the current state of the task FSA is always represented by the marked place. Therefore, there are also FSA to represent the tasks.

The above construction of task FSA from the PN model is not the best for our purposes, however. To see that the combination of the PNs of the tasks can be represented using a task product, one must show how the communication can be achieved using shared transitions instead of using intermediate places, since the former is the way the task product synchronizes events, that is, by having them in the intersection of the alphabets. We will only treat translations using the rules in Figure 17.13 which are crucial for communication. For the names of places and transitions in the following, please refer to Figure 17.13.

We will first treat the model of the entry call. This introduces a wait-ack place making the ⟨entry⟩ and end-accept transitions have more than one output and input place, respectively. This problem is easily solved, however, since the wait-ack place is *redundant*. It is never the only one to disable the end-entry transition, so it can be simply removed together with the incident arcs [22]. The reachability graph of the resulting net will be isomorphic to the original.

Recall that the translation of the **select** statement assumes there are only **accept** choices. The select transitions can be removed if the accept places of these **accept** statements are merged with the select place. This is one of the transformations mentioned above to remove an intermediate state and it does in a broad sense preserve the behavior of the net. By the structure of the net, the accept transition in any branch of the net before the transformation is not in conflict with any transition other than the corresponding **select** transition. The two transitions are obviously never both enabled in any reachable state (otherwise the net would not be safe), so the latter transition cannot be prevented from firing once enabled. Therefore, the two transitions can be merged into one with the same net effect unless one is specifically interested in the intermediate state in question, e.g., [33,34]. There should be no need to be interested in the state, since there need not be a counterpart for it in the semantics of the **select** statement.

The translation of an **accept** statement involves the ⟨entry⟩-ex places that were used to maintain information about which entry call statement was actually being serviced. These places are actually redundant in the example, since the call statement is always unique. In any case, there will be, for any **accept** statement in the task, a unique accept transition, a unique ⟨entry⟩-ex place and a unique end-accept transition for each entry call statement calling the entry of the **accept** statement. Consider now any particular **accept** and a particular entry call statement for the entry of the **accept**, and, furthermore, the unique transition-place-transition triplet corresponding to this chosen pair. Split the transitions of the triplet into two, and connect the copies so that

- one copy of the accept transition has the ⟨entry⟩ place as its unique input place and the ⟨entry⟩-ex place as its unique output place,
- the other copy of the accept transition has the accept place, perhaps one merged with a select place in the previous step, as its unique input place and the first place of the body of the **accept** statement translation as its unique output place,
- one copy of the end-accept transition has the ⟨entry⟩-ex place as its unique input place and the ack-⟨entry⟩ place as its unique output place, and
- the other copy of the end-accept transition has the last place of the body of the **accept** as its unique input place and the first place of the following statement as its unique output place.

Both pairs of transition copies should be labeled to reflect that they are parts of the same transition. These will become elements in the intersection of the alphabets of a calling task and the task accepting the call. The changes to the translation of the **accept** without a body are a simplified version of this.

After applying these transformations, we have separated each of the tasks into a PN where each transition has one input and one output place. For the net in Figure 17.14 the resulting net is given in Figure 17.31. Therefore, we can replace the transitions with arcs, giving us a collection of task FSA. The original Petri net can be retrieved by reversing the steps, which fairly closely corresponds to applying the task product, with the exception of the removal of the select transition and the wait-ack place, neither of which was strictly necessary in the first place. Since the begin place never gets duplicated or split, the initial state of each task FSA is well defined.

A FSA can obviously be represented as a PN belonging to the subclass of state machines with the initial marking consisting of exactly one token. Any transition is then effectively an arc between these two places. The arc labels of the FSA can be represented as the set of transitions by making a distinct transition for each occurrence of each arc label on an arc in the FSA.

Constrained Expressions

The constrained expressions are the model in a sense closest to FSA. The three differences are: the use of shuffle instead of the task product, the use of constraints, and, further, the dagger operator † employed in them. For the cases where the dagger is present and truly unavoidable, the constrained expressions cannot be modeled using FSA, since the dagger can be used to describe languages not accepted by FSA. The dagger is not needed, however, if there is an upper bound on the number of concurrent actions, since in this case it can be replaced by an expression containing sufficiently many shuffle operators. Since the number of tasks clearly limits the concurrency and is assumed to be fixed, there clearly is such a bound for any particular program. Even then, the dagger still serves a purpose in separating concerns in modeling, since it can be used to make a constraint independent of the particular program, specifically, the number of tasks of the program in this case. So, any Ada program of interest for static analysis can be represented without dagger, but it can be convenient to be able to use this in constraints and only substitute it for a relevant number of shuffles when applied to a particular program.

Each of the task expressions can be represented as FSA; so can the shuffle of these, too. Therefore, there is a FSA recognizing the language of the system expression. This FSA can be made to recognize the prefixes of its language by making all of its states final. The constraints without the dagger can also be represented as FSA. It should not be a surprise either that combining the resulting prefix FSA and the constraints can be done using the task product of FSA: the constraints were said to restrict the language of the system expressions to those prefixes that the constraint expressions also accept after the alphabet is projected. This is a property of the task product that was briefly mentioned above. The relation to products of FSA is in fact described in [25] when discussing the analysis tool set.

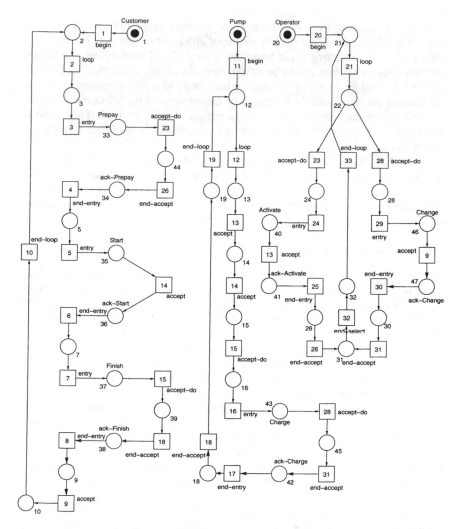

Figure 17.31. State machines obtained from the PN of Figure 17.14.

17.8 DISCUSSION AND RELATED WORK

All the presented models for static analysis of Ada tasking programs have been shown above to be basically equivalent to FSA for this purpose. This provides a better understanding of each of the models and of the relationships between the models. The FSA provide a bridge for ideas conceived for one model to be transferred to the other models. Through FSA, all the models can be related to the best results of all the other models.

With any model there are two dimensions for its performance: modeling convenience and analysis capabilities. Usually there is also a trade-off between the two; a more general model will have to pay for its generality in its analysis performance. Due to the equivalence of the models, none of them will have different analysis possibilities, so the only restrictions on analysis are the performance aspects and whether a particular analysis technique has been implemented or not. Both of these will vary with time, perhaps even drastically.

There have been many suggestions that attempt to reduce the amount of effort needed to perform the reachability analysis.

- The symmetries of a program can be used to reduce effort: references [35–37] use symmetries in Petri nets to generate only part of a reachability graph when symmetric parts are guaranteed to exist. Some authors have suggested extensions to this idea based on *parameterization* as the way of expressing the equivalence of markings [38,39].
- McDowell [4] has introduced the idea of using so-called *clans*: these are a way of not fixing the identity of a task chosen among identical ones until necessary for the analysis. The number of tasks in each clan and the set from which these have been picked are maintained during the analysis. Clans are potentially useful if the system consists of a number of identical tasks.
- Valmari's stubborn sets [34] are a way of exploiting concurrency as a form of *well-behaved nondeterminism* for the purpose of finding all the deadlocks of the program: roughly, there is little point in considering all the interleavings of transitions that cannot possibly disable each other. This can lead to exponential savings in the number of states in the reachability graph in the cases where the tasks are relatively independent. The method has been extended to be able to verify or disprove any stuttering-free formula of linear temporal logic given prior to the reachability analysis. Valmari names Overman [40] as one who has first presented ideas related to his method. Another similar but differently motivated is Godefroid's method [41], which is based on maintaining a Mazurkiewicz trace [42] to each state instead of a sequence of events. These have later expanded to a collection of methods sometimes called *partial order methods*, since they purport to avoid generating all the interleavings of concurrent, partially ordered events, only generating those relevant to finding deadlocks.
- System reductions such as the ones used to find deadlocks in PN models mentioned above, can be used to reduce the size of the model and the number of states in the state space. Damerla [15] has suggested a new class of PNs that would complement the PN reduction scheme sketched.

This requires a specifically designed program for performing the reachability analysis.

- Burch et al. [43] use a data structure for binary decision diagrams that allows the manipulation of sets of states at a time. The transition relation among states is also represented as the set of pairs, so that a new set of "current" states can be computed using a few operations on the data structure. This results in a set-parallel, breadth-first search of the state space. The method is best suited for synchronous systems, such as clocked hardware circuits [44,45]. This assumes the system to have binary state variables, though later work has considered relaxing this assumption.

- Several authors have suggested the use of hierarchical verification methods [32,46,47]. These attempt to perform a reachability analysis of a part of the program, i.e., apply the task product only among some tasks leaving **accept**s open for other tasks, reduce its size while maintaining relevant properties, and repeat the process hierarchically. Any gain in the number of states on a lower level in the analysis hierarchy can potentially save many states on a higher level. The savings depend heavily on the choice of tasks to combine. All should significantly reduce the possible behaviors of the others they are combined with [31].

- There are also ways to perform analysis of programs based on linear algebraic methods. The method for analyzing deadlocks for constrained expressions briefly described above is one example of these. For PNs the best known approach involves embedding the Petri net into a linear system of equations and proving the property for this, see, e.g., [48]. Murata et al. [5] have used so called *S-* and *T-invariants* of PNs for finding deadlocks. Use of invariants or constraints may result in large reduction in the size of the state space that must be generated, since they can be used to guide the search to reach particular states such as deadlocks.

Flowgraphs

One of the problems of the flowgraph model is that the Ada semantics is explicitly referred to in the definitions. The complexity of the semantics makes the model hard to grasp, the analysis programs harder to write, and the definitions more or less informal. It is technically better to present a model as a separate entity with the abstractions (omissions) necessary to obtain the model from the program stated and discussed, with the abstraction (translation) process separately justified, than to make the semantics of Ada a part of the model. This would make the approach more transparent, easing the design of computer programs to aid in the analysis and providing a clearer "audit-trail" for the verification of the analysis results. Naturally, these comments are minor quibbles since programs to generate concurrency graphs already exist. Development of other analysis methods would, however, definitely benefit from separating the Ada semantics from the definition of concurrency graphs.

Task Interaction Graphs

For small examples the TICGs tend to be distinctly smaller than the concurrency graphs, the difference increasing with more tasks. This is partly a result of the removal of the initialization of each of the tasks.

The regions as given present an application of the theory of *virtual coarsening* of atomic actions, originally described by Ashcroft and Manna [11,33]. The idea of virtual coarsening is simply that it is of no concern for the verification of concurrent behavior where within a non-interruptible internal computation the control of a task resides. It is therefore quite reasonable to extend the atomic actions (here, regions) to their widest possible extent. The coarsening is intuitively safe until there is at most one synchronizing or choice action in a region. In fact, the regions could be extended to include more than one of these under some conditions [11].

The task interaction graphs include also a feature called *edge groups*, which we have omitted to more concisely present the model. In a TIG, an edge represents a possible transition between two regions, labeled with a relevant synchronization action. Now, a collection of edge groups is defined for each region such that if one of the edges in a given group can be taken to reach another region (as far as the task containing the code comprising the region is concerned), then so can any one of the other edges in the same group. This concept would allow the modeling of Boolean guards on **accept** or **select** by having all the edges labeled with the start of a rendezvous correspond to edge groups that could be open at some time. Using these edge groups one could then determine, whether there is a chance that the region represents a deadlock even though it has some edges out of it.

Petri Nets

The primary advantage of PNs is that they are an intuitively appealing, well-known, widely applied, and extensively studied formalism. The simplicity, even austerity, of the basic concepts makes the model easy to treat accurately, giving a good basis to develop ideas. Reachability analysis programs for PNs have existed for years. Indeed, it does not require much effort to write your own. Any reachability analysis program could in principle be used for the analysis of Ada tasking programs once these have been translated to PNs. This gives the PN a distinct advantage as a tool for further research on the subject, since the initial time and effort investment in getting the tools is small [10].

Constrained Expressions

The constrained expression formalism offers additional convenience by separating the system expressions and the constraints and modeling power through the dagger operator. Otherwise, the presented view of the equivalence of the models through FSA is basically a demonstration of the power of constrained expressions. There are differences, however. Note, for example, that the shuffle of the languages denoted by two regular expressions is *not* necessarily that recognized by the task product or by a semi-product.

Process Algebras

Other models suggested for describing and analyzing Ada tasking programs include the process algebras [32], specifically one called ACP-η [49]. These build on the work on path expressions, COSY, CCS (Calculus of Communicating Systems) by Milner [16,17], and Theoretical CSP (Communicating Sequential Processes) by Hoare et al. [50,51]. The basic idea is to represent the future behavior of a program (called a *process*) by an expression involving an alphabet of events, prefixing a process by an event, choice among events (either internal or external choice), parallel composition (having the subexpressions operate in parallel), renaming of events, and *hiding*, (or *restriction* which has a different details) that is, making some events not "visible" beyond a boundary. The expression can then evolve by performing any one of some set of events and can transform to another expression. This can involve a joint event by some component expressions combined using the parallel composition. Repetitions are usually achieved by an explicit recursion operator that names "process variables" that once met restart the behavior from the beginning, or by stating equations that describe the behavior. An example of the first could be $\mu X : a.b.X$ that could describe a process that could first do an a followed by a b before repeating its behavior. The same could be denoted by a (fix-point) equation $X = a.b.X$. The operator "." corresponds to prefixing a process with an event in both of these. The details as to what kind of events can cooperate and what kind of effect the cooperation has on the expression depends very much on the particular kind of algebra.

One of the basic problems of concern for the process algebras is that of *equivalence* and, further, of *congruence* [16]. Since the equality of the languages is not strong enough to distinguish a deadlocking process from one that does not, when should the processes be considered equivalent? The problem is also intuitively understandable, since some processes are obviously "equal", though they look different, like $a.STOP$ and $a.STOP \parallel STOP$, where $STOP$ is a process that can do nothing and $\parallel$ denotes the parallel composition or processes. Research on the subject has produced a myriad of different equivalences. An interesting criterion is whether the equivalence is a congruence over the operations involved in the expressions. Recall that an equivalence partitions any set to disjoint blocks, the *equivalence classes*, that do not overlap, but cover the whole set. An equivalence is a congruence over an operation *iff* the similar operation can be defined on the equivalence classes by picking arbitrary representatives of each class, performing the original operation on the representatives, and finally taking the equivalence class of the result. For a unary operator $f : A \rightarrow A$ for some set A, this can be written as

$$(x \equiv y) \Rightarrow (f(x) \equiv f(y)),$$

which says that for $\equiv$, x can be replaced by y. For a congruence the above must hold for any $x, y \in A$, which basically says that equivalent elements can be replaced with each other without changing a thing as far as the equivalence is concerned. In this case, we can define $f([x]) = [f(x)]$ regardless of which x we want to pick. Here $[x]$ denotes the equivalence class of x.

For a binary operator, say +, we can define the corresponding operation on the equivalence classes by

$$[x] + [y] = [x + y]$$

for any $x, y \in A$, *iff* $\equiv$ is a congruence. For example, to define, say, the addition in arithmetic *modulo* 3, we define an equivalence relation $\equiv$ by saying that two numbers are equivalent *modulo* 3 *iff* the positive residues after dividing both by 3 are equal. This gives us three equivalence classes, [0], [1], and [2], and addition among these equivalence classes is defined by

$$[x] + [y] = [x + y] \ (mod \ 3),$$

which is known to work. The fact that this works is proven by showing that the equivalence is a congruence over addition. In fact, this is where the term congruence comes from, since the equivalence relation here is called "congruence *modulo* 3", 22 is congruent to 4 *modulo* 3, for example.

Thus, to be able to substitute equivalent things for other equivalent things, and to perform the operations on arbitrary representatives without missing anything, the equivalence must be a congruence over all the relevant operations.

The importance of these to static analysis of Ada tasking is the following. Any finite state process, that is, a process that can only reach a finite number of states, can be represented by a regular expression and, therefore, by a FSA. Choices in the process become choices among subexpressions, with λ-moves or not, parallel composition is very close to the task product, but might need some substitutions depending on the process algebra in question, renaming and hiding (restriction) correspond also to substitutions, and repetition to a suitable use of the closure operators $(\ldots)^*$ and $(\ldots)^+$. All the states of the FSA will be final so that any prefix is in the language accepted by it. This makes the process algebras having finite state spaces (again) equivalent to FSA. Suppose there is an equivalence on process algebras that

- is a congruence over the relevant operations,
- considers two processes equivalent only if one can deadlock after a sequence of events exactly when the other can,
- the algebra can easily model the Ada tasking programs, and

- there is an algorithm to find a smallest FSA that is equivalent to a given one.

Then this equivalence can be used to do hierarchical analysis of Ada tasking programs. The analysis involves combining some task FSA using the appropriate version of task product and then minimizing the result with respect to the equivalence. The result is again a FSA that can be combined further, providing for the hierarchical analysis. Here we shall simply name one candidate for such an equivalence, the Chaos-Free Failures-Divergences (CFFD) equivalence by Valmari and Tienari [53]. This is based on the failure semantics of Theoretical CSP [51,54]. The translation of Ada tasking programs into the slightly extended Basic LOTOS [55] that Valmari and Tienari are using has not been defined, but is hardly a difficult problem, assuming the abstractions for static analysis are employed.

An important theoretical step in utilizing a congruence relation is proving some relevant properties that state when two expressions are equivalent. These amount to reduction rules among the process expressions. Reduction rules open up a way of proving that a system, given as an expression, implements a specification (service), given as another expression, up to the congruence, by showing how one can be reduced to the other. This kind of reasoning is a thrust in the presentation of Theoretical CSP in [51], for example.

Expressions of process algebras can usually be given an interpretation as Labeled Transition Systems (LTSs), a generalization of state machines, not necessarily finite. In fact, we could have used LTSs instead of FSA in this paper with little difficulty.

Future directions

Where is the static analysis of Ada tasking programs heading? Some effort should probably go to incorporating the best ideas of any one model into the other models. Extending the class of programs that can be treated will involve being able to treat more of the syntactic structures of Ada [9,10]. But after these there will be a definite push needed to extend the scope of the analysis techniques.

An idea to improve analysis methods is to admit the insertion of *redundancy* into the description of the program. This could involve data invariants, program invariants, anything that would present a usable description of what the program *should* do as opposed to the program text that describes what it does do. This can then be used to restrict the search of anomalies by letting the analysis program immediately notify of any contradictions between the actual and intended behavior. Because of this ability to stop early during the analysis, these are at times referred to as *"on-the-fly"* verification techniques. These incur a benefit if a bulk of a reachability analysis would be spent on states that become reachable only as a consequence of an error.

A natural step is to include, at least to some extent, the variables that have been ignored. At least two interesting problems are apparent in this [52]. First, the number of possible states associated with variables can be much larger than with control flow. Note that any state of the first PN model in Figure 17.14 can be represented using a bit for each place at most, since there will be at most one token in a place[5]. A single integer variable in an Ada tasking program, never mind a more complicated data structure, can contain that many bits of information. Furthermore, some of the time the information is purely redundant to the tasking behavior. The value of the variable can make the analysis distinguish two program states even if the difference is totally irrelevant. Obviously, there must be some research done on extracting an equivalence relation out of a program such that it allows the analysis to equate the two seemingly different states. The equivalence relation can then be used to collapse all the equivalent states into one, a representative of the class. Some headway has already been made in this direction, e.g., [56]. We will call these problems associated with the introduction of variables the *secondary* state explosion to distinguish the effect from that of the nondeterminism and concurrency introduced by the Ada tasking constructs.

A related interesting problem is that the assignment statement, the main means to change the state of the variables, is in general a nonreversible operation, e.g., $X := 0$ leaves little idea about the prior value of X. This is a problem especially apparent for PNs, since the PN model will have a transition for each possible value in the range of X. The transition fired and the resulting marking uniquely determine the previous marking in a PN, and since nothing is known about the prior value of X, there has to be a transition for any value. This is discussed in [52], where also a solution employing yet another model is proposed. We will not go into this further, since there is another well-known alternative, the use of high-level nets. There, any local variables can be encoded as an attribute of a token representing the location of the control of a task. Any shared variable could be represented as a single token in a shared place. Since the transitions can modify the attributes in complicated ways, even change the number of these, this provides a way to model even declarations of variables in an Ada program. This does not, of course, solve the problem of the secondary state explosion.

For the FSA or process algebras the same effect can be achieved by indexing the states of the FSA (process variables for the algebras) by the value of the variable. This is in fact the same device that the high-level PNs use since the range of attributes of some token can be seen as indices on the place where the token resides. However, there must be a way of representing the attributes and operations on the high level. This forces a choice of notation that can never satisfy all the interested. Moreover, it makes writing the analysis programs more of a chal-

---

[5] Since this is a model of a sequential task, an abstract program counter that names the place with the token is enough. This needs $O(\log |P|)$ bits.

lenge since these must be able to perform or at least react to all the necessary operations.

Finally, we have chosen to abstract away the real-time aspects of the Ada program. This is not an option for those systems where the real-time behavior is crucial. To treat such systems, one would need a model that is able to represent the relevant real-time properties of the program, see, e.g., [9].

REFERENCES

1. Taylor RN: A General Purpose Algorithm for Analyzing Concurrent Programs. CACM 26 (1983) 5, 362–376.

2. Dillon LK, Avrunin GS, Wileden JS: Constrained Expressions: Toward Broad Applicability of Analysis Methods for Distributed Software Systems. ACM Transactions on Programming Languages and Systems 10 (1988) 3, 374–420.

3. Long DL, Clarke LA: Task Interaction Graphs for Concurrency Analysis. Proceedings of the 11th International Conference on Software Engineering, Pittsburgh, May 1989.

4. McDowell CE: Representing Reachable States of a Parallel Program. Technical report 89–17, Computer Research Laboratory, University of California, Santa Cruz, California, 1989.

5. Murata T, Shenker B, Shatz SM: Detection of Ada Static Deadlocks Using Petri Net Invariants. IEEE Transactions on Software Engineering SE–15(1989)3, 314–326.

6. Shatz SM, Cheng WK: A Petri Net Framework for Automated Static Analysis of Ada Tasking Behavior. The Journal of Systems and Software 8 (1988), 343–359.

7. Shatz SM, Tu S, Murata T, Duri S: An Application of Petri Net Reduction for Ada-Tasking Deadlock Analysis. IEEE Transactions on Parallel and Distributed Systems 7 (Dec. 1996) 12, 1307–1322.

8. Pezze M, Taylor RN, Young M: Graph models for reachability analysis of concurrent programs. ACM Transactions on Software Engineering and Methodology (Apr. 1995) 171–213.

9. Burns A, Wellings AJ: How to verify concurrent Ada programs—the application of model checking, Ada Letters, 19 (1999) 2, 78–83.

10. Burns A, Wellings AJ, Burns F, Koelmans AM, Koutny M, Romanovsky A, Yakovlev A: Toward modeling and Verification of concurrent Ada programs using Petri nets. Proceedings of Workshop on Software Engineering and Petri Nets, pre-Workshop of

International Conference On Application and Theory of Petri Nets, Aarhus, Denmark, June 2000, 115–134.

11. Pnueli A: Applications of Temporal Logic to the Specification and Verification of Reactive Systems: A Survey of Current Trends. Lecture Notes in Computer Science 224: Current Trends in Concurrency, Overviews and Tutorials 1986, deBakker JW, deRoever W-P, Rozenberg G (*eds.*), Springer-Verlag, Berlin 1986, 510–584.

12. Clarke EM, Emerson EA, Sistla AP: Automatic Verification of Finite-State Concurrent Systems Using Temporal Logic Specifications. ACM Transactions on Programming Languages and Systems 8 (1986) 2, 244–263.

13. Mendelson E: Introduction to Mathematical Logic. Wadsworth & Brooks / Cole Advanced Books & Software, Monterey, California 1987, 341 p.

14. Helmbold DP, Luckham D: Debugging Ada Tasking Programs. IEEE Software 2 (1985) 2, 47–57.

15. Damerla S: Concurrent Program Analysis for State Space Generation and Complexity Evaluation. Ph.D. Thesis, Dept of Electrical Engineering and Computer Science, Univ. of Illinois at Chicago 1991, 96 p.

16. Milner R: A Calculus of Communicating Systems. Lecture Notes in Computer Science 92, Springer-Verlag 1980.

17. Milner R: Communication and Concurrency. Prentice-Hall 1989, 260 p.

18. Petri CA: *Kommunikation mit Automaten. Schriften des IIM* Nr. 2 (1962), *Institut für Instrumentelle Mathematik*, Bonn. English translation: *Communication with Automata*. Technical Report RADC–TR–65–377, Vol. 1, Suppl. 1, Griffith Air Force Base, New York 1966.

19. Petri CA: State-Transition Structures in Physics and in Computation. International Journal of Theoretical Physics 21 (1982) 12, 979–992.

20. Taylor RN, Levine DL, Kelly CD: Structural Testing of Concurrent Programs. IEEE Transactions on Software Engineering SE–18 (1992) 3, 206–215.

21. Sermersheim B: Enhancements, Optimizations, and Testing of Software in the TOTAL System. Master's Project, University of Illinois at Chicago 1990.

22. Berthelot G, Roucairol G: Reduction of Petri Nets. Lecture Notes in Computer Science Vol. 45: Mathematical Foundations of Computer Science 1976, Mazurkiewicz A (*ed.*), Springer-Verlag, Berlin 1976, 202–209.

23. Ginsburg S: The Mathematical Theory of Context-Free Languages. McGraw-Hill Publishing Company, New York 1966.

24. Avrunin GS, Dillon, LK, Wileden JC, Riddle WE: Constrained Expressions: Adding Analysis Capabilities to Design Methods for Concurrent Software Systems. IEEE Transactions on Software Engineering, SE–12 (1986) 2, 278–291.

25. Avrunin GS, Buy UA, Corbett JC, Dillon LK, Wileden JC: Automated Analysis of Concurrent Systems with the Constrained Expression Toolset. Technical Report 90–116, Department of Computer and Information Science, University of Massachusetts, December 1990, 51 p.

26. Lauer PE, Shields MW, Best E: Formal Theory of the Basic COSY Notation. TR 143, Computing Laboratory, University of Newcastle upon Tyne 1978.

27. Lauer PE, Torrigiani PR, Shields MW: COSY—A System Specification Language Based on Paths and Processes. *Acta Informatica* 12 (1979), 109–158.

28. Best E: COSY: Its Relation to Nets and to CSP. Petri Nets: Applications and Relationships to Other Models of Concurrency, Advances in Petri Nets 1986, Part II, Proceedings of an Advanced Course, Bad Honnef, September 1986, Brauer W, Reisig W, Rozenberg G (*eds.*), Lecture Notes in Computer Science 255, Springer-Verlag 1987, 416–440.

29. Campbell RH, Habermann AN: The Specification of Process Synchronization by Path Expressions. Lecture Notes in Computer Science 16, Springer-Verlag 1974, 89–102.

30. Hopcroft JE, Ullman JD: Introduction to Automata Theory, Languages, and Computation. Addison-Wesley 1979, 418 p.

31. Graf S, Steffen B: Compositional Minimization of Finite Sate Processes. Proceedings of the Workshop on Computer-Aided Verification, Rutgers University, June 1990, DIMACS Technical Report 90–31, Vol.I.

32. Yeh WJ, Young M: Compositional Reachability Analysis Using Process Algebra. 4th ACM Symposium on Testing, Analysis, and Verification, October 91, 49–59.

33. Ashcroft E, Manna Z: Formalization of Properties of Parallel Programs. Machine Intelligence 6 (1971), Meltzer B, Michie D (*eds.*) Edinburgh, 17–41.

34. Valmari A: Stubborn Attack on State Explosion. Computer-Aided Verification 90, Series in Discrete Mathematics and Theoretical Computer Science, Vol. 3, American Mathematical Society, Providence, Rhode Island, 1991.

35. Huber P, Jensen AM, Jepsen LO, Jensen K: Towards Reachability Trees for High-Level Petri Nets. Lecture Notes in Computer Science Vol.188: Advances in Petri Nets 1984, Rozenberg, G (*ed.*), Springer-Verlag, 215–233.

36. Starke PH: Reachability Analysis of Petri Nets Using Symmetries. *Systeme: Analysis, Modellierung, Simulation* 8 (1991) 4/5, 293–303.

37. Schmidt K, Starke PH: An Algorithm to Compute the Symmetries of Petri Nets. Petri Net Newsletter 40 (Dec. 1991), 25–30.

38. Dutheillet C, Haddad S: Regular Stochastic Petri Nets. Supplement to the Proceedings of the 10th International Conference on Application and Theory of Petri Nets, June 28–30, 1989, Bonn, Federal Republic of Germany, 43–62.

39. Lindqvist M: Parameterized Reachability Trees for Predicate/Transition Nets. *Acta Polytechnica Scandinavica*, Mathematics and Computer Science, No. 54 (1989).

40. Overman WT: Verification of Concurrent Systems: Function and Timing. Ph.D. dissertation, University of California, Los Angeles 1981, 174 p.

41. Godefroid P: Using Partial Orders to Improve Automatic Verification Methods. Proceedings of Workshop on Computer Aided Verification, Rutgers University, June 1990, DIMACS Technical Report 90–31.

42. Mazurkiewicz A: Trace Theory. Petri Nets: Applications and Relationships to Other Models of Concurrency, Advances in Petri Nets 1986, Part II, Proceedings of an Advanced Course, Bad Honnef, September 1986, Brauer W, Reisig W, Rozenberg G (*eds.*), Lecture Notes in Computer Science 255, Springer-Verlag 1987, 279–324.

43. Burch JR, Clarke EM, McMillan KL, Dill DL, Hwang J: Symbolic Model Checking: 10^{20} States and Beyond. Proceedings of the Fifth Annual IEEE Symposium on Logic in Computer Science, June 1990.

44. Burch JR, Clarke EM, Long DE: Symbolic Model Checking with Partitioned Translation Relations. Proc. VLSI 91, Edinburgh, Scotland, 1991.

45. Clarke EM, Burch JR, Grumberg O, Long DE, McMillan KL: Automatic Verification of Sequential Circuit Designs. Philosophical Transactions of the Royal Society, Series A, 339, 1652, Apr. 15, 1992, 105–120.

46. Valmari A: Compositional State Space Generation. 11th International Conference on Application and Theory of Petri Nets, Paris, France, June 27–29, 1990, 43–62.

47. Notomi M, Murata T: Hierarchical Reachability Graph of Bounded Petri Nets for Concurrent-Software Analysis. IEEE Transactions on Software Engineering 20 (May 1994) 5, 325–336.

48. Murata T: Petri Nets: Properties, Analysis and Applications. Proceedings of the IEEE 77 (1989) 4, 541–580.

49. Baeten JCM, van Glabeek RJ: Another Look at Abstraction in Process Algebra. Proceedings of the 14th International Colloquium on Automata Languages, and Programming (ICALP), Karlsruhe, Germany, July 1987, 84–94.

50. Brookes SD, Hoare CAR, Roscoe AW: A Theory of Communicating Sequential Processes. Journal of the ACM 31 (1984) 7, 560–599.

51. Hoare CAR: Communicating Sequential Processes. Prentice-Hall 1985, 256 p.

52. Tiusanen M, Valmari A: A Graph Model for Efficient Reachability Analysis of Description Languages. Research report B34, Helsinki University of Technology, Digital Systems Laboratory 1986, 17 p.

53. Valmari A, Tienari M: An Improved Failures Equivalence for Finite-State Systems with a Reduction Algorithm. Proceedings of IFIP WG 6.1 Protocol Specification, Testing, and Verification, Stockholm, June 1991.

54. Brookes SD, Roscoe AW: An Improved Failures Model for Communicating Sequential Processes. Proceedings NSF-SERC Seminar on Concurrency, Lecture Notes in Computer Science, Springer-Verlag, New York 1985.

55. Bolognesi T, Brinksma E: Introduction to the ISO Specification Language LOTOS. Computer Networks and ISDN Systems 14 (1987), 25–59. Also in: The Formal Description Technique LOTOS, North-Holland 1989, 25–73.

56. Buy U, Moll R: Liveness Analysis and the Automatic Generation of Concurrent Programs. Computer-Aided Verification 90, Series in Discrete Mathematics and Theoretical Computer Science, Vol. 3, American Mathematical Society, Providence, Rhode Island, 1991.

18

Deadlock Handling in Database Systems

Mathias Weske
Hasso Plattner Institute at University of Potsdam Potsdam, Germany.

Abstract

Synchronization of concurrent transactions in database systems using the well-known 2-phase-locking protocol may result in waiting conditions involving database transactions and, in case of circular waiting conditions, deadlock. All transactions involved in a deadlock come to a halt, a clearly very undesirable situation. In this chapter, the deadlock problem in database systems is characterized using a set of generic deadlock conditions. We show that a set of transactions encounter a deadlock situation if these conditions are met. In general, there are fundamentally different approaches to deadlock handling: deadlock prevention, deadlock avoidance, and deadlock detection. We discuss algorithms for each of these approaches. Finally, deadlock detection in distributed database systems is treated in more detail. In distributed database systems transactions may span multiple sites. Hence, distributed deadlocks cannot be detected using local knowledge of one site only; on the contrary, sites have to communicate according to deadlock detection algorithms, to identify distributed deadlock cycles, and to resolve them allowing transactions to resume operation. In this chapter, the deadlock problem in distributed database systems is introduced, and a set of algorithms to detect and resolve distributed deadlocks are presented.

18.1   Introduction

Database management systems are software systems for managing large amounts of enterprise data. These systems are well equipped to provide integrated access to, as well as safe storage and efficient and convenient access to data. A number of excellent textbooks on database systems are available, including [ONeil2000, RaGe2000, ElNa2000].

Among a variety of other aspects not in the scope of this monograph (for example, query processing and integrity constraints checking), database management systems are responsible for the correct execution of concurrent application programs, also called transaction synchronization or concurrency control. Most database products nowadays use some variant of the 2-phase-locking protocol to ensure transaction synchronization [BeHaGo1987]. It can be shown that locking protocols provide very good performance while ensuring isolation between concurrent transactions. However, using locking protocols for synchronizing concurrent transactions may result in waiting conditions between transactions and, in case of circular waiting conditions, deadlock. All transactions involved in a deadlock come to a halt, a very undesirable situation. In this chapter, the deadlock problem in database systems is introduced, and a set of algorithms to handle deadlocks in database systems are presented.

We point out that the occurrence of a deadlock is a random and often even rare event. There might be hundreds or even thousands of executions of a set of application programs and only once a deadlock occurs, due to particular runtime behavior of the transactions involved. If a decent deadlock handling mechanism is missing in a given database system, it might be the case that once a week or once a month by accident, a deadlock occurs. In this case, the operator apologizes to you that your request cannot be answered "because our computer system is down."

The remainder of this chapter is organized as follows. In Section 18.2, the foundations of database transaction processing are introduced. Rather than presenting a thorough study of the topic, we focus on the aspects that are relevant for the issue addressed, i.e., the question why waiting conditions involving transactions are possible in database transaction processing. The deadlock problem in database systems is introduced in Section 18.3. It is shown that a set of generic deadlock conditions are met in the database context. Deadlock handling is addressed in Section 18.4, where algorithms for preventing, avoiding and detecting database deadlocks are provided, and their advantages and disadvantages are discussed. Section 18.5 is devoted to distributed deadlock detection. The specific issues in distributed deadlock detection as opposed to centralized deadlock detection are characterized, and a set of algorithms for detecting and resolving deadlocks spanning multiple sites of a distributed database system are presented. Concluding remarks complete this chapter.

18.2 Database Transaction Processing

Programmers involved in database application development can concentrate on application-specific issues, rather than take into account technical details of data management. High-level descriptive query languages are provided for convenient and efficient access to data stored in a database, such as the Structured Query Language (SQL). Database management systems provide ad-hoc query facilities that support complex queries without writing a program. However, SQL provides efficient access at the price of restricted expressive power. Therefore, application programmers may access the database from within general purpose programming languages such as C, C++ or Java. In particular, application programs may use specific interfaces to the database, in particular call level interface (such as Java Database Connectivity, JDBC) or system level interface (Embedded SQL). In the former approach, queries against the database are constructed at run-time of the application program, and prefabricated library functions are used to run the queries against the database. In the statement level interface approach, queries may be constructed at compile time, i.e., statically. In this case, the application program contains parts which are expressed in the database query language, typically SQL. A precompiler transforms these parts into the host language. Just like in the call level interface approach, library functions are linked to generate the executable code of the application program.

In any case, programs access the database using read and write operations. To abstract away from the specific properties of memory organization and management of specific database management systems, the read/write model is introduced. It is a strong abstraction of typical real world situations, nevertheless very useful and appropriate for database transactions. The read/write model rules are that programs access the database via read and write operations on atomic data. Hence, page sizes, block sizes, the size of physical main memory are irrelevant for conceptual discussion of transaction processing. In addition to read and write operations to atomic data, transactions can execute a commit or abort operation. Each transaction executes either commit or abort as its last operation. Executing commit completes the transaction successfully, and modified data is entered into the database, whereas abort stands for an unsuccessful termination. In this case, the modifications of the transaction are withdrawn. In the remainder of this chapter we will assume the read/write model.

Correct concurrent executions in the presence of system failures are called transactions. Transactions are characterized by the ACID properties, which is an acronym for the following properties:

- *Atomicity*: Each transaction is executed completely or not at all. Partial executions of transactions are not possible.

- *Consistency*: Transactions are correct in the sense that they transfer a consistent database state in (typically different) consistent database state.

- *Isolation*: Concurrent transactions are executed in isolation from each other. This means that a transaction can read data from other transactions only after the latter have completed.

- *Durability*: The effects of completed transactions are durable and survive future system failures.

It can be shown that the order of read and write operations is crucial when it comes to correctness of interleaved operations. The sequence of all read, write, commit and abort operations that are being executed in a database transaction processing system is called a schedule. The scheduler is the system component that is responsible for ordering operations in a way that synchronization issues are solved. It can be shown that the order of operations p and q is significant (i.e., changing the order in general results in different values for the data stored in the database) if and only if both operations access the same data object and belong to different transactions. In this case we say p and q are in conflict with each other or p and q are conflicting. The basis of transaction synchronization is based on a notion of equivalence between schedules. One form of equivalence is conflict equivalence. Two schedules are conflict equivalent if and only if they have the same set of operations and they agree on the order of all operations in conflict. A schedule S is conflict serializable, if there exists a sequential schedule S' (one in which all transactions are executed in sequential order) that is conflict equivalent to S. Database transaction processing has generated a large body of literature in recent years; see [WeiVo2001] for an excellent reference book transaction processing in database systems.

One of the results from transaction processing that has the largest practical implications is the fact that a scheduler is guaranteed to generate only conflict-serializable schedules, if it uses the so called 2-phase locking protocol or 2PL. This protocol is defined by the following rules:

- *R1*: Before a read or write operation on a data item can be performed, the transaction has to hold the respective lock on that data item.

- *R2*: At each instant, there is at least one of two conflicting locks set on a given data item.

- *R3*: After the first unlock operation by a transaction, this transaction is not permitted to issue another lock operation (2 phase rule)

- *R4*: After a transaction has issued a commit or abort operation, all locks are released.

Most database systems today use some variant of 2PL to ensure correct execution of concurrent transactions.

18.3   Database Deadlock Problem

The good news is that locking protocols ensure conflict serializable schedules. However, by locking data objects, waiting conditions between transactions may form dynamically. In addition, circular waiting conditions result in deadlock. All transactions involved in a deadlock situation come to a standstill and cannot proceed execution. Before discussing the deadlock problem in database systems, a set of generic deadlock conditions are introduced. Deadlock conditions are generic in the sense that they are applicable to deadlocks in different kinds of computer systems, including operating systems and database systems. The deadlock conditions are as follows:

- *Mutual Exclusion*: The resources are exclusive in the sense that at each point in time at most one process may hold a given resource.

- *Nonpreemption*: It is not possible to preempt processes, i.e., to withdraw resources from processes.

- *Waiting Condition*: It must be possible for a process to hold resources while requesting additional resources.

- *Circular Wait*: A circular waiting condition between processes is possible.

These generic deadlock conditions have been developed in the context of deadlocks in operating systems. While being developed for operating systems deadlocks, it turns out that the following conditions are well suited to characterize deadlocks in database systems:

- *Mutual Exclusion*: The resources under consideration in the database context are locks; in particular, conflicting locks. The mutual exclusion condition is satisfied in database systems, since at each instant at most one transaction can hold one of two conflicting locks. Hence, conflicting locks are exclusive.

- *Nonpreemption*: As discussed above, correct synchronization of concurrent transactions is only possible if the 2-phase rule is satisfied. This means that the database management system may not withdraw a lock from a transaction, once the lock is requested by another transaction. In contrast, the transaction has to execute an unlock operation on its behalf, once it completes. Hence, the nonpreemption rule is satisfied for database transaction processing systems based on 2PL.

- *Waiting Condition*: It is possible for a transaction to hold a lock on a data item while requesting a lock on an additional data item. This makes perfect sense, since a transaction issues a lock on a data object only if and when the transaction needs to access it. Hence, the waiting condition is also satisfied.

- *Circular Wait*: Since a priori there is no limit on which transactions access which data, any waiting condition may dynamically arise. If a circular waiting condition arises, a deadlock is formed.

To explain a deadlock situation in more detail, consider a simple example involving two transactions. Transaction T_1 wants to access data objects x and y (x followed by y), while transaction T_2 wishes to access the same data items in opposite order. If both transactions execute sequentially, no problems occur. Sequential execution means that one transaction completes and releases its locks before the second transaction starts execution, i.e., before it sets the first lock on a data item. However, if both transactions execute concurrently, the following situation may occur: T_1 has set a lock on x and T_2 has set a lock on y. Both transactions access the locked data and proceed. However, at this instant, it is clear that they will run into a deadlock situation because none of them is able to set the lock on the next data object.

Assume T_1 has accessed x and now wants to proceed. Therefore, it has to lock data object y. T_1 issues a lock request to the scheduler. The lock cannot be granted by the scheduler, since there is a conflicting lock (set for T_2) on the data item requested. Therefore T_1 enters a waiting condition. In particular, T_1 waits until the lock on y can be granted. However, that lock can only be granted after T_2 has released the lock on y. Analogously, T_2 now tries to lock x, which also fails.

This situation can be characterized as follows: T_1 waits for the lock on y and T_2 waits for the lock on x. Will any of the transactions ever be able to proceed? The answer is No! This is due to the 2 phase rule, which states that a transaction cannot lock additional data items after the first unlock operation. As a result, none of the locks set can be released: T_1 waits for T_2 to unlock y, while T_2 waits for T_1 to unlock x. Effectively, T_1 waits for T_2 to commit (and release its locks) and vice versa. However, none of the transactions can commit, since additional locks are required until commit can be executed. This example shows how deadlocks in database systems can occur. It is obvious that this situation extends to circles involving multiple transactions. In general, a deadlock cycle may consist of transactions $T_1, T_2, \ldots, T_n$ where T_1 waits for T_2, T_2 waits for T_3 and, eventually, T_n waits for T_1.

18.4 Handling Database Deadlocks

In general, there are different ways to deal with deadlocks: deadlock prevention, deadlock avoidance and deadlock detection. In deadlock prevention, the underlying processing is restricted in a way that deadlocks can never occur. In this case, no additional tests at run-time have to be done to handle deadlocks. In deadlock avoidance, before each request to a resource is granted, the system has to make sure that granting that particular resource request will not lead to a deadlock, not even later. Therefore, run-time checks have to be used in order to restrict resource allocation in a way that deadlocks cannot occur. Finally, deadlock detection deals with monitoring waiting conditions that arise during run-time. These waiting conditions are checked for deadlock cycles. Once a deadlock is found, one of the processes involved is terminated and the resources the process held are released. By using the released resources, other processes involved in the deadlock can proceed, breaking the deadlock cycle. As this discussion illustrates, deadlock detection is the most advanced concept, since complex waiting conditions have to be monitored and deadlock cycle detection algorithms have to be in place to ensure all deadlocks are detected. We remark that deadlock detection and resolution is possible only if the computer system permits the termination of processes without harming the system altogether.

18.4.1   Preventing Database Deadlocks

Deadlock prevention in general is done by restricting the normal processing in a way that deadlocks cannot occur. The deadlock conditions introduced above are a very good tool to design deadlock prevention algorithms. The general approach is as follows: If the processing of the computer system can be restricted in a way that one of the deadlock conditions can never occur, then deadlocks are prevented. This general approach is also feasible in the context of database deadlocks. By restricting database transaction processing using locking protocols in a way that one deadlock condition cannot occur, deadlocks can never occur. We now investigate the possibility of negating the deadlock conditions. In particular, for each deadlock condition we explain what negating means, and we discuss ways to do so.

Dropping the mutual exclusion condition means that multiple transactions can hold conflicting locks on a given data item at a given instant. As a result, these transactions can access the data item without any restrictions. Obviously this cannot be permitted in database transaction processing, since the goal of isolation between concurrent transactions cannot be reached by dropping the mutual exclusion condition.

Analogous considerations apply to the nonpreemption condition. Negating this condition means that transactions release locks on data item, followed by setting locks on other data items. As considerations in database transaction processing show [BeHaGo1987], the 2 phase rule cannot be violated. In particular, concurrent transactions are not executed in isolation if they do not meet the 2 phase rule.

The waiting condition can be negated by setting all locks a transaction will ever need when the transaction starts. This variant of the 2-phase locking protocol is called conservative locking. If one or more locks cannot be set, then no lock will be set and the transaction tries again later. It is obvious that the waiting condition cannot be satisfied in this setting, since if a transaction holds locks then it can proceed to its end and release the locks. Also notice that the 2-phase rule is satisfied in conservative locking, since there is no lock operation after an unlock operation for a given transaction. However, two major problems result from this approach:

1. Locks are held longer than necessary. To see this point, consider a transaction which requires four data objects. However, it requires one object in the beginning and the other three objects a short time before its termination, for example to write results of complex operations performed on the data item locked first. This means that data items (numbers two, three and four) are locked much longer than they have to, which in turn considerably lowers the degree of concurrency the database transaction processing system permits.

2. The second issue involved here is related to the first one. Since a transaction can only start if and when all locks are set, the degree of concurrency between transactions is lowered, since no two transactions can overlap in time if they involve common data objects.

We illustrate the second observation by the following example. Assume there is an additional transaction involving data item two (accessed by the first transaction only briefly before termination, but locked right in the beginning due to the conservative locking approach). Transaction two has to wait for the first transaction to commit and release its locks, although it may use data item two only in its beginning. An unrestricted execution of these transactions would allow both transactions to execute concurrently until the first transaction requests the second data item (very late). This means that the overall processing time of the transactions can be reduced considerably without predeclaring locks.

Finally, the circular waiting condition can be negated by defining an order on the data items. Transactions are allowed to request locks on data items only in the order defined on the data items. This means that transactions are restricted with respect to the order in which data items are locked. In particular, the data item that stands lowest in the data object order has to be locked first, independent of the time the data item is actually required by the transaction. Similar issues which we already encountered in the predeclaration approach apply in this case; however, the limitations are weaker, since not all locks have to be held during the complete life time of the transaction; rather the order in which locks are set is restricted, which can also lead to holding locks longer than required. A variant of this approach is the tree locking protocol, in which a hierarchical tree structure is defined on the data objects, and transactions can only request locks in the order that is specified by the tree. The tree locking protocol is described in [BeHaGo1987].

We now motivate why this approach prevents deadlocks; the argument is by contradiction: consider a deadlock cycle $T_1 \to T_2 \to \ldots \to T_n \to T_1$. We look at waiting condition $T_{n-1} \to T_n$. From the fact that locks on data items can only be set in the order defined on the data items, it follows that T_n holds a lock on a data item x, which is higher in the data item order than any data item held by T_{n-1}. This argument is applied inductively to the other waiting conditions involved in the deadlock. Finally it follows that T_n holds a lock on a data item which stands higher in the data object hierarchy than any lock held by (that very transaction) T_n! This contradiction shows that the assumption was wrong. Hence, deadlocks cannot occur if all transactions request locks on data items only according to the order of the data items.

18.4.2   Avoiding Database Deadlocks

Deadlock avoidance in general puts no limits on the processing; rather at run-time there are additional algorithms employed which make sure that deadlocks cannot occur. In particular, each resource request is analyzed and granted only if it does not lead to a deadlock. Since the algorithms do not check for deadlocks (as deadlock detection algorithms do), they guess if deadlocks can occur. Since they always have to be "on the right side," waiting conditions are rejected although they do not result in a deadlock! Besides run-time costs of the algorithms, the main cost of these algorithms is aborting and restarting processes, which would not lead to deadlock.

We investigate the possibility to negate the circular wait deadlock condition. As it turns, this condition can be negated by allowing only certain types of waiting conditions. In particular, only linear waiting conditions are allowed. This idea can be implemented easily by allowing a waiting condition $T_i \to T_j$ only if $i < j$, where its subscripts denote the identifier of the transaction. If a waiting condition occurs which does not satisfy this criterion, then one of the participating transactions is aborted. Hence, waiting conditions can only be linear but never cyclic. To see this reconsider the above mentioned deadlock cycle $T_1, T_2, \ldots, T_n$ where T_1 waits for T_2, T_2 waits for T_3 and, eventually, T_n waits for T_1. We now show that this deadlock cycle cannot occur in this approach. From the specification of the possible waiting conditions follows that $T_1 < T_2 < \ldots < T_n$; in particular $T_1 < T_n$. If that were a cycle then T_n would wait for T_1, which means $T_n < T_1$. This contradicts the above statement $T_1 < T_n$. Hence, deadlock cycles are not possible if waiting conditions $T_1 \to T_j$ can only be allowed if $i < j$. As with the approaches mentioned above, the concurrent execution of transactions are limited, because not all waiting conditions can be allowed. However, the overall limitation of this approach seems weaker than the other approaches mentioned so far.

Concrete examples based on this approach are timestamp based deadlock avoidance algorithms. Two famous algorithms in this context are the Wound-Wait algorithm and the Wait-Die algorithm. Both algorithms are explained next. Each transaction T receives a unique timestamp $ts(T)$ when it starts. Timestamps are unique, and a total order is defined on the timestamps. Timestamps are assigned in ascending order, which means that $ts(T) < ts(T')$ iff T started before T'. The above mentioned algorithms differ with respect to what kinds of waiting conditions can be permitted:

- *Wait-Die*: Older transactions are allowed to wait for younger transactions. This means that a waiting condition $T_i \to T_j$ can be allowed iff $ts(T_i) < ts(T_j)$. If a younger transaction requests a lock held by an older transaction, the younger transaction is aborted, the transaction "dies."

- *Wound-Wait*: If an older transaction requests a lock held by a younger transaction, the younger transaction is aborted. Hence, the older transaction "wounds" the younger one. If a younger transaction waits for a lock held by an older one, it is allowed to wait for the older one to release its locks.

The algorithms are detailed as follows: notice that in both cases linear waiting conditions are only permitted. Circular waiting conditions are not possible. To illustrate the difference between those algorithms, consider the following example, involving transactions T_5, T_7 and T_8, such that T_5 is

Wait-Die:

if $ts(T_i) < ts(T_j)$ **then**

  T_i waits // older tx waits

else

  abort T_i // younger tx dies

Wound-Wait:

if $ts(T_i) < ts(T_j)$ **then**

  abort T_j // older tx wounds younger

else

  T_i waits // younger tx waits

Figure 18.1. Deadlock Avoidance on $T_i \rightarrow T_j$.

the oldest transaction, followed by T_7 and T_8. Assume a waiting condition $T_5 \rightarrow T_7$ occurs. In the Wait-Die algorithm, this waiting condition can be allowed, since an older transaction is allowed to wait for a younger one. If a waiting condition $T_8 \rightarrow T_7$ occurs, a younger transaction requests a lock from an older one. In this case, the younger transaction is aborted and dies. Considering the Wound-Wait algorithm, the younger transaction is allowed to wait for the older to complete and release its locks.

Both algorithms guarantee freedom from deadlocks, as the following discussion shows. Similar to the argument above, we show the correctness of the algorithms by contradiction. Assume a deadlock cycle $T_1 \rightarrow T_2 \ldots \rightarrow T_n \rightarrow T_1$ exists. From the definition of the Wait-Die algorithm it follows that

$$ts(T_1) < ts(T_2) < \ldots < ts(T_n) < ts(T_1)$$

Due to transitivity of the $<$ relation, the contradiction $ts(T_1) < ts(T_1)$ can be deduced. Hence, no such cycle can exist. Therefore, the algorithm guarantees freedom from deadlocks. The correctness of the Wound-Wait algorithm can be shown analogously.

18.4.3   Detecting Deadlocks

The third approach to deadlock handling is detection of deadlock cycles. The advantage of this approach is that there are no limitations on transaction processing, i.e., transaction processing performance is not hampered by deadlock handling. However, additional algorithms have to be in place to maintain information on the current waiting conditions and to check them for deadlocks. In deadlock detection, there is a considerable difference between centralized deadlock detection and distributed deadlock detection.

In this section we will briefly discuss deadlock detection in the centralized case; distributed deadlock detection will be discussed in Section 18.5.

We start the discussion of deadlock detection by a way to maintain information on waiting conditions between transactions. Typically, a directed graph is used to represent waiting conditions, known as the waits-for-graph. The nodes of the waits-for-graph are the transactions of the system, and whenever a transaction T waits for a data item currently locked by a transaction T', an edge from T to T' is inserted in the edge set of the waits-for-graph. Notice that each deadlock is represented by a cycle in that graph. Hence, deadlock detection boils down to detecting cycles in the waits-for-graph.

Cycle checking algorithms in directed graphs are widely available, as are efficient implementations. When a deadlock cycle is found, one of the transactions participating in the deadlock is selected to be aborted. This transaction is called deadlock victim. Aborting the deadlock victim results in releasing all locks that the transaction held. Since it took part in a deadlock cycle, there must be a transaction, which can now proceed. As a result, the deadlock cycle is broken. Notice that the transaction involved in the deadlock cycle under consideration can again be involved in a deadlock. That particular deadlock is resolved by aborting a single transaction after the system checks the waits-for-graph and finds a cycle representing that newly formed deadlock.

Deadlock detection in centralized database systems is rather easy to handle, since all information on waiting conditions between transactions is available locally. Hence, a database system designer has the choice to decide when the waits-for-graph is checked for deadlock cycles. Typically, these checks are performed periodically. Another choice would be to check after each lock request by a transaction that cannot be granted. However, on high transaction loads this approach would lead to large overhead, so that periodic checks are a better approach. Depending on the deadlock probability of a particular database system and its applications, the time period between checks can vary from seconds to minutes. In any case, deadlocks in centralized database systems can be detected and resolved with limited overhead.

18.4.4   Assuming Deadlocks

An approach related to deadlock detection is assuming deadlock. By assuming deadlocks, the system does not exactly detect deadlock situations, but based on observations, the system assumes that a deadlock was responsible for the observations. Assuming deadlocks is a rather vivid naming for a very simple approach, based on a timeout mechanism. For each waiting condition a timer is started. If the waiting condition lasts longer than a predefined timeout value, the system assumes that the waiting condition is part of a deadlock cycle. As a result, the waiting condition is deleted by aborting one of the participating transactions. This very simple algorithm will break deadlocks after the timeout value has elapsed. However, the approach is rather brute force than elegant, and selecting the timeout value is a typical trade-off situation.

- *High timeout value*: The transactions are allowed to stay in waiting conditions a long time. As a result, deadlocks are detected only after long periods of time have elapsed. However, few waiting conditions are deleted (by aborting transactions) that do not belong to a deadlock cycle. With growing timeout value, the probability to abort a transaction that does not belong to a deadlock is approaching zero. On the other hand, deadlocks remain undetected for a long time.

- *Low timeout value*: Selecting a low timeout value, transactions involved in waiting conditions are aborted after short periods of time. This means that deadlocks are resolved quickly. That is the good news. However, it can even happen that no deadlock cycles form, since waiting conditions are deleted before a deadlock can even form. While this situation seems beneficial, one must take into account the cost that is incurred by aborting and restarting transactions that encounter waiting conditions, which would never lead to a deadlock.

18.5   Distributed Deadlock Detection

Distributed database systems consist of a set of local database systems that contain logically related data. A sample setting of a distributed database system is a multi-national company with branches in different states. Each of these branches run a local database system and is responsible for the data at its local site. However, the headquarter may run transactions involving multiple local database systems of the distributed database system. A transaction that accesses data in one local site is called a local transaction. A transaction that accesses data in multiple sites is called a distributed transaction. The issues of distributed deadlock detection stem from distributed transactions.

Loosely speaking, distributed deadlock detection is hard because waiting conditions are spread over many sites, which do not share memory. Each site may encounter locally only acyclic waiting conditions. However, the global view involving waiting conditions in all sites of the distributed database system contains a deadlock. Since each local sites only sees local waiting conditions and the sites do not share memory, the sites have to communicate in order to detect the global deadlock situation. We assume that sites communicate by sending and receiving messages. Messages are assumed to arrive in the order sent, and messages arrive after finite time in good shape, i.e., they are not lost or corrupted. Computer network technology is able to fulfill these assumptions.

Deadlock detection in distributed database systems has received much attention over the years [Knapp1987, SiNa1989]. It is one of the few areas, where algorithms were proven correct by the authors, and some issues later, the journal published an erratum written by colleagues who found an error. For example, the the deficiency of [MeMu1979, Obermark1982, SiNa1985, Chou1989] was pointed out in [GliSha1980, Elma1986, Chou1989, KshSi1991], respectively.

In the remainder of this chapter we introduce edge-chasing algorithms, a particular class of deadlock detection algorithms. The name of the class of algorithms stems from their approach to send (chase) small messages along the edges of the global waits-for-graph. Notice that the global waits-for-graph is not explicitly constructed; rather the graph is implicitly constructed by sending messages over its edges.

Edge-chasing algorithms are described more precisely as follows. When a transaction gets blocked, a special message (called *probe*) is sent to the transaction it is blocked by. Probes carry transaction identifiers (e.g., the transaction timestamp). When a transaction receives a probe, it checks whether the probe's identifier equals its transaction identifier, in which case a deadlock is detected. The reason is quite clear: since transaction identifiers are unique, the message must be created by the transaction receiving the probe. Since the transaction receives that message and messages are sent along the edges of the global waits-for-graph, it can be deduced that the message traveled a cycle in the waits-for-graph before being received by the transaction. Since there is a cycle in the waits-for-graph, a global deadlock can be detected. In a first approach, the transaction that detects deadlock is aborted to resolve the deadlock.

Assuming the identifier of the probe does not match the identifier of the transaction receiving it, two cases have to be considered. If the receiving transaction is blocked, it propagates the probe — possibly modified — to the transaction(s) it is blocked by. This is how probes travel along the edges of the global waits-for-graph. If, however, the receiving transaction is not blocked, the probe is simply discarded. To make sure each deadlock is detected by a single transaction, when propagating a probe, a transaction updates the probe identifier to hold the maximum of its own identifier and the identifier of the received probe. The algorithm is symmetric and distributed in the sense that all transactions run identical copies of the algorithm and transactions communicate only by sending and receiving messages.

The basic algorithm is an immediate implementation of these ideas [Moss1981]; it is given in Figure 18.2. The algorithm is described using an event-based notation. In particular, $(T_i \rightarrow T_j)$ represents the occurrence of a waiting condition between the transactions involved. This event is called blocking event. Sending of messages is characterized by $(T_i : s(i, T_j))$, meaning that transaction T_i sends a message with identifier i to transaction T_j. The corresponding receive event is denoted by $(T_j : r(i, T_i))$. In the algorithm, a blocking event causes the sending of a probe, and a receive event causes either an abort of the transaction (if deadlock is detected) or a probe propagation. A broadcast of message M to a set X of transactions is represented by $(T_i : s(M, X))$. Note that no message is sent if $X = \{\}$.

Consider Figure 18.3. If (T_5, T_1) is closing edge of $d = (T_1, T_4, T_6, T_2, T_3, T_5)$ then T_5 initiates a probe in event $(T_5 : s(5, T_1))$. T_1 receives the probe in $(T_1 : r(5, T_5))$. Since the received probe carries a larger identifier than the receiving transaction, T_1 propagates the original probe to T_4, which propagates it to T_6. T_6, in contrast, changes the probe identifier from 5 to 6 to generate send event $(T_6 : s(6, T_2))$. This probe is propagated by all transactions participating in the deadlock, leading to the eventual detection and resolution of the deadlock by aborting T_6 (event a_6), following event $(T_6 : r(6, T_4))$. Note that no other transaction can detect the deadlock, since T_6 would not propagate the probe.

Rather than formally proving the correctness of the algorithm, we mo-

$$(T_i \rightarrow T_j) \Rightarrow (T_i : s(i, T_j))$$

$$(T_i : r(j, T_l)) \Rightarrow$$
$$\textbf{if } (i = j)$$
$$(a_i)$$
$$\textbf{else}$$
$$(T_i : s(max(i, j), \text{WS}_i))$$

Figure 18.2. Basic edge-chasing algorithm.

tivate its correctness by an example. Consider a deadlock cycle involving transactions $T_1, T_2, \ldots, T_6$. To see why the basic edge-chasing algorithm detects this deadlock, assume that $T_1 \rightarrow T_2$ is the last edge that forms. Following that blocking event, a probe is generated and sent with identifier 1 to T_2. Since this is the closing edge, T_2 is blocked when the probe arrives there. Therefore, $max(1, 2) = 2$ is propagated to the outgoing edges of T_2, i.e., to T_3, where a probe message with identifier 3 is propagated. Finally, a probe with identifier 6 is generated, which travels the deadlock cycle and leads to the detection of the deadlock by transaction 6. That transaction is aborted to resolve that deadlock. Notice that no other transaction $i \neq 6$ involved in that deadlock can detect the deadlock, since T_6 would not propagate that identifier.

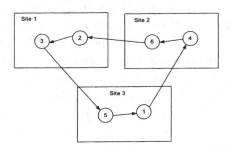

Figure 18.3. Example of a Global Deadlock Situation.

The correctness of the basic algorithm is based on the observation that each deadlock is detected at the latest by the transaction with maximum transaction identifier using the probe that was generated by the deadlock's

$$(T_i \rightarrow T_j) \Rightarrow$$
$$\textbf{if } (i > j)$$
$$(T_i : s(i, T_j))^+$$

$$(T_i : r(j, T_l)) \Rightarrow$$
$$\textbf{if } (i = j)$$
$$(a_i)$$
$$\textbf{else if } (i < j)$$
$$(T_i : s(j, \text{WS}_i))$$

Figure 18.4. Priority Algorithm

closing event. This observation leads to the idea to initiate a probe on blocking event $(T_i \rightarrow T_j)$ only if it may detect a deadlock later. Since the transaction with maximum identifier detects deadlock, a probe must be generated only if $i > j$. Furthermore, node T_k has to propagate a probe (i) only if the incoming probe carries a larger identifier than T_k, i.e., if $i > k$.

However, the argument that the closing-edge-probe detects the deadlock is no longer valid, since probes necessary for deadlock detection may get lost in currently unblocked nodes. Reinitiating probes ensures correctness without violating the edge-chasing paradigm. It is based on the observation that (i) deadlocks are permanent, and (ii) a probe is initiated at a time the deadlock exists. This probe leads to the detection of the deadlock eventually. One might argue that this approach incurs a lot of communication overhead. However, the actual overhead is widely determined by the reinitiation period. Furthermore, this parameter provides a useful means for tuning system performance and enhances robustness. The priority algorithm implements these ideas; it is given in Figure 18.4. (The periodical sending of a message M from T_i to T_j is specified by $(T_i : s(M, T_j))^+$.)

The algorithm is illustrated using the global waits-for-graph depicted in Figure 18.3. Assume T_5 sends probe (5) to T_1. If T_1 is not blocked when receiving the probe, the probe is discarded. However, probe reinitiation ensures that the probe is received by T_1 at a time the deadlock holds. Then, since the received probe carries a larger identifier than the receiving transaction, T_1 propagates the probe to T_6. On receiving the probe in T_6, the probe is discarded — it cannot lead to the detection of deadlock in which T_6 participates. Reinitiation of probe (6) by transaction T_6 ensures that the deadlock is eventually detected and resolved.

The algorithms introduced so far detect deadlock after the maximum probe has traversed the deadlock cycle completely. Moreover the system is aware of just a single node participating in the detected deadlock. It may be of crucial importance for efficient deadlock resolution to know the identity of more than one deadlocked transaction (to elect the cheapest-restart transaction deadlock victim).

The following algorithm is based on the idea to aggregate identifiers in probes, as they travel the paths of the waits-for-graph [Moss1981]. In particular, a probe consists of a list L of identifiers, allowing a transaction T_i to append its identifier to the list when propagating the probe (represented by $\langle L, i \rangle$). Hence, the list of a probe traces back the path that the probe traveled. Clearly on receiving L in T_i, a deadlock is detected if and only if the list holds the identifier of the receiving transaction. ($is\_member(i, L)$ returns true, if and only if the identifier i is in the list L.)

Note that an arbitrary transaction participating in a deadlock may detect it (not necessarily the one with maximum identifier), leading to timely deadlock detection. However, additional computations are necessary to ensure correctness. The transactions detecting a deadlock must agree on a common deadlock victim, which is done by electing the transaction with maximum identifier deadlock victim. Since all transactions detecting the deadlock are aware of the identity of all participating transactions, this agreement is guaranteed. After detecting a deadlock by T_k, the transaction sends a *do_abort* message to the transaction with maximum identifier telling it to abort itself. In the distributed computation model the behavior of a transaction T_i receiving such a message from a transaction T_k is specified by $(T_i : r(do\_abort, T_k)) \Rightarrow (a_i)$. The aggregate algorithm is given in Figure 18.5.

Both extensions of the basic algorithm can be integrated to a priorized / aggregative version in Figure 18.6. The idea of this algorithm is to priorize probe initiation and to aggregate transaction identifiers during probe propagation, marrying the advantates of the two previous algorithms.

To prove the correctness of that algorithm, we first show that on receiving a probe list L, a path is visible with the head of the list the maximum identifier. The proof is based on induction over the length of the path. Since a probe is propagated by transaction T_{i_j} only if $i_j < i_1$, the first element always holds the largest identifier. Since each propagating transaction appends its identifier to the end of the list, the list represents a path

$$(T_i \rightarrow T_j) \Rightarrow$$
$$(T_i : s(\langle i \rangle, T_j))$$

$$(T_i : r(L, T_l)) \Rightarrow$$
$$\textbf{if } (is\_member(i, L))$$
$$/ * \ L = \langle i_1, \ldots, i_n \rangle \ * /$$
$$i_{max} = max_{m=1}^{n}(i_m)$$
$$(T_i : s(do\_abort, T_{i_{max}}))$$
$$\textbf{else}$$
$$(T_i : s(\langle L, i \rangle, \mathrm{WS}_i))$$

Figure 18.5. Aggregate algorithm.

Algorithm	Priorization	Aggregation
Basic	-	-
Priorized	•	-
Aggregative	-	•
PA	•	•

Table 18.1. Overview of deadlock algorithms.

of the waits-for-graph.

To summarize, the basic algorithm is an immediate implementation of the edge-chasing paradigm. The priorized version reduces the number of probe propagations that do not lead to deadlock detection. By introducing the reinitiation period as a tunable system parameter, the number of messages sent can be tuned against timely deadlock detection. Furthermore, reinitiating probes makes the algorithm tolerate the loss of messages and thus increases its robustness. The aggregative version provides the system with additional information on transactions participating in a detected deadlock and can therefore lead to more efficient deadlock resolution. The priorized/aggregative version combines the advantages of tunability and robustness with efficient deadlock resolution. The algorithms are summarized in Table 18.1.

$$(T_i \rightarrow T_j) \Rightarrow$$
$$\mathbf{if}\ (i > j)$$
$$(T_i : s(\langle i \rangle, T_j))^+$$

$$(T_i : r(L, T_l)) \Rightarrow$$
$$\mathbf{if}\ (is\_member(i, L))$$
$$(a_i)$$
$$\mathbf{else}\ /*\ L = \langle i_1, \ldots, i_k \rangle\ */$$
$$\mathbf{if}\ (i < i_1)$$
$$(T_i : s(\langle L, i \rangle, \mathrm{WS}_i))$$

Figure 18.6. Priority/aggregate algorithm.

18.6 Summary

In this chapter we have discussed deadlock handling in database systems. Deadlocks can occur because of the 2-phase locking protocol used for synchronizing concurrent transactions. It is interesting to notice that generic deadlock conditions initially developed for deadlocks in operating systems are very well applicable to database deadlocks. Deadlocks in database systems can be prevented by restricting the usual transaction processing, for example, by predeclaring locks as is done in conservative 2PL. Deadlocks can be avoided by checking on each lock request issued by a transaction against a lock manager if that particular lock request can be granted. Typical algorithms for deadlock avoidance are the Wait-Die and the Wound-Wait algorithms. Finally we have focused on deadlock detection, which is particularly interesting in distributed database systems. A set of distributed deadlock detection algorithms of the edge-chasing class have been presented and illustrated using an example of a global deadlock.

Bibliography

[BeHaGo1987] P.A. Bernstein, V. Hadzilacos, and N. Goodman. *Concurrency Control and Recovery in Database Systems*. Addison-Wesley, Reading, MA, 1987.

[Chou1989] A.N. Choundhary, W.H. Kohler, J.A. Stankovic, and D. Towsley. *A Modified Priority Based Algorithm for Distributed Deadlock Detection and Resolution*. IEEE Transactions on Software Engineering, 15(1):10–17, 1989.

[Elma1986] A.K. Elmagarmid. *A Survey of Distributed Deadlock Detection Algorithms*. ACM SIGMOD, 15(3):37–45, 1986.

[ElNa2000] R. Elmasri and S. Navathe. *Fundamentals of Database Systems. Third edition*. Addison-Wesley, Reading, MA, 2000.

[GliSha1980] V.D. Gligor and S.H. Shattuck. *On Deadlock Detection in Distributed Systems*. IEEE Transactions on Software Engineering, 6(5):435–440, 1980.

[Knapp1987] E. Knapp. *Deadlock Detection in Distributed Databases*. ACM Computing Surveys, 19(4):303–328, 1987.

[KshSi1991] A.D. Kshemkalyani and M. Singhal. *Invariant-Based Verification of a Distributed Deadlock Detection Algorithm*. IEEE Transactions on Software Engineering, 17(8):789–799, August 1991.

[MeMu1979] D. Menasce and R. Muntz. *Locking and Deadlock Detection in Distributed Data Bases*. IEEE Transactions on Software Engineering, 5(3):195–202, 1979.

[Moss1981]   J.E.B. Moss. *Nested Transactions: An Approach to Reliable Distributed Computing.* PhD thesis, Dept. of Electrical Engineering and Computer Science, Massachusetts Institute of Technology, Cambridge, MA, April 1981.

[Obermark1982] R. Obermarck. *Distributed Deadlock Detection Algorithm.* ACM Transactions on Database Systems, 7(2):187–208, 1982.

[ONeil2000]   P. O'Neil and E. O'Neil. *Databases: Principles, Programming, and Performance.* Morgan Kaufmann, San Francisco, second edition edition, 2000.

[RaGe2000]   R. Ramakrishnan and J. Gehrke. *Database Management Systems.* McGraw-Hill, New York, second edition edition, 2000.

[SiNa1989]   M. Singhal. *Deadlock Detection in Distributed Systems.* IEEE Computer, 22(11):37–48, 1989.

[SiNa1985]   M.K. Sinha and N. Natarajan. *A Priority Based Distributed Deadlock Detection Algorithm.* IEEE Transactions on Software Engineering, 11(1):67–80, 1985.

[WeiVo2001]   G. Weikum and G. Vossen. *Transactional Information Systems: Theory, Algorithms, and the Practice of Concurrency Control and Recovery.* Morgan Kaufmann, San Francisco, 2001.

Index